14th International Conference on Strategic Management and its Support by Information Systems 2021

Ostrava, Czech Republic
25-26 May 2021

Editors:

Radek Němec
Lucie Chytilová

ISBN: 978-1-7138-4230-9

Printed from e-media with permission by:

Curran Associates, Inc.
57 Morehouse Lane
Red Hook, NY 12571

Some format issues inherent in the e-media version may also appear in this print version.

Printed with permission by Curran Associates, Inc. (2021)

For permission requests, please contact VŠB - Technical University of Ostrava at the address below.

VŠB - Technical University of Ostrava
17. Listopadu 15/2172
708 33 Ostrava - Poruba
Czech Republic

Phone: +420 597 325 278
Fax: +420 596 918 507

university@vsb.cz

Additional copies of this publication are available from:

Curran Associates, Inc.
57 Morehouse Lane
Red Hook, NY 12571 USA
Phone: 845-758-0400
Fax: 845-758-2633
Email: curran@proceedings.com
Web: www.proceedings.com

VŠB - Technical University of Ostrava
Faculty of Economics
Department of Systems Engineering

Proceedings of the 14th International Conference

SMSIS

Strategic Management

and its support by

Information Systems 2021

Radek Němec, Lucie Chytilová (eds.)

Ostrava
May 25-26, 2021
Czech Republic

DESIGN Radek Němec *(background graphic is free for commercial use image, designed by BSGStudio – attribution URL)*

Editors	Radek Nemec, Lucie Chytilova
Department	Department of Systems Engineering
Title	Proceedings of the 14th International Conference on Strategic Management and its Support by Information Systems 2021
PUBLICATION YEAR	2021
Number of pages	346
Publisher	VŠB-Technical University of Ostrava, Faculty of Economics, Department of Systems Engineering, Czech Republic
@ COPYRIGHT	the author/authors of each paper
ISSN	**2570-5776**
Production	Department of Systems Engineering

PAPER CITATION EXAMPLE:

Author, A. (2021). 'Title of the paper'. In: Nemec, R. and Chytilova, L. (eds.) *Proceedings of the 14th International Conference on Strategic Management and its Support by Information Systems 2021*, May 25-26, 2021, Ostrava, Czech Republic, pp. x-y.

All papers published in the proceedings have been peer-reviewed by 2 independent reviewers. Editors are not responsible for the grammar and language used in papers.

VSB TECHNICAL UNIVERSITY OF OSTRAVA | FACULTY OF ECONOMICS

SMSIS

PROGRAMME COMMITTEE

ORGANIZING COMMITTEE

Chair **Lucie Chytilová**

VŠB – Technical University of Ostrava, Czech Republic

Members

Radek Němec, Miroslav Hudec, Blanka Bazsová, Miloš Švaňa

VŠB – Technical University of Ostrava, Czech Republic

Conference website

http://www.ekf.vsb.cz/smsis/

PREFACE

Two years have passed again, and we are happy to welcome you at the conference on Strategic Management and its Support by Information Systems (SMSIS). This year, the conference is held for the 14th time in a row, we are glad for the support from the dean of the Faculty of Economics, VŠB – Technical University of Ostrava, Assoc. prof. Vojtěch Spáčil.

In the last almost two years, the whole world is heavily affected by the pandemic strike and during this time, and the scientific conferences are not exceptions. We are really sorry that we were forced to switch from the regular "physical" conference to the online mode, because we are convinced that the social aspect of the meeting plays almost as important role as knowledge sharing. Or it is better to say that these two roles are in perfect symbiosis. On the other hand, we are trying to look at the bright sight of this situation. Namely, we can listen to the interesting talks of people who are currently anywhere in the world. We can also record the talks and play them again later if necessary. We firmly hope that, despite we meet only virtually this year, you will enjoy the conference and its prepared program. Probably all of us wish that in two years, we will meet again in person and everything will get back to normal.

The conference program is split according to the topics of contributions as follows:

- strategic management,
- quantitative methods and their applications in management issues,
- trends and issues in information systems design, management and security,
- and applications of new media and intelligent tools in the Digital Economy.

This year, you can again look forward to the hot topics in the given fields, including the impact of the COVID pandemic.

The SMSIS 2021 conference is organized in cooperation with the Czech Society for Operations Research (ČSOV) and three Czech universities: VŠB – Technical University of Ostrava (Faculty of Economics), University of Economics in Prague (Faculty of Informatics and Statistics) and Masaryk University in Brno (Faculty of Informatics).

We are pleased that we can publish almost 40 high-quality studies written by researchers from the Czech Republic, Slovakia, Germany, and Spain. All papers were carefully double-blind reviewed by programme committee members and recognized experts in the given fields. This year, the programme is enriched with 4 invited speakers: Stanislav Tvrz, Ph.D. (Czech National Bank), prof. Michal Černý (University of Economics, Prague), prof. Mario Koeppen (Kyushu Institute of Technology, Japan), Henri Pirkkalainen (Tampere University, Finland).

Finally, I would like to thank all organizers and reviewers for their hard work and excellent cooperation, as well as the authors of contributions for not being discouraged by the current troublesome time and submitted high-quality papers.

To a successful conference!

On behalf of the program and organizing committee *František Zapletal*

May 2021

Regular papers

KEYNOTE SPEECHES

(ABSTRACTS)

Some open problems in linear programming

Michal Černý[1]

Abstract. Linear programming (LP) is a mature discipline of optimization. It is of great importance both in theory and in practice, namely due to the fact that most optimization problems solved in business and industry are formulated as mixed-integer LPs. The solution methods for them require efficient LP algorithms as the crucial subroutine. Still, LP is a source of difficult open problems in theory, remaining unsolved for a long time. Namely, it is the problem of computational complexity of the Simplex Algorithm (SA). The question is whether there exists a pivotage strategy making SA work in polynomial time. A positive answer, under further assumptions, would settle another important problem whether or not LP has a strongly polynomial algorithm. All of the currently known efficient algorithms, such as Khachyian's Ellipsoid Method (which is polynomial in theory but hard-to-implement in practice) or Interior Point Methods (which are efficient both in theory and in practice) are weakly polynomial only, meaning that their iteration bounds depend on the so-called Big-L measure of the size of input data. We also point out some recent results on the polynomial version of the Hirsch hypothesis, which plays an essential role in the analysis of SA and is a long-standing open problem in polyhedral geometry. And, finally, we will summarize some results on the average-time complexity of SA, trying to explain why the difficult instances for SA, such as Klee-Minty's LPs, seem to occur so rarely.

Michal Černý is a full professor of Econometrics & Operations Research at Department of Econometrics, University of Economics, Prague, Czech Republic. He graduated from Faculty of Mathematics and Physics, Charles University, Prague and Faculty of International Relations, University of Economics, Prague. His research interests include special optimization problems, optimization problems with inexact inputs, optimization problems in statistics and statistical analysis of special kinds of data (such as streaming data or interval-valued data). He currently works on the CSF grant project Financial data streams and related identification and optimization problems.

[1] University of Economics, Prague, Faculty of Informatics and Statistics, Department of Econometrics, nam. W. Churchilla 4, 130 67 Prague 3, Czech Republic, cernym@vse.cz

Smart Farming Documentation System

Mario Koeppen[2]

Abstract. These days, complex food supply chains, characterized by the production, distribution, transport, processing, retail and consumption of food get more and more entitled to various risks and hazards: contamination, domino effects, contamination propagation (incl. virus spread), resource depletion, origination and quality disputes. Here, farming is not only farm production of food at some location, but has to be seen by its effects on the whole chain. This is a challenge that needs proper reflection in any concept of Precision Agriculture. Here, we want to discuss the various stages and the related technology challenges.

The novel viewpoint here is to start on the documentation of the whole system. Bullet items of such a documentation are: new sensors data logs, incl. polarization, thermal, acoustic, multi-spectral imaging and wearables (monitor farmer condition and status) integration, incl. hierarchical classification and prediction tasks; security, esp. the tracking of ingredients mixtures, or the special multi-factor and small scale modality of blockchain technology. Further on, we need to explore new computational intelligence solutions for the task of retrieval of data to give it into the hand of consumers, a broad avenue for fuzzy information processing. Novel optimization approaches are needed for the interplay of the various optimization modalities of the food system: farmers' "look after things" as a correction-driven cognitive ability of humans brought into the AI domain, scheduling with respect to distribution and transport stage, efficiency and non-physical optimization for the processing and manufacturing stage, and the price-driven retail and consumption stage. All those tasks have been studied in perfect isolation so far, but to keep them in a global balance poses new requirements on optimization algorithms flow. We might take inspiration from the microbiome and how it achieves its task to keep an organism up and running. As a last step, how about moving the food system from a chain to a circle and base it on circular economy, to tackle the problem of incentives driving the system and avoid future harm caused by the classical domino effect?

The whole story has just opened its first chapter. But we have already promising technology at hand, incl. Big Data and IoT, global communication, low-cost sensors, and Computational Intelligence. Those can surely support to move away from the isolated efficiency race per food system stage to the safety-oriented, open, holistic and versatile documentation point of view towards the design and conception of a future smart farming system.

Mario Koeppen is a full professor at the Department of Computer Science and Electronics, at Graduate School for Creative Informatics, KYUSHU INSTITUTE OF TECHNOLOGY. Prof. Koeppen's research interests include: Pattern Recognition, Image Processing, Soft Computing, Computational Intelligence, Security Technologies, (Multi-Objective) Optimization, and Algorithm Theory.

[2] Kyushu Institute of Technology, Kitakyushu, Japan, mkoeppen@ci.kyutech.ac.jp

Value creation with Social Extended Reality: Insights on technology adoption

Henri Pirkkalainen[3]

Abstract. New extended reality technologies, including virtual, augmented and mixed realities have recently matured as a technology and are increasingly adopted for industries. The major beneficial use cases are now witnessed for remote collaboration due to overriding the limitations of traditional IT tools, bringing the collaborators in the same shared space and collaborating over 3D content, similar than in face to face settings. This is referred to as Social Extended Reality (SXR), which allows multiple users to interact with each other simultaneously in an immersive way in the same virtual space via avatars. SXR has the potential to increase organizational performance by improving collaboration between different stakeholders in industry value chains and by enabling efficient collaboration in situations in which physical meetings are not possible. The presentation will focus on insights about the potentials of SXR and discuss factors that either enable or disrupt its adoption.

Henri Pirkkalainen is an associate professor of Information and Knowledge Management in Tampere University. His research interest is in technology adoption, dark side of information systems use and knowledge management. Pirkkalainen manages national projects on AR and VR by collaborating actively with the leading technology companies in Finland. These national, company-funded projects are specifically related to adoption of AR and VR in industries. The team of Assistant Professor Pirkkalainen is currently working on new types of social VR application and scenarios which enable multiple users to collaborate and educate each other in VR environments. Pirkkalainen has published in many of the leading journals listed by the Association for Information Systems (AIS) and has chaired and acted as an associate editor for many AIS conferences.

[3] Tampere University, Faculty of Management and Business, henri.pirkkalainen@tuni.fi

CNB's forecasting process in the period of global pandemic

Stanislav Tvrz[4]

Abstract. Recent developments related to the coronavirus pandemic present many challenges to the forecasting institutions in the whole world. National governments react to the changing situation by a continual stream of quarantine measures and accommodative policies. These decisions as well as the response of households and firms in the economy may be hard to predict. The unprecedented nature of the pandemic shock is also accompanied with excessive data uncertainty. This constitutes extraordinary conditions and challenges also for the forecasting at the central banks, including the Czech National Bank. Since the CNB operates in the inflation targeting regime, it relies on its macroeconomic forecast. The „g3+" DSGE model remains at the core of the forecasting process. However, new instruments and approaches have been employed during the pandemic period as well. This presentation describes the main innovations in the forecasting process at the CNB adopted in response to abovementioned challenges. It also explains and highlights the usefulness of the „g3+" model even in these extraordinary times.

Stanislav Tvrz works as a senior macroeconomic analyst in the forecasting team of the Monetary Department at the Czech National Bank. Last year, when the Covid-19 pandemic repeatedly hit the economy, he lead the forecasting team at the CNB. Previously, he also worked at the Monetary Department of the National Bank of Slovakia. He earned his Ph. D. in economic policy at the Faculty of Economics and Administration of Masaryk University in Brno. Moreover, he studied applied mathematics at the Faculty of Science of Masaryk University. In his research, he focuses on applying structural models for economic modelling and forecasting with DSGE models.

[4] Czech National Bank, Masaryk University, Stanislav.Tvrz@econ.muni.cz

REGULAR PAPERS

Risk management of cloud environments

Jan Andraščík[1]

Abstract. There are many information security risk assessment approaches present on the market – some generic, some cloud oriented. But which information security risk assessment method should be used when a company decides to use a cloud-hosted system? This paper uses the CURF framework to compare existing information security risk assessment methods to identify the ideal method to use for a cloud-hosted adoption. Several methods both generic and cloud specific were selected for the comparison.
Even though there are several cloud specific risk assessment methods, they are not so comprehensive to fully cover the risk assessment process. To perform a comprehensive analysis, they should be combined with the generic approaches as well.

Keywords: cloud, risk management, security, risk analysis, risk assessment.

JEL Classification: C88

1 Introduction

Cloud computing is claimed to be the most revolutionary information delivery model since the introduction of the internet (Kajiyama, Jennex and Addo, 2017). Cloud can be viewed as a pool of computing resources (Mackita, Shin and Choe, 2019) which companies can access over the internet and use them from anywhere in the world. Many organizations, be it SMEs or large enterprises, therefore move their operations of information systems towards clouds (VERIZON, 2020).

Clouds offer many benefits such as scalability and cost-effectiveness when compared with having all the services hosted on-premise (Madria, 2016). Moreover, it reduces the need to carry sensitive data on potentially fragile storage devices, it can provide a low-cost disaster recovery solution and overall can provide better utilization of hardware when compared with on-premise solutions (Kajiyama, Jennex and Addo, 2017). Despite those benefits, clouds also pose some cloud-specific risks, which makes companies delay their activities in the cloud. Overall, companies fear risks related to security of the cloud environments and privacy controls applied (or not applied) in such environments (Madria, 2016). Attacks on various cloud services also grow in count and magnitude (VERIZON, 2020) as the usage of cloud services raises.

In order to identify specific risks which they would face within the cloud environment, an in-depth risk analysis should be performed on the cloud service(s) they would like to use. Such analysis should cover various aspects of risks – security, privacy, compliance, general IT risks etc. On the market, there are several methodologies for performing risk assessments going more or less into detail of individual risks. Some are more general; some are more security related. But both such types can be used to perform the risk assessment.

In order for a risk assessment methodology to be used for a cloud service, it should ideally be able to identify risks which are specific for that kind of environment (Mackita, Shin and

[1] The Prague University of Economics and Business, Department of Systems Analysis, W. Churchill Sq. 1938/4, 130 67 Praha 3 – Zizkov, xandj19@vse.cz

Choe, 2019). Risk assessments aimed at cloud services should take into account specific technologies of the cloud environments which are widely used, e.g., AWS and MS Azure and from them get the basic idea of risks cloud services face and use such data when analyzing other similar cloud services.

Correctly performed risk assessment should provide companies and their management an insight into possible risk scenarios related to the use of selected cloud services. Such insight should be a base of a management decision with regards to the use of a particular cloud service *before* the services is actually procured. However, risk assessment should not be a one-time thing used only when selecting a proper cloud service, it should be performed continuously throughout the cloud service lifecycle, as cloud services evolve and risks they can face evolve with them.

The aim of this work is therefore to analyze existing risk assessment methodologies and evaluate their possible usage in cloud environments. The assessment is based on an overall process of the risk assessment as well as depth of the actual analysis performed.

The main contributions of this work are:

- Evaluation of existing risk assessment method taking into account specifics of the cloud environments,
- Identification of a suitable existing risk assessment method for cloud environments.

The remainder of this work is organized as follows:

- Part 2 introduces the risk assessment, its fundamentals, existing risk assessment methods and a method for comparing risk assessment methods,
- Part 3 presents the results of the analysis of risk assessment methods,
- Part 4 provides a summary of the research.

2 Background and related work

This section presents a summary of fundamental concepts of risk assessment and existing methods/methodologies which could be used for the assessment in the cloud. Moreover, a comparison method of risk assessment is introduced.

2.1 Risk assessments

Overall goal of a risk assessment should be to identify and recognize risks at an early stage of adoption of a cloud service and help mitigate or minimize such risks (Elzamly *et al.*, 2016) to a level which would be acceptable for a company and its management. During the process of identification of risks, key risks should be identified and prioritize in order to produce an adequate mitigation plan and a basis for management decision. (Mackita, Shin and Choe, 2019).

Overall, risks are defined as a product of an impact of an incident resulting from a threat abusing an existing vulnerability of a service and a likelihood or a probability of such incident happening in the respective environment (ISO/IEC JTC 1/SC 27, 2018).

A good cloud risk assessment method should therefore take into account potential vulnerabilities of cloud technologies and vulnerabilities they can contain. The method should also be flexible enough to dynamically adapt to everchanging cloud technologies.

2.2 Existing risk assessment methods

Below there is a list of selected information security risk assessment methods. Generic information security risk assessment methods - ISO/IEC 27005:2018 and OCTAVE were selected as a baseline for comparison. Moreover, three existing cloud specific information security risk assessment methods were added to include the cloud area – risk assessment by ENISA, Cloud Octagon Model and Microsoft Cloud Risk Decision Framework.

ISO/IEC 27005:2018

This standard was prepared by The International Organization for Standardization and provides a general approach to information security risk management. The standard provides a description of a risk management process which can be applied to any environment not specifying and particular risks for specific technologies. It does, however, provide a list of general risks. (ISO/IEC JTC 1/SC 27, 2018)

Operationally Critical Threat, Asset, and Vulnerability Evaluation (OCTAVE)

Software Engineering Institute of Carnegie Mellon University prepared a framework focused on information security risk management called Operationally Critical Threat, Asset, and Vulnerability Evaluation or OCTAVE for short. There are currently three distinct versions of OCTAVE all with different level of detail analyzed. (Caralli *et al.*, 2007)

ENISA

In 2009 The European Network and Information Security Agency (ENISA) introduced its framework for risk assessment of cloud environments where 35 risks were identified in four major categories mapping the most common risks for cloud services (ENISA, 2009)

Cloud Octagon Model

Cloud Octagon Model was released by Cloud Security Alliance (CSA) in 2019 to address risk management of SaaS services in companies. It does not solely focus on information security, it also includes areas such as procurement, IT governance, architecture, development and engineering, service providers, risk processes, data classification, etc. (Cloud Security Alliance, 2019)

Microsoft Cloud Risk Decision Framework

Microsoft also prepared its risk management framework inspired by ISO 31000. The framework provides a high level description of a risk management process and identified a basic set of risk not only limited to information security risks. (Stone and Noel, 2015)

2.3 Comparison methodology

To assess individual risk assessment methods the Core Unified Risk Framework (CURF) has been chosen. The framework provides a bottom-up approach for comparing risk assessment methods. Using the CURF framework, individual tasks within the analyzed methods need to be evaluated. The ISO/IEC 27005 model has been used as a reference for evaluation. The core activities of the CURF model consist of risk identification, risk estimation and risk evaluation. The CURF uses three scores for evaluation of tasks: fully addressed, i.e., with clear description of how to solve a specific task, partially addressed, i.e., when task is suggested but not described, and not addressed, i.e., when not mentioned in a specific method at all. (Wangen, Hallstensen and Snekkenes, 2018). To simplify, a score of 0 to 2 was assigned to individual aforementioned scores. 0 has been assigned to "not addressed", while 2 was assigned to "fully addressed".

3 Risk assessment methods analysis

This part applies the CURF framework described above to individual risk assessment methods. Authors of the CURF framework evaluated ISO/IEC 27005, OCTAVE and Microsoft framework in the paper introducing the framework according to chapter 2.3 (Wangen, Hallstensen and Snekkenes, 2018), to score the remaining method, the author of this paper analyzed the methods and scored them according to the same methodology. Table 1 is an overview of the results for all the methods.

Area	ISO/IEC 27005:2018	OCTAVE	ENISA	Cloud Octagon Model	Microsoft Cloud Risk Decision Framework
Risk identification					
Preliminary assessment	0	2	0	1	1
Risk criteria determination	2	2	0	0	2
Cloud-specific considerations	0	0	2	2	2
Business objective identification	2	2	0	0	1
Key risk indicators	0	0	0	0	0
Stakeholder identification	2	1	0	1	2
Stakeholder analysis	0	0	0	0	0
Asset identification	2	2	1	0	0
Mapping of personal data	1	1	0	1	0
Asset evaluation	1	1	2	0	0
Asset owner and customer	2	2	1	1	0
Asset container	0	2	0	0	0
Business process identification	2	0	0	0	0
Vulnerability identification	2	1	2	1	1

Vulnerability assessment	2	0	1	1	0
Threat identification	2	2	0	1	0
Threat assessment	2	2	0	1	0
Control identification	2	1	0	1	2
Control assessment	2	0	0	1	0
Outcome identification	2	2	0	0	2
Outcome assessment	2	1	0	0	2
Risk estimation					
Asset identification and evaluation	0	0	0	0	1
Threat willingness/motivation	2	2	1	1	0
Threat capability (know how)	1	0	0	1	0
Threat capacity (Resources)	1	1	0	1	0
Threat attack duration	0	0	0	0	2
Vulnerability assessment	0	0	1	1	0
Control efficiency assessment	1	0	0	0	2
Subjective P Est. for event	2	1	1	1	2
Quantitative P Est. for event	2	0	0	0	1
Subjective impact estimation	2	2	1	1	2
Quantitative impact estimation	2	1	0	0	1
Privacy risk estimation	0	0	0	0	0
Utility and incentive calc.	0	0	0	0	0
Cloud vendor assessment	0	0	0	0	2
Opportunity cost	1	0	0	0	0
Level of risk determination	2	0	2	0	1
Risk aggregation	2	1	0	0	0
Risk evaluation					
Risk criteria assessment/revision	1	1	0	0	0
Risk prioritization/evaluation	2	2	1	0	2

Risk treatment recommendation	0	2	0	0	0
Total	51	37	16	18	31

Table 1 Comparison of methods

ISO/IEC 27005:2018

The ISO standard for information security risk management well describes the overall risk management process from risk identification to risk treatment. The standard itself also provides a catalogue of risks which can be used as a guide when performing the risk assessment. However, the risk catalogue contains only risks related to information security therefore all other risks would need to be assessed using a different approach or obtained from different sources. Also, since it is a generic approach to risk management, it can be easily tailored to cloud environments.

Operationally Critical Threat, Asset, and Vulnerability Evaluation (OCTAVE)

The OCTAVE method provides a comprehensive risk management process with a lot of supporting documentation, guides and checklists helping with the assessment itself. While it does not always provide guidance on all assessment areas, the described areas provide a thorough guidance. However, the method itself does not provide any list of potential risks which can be identified using it. Although many risks can be deduced from all the supporting documentation. Moreover, just like ISO/IEC 27005:2018, OCTAVE is a generic approach which could easily be tailored to suit cloud environment assessments.

ENISA

Method suggested by ENISA contains a wide list of risks and vulnerabilities directly connected to cloud environments. Using the list can therefore simplify performance of a cloud risk assessment. However, the method was introduced in 2009 and was not updated ever since, therefore some of current risks may not be covered by the method and some of the risks covered by the method may not be adequately evaluated according to the current situation. Moreover, it does not fully cover all areas of risk assessment processes.

Cloud Octagon Model

The Cloud Octagon Model CSA uses the processes designed by ISO 31000 and extends risk identification and risk estimation areas for cloud environments. In these specific areas the Model provides high level guidance on risk areas related to cloud environment. However, the model itself does not contain any risk catalogue except of the high-level risk areas. Also, since it was introduced in 2019 it can cover current risks. Unfortunately, the Model itself focuses on SaaS clouds only, therefore it is not that flexible as it does not cover IaaS and PaaS environments. The model itself does not provide guidance on specific risk assessment processes. Rather it refers to other frameworks.

Microsoft Cloud Risk Decision Framework

Microsoft, like CSA, derived its framework from ISO 31000. It extends the risk management processes in individual areas of risk management. The framework also provides a list of risks in individual areas including estimated impact and likelihood.

4 Summary and conclusion

To conclude this paper, based on the results of the analysis, the most suitable methods for risk assessment of cloud environments would be ISO/IEC 27005:2018 and OCTAVE, followed by the Microsoft Cloud Risk Decision Framework. These methods provide most comprehensive approaches to the process. While the ISO/IEC 27005:2018 can also help with a risk catalogue, OCTAVE can provide a comprehensive guidance on identification of specific risks. Microsoft Framework can provide an approach more tailored to cloud environments.

Since both ISO/IEC 27005:2018 and OCTAVE provide generic approach to risk assessment, it is advisable to select one of them and combine it with a cloud specific risk assessment method such as Microsoft Cloud Risk Decision Framework.

This work examined selected risk assessment methods from the view of cloud environments. The methods were analyzed based on applicability for cloud, details of their process description etc. The methods were selected based on their popularity and authoring organization applicability for the subject matter.

For future work, it is planned to perform more detailed analysis of individual methods and propose a method which would combine advantages of selected methods for maximum usage. Companies could then use such method when selecting new cloud services and overall management of risks of their cloud services during their whole lifecycle.

Acknowledgements

Paper was processed with support from institutional-support fund for long-term conceptual development of science and research at the Faculty of Informatics and Statistics of the Prague University of Economics and Business (IP400040).

5 References

Caralli, R. A. *et al.* (2007) *Introducing OCTAVE Allegro: Improving the Information Security Risk Assessment Process*. Software Engineering Institute. Available at: https://doi.org/10.1184/R1/6574790.v1 (Accessed: 15 December 2020).

Cloud Security Alliance (2019) *Cloud Octagon Model, Cloud Security Alliance*. Available at: https://cloudsecurityalliance.org/artifacts/cloud-octagon-model/ (Accessed: 10 December 2020).

Elzamly, A. *et al.* (2016) 'A new conceptual framework modelling for cloud computing risk management in banking organizations', *International Journal of Grid and Distributed Computing*, 9(9), pp. 137–154. doi: 10.14257/ijgdc.2016.9.9.13.

ENISA (2009) *Cloud Computing - Benefits, risks and recommendations for information security*. Available at: https://www.enisa.europa.eu/publications/cloud-computing-risk-assessment (Accessed: 11 December 2020).

ISO/IEC JTC 1/SC 27 (2018) 'ISO/IEC 27005:2018 Information technology — Security techniques — Information security risk management'. Available at: https://www.iso.org/cms/render/live/en/sites/isoorg/contents/data/standard/07/52/75281.html (Accessed: 10 December 2020).

Kajiyama, T., Jennex, M. and Addo, T. (2017) 'To cloud or not to cloud: how risks and threats are affecting cloud adoption decisions', *Information & Computer Security*, 25(5), pp. 634–659. doi: 10.1108/ICS-07-2016-0051.

Mackita, M., Shin, S.-Y. and Choe, T.-Y. (2019) 'ERMOCTAVE: A risk management framework for IT systems which adopt cloud computing', *Future Internet*, 11(9). doi: 10.3390/fi11090195.

Madria, S. K. (2016) 'Security and Risk Assessment in the Cloud', *Computer*, 49(9), pp. 110–113. doi: 10.1109/MC.2016.280.

Stone, G. and Noel, P. (2015) *Cloud Risk Decision Framework*. Microsoft.

VERIZON (2020) *2020 Data Breach Investigations Report*. Available at: https://enterprise.verizon.com/resources/reports/2020-data-breach-investigations-report.pdf (Accessed: 1 December 2020).

Wangen, G., Hallstensen, C. and Snekkenes, E. (2018) 'A framework for estimating information security risk assessment method completeness: Core Unified Risk Framework, CURF', *International Journal of Information Security*, 17(6), pp. 681–699. doi: 10.1007/s10207-017-0382-0.

A universal theorem of the alternative

David Bartl[1]

Abstract. We present a particular theorem of the alternative for finite systems of linear inequalities. The theorem is universal in the sense that other classical theorems of the alternative (Motzkin's Theorem and Tucker's Theorem) are implicit in it; the theorem itself is an extension of Farkas' Lemma. The presented result also generalizes and unifies both Dax's new theorem the alternative [Dax, A. (1993). *Annals of Operations Research*, 46, 11–60] and Rohn's residual existence theorem for linear equations [Rohn, J. (2010). *Optimization Letters*, 4, 287–292]. The universal theorem of the alternative is established by using Farkas' Lemma in the setting of a vector space over a linearly ordered (commutative or skew) field.

Keywords: Theorems of the alternative, systems of linear inequalities, Farkas' Lemma, linearly ordered vector spaces, linearly ordered fields.

JEL Classification: C65

1 Introduction

In this note, we present a universal theorem of the alternative which unifies both Dax's new theorem of the alternative (Dax, 1993) and Rohn's residual existence theorem for linear equations (Rohn, 2010). Moreover, the universal theorem contains Motzkin's Theorem of the alternative (Motzkin, 1934) and Tucker's Theorem of the alternative (Tucker, 1956) implicitly in it. The theorem is established by using Farkas' Lemma (Farkas, 1902), which has proved to be a result of importance in optimization and also in economics (Vohra, 2006). Short proofs of Farkas' Lemma include those given by Dax (1997), Broyden (1998; Roos and Terlaky, 1999), Komornik (1998), Scowcroft (2006, pp. 3535–3536, in the Introduction) and Bartl (2012a). See Fujimoto et al. (2018) for another proof; see also the references therein for further discussion of earlier proofs. Considering natural numbers $m, n, v \in \mathbb{N}$, recall the original results in the setting of the finite-dimensional vector space $\mathbb{R}^N$, where $N \in \mathbb{N}$ is a natural number.

Farkas' Lemma (Farkas, 1902). *Let $\boldsymbol{A} \in \mathbb{R}^{m\times N}$ be a matrix and let $\boldsymbol{c}^{\mathrm{T}} \in \mathbb{R}^{1\times N}$ be a row vector. It holds*

$$\forall \boldsymbol{x} \in \mathbb{R}^N\colon\ \boldsymbol{A}\boldsymbol{x} \leq \boldsymbol{0} \Longrightarrow \boldsymbol{c}^{\mathrm{T}}\boldsymbol{x} \leq 0$$

if and only if

$$\exists \boldsymbol{u}^{\mathrm{T}} \in \mathbb{R}^{1\times m},\ \boldsymbol{u}^{\mathrm{T}} \geq \boldsymbol{0}^{\mathrm{T}}\colon\ \boldsymbol{c}^{\mathrm{T}} = \boldsymbol{u}^{\mathrm{T}}\boldsymbol{A}.$$

Dax's new theorem of the alternative (Dax, 1993, Sections 5.1 and 5.4). *Let $\boldsymbol{c}^{\mathrm{T}} \in \mathbb{R}^{1\times N}$ be a row vector, let $\boldsymbol{B}_1, \dots, \boldsymbol{B}_n \in \mathbb{R}^{1\times N}$ be one-row matrices, and let $w_1, \dots, w_n \in \mathbb{R}$ be positive weights. It holds*

$$\forall \boldsymbol{x} \in \mathbb{R}^N\colon\ \boldsymbol{c}^{\mathrm{T}}\boldsymbol{x} \leq w_1|\boldsymbol{B}_1\boldsymbol{x}| + \dots + w_n|\boldsymbol{B}_n\boldsymbol{x}|$$

if and only if

$$\exists v_1 \in \mathbb{R},\ -w_1 \leq v_1 \leq w_1,\ \dots,\ \exists v_n \in \mathbb{R},\ -w_n \leq v_n \leq w_n\colon\ \boldsymbol{c}^{\mathrm{T}} = v_1\boldsymbol{B}_1 + \dots + v_n\boldsymbol{B}_n.$$

Rohn's residual existence theorem for linear equations (Rohn, 2010, Theorem 2). *Let $\boldsymbol{c}^{\mathrm{T}} \in \mathbb{R}^{1\times N}$ be a row vector, let $\boldsymbol{Z} \in \mathbb{R}^{p\times N}$ be a matrix, and let $\{\boldsymbol{b}_1^{\mathrm{T}}, \dots, \boldsymbol{b}_v^{\mathrm{T}}\} \subseteq \mathbb{R}^{1\times p}$ be any collection of row vectors. It holds*

$$\forall \boldsymbol{x} \in \mathbb{R}^N\colon\ \boldsymbol{c}^{\mathrm{T}}\boldsymbol{x} \leq \max\{\boldsymbol{b}_1^{\mathrm{T}}\boldsymbol{Z}\boldsymbol{x}, \dots, \boldsymbol{b}_v^{\mathrm{T}}\boldsymbol{Z}\boldsymbol{x}\}$$

if and only if

$$\exists v_1, \dots, v_v \in \mathbb{R},\ v_1, \dots, v_v \geq 0,\ v_1 + \dots + v_v = 1\colon\ \boldsymbol{c}^{\mathrm{T}} = (v_1\boldsymbol{b}_1^{\mathrm{T}} + \dots + v_v\boldsymbol{b}_v^{\mathrm{T}})\boldsymbol{Z}.$$

[1] Silesian University in Opava, School of Business Administration in Karviná, Department of Informatics and Mathematics, Univerzitní náměstí 1934/3, 733 40 Karviná, Czech Republic, bartl@opf.slu.cz

Motzkin's Theorem (Motzkin, 1934; Motzkin, 1952, Theorem D6, p. 60). *Let* $\boldsymbol{A} \in \mathbb{R}^{m\times N}$ *and* $\boldsymbol{B} \in \mathbb{R}^{\nu\times N}$ *be matrices. It holds*

$$\nexists \boldsymbol{x} \in \mathbb{R}^N\colon\ \boldsymbol{Ax} \leq \boldsymbol{0} \wedge \boldsymbol{Bx} < \boldsymbol{0}$$

if and only if

$$\exists \boldsymbol{\lambda}^{\mathrm{T}} \in \mathbb{R}^{1\times m},\ \boldsymbol{\lambda}^{\mathrm{T}} \geq \boldsymbol{0}^{\mathrm{T}},\ \exists \boldsymbol{\mu}^{\mathrm{T}} \in \mathbb{R}^{1\times \nu},\ \boldsymbol{\mu}^{\mathrm{T}} \geq \boldsymbol{0}^{\mathrm{T}},\ \mu_1 + \cdots + \mu_\nu = 1\colon\ \boldsymbol{\lambda}^{\mathrm{T}}\boldsymbol{A} + \boldsymbol{\mu}^{\mathrm{T}}\boldsymbol{B} = \boldsymbol{o}^{\mathrm{T}},$$

where $\boldsymbol{o}^{\mathrm{T}} \in \mathbb{R}^{1\times N}$ *is the row vector consisting of N zeros and* $\mu_1, \dots, \mu_\nu \in \mathbb{R}$ *are the components of* $\boldsymbol{\mu}^{\mathrm{T}}$.

Tucker's Theorem (Tucker, 1956, Corollary 2A part (i)). *Let* $\boldsymbol{A} \in \mathbb{R}^{m\times N}$ *and* $\boldsymbol{B} \in \mathbb{R}^{n\times N}$ *be matrices, where the matrix* $\boldsymbol{B}$ *consists of the rows* $\boldsymbol{b}_1, \dots, \boldsymbol{b}_n \in \mathbb{R}^{1\times N}$. It holds

$$\nexists \boldsymbol{x} \in \mathbb{R}^N\colon\ \boldsymbol{Ax} \leq \boldsymbol{0} \wedge \boldsymbol{Bx} \leq \boldsymbol{0} \wedge \boldsymbol{b}_1\boldsymbol{x} + \cdots + \boldsymbol{b}_n\boldsymbol{x} = -1$$

if and only if

$$\exists \boldsymbol{\lambda}^{\mathrm{T}} \in \mathbb{R}^{1\times m},\ \boldsymbol{\lambda}^{\mathrm{T}} \geq \boldsymbol{0}^{\mathrm{T}},\ \exists \boldsymbol{\mu}^{\mathrm{T}} \in \mathbb{R}^{1\times n},\ \boldsymbol{\mu}^{\mathrm{T}} > \boldsymbol{0}^{\mathrm{T}}\colon\ \boldsymbol{\lambda}^{\mathrm{T}}\boldsymbol{A} + \boldsymbol{\mu}^{\mathrm{T}}\boldsymbol{B} = \boldsymbol{o}^{\mathrm{T}},$$

where $\boldsymbol{o}^{\mathrm{T}} \in \mathbb{R}^{1\times N}$ *is the row vector consisting of N zeros.*

2 Notation and Farkas' Lemma

Let F be a linearly ordered (commutative or skew) field. Additionally, let V be a linearly ordered vector space over the linearly ordered field F. The relation of the linear ordering of the field F and vector space V will be denoted by the symbol $\leq$ and $\preccurlyeq$, respectively. Recall that an element $\lambda \in F$ is *positive* and *non-negative* if and only if $\lambda > 0$ and $\lambda \geq 0$, respectively. These two concepts are analogously defined for the elements of the vector space V. Finally, let W be a vector space over the field F.

For non-negative natural numbers m and n, and for positive natural numbers $\nu_1, \dots, \nu_n$, let $\alpha_1, \dots, \alpha_m\colon W \to F$ and $\beta_{j1}, \dots, \beta_{j\nu_j}\colon W \to F$ be linear forms, which make up the linear mappings $A\colon W \to F^m$ and $B_j\colon W \to F^{\nu_j}$, respectively, for $j = 1, \dots, n$. (The mappings $A\colon W \to F^m$ and $B_j\colon W \to F^{\nu_j}$ generalize the concept of the matrices $\boldsymbol{A} \in \mathbb{R}^{m\times N}$ and $\boldsymbol{B}_j \in \mathbb{R}^{\nu_j\times N}$, which we could see in the Introduction. Additionally, the linear forms $\alpha_1, \dots, \alpha_m\colon W \to F$ and $\beta_{j1}, \dots, \beta_{j\nu_j}\colon W \to F$ correspond to the rows $\boldsymbol{a}_1, \dots, \boldsymbol{a}_m$ and $\boldsymbol{b}_{j1}, \dots, \boldsymbol{b}_{j\nu_j}$ of the matrix $\boldsymbol{A}$ and $\boldsymbol{B}_j$, respectively, for $j = 1, \dots, n$.)

For any elements $\lambda, \mu \in F$ and for any vector $u \in V$, we put $\iota\lambda\mu = \mu\lambda$ and $\iota u\lambda = \lambda u$. In other words, the symbol 'ι' (Greek letter iota) means that the next two entities are to be transposed and multiplied in the new order.

Now, let m and ν be a non-negative and positive, respectively, natural number. As above, consider the linear mappings $A\colon W \to F^m$ and $B\colon W \to F^\nu$. For any $\boldsymbol{u} \in V^m$ and $\boldsymbol{v} \in V^\nu$, we stipulate that they consist of the components $u_1, \dots, u_m$ and $v_1, \dots, v_\nu$, respectively. Moreover, we define the linear mappings $\iota\boldsymbol{u}^{\mathrm{T}}A\colon W \to V$ and $\iota\boldsymbol{v}^{\mathrm{T}}B\colon W \to V$ by $\iota\boldsymbol{u}^{\mathrm{T}}Ax = \sum_{i=1}^{m}(\alpha_i x)u_i$ and $\iota\boldsymbol{v}^{\mathrm{T}}Bx = \sum_{k=1}^{\nu}(\beta_k x)v_k$, respectively, for every $x \in W$. The symbol $\boldsymbol{0}$ denotes the column vector consisting of m zeros of the field F. Additionally, the symbol $\boldsymbol{0}^{\mathrm{T}}$ denotes the row consisting of ν zeros of the vector space V. The inequalities $Ax \leq \boldsymbol{0}$ and $\boldsymbol{u}^{\mathrm{T}} \succcurlyeq \boldsymbol{0}^{\mathrm{T}}$ are understood componentwise, that is $\alpha_i x \leq 0$ for every $i = 1, \dots, m$ and $u_k \succcurlyeq 0$ for every $k = 1, \dots, \nu$, respectively. The symbol $\boldsymbol{e}$ denotes the column vector consisting of ν ones of the field F. We then have $\iota\boldsymbol{v}^{\mathrm{T}}\boldsymbol{e} = \iota v_1 1 + \cdots + \iota v_\nu 1 = v_1 + \cdots + v_\nu$. The symbol o denotes the zero linear mapping $o\colon W \to V$. If $m = 0$, then $\iota\boldsymbol{u}^{\mathrm{T}}A = o$ and the inequalities $Ax \leq \boldsymbol{0}$ and also $\boldsymbol{u}^{\mathrm{T}} \succcurlyeq \boldsymbol{0}^{\mathrm{T}}$ are logically true by convention.

Finally, let $\gamma: W \to V$ be any linear mapping. (The mapping $\gamma: W \to V$ generalizes the concept of the row vector $\boldsymbol{c}^{\mathrm{T}} \in \mathbb{R}^{1\times N}$, which we could see in the Introduction.)

Considering a non-negative natural number m, we now recall the following generalization of Farkas' Lemma formulated in the setting of a (possibly infinite-dimensional) vector space W over a (commutative or skew) linearly ordered field F, see Bartl (2007, Lemma 4.1).

Lemma 1 (Farkas' Lemma). *Let F be a linearly ordered (commutative or skew) field, let W be a vector space over the field F, and let V be a linearly ordered vector space over the linearly ordered field F. Let $A: W \to F^m$ and $\gamma: W \to V$ be linear mappings. It then holds*

$$\forall x \in W:\ Ax \le \mathbf{0} \implies \gamma x \preccurlyeq 0$$

if and only if

$$\exists \boldsymbol{u} \in V^m,\ \boldsymbol{u}^{\mathrm{T}} \succcurlyeq \mathbf{0}^{\mathrm{T}}:\ \gamma = \iota\boldsymbol{u}^{\mathrm{T}}A\,.$$

See Bartl (2012a) for a very short proof. The original version of Farkas' Lemma presented in the Introduction is obtained by considering the field $F := \mathbb{R}$ of the real numbers, the finite-dimensional vector space $W := \mathbb{R}^N$, and the one-dimensional real line $V := \mathbb{R}^1$.

3 A universal theorem of the alternative

Considering non-negative natural numbers m and n and also positive natural numbers $\nu_1, \dots, \nu_n$, we present a new universal theorem of the alternative.

Theorem 2 (universal theorem of the alternative). *Let F be a linearly ordered (commutative or skew) field, let W be a vector space over the field F, and let V be a linearly ordered vector space over the linearly ordered field F. Let $A: W \to F^m$ be a linear mapping, let $B_1: W \to F^{\nu_1}$, ..., $B_n: W \to F^{\nu_n}$ be linear mappings consisting of the linear forms $\beta_{11}, \dots, \beta_{1\nu_1}: W \to F$, ..., $\beta_{n1}, \dots, \beta_{n\nu_n}: W \to F$, respectively, let $w_1, \dots, w_n \in V$ be non-negative weights, and let $\gamma: W \to V$ be a linear mapping. It then holds*

$$\forall x \in W:\quad Ax \le \mathbf{0} \implies \gamma x \preccurlyeq \iota w_1 \max\{\beta_{11}x, \dots, \beta_{1\nu_1}x\} + \dots + \iota w_n \max\{\beta_{n1}x, \dots, \beta_{n\nu_n}x\}$$

if and only if

$$\exists \boldsymbol{u} \in V^m,\ \boldsymbol{u}^{\mathrm{T}} \succcurlyeq \mathbf{0}^{\mathrm{T}},$$
$$\exists \boldsymbol{v}_1 \in V^{\nu_1},\ \boldsymbol{v}_1^{\mathrm{T}} \succcurlyeq \mathbf{0}^{\mathrm{T}},\ \iota\boldsymbol{v}_1^{\mathrm{T}}\boldsymbol{e} = w_1,\ \dots,\ \exists \boldsymbol{v}_n \in V^{\nu_n},\ \boldsymbol{v}_n^{\mathrm{T}} \succcurlyeq \mathbf{0}^{\mathrm{T}},\ \iota\boldsymbol{v}_n^{\mathrm{T}}\boldsymbol{e} = w_n:\quad \gamma = \iota\boldsymbol{u}^{\mathrm{T}}A + \iota\boldsymbol{v}_1^{\mathrm{T}}B_1 + \dots + \iota\boldsymbol{v}_n^{\mathrm{T}}B_n\,.$$

Proof. The implication

$$Ax \le \mathbf{0} \implies \gamma x \preccurlyeq \iota w_1 \max\{\beta_{11}x, \dots, \beta_{1\nu_1}x\} + \dots + \iota w_n \max\{\beta_{n1}x, \dots, \beta_{n\nu_n}x\}$$

holds for every $x \in W$ if and only if the implication

$$Ax \le \mathbf{0} \wedge B_1x \le \boldsymbol{e}y_1 \wedge \dots \wedge B_nx \le \boldsymbol{e}y_n \implies \gamma x \preccurlyeq \iota w_1 y_1 + \dots + \iota w_n y_n$$

holds for every $x \in W$ and for every $y_1, \dots, y_n \in F$, which equivalently means that

$$\forall \begin{pmatrix} x \\ y_1 \\ \vdots \\ y_n \end{pmatrix} \in W \dot{\times} F^n:\ \begin{Bmatrix} Ax & & & \le 0 \\ B_1x + \boldsymbol{e}y_1 & & & \le 0 \\ \vdots & & \ddots & \vdots \\ B_nx & & + \boldsymbol{e}y_n & \le 0 \end{Bmatrix} \implies \gamma x + \iota w_1 y_1 + \dots + \iota w_n y_n \preccurlyeq 0\,.$$

By Farkas' Lemma 1, with the vector space W replaced by $W \dot{\times} F^n$, it equivalently holds that

$$\exists \begin{pmatrix} \boldsymbol{u} \\ \boldsymbol{v}_1 \\ \vdots \\ \boldsymbol{v}_n \end{pmatrix} \in V^m \dot{\times} V^{\nu_1} \dot{\times} \dots \dot{\times} V^{\nu_n},\ \begin{pmatrix} \boldsymbol{u} \\ \boldsymbol{v}_1 \\ \vdots \\ \boldsymbol{v}_n \end{pmatrix}^{\mathrm{T}} \succcurlyeq \begin{pmatrix} \mathbf{0} \\ \mathbf{0} \\ \vdots \\ \mathbf{0} \end{pmatrix}^{\mathrm{T}}:\quad \iota\begin{pmatrix} \boldsymbol{u} \\ \boldsymbol{v}_1 \\ \vdots \\ \boldsymbol{v}_n \end{pmatrix}^{\mathrm{T}} \begin{pmatrix} A & & & \\ B_1 & \boldsymbol{e}\iota & & \\ \vdots & & \ddots & \\ B_n & & & \boldsymbol{e}\iota \end{pmatrix} = (\gamma \quad \iota w_1 \quad \dots \quad \iota w_n)\,.$$

It is thus equivalent to say that there exist a non-negative $\boldsymbol{u} \in V^m$ and a non-negative $\boldsymbol{v}_1 \in V^{\nu_1}$, ..., a non-negative $\boldsymbol{v}_n \in V^{\nu_n}$ such that $\iota\boldsymbol{v}_1^{\mathrm{T}}\boldsymbol{e}\iota = \iota w_1$, ..., $\iota\boldsymbol{v}_n^{\mathrm{T}}\boldsymbol{e}\iota = \iota w_n$, which equivalently means that $\iota\boldsymbol{v}_1^{\mathrm{T}}\boldsymbol{e} = w_1$, ..., $\iota\boldsymbol{v}_n^{\mathrm{T}}\boldsymbol{e} = w_n$, and also $\gamma = \iota\boldsymbol{u}^{\mathrm{T}}A + \iota\boldsymbol{v}_1^{\mathrm{T}}B_1 + \dots + \iota\boldsymbol{v}_n^{\mathrm{T}}B_n$, which concludes the proof. ∎

4 Special cases of the universal theorem of the alternative

We discuss some special cases of the universal theorem of the alternative (Theorem 2) in this section.

4.1 Farkas' Lemma

In the previous section, we used Farkas' Lemma 1 to prove Theorem 2. At the same time, Farkas' Lemma 1 is also a special case of Theorem 2 when $n = 0$. In particular, if $n = 0$, then the empty sum $\iota w_1 \max\{\beta_{11}x, \dots, \beta_{1v_1}x\} + \cdots + \iota w_n \max\{\beta_{n1}x, \dots, \beta_{nv_n}x\} = 0$, the zero of the vector space V, by convention. The remaining terms '$\exists \boldsymbol{v}_j \in V^{v_j}$, $\boldsymbol{v}_j^{\mathrm{T}} \succcurlyeq \boldsymbol{0}^{\mathrm{T}}$, $\iota \boldsymbol{v}_j^{\mathrm{T}} \boldsymbol{e} = w_j$' and '$\iota \boldsymbol{v}_j^{\mathrm{T}} B_j$' vanish in Theorem 2 if $n = 0$, whence the conclusion is easy to see.

4.2 Dax's new theorem of the alternative

The version of Dax's new theorem of the alternative which was given in the Introduction can be found in Dax (1993, Sections 5.1 and 5.4). A generalized version can be found in Dax (1990). Here, we obtain the following generalization of Dax's new theorem of the alternative, where m and n are non-negative natural numbers, as a special case of Theorem 2.

Theorem 3 (Dax's new theorem of the alternative). *Let F be a linearly ordered (commutative or skew) field, let W be a vector space over the field F, and let V be a linearly ordered vector space over the linearly ordered field F. Let $A: W \to F^m$ be a linear mapping, let $B_1: W \to F$, ..., $B_n: W \to F$ be linear forms, let $w_1, \dots, w_n \in V$ be non-negative weights, and let $\gamma: W \to V$ be a linear mapping. It then holds*

$$\forall x \in W: \quad Ax \leq \boldsymbol{0} \implies \gamma x \preccurlyeq \iota w_1 |B_1 x| + \cdots + \iota w_n |B_n x|$$

if and only if

$$\exists \boldsymbol{u} \in V^m,\ \boldsymbol{u}^{\mathrm{T}} \succcurlyeq \boldsymbol{0}^{\mathrm{T}},$$
$$\exists v_1 \in V,\ -w_1 \preccurlyeq v_1 \preccurlyeq w_1,\ \dots,\ \exists v_n \in V,\ -w_n \preccurlyeq v_n \preccurlyeq w_n: \quad \gamma = \iota \boldsymbol{u}^{\mathrm{T}} A + \iota v_1 B_1 + \cdots + \iota v_n B_n .$$

Proof. In Theorem 2, consider $v_1 = \cdots = v_n = 2$ with $\beta_{11} = B_1, \beta_{12} = -B_1, \dots, \beta_{n1} = B_n, \beta_{n2} = -B_n$. Observe that the absolute value $|B_j x| = \max\{B_j x, -B_j x\} = \max\{\beta_{j1}x, \beta_{j2}x\}$ for every $x \in W$ for $j = 1, \dots, n$. Moreover, we have for any $v_j \in V$ that $-w_j \preccurlyeq v_j \preccurlyeq w_j$ if and only if $v_j = v_{j1} - v_{j2}$ for some non-negative $v_{j1}, v_{j2} \in V$ such that $v_{j1} + v_{j2} = w_j$ for $j = 1, \dots, n$. Finally, notice that $\iota v_j B_j = \iota(v_{j1} - v_{j2})B_j = \iota v_{j1}\beta_{j1} + \iota v_{j2}\beta_{j2}$ for $j = 1, \dots, n$. The equivalence is easy to see now. ■

The original version due to Dax (1993, Sections 5.1 and 5.4), presented in the Introduction, is obtained by considering the field $F := \mathbb{R}$ of the real numbers, the finite-dimensional vector space $W := \mathbb{R}^N$, the one-dimensional real line $V := \mathbb{R}^1$, and by letting $m := 0$.

4.3 Rohn's residual existence theorem for linear equations

Rohn's residual existence theorem for linear equations (Rohn, 2010, Theorem 2), which was presented in the Introduction, says in words that the system of linear equations $\boldsymbol{c}^{\mathrm{T}} = \boldsymbol{\xi}^{\mathrm{T}} \boldsymbol{Z}$ has a solution $\boldsymbol{\xi}^{\mathrm{T}} \in \mathbb{R}^{1 \times p}$ in the convex hull of the set $\{\boldsymbol{b}_1^{\mathrm{T}}, \dots, \boldsymbol{b}_v^{\mathrm{T}}\}$ if and only if $\boldsymbol{c}^{\mathrm{T}} \boldsymbol{x} \leq \max\{\boldsymbol{b}_1^{\mathrm{T}} \boldsymbol{Z} \boldsymbol{x}, \dots, \boldsymbol{b}_v^{\mathrm{T}} \boldsymbol{Z} \boldsymbol{x}\}$ for every $\boldsymbol{x} \in \mathbb{R}^N$. We obtain the following generalization of Rohn's residual existence theorem for linear equations, where m and v is a non-negative and positive, respectively, natural number, as a special case of Theorem 2.

Theorem 4 (Rohn's residual existence theorem for linear equations). *Let F be a linearly ordered (commutative or skew) field, let W be a vector space over the field F, and let V be a linearly ordered vector space over the linearly ordered field F. Let $A: W \to F^m$ be a linear mapping, let $\beta_1, \dots, \beta_v: W \to F$ be linear forms, let $w \in V$ be a non-negative weight, and let $\gamma: W \to V$ be a linear mapping. It then holds*

$$\forall x \in W: \quad Ax \leq \mathbf{0} \implies \gamma x \preccurlyeq \iota w \max\{\beta_1 x, \dots, \beta_\nu x\}$$

if and only if

$$\exists \boldsymbol{u} \in V^m,\ \boldsymbol{u}^{\mathrm{T}} \succcurlyeq \mathbf{0}^{\mathrm{T}},\ \exists v_1, \dots, v_\nu \in V,\ v_1, \dots, v_\nu \succcurlyeq 0,\ v_1 + \dots + v_\nu = w: \quad \gamma = \iota \boldsymbol{u}^{\mathrm{T}} A + \iota v_1 \beta_1 + \dots + \iota v_n \beta_n .$$

Proof. Consider Theorem 2 with $n = 1$. ∎

The original version of Rohn's residual existence theorem for linear equations (Rohn, 2010, Theorem 2), presented in the Introduction, is obtained by considering the field $F := \mathbb{R}$ of the real numbers, the finite-dimensional vector space $W := \mathbb{R}^N$, the one-dimensional real line $V := \mathbb{R}^1$, by letting $m := 0$ and $n := 1$, and by taking the weight $w := 1$. Then, given the row vector $\boldsymbol{c}^{\mathrm{T}} \in \mathbb{R}^{1\times N}$, the matrix $\boldsymbol{Z} \in \mathbb{R}^{p\times N}$, and the row vectors $\boldsymbol{b}_1^{\mathrm{T}}, \dots, \boldsymbol{b}_\nu^{\mathrm{T}} \in \mathbb{R}^{1\times p}$, consider the mapping $\gamma: \mathbb{R}^N \to \mathbb{R}^1$ and the linear forms $\beta_1, \dots, \beta_\nu: \mathbb{R}^N \to \mathbb{R}$ defined by $\gamma: \boldsymbol{x} \mapsto \boldsymbol{c}^{\mathrm{T}}\boldsymbol{x}$ and $\beta_k: \boldsymbol{x} \mapsto \boldsymbol{b}_k^{\mathrm{T}}\boldsymbol{Z}\boldsymbol{x}$ for $k = 1, \dots, \nu$, respectively, for every $x \in \mathbb{R}^N$.

More generally, given the row vector $\boldsymbol{c}^{\mathrm{T}} \in \mathbb{R}^{1\times N}$, the matrix $\boldsymbol{Z} \in \mathbb{R}^{p\times N}$, and the set $\{\boldsymbol{b}_1^{\mathrm{T}}, \dots, \boldsymbol{b}_\nu^{\mathrm{T}}\} \subseteq \mathbb{R}^{1\times p}$, consider yet a set $\{\boldsymbol{a}_1^{\mathrm{T}}, \dots, \boldsymbol{a}_m^{\mathrm{T}}\} \subseteq \mathbb{R}^{1\times p}$. Then, by Theorem 4, the system of linear equations $\boldsymbol{c}^{\mathrm{T}} = \boldsymbol{\xi}^{\mathrm{T}}\boldsymbol{Z}$ has a solution $\boldsymbol{\xi}^{\mathrm{T}} \in \mathbb{R}^{1\times p}$ of the form $\boldsymbol{\xi}^{\mathrm{T}} = u_1\boldsymbol{a}_1^{\mathrm{T}} + \dots + u_m\boldsymbol{a}_m^{\mathrm{T}} + {} + v_1\boldsymbol{b}_1^{\mathrm{T}} + \dots + v_\nu\boldsymbol{b}_\nu^{\mathrm{T}}$ for some $u_1, \dots, u_m \geq 0$ and for some $v_1, \dots, v_\nu \geq 0$ such that $v_1 + \dots + {} + v_\nu = 1$, that is in the Minkowski sum (the convex hull of $\{\boldsymbol{b}_1^{\mathrm{T}}, \dots, \boldsymbol{b}_\nu^{\mathrm{T}}\}$ plus the convex conical hull of $\{\boldsymbol{a}_1^{\mathrm{T}}, \dots, \boldsymbol{a}_m^{\mathrm{T}}\}$) if and only if $\boldsymbol{a}_1^{\mathrm{T}}\boldsymbol{Z}\boldsymbol{x}, \dots, \boldsymbol{a}_m^{\mathrm{T}}\boldsymbol{Z}\boldsymbol{x} \leq 0$ implies $\boldsymbol{c}^{\mathrm{T}}\boldsymbol{x} \leq \max\{\boldsymbol{b}_1^{\mathrm{T}}\boldsymbol{Z}\boldsymbol{x}, \dots, \boldsymbol{b}_\nu^{\mathrm{T}}\boldsymbol{Z}\boldsymbol{x}\}$ for every $\boldsymbol{x} \in \mathbb{R}^N$. See Bartl (2012b, Theorem 5) for further generalization in this direction.

4.4 Motzkin's Theorem of the alternative

Motzkin's Theorem of the alternative (Motzkin, 1934; Motzkin, 1952, Theorem D6 [in Chap. III, § 13, par. 73], p. 60; cf. Tucker, 1956, Corollary 2A part (i)) is used to establish optimality conditions in non-linear optimization, see, e.g., Mangasarian (1994), Birbil et al. (2007). Notice that, depending upon the approach, Farkas' Lemma can be used to establish optimality conditions in non-linear optimization directly, see, e.g., Franklin (2002). Below, we obtain the following generalization of Motzkin's Theorem of the alternative, where m and ν is a non-negative and positive, respectively, natural number and 0 denotes the zero vector of the space V, as a special case of Theorem 2; it is a special case of Theorem 4 actually.

Theorem 5 (Motzkin's Theorem of the alternative). *Let F be a linearly ordered (commutative or skew) field, let W be a vector space over the field F, and let V be a linearly ordered vector space over the linearly ordered field F. Let $A: W \to F^m$ be a linear mapping, let $\beta_1, \dots, \beta_\nu: W \to F$ be linear forms, and let $w \in V$ be a non-negative weight. It then holds*

$$\nexists x \in W: \quad Ax \leq \mathbf{0} \wedge \iota w \max\{\beta_1 x, \dots, \beta_\nu x\} \prec 0$$

if and only if

$$\exists \boldsymbol{u} \in V^m,\ \boldsymbol{u}^{\mathrm{T}} \succcurlyeq \mathbf{0}^{\mathrm{T}},\ \exists v_1, \dots, v_\nu \in V,\ v_1, \dots, v_\nu \succcurlyeq 0,\ v_1 + \dots + v_\nu = w: \quad \iota \boldsymbol{u}^{\mathrm{T}} A + \iota v_1 \beta_1 + \dots + \iota v_n \beta_n = o .$$

Proof. There is no $x \in W$ such that $Ax \leq 0$ and $\iota w \max\{\beta_1 x, \dots, \beta_\nu x\} \prec 0$ if and only if $Ax \leq 0$ implies $0 \preccurlyeq \iota w \max\{\beta_1 x, \dots, \beta_\nu x\}$ for every $x \in W$. Now, conclude the proof by considering Theorem 4 with $\gamma = o$, the zero linear mapping $o: W \to V$. ∎

Remark 1. It holds $\max\{\beta_1 x, \dots, \beta_\nu x\} < 0$ if and only if $Bx < \mathbf{0}$, cf. Motzkin's Theorem in the Introduction.

By identifying the vector space V with the one-dimensional line F^1, i.e. by taking $V := F^1$, and by considering the weight $w := 1$ and also Remark 1, we obtain the generalization of Motzkin's Theorem due to Bartl (2007, Theorem 5.1).

To obtain the original formulation of Motzkin's Theorem (Motzkin, 1934; Motzkin, 1952, Theorem D6, p. 60; see Birbil et al., 2007, Lemma 2.2, for another equivalent formulation), presented in the Introduction, consider the field $F := \mathbb{R}$ of the real numbers, the finite-dimensional vector space $W := \mathbb{R}^N$, the one-dimensional real line $V := \mathbb{R}^1$, the weight $w := 1$, and Remark 1.

4.5 Tucker's Theorem of the alternative

Tucker's Theorem of the alternative (Tucker, 1956, Corollary 2A part (ii)) is dual to Motzkin's Theorem of the alternative; compare both theorems in the Introduction to see this. The following generalization of Tucker's Theorem of the alternative, where m and n are non-negative natural numbers and 0 denotes the zero vector of the space V, is a special case of Theorem 2.

Theorem 6 (Tucker's Theorem of the alternative). *Let F be a linearly ordered (commutative or skew) field, let W be a vector space over the field F, and let V be a linearly ordered vector space over the linearly ordered field F. Let $A: W \to F^m$ be a linear mapping, let $B: W \to F^n$ be a linear mapping consisting of the linear forms $\beta_1, \dots, \beta_n: W \to F$, and let $\mathbf{w} \in V^n$ be a column vector of non-negative weights $w_1, \dots, w_n \in V$. It then holds*

$$\nexists x \in W: \quad Ax \leq \mathbf{0} \wedge Bx \leq \mathbf{0} \wedge \iota w_1\beta_1 x + \cdots + \iota w_n\beta_n x \prec 0$$

if and only if

$$\exists \boldsymbol{u} \in V^m, \boldsymbol{u}^{\mathrm{T}} \succcurlyeq \mathbf{0}^{\mathrm{T}}, \exists \boldsymbol{v} \in V^n, \boldsymbol{v}^{\mathrm{T}} \succcurlyeq \boldsymbol{w}^{\mathrm{T}}: \quad \iota\boldsymbol{u}^{\mathrm{T}}A + \iota\boldsymbol{v}^{\mathrm{T}}B = o\,.$$

Proof. There is no $x \in W$ such that $Ax \leq \mathbf{0}$ and $Bx \leq \mathbf{0}$ and also $\iota w_1\beta_1 x + \cdots + \iota w_n\beta_n x \prec 0$ if and only if

$$\forall x \in W: \quad \binom{A}{B} x \leq \binom{\mathbf{0}}{\mathbf{0}} \quad \Rightarrow \quad 0 \preccurlyeq \iota w_1\beta_1 x + \cdots + \iota w_n\beta_n x\,.$$

By Theorem 2, with $\nu_1 = \cdots = \nu_n = 1$ and $\gamma = o$, the zero linear mapping $o: W \to V$, and also with the linear mapping $A: W \to F^m$ replaced with the linear mapping $\binom{A}{B}: W \to F^m \dot{\times} F^n$, it equivalently holds that

$$\exists \boldsymbol{u} \in V^m, \boldsymbol{u}^{\mathrm{T}} \succcurlyeq \mathbf{0}^{\mathrm{T}}, \exists \overline{\boldsymbol{v}} \in V^n, \overline{\boldsymbol{v}}^{\mathrm{T}} \succcurlyeq \mathbf{0}^{\mathrm{T}}: \quad \iota\boldsymbol{u}^{\mathrm{T}}A + \iota\overline{\boldsymbol{v}}^{\mathrm{T}}B + \iota w_1\beta_1 + \cdots + \iota w_n\beta_n = o\,.$$

We have $\iota\overline{\boldsymbol{v}}^{\mathrm{T}}B + \iota w_1\beta_1 + \cdots + \iota w_n\beta_n = \iota\overline{\boldsymbol{v}}^{\mathrm{T}}B + \iota\boldsymbol{w}^{\mathrm{T}}B = \iota(\overline{\boldsymbol{v}} + \boldsymbol{w})^{\mathrm{T}}B$. By considering $\boldsymbol{v} = \overline{\boldsymbol{v}} + \boldsymbol{w}$, it is equivalent to say that $\iota\boldsymbol{u}^{\mathrm{T}}A + \iota\boldsymbol{v}^{\mathrm{T}}B = o$ for some non-negative $\boldsymbol{u} \in V^m$ and for some $\boldsymbol{v} \in V^n$ such that $\boldsymbol{v}^{\mathrm{T}} \succcurlyeq \boldsymbol{w}^{\mathrm{T}}$, which means we are done. ∎

Remark 2. If the weights $\boldsymbol{w} \in V^n$ are positive, then $\boldsymbol{v}^{\mathrm{T}} \succcurlyeq \boldsymbol{w}^{\mathrm{T}} \succ \mathbf{0}^{\mathrm{T}}$, cf. Tucker's Theorem in the Introduction.

By identifying the vector space V with the one-dimensional line F^1, i.e. by taking $V := F^1$, and by considering the weights $w_1 := \cdots := w_n := 1$, we obtain the generalization of Tucker's Theorem due to Bartl (2007, Theorem 5.2).

To obtain the original formulation of Tucker's Theorem (Tucker, 1956, Corollary 2A part (ii)), presented in the Introduction, consider the field $F := \mathbb{R}$ of the real numbers, the finite-dimensional vector space $W := \mathbb{R}^N$, the one-dimensional real line $V := \mathbb{R}^1$, and the weights $w_1 := \cdots := w_n := 1$.

5 Concluding remarks

We presented a new universal theorem of the alternative (Theorem 2). We proved this result by using Farkas' Lemma 1. We then showed that many other theorems of the alternative (Farkas' Lemma itself, Dax's new theorem of the alternative, Rohn's residual existence theorem for linear equations, Motzkin's Theorem of the alternative and Tucker's Theorem of the alternative) are special cases of the universal theorem of the alternative (Theorem 2).

Fan (1956) and Chernikov (1968) also considered (finite) systems of linear inequalities and theorems of the alternative from the algebraic point of view, i.e. in a vector space of arbitrary dimension. Fan (1956) studies linear inequalities in a vector space over the field of real numbers $\mathbb{R}$ and also over the field of the complex numbers $\mathbb{C}$. Chernikov (1968) presents a theory of linear inequalities in a vector space over a linearly ordered commutative field F. In this paper, we consider any linearly ordered (commutative or skew) field F, a vector space W over the field F, and a linearly ordered vector space V over the linearly ordered field F.

Let the linear mappings $B_1: W \to F^{\nu_1}$, ..., $B_n: W \to F^{\nu_n}$ and the non-negative weights $w_1, \ldots, w_n \in V$ be as in Theorem 2. Notice that the mapping $p: W \to V$ defined by

$$p: x \longmapsto \iota w_1 \max\{\beta_{11}x, \ldots, \beta_{1\nu_1}x\} + \cdots + \iota w_n \max\{\beta_{n1}x, \ldots, \beta_{n\nu_n}x\}$$

is sublinear, that is $p(\lambda x) = \lambda p(x)$ for all positive $\lambda \in F$ and for all $x \in W$ and also $p(x + y) \preccurlyeq$ $\preccurlyeq p(x) + p(y)$ for all $x, y \in W$. It seems that Theorem 2 can be used to obtain optimality conditions for some optimization problems with a non-smooth objective function of a special form.

By using a discrete variant of Farkas' Lemma (Bartl, 2020), we could achieve analogous results in the discrete setting of a module over a non-trivial linearly ordered commutative ring.

Finally, by using an extended variant of Farkas' Lemma, which allows the system '$Ax \leq \mathbf{0}$' to be infinite, we could generalize the results even further.

Acknowledgements

This work was supported by the Czech Science Foundation under grant number GAČR 21-03085S, and by the Ministry of Education, Youth and Sports of the Czech Republic within the Institutional Support for Long-Term Development of a Research Organization in 2021.

References

Bartl, D. (2007). 'Farkas' Lemma, other theorems of the alternative, and linear programming in infinite-dimensional spaces: a purely linear-algebraic approach'. *Linear and Multilinear Algebra*, 55 (4), pp. 327–353.

Bartl, D. (2012a). 'A very short algebraic proof of the Farkas lemma'. *Mathematical Methods of Operations Research*, 75 (1), pp. 101–104.

Bartl, D. (2012b). 'Separation theorems for convex polytopes and finitely-generated cones derived from theorems of the alternative'. *Linear Algebra and its Applications*, 436 (9), pp. 3784-3789.

Bartl, D. (2020). 'A discrete variant of Farkas' lemma and related results'. *Optimization*, DOI: 10.1080/02331934.2020.1768535.

Birbil, Ş. İ., Frenk, J. B. G. and Still, G. J. (2007). 'An elementary proof of the Fritz-John and Karush–Kuhn–Tucker conditions in nonlinear programming'. *European Journal of Operational Research*, 180 (1), pp. 479–484.

Broyden, C. G. (1998). 'A simple algebraic proof of Farkas' lemma and related theorems'. *Optimization Methods and Software*, 8 (3–4), pp. 185–199.

Chernikov, S. N. (1968). *Linear inequalities.* Moscow: Nauka. [In Russian. Черников, С. Н. (1968). *Линейные неравенства.* Москва: Наука. (Современная алгебра).]

Dax, A. (1990). 'A new theorem of the alternative'. *Mathematical Programming*, 47 (1–3), 297–299.

Dax, A. (1993). 'The relationship between theorems of the alternative, least norm problems, steepest descent directions, and degeneracy: A review'. *Annals of Operations Research*, 46 (1), pp. 11–60.

Dax, A. (1997). 'An elementary proof of Farkas' lemma'. *SIAM Review*, 39 (3), pp. 503–507.

Fan, K. (1956). 'On systems of linear inequalities'. In Kuhn, H. W. and Tucker, A. W. (eds.) *Linear Inequalities and Related Systems.* Princeton: Princeton University Press, pp. 99–156. (Annals of Mathematics Studies; no. 38).

Farkas, J. (1902). 'Theorie der einfachen Ungleichungen'. *Journal für die reine und angewandte Mathematik*, 124 (1), pp. 1–27.

Franklin, J. N. (2002). *Methods of mathematical economics: Linear and nonlinear programming, fixed-point theorems.* Philadelphia: SIAM. ISBN 0-89871-509-1.

Fujimoto, T., Perera, B. B. U. P. and Giorgi, G. (2018). 'A proof of the Farkas–Minkowski theorem by a tandem method'. *Metroeconomica*, 69 (1), pp. 142–150.

Komornik, V. (1998). 'A simple proof of Farkas' lemma'. *The American Mathematical Monthly*, 105 (10), pp. 949–950.

Mangasarian, O. L. (1994). *Nonlinear programming.* Philadelphia: SIAM. ISBN 0-89871-341-2.

Motzkin, T. S. (1934). *Beiträge zur Theorie der linearen Ungleichungen.* Basel: University of Basel. Doctoral dissertation. Published also in Jerusalem: Azriel, 1936.

Motzkin. T. S. (1952). *Contributions to the theory of linear inequalities.* [A translation of Motzkin (1934) by Fulkerson, D. R.] Santa Monica: RAND Corporation, 7 March 1952. RAND Corporation Translation 22. Reprint in: Cantor, D., Gordon, B. and Rothschild, B. (eds.) *Theodore S. Motzkin: Selected Papers.* Boston: Birkhäuser, 1983, pp. 1–80. (Contemporary Mathematicians). ISBN 3-7643-3087-2.

Rohn, J. (2010). 'A residual existence theorem for linear equations'. *Optimization Letters*, 4 (2), pp. 287–292.

Roos, C. and Terlaky, T. (1999). 'Note on a paper of Broyden'. *Operations Research Letters*, 25 (4), pp. 183–186.

Scowcroft, P. (2006). 'Nonnegative solvability of linear equations in certain ordered rings'. *Transactions of the American Mathematical Society*, 358 (8), pp. 3535–3570.

Tucker, A. W. (1956). 'Dual systems of homogeneous linear relations'. In Kuhn, H. W. and Tucker, A. W. (eds.) *Linear Inequalities and Related Systems.* Princeton: Princeton University Press, pp. 99–156. (Annals of Mathematics Studies; no. 38).

Vohra, R. V. (2006). 'The ubiquitous Farkas lemma'. In Alt, F. B., Fu, M. C. and Golden, B. L. (eds.) *Perspectives in Operations Research.* Boston: Springer, pp. 199–210. (Operations Research/Computer Science Interfaces Series; vol. 36). ISBN 0-387-39934-8.

Development of the traffic accidents in the Moravian-Silesian Region

Blanka Bazsová[1], Lucie Chytilová[2]

Abstract The growing media interest and effective preventive action are helping to reduce road accidents. However, the question is whether this trend will last into the future. The aim of the paper is to analyze and then predict the number of accidents, specifically in the Moravian-Silesian Region. For this reason, it is necessary to identify the variables that affect the number of accidents in the Moravian-Silesian Region. Correlation and regression analysis are used to determine the relationships between variables and create a model, which is then used for the prediction. The results show that the explanatory variables are two - the number of people and the number of cars. The results also confirmed the continuing trend in the development of the number of traffic accidents in the Moravian-Silesian Region for the next three time periods.

Keywords: accidents, population, prediction, regression analysis.

JEL Classification: C32

1 Introduction

The Czech lands are among the pioneers of motoring more than a century of tradition. With the development and increase of motoring, the accident rate also started to increase. It was therefore necessary to start addressing security. In modern history, the end of the 1960s can be considered the beginning of systematic road safety care. As expected, motor vehicle drivers have a dominant position among the perpetrators of traffic accidents in the Czech Republic - three out of four accidents occurred in passenger cars and one in six accidents in truck drivers (CZSO, 2020). The development of accidents in transport between 1989 and 2019 is displayed in Figure 1. The development of accidents in transport between 1989 and 2019 is displayed in Figure 1. The highest number of traffic accidents was reached in the Czech Republic in 1999. After that it decreased, but again this number climbed to 200,000 accidents in 2005. In the following period, the number of accidents decreased again until 2009 and from 2010 this number increases slightly again (see Figure 1).

[1] VSB - Technical University of Ostrava/Faculty of Economics, Department of Systems Engineering, 17. listopadu 15, 709 00 Ostrava, blanka.bazsova@vsb.cz.

[2] VSB - Technical University of Ostrava/Faculty of Economics, Department of Systems Engineering, 17. listopadu 15, 709 00 Ostrava, lucie.chytilova@vsb.cz.

Figure 1 Development of traffic accidents in the Czech Republic between 1989-2019. (CSO, 2020)

In 2011, motor vehicle drivers caused almost 83% of accidents. These accidents are more serious, as evidenced by the fact that their drivers killed 92% of the victims of all accidents and accounted for 86% of the total number of accidents (CSO, 2020). The development of the injured and killed people in the Czech Republic between 1989-2019 is displayed in Figure 2. While the number of people injured is around 250,000, the number of people killed is decreasing. Traffic accidents are classified according to many aspects - accidents by type and location of accident, due to excessive speed, etc.

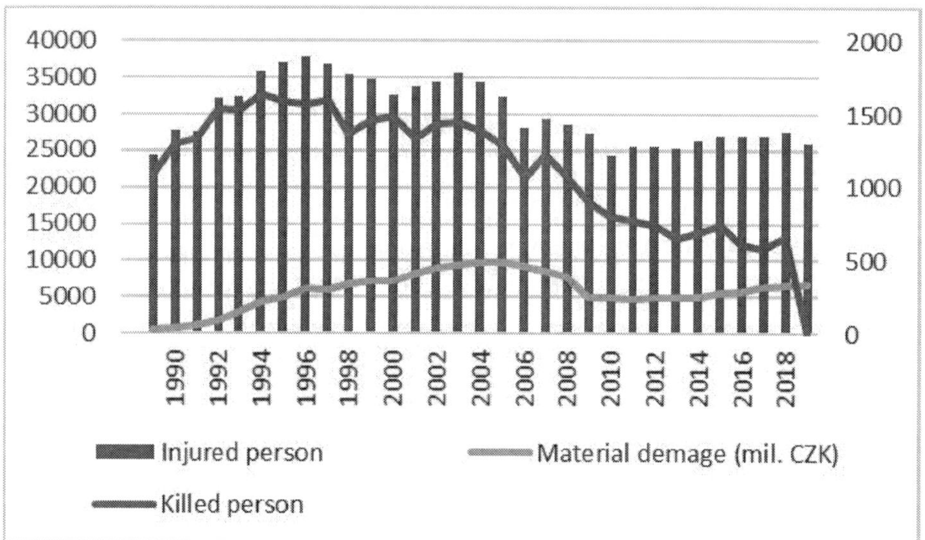

Figure 2 Development of injured people in the Czech Republic between 1990-2018. (CSO, 2020)

One of the disadvantages of assessing road safety on the basis of traffic accident statistics is the fact that accidents that have already occurred are being assessed, as state FAST, VSB-TU Ostrava (2009). Their project analysis the traffic accidents on specific roads and their models predicting the number of accidents in the most congested places. They use the Smeed's model of the probable number of people killed or other models for predicting the number of accidents. The safety factor method is one of the simpler methods of assessing road safety. It is based on the basic assumption that the main characteristic of a vehicle driving mode is its speed.

Another method is the aggregate accident coefficient method can be used to define potential accident sites or locations on a given section of road. The principle of the method consists in determining the coefficient of the total accident by the product of individual partial coefficients, which express the effects of traffic intensity, speed or geometric arrangement of the road. The values of partial coefficients represent the ratio between the total number of traffic accidents on the assessed road section and the average number of accidents on the so-called comparison section (Fakulta strojní, VSB-TU Ostrava, 2009). Ghassedi (2021) provided the prediction and analysis by using of the Severity and Number of Suburban Accidents. He used the logit model, factor analysis and machine learning in the developed countries. Xie et al. (2021) proposed the self-trajectory model and an improved trajectory prediction framework, which could significantly enhance traffic safety in transportation systems. By the prediction they used the two-step clustering method. Nejedlova (2016) investigated the weather, travel accidents and the level of economic damage in the Czech Republic for the prediction by using the neural network.

Authors of this paper follows the aim to predict the number of accidents in the smaller unit – Moravian-Silesian Region by using regression analysis and in another way using basic known information. The research question is what variables influence the number of accidents in Moravian-Silesian region and what is their relationship. The relationship will be examined by correlation matrix and after the confirmation of the right assumptions will be involved in the regression model, which shows the development of the accidents.

2 Data

As already mentioned, the authors aimed to make a model for the number of accidents based on data that is easy to obtain and does not require special projects. The authors included among the variables that could be used mean population, GDP, population, employment, average wage or number of vehicles.

Thus, accident numbers (*NUA*) were identified as the explanatory analysis. And after a thorough analysis and analysis of the correlation matrix, only two explanatory variables were identified as statistically significant and usable for the analysis, more precisely:

- number of people (mean population - *NUP*);
- number of cars (*NUC*).

As the analysis is done in time, the time series are used. Collected time series were analyzed using IBM SPSS Statistics. Data analyses included descriptive statistics, correlation analysis, regression analysis and analysis of variance (ANOVA). The number of people and number of cars is decreasing in the period 1999 – 2019 (see Figure 3).

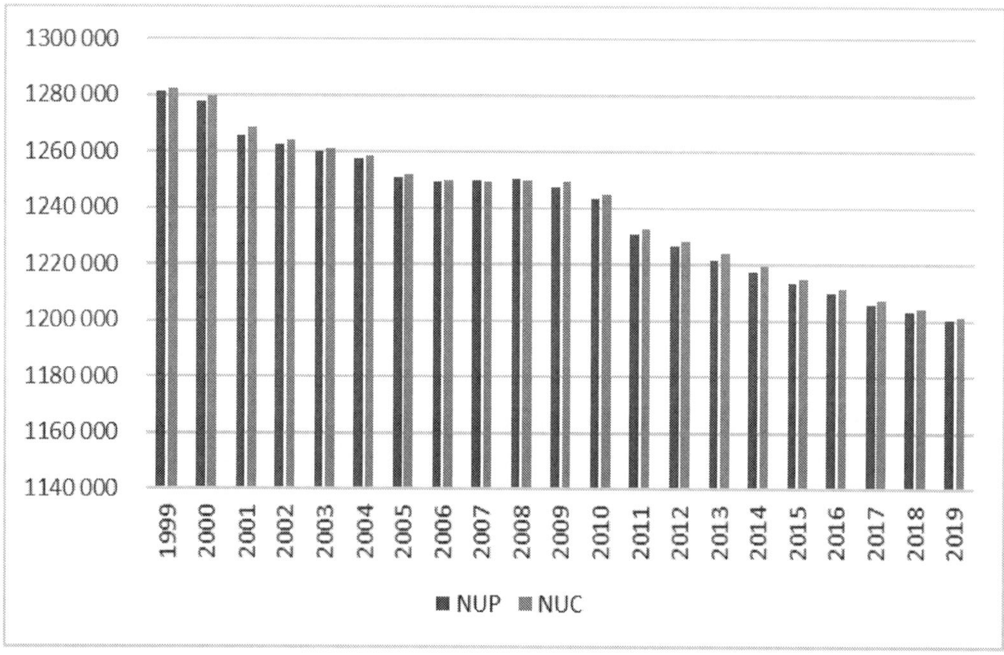

Figure 3 Development of people and cars in the Moravian-Silesian region during the period 1999-2019. (CSO, 2020)

Descriptive statistics of all data are seen in Table 1. It is seen that there are no missing values and the analysis is done for 21 observations (years – 1999-2019). Table 1 shows also mean values, standard deviation, minimum and maximum values.

	NUP	NUC	NUA
#	21	21	21
Mean Value	$1.239 \cdot 10^6$	$1.241 \cdot 10^6$	13689
Std. Deviation	24810	24752	5362
Minimum	$1.201 \cdot 10^6$	$1.201 \cdot 10^6$	7902
Maximum	$1.281 \cdot 10^6$	$1.283 \cdot 10^6$	21432

Table 1 Descriptive Statistics. (own calculation)

3 A Brief review of the regression analysis

The regression analysis is a statistical tool for the investigation of relationships between variables. The usual goals of regression are to predict and control. Regression analysis gives an information about relationship between the chosen dependent variable (denoted as Y) by filling in values for the independent variables (X) in an equation estimated from data. Regression analysis also offers a measure of the probable accuracy of the predictions. The use of regression analysis for control implies that it could be manipulated with one or more independent variables with the aim of changing the value of the dependent variable.

Multiple regression analysis is based on the principle of a classical linear equation, which has the form (Kuhn and Johnson, 2013):

$$Y_t = \beta_0 + \beta_1 X_{1,t} \dots \beta_k X_{k,t} + \mu_t, \qquad (1)$$

where Y_t ... dependent variable (predicate), $X_{i,t}$ ... independent variables (predictors), β_i ... regression coefficients of independent variables (β_0 is a constant) and μ_t ... expresses the error of the equation, model, noise, measurement error, or the sum of the factors not included.

The dependent and independent variables may be transformed during the regression analysis (logarithm, differentiate, etc.). Regression coefficient estimates indicating the expected marginal impact of a unit change in each independent variable of her or another independent variable are at average levels.

The regression analysis has the following assumptions for the equation (1). The assumptions that complete this multiple regression model are following:

1) the independent variables $X_1, X_2, \dots, X_k$ are non-stochastic;
2) the random errors are normally distributed, i.e., $\mu_t \sim N(0; \sigma^2)$, that is the normality of residues;
3) the mean of random errors μ_t is zero, i.e. $E(\mu_t) = 0$;
4) the variance of random errors μ_t is constant, i.e. $Var(\mu_t) = \sigma^2$, that is the homoscedasticity;
5) the random errors μ_t are uncorrelated, i.e. $Cov(\mu_i; \mu_j) = 0$ for $i \neq j$, that means that model is not autocorrelated;
6) independent variables $X_1, X_2, \dots, X_k$ are collinear, i.e. there is no multicollinearity.

4 Results

Formulation of the first stochastic regression model according to the above-mentioned topic is as follows:

$$NUA_t = \beta_0 + \beta_1 NUP_t + \beta_2 NUC_t + \mu_t. \qquad (2)$$

The secondary aims of the analysis are the relationships between the dependent variable *NUA* and each independent variable (*NUP* and *NUC*) as it is seen in equation (2). These relationships (partial hypothesis) may be as follows:

- $NUA_t = f(NUP_t)^+$ so the regression coefficients is $\beta_1 > 0$,
- $NUA_t = f(NUC_t)^+$ so the regression coefficients is $\beta_2 > 0$,

where + sign means the positive dependency.

Due to the fact that in the model (2) has a problem with correlation and stationarity, there had been done a transformation by time difference (annual change) and shift of dependent variables by the cross-transformation. The second model is defined as follows:

$$dNUA_t = \beta_0 + \beta_1\ dNUP_{t-2} + \beta_2\ dNUC_{t+3} + \mu_t, \qquad (3)$$

where these transformations and displacements can be generally interpreted: $dNUP_{t-2}$ means the predicted variable population shifted backwards by 2 years, $dNUC_{t+3}$ predicted variable number of cars with a shift of 3 years and $dNUA_t$ express predicted number of accidents in Moravia-Silesian region.

The estimated model is as follows:

$$dNUA_t = -1542.93 - 0.125\ dNUP_{t-2} + 0.053_2\ dNUC_{t+3} + \mu_t, \qquad (4)$$

where again a discrepancy with secondary analyzes can be seen - this can be caused by other influences, such as commuting to work, etc. However, this model has stationary time series, there is an analogy between correlation analysis and regression coefficients. Model statistically specified at the 5% level of significance. The model also meets all the assumptions of regression analysis at the 5% level of significance, only the assumption of normalization is not met due to the small number of measurements. The model is 45% correctly specified. The model as a whole is therefore suitable for prediction. The prediction is seen in Figure 4.

From Figure 4 it can be seen that this model promises that the number of accidents has more or less stabilized at a constant value. This corresponds to the trend today - more cars are not bought at the moment, because there is not much money in the Moravian-Silesian Region, there are new regulations regarding environmental standards which keep the number of cars stable, etc. However, it is true that this analysis may be skewed by the ongoing COVID-19 pandemic. People traveled and therefore crashed less.

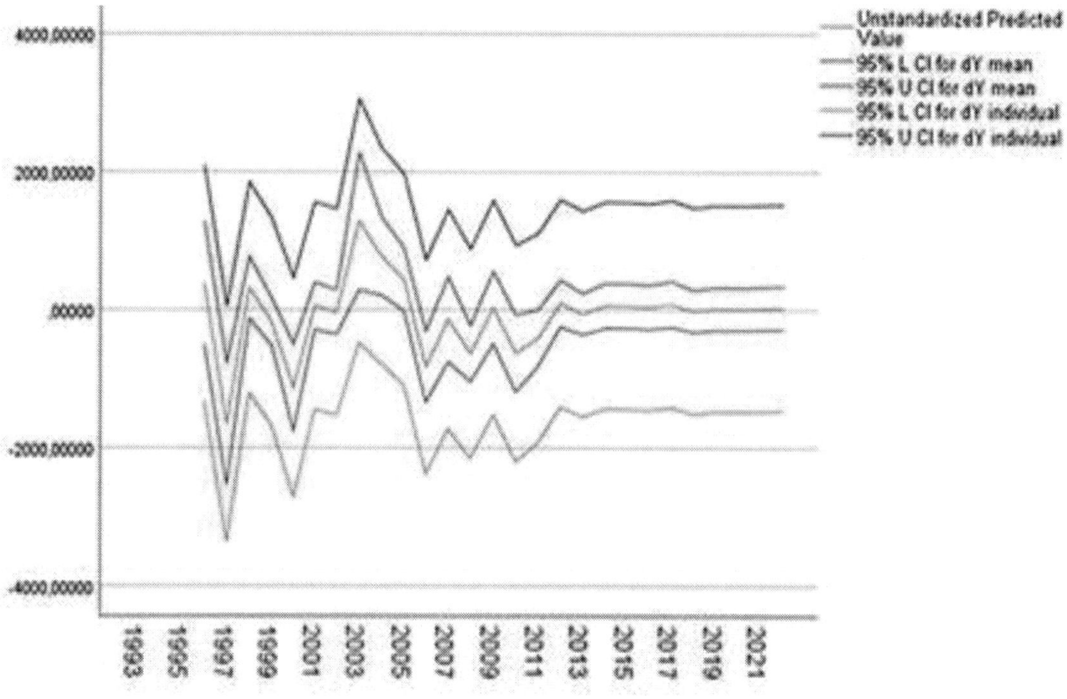

Figure 4 Prediction of the mean number of accidents. (Own processing)

5 Conclusion

The proposed stochastic regression model of the number of accidents in the Moravian-Silesian region confirmed the possibility how to another way express the safety in this region. There were identified variables which influence the number of accidents in the Moravian-Silesian Region, the number of people, and the number of cars. The prediction was provided by the modified variables - delayed number of people in the Moravian-Silesian region and delayed number of cars. The prediction provided in Figure 4 showed that the predicted mean number of accidents moves around its means value. It is explained with 45 % probability. For further research and development of this model, it would be useful to specify and analyze the socio-demographic factors in Moravian-Silesian region, not only their development, but also the mutual causality of these relationships. The authors further study these factors in more detail and create a more comprehensive model that would consider the above-mentioned facts.

Acknowledgements

This paper was supported within SGS Project 51/2021 „Complex use of quantitative methods in economic disciplines“.

References

Czech Statistical Office (2020). *Statistical yearbook of the Moravsko-slezský region,* [On-line]. Available at: https://www.czso.cz/documents/10180/121739370/33010020.pdf/895e710c-bf00-4472-b64e-4e595ebb077c?version=1.1.

Fakulta strojní, VSB-TU Ostrava (2009). *Dopravní nehodovost,* [On-line]. Available at: http://projekt150.ha-vel.cz/node/98.

Ghasedi (2021) Prediction and Analysis of the Severity and Number of Suburban Accidents Using Logit Model, Factor Analysis and Machine Learning: A case study in a developing country. *SN APPLIED SCIENCES* 3(1).

Kuhn, M. and Johnson, K. (2013). *Applied predictive modelling*. New York: Springer.

Nejedlova, D. (2016). Prediction of Daily Traffic Accident Counts and Related Economic Damage in the Czech Republic. *Proceedings of the 34th International Conference Mathematical Methods in Economics (MME)*, 2016, pp. 606-611.

Xie, B. et al. (2021). Self-adaptive trajectory prediction for improving traffic safety in cloud-edge based transportation systems. *Journal of Cloud Computing-Advances Systems and Applications*, 10(1).

Decision Support Systems and Their Influence on Decision Choices and Results

Petra Bláhová[1], Michal Škoda[2]

Abstract. It is hard to imagine a main industry where decision support systems would not play an important role, especially with regards to the rapid digitalization and development of information technologies. This article focuses on analysis and quantification of decision support systems (DSS) effects on investment decision-making. A questionnaire survey research method was used to collect data. Target population of the research were experienced managers, mostly with 10 – 20 years of experience, from tactical or strategic management level, large enterprises and from various industries and functional departments. For purposes of the study, the sample was divided into two groups, where only the first group had access to the decision support system (DSS) output to support their investment decision. Major findings of this research include that the usage of the DSS during the decision-making process leads to a different selection of the investment portfolio, increases a level of certainty of a decision-maker and decision-makers rely on the information provided in DSS output.

Keywords: Decision Support Systems, decision-making, survey, investment, management.

JEL Classification: C83, D81, D83

1 Introduction

The modern economy is creating a competitive environment which leads to more and more pressure on organizations. Due to this pressure the organizations are seeking new possibilities how to gain a competitive advantage and are forced to make strategic decisions in highly competitive environment, with instantly changing information and increasing amount of information. In the area of strategic management, quality decisions are impossible without effective information and analytical support. Strategic management decisions are complex purposeful activities and the effectiveness of performing this complex task greatly depends on decision-making methods which improvement is depending on integrated automation and informatization (Alieinykov et al., 2019).

With appropriate and well-designed and high-performance decision support, the net result of the interactions should improve decision quality (Phillips-Wren, Power and Mora, 2019). Quality and correctness of information are a key aspect of DSS. Quality of the data are important aspect of making quality decisions. If data are poor quality, decisions are likely to be unsound (Karkouch et al., 2016).

Most recently increase of mobile devices usage created new challenges for DSS development, included in the recent research work (Gao, 2013). Trends include the increasing impact of social media and mobile computing on DSS research, as well as the knowledge management DSS (Hosack *et al.*, 2012). There is wide reported implementation of DSS outside

[1] Czech University of Life Sciences Prague, Department of Systems Engineering, Prague, Czech Republic, blahovap@pef.czu.cz
[2] Czech University of Life Sciences Prague, Department of Systems Engineering, Prague, Czech Republic, mskoda@pef.czu.cz

of business corporations in medical and environmental area, for example in landscape and environmental management (Zasada et al., 2017), or in strategic flood risk management (van der Most, Asselman and Slager, 2018).

Specifically, in investment DSS, decision variable could be a set of presented investment alternatives and amounts, together with duration of each possible investment and starting time of the investment. The model parameters could be the inflation rate, and the competition. The result variables could be total profit and risk (Ponis and Christou, 2013). Experiments show that the evaluation indexes of prediction model are mainly used to judge the quality of investment of commercial enterprises. Based on this deep learning models, various index data of enterprises are analyzed, which can assist investors in decision-making (Lei, 2020).

Research methods in the area of DSS include building an experimental DSS system with interactions of participants in multiple and repeated rounds of decisions with measuring a task motivation and tracking of unsafe (Chan et al., 2017) and experimental design of DSS that study how participants revise their initial decision (Burkart, Robert and Huber, 2020).

The main goal of this study is to explore the impact of DSS information output during decision-making process of two groups of respondents, where one group will have the access to the DSS outputs, and the other group will be left without them. Decision problem has been constructed so that the results can be measured and compared. The target respondents are experienced managers from various organizations as managers need to master DSS software products relevant to their jobs and in some situations, managers need to be able to develop small-scale DSS applications (Power, 2005).

The structure of the paper is as follows: the second chapter describes the used materials and methods including description of DSS output and structure of survey questionnaire, third chapter provides results of the research, fourth chapter presents discussion and is followed by conclusions in chapter five.

2 Material and Method

A survey including a decision situation for managers from various business backgrounds and sizes was conducted. A decision problem, on which the evaluation of influence of DSS outputs will be done, was defined as an investor's portfolio decision.

Portfolio consisted of five investment options. The goal for the respondents was to maximize profit by dividing the amount of $100 000 between the individual assets of the portfolio. The respondents were divided into two groups where first group was instructed to make decision without any information provided (Group A) and second group received a relevant information in a form of a DSS output to support their decision (Group B). Czech managers across the areas of human endeavor were selected as the respondents. The requirement for the managers was to have at least two years of experience in management without extensive experience in investment. A questionnaire survey was chosen as the research method. Surveys are designed to provide a picture of how things are at a specific time. There is no possibility for respondents to control conditions or manipulate variables (Kelley et al., 2003).

The survey was divided into three parts where first part was identical for both groups, second part including decision about investment portfolio was prepared with specific instructions and information for each group and third part examined mainly level of decision certainty and questions regarding a completeness of information.

Specifically, first part of the survey examined relevant characteristics of participants: gender, years of experience in managerial role, level of management, functional department, industry, and size of an organization. It was important to have diversified respondents from management pool since each industry and functional department typically require specific decisions.

In the second part, both groups were asked to invest $100 000 into 5 investment options: silver, crude oil, cocoa, Apple Inc. stocks and Boeing company stocks with the goal to maximize profit over a given period from 1st of December 2020 to 31st of March 2021. The specific instructions and information were defined as follows: Respondents belonging to Group A were not provided with any information to support their decision. Respondents belonging to Group B was provided with information in a form of DSS output designed to support their investment decisions as much as possible.

In the third part, the semantic differential scale question was used to rate respondents' certainty with the decision on the scale from one to ten where ten meant absolutely certain. Lastly a completeness of information was examined, where Group A was asked to select or fill in one or more information types they would like to have in order to make better decision and Group B was asked if provided DSS output included sufficient and complete information.

The abbreviated version of the additional information provided to Group B in the form of a possible DSS output can be seen in the Table 1. Actual price of investment items was as of Nov 30, 2020. All responses were gathered in a short time period from Dec 1st to Dec5th 2020 to make sure possible stock market changes do not influence decision-makers.

Invest Option	**Current Unit Price**	**Summary of DSS output**	**Estimated Price Change**
Silver	$22.59	Metal Focus analyst expects $30 at the end of 2021, but warns before short-term volatility due to increased unemployment. Short-term the commodity can reach $28 at Q4 2020.	24%
		JP Morgan predicts decreasing trend ending 1Q 2021 $20.17.	-11%
Cocoa	$2 739.00	Walletinvestor.com expects price increase to $2800 per tun at the end of 2021, which indicates price stagnation.	0% 10%
Oil	$45,34	Bank of America expects stagnation at $45 per barrel at the end of the year 2020.	0%
		Analysts agree that increasing trend is expected in 2nd half of the year 2021. Alexander Dyukov, CEO Gazprom Neft, believes the price will reach pre-pandemic level $50 per barrel during 2nd half of 2021	10%
Boeing	$210,71	November increased by 45,9% due to granted license for Boeing 737 MAX. If the share price returns to pre-pandemic level to $250, the potential evaluation is 19%.	19%

Apple Inc.	$119,05	Last week of November, Apple was top performer of Dow Jones index and continues to increase thanks to message from Wall Street about deal between Amazon and Apple. Reported EPS 1Q, 2Q a 3Q exceeded expectations of analysts by 9,83%, 13,29% a 25,63% , revenues increased by 5,46% and profit by 21,23%. Analysts middle estimation is $133 per share.	12%

Table 1 Information provided to Group B in a form of DSS output

3 Results

A total of 14 respondents, who met the specified requirements, completed the survey. The first part of the survey focused on relevant characteristics of participants in terms of their managerial role, level and experience. The detailed answers can be seen in Table 2. Main results show that 71% of respondents have more than 6 years of experience in managerial role and 57 % of them is in the range of 11-20 years of experience. As for management level 64% of respondents stated tactical or strategic level and the majority of respondents work in the large organization. With exception of gender, similar distribution of respondent's characteristics applies for both groups.

Characteristics	Value	Group A		Group B		Total	
		n	%	n	%	n	%
Gender	Female	5	71%	1	14%	6	43%
	Male	2	29%	6	86%	8	57%
Years of experience	<2	0	0%	0	0%	0	0%
	2-5	2	29%	2	29%	4	29%
	6-10	1	14%	1	14%	2	14%
	11-15	2	29%	1	14%	3	21%
	16-20	2	29%	3	43%	5	36%
	>20	0	0%	0	0%	0	0%
Level of management	Operative	3	43%	2	29%	5	36%
	Tactical	2	29%	4	57%	6	43%
	Strategic	2	29%	1	14%	3	21%
Size of organization	Small	1	14%	1	14%	2	14%
	Medium	1	14%	2	29%	3	21%
	Large	5	71%	4	57%	9	64%

Table 2 Managerial Scope and Experience and Gender

Company industry and organization functional department was examined to obtain information about diversity of research sample of respondents. As outlined in Table 3, all functional departments and large spectrum of company industries were covered and there is no single industry or functional department with majority.

Characteristics	Value	Group A		Group B		Total	
		n	%	n	%	n	%
Function/Department	Finance	1	14%	1	14%	2	14%
	HR	1	14%	0	0%	1	7%
	Marketing	1	14%	0	0%	1	7%
	IT	2	29%	0	0%	2	14%
	Production	0	0%	3	43%	3	21%
	Sales	1	14%	1	14%	2	14%
	Management	1	14%	2	29%	3	21%
Industry	Banking and finance	1	14%	2	29%	3	21%

IT and communication	2	29%	1	14%	3	21%
Construction	1	14%	1	14%	2	14%
Production	0	0%	1	14%	1	7%
Food and accommodation	1	14%	1	14%	2	14%
Logistics and transport	0	0%	1	14%	1	7%
Media and culture	2	29%	0	0%	2	14%

Table 3 Functional Department and Industry Distribution

The investment decision about portfolio in $ and portfolio share of each group is stated in Figure 1. It shows that Group A invested more into Silver, Oil and Cocoa as total portfolio share 55% than Group B 27%. Group B invested 73% of their portfolio into Boeing and Apple.

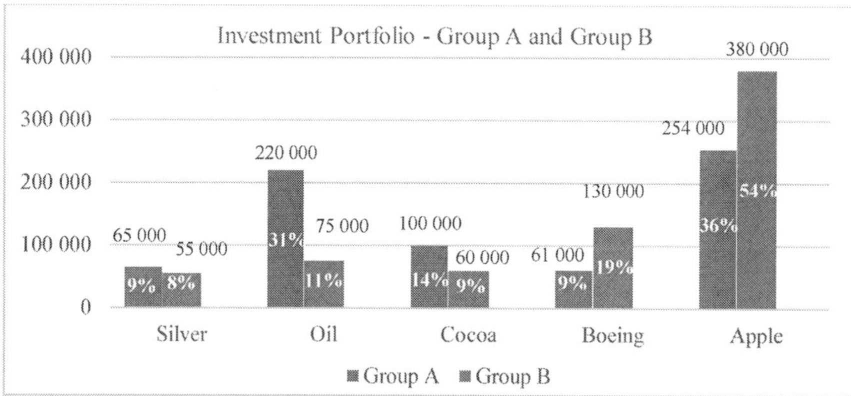

Figure 1 Investment Portfolio Chart – Group A and Group B

In the third part of the survey the evaluation of the level of certainty with decision, past investment existence and completeness of the DSS information output provided following results. As outlined in Figure 2, level of certainty of each group is distributed towards opposite side of the spectrum. Members of Group A tend to be less certain with their decision. Contrariwise, members of Group B provided with DSS output tend to be more certain with their decision. In Group A, only one person indicated high level of certainty with the decision, 9 on the scale from 1-10. On the contrary, 86% of members of Group B saw their level of certainty on the upper half of the scale.

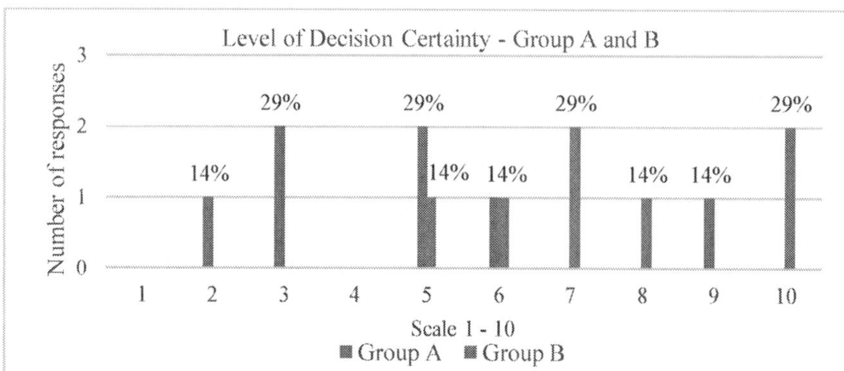

Figure 2 Level of certainty with decisions of respondents

Evaluation of completeness of provided information showed that in Group B 86 % of respondents confirmed that provided information were complete and sufficient for them. The information that would respondents in Group A need to support their decision were evaluated based on multiple check-box question with possibility to fill in the question. Listed options and responses are showed in Table 4.

Type of Information	Frequency	
Current price of the investment item	3	43 %
Historical price evolution	6	86 %
Future price prediction	5	71 %
Analyst recommendations	4	57 %

Table 4: Information needed by Group A

Portfolio profitability represents interim results as of January 29 as outlined in Table 5. At this stage of the research, both groups gaining profit, while respondents in Group B together gained $33 125 the respondents in Group A managed to gain about $9 796 more.

	Price			Profit		
Portfolio	**Nov 30**	**Jan 29**	**Change**	**Group A**	**Group B**	**Difference**
Silver	$29,42	$26,91	-9%	-$5 533	-$4 681	$851
Oil	$45,34	$52,20	15%	$33 286	$11 348	-$21 939
Cocoa	$2 739,00	$2 531,00	-8%	-$7 594	-$4 556	$3 038
Boeing	$210,71	$194,19	-8%	-$4 782	-$10 192	-$5 410
Apple	$119,05	$131,96	11%	$27 544	$41 208	$13 664
				$42 921	$33 125	-$9 796

Table 5 Portfolio profitability comparison

4 Discussion

The findings show valuable information about decision-making process where decision-makers have and have not had access to the data (the DSS outputs). Based on our research sample, assumptions can be made that having a DSS output is influencing decision of respondents about investment portfolio. Survey questionnaire was chosen as a research method as it is easy to use, unexpensive and enables instant distribution to participants (Kelley et al., 2003). Additionally, a non-contact form of research was preferred with regard to the restrictions due to the coronavirus crisis.

This research could provide more valuable results if a sample of respondents would be larger. It would allow to identify patterns of decisions in each group and between groups more reliably. As Kelley et al. (2003) confirm, larger samples give a better estimate of the target population, but it can be difficult to obtain an adequate number of responses. Further validation of decision-making questionnaire as described by Sanz de Acedo Lizarraga et al. (2009) shall be performed in order to examine the factors that affect decision making in this research.

Investment decision about investment portfolio and portfolio profit results

Decision about investment portfolio shows significantly different investment decisions between Group A and Group B. Group B, who was using information in a form of DSS output, invested significantly more into Apple Inc. and Boeing company stocks. Group B decision was aligned with the information provided in DSS output, indicating Apple shares to gain 12% profit and Boeing to gain 19% if the prices reach pre-pandemic level, estimated only after Q1, which is after the end of investment period. Boeing information also indicated declining financial results of the company.

So far Group A that was not provided with DSS output gained higher profit than Group B and therefore from this interim result of this research we cannot prove that using DSS in this specific decision problem is having positive effect on the decision results.

Users of DSS in our research made decisions in according to the DSS recommendations and they stated higher level of certainty indicating trusting the information in DSS output. So far, the interim analysis of the DSS output shows, that future price prediction information was overstated for Boeing causing loss, other items did not affect profit significantly. Largest effect on portfolio profitability was driven by Crude Oil investments in Group A. Group A gained almost $22 000 more profit in Crude Oil than Group B which resulted into profit difference $9 796 between groups.

Level of certainty

Provided information in the form of DSS output effected level of certainty of the respondents. Level of certainty, which was examined on a 1 to 10 scale, shows opposite results between the two groups of respondents. Respondents without information stated low level of certainty; selecting lower half of the scale, and respondents with information in a form of DSS output stated high level of certainty with their decision; selecting only upper half of the scale. It can therefore be assumed that the availability of relevant information plays a crucial role in relation to the level of certainty of the respondents.

It would be appropriate to make a next research in the area of DSS information trust and acceptance by respondents, on similar decision situations. Measuring trust into provided information where also confidence was measured by determining the difference between the prediction of the prediction model and the prediction of the participant (Burkart, Robert and Huber, 2020) was researched.

Completeness and quality of the information

Completeness and quality of provided information in a form of DSS output was examined. Group A indicated that they would need exactly the same information type as were provided to Group B and Group B made their investment choices in accordance to information provided in DSS output. This leads us to confirmation that our information in a form of potential DSS output was constructed correctly and supported decision of respondents in Group B.

5 Conclusion

The research suggests decision support systems usage is impacting the decision-making process and the decision results. Analyzing the impact of DSS output on the decision results was proposed in order to provide quantification of such impact, in this case by comparing two groups (group A and B) of respondents where only Group B had access to information in a form of DSS output. Investment portfolio choices were different between the groups, out of five investment options (Silver, Cocoa, Crude Oil, Boeing, Apple), Respondents of Group A invested more into Silver, Cocoa and Crude Oil; 55% of their total portfolio and respondents of Group B invested more into Apple and Boeing; 73% of total portfolio. Decisions of respondents in the Group B were aligned with the provided information in DSS output,Respondents in Group B also stated higher level of certainty with their decisions; on average 7,6 on the scale 1-10 compared to respondents in Group A with 4,7. In the next research it is planned to expand the sample of participants and focus on non-investment scenarios in order to avoid possible problems with market volatility.

Acknowledgements

The authors are grateful for the support provided by the University of Life Sciences Prague and for the valuable comments and suggestion from the respected reviewers.

References

Alieinykov, I. et al. (2019) 'Development of a method of fuzzy evaluation of information and analytical support of strategic management', Eastern-European Journal of Enterprise Technologies, 6(2–102), pp. 16–27. doi: 10.15587/1729-4061.2019.184394.

Arnott, D. and Gao, S. (2019) 'Behavioral economics for decision support systems researchers', Decision Support Systems, 122(May). doi: 10.1016/j.dss.2019.05.003.

Arnott, D. and Pervan, G. (2005) 'A critical analysis of decision support systems research', Journal of Information Technology. doi: 10.1057/palgrave.jit.2000035.

Burkart, N., Robert, S. and Huber, M. F. (2020) 'Are you sure? Prediction revision in automated decision-making', Expert Systems, (April 2020), pp. 1–19. doi: 10.1111/exsy.12577.

Chan, S. H. et al. (2017) 'Decision support system (DSS) use and decision performance: DSS motivation and its antecedents', Information and Management, 54(7), pp. 934–947. doi: 10.1016/j.im.2017.01.006.

Gao, S. (2013) 'Mobile decision support systems research: A literature analysis', Journal of Decision Systems, 22(1), pp. 10–27. doi: 10.1080/12460125.2012.760268.

Hosack, B. et al. (2012) 'A look toward the future: Decision support systems research is alive and well', Journal of the Association for Information Systems. doi: 10.17705/1jais.00297.

Karkouch, A. et al. (2016) 'Data quality in internet of things: A state-of-the-art survey', Journal of Network and Computer Applications, 73, pp. 57–81. doi: 10.1016/j.jnca.2016.08.002.

Kelley, K. et al. (2003) 'Good practice in the conduct and reporting of survey research', International Journal for Quality in Health Care, 15(3), pp. 261–266. doi: 10.1093/intqhc/mzg031.

Lei, Z. (2020) 'Research and analysis of deep learning algorithms for investment decision support model in electronic commerce', Electronic Commerce Research, 20(2), pp. 275–295. doi: 10.1007/s10660-019-09389-w.

van der Most, H., Asselman, N. and Slager, K. (2018) 'Experiences in developing and applying decision support systems for strategic flood risk management', International Journal of River Basin Management, 16(3), pp. 371–378. doi: 10.1080/15715124.2017.1411925.

Phillips-Wren, G., Power, D. J. and Mora, M. (2019) 'Cognitive bias, decision styles, and risk attitudes in decision making and DSS', Journal of Decision Systems, 28(2), pp. 63–66. doi: 10.1080/12460125.2019.1646509.

Ponis, S. T. and Christou, I. T. (2013) 'Competitive intelligence for SMEs: A web-based decision support system', International Journal of Business Information Systems, 12(3), pp. 243–258. doi: 10.1504/IJBIS.2013.052449.

Power, D. J. (2002). Decision support systems: Concepts and resources for managers. Westport CT: Quorum Books.

Power, D. J. (2005). Decision support systems: frequently asked questions. Lincoln, NE: iUniverse, Inc.

Sanz de Acedo Lizarraga, M. L. et al. (2009) 'Development and validation of a decision-making questionnaire', British Journal of Guidance and Counselling, 37(3), pp. 357–373. doi: 10.1080/03069880902956959.

Zasada, I. et al. (2017) 'What do we know about decision support systems for landscape and environmental management? A review and expert survey within EU research projects', *Environmental Modelling and Software,* 98, pp. 63–74. doi: 10.1016/j.envsoft.2017.09.012.

Evaluation of the impact of the COVID-19 pandemic on the management strategy of innovative SME´s enterprises in the Czech Republic and Poland

Katarzyna Czerná[1], Hana Štverková [2]

Abstract. Through a dynamic business environment, innovations are frequently transforming into a crucial determinant in improving and creating competitive advantage and the survival of an enterprise on the market. In times of pandemic, this trend is becoming increasingly apparent as various enterprises, especially SMEs, have been forced to modify the business model to survive. This paper aims to evaluate the impact of the COVID 19 pandemic on the strategic management of innovation in SMEs in Poland and the Czech Republic, as two regions similar economically and historically. Through research in SMEs in both countries, the evaluation of the rate of change caused by a pandemic and the main problems in innovative business management were identified. Based on the obtained data, the surveyed companies were divided into four groups according to innovation potential, which will offer a further international comparison.

Keywords: innovation, innovation potential, SMEs, COVID 19.

JEL Classification: M10, O31, O36

1 Introduction

During globalization, innovations are increasingly converting into a fundamental factor in developing and building competitive advantage and the survival of an enterprise on the market, especially today when the pandemic of COVID 19 efficiently slowed down economic development and brought uncertainty to the business environment. Many enterprises, especially SMEs, have been forced to rapidly transform their business model and fight for survival, often through innovation. In these conditions, one of the main challenges facing the enterprise is to develop an appropriate innovation management strategy, together with adaptation of resource management systems related to innovative activities to the requirements of the modern market. SMEs play a crucial role in most countries' national economies to create a robust business environment. These enterprises are essential for the growth of the national economy and cities and whole regions, represent 99 % of all companies in the EU. In this paper, SMEs are viewed in EU Recommendation 2003/361; see Table 1.

Company category	Staff	Turnover	or	Balance Sheet Total
Medium-sized	<250	≤ € 50 m		≤ € 43 m
Small	< 50	≤ € 10 m		≤ € 10 m

Table 1 Typology of SMEs [EU Recommendation 2003/361]

They co-create a viable market ecosystem and improve market dynamism. This trend is also evident in Poland and the Czech Republic, neighboring countries, which are characterized by similar post-communist developments, especially in business. Companies, including SMEs, are

[1] Department of Business Administration, VŠB – TU Ostrava, Sokolská tř. 33, 70200, Czech Republic, katarzyna.czerna@vsb.cz.
[2] Department of Business Administration, VŠB – TU Ostrava, Sokolská tř. 33, 70200, Czech Republic, hana.stverkova@vsb.cz.

currently handling the difficulties linked with the continuing COVID-19 pandemic, which has changed all countries' markets. Managers and owners cannot predict its consequences with confidence. Due to their flexibility, SMEs could respond to the crisis development caused by COVID 19 and transform their business into working concepts. Before the crisis has occurred, previously Freeman (1997) understood that innovative SMEs' effectiveness might be more prominent than the large ones, as small entities can produce more innovations per unit of R&D expenditure. Therefore, this paper aims to evaluate the coronavirus pandemic's impact on innovation management strategies in small and medium-sized enterprises in both the Czech Republic and Poland. Based on the Oslo manual (2018), an innovative enterprise is understood as an enterprise implement one or more innovations during the observation period. This statement applies equally to enterprises responsible for a given innovation individually and jointly with other entities. Innovative activity may be continued, suspended, completed, or abandoned. These companies were selected from Associations of Innovative Entrepreneurship database in both countries. It builds on previous research on comparing innovative companies' innovation activities in Poland and the Czech Republic, especially innovation management models. However, this time, attention is paid to the changes that have occurred in the strategic management of these companies' innovation activities due to the global pandemic. The secondary objective is to identify and describe a particular survival model that could guide other innovative SMEs in transforming their management strategy. Simultaneously, the surveyed companies will be evaluated in terms of their further innovation potential according to the aggregate indicator and divided into four primary groups: weak potential; medium potential; significant potential, leader based on the level of metrics achieved.

2 Literature review

The theory of innovation is often connected with economic activity development and compared to modernity, while the conceptual frameworks for innovation measuring are acquired primarily from disciplines such as management and economics (Smith, 2006). The management approach to innovation reflects how innovation can improve a company's market position and generate innovative ideas. On the other hand, economic-based approaches explore the circumstances that drive organizations to innovate, encourage and limit innovation, and the macroeconomic effects of innovation on the industry, the market, or the economy. Innovation in a general understanding is defined as any change consisting of the acquisition of obtained knowledge. However, in a narrow sense, as Schumpeter (1987) described, it defines a change in production methods and products (possibly in the organization of the production process) based on new or previously used knowledge. Innovation theories such as innovation systems theory (Lundvall, Chaminade and Haneef, 2018; Borrás, 2004; OECD, 2018) indicate that innovation is not a straight, constant process, but involves many interactions and feedback in the process of creating and using knowledge.

Moreover, innovation is based on a learning process that uses many sources and requires constant problem-solving. The evaluation of the theory of innovation registers four dimensions of innovation that can become a source of recommendations in measurement: knowledge, novelty value, implementation, and value creation. According to Valenta (2001), nine innovation codes are divided into rationalization, qualitative innovation, and technological breakthrough. The OECD definition (2018) declaims the introduction of a new or significantly improved product and the use of a new or significantly improved process in the production company's internal environment. This theory completed Tidd and Bessant (2016) with need develop them into practical use through the designed and implemented innovation management strategy. Breunig and Skjølsvik (2020), talked about a detailed classification of innovative strategies, which are classified according to goals, innovation factors, implementing innovations, references to ecological problems, and ways of influencing the market. Generally, an appropriate innovation strategy dictates reactions to the questions about value for customers, value for a company, what resources each type of innovation needs. To shape their innovation strategies, companies need to absorb new information from the environment and use it internally (Borowski, 2021). It also includes an innovative culture, which the authors describe as creating a friendly and motivating environment (outside and inside the company) for "blowing innovative ideas." The innovation culture then contains many elements, such as knowledge, handling know-how, motivating employees, digitization.

In order to forecast the development of innovation and at the same time adapt the innovation management strategy, it is necessary to quantify the innovation potential of the company. Zastempowski (2013) incorporates in the innovation potential of enterprises all their material and immaterial resources and distinguishes the following ten areas: production, personnel, logistics, research and development, organization and administration, quality management, marketing, invisible resources, finance, information, and communication. Roszko-Wójtowicz and Białek (2017) defined innovative potential as a quality of the socio-economic system, characterizing the acceptability (feasibility) and the maximum achievable result of a planned action to change the structural and functional properties of this system.

The COVID-19 pandemic has swung the market environment, and many SMEs were forced to handle the issue of whereby to endure and refresh their activities. Paradoxically, the ongoing pandemic can positively affect SMEs' innovation activities in terms of providing the traction to initiate innovation (Urbaniková et al, 2020). The authors (Kristinae et al, 2020; Priyono et al, 2020) mention the attitude and level of digitization or business strategy focused on continuous innovation as crucial success elements.

3 Methodology and Data

The needed empirical data were obtained through an online questionnaire conducted in 2020 (The companies were contacted during June and July; the answers themselves were obtained from mid-October to the end of November and evaluated in December.), which targeted innovative small and medium-sized enterprises in Poland and the Czech Republic to obtain the results of appropriate comparisons.

The nature of innovation ensured companies' selection from the Associations of Innovative Entrepreneurship database, both on the Czech and Polish sides. A total of 300 companies were contacted, 150 on the Czech and similarly 150 on the Polish side. Two hundred ten companies answered the questions, 105 on the Czech and similarly 105 on the Polish side, resulting in a response rate of 70%. In terms of classification of the research sample, these were mainly manufacturing companies (39% CZ, 52% PL), then software (34% CZ, 31% PL). Only 27% of

CZ and 17% of PL companies of the research sample were service companies. Simultaneously, the surveyed companies are domestically owned (84% CZ, 87% PL). Based on a thorough study of the literature and previous research, the questionnaire contains three essential parts: an identification part (9 questions), pandemic management challenges (12 questions), the potential for innovation management (10 indicators). The first part focused on the classification of the surveyed companies in terms of field of activities and critical aspects of innovation management. The second part contained questions related to changes in the strategy of innovative companies strategy, and these were closed questions from the possibility of multiple choices. In the last part, all constructs were measured through [0, 1] scale, where 1 meant the occurrence of a particular statement in the company, while 0 meant no occurrence. The individual indicators were created not only based on previous research in the field but also concerning the Oslo Manual 2018 while taking into account the sequence of steps in the strategic innovation management process. The importance of indicators was graded based on the determination of weights using the Saaty´s method (Ramík, 1999), where:

$$w_i = \frac{\left[\prod_{j=1}^{k} s_{ij}\right]^{1/k}}{\sum_{i=1}^{k}\left[\prod_{j=1}^{k} s_{ij}\right]^{1/k}}, \; i = 1, \dots, k \qquad (1)$$

It was then calculated aggregate indicator *Potential for innovation management*, the value of which is the sum of the products of factors and individual weights determining the significance of a given factor.

4 Results

The presentation of the results for the needs of this paper will be divided into two essential parts. The first of them describes the pandemic's impact on the innovation management strategy in the monitored companies. The second part focuses on the potential of innovation management.

4.1 Challenges of strategic innovation management in the pandemic period

Although innovations are incorporated into the company's philosophy within the monitored companies, both in Poland and the Czech Republic, most do not have their research and development departments. Of interest is the different approach of both countries to a corporate innovation culture. In the Czech Republic, up to 56% of SMEs innovative enterprises identify it within their corporate philosophy, but only 39% in Poland. Although the digitization of business processes is considered part of the innovation culture, only 48% of companies have talked about existing innovation culture in the Czech Republic. In Poland, on the contrary, up to 57% of SMEs. From the methods of solving innovation problems, the most frequently monitored companies in both countries choose their methods, often unstructured and brainstorming. Only in Poland, the monitored small and medium-sized enterprises (21% of cases) use a comprehensive system for generating and selecting innovative solutions, namely WOIS. These results are shown in Table 1.

Country	Innovation - corporate philosophy	Innovation culture	Digitalization of processes	Unstructured method	Brainstorming	Complex method
CZ	67%	56%	48%	54%	35%	4%
PL	43%	39%	57%	49%	29%	21%

Table 2 Innovation background

Before the pandemic onset, Czech small and medium-sized companies operated mainly on the national market (41%) and the world market (35%). In Poland, innovative SMEs focused on developing their business globally (46%) and national (35%) markets. After the onset of the pandemic in Czech innovative SMEs, attention began to focus on the national market (49%), but there is already an increase in the regional market's importance (30%). In Poland, this trend is more substantial, with up to 46% of innovative SMEs focusing on regional markets after the onset of the pandemic and the national market (44%). Only 10% of the surveyed companies remained on the world market. The issue of detailed market characteristics is also related to this topic. Before COVID 19 in Poland and the Czech Republic, the mass market's predominance was recorded (53% CZ, 48% PL). Czech and Polish SMEs of an innovative nature also focused on a diversified market with different groups of customers with different needs and problems (19% CZ, 29% PL). The Polish SMEs surveyed of an innovative nature showed minimal interest in the multilateral market, which focuses on the two most interconnected customer segments (3%). On the other hand, in the Czech Republic, the least interest was recorded in the niche market (12 %), groups of customers with particular needs. With the onset of the coronavirus pandemic, the Czech companies surveyed began to focus on the mass market (35%) and the diversified market. In addition to the diversified market (45%), the Polish companies surveyed showed interest in developing the niche market (34%). The mass market here accounted for only 19% of monitored companies' portfolio. It was found that the monitored companies did not interrupt innovation activities due to the pandemic. During the crisis, they changed the focus of innovation, focusing on business process innovation (e.g., logistics, distribution, marketing). In the case of crucial partnerships, in the pandemic period, the Czech monitored companies established relations mainly of a buyer-supplier nature to ensure reliable supplies (37%) and made strategic alliances between non-competing entities (26%). In the Polish companies surveyed, the answers pointed not only to strategic alliances (34%) but also to cooperation with the academic environment.

The research areas were also business problems, which most often arose during the pandemic in individual areas of innovative enterprise management. During the monitoring of signals from the environment, the monitored Polish and Czech companies most often face non-existent forecasting of innovations (29% CZ, 32% PL). In the Czech companies, flawed market research (24 %) or missing knowledge from marketing analyzes (18 %) also appear to be a problem. On the other hand, Poland addresses the unavailability of data to map the environment (21 %) and the lack of knowledge from basic and applied research (19 %). The problem in the implementation of ideas is the lack of employees' experience (49 % CZ, 52 % PL) and the long-term nature of implementation (34 % CZ, 28 % PL). During the implementation of production activities, the Czech Republic's monitored companies most often face low-quality input raw materials (38 %), high product costs (23 %). In Poland, the problems are insufficient production workers' qualifications (34 %), growing energy prices (23 %), and a lack of reporting on production activities (19 %). The monitored companies in both countries during the pandemic were forced to face low profitability of sales (54% CZ, 53% PL) and lack of sales profitability (35 %CZ, 29 % PL). In the human resources management, the survey in both countries shows struggling with a shortage of skilled labor (59% CZ, 55% PL). Furthermore, the problems are different: the Czechs face high levels of staff turnover (26 %) and high human resource management costs (18 %), while in Poland they have to overcome obstacles in the form of workers' reluctance to train (25 %) or low staff involvement (creative thinking – 19 %).

4.2 Potential for innovation management

Based on the authors' previous research, and also taking into account the recommendations of the Oslo Manual (2018), a list of 9 indicators has been compiled, the occurrence [1] or absence [0] of which determines the potential for innovation management, while maintaining the sequence within the process of strategic innovation management (from the collection of ideas to the protection of know-how), namely: a systematic evaluation of innovation ideas and setting priorities (1), standardization of innovation activities (2), selection of methods for resource allocation within innovation activities gradually depending on progress (3), management of innovation activities in cooperation with external partners (4), creation of innovation groups in the company (5), integration of external knowledge and other external elements into innovation activity (6), rewarding innovators and results activities before completion unless specific objectives are met (7), temporary involvement of employees from various fields in innovative projects (8), protection of knowledge of assets related to innovation activities (9). The weights of individual indicators were determined using the Saaty´s method: individual indicators' preferences were determined based on interviews (ongoing during January and February) with 70 managers of the surveyed companies (35 PL and 35 CZ). The following elements were found to be most important for the potential of innovation management: rewarding innovators and the results of innovative activities; standardization of different types of innovation activities; creating innovation groups in the company. The scales

	1	2	3	4	5	6	7	8	9	The geometric diameter of lines	w_i
1	1	0,2	1	0,33	0,2	1	0,2	0,33	0,5	0,424	0,037
2	5	1	3	2	1	3	1	2	3	2,012	**0,173**
3	1	0,33	1	0,2	0,33	1	0,17	0,2	0,33	0,397	0,036
4	3	0,5	5	1	0,5	2	0,5	1	2	1,251	0,108
5	5	1	3	2	1	0,33	1	2	3	1,576	**0,152**
6	1	0,33	1	0,5	3	1	0,14	0,2	0,5	0,577	0,08
7	5	1	6	2	1	7	1	2	3	2,387	**0,214**
8	3	0,5	5	1	0,5	5	0,5	1	2	1,385	0,131
9	2	0,33	3	0,5	0,33	2	0,33	0,5	1	0,783	0,07
											1,001

GCI = 0,13

are shown in Figure 1.

Figure 1 The importance of the indicators

Based on the responses of individual monitored companies, these indicators were aggregated into a single indicator of the potential of innovation management, and companies were included in individual groups according to the level of the indicator shown in Table 3.

Indicator level	Group of potential
≤ 0,3	Weak potential
0,31 – 0,6	Slight potential
0,61 – 0,9	Strong potential
>0,9	Leader in potential

Table 3 Groups of potential

The most monitored companies in the Czech Republic belong to the strong potential group, 46%, followed by a group of moderate potential (33 %). The remaining 21% of the companies surveyed are on opposite sides of the spectrum: 10% belong to the group of leaders in terms of potential, but 11% are in the group of weak potential. The situation is different in Poland. The most numerous group are companies belonging to the group of moderate potential (49%), followed by high potential with 28% of the surveyed companies. Only 4% of companies are in the group with the lowest score, and the remaining 19% are among the leaders.

5 Discussion

The research showed that although the Czech Republic and Poland are neighboring countries and are characterized by similar historical and economic developments, there are several differences in innovative SMEs. Although the addressed Polish small and medium-sized enterprises are described as innovative enterprises according to the Oslo Manual, their understanding of innovation is not conceptual and institutionalized. They do not have a defined innovation culture; at the same time, innovation is not included in their corporate philosophy. On the other hand, they apply many methods and practices that typically belong to innovation culture and philosophy, such as the digitization of business processes or methods to select innovative ideas. Czech companies are already learning to work with the conceptualization of innovation strategies. Simultaneously, the results support the opinion that small and medium-sized enterprises (CZ and PL) do not have an excellent financial base, to tighten their research and development departments. Innovations are therefore carried out within existing departments, often by teams of workers from different sections. At the same time small and medium-sized enterprises, regardless of the country surveyed, can respond to times of crisis (this time caused by the COVID 19 pandemic) and thus fight flexibly and effectively to survive. They were able to assess the situation and transform into another market, which guaranteed them either the maintenance of a competitive position on the market or, at the very least, their survival. The establishment of strategic partnerships also showed an effort to apply open innovations, i.e., in cooperation with the external environment. In the Czech Republic, however, there is a tendency to create a reliable logistics chain (which in times of pandemic can mean security of supply of goods to the client). Poland focuses on gaining experience from other non-competing fields but also on cooperation with academic world.

The pandemic slowed down economic development, not only in both countries studied. Therefore, it is not surprising to find that the surveyed SMEs faced low profitability of sales (caused by a change in the market - smaller orders). A certain peculiarity may be the absence of a problem with high indebtedness of companies, so an explanation is offered that innovative companies are healthy; they examine the level of indebtedness and finance innovations from diversified sources. The next step would be to compare the pandemic crisis on innovation in SMEs in all V4 and EU countries. Further research will focus on this comparison, as the lack of data from 2020 from various countries has been limiting at present. However, it can be predicted that SMEs, thanks to adequately set process management, streamlined their performance and strengthened their market position. Businesses that did not innovate got into trouble and had to close down.

6 Conclusions

Innovation in today's turbulent and uncertain crisis caused by the COVID 19 can be seen as a way for the survival of businesses, especially SMEs, which do not have financial and infrastructural support similar to large corporations but are more flexible in responding to possible changes and trends in the markets. This paper aimed to evaluate the impact of the COVID 19 pandemic on the strategic management of innovation in SMEs in Poland and the Czech Republic. It was found that this effect was very significant, as the pandemic caused a change in the focus of the companies surveyed, both in terms of geography and portfolio. At the same time, it was found that the innovative researched enterprises in Poland and the Czech Republic understand the innovation potential; they include several elements of strategic innovation management in their business activities, but not yet in full force. This indicates how innovations are incorporated into the corporate philosophy and, above all, the number of companies in the group with moderate or even weak potential for innovation management. The pandemic crisis caused an increase in innovations in business process management in both monitored countries. Thanks to this crisis period, which led to a reduction in the connection between companies and customers, innovative companies, especially leaders, focused on increasing their innovation potential and gaining more outstanding market share. It is quite clear that even a pandemic crisis can positively affect the competitiveness of small and medium-sized enterprises if the processes are set up correctly, which will enable them to function effectively in times of crisis.

Acknowledgements

Financial support of the Student Grant Competition – project "SP2020/107".

References

Borrás, S, (2004). System of innovation theory and the European Union. *Science and Public Policy,* 31 (6), pp. 425-433).

Borowski, P. F. (2021). Innovation strategy on the example of companies using bamboo. *Journal of Innovation and Entrepreneurship,* 10 (1), pp. 1-17.

Breunig, K. J and Skjølsvik, T. (2020). Understanding the Strategy-Innovation Link in an Era of Disruptions. *Technology Innovation Management Review,* 10 (8), pp. 4-13.

European Commission. Entrepreneurship and Small and medium-sized enterprises (SMEs), [Online]. Available at: https://ec.europa.eu/growth/smes/sme-definition [cited 2020-02-10].
Freeman, Ch. (1997). The Economics of Industrial Innovation, 3rd ed. Cambridge: The MIT Press.
Kristinae, V., Wardana, I., Giantari, I and Rahyuda, A. (2020). The role of powerful business strategy on value innovation capabilities to improve marketing performance during the COVID-19 pandemic. Uncertain Supply Chain Management, 8(4), pp. 675-684.
Lundvall, B. A., Chaminade, C. and Haneef, Sh. (2018). *Advanced Introduction to National Innovation Systems,* Cheltenham: Edward Elgar Publishing.
OECD (2018). Oslo Manual 2018, [Online]. Available at: https://www.oecd.org/sti/oslo-manual-2018-9789264304604-en.htm [cited 2021-02-10].
Priyono, A., Moin, A. and Putri, V.N.A.O. (2020). Identifying Digital Transformation Paths in the Business Model of SMEs during the COVID-19 Pandemic. *Journal of Open Innovation: Technology, Market, and Complexity,* 6(4), pp. 104.
Ramík, J. (1999). *Vicekriteriální rozhodování – analytický hierarchický process.* Karviná: Slezská univerzita.
Roszko-Wójtowicz, E. and Białek, J. (2017). Evaluation of the EU countries´ innovative potential – multivariate approach. *Statistics in Transition New Series,* 18 (1), pp. 167-180.
Schumpeter, J. A. (1987). Theory of Economic Development. The New Palgrave, 1987.
Smith, K. (2006). Measuring innovation, in *The Oxford Handbook of Innovation*, Oxford: University Press.
Tidd, J. and J. Bessant (2016). Managing Innovation: Integrating Technological, Market and Organizational Change. Chichester: Wiley.
Urbaníková, M. et al. (2020). Analysis of Innovation Activities of Slovak Small and Medium-Sized Family Businesses. *Administrative Sciences*, 10(4), pp. 80.
Valenta, F. (2001). Inovace v manažerské praxi. Praha: Velryba.
Zastempowski, M. (2013). Potencjał innowacyjny małych i średnich przedsiębiorstw na tle liderów polskiej gospodarki w świetle badań empirycznych. *Współczesne Zarządzanie,* 2, pp. 68-75).

Information Support for Brownfield Revitalisation Projects and Other Tasks in Environmental Areas

Roman Danel [1], Ivana Čermáková [2], Jakub Chlopecký [3]

Abstract. This paper presents results achieved in the field of information support using information technology to solve projects on brownfield revitalisation, and modelling and visualisation of the landscape. The initial task was to analyse and design a database of brownfields with relevant information for project managers. This was solved as a partial task within the international project COBRAMAN2. The described solution was then combined with the method of landscape modelling and visualisation, using information technology designed by Associate Professor Zdeněk Neustupa - a combination of Computer-aided Design (CAD) and Geographic Information System (GIS) tools with virtual reality capability. The result of many years of research is an original procedure for processing environmental data with the resultant output available for professionals in the field, who may not have knowledge of information and communication technology (IT/ICT) but require information support in their work. An example of the implementation of this procedure is the Czech-Polish project INVARO dealing with mapping the spread of invasive plants.

Keywords: Brownfield, landscape modelling, landscape visualization, COBRAMAN.

JEL Classification: O3, L86

1 Introduction

There are many locations in the world where heavy industry was the basis of economic development. With the retreat of heavy industry, we increasingly encounter the issue of solving the problem of so-called brownfields and projects to revitalise landscapes affected by industrial activity. The utilisation of information technology and technologies for modelling landscapes affected by industrial activity, raw material gathering or mining, is a part of the long-term research activities. In this article, we describe information support for environmental projects, especially in the form of a brownfield database design containing relevant information for project managers of revitalisation.

2 Literature Review and Problem Statement

The Organisation for Economic Co-operation and Development (OECD) defines urban brownfield sites as 'vacant, derelict, underused lots in urban areas, with actual soil contamination or risk of soil contamination'. The Concerted Action on Brownfield and Economic Regeneration Network (CABERNET) defines brownfield sites as 'sites that have been affected by the former uses of the site or surrounding land, are derelict or underused, are

[1] VŠB Technical University of Ostrava, Faculty of Economics, Department of Applied Informatics, Sokolská třída 33, Ostrava, roman.danel@vsb.cz.
[2] VŠB Technical University of Ostrava, Faculty of Economics, Department of Applied Informatics, Sokolská třída 33, Ostrava, ivana.cermakova@vsb.cz.
[3] Cevyko, a.s.., Svornosti 86/2, Havířov, chlopecky@cevyko.cz.

mainly in developed urban areas, require intervention to bring them back to beneficial use and may have real or perceived contamination problems' (CABERNET, 2019).

There is already evidence of a number of brownfield solutions in the form of freely accessible or paid web projects.

For example, brownfield databases managed by the municipalities of Ústí and Labem or Pardubice in the Czech Republic, Thessaloniki in Greece or Stuttgart in Germany exist but they were built upon a different philosophy (Ertel and Bořecký, 2012). The focus on specific regions and the fact that the databases are built in local languages result in them being unusable for the international public. The above-mentioned databases mainly specialise in collecting foundational descriptive information extended with a GIS layer.

The brownfield database created by CzechInvest specifically focuses on areas of commercial use (CZECHINVEST, 2020). Typical representant of this group can be a Pardubice region brownfield website. Pardubice city had the brownfield website, which was permanent and did not change. In these days, Pardubice city has a website informs about actual available brownfields whose can be revitalized to other type of buildings/usage. The website distributes basic info about each brownfield, e. g. area or type of brownfield, position on map, photos and contact on interested person (Brownfieldy Pardubického kraje, 2020).

The problem with many existing brownfield databases is that they were created during a project but not updated after the project ended. As a result, their information value gradually decreases over time. In order for databases to be used and to benefit interested professionals, it is necessary for them to be maintained and continuously updated. The initial design of the brownfield database was created within the international project Manager Coordinating Brownfield Redevelopment Activities (COBRAMAN, European Union project 1CE014P4 – Central Europe Programme co-financed by the European Regional Development Fund) as one of the outputs of the project. The aim of the database solution is to provide information for managers of brownfield revitalisation projects in the form of best practices observed from already implemented projects (Cobraman, 2019).

Paper (Ganser and Williams, 007) describes strategies to reuse of urban brownfield sites in England and Germany with explores their shortcomings and highlights implementation problems. (Rizzo et al., 2015) presents a comprehensive study providing an overview of brownfield regeneration stakeholders' perceptions, concerns, attitudes and information needs from five European countries to develop a system to support the categorisation of the needed information and to support the understanding of which typology of information is the most relevant for specific categories of stakeholders. (Thornton et al, 2007) presents the existing incentives on a European Union level, in Germany, the UK, and France to make brownfield regeneration more attractive but rarely consider their sustainability. The paper discusses the effects and gaps; and makes suggestions for more effective instruments for the promotion of sustainable brownfield regeneration.

The requirements of the design and planning of revitalisation brownfield projects demanded the creation of visualisation of possible solutions, especially the modelling and visualisation of landscapes (Hudeček and Mikoláš, 2014). To satisfy this demand, we used the results of many years of experience with modelling and visualisation of landscapes affected by mining activities, conducted by a team led by Associate Professor Zdenek Neustupa from the Institute of Economics and Control Systems, Faculty of Mining and Geology, VŠB - Technical University of Ostrava (Neustupa, 2006; Neustupa, 2003; Maršolek, Neustapa and Řepka, 2006).

Project managers solving brownfield revitalisation need an overview of all project-related topics and activities, and they need fast and easy access to the relevant data (Kozel and Chuchrová, 2015). The greatest need for information in the process of redevelopment occurs in stages of preparation and planning, when key decisions are undertaken. The appropriate information reduces any associated risks.

3 Methodology

The database structure design was based on the study of existing brownfield databases, data sources, user demand analysis and surveys of potential users. The existing solutions of applications dealing with the evidence of brownfields were also studied.

An Excel form was used for data collection from individual locations during the first phase of building the database. However, inconsistent form filling, additional data insertion by individual users and failure to follow the structure of the form made deployment of automated form processing impossible to execute. Therefore, a web interface, a PHP (PHP is a general-purpose scripting language especially suited to web development) application, using forms for data collection has been created. Not only does the interface force users to follow the form structure, it also enables verification of the input data. The interface also provides the capability to insert figures, photos and other related documents.

In addition to the problem of the variety of data formats, images and miscellaneous information, there was also a significant problem with some brownfield owners and project managers who were reluctant to share their data. Revitalisation projects completed by private companies on private sites can provide know-how, but in some cases the implementers were not willing to disclose the information. This fact resulted in incomplete data collection on some brownfield sites.

After the completion of project COBRAMAN, the database continues to be further developed. Since 2017, it has been supplemented by a section detailing local brownfields in the Moravian-Silesian Region. To create a list of brownfields at individual locations, diploma theses of students from the environmental engineering study programme were successfully employed.

Landscape modeling and visualization used to support the planning of brownfield revitalization projects was established by Associate Professor Zdeněk Neustupa from the Institute of Economics and Control Systems at the VŠB-Technical University of Ostrava. He and his team specialise in landscapes affected by deep mining, where landscapes suffer from significant subsidence, and open-pit mining where a large area is affected. An example of a successful landscape modelling and visualisation project is the visualisation of a brownfield that resulted from brown coal mining in northern Bohemia, and was transformed into an artificial lake, near the town of Most (Neustupa and Stalmachová, 2006).

The following methods were used to solve the results presented in this paper:

- data collection using an Excel form
- data collection using a form in a web application
- analysis - study of documentation, interviews with potential system users, interviews with managers, study of implemented projects
- design of database structures based on the performed analysis (including creation of ERD model)
- the methodology of creating landscape models using ArcGIS and AutoCAD software created by doc. Zdeněk Neustupa

4 Solutions and Results

4.1 Database of Brownfields Created Within Project COBRAMAN

The COBRAMAN brownfield revitalisation projects database has met the following objectives:

- To collect relevant information relating to significant projects on brownfield revitalisation in Central European countries.
- To provide an information bank for the scientific community and offices concerned with brownfield redevelopment.
- To provide study materials for students of the master's course European School for Brownfield Redevelopment at the VŠB-Technical University of Ostrava, in the Czech Republic.
- To provide public access to the descriptions and solutions of brownfield revitalisation projects.
- To make the information accessible to the international scientific community by using English for all data stored in the database (Cobraman, 2019).

The fundamental block of the database is a brownfield card. It contains basic information about the brownfield type, area, topology, location and essential characteristics. Significant information about a revitalisation project is connected with each brownfield card: objectives; budget; deadlines; the most important experience; the owner at the time of the project; the owner of the project after implementation; funding sources; the stages of the project. Additional brownfield information, such as transport accessibility and the condition of infrastructure, is recorded. Data on pollution types and levels are available for each site. The projects are complemented with best practices, lessons learned, specific project tools, pictures of the site, external information sources, illustrations and contact information. This allows the user to read the full details on projects carried out under similar conditions (Cobraman, 2019).

The specific tools used in projects were divided into the following categories: environmental (mainly related to environmental protection and its regeneration and sustainable urban planning); economic and financial (to support financing of the project); management (designed to overcome organisational barriers); legal (mainly the specific regulations related to the project); society (a group of tools serving the achievement of meeting social objectives of regeneration); heritage (associated with the protection of cultural property); technical (specific, innovative technical solutions applied in the project); marketing (responsible for the promotion and market success of the project) (Cobraman, 2019). The database application allows browsing, using identified tools and concepts, in European post-industrial revitalisation projects and is organised into categories. The user may find information concerning the main benefits of specific tools and practical implications of an applied tool on a project's success.

The same groups were separated in the area of best practice. They represent a more general category than project tools, making it easier to refer to them in new projects. The activities described in best practice can be proven elements of the classic approach to the process of revitalisation, as well as highly innovative elements.

The database also contains spatial information and geographic coordinates, making it possible to visualise the deployment of projects on a map. The project website uses Google Maps.

The brownfield card additionally provides access to a brownfield website. A keyword search and the project-filtering system using areas, specific tools, brownfield types or best practices criteria are available. There is the ability to search the descriptions of a project within various categories, using keywords. It is possible to search for information using the project description (region, city, name, idea, description, context, objectives, key experiences, stages) and the different areas of specific project tools and best practices (Cobraman, 2019).

A detailed description of the database and the results of the COBRAMAN project, such as the Guide for Brownfield Managers, were published on the project website http://www.cobraman-ce.eu. Unfortunately, these pages have not been publicly available since the end of the project.

Based on the experience of working on the brownfield database and further similar projects, we put together the following recommendations:

- The collection of data via an Excel form is not recommended as users have a tendency to expand and adjust the form. This creates difficulty in processing the form. The solution is to prepare a web interface, with input verification, to store data directly into the database.
- The interface language depends on the target group. English should be used for an international audience, while a local language is more suitable for professionals from regional business.
- Linking the GIS layer with a national cadastral database is very effective, if the cadastre is open to the public. For example, this is possible in the Czech Republic but not in Germany.
- GIS is important for the web-based visualisation of data for citizens, investors and other interested stakeholders. This helps to establish appropriate contact with the responsible brownfield manager at the municipality.

The database became a promotional tool, illustrating successful revitalisation projects and lessons learned, and increasing the chance of attracting investors. At the same time, it offers inventorial and statistical data for individuals with an interest in investment. The database is a significant asset during the planning of specific activities to be carried out in the process of revitalisation. It allows common elements to be identified, analogies to be found, and the selection of actions and tools that were successfully applied in other projects. The database can also be used for educational purposes, such as during the process of training personnel for the revitalisation of brownfields or landscapes affected by industrial activities.

An added value that the solution of this database and application has, differentiating it from other projects presenting brownfield evidence, is that we obtained information from unsuccessful projects; projects where the deadline was not met or where the funds did not cover the financing of all necessary work. These failed projects, under applicable conditions, serve as what not to do lessons for managers.

4.2 Modelling and Visualisation of Landscapes

A separate task for the information support of brownfield revitalisation is to visualise the appearance of the site as it will look after the revitalisation process.

The scheme of the information system for landscape modelling is shown in Figure 1. We have expanded the procedure using GIS systems and design and graphical programs to create a digital landscape model which enables landscape visualisation; from simple models to three-dimensional formats or landscape and building presentations using virtual reality tools. This is a general procedure enabling computer modelling of brownfield landscapes.

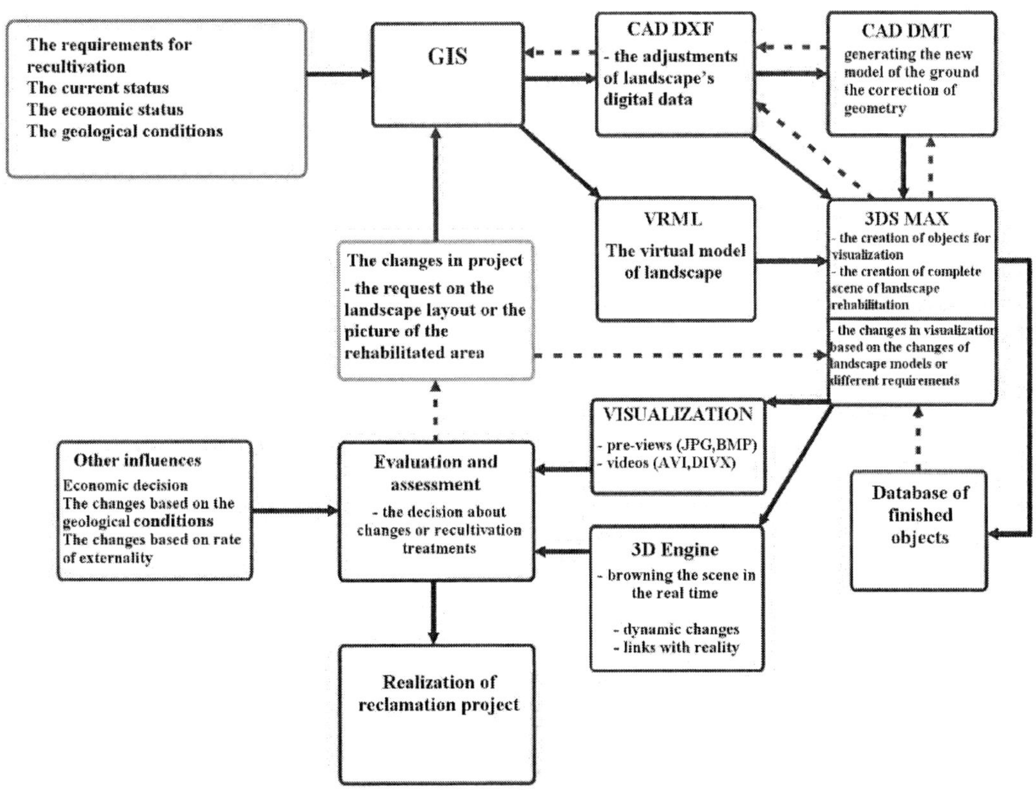

Figure 1 The Block Diagram of the Procedure for Building the Information System for Landscape Modelling (Danel and Neustupa, 2016)

We create landscape models for the following purposes:

- Visualisation of the current status of a location, including connection to GIS data (hydrogeological aspects, meteorological data, geological aspects, contamination and pollution, land registry data, transport accessibility...).
- Visualisation of the impact of each applied reclamation method to facilitate the selection of various solutions.
- Simulation of the future appearance of the landscape for visualisation of the impact of mining on the landscape.

For example, for brownfield sites which are a consequence of underground mining, it is necessary to perform the following activities:

- Landscape analysis during and after mining activities.
- Analysis of the intended use of areas remaining after mining activities.
- Solution of subsidence issues.
- Management of moving large volumes of material.
- Limits and options of landscaping solutions.
- Modelling landscapes, landscape components and segments.
- Modelling ecological aspects for functional regeneration of the landscape.
- Monitoring and modelling biological reclamation.

A component task, which was partly solved in the form of a student diploma thesis, was the analysis of available public data sources, free or paid, providing data usable for landscape modelling. An overview of available resources was published at a conference dedicated to brownfields, which took place at the VŠB - Technical University of Ostrava in March 2016 (Danel and Neustupa, 2016). However, it should be kept in mind that the available data sources and formats vary greatly from country to country. The requirements resulting from national legislation are also different.

The previously mentioned landscape modelling procedures were used, except for the final part of the design based on virtual reality tools, in the Czech-Polish co-operation project (2014–2016), addressing the effects of mining activities on the landscape and the issue of mining waste landfills in the Silesia region (Danel et al, 2014).

Our knowledge of building brownfield databases, collecting geographically oriented data and landscape modelling was used in the Czech-Polish cross-border co-operation project called INVARO; led by Associate Professor Barbara Stalmachová from the VŠB-Technical University of Ostrava in co-operation with the GIG - Głowny Instytut Górnictwa, Katowice, Poland (Main Mining Institute). The project took place in the years 2016–2019 and its goal was to map the spread of invasive plants on the Czech-Polish border and then determine the strategy for preventing further spread. Data on the occurrence of individual plant species were collected using drones and research on the terrain. The spread of invasive plants in the mapped area was modelled using a GIS system based on data in the database. Selected sites were photographed using drones for three consecutive years and changes were evaluated using GIS. The investigated location consists of densely populated and industrial areas, which created problems with imaging, as drones are not permitted to fly over built-up areas. The main output of the project was the 'Plan for Reducing the Risks Associated with Invasive Plant Species'. The results of the project and publications created within it are available at http://invaro.vsb.cz/, in Czech and Polish, and were published in 2018 (Olszewski et al, 2018).

5 Discussion and Future Direction

From our experience with building brownfield databases, we can say that due to the variability of the recorded data, it would be appropriate to use a NoSQL database instead of a relational database. The MongoDB document database seems to be a suitable candidate. One of the planned steps of further development is testing the use of the NoSQL database for processing unstructured brownfield data.

The next step, which is planned in the near future, is the use of advanced tools for information retrieval. The existing solution based on SQL queries is unsatisfactory due to the considerable variability of data. At the moment, the possible use of the Elasticsearch search engine is being explored in the form of a student's master's thesis.

6 Conclusion

This paper presents solutions for processing unstructured data, typically found in environmental engineering. We have been dealing with the issue of information support for a long time. The result is several implemented solutions, such as the COBRAMAN project database mentioned in this article and the solution used in the Czech-Polish co-operation projects, which focused on the Silesian region with has significant influences from heavy industry, especially mining. We want to continue working with these solutions in the future, using advanced information technology such as NoSQL databases or search engines. We also plan to create an expert system that will be able to recommend the most suitable revitalisation process for a described brownfield site based on data in the knowledge bank.

Acknowledgements

Paper was supported from SP2021/51 grant of VSB – Technical University of Ostrava.

References

Brownfieldy Pardubického kraje. (2020) [online]. Available at: https://www.brownfieldy-pk.cz://. [cited 2021-02-01].

CABERNET (2019). Brownfield definition, [online]. Available at: http://www.cabernet.org.uk/index.asp?c=1134 [cited 2020-11-14].

Cobraman (2019). Brownfield regeneration management: From education to practice – final brochure [Online]. Available at: http://www.cobraman-ce.eu/Portals/0/CM%20newsletter/Cobraman%2006_Newsletter_%20FINAL%20brochure.pdf. [cited 2020-11-01].

CZECHINVEST. (2020) About CzechInvest. [online]. http://www.czechinvest.org/en. [cited 2020-12-22].

Danel, R. and Neustupa, Z. (2016). 'Summary of spatial data sources in the Czech Republic usable for brownfield revitalization projects'. *International Conference of Brownfields Management and Redevelopment,* Ostrava, VŠB–Technical University of Ostrava, Czech Republic.

Danel, R., Neustupa, Z., Lacková, E. and Urbancová, L. (2014). 'An Information System for the Support of Land-Use Solutions for Areas Affected by Mining Activities in the Region of Upper Silesia'. *14th SGEM GeoConference on Informatics, Geoinformatics And Remote Sensing, - SGEM 2014,* Bulgaria. pp. 19–26.

Ertel, T. and Bořecký, K. (2012). *Best practices in brownfield management, City of Most.* ISBN 978-80-260-3585-5.

Ganser, R. and Williams, K. (2007). 'Brownfield development: Are we using the right targets? Evidence from England and Germany'. *European Planning Studies*, 15 (5), pp. 693-622.

Hudeček, V. and Mikoláš, M. (2014). 'Condition of localities in post-mining areas in the Czech-Polish borderland with focus on the Ostrava-Karvina coalfield'. *14th International Multidisciplinary Scientific Geoconference and EXPO - SGEM 2014*, Albena, Bulgaria. pp. 147–153.

Kozel, R. and Chuchrová, K. (2015). 'Creation of System Support for Decision-Making Processes of Managers'. *IDIMT-2015: Information Technology and Society - Interaction and Interdependence - 23rd Interdisciplinary Information Management Talks*. Poděbrady, Czech Republic. Linz: Universitatsverlag Rudolf Trauner, pp.163–170.

Maršolek, M., Neustupa, Z. and Řepka, M. (2006). 'Control and visualization of open pit physical model'. *7th International Carpathian Control Conference,* Czech Republic, pp. 357–360.

Neustupa, Z. (2003). 'Opencast Mining Technology Visualization'. *19th World Minig Congress*, New Delhi, India, pp. 1669–1676.

Neustupa, Z. and Stalmachová, B. (2006). 'Modelling and visualization of water ecosystems for post-mining landscape'. *7th International Carpathian Control Conference*, Czech Republic, pp. 397-400.

Olszewski, PP., Grabowski, J., Stalmachová, B., Švehláková, H. and Nováková, J. (2018). 'Risks concerning invasive plant species in an industrial-agricultural community'. *18th International Multidisciplinary Scientific Geoconference, SGEM 2018,* Albena, Bulgaria, pp. 753–760.

Rizzo, E., Pesce, M., Pizzol, L., Alexandrescu, F, Giubilato, E., Critto, A., Marcomini, A. and Bartke, S. (2015). 'Brownfield regeneration in Europe: Identifying stakeholder perceptions, concerns, attitudes and information needs'. *Land Use Policy*, vol. 48, pp. 437-453.

Thornton, G., Franz, M., Edwards, D., Pahlen, G. and Nathanail, P. (2007). 'The challenge of sustainability: incentives for brownfield regeneration in Europe'. *Environmental Science & Policy*, 10 (2), pp. 116-134.

Strategic management of project portfolios

Petr Fiala[1], Renata Majovská[2]

Abstract. The use of project portfolio management is increasingly becoming a tool for promoting the strategy of the organization. Project opportunities come in time and it is necessary to decide which will be accepted for creating a dynamic portfolio of projects and which will be rejected. Using sophisticated quantitative tools becomes a significant competitive advantage for project portfolio management. Project portfolio management is a dynamic multi-criteria decision-making problem under risk. The paper presents new approaches for analyzing the problem. A dynamic version of the Analytic Network Process (ANP) captures the network, multicriteria and dynamic structure of the problem. Multicriteria decision trees analyze risk of project portfolios. Possible projects are characterized by sets of inputs and outputs, where inputs are resources for project realization and outputs measure multiple criteria of goals of the organization. The Data Envelopment Analysis (DEA) is an appropriate approach to select efficient project portfolios.

Keywords: project portfolio, multiple criteria, dynamics, risk, efficiency.

JEL Classification: M00, C44

1 Introduction

Most project organizations exist in a multi-project environment. This environment creates the problems of project interdependency and the need to share resources. Strategic alignment of projects is of major importance to effective use of organization resources. Selection criteria need to ensure each project is prioritized and contributes to strategic goals. There is a very extensive literature on the management of individual projects and project portfolios (Fiala, 2003, Larson and Gray, 2013).

Management of the project portfolio ensures that only the most valuable projects are approved and managed. All of the projects selected become part of a project portfolio that balances the total risk for the organization. The key to success in project portfolio management is to select the right projects at the right time (Levine, 2005). Portfolio management is a process evaluated by multiple criteria.

To select a portfolio of projects are basically two approaches, one is based on standard methods used in practice, the second approach is based on searching and applying new sophisticated methods based on quantitative analysis. Lot of professionals tried to find sophisticated way to improve techniques for project portfolio management in different ways.

The paper focuses on the problem of strategic management of project portfolios solved by applying sophisticated models. It is generally expected that the portfolio should be designed in such a way as to maximize the possibility of achieving the strategic goals of the company. This

[1] Prague University of Economics and Business, Department of Econometrics, W. Churchill Sq. 4, 130 67 Prague 3, Czech Republic, pfiala@vse.cz

[2] University of Finance and Administration, Prague, Department of Computer Science and Mathematics, Estonská 500, 101 00 Praha 10, Czech Republic, renata.majovska@mail.vsfs.cz

is consistent with the notion that portfolio selection problem is a multi-criteria decision making. The aim is to develop a general model, which would be completed for the specific needs of problems. This paper aims to verify the ability to model and solve the problem of dynamic project portfolio using the Analytic Network Process (ANP) model. The organization must decide under risk whether to assign all available resources to present proposals or to reserve a portion of the funds unused for some time and wait for better alternatives that may occur later. We propose to complete our ANP model by a decision tree with multiple criteria and interactive multi-criteria analysis for solving this problem. Efficiency of project portfolio is measured by proposed method based on Data Envelopment Analysis (DEA) approach.

Project portfolio is set all projects that are implemented in the organization at that time. Project opportunities come in time and it is necessary to decide which will be accepted for creating a dynamic portfolio of projects and which will be rejected (Fig. 1).

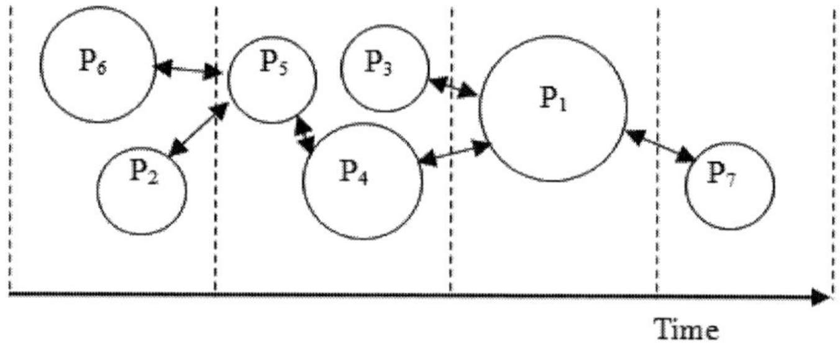

Figure 1 Dynamic flow of projects [Authors]

2 ANP model

The Analytic Network Process (ANP) is the multi-criteria method (Saaty, 2001) that makes it possible to deal systematically with all kinds of dependence and feedback in the performance system. The ANP approach seems to be very appropriate instrument for project portfolio management. Another issue is the appropriate selection of clusters, which would be the basis of the basic model and their fulfilment by system elements. Another specific problem is the creation of sub - networks in the ANP model characterizing the specific important circumstances of the model. The current economic environment is characterized by significant changes. An important problem of the model will be to capture the dynamics that would represent appropriate changes. Time dependent priorities play an increasingly important role in a rapidly changing environment of network systems. Long-term priorities can be based on time dependent comparisons of system elements.

The structure of the ANP model for dynamic project portfolio (DPP) is described by clusters of elements connected by their dependence on one another. A cluster groups elements (projects, resources, criteria, time) that share a set of attributes. At least one element in each of these clusters is connected to some element in another cluster. These connections indicate the flow of influence between the elements (see Fig. 2).

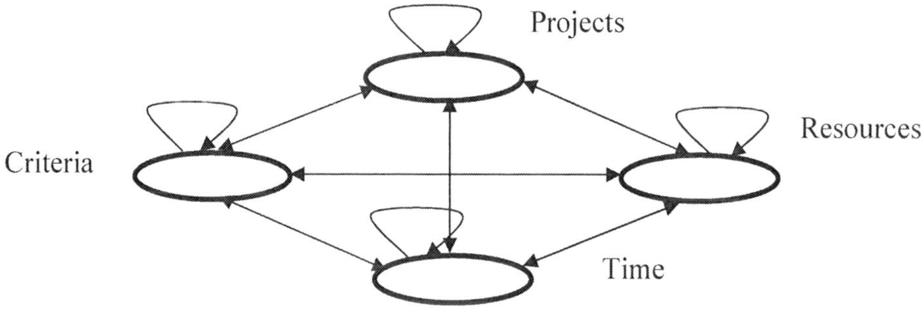

Figure 2 Flows of influence between the elements [Authors]

The ANP model consists of four basic clusters with their elements and influences:

Projects: This cluster consists of potential alternatives of projects of which will be selected a dynamic portfolio. There are priorities among projects for inclusion in the portfolio. The cluster has connections to all other clusters.

Resources: Resources are necessary for the implementation of projects. Main resources are human resources between which are relations important for creating project teams. The cluster has connections to all other clusters.

Criteria: Projects are evaluated according to criteria which include benefits, opportunities, costs, and risks (BOCR). The cluster has connections to all other clusters.

Time: Time is measured in discrete units. Elements of other clusters vary in time and theirs values depend on the values in previous time periods.

The basic ANP model is completed by specific sub-networks. The sub-networks are used to model important features of the DPP problem. The most important features in our ANP-based framework for DPP management are captured in sub-networks: dynamic flow of projects, time dependent resources.

Dynamic flow of projects: Project opportunities come in time and it is necessary to decide which will be accepted for creating a dynamic portfolio of projects and which will be rejected. The sub-network connects clusters: time and projects.

Time dependent resources: A specific sub-network is devoted to model time dependent amounts of resources. The time dependent amount of resources is given by. The sub-network connects clusters: time, resources and projects.

Time dependent priorities in the ANP model can be expressed by forecasting using pairwise comparison functions (Fiala, 2006, Saaty, 2007). Dynamic extensions of ANP method can work with time-dependent priorities in a networked system. There are two approaches for time-dependent pairwise comparisons: structural, by including scenarios, functional by explicitly involving time in the judgment process. Judgment matrix in dynamic form can be formulated

$$A(t) = \begin{bmatrix} a_{11}(t) & a_{12}(t) \dots & a_{1k}(t) \\ a_{21}(t) & a_{22}(t) \dots & a_{2k}(t) \\ \vdots & \vdots & \vdots \\ a_{k1}(t) & a_{k2}(t) \dots & a_{kk}(t) \end{bmatrix}.$$

3 Risk of project portfolios

In each period, the project portfolio is reviewed in line with the strategic objectives of the organization. Management may decide to initiate new projects, but also to end of some others that are currently being implemented. The organization must decide under risk whether to assign all available resources to present proposals or to reserve a portion of the funds unused for some time and wait for better alternatives that may occur later. We propose to use a decision tree with multiple criteria and interactive multi-criteria analysis for solving this problem.

3.1 Decision trees

Sequences of partial decisions which follow one another frequently occur in assessing potential projects. They are multi-stage decision processes. The task of the decision maker is to select one of the possible sequences that leads to the best final goal solution. Decision-making takes place in periods $t = 1, 2, \ldots, T$. The decision trees are used to solve these problems successfully.

Solution of multi-stage decision problems proceed in two phases. The first phase is the construction of a decision tree and the second phase is its evaluation. The graph tree structure is used by the construction of decision trees that appropriately models the branching options. Two types of nodes are considered, decision and chance nodes. The edges of the tree represent branching of decision and chance possibilities. We start with the decision node from which they emanate lines that represent the possible decisions a_i. The ends of these edges are chance nodes on which they rely edges representing s_j possible situations that may occur with conditional probabilities p_j. These edges can be followed by another decision nodes with possible decisions, as well as chance nodes with possible situations, etc. End edges, which are not followed by further decision and chance nodes, represent the possible end sequences of partial decisions that are evaluated.

Evaluation of the decision trees proceed in the opposite direction from the end edges back to the starting node of the decision. The decision-maker selects the decision that cannot affect the occurrence of situations and must consider all situations with their conditional probabilities of occurrence. The decision from possible decisions is always chosen that delivers a better evaluation. Principle of maximizing the expected value is used in the selection. The optimal sequence of decisions is obtained in this manner.

3.2 Multi-criteria analysis

Multi-criteria decision trees (Haimes and Tulsiani, 1990, Nowak and Nowak, 2013) are used to select the most suitable strategy for a dynamic project portfolio management. We use standard methods of multi-criteria decision-making for their analysis. We will seek a final compromise strategy for dynamic project portfolio selection. This strategy should be called effective. Effective multi-criteria strategy is one to which no exists other alternative strategy that would be better at least under one criterion, and not worse under other criteria. Multi-criteria analysis is at two levels: identification of all effective strategies for dynamic portfolio selection, interactive procedure for determining the final compromise strategy for dynamic portfolio selection.

The following simple procedure can be applied for the identification of effective strategies:
Step 1: Starting from the last period $t = T$, identify sub-effective strategy for all decision nodes of the period T.
Step 2: Go to the previous period $t = t - 1$.
Step 3: Identify strategies that meet the conditions of effectiveness for each decision node of the period t.
Step 4: If $t > 1$, go to step 2, otherwise the procedure stops.

Number of effective strategies can be large. It is possible to use a simple interactive process between the decision maker and solver for the selection of the final compromise strategy from the set of all effective strategies. In each iteration q, a set of strategies $S(q)$ is analysed and the ideal alternative $\mathbf{H}(q)$ (vector of best values according to each criterion) and the anti-ideal alternative $\mathbf{D}(q)$ (vector of worst values according to each criterion) are determined. The decision maker compares between such values may vary criteria values. The decision maker is asked about the aspiration levels of criteria $\mathbf{A}(q)$, which he would accept as a compromise strategy. If the decision-maker is satisfied with the proposed strategy, the process stops.

Interactive process to determine the final compromise strategy has the following steps.
Step 1: Iteration $q = 1$, the set of all analysed strategies $S(1)$ is equal to the set of all effective strategies.
Step 2: Determine the ideal alternative $\mathbf{H}(q)$ and the anti-ideal alternative $\mathbf{D}(q)$.
Step 3: Decision-maker is asked to accept anti-ideal values. If yes, go to Step 8.
Step 4: The decision-maker is asked to propose the aspiration levels $\mathbf{A}(q)$. If not, go to step 6.
Step 5: The decision-maker enters aspiration levels $\mathbf{A}(q)$ and he determines the corresponding set of acceptable strategies $S(q + 1)$. If $S(q + 1) = \emptyset$, go to step 4, otherwise to step 7.
Step 6: The decision-maker is asked which anti-ideal value is unacceptable for him. A new set of strategies is defined $S(q + 1)$which exceed the unacceptable anti-ideal value.
Step 7: Set $q = q + 1$, go to step 2.
Step 8: The decision-maker is asked which criterion should reach the ideal value. The strategy that maximizes this criterion is the resulting compromise one.

4 Efficiency of project portfolios

We propose a new approach for efficient project portfolio designing based on a Data Envelopment Analysis (DEA). Possible projects are characterized by sets of inputs and outputs. Inputs are resources for project realization and outputs are criteria. Charnes, Cooper, and Rhodes (1978) developed the first DEA model. The DEA model is based on the reduction of the multiple inputs and multiple outputs to that of a single "virtual" input and a single "virtual" output using weights. The model searches for the set of weights which maximize the efficiency of the project. The DEA may be characterized as a method of objective weight assessment. The DEA includes a number of models and methods to evaluating performance (Charnes et al, 2013).

4.1 Efficient individual projects

For our problem, there is supposed a set $P = \{P_1, P_2, \dots, P_n\}$ of n projects each consuming r inputs and producing s outputs; (r, n)-matrix X and (s, n)-matrix Y are observed input and output measures. The CCR (Charnes, Cooper, and Rhodes) model with supposed constant return to scale was used for project evaluations. For a particular project, the ratio of the single output to the single input provides a measure of efficiency that is a function of the weight multipliers (u,v). The relative efficiency e_k of the project P_k is maximised to the condition that the relative efficiency of each project is less than or equal to one.

A DEA-based approach allows each project to evaluate itself, relative to all the projects under consideration. The formulation leads to a linear fractional programming problem.

$$e_k = \frac{\sum_{i=1}^{s} u_i y_{ik}}{\sum_{j=1}^{r} v_j x_{jk}} \to max, \qquad k = 1, 2, \dots, n \tag{1}$$

$$\frac{\sum_{i=1}^{s} u_i y_{ih}}{\sum_{j=1}^{r} v_j x_{jh}} \leq 1, h = 1, 2, \dots, n \tag{2}$$

$$u_i, v_j \geq 0, i = 1, 2, \dots, s, \qquad j = 1, 2, \dots, r \tag{3}$$

If it is possible to find a set of weights for which the efficiency ratio of the project P_k is equal to one, the project P_k will be considered as efficient otherwise it will be considered as inefficient. The set of efficient projects is designed in this way.

Solving this nonlinear nonconvex problem directly is not an efficient approach. The following linear programming problem with new variable weights (u, v) that results from the Charnes - Cooper transformation gives optimal values that will also be optimal for the fractional programming problem.

$$e_k = \sum_{i=1}^{s} u_i y_{ik} \to max, \quad k= 1, 2, \dots, n, \tag{4}$$

$$\sum_{j=1}^{r} v_j x_{jk} = 1 \tag{5}$$

$$\sum_{i=1}^{s} u_i y_{ih} - \sum_{j=1}^{r} v_j x_{jh} \leq 0, h = 1, 2, \dots, n \tag{6}$$

$$u_i, v_j \geq 0, \qquad i = 1, 2, \dots, s, \qquad j = 1, 2, \dots, r \tag{7}$$

The efficiency scores e_k might be used to rank the projects. Implementing the most effective projects until resources are consumed will not always lead to the most effective portfolio. The reason is the same as for the knapsack problem.

4.2 Efficient portfolios

A portfolio as a subset C of the set of possible projects P $(C \subseteq P)$ can be taken as a single combined project. The combined project is defined by combinations of outputs and combinations of inputs. The combination vector is $\lambda = (\lambda_1, \lambda_2, \dots, \lambda_n)$ where $\lambda_i = 1$ (the individual project P_i is included in the portfolio) or $\lambda_i = 0$ (the individual project P_i is not included in the portfolio). Total inputs of the combined project denoted as $x_j(C) = \sum_{h=1}^{n} \lambda_h x_{jh}$, $j = 1, 2, \dots, r$, and total outputs denoted as $y_i(C) = \sum_{h=1}^{n} \lambda_h y_{ih}$, $i = 1, 2, \dots, s$, are determined by the combination vector λ. The set of all combined projects is the so-called power set of P and the set is denoted as $R(P)$ where the number of elements in $R(P)$ is $2^n - 1$.

DEA-approach can be used for evaluation of each combined project relative to the power set $R(P)$.

$$e_C = \sum_{i=1}^{s} u_i \sum_{h=1}^{n} \lambda_h y_{ih} \rightarrow max \tag{8}$$

$$\sum_{j=1}^{r} v_j \sum_{h=1}^{n} \lambda_h x_{jh} = 1 \tag{9}$$

$$\sum_{i=1}^{s} u_i \sum_{h=1}^{n} \lambda_h y_{ih} - \sum_{j=1}^{r} v_j \sum_{h=1}^{n} \lambda_h x_{jh} \leq 0,\ C \in R(P) \tag{10}$$

$$\lambda_h \in \{0, 1\}, h = 1, 2, \dots, n \tag{11}$$

$$u_i, v_j \geq 0, \qquad i = 1, 2, \dots, s, \qquad j = 1, 2, \dots, r \tag{12}$$

The model (8)-(12) is a non-linear one with variables λ_h, u_i ,v_j where λ_h are elements of an unknown project combination vector and u_i ,v_j are weights of outputs and inputs. Due to the large number of constraints (10) it is difficult to solve.

Introducing new variables

$$c_{ih} = u_i \lambda_h,\ d_{jh} = v_j \lambda_h, i = 1, 2, \dots, s,\ j = 1, 2, \dots, r,\ h = 1, 2, \dots, n \tag{13}$$

linearizes this problem. The portfolio total inputs and outputs are compared against the set of all portfolios $R(P)$ but it is easy to see that the general constraints (10) are additive combination of constraints for individual projects and it is sufficient to compare them with individual projects from the set P given by the constraint (16) (Cook and Green, 2000). Constraints for combined projects are redundant. The constraints (19) and (20) link new variables c_{ih}, d_{jh} and old variables u_i, v_j, λ_h, where M is a large number. The constraint (19) links the variables c_{ih}, u_i, λ_h. If the binary variable $\lambda_h = 1$, then $0 \leq c_{ih} \leq M, u_i = c_{ih}$ and if the binary variable $\lambda_h = 0$, then $0 \leq u_i \leq M, c_{ih} = 0$. The constraint (20) analogically links the variables d_{jh}, v_j, λ_h.

The problem is then formulated as follows:

$$e_C = \sum_{i=1}^{s} \sum_{h=1}^{n} c_{ih} y_{ih} \rightarrow max \tag{14}$$

$$\sum_{j=1}^{r} \sum_{h=1}^{n} d_{jh} x_{jh} = 1 \tag{15}$$

$$\sum_{i=1}^{s} u_i y_{ih} - \sum_{j=1}^{r} v_j x_{jh} \leq 0, h = 1, 2, \dots, n \tag{16}$$

$$\lambda_h \in \{0, 1\}, h = 1, 2, \dots, n \tag{17}$$

$$u_i, v_j \geq 0, \qquad i = 1, 2, \dots, s, \qquad j = 1, 2, \dots, r, \tag{18}$$

$$c_{ih} \geq 0, c_{ih} \leq M\lambda_h,\ u_i \geq c_{ih}, u_i \leq c_{ih} + M(1 - \lambda_h), i = 1, 2, \dots, s, h = 1, 2, \dots, n \tag{19}$$

$$d_{jh} \geq 0, d_{jh} \leq M\lambda_h,\ v_j \geq d_{jh}, v_j \leq d_{jh} + M(1 - \lambda_h), j = 1, 2, \dots, r, h = 1, 2, \dots, n \tag{20}$$

5 Conclusion

The aim of the paper was to capture new trends in project portfolio management. These new trends are analyzed using sophisticated quantitative approaches. Popular approaches such as Analytic Network Process (ANP), multicriteria analysis, decision trees and Data Envelopment Analysis (DEA) were used for the analysis. These procedures have been adapted specifically for project portfolio management.

The proposed portfolio management procedure respects the characteristics of the problem:

- network structure;
- multi-criteria evaluation;

- dynamics;
- risk;
- efficiency.

The procedure is flexible and can be modified and generalized. For example, analyzing risk and efficiency by imprecise DEA (Smirlis et al, 2004), to use other options for capturing the network structure, other methods of multi-criteria analysis, other principles for measuring risk and capturing dynamics, other ways of measuring the performance of project portfolios may be used. Experimental results will affect the specification, completing and extending the model.

Acknowledgements

This work was supported by the grant No. IGA F4/42/2021, Faculty of Informatics and Statistics, Prague University of Economics and Business. The paper is a result of an institutional research project no.7429/2020/02 "System approach to selected ICT trends" supported by University of Finance and Administration, Prague.

References

Charnes, A., Cooper, W. W., Rhodes, E. (1978). Measuring Efficiency of Decision Making Units. *European Journal of Operation Research*, 1 (3), pp. 429-444.

Charnes, A., Cooper, W. W., Lewin, A.Y. and Seiford, L. M. (Eds) (2013). *Data envelopment analysis: Theory, methodology, and applications*. New York: Springer Science & Business Media.

Fiala, P. (2003). *Projektové řízení - modely, metody, analýzy*. Praha: Professional Publishing.

Fiala, P. (2006). An ANP/DNP analysis of economic elements in today's world network economy. *Journal of Systems Science and Systems Engineering*. 15 (2), pp. 131-140.

Fiala, P. (2008*). Modely a metody rozhodování*. Praha: Oeconomica.

Fiala, P. (2018). Project portfolio designing using data envelopment analysis and De Novo optimisation. *Central European Journal of Operations Research*, 26 (4), pp. 847-859.

Fiala, P. and Majovská, R. (2019) Project portfolio designing under risk. In: *37th International Conference on Mathematical Methods in Economics 2019*. České Budějovice: Jihočeská univerzita v Českých Budějovicích, pp. 566–571.

Fiala, P. and Majovská, R. (2020). New trends in project portfolio management. *Trendy v podnikání,* 10 (3), pp. 4–11.

Haimes, Y., Li, D. and Tulsiani, V. (1990). Multiobjective decision tree method. *Risk Analysis,* 10 (2), pp.111-129.

Larson, E. W. and Gray, C. (2013). *Project Management: The Managerial Process with MS Project*. New York: McGraw-Hill,

Levine, H. A. (2005*). Project Portfolio Management*. San Francisco: Jossey-Bas.

Nowak, M., and Nowak, B. (2013). An application of the multiple criteria decision tree in project planning, *Procedia Technology,* 9 (4), pp. 826-835.

Saaty, T. L. (2001). *Decision making with Dependence and Feedback: The Analytic Network Process*. Pittsburgh: RWS Publications.

Saaty, T. L. (2007). Time dependent decision making; dynamic priorities in the AHP/ANP: Generalizing from points to functions and from real to complex variables. *Mathematical and Computer Modeling*, 46 (5), pp. 860-891.

Smirlis, Y. G., Despotis, D. K., Jablonský, J. and Fiala, P. (2004). Identifying „Best-Buys" in the Market of Prepaid Mobile Telephony: an Application of Imprecise DEA. *International Journal of Information Technology & Decision* Making, 3(1), pp. 167–177.

Fuzzy rating of a country travel and tourism competitiveness with respect to tourism sustainability

Simona Hašková[1]

Abstract. Country tourism competitiveness with respect to sustainable development can be partly expressed by different indicators (environment, services, safety, etc.). The paper reflects three main indicators from the viewpoint of travelling persons to construct a fuzzy score of a country sustainable travel and tourism competitiveness. The fuzzy approach was used to reflect the vague character of input parameters and the fact that this method provides a space for application of the human factor. Results enabled to distinguish two groups of European and Asian countries; they are ranked between the highly competitive and conditional competitive countries based on the fuzzy score calculation.

Keywords: Fuzzy score, country tourism competitiveness, sustainable tourism, fuzzy approach, vague input parameters, human factor.

JEL Classification: C51, L8, R15

1 Introduction

Among the current world trends in the development of tourism, the concept of sustainable development of tourism occupies an important place. The need for the transition of the tourism sphere to the principles of sustainability under current conditions of globalization and informatization of societies is obvious. The actual tourism crisis caused by the Covid-19 pandemic only reinforces this trend. Now it is not "just" about the uncontrolled growth of tourism, the aim of which is a quick profit, the negative consequences of which can be reflected in environmental damage, which destroys the essence that is crucial for the functioning and successful development of tourism, nowadays it is also about hygienic safety (Tian et al, 2020).

Management in the tourism sector is a system of activities, the elements of which are different types of actions performed by managing entities. International organizations are proposing different approaches to assessing the sustainable development of tourism (Ziyadin et al., 2019). The European Commission has set up its own European system of tourism indicators (ETIS), a tool for managing the sustainability of destinations; so far it contains 27 basic and 40 additional indicators structured into four sections: management, social and cultural influence, economic value, environmental impact (European Commission, 2021).

The paper aims to construct an indicator of sustainable tourism development in the form of fuzzy rating utilizing the fuzzy procedure. The source of inputs are the individual rankings of Travel & Tourism Policy and Enabling Conditions, Natural and Cultural Resources, and Safety and Security compiled on the evaluation of traveling persons and published by Calderwood and Soshkin (2019). The main objective of the paper is to evaluate the comprehensive degree of country travel & tourism competitiveness with respect to sustainable tourism development in some European and Asian countries.

[1] Institute of Technology and Business in České Budějovice, School of Expertness and Valuation, Okružní 10, 370 01 České Budějovice, haskovas@post.cz.

This expert management problem deals with vaguely defined concepts that are usually presented by means of linguistic variables and their linguistic values (i.e. terms). Desirable relationships between combinations of terms of input linguistic variables and terms of an output linguistic variable are given by a set of rules. Therefore, the fuzzy set theory and the fuzzy approach based on it serves our purpose very well.

Moreover, the fuzzy approach provides space for application of the human factor (individual knowledge, skills, and experience of an expert). It is based on the assumption that key elements of human thinking are not numbers, but intuitive concepts, the contents of which can be modelled by fuzzy sets (Zadeh, 1999). The ubiquity of fuzziness in the processes of human thinking suggests that most of the logic behind it is the logic with continuous fuzzy truths, fuzzy connections, and fuzzy derivation rules. The ability to manipulate intuitive concepts and subsequent summarization in the sense of summarizing data is one of the most important advantages of the human mind, which is also its fundamental characteristic (Zadeh, 1973).

2 Formal description of fuzzy approach

Let the set U be a field of consideration or discussion. Let $\mu_{\underline{A}}: U \rightarrow \langle 0,1 \rangle$ be a membership function and let $\underline{A} = \{(y, \mu_{\underline{A}}(y)): y \in U\}$ be a set of all pairs $(y, \mu_{\underline{A}}(y))$ in which the numbers $0 \leq \mu_{\underline{A}}(y) \leq 1$ assign to the given $y \in U$ a membership degree of the pair $(y, \mu_{\underline{A}}(y))$ to the set $\underline{A}$. Then $\underline{A}$ is a *fuzzy subset* on the universe U. The significant characteristic of fuzzy subset $\underline{A}$ is its support $U_{\underline{A}} = \{y: 0 < \mu_{\underline{A}}(y) \leq 1, y \in U\} \subset U$. In terms of fuzzy logic $\mu_{\underline{A}}(y) = |y \in U_{\underline{A}}|$. The element $y \in U$ with $\mu_{\underline{A}}(y) = 0.5$ is called the *crossover point* in $\underline{A}$. In the case of values greater than 0.5, the element y rather belongs to $U_{\underline{A}}$, in the case of the smaller ones it rather does not belong to it (Dubois and Prade, 1996).

In this paper, the numerical fuzzy sets are formal representations of terms of linguistic variables. For our purpose, the model with one internal and two border fuzzy sets for the terms *low* ($\underline{L}$), *common* ($\underline{M}$), and *high* ($\underline{H}$) value is suitable. Interval U is divided with the points a, b, c, d into five sections with the following membership functions (1) (for graphical interpretation see the behaviour of functions $\mu_{\underline{L}}$, $\mu_{\underline{M}}$ and $\mu_{\underline{H}}$ in Figure 1):

$$(\underline{L}) \quad \begin{aligned} &\mu_{\underline{L}}(y) = 1 \text{ for } y < \mathrm{a}, \\ &\mu_{\underline{L}}(y) = (\mathrm{b} - y) / (\mathrm{b} - \mathrm{a}) \text{ for } \mathrm{a} \leq y < \mathrm{b}, \\ &\mu_{\underline{L}}(y) = 0 \text{ otherwise.} \end{aligned}$$

$$(\underline{M}) \quad \begin{aligned} &\mu_{\underline{M}}(y) = (y - \mathrm{a}) / (\mathrm{b} - \mathrm{a}) \text{ for } \mathrm{a} \leq y < \mathrm{b}, \\ &\mu_{\underline{M}}(y) = 1 \text{ for } \mathrm{b} \leq y < \mathrm{c}, \\ &\mu_{\underline{M}}(y) = (\mathrm{d} - y) / (\mathrm{d} - \mathrm{c}) \text{ for } \mathrm{c} \leq y < \mathrm{d}, \\ &\mu_{\underline{M}}(y) = 0 \text{ otherwise.} \end{aligned} \qquad (1)$$

$$(\underline{H}) \quad \begin{aligned} &\mu_{\underline{H}}(y) = 0 \text{ for } y < \mathrm{c}, \\ &\mu_{\underline{H}}(y) = (y - \mathrm{c}) / (\mathrm{d} - \mathrm{c}) \text{ for } \mathrm{c} \leq y < \mathrm{d}, \\ &\mu_{\underline{H}}(y) = 1 \text{ otherwise.} \end{aligned}$$

The role of the experts is to determine the position of the points a, b, c and d in the universe U. In the case of their regular distribution, we get the courses of the functions μ shown in Figure 1 (part 3.2). From it we see that the linguistic variable acquires the values at two levels: at the level of the basal values y in the universe U and at the level of terms (intuitive concepts) as fuzzy subsets of $\underline{L}$, $\underline{M}$, $\underline{H}$ in the universe U. Each of these terms are defined by its membership function $\mu_{\underline{L}}$, $\mu_{\underline{M}}$, $\mu_{\underline{H}}$ over the field of its support, which is a subset of U.

Another important tool of the fuzzy set theory is the *rule*. In our considered model with n input linguistic variables and one output linguistic variable it is an element $((\underline{A}_1,...,\underline{A}_n), \underline{C})$ of the relation $F \subset (\{\underline{L}_1, \underline{M}_1, \underline{H}_1\}\times...\times\{\underline{L}_n, \underline{M}_n, \underline{H}_n\})\times\{\underline{L}, \underline{M}, \underline{H}\}$, which is a projection F: $(\{\underline{L}_1, \underline{M}_1, \underline{H}_1\}\times...\times\{\underline{L}_n, \underline{M}_n, \underline{H}_n\}) \rightarrow \{\underline{L}, \underline{M}, \underline{H}\}$ in the form of $F(\underline{A}_1,...,\underline{A}_n) = \underline{C}$, where $\underline{C} \in \{\underline{L}, \underline{M}, \underline{H}\}$ and $\underline{A}_i \in \{\underline{L}_i, \underline{M}_i, \underline{H}_i\}$, i = 1,…, n. The n-tuple of terms $(\underline{A}_1,...,\underline{A}_n)$ is the left side of the rule, the term $F(\underline{A}_1,...,\underline{A}_n)$ is the right side of the rule. The relation F has a maximum of n^3 elements. We call it a set of *inferential* rules (Běhounek and Cintula, 2006).

One of the basic concepts of the fuzzy set theory is the so-called extension principle (in detail see Kahraman, 2008). Our modification of the extension principle is based on the following steps:

1. The *fuzzification* of the numerical vector $x = (x_1, ..., x_n)$ entering the relation in which the vector x selects inferential rules relevant to its multi-criteria evaluation. These are the rules $((A_{1i},...,A_{nj}), B_k) \in P$, in which terms´ formalizations $A_{1i},...,A_{nj}$ of the left side are all nonzero numbers $\mu_{\underline{A}1i}(x_1),..., \mu_{\underline{A}nj}(x_n)$.
2. Moving from the *symbolic notation* $((A_{1i},...,A_{nj}), B_k)$ of the selected inference rule to its *logic notation* dependent on x in the form of $(\min\{\mu_{\underline{A}1i}(x_1),..., \mu_{\underline{A}nj}(x_n)\}, \mu_{\underline{B}k}) = (\mu_{\underline{A}^*}(x), \mu_{\underline{B}k})$, we obtain a number $\mu_{\underline{A}^*}(x)$ indicating not only the degree of truthfulness that the situation characterized by the vector x actually occurred, and therefore, the degree of eligibility of the rule selection $((A_{1i},...,A_{nj}), B_k)$ to its solution, but also the degree of significance of the term B_k in the multi-criteria evaluation of the vector x. $\mu_{\underline{B}k}: Y \rightarrow \langle 0,1\rangle$ is the standard membership function of the elements $y \in Y$ to the fuzzy set $\underline{B}_k$. On the other hand, $\mu_{\underline{B}k}^*: Y \rightarrow \langle 0,1\rangle$ in the form of $\mu_{\underline{B}k}^*(y) = \min\{\mu_{\underline{A}^*}(x), \mu_{\underline{B}k}(y)\}$ limits from above the function $\mu_{\underline{B}k}$ by means of the number $\mu_{\underline{A}^*}(x)$.
3. The components of the relation K will then be the elements of the set $Px = \{B_k: \exists y: (\min\{\mu_{\underline{A}^*}(x), \mu_{\underline{B}k}(y)\} > 0), ((A_{1i},...,A_{nj}), B_k) \in P, y \in Y\}$. These are the partial intermediate results by which *aggregation* (logical sum) we obtain the formalized term $\underline{B}_{agg} = \{(y, \mu_{agg}(y)): y \in Y\}$ on Y, for which it holds that (2)

$$\mu_{agg}(y) = max\left\{min\{\mu_{\underline{A}^*}(x), \mu_{\underline{B}k}(y)\}: \left((A_{1i}, ..., A_{nj}), B_k\right) \in P, y \in Y\right\} \qquad (2)$$

4. The final phase of the fuzzy approach is *defuzzification*, whose last step provides the output value y_x of the multicriteria model of an alternative evaluation $(a_1,...,a_c) \in A$ as the mean value of the elements $y \in \underline{B}_{agg}$ weighted by the values $\mu_{agg}(y)$ of their significance. Therefore

$$y_x = \int y \cdot \mu_{agg}(y)dy / \int \mu_{agg}(y)dy \qquad (3)$$

where ∫ is the symbol of a definite integral over the universe Y – more in detail in Dubois and Prade (1996).

Since the resulting constant y_0 is largely the result of the subjective experience and opinions of experts who create the model, we call it a *subjectively* expected value.

3 Application

The fuzzy procedure of a country travel and tourism competitiveness evaluation with respect to sustainable tourism development is applied from the viewpoint of travelling persons. The fuzzy approach takes into account the uncertainty of the input data contained in the indexes of ratings (Manns, 2013) and the uncertainty and complexity of vague sociological and psychological factors (Morim et al., 2017) as well as expert knowledge and experience.

3.1 Problem setting and data

Based on the values of Travel & Tourism Policy and Enabling Conditions (P), Natural and Cultural Resources (R) and Safety and Security (S) published by Calderwood & Soshkin (2019) - see Table 1, the selected European and Asian countries can be divided into three categories (countries with high travel & tourism competitiveness, countries with conditional travel & tourism competitiveness, and countries with low travel & tourism competitiveness) based on the perception of travelling persons obtained from Executive Opinion Survey and quantitative data obtained from other sources.

Country/Index	Travel & Tourism Policy and Enabling Conditions (P) Score / Percentage rate (%)	Natural and Cultural Resources (R) Score / Percentage rate (%)	Safety and Security (S) Score / Percentage rate (%)
Albania	4.3 / 61	2.0 / 29	5.8 / 83
Bosnia and Herzegovina	4.1 / 59	1.7 / 24	5.4 / 77
China	4.3 / 61	6.1 / 87	5.6 / 80
Czech Republic	4.7 / 67	2.5 / 36	6.1 / 87
Japan	4.8 / 69	5.3 / 76	6.2 / 89
Singapore	5.0 / 71	2.4 / 34	6.4 / 91
Slovak Republic	4.6 / 66	2.2 / 36	5.6 / 80
Spain	4.9 / 70	5.7 / 80	6.1 / 87
Russia	4.4 / 60	3.8 / 54	5.1 / 73
Turkey	4.5 / 64	3.3 / 47	3.4 / 49

Source: Calderwood & Soshkin, 2019; own processing. Note: Rating data are at the evaluation scale 1 - 7, where 1 represents the worst and 7 the best score; for the purpose of further processing, the absolute values are converted to a percentage scale at the interval ⟨0, 100⟩ %.

Table 1 Values of indexes of Travel & Tourism Policy and Enabling Conditions, Natural and Cultural Resources and Safety and Security of selected countries in 2019

A direct relationship between the values of the indexes and the level of travel and tourism sustainable competitiveness of a country is not known. However, a vague practice – the fuzzy procedure – exists for estimating the level of travel and tourism competitiveness from the values of these determinants. Its implementation allows us to solve the given task as follows: the first step is the fuzzy estimation of travel and tourism sustainable competitiveness; the second step utilizes the estimation results to allocate the country into a category according to popularity from the viewpoint of travelling persons.

3.2 Results

The task is solved using the established fuzzy approach described in part 2, which captures the individual steps within the fuzzy process. This is preceded by a phase of a fuzzy model formulation, which is specified as follows:

Let us consider three input linguistic variables Ai, i ∈ {P, R, S} with value domains $U_{Ai} = \langle 0, 100 \rangle$ %, the identified basis values of which are the numbers presented in separate columns of Table 1. The task is to estimate the individual basic value of output linguistic variable B (travel and tourism sustainable competitiveness level) at the value domain $U_B = \langle 0, 100 \rangle$ %. For linguistic terms Aik of the variable Ai, and Bj of the variable B and for their formalized terms (fuzzy sets) $\underline{Aik}$, and $\underline{Bj}$ it holds true that j = k, k ∈ {L, M, H}. For practical reasons, Ai, Aik, and $\underline{Aik}$ will be replaced by i, ki, and $\underline{ki}$, B and $\underline{Bj}$ by O and $\underline{kO}$.

The files of fuzzy sets $\underline{ki} = \{\{(x, \mu_{ki}(x)): x \in U_i\}$, k ∈ {L, M, H}, I ∈ {P, R, S} or the file $\underline{kO} = \{(p, \mu_{kO}(p)): p \in U_O\}$ can be an acceptable choice, in which the designation L means a low value of linguistic variable, M a mean value and H a high value, defined by trapezoidal membership functions $\mu_{ki}(x)$, respectively $\mu_{kO}(p)$ drawn in Fig. 1. To describe the procedure of the task, all linguistic variables are assumed to have the same distribution and uniformity. This distribution can vary according to the experts who decide on its parameters.

Another step is a compilation of a set of inference rules of type $((\underline{k_1P}, \underline{k_2R}, \underline{k_3S}), \underline{kO})$ for assigning three output terms to total 27 various triplets α_3 of input terms, where k_1, k_2, k_3, k ∈ {L, M, H}. The basic strategy is the choice of $\underline{kO}$ with the k, which prevails in the triplet $(\underline{k_1P}, \underline{k_2R}, \underline{k_3S})$. If none of them prevails, $\underline{MO}$ is chosen. This selection strategy assigns $\underline{MO}$ to thirteen triplets of input terms in total; $\underline{LO}$, respectively $\underline{HO}$, is assigned in seven of the remaining cases – see Table 2 presenting the rules compiled on the basis of this strategy, which is determined by the experts and decision makers.

LLL→L	**LLH→L**	**LMH→M**	**MMM→M**	**MLL→L**	**MHM→M**	**HHH→H**	**HLH→H**	**HHM→H**
LLM→L	LHL→L	LMM→M	MLM→M	MLH→M	MHH→H	HLL→L	HMM→M	HLM→M
LML→L	LHM→M	LHH→H	MML→M	MMH→M	MHL→M	HHL→H	HMH→H	HML→M

Source: Author

Table 2 Set of twenty-seven inference rules (in the form $k_1k_2k_3 \rightarrow k$)

The specific procedure related to the fuzzy model solution will be explained on the example of the construction of the y_0 parameter for the Slovak Republic. For the purpose of the demonstrative calculations, the differences in the distribution of values of individual indices will be ignored (i.e., for each of them the parameters of membership functions to terms it holds a = 20%, b = 40%, c = 60%, d = 80%).

From a triplet of input basis values (66, 36, 80) – see Table 1, it follows that (the formulas for calculation are specified in part 2):

- $66 \in S_{MP}$ with the truth $|66 \in S_{MP}| = \mu_{MP}(66) = 0.7$
- $66 \in S_{HP}$ with the truth $|66 \in S_{HP}| = \mu_{HP}(66) = 0.3$
- $36 \in S_{LR}$ with the truth $|36 \in S_{LR}| = \mu_{LR}(36) = 0.2$
- $36 \in S_{MR}$ with the truth $|36 \in S_{MR}| = \mu_{MR}(36) = 0.8$
- $80 \in S_{HS}$ with the truth $|87 \in S_{HS}| = \mu_{HP}(80) = 1$.

The assigned input values (66, 36, 80) put in the fuzzification process enabled us to construct four triplets α_3 in the symbolic notation $\alpha_{MMH} = (\underline{MP}, \underline{MR}, \underline{HS})$, $\alpha_{MLH} = (\underline{MP}, \underline{LR}, \underline{HS})$, $\alpha_{HMH} = (\underline{HP}, \underline{MR}, \underline{HS})$ and $\alpha_{HLH} = (\underline{HP}, \underline{LR}, \underline{HS})$; in the logic notation $\alpha_{MMH}^* = (66 \in S_{MP}) \wedge (36 \in S_{MR}) \wedge (80 \in S_{HS})$, $|\alpha_{MMH}^*| = \min\{0.7, 0.8, 1\} = 0.7$; $\alpha_{MLH}^* = (66 \in S_{MP}) \wedge (36 \in S_{LR}) \wedge (80 \in S_{HS})$, $|\alpha_{MLH}^*| = \min\{0.7, 0.2, 1\} = 0.2$; $\alpha_{HMH}^* = (66 \in S_{HP}) \wedge (36 \in S_{MR}) \wedge (80 \in S_{HS})$, $|\alpha_{HMH}^*| = \min\{0.3, 0.8, 1\} = 0.3$; $\alpha_{HLH}^* = (66 \in S_{HP}) \wedge (36 \in S_{LR}) \wedge (80 \in S_{HS})$, $|\alpha_{HLH}^*| = \min\{0.3, 0.2, 1\} = 0.2$.

By the application of inference rules on the symbolic notation of triplets, the outputs $\underline{MO}$ and $\underline{HO}$ were traced by the rules $((\underline{MP}, \underline{MR}, \underline{HS}), \underline{MO})$, $((\underline{MP}, \underline{LR}, \underline{HS}), \underline{MO})$, $((\underline{HP}, \underline{MR}, \underline{HS}), \underline{HO})$ and $((\underline{HP}, \underline{LR}, \underline{HS}), \underline{HO})$. Then AGG $= (\alpha_{MMH}^*, p \in S_{MO}) \vee (\alpha_{MLH}^*, p \in S_{MO}) \vee (\alpha_{HMH}^*, p \in S_{HO}) \vee (\alpha_{HLH}^*, p \in S_{HO})$ and $\mu_{agg} = |\text{AGG}| = \max\{\min\{|\alpha_{MMH}^*|, \mu_{MO}(p)\}, \min\{|\alpha_{MLH}^*|, \mu_{MO}(p)\}, \min\{|\alpha_{HMH}^*|, \mu_{HO}(p)\}, \min\{|\alpha_{HLH}^*|, \mu_{HO}(p)\}\} = \max\{\min\{0.7, \mu_{MO}(p)\}, \min\{0.3, \mu_{HO}(p)\}\}$. Then $\mu_{AGG}(y) = 0$ for $y < 20$, $\mu_{AGG}(y) = (y_i - 20) / 20$ for $20 \leq y < 34$, $\mu_{AGG}(y) = 0.7$ for $34 \leq y < 66$, $\mu_{AGG}(y) = (80 - y_i) / 20$ for $66 \leq y < 74$ and $\mu_{AGG}(y) = 0.3$ for $y \geq 74$ (see the bold line in Figure 1).

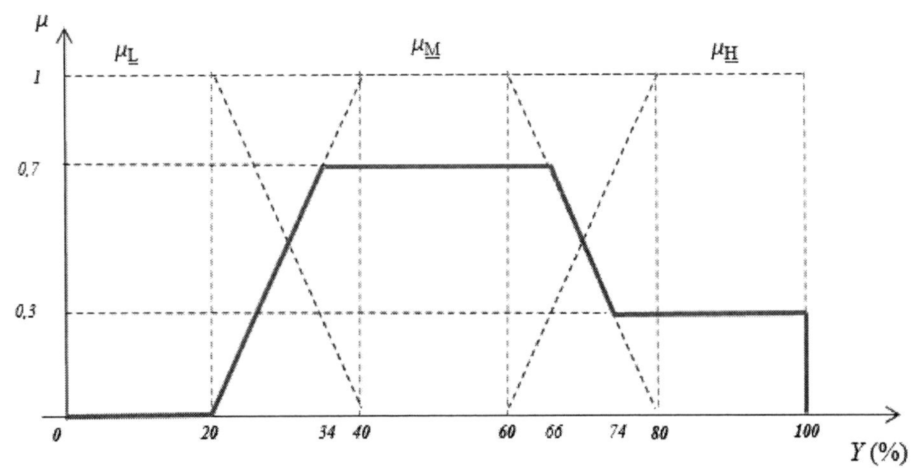

Source: Author

Figure 1 Graph of function μ_{agg}

For the value y_0 given by formula (3) it holds: $y_0 = \int y \cdot \mu_{agg}(y)dy / \int \mu_{agg}(y)dy \approx 2\,444.8 / 39.1 \approx 62.5$ %. After recalculation y_0 to the fuzzy score we get the fuzzy evaluation of travel and tourism sustainable competitiveness of the Slovak Republic = (62.5 · 7 / 100) = 4.375. The resulting values of y_0 for all examined countries are summarized in Table 3.

Country	Fuzzy score / Index y_0 in %
China	5.9 / 84.2
Spain	5.76 / 82.3
Japan	4.94 / 70,56
Czech Republic	4.56 / 65.14
Singapore	4.39 / 62.7
Slovak Republic	4.375 / 62.5
Albania	4.03 / 57,5
Russia	3.5 / 50
Bosnia and Herzegovina	3.5 / 50
Turkey	3.5 / 50

Source: Author

Table 3 Values of travel and tourism competitiveness index y_0 in %

4 Discussion

The boundaries distinguishing the countries with high travel & tourism competitiveness (highly popular destinations), conditional travel & tourism competitiveness (conditionally popular destinations), and low travel & tourism competitiveness (low popular destinations) lie at the points Y_1 = 30 percent and Y_2 = 70 percent. The results summarized in Tab. 3 indicate that China, Japan, Spain are ranked as countries with high travel & tourism competitiveness (very popular tourist destinations). The countries with conditional travel & tourism competitiveness include the rest of the examined countries, i.e., Singapore, Czech Republic, Slovak Republic, Russia, Albania, Bosna and Hercegovina, and Turkey, which are medium popular with travelling persons.

5 Conclusions

The objective of the paper was to evaluate the level of travel & tourism competitiveness with respect to sustainability in tourism of selected European and Asian countries based on the subjective rankings of travelling persons. The rankings used are the representative indicators of sustainable tourism development. Due the character of these input parameters the task was dealt with the fuzzy approach method, which provides space for the application of the human factor. For the purposes of the demonstrative task, necessary calculations were, without loss of generality, minimized by the assumption of identical courses of membership functions of formalized terms of input linguistic variables. Regardless of this simplification, the solved specific task is a useful illustration of the presented method.

The resulting fuzzy score enabled to identify two groups of countries – the highly competitive group (China, Japan, Spain) and conditionally competitive group (Singapore, Czech Republic, Slovak Republic, Russia, Albania, Bosna and Hercegovina, and Turkey).

References

Běhounek, L., & Cintula, P. (2006). From fuzzy logic to fuzzy mathematics: A methodological manifesto. *Fuzzy Sets and Systems*, *157*(5), 642-646. https://doi.org/10.1016/j.fss.2005.10.011.

Calderwood, L. U., & Soshkin, M. (2019). The travel & tourism competitiveness report 2019. In K. Schwab, A. Menon & C. Wolff (Eds.), *World Economic Forum* (pp. 1-112). Geneva: The World Economic Forum. http://www3.weforum.org/docs/WEF_TTCR_2019.pdf.

Dubois, D., & Prade, H. (1996). What are fuzzy rules and how to use them. *Fuzzy sets and systems*, *84*(2), 169-185. https://doi.org/10.1016/0165-0114(96)00066-8.

European Commission, European Tourism Indicators System for sustainable destination management, Available: https://ec.europa.eu/growth/industry/sustainability_en (accessed: 19.1.2021).

Kahraman, C. (Ed.). (2008). Fuzzy multi-criteria decision making: theory and applications with recent developments (Vol. 16). Springer Science & Business Media.

Manns, J. (2013). Downgrading rating agency reform. *George Washington Law Review*, *81*(3), 749. https://papers.ssrn.com/sol3/papers.cfm?abstract_id=2174802.

Morim, A., Fortes, E. S., Reis, P., Cosenza, C., Doria, F., & Gonçalves, A. (2017). Think fuzzy system: developing new pricing strategy methods for consumer goods using fuzzy logic. Int. J. Fuzzy Logic Syst. IJFLS, 7(1), 1-15.

Tian, C., Peng, J., Zhang, W., Zhang, S., & Wang, J. (2020). Tourism environmental impact assessment based on improved AHP and picture fuzzy PROMETHEE II methods. *Technological and Economic Development of Economy*, *26*(2), 355-378. https://doi.org/10.3846/tede.2019.11413.

Ziyadin, S., Borodin, A., Streltsova, E., Suieubayeva, S., & Pshembayeva, D. (2019). Fuzzy logic approach in the modeling of sustainable tourism development management. *Polish Journal of management studies*, *19*.

Zadeh, L. A. (1973). Outline of a new approach to the analysis of complex systems and decision processes. *IEEE Transactions on systems, Man, and Cybernetics*, (1), 28-44. https://doi.org/10.1109/TSMC.1973.5408575.

Zadeh, L. A. (1999). Fuzzy logic = computing with words. In L. A. Zadeh & J. Kacprzyk (Eds.), *Computing with Words in Information/Intelligent Systems 1* (pp. 3-23). Heidelberg: Physica, Springer. https://doi.org/10.1007/978-3-7908-1873-4_1.

On transformations in interval linear programming: just be careful!

Milan Hladík [1]

Abstract. We deal with linear programming problems the input data of which are uncertain. The only information we have about the uncertainty are the lower and upper bounds on the values; this yields interval enclosures of the uncertain coefficients. Interval linear programming is an established discipline with many results and open problems, too. We focus on the transformations of the constraints, which are standard in the real case, and point out the pitfalls appearing in the interval case. We will see that under general assumptions they bring fundamental changes of the problem – either they cause infeasibility or huge overestimation.

Keywords: interval analysis, interval matrix, linear programming, optimization, uncertainty.

JEL classification: C44, C61

1 Introduction

Linear programming (LP) is a common tool to solve many real-life problems. Since the input data of practical models are often subject to various types of uncertainty (such as inexactness of measurements, estimations, missing data etc.), we have to reflect it in the linear programming theory. In particular, in this paper we assume that (possibly all) input data are known with some precision only, that is, we know intervals covering the true data. This gives rise to interval linear programming (Fiedler et al., 2006; Hladík, 2012). Before stating the problem, we have to introduce basic interval concepts first.

Interval objects. An interval matrix is a set of matrices

$$\mathbf{A} = \{A \in \mathbb{R}^{m\times n} \underline{A} \leq A \leq \overline{A}\},$$

where $\underline{A}, \overline{A} \in \mathbb{R}^{m\times n}$ are given matrices and the inequality is meant entrywise. Interval vectors are defined analogously. The midpoint A_c and the radius A_Δ of $\mathbf{A}$ respectively read

$$A_c = \frac{1}{2}(\underline{A} + \overline{A}), \quad A_\Delta = \frac{1}{2}(\overline{A} - \underline{A}).$$

The set of all $m \times n$ interval matrices is denoted by $\mathbb{IR}^{m\times n}$. Interval vectors are introduced accordingly.

Interval linear programming. Let $\mathbf{A} \in \mathbb{IR}^{m\times n}$, $\mathbf{b} \in \mathbb{IR}^m$ and $\mathbf{c} \in \mathbb{IR}^n$. By an *interval LP problem* we mean a family of LP problems

$$f(A, b, c) = \min\ c^T x \text{ subject to } Ax = b,\ x \geq 0, \tag{1}$$

[1] Charles University, Faculty of Mathematics and Physics, Department of Applied Mathematics, Malostranské nám. 25, 11800, Prague, Czech Republic, hladik@kam.mff.cuni.cz

where $A \in \mathbf{A}$, $b \in \mathbf{b}$ and $c \in \mathbf{c}$. In short, we write the interval LP problem as

$$\min\ c^T x \text{ subject to } \mathbf{A}x = \mathbf{b},\ x \geq 0. \tag{2}$$

By the *(feasible) solution set* we mean the the union of feasible solutions over all realizations.

There are several issues related to the interval LP problem. *The optimal value range* (Garajová et al., 2019b; Hladík, 2014; Mohammadi and Gentili, 2019; Mostafaee et al., 2016)) aims at computing the best and the worst case optimal values. Formally, it is an interval $\mathbf{f} = [\underline{f}, \overline{f}]$, where

$$\underline{f} = \min\ f(A, b, c) \text{ subject to } A \in \mathbf{A},\ b \in \mathbf{b},\ c \in \mathbf{c},$$
$$\overline{f} = \max\ f(A, b, c) \text{ subject to } A \in \mathbf{A},\ b \in \mathbf{b},\ c \in \mathbf{c}.$$

The optimal solution set $\mathcal{S}$ is the union of all optimal solutions of all realizations of interval data, that is

$$\mathcal{S} = \cup\{S(A, b, c); A \in \mathbf{A},\ b \in b,\ c \in c\},$$

where $S(A, b, c)$ is the set of optimal solutions associated with the particular realization (1). Many tasks related to $\mathcal{S}$ are hard, including an explicit characterization of $\mathcal{S}$, its tight approximation etc. Many scholars focus on the optimal value range problem, so there are also considerably less results related to $\mathcal{S}$; for some of them see Allahdadi and Nehi (2013); Garajová and Hladík (2019); Li et al. (2015); Rada et al. (2019).

Our objectives. Besides (2), one can consider an interval LP problem in the form

$$\min\ c^T x \text{ subject to } \mathbf{A}x \leq \mathbf{b},\ x \geq 0,$$

or in the form

$$\min\ c^T x \text{ subject to } \mathbf{A}x \leq b.$$

In the real case, usually just one form is considered since other forms are easily reduced to the basic one by simple transformations (in particular, splitting equations to double inequalities and imposing nonnegativity of variables). Nevertheless, in the interval case, such transformations are no more equivalent and they do change many properties of the problem.

Our aim is to show the pitfalls associated with such transformations. We will observe that under very mild assumptions the standard transformations produce substantial change in the problem – one of them causes infeasibility and another one redundancy.

Besides the aforementioned two transformations, we will also inspect an (invertible) substitution. It is another kind of transformation of the model which is often used in practice. We will see that for an interval valued problem, it can give rise to an arbitrarily large expansion of the range of optimal values.

2 Transformations in action

In the following subsections, we discuss three common transformation of linear systems. We will see, however, that in the interval setting the transformations are no more equivalent and, even more, the may lead to substantial change of the problem.

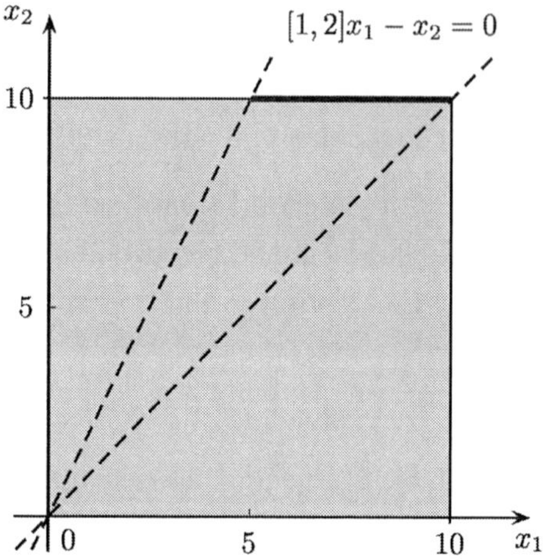

Figure 1 (Example 1) Illustration of the interval LP problem.

2.1 Splitting equations to double inequalities

Transformation of interval equation

$$\mathbf{A}x = \mathbf{b} \tag{3}$$

into inequalities

$$\mathbf{A}x \leq \mathbf{b}, \ \ \mathbf{A}x \geq \mathbf{b} \tag{4}$$

is not an equivalent procedure in general. The reason is that the latter system is corrupted with dependencies. Considering interval parameters as independent quantities, it contains real valued systems in the form of

$$A_1 x \leq b_1, \ \ A_2 x \leq b_2,$$

where $A_1, A_2 \in \mathbf{A}$ and $b_1, b_2 \in \mathbf{b}$. In general, such systems origin from no realization of $\mathbf{A}x = \mathbf{b}$.

Surprisingly, in view of Hladík (2017); Li (2015), both systems (3) and (4) have the same feasible solution set. As a consequence, the value of $\underline{f}$ remains unchanged (Garajová et al., 2019a). On the other hand, the optimal solution set $\mathcal{S}$ and the whole optimal value range f may be changed, in particular $\overline{f}$ may increase. Our aim is to show that under general assumptions the overestimation caused by the transformation is tremendous.

Example 1. Consider the interval LP problem

$$\min \ -x_1 \text{ subject to } [1,2]x_1 - x_2 = 0, \ 0 \leq x \leq 10.$$

By inspection, we see that the optimal values range in the interval $f = [-10, -5]$. The optimal solution set $\mathcal{S}$ consists of the line segment between points $(5, 10)^T$ and $(10, 10)^T$. See illustration in Figure 1.

The transformation yields the interval LP problem

$$\min \ -x_1 \text{ subject to } [1,2]x_1 - x_2 \geq 0, \ [1,2]x_1 - x_2 \leq 0, \ 0 \leq x \leq 10.$$

The realization

$$\min\ -x_1 \text{ subject to } x_1 - x_2 \geq 0,\ 2x_1 - x_2 \leq 0,\ 0 \leq x \leq 10$$

has only one feasible point, the origin. As a consequence, the optimal value range is $f' = [-10, 0]$. Not every value in this interval is, however, attained as the optimal value of a certain realization. The actual set of optimal values is $[-10, -5] \cup \{0\}$. The optimal solution set $\mathcal{S}'$ is disconnected, too. We have $\mathcal{S}' = \mathcal{S} \cup \{(0,0)^T\}$.

Even more, the transformation may change emptiness of the optimal solution set.

Example 2. Consider a modified example from Garajová et al. (2019a)

$$\min\ -x_1 \text{ subject to } [0,1]x_1 - x_2 = 0,\ x_1, x_2 \geq 0.$$

Every realization is unbounded, so $\mathcal{S} = \emptyset$. Transforming the equation into double inequalities gives the ILP problem

$$\min\ -x_1 \text{ subject to } [0,1]x_1 - x_2 \leq 0,\ [0,1]x_1 - x_2 \geq 0,\ x_1, x_2 \geq 0.$$

Now, the optimal solution set is not empty since, for instance, the realization

$$\min\ -x_1 \text{ subject to } 1x_1 - x_2 \leq 0,\ 0x_1 - x_2 \geq 0,\ \ x_1, x_2 \geq 0$$

has the optimal solution $(0,0)^T$.

We say that an interval system of equations or inequalities is *infeasible* (*feasible*) if there is an infeasible (feasible) realization. The following observation shows that under very general assumptions the transformation produces infeasible systems.

Proposition 1. *The transformation of one interval linear equation*

$$\mathbf{a}^T x = \mathbf{b} \quad \rightarrow \quad \mathbf{a}^T x \leq \mathbf{b},\ \mathbf{a}^T x \geq \mathbf{b}$$

leads to an infeasible system provided at least one of the following conditions holds

1) $b_\Delta > 0$;

2) $a_\Delta > 0$ *and* $x = 0^T$ *is not a common feasible solution to every realization.*

Proof. 1) If $b_\Delta > 0$, then the system $\mathbf{a}^T x \leq \mathbf{b},\ \mathbf{a}^T x \geq \mathbf{b}$ contains the realization $a^T x \leq \underline{b},\ a^T x \geq \overline{b}$, from which

$$\underline{b} \geq a^T x \geq \overline{b} > \underline{b}.$$

Therefore the realization is infeasible.

2) If $a_\Delta > 0$, then the system $\mathbf{a}^T x \leq \mathbf{b},\ \mathbf{a}^T x \geq \mathbf{b}$ contains the realization $\overline{a}^T x \leq b,\ \underline{a}^T x \geq b$, from which

$$\overline{a}^T x \leq b \leq \underline{a}^T x < \overline{a}^T x$$

in view of $x \neq 0$. Therefore the realization is infeasible. □

2.2 Imposing nonnegativity

If x_is are free (i.e., sign unrestricted) variables, then we simply impose nonnegativity of variables by the substitution $x := x^1 - x^2$, $x^1, x^2 \geq 0$. In the model, however, this transformation causes dependencies because $\mathbf{A}x$ is replaced by $\mathbf{A}x^1 - \mathbf{A}x^2$. This is basically the same for equations or inequalities,

$$\mathbf{A}x = b \quad \rightarrow \quad \mathbf{A}x^1 - \mathbf{A}x^2 = b,\ x^1, x^2 \geq 0,$$
$$\mathbf{A}x \leq b \quad \rightarrow \quad \mathbf{A}x^1 - \mathbf{A}x^2 \leq b,\ x^1, x^2 \geq 0.$$

It is known (Garajová et al., 2019a) that the transformation preserves the value of $\overline{f}$. On the other hand, the transformation can change the optimal solution set and the optimal value range. Our aim is to show that the negative effect can be huge. In fact, we show that imposing nonnegativity eliminates basically all interval constraints, which leads possibly to tremendous overestimation.

Proposition 2. *The transformation applied to an interval linear constraint with at least one interval entry in left-hand side makes the constraint redundant. In particular, let* $\mathbf{a} \in \mathbb{IR}^n$, $a_\Delta \neq 0$, *and* $\mathbf{b} \in \mathbb{IR}$. *Then*

1) $\mathbf{a}^T x = \mathbf{b}$ *is transformed to* $\mathbf{a}^T x^1 - \mathbf{a}^T x^2 = \mathbf{b}$, $x^1, x^2 \geq 0$, *the solution set of which is* $\mathbb{R}^n$*;*

2) $\mathbf{a}^T x \leq \mathbf{b}$ *is transformed to* $\mathbf{a}^T x^1 - \mathbf{a}^T x^2 \leq \mathbf{b}$, $x^1, x^2 \geq 0$, *the solution set of which is* $\mathbb{R}^n$.

Proof. We will focus on the interval linear inequality $\mathbf{a}^T x \leq \mathbf{b}$ only; equations are handled analogously. Imposing nonnegativity results in the inequalities $\mathbf{a}^T x^1 - \mathbf{a}^T x^2 \leq \mathbf{b}$, $x^1, x^2 \geq 0$. The solution set is characterized by the Vajda Theorem (Vajda, 1961) as

$$\underline{a}^T x^1 - \overline{a}^T x^2 \leq \overline{b}, \quad x^1, x^2 \geq 0,$$

or

$$a_c^T (x^1 - x^2) - a_\Delta^T (x^1 + x^2) \leq \overline{b}, \quad x^1, x^2 \geq 0.$$

Notice that the original variables read $x = x^1 - x^2$ and $a_\Delta \neq 0$. Thus, for any $x \in \mathbb{R}^n$ we can take $x^1 := \max(x, 0) + \alpha e$, $x^2 := \max(-x, 0) + \alpha e$, where $\alpha > 0$ is sufficiently large. □

Example 3. Consider the interval LP problem

$$\min\ x_2 \text{ subject to } x_1 + x_2 \geq 10,\ -[1,2]x_1 + [0,1]x_2 \geq 0.$$

The optimal value range reads $\boldsymbol{f} = [5, 10]$. Substituting $x := x^1 - x^2$, $x^1, x^2 \geq 0$, we obtain the interval LP problem

$$\begin{aligned} \min\ x_2^1 - x_2^2 \text{ subject to } & x_1^1 - x_1^2 + x_2^1 - x_2^2 \geq 10, \\ & -[1,2]x_1^1 + [1,2]x_1^2 + [0,1]x_2^1 - [0,1]x_2^2 \geq 0. \end{aligned}$$

The realization

$$\begin{aligned} \min\ x_2^1 - x_2^2 \text{ subject to } & x_1^1 - x_1^2 + x_2^1 - x_2^2 \geq 10, \\ & -x_1^1 + 2x_1^2 + x_2^1 \geq 0 \end{aligned}$$

is unbounded. So the optimal value range is $f' = (-\infty, 10]$. This confirms that $\overline{f}$ was preserved, but $\underline{f}$ changed. Moreover, the change of $\overline{f}$ from the finite value of 5 to $-\infty$ is crucial from many perspectives.

Proposition 3. *Suppose that $(c_\Delta)_i > 0$ for some i, and suppose that the interval LP problem is feasible. Then for the optimal value range f' after the transformation we have $\underline{f}' = -\infty$.*

Proof. Consider the ith variable x_i, which is substituted by the transformation as $x_i := x_i^1 - x_i^2$, $x_i^1, x_i^2 \geq 0$. The corresponding term $\mathbf{c}_i x_i$ in the objective function changes to $\mathbf{c}_i x_i^1 - \mathbf{c}_i x_i^2$. Consider the realization with the term $\underline{c}_i x_i^1 - \overline{c}_i x_i^2$; the other objective function coefficients can be chosen arbitrarily. Concerning the constraints, consider the realization that results from the feasible realization of the original constraints by applying the transformation.

For any feasible solution x^1, x^2 (notice there is at least one by the assumptions) we can take $x_i^1 := x_i^1 + \alpha$, $x_i^2 := x_i^2 + \alpha$, where $\alpha > 0$. The feasibility is preserved and the objective function decreases by $2\alpha(c_\Delta)_i$, so it tends to $-\infty$ as $\alpha \to \infty$. □

2.3 Substitution

Substitution is another commonly used transformation of variables (basically, imposing non-negativity is also a kind of substitution). For the sake of simplicity, consider a substitution of variables $x := Sy$ represented by a nonsingular matrix $S \in \mathbb{R}^{n \times n}$. Thus a vector of variables x is substituted for a vector of variables y of the same size. Again, in the real case, the substitution is equivalent. In the interval case, it is equivalent only if S is diagonal or a permuted diagonal matrix.

In the interval case, the transformation works as illustrated on the example: The interval system $\mathbf{A}x \leq b$ is replaced by $(\mathbf{A}S)y \leq b$. So the novel constraint interval matrix is $\mathbf{A}S$, as evaluated by interval arithmetic.

Let f be the original optimal value range and f' after the substitution. By the properties of interval arithmetic we always have $f \subseteq f'$. The inclusion can be strict (and in nontrivial cases it usually is). As the example presented in the proof of Proposition 4 shows, the overestimation can be arbitrarily large (from zero radius to positive radius).

Proposition 4. *Let S be such that it is not a permuted diagonal matrix. Then there is an interval LP problem for which $\underline{f}' < \underline{f} \leq \overline{f} < \overline{f}'$.*

Proof. Consider the interval LP problem

$$\min \mathbf{c}^T x \text{ subject to } x = e_1,$$

where

$$\mathbf{c} = (0, [-1, 1], \ldots, [-1, 1])^T, \quad e_1 = (1, 0, \ldots, 0)^T.$$

Obviously, $f = 0$. The substitution transforms the problem to

$$\min (\mathbf{c}^T S)y \text{ subject to } Sy = e_1,$$

so that $f' = (\mathbf{c}^T S)S^{-1}e_1$. Due to the assumption, in at least one column of S there are two or more nonzero entries. Hence all entries of the interval vector $\mathbf{c}^T S$ are intervals with positive radius. Since $S^{-1}e_1 \neq 0$, the resulting interval f' has positive radius, too. Due to symmetry of c around zero, f' is symmetric around zero as well. Therefore $\underline{f}' < \underline{f} = 0 = \overline{f} < \overline{f}'$. □

3 Conclusion

In this paper, we discussed the basic transformations of constraints and variables of LP problems in the case the input coefficients are interval valued. It is known (Garajová et al., 2019a) that the transformations are correct in the interval setting only in certain situations, but often they produce a problem that is not equivalent to the original one.

Indeed, we demonstrated by examples as well as by theoretical results that one has to be vary careful when handling an interval-valued model. We saw that even a simple transformation of the constraints may lead to a drastic change of the model properties and outputs. This also confirms that we have to maximally utilize the original structure of the data and avoid unprofessional manipulation with the data and the model.

Acknowledgements

The author was supported by the Czech Science Foundation Grant P403-18-04735S.

References

M. Allahdadi and H. Mishmast Nehi. The optimal solution set of the interval linear programming problems. *Optim. Lett.*, 7(8):1893–1911, 2013.

M. Fiedler, J. Nedoma, J. Ramík, J. Rohn, and K. Zimmermann. *Linear Optimization Problems with Inexact Data*. Springer, New York, 2006.

Elif Garajová and Milan Hladík. On the optimal solution set in interval linear programming. *Comput. Optim. Appl.*, 72(1):269–292, 2019.

Elif Garajová, Milan Hladík, and Miroslav Rada. Interval linear programming under transformations: optimal solutions and optimal value range. *Cent. Eur. J. Oper. Res.*, 27(3):601–614, 2019a.

Elif Garajová,MilanHladík, and Miroslav Rada. Thebest,theworstandthesemi-strong: optimal values in interval linear programming. *Croat. Oper. Res. Rev.*, 10(2):201–209, 2019b.

Milan Hladík. Interval linear programming: A survey. In Zoltán Ádám Mann, editor, *Linear Programming - New Frontiers in Theory and Applications*, chapter 2, pages 85–120. Nova Science Publishers, New York, 2012. ISBN 978-1-61209-579-0.

Milan Hladík. On approximation of the best case optimal value in interval linear programming. *Optim. Lett.*, 8(7):1985–1997, 2014.

Milan Hladík. Transformations of interval linear systems of equations and inequalities. *Linear Multilinear Algebra*, 65(2):211–223, 2017.

Wei Li. A note on dependency between interval linear systems. *Optim. Lett.*, 9(4):795–797, 2015.

Wei Li, Xiao Liu, and Haohao Li. Generalized solutions to interval linear programmes and related necessary and sufficient optimality conditions. *Optim. Methods Softw.*, 30(3):516–530, 2015.

Mohsen Mohammadi and Monica Gentili. Bounds on the worst optimal value in interval linear programming. *Soft Comput.*, 23(21):11055–11061, 2019.

Amin Mostafaee, Milan Hladík, and Michal Černý . Inverse linear programming with interval coefficients. *J. Comput. Appl. Math.*, 292:591–608, 2016.

Miroslav Rada, Milan Hladík, and Elif Garajová. Testing weak optimality of a given solution in interval linear programming revisited: NP-hardness proof, algorithm and some polynomially-solvable cases. *Optim. Lett.*, 13(4):875–890, 2019.

S. Vajda. *Mathematical Programming*. Addison-Wesley, Reading Mass., USA, 1961.

Robust Steiner Tree with uncertain edge costs

Robert Hlavatý[1], Tereza Vudarčíková[2]

Abstract. Steiner Tree problem is a problem of combinatorial optimization and a special case of minimum spanning tree problem. Similarly to the minimum spanning tree, we are looking for a minimum connection of vertices while in the case of Steiner tree, some additional vertices may be used to achieve an improvement in the objective function. In this paper, we consider a situation where some of the edge costs are not specifically set and ranging in a predefined symmetrical interval instead. The problem is formulated as an integer linear program and a way of building the robust equivalent of the model is described using the gamma-robustness approach. The proposed approach is demonstrated on a semi-artificial case of an electrical grid for different degrees of uncertainty measured by algebraic function. The results justify the profitability of using Steiner vertices in the model and the expected increase in the costs related to different degrees of uncertainty is calculated.

Keywords: Graph theory, optimization, robustness, Steiner tree.

JEL Classification: C44, C61

1 Introduction

We revisit the classical problem of combinatorial optimization and graph theory called the Steiner tree problem. The history of the problem goes back to the early 19th century and the attribution to Jakob Steiner is considered quite misleading since many mathematicians were involved in discussing this problem (Brazil et al., 2013). Still, the name of the problem after Jakob Steiner got established in textbooks and among the scientific community. Extensive work exists on the topology, solution techniques and geometry analysis of the problem which is documented by the extensive survey by Hwang, Richards and Winter (1992).

The Steiner tree problem has been approached by many researchers and various algorithms were developed for the exact solution of the problem. An overview of exact algorithms (for Euclidean case) is provided by Fampa, Lee and Maculan (2015). The exact solution to the problem is known to be NP-hard (Garey, Graham and Johnson, 1977) and that is why many researchers focused on developing polynomial approximations of the problem. A survey of approximation algorithms is provided by Gröpl et al. (2001).

Regardless of the exactness of the algorithm, there is an issue to be dealt with coming from practical applications of the Steiner tree problem. That is, the data input describing some particular Steiner tree is incomplete or uncertain. Specifically, the edge costs of the given graph may not be given for various reasons, whenever the exact evaluation is not possible or is possible only ex-post. It is possible to overcome this issue by taking a probabilistic approach like Gupta and Pál (2005) or a fuzzy approach like Šeda (2008). Another way of dealing with uncertainty is the robust approach which allows performing an efficient worst-case analysis of different scenarios. Bertsimas and Sim (2003) made this a very popular approach by developing their concept of gamma-robustness. This concept has already been applied to Steiner tree

[1] CZU Prague, Department of Systems Engineering, Kamýcká 129, 165 00, Prague, hlavaty@pef.czu.cz

[2] CZU Prague, Department of Systems Engineering, Kamýcká 129, 165 00, Prague, xvudt001@studenti.czu.cz

problem in the study of Álvarez-Miranda, Ljubić and Toth (2013). In our paper, we use the gamma-robustness approach for a different and simpler version of the problem, which is more straightforward and we consider a different integer linear programming formulation of the problem.

The rest of the paper is organized as follows: we start with the definition of the Steiner tree problem and formulate the problem as an integer linear programme. The overview of gamma-robustness follows. Our result is embedding the gamma-robustness into the integer programming formulation of the Steiner tree problem and explain the approach usefulness in a semi-real case.

2 Materials and methods

The section is divided into two main subparts. After the definition of the Steiner tree problem, we first describe one of the possible formulations of the Steiner tree problem as integer linear programming (ILP) and consequently, we briefly introduce the concept of gamma-robustness. This concept of robustness will be used to build a robust counterpart of the Steiner tree problem.

2.1 Problem definition

We consider the following definition of the Steiner tree problem, inspired by Siebert, Ahmed and Nemhauser (2020): An undirected graph $G = (V, E)$ is given with the set of vertices V and the set of edges E with no multiple edges considered. A subset $R \subseteq V$ is a set of *terminal vertices* and the edges are evaluated with nonnegative costs $c_{ij} \geq 0$, for all edges $(i, j) \in E$. A Steiner tree is a subgraph of G in which all terminal vertices are connected while the tree may contain vertices $v \in V \setminus R$ which are called *Steiner vertices*. The Steiner tree problem is to find such a tree that minimizes the sum of all edge costs over all edges in the tree.

2.2 Formulation of Steiner tree as ILP

There are various possibilities of formulating the Steiner tree problem as ILP. We choose the formulation of Diané and Plesnik (1993) for the purposes of this paper, although the choice is not exclusive and other formulations might be used similarly. The aforementioned approach is based on the following assumptions. We set $V = \{v_1, \dots, v_n\}$ and $R = \{v_1, \dots, v_p\}$ and pick an arbitrary vertex $v_1 \in R$. A new digraph $\bar{G}(V, \bar{E})$ is constructed, which is obtained from G by duplicating each edge (i, j) by two edges (i, j) and (j, i) of opposite direction with the same cost c_{ij}. We further denote a set of indices $V' := \{i \in V | (i, j) \in \bar{E}\}$ to create a set of indices that actually exist in the created digraph since we do not assume $G(V, E)$ or consequently $G(V, \bar{E})$ to be a complete graph.

Then the following formulation describes the minimum Steiner tree problem:

$$\min \sum_{(i,j) \in \bar{E}} c_{ij} x_{ij} \tag{1}$$

subject to

$$\sum_{i \in V'} x_{ij} \leq 1 \,, \forall j \in V \backslash \{1\}$$

$$n \sum_{i \in V'} x_{ij} \geq u_j + 1, \forall j \in V \backslash \{1\}$$

$$(n+1) \sum_{i \in V'} x_{ij} \geq n(u_j + 1), \forall j \in V \backslash \{1\}$$

$$1 - n(1 - x_{ij}) \leq u_j - u_i \leq 1 + n(1 - x_{ij}) \,, \forall (i,j) \in \bar{E}$$

$$x_{ij} \in \{0,1\} \,, \forall (i,j) \in \bar{E}$$

$$u_1 = 0$$

$$u_i \geq 0, \forall i \in R \backslash \{1\}$$

Model (1) minimizes the costs over all edges in the given graph represented by binary variables x_{ij} and the resulting Steiner tree is formed by all edges such that $x_{ij} = 1$. The constraints preserve that at most one edge enters any vertex and that each *terminal vertex* is reached by an edge for which $x_{ij} = 1$. The auxiliary variables u_i express the distance (=number of 1-edges) of any vertex $v_i \in V \backslash \{1\}$ from the chosen vertex $v_1 \in R$ which acts as a root in the created tree. Through these distances, it is secured that an edge is $(x_{ij} = 1)$ or is not $(x_{ij} = 0)$ a part of the resulting Steiner tree. We refer a reader to Diané and Plesnik (1993) for a detailed explanation of the approach and proof.

2.3 Building a robust counterpart for generic ILP

In the following section, we present a brief overview of the approach of Bertsimas and Sim (2003) commonly known as gamma-robustness. The name gamma-robustness is due to the presence of parameter Γ in this approach that acts as a control parameter for a degree of uncertainty for a decision-maker. The purpose of this chapter is to show how to turn a generic ILP model into its *robust counterpart*. A robust counterpart is a form of the original model that allows one to search worst-case scenarios for a given degree of uncertainty that a decision-maker lays upon the input parameters of the ILP model.

We assume the following generic ILP model (2). We notify a reader that the indices used in this section (2.3) do not relate to indices in (2.2). We use the same symbols i and j to avoid overload of notation.

$$\max \sum_{j=1}^{n} c_j x_j \quad \text{s.t.} \quad \sum_{j=1}^{n} a_{ij} x_j \leq b_i \,, i = 1, \dots, m \quad x_j \in \mathbb{Z}, \forall j \qquad (2)$$

$$\max \sum_{j=1}^{n} (c_j \pm \delta_j^c) x_j \quad \text{s.t.} \quad \sum_{j=1}^{n} a_{ij} x_j \leq b_i \,, i = 1, \dots, m \quad x_j \in \mathbb{Z}, \forall j \qquad (3)$$

In model (2), no uncertainty on the input is considered and all parameters attain given exact values. Unlike in model (3), wherein it is considered that the objective function coefficients can deviate by a given $\delta_j^c > 0$. We specifically consider changes only in the objective function coefficients in this paper, however, a similar approach can be applied to any other coefficient (a_{ij}, b_i). The value δ_j^c is to be set by a decision-maker and a way of setting the value is discussed in the discussion chapter. We next show, how to turn model (3) into its robust version called robust counterpart. We introduce a parameter Γ, $0 \leq \Gamma \leq |\mathrm{P}|$ and $\mathrm{P} = \{j | \delta_j^c > 0\}$ describes the set of objective function coefficients that can deviate from its original (expected) value. The parameter Γ controls the degree of uncertainty in the objective function. If Γ is set to $\Gamma = 0$, then no deviations are expected. If Γ is set $0 < \Gamma \leq |\mathrm{P}|$, then a certain number Γ of coefficients c_{ij} is expected to deviate from its expected value by δ_j^c while it is not specifically told which particular coefficients will deviate. In this sense, Γ serves as a control parameter to set the percentage of coefficient in the objective that could "go wrong".

Introducing Γ and $\mathcal{U}$ allows reformulation of the problem (3) into the following ILP (4):

$$\max \sum_{j=1}^{n} c_j x_j - \max_{\{P | \Gamma \leq |P|\}} \left\{ \sum_{j \in \mathcal{U}} \delta_j^c x_j \right\}$$
$$\text{s.t.}$$
$$\sum_{j=1}^{n} a_{ij} x_j \leq b_i, i = 1, \ldots, m \tag{4}$$
$$x_j \in \mathbb{Z}, \forall j$$

Problem (4) seeks to maximize the original objective while maximizing possible deviations in the opposite direction to the original objective. Problem (4) constitutes a combinatorial max-min problem that is generally not easy to be solved. This is where Bertsimas and Sim (2003) propose an approach to overcome this difficulty. Model (4) is first reformulated as a knapsack problem and the dual of the knapsack problem is consequently created. By inserting chosen constraints from the dual model into (4), they define the robust counterpart that solves the problem (4) as ILP. The robust counterpart is defined as:

$$\max \Phi$$
$$\text{s.t.}$$
$$\sum_{j=1}^{n} a_{ij} x_j \leq b_i, i = 1, \ldots, m$$
$$-\sum_{j=1}^{n} c_j x_j + \Gamma z + \sum_{j \in P} p_j + \Phi \leq 0 \tag{5}$$
$$z + p_j \geq \delta_j^c x_j, \forall j \in P$$
$$z \geq 0$$
$$p_j \geq 0, \forall j \in P$$
$$x_j \in \mathbb{Z}, \forall j$$

We notify the reader that formulation (5) is slightly different from the original formulation of Bertsimas and Sim (2003) which is more general. We only assume changes in objective function coefficients because only these deviations are sensible in the case of the Steiner tree problem. In our formulation (5), the objective function is turned into constraint and bounded from below by auxiliary function Φ. This can be done also for an ILP with minimizing objective in a similar way as we have demonstrated in our previous work (Hlavatý and Brožová, 2018).

Model (5) minimizes the original objective while taking into consideration possible Γ deviations in the objective coefficients. Variables p_j and z are originating from the dual model of (4) and P is the set of indices j for those c_j that are expected to deviate by δ_j^c. The optimal solution of (5) provides the best guaranteed (=robust) solution with the possible deviations considered.

3 Results

The results are divided into two subparts. First, we show how to use a general approach from 2.3 to build a robust counterpart of the model (1). Afterwards, we demonstrate the applicability of this approach in the semi-real case.

3.1 Robust formulation of Steiner tree problem

We now take the ILP formulation of the Steiner tree problem (1) and using the approach described in 2.3, we construct a robust counterpart of (1). Specifically, we turn the objective function of (1) into constraint and in addition to the original constraints of (1), new constraints according to (5) must be added as well to create the robust version. The following formulation (6) describes the robust Steiner tree problem:

$$
\begin{gathered}
\min \Phi \\
\text{s.t.} \\
\sum_{(i,j)\in\bar{E}} c_{ij}x_{ij} + \Gamma z + \sum_{(i,j)\in P} p_{ij} - \Phi \leq 0 \\
z + p_{ij} \geq \delta_{ij}^c x_{ij}, \forall (i,j) \in P \\
z \geq 0 \\
p_{ij} \geq 0, \forall (i,j) \in P \\
\sum_{i\in V'} x_{ij} \leq 1, \forall j \in V\backslash\{1\} \\
n\sum_{i\in V'} x_{ij} \geq u_j + 1, \forall j \in V\backslash\{1\} \\
(n+1)\sum_{i\in V'} x_{ij} \geq n(u_j + 1), \forall j \in V\backslash\{1\} \\
1 - n(1 - x_{ij}) \leq u_j - u_i \leq 1 + n(1 - x_{ij}), \forall (i,j) \in \bar{E} \\
x_{ij} \in \{0,1\}, \forall (i,j) \in \bar{E} \\
u_1 = 0 \\
u_i \geq 0, \forall i \in R\backslash\{1\}
\end{gathered}
\tag{6}
$$

Model (6) is created as a combination of (1) and (5). Because of the converse objective (minimization), the first constraint in (6) was adjusted in comparison with (5). Now, we seek the connection of all terminal vertices from R with the possible use of Steiner vertices from $V \backslash R$ and minimize the connection over all $\{i, j\} \in E$. In the robust counterpart (6), it is considered that a number Γ of unspecified cost coefficients c_{ij} can deviate by predefined values δ_{ij}^{c}. Model (6) finds a minimum guaranteed Steiner tree if the possible deviations are considered.

3.2 Illustrative case

We present a brief example that can illustrate the possible use of the robust Steiner tree for planning in practice. The case study is based on Vudarčíková (2020) and details are omitted here due to page restrictions. In the case study, we consider a real development project in Prague. The developer company has no real connection to this case study and all data were collected from public sources (IPR Praha). The developer plans to build a new block of buildings in the given area and the building must be connected to the electrical grid. The electrical grid must be established before the buildings are built. The layout is depicted in Figure 1:

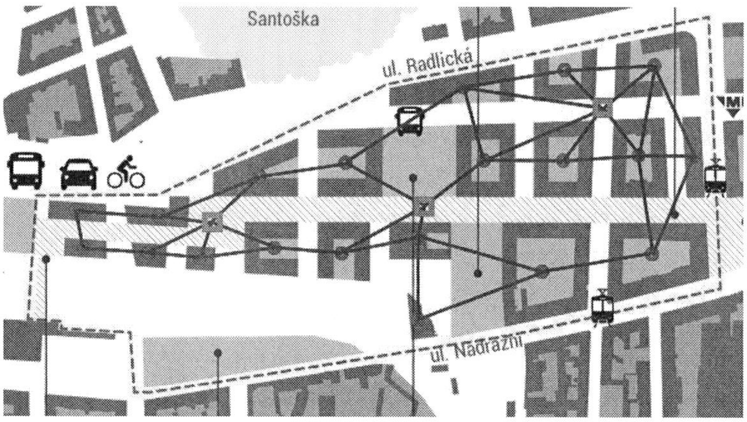

Figure 1 The building site with electrical grid [IPR Praha, 2015]

The position of the buildings is based on the real project, however, the electrical grid is artificial and simplified for illustrative purposes. The red dots represent the connection points in the buildings and green squares represent the additional junctions that would be placed between the buildings to make the connection more effective. The blue lines represent the wiring between the individual connection points. For the sake of simplicity, we consider the graph consisting of red points, green points and blue arcs to be Euclidean. The entire blue grid subsystem would be eventually connected to the city grid through one of the points. The task is to find a minimal connection of all red points (terminal vertices) with the possible use of green points (Steiner vertices). The connection costs c_{ij} are based on the real costs incurred in the process of digging, labour and prices of materials (detailed calculation in Vudarčíková 2020).

We first show the solution to the problem with no deviations from the expected value considered. The model is solved as a normal Steiner tree problem (1). The solution of the model is shown in Figure 2

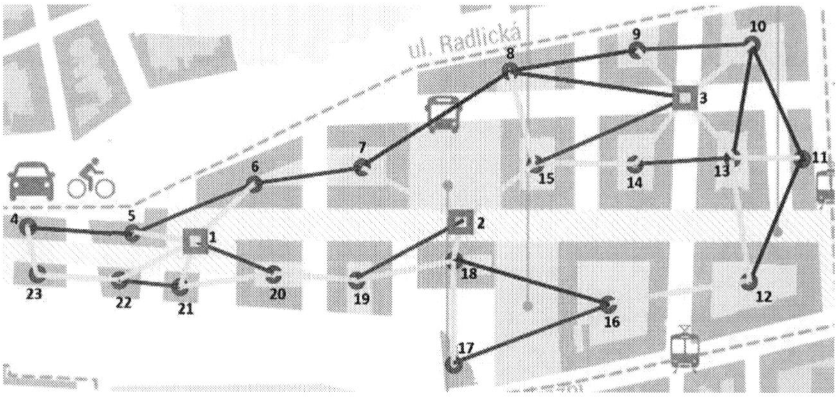

Figure 2 The minimum Steiner tree with no deviations considered ($\Gamma = 0$) [Vudarčíková, 2020]

The solution in Figure 2 shows the minimum (cheapest) connection of all terminal vertices with yellow lines. Note that also each Steiner vertex is connected to the tree. The blue connections would not be used. This model is valid only in the case that the real costs of connections are the same as the expected costs, which is hard to be achieved in practice. Therefore, we suggest using the robust Steiner tree formulation which takes into consideration possible deviations from the expected costs. The deviations in expected costs are mainly caused by extra activity required due to characteristics of the terrain. This consequently causes delays and the requirement of extra labour and material. It was estimated by Vudarčíková (2020) that the costs could worsen by 10% for connections leading through normal terrain and by 16% for connections through already complicated terrain (where the old buildings previously stood and were demolished).

Let us now show the robust solution, i.e. the best-guaranteed connection of terminal vertices when a number Γ of the unspecified coefficient c_{ij} deviate by 10% (or 16% depending on each edge). Let us set $\Gamma = 13$ meaning that we expect that one third (13 out of 39 edges) of the c_{ij} the coefficient will worsen by 10% (16%). Figure 3 shows the robust solution:

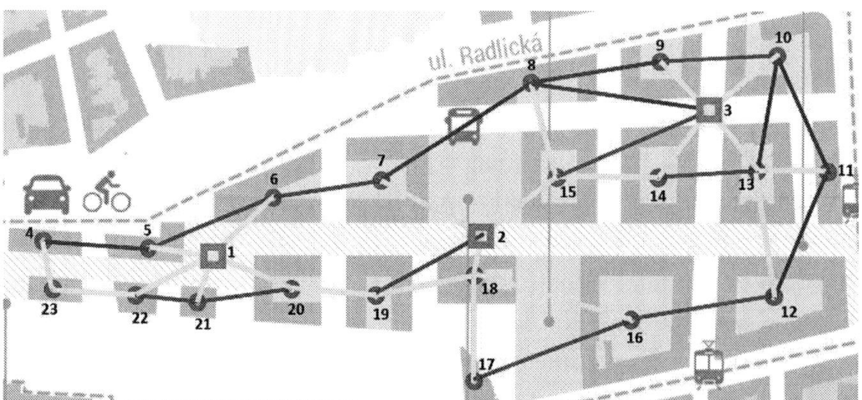

Figure 3 The minimum Steiner tree with one-third of the coefficients deviating ($\Gamma = 13$) [Vudarčíková, 2020]

Note that the resulting Steiner tree has a slightly different structure, the edge 20_1 is used instead of 20_21 and 16_18 instead of 12_16 in comparison with Figure 2. This is indeed caused by the robust solution in which, it is more profitable to change the structure of connections. Apart from the different connection with the best-guaranteed price considering the possible deviations, the objective will worsen as well. Figure 4 shows how the expected total costs of building the connection grow when more uncertainty is imposed on the robust model through the parameter Γ.

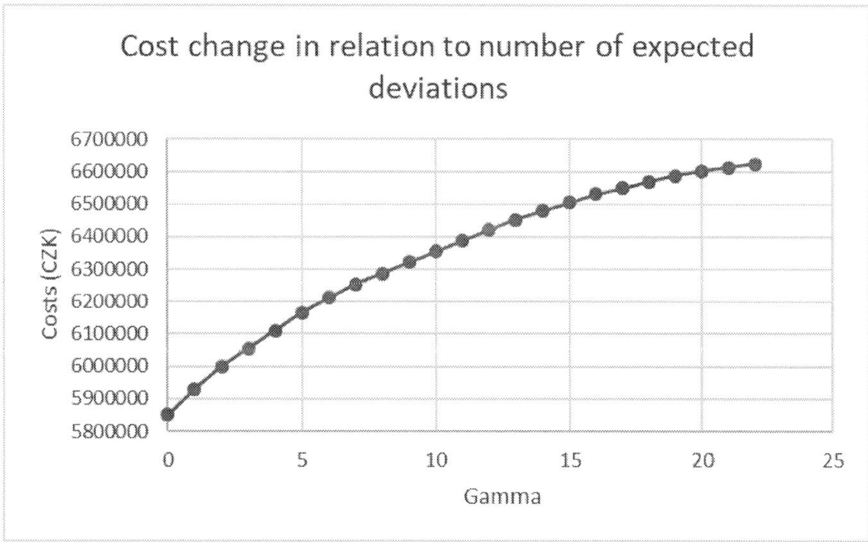

Figure 4 Cost change depending on the number of deviations

The trend is shown for $\Gamma = 0$ (no deviations expected) up to $\Gamma = 22$. The value of 22 is given by the size of the graph. Since our case has $|V| = 23$ the spanning tree will consist of $|V| - 1$ edges (and Steiner tree of at least $|R| - 1$ edges in general). The value $\Gamma = 22$ is the maximum since any additional change in the graph for $\Gamma > 22$ will not have any effect on the objective. The scenario with $\Gamma = 22$ lead to an increase of the cost by more than 13%, which is expected because this scenario represents the situation with all edges of the Steiner tree deviating by 10% or 16% and so the objective worsens by a similar amount.

4 Discussion

All calculations were carried out on *Intel® Core™ i7-7700 CPU, 3.60GHz, 16GB RAM* using *OpenSolver (COIN-OR CBC linear solver)* environment in *MS Excel*. The representation of the case study (3.2) based on model (6) consisted of 175 variables and 487 constraints and all scenarios were solved in negligible running times up to 5 seconds at most. The gamma-robustness approach allows us to find efficiently the guaranteed objective for the small instance of the problem like in our case (3.2). In a combinatorial sense, finding the minimal guaranteed tree for the problem in figure 3 would mean inspecting and comparing C_{13}^{39} (over 8.10^9) different graphs, should the brute force approach be used. This is the strength of the robust optimization, considering the instance of the problem is solvable as ILP in a reasonable time. Making a robust counterpart of the ILP problem does not affect the complexity factor adversely and only increases the input size of the initial ILP problem.

The solution of the similar problem has already been presented and discussed before by Álvarez-Miranda, Ljubić and Toth (2013) who consider the prize-collecting variant of the Steiner tree problem. This variant minimizes also the cost of Steiner vertices to be placed which is not considered in this paper. We also present a different ILP formulation than Miranda, Ljubić and Toth (2013) based on Diané and Plesnik (1992) which is smaller in size and the variables in our model are not strictly binary. We do not discuss the computational quality of our approach in comparison with other formulations. We consider its straightforward formulation to be an advantage for practitioners.

The individual scenarios in figure 4 not only show the guaranteed expected cost but also carry information about the critical components of the network. Running different scenarios for different Γ values shows that some of the edges appear repeatedly in the solution trees than others and therefore can be considered of greater importance and should be a focus of a decision-maker. Running the different scenarios also proves the usefulness of the Steiner vertices placed in the network, as they are all part of the solution. Without these vertices, the total cost of the connection would be worse.

5 Conclusion

We presented the ILP model formulation of the robust Steiner tree problem. Our model represents an approach to handling uncertain data without involving stochastic tools. The robust approach is based on the efficient finding of the worst-case scenarios under the given degree of uncertainty and predefined deviations from originally expected values. The approach was demonstrated in the case of planning electrical grids but can be applied in any situation which can be represented as the Steiner tree problem, such as wireless networks, broadcasting schemes or circuit layouts. We aim to extend our work further by defining a methodology of identifying critical components of the Steiner tree based on robust optimization.

Acknowledgements

This paper was supported by the Czech Science Foundation (GAČR) project No. P403-18-04735S

References

Álvarez-Miranda, E., Ljubić, I. and Toth, P. (2013). 'Exact approaches for solving robust prize-collecting Steiner tree problems', *European Journal of Operations Research*, 229 (3), pp. 599-612. https://doi.org/10.1016/j.ejor.2013.03.037

Bertsimas, D. and Sim, M. (2003). 'Robust discrete optimization and network flows'. *Mathematical Programming Series B,* 98, pp. 49–71. https://doi.org/10.1007/s10107-003-0396-4

Brazil, M., Graham, R.L., Thomas, D.A. and Zachariasen, M. (2014). 'On the history of the Euclidean Steiner tree problem'. *Archive for History of Exact Sciences,* 68, pp. 327–354. https://doi.org/10.1007/s00407-013-0127-z

Diané, M. and Plesník, J. (1993). 'An Integer Programming Formulation of the Steiner Problem in Graphs'. *Methods and Models of Operations Research,* 37, pp. 107-111.

Fampa, M., Lee, J. and Maculan, N. (2016). 'An overview of exact algorithms for the Euclidean Steiner tree problem in n-space'. *International Transactions in Operations Research,* 23, pp. 861-874. https://doi.org/10.1111/itor.12207

Garey, M.R., Graham, R.L. and Johnson, D.S. (1977). 'The Complexity of Computing Steiner Minimal Trees'. *SIAM Journal of Applied Mathematics,* 32, pp. 835-859.

Gröpl C., Hougardy S., Nierhoff T. and Prömel H.J. (2001). *Approximation Algorithms for the Steiner Tree Problem in Graphs*. In: Cheng X.Z., Du DZ. (eds) Steiner Trees in Industry. *Combinatorial Optimization*, 11. Boston, MA: Springer. https://doi.org/10.1007/978-1-4613-0255-1_7

Gupta A. and Pál M. (2005). *Stochastic Steiner Trees Without a Root*. In: Caires L., Italiano G.F., Monteiro L., Palamidessi C., Yung M. (eds) Automata, Languages and Programming. ICALP 2005. *Lecture Notes in Computer Science*, 3580. Heidelberg: Springer. https://doi.org/10.1007/11523468_85

Hlavatý, R. and Brožová, H. (2018). 'Matrix Games with Uncertain Entries: A Robust Approach'. *Proceedings of 36th International Conference Mathematical Methods in Economics,* Jindřichův Hradec, Czech Republic, pp. 139-144.

Hwang, F.K., Richards, D.S. and Winter, P. (1992). *The Steiner Tree Problem,* 1st ed. North Holland: Elsevier.

IPR Praha – Institut plánování a rozvoje hlavní města Prahy (2015). *Vyzvaná architektonická soutěž Smíchov City Sever*. Praha: IPR/SDM.

Siebert, M., Ahmed, S. and Nemhauser, G. (2020). 'A linear programming based approach to the Steiner tree problem with a fixed number of terminals'. *Networks,* 75, pp. 124–136. https://doi.org/10.1002/net.21913

Šeda, M. (2008). 'Fuzzy Shortest Path Approximation for Solving the Fuzzy Steiner Tree problem in Graphs'. *International Journal of Applied Mathematics and Computer Sciences,* 1 (3).

Vudarčíková, T. (2020). 'Robustní Steinerův strom'. (Master's degree thesis, CZU Prague). *Registr kvalifikačních prací,* vskp.czu.cz.

The strategic analysis of the external and internal environment of the new waste treatment company

Jakub Chlopecký[1], Roman Danel[2], Šárka Vilamová[3], Omar Ameir[4]
Adam Pawliczek[5]

Abstract. The uncertain business environment after the escalation of the COVID 19 pandemics places more importance on sound strategic business decisions. For the right strategic decisioning in the medium term, quality theoretical training is needed in the external analysis of the company. The presented paper includes external analysis for CEVYKO, a.s. and sets out proposals for strategies of the given areas of company's operation. The company CEVYKO, a.s. is a purely municipal project. Although publicly owned companies do not have the primary goal of maximizing profit and market share, the basic principles of strategic management apply to them too. These principles must be reflected in the proper strategic management of the company and in the provision of services to citizens. The company CEVYKO, a.s. is a unique project in the Czech Republic and the results of this contribution can be applied in the future also in comparable companies of a similar type of business.

Keywords: Strategic management, waste management, external and internal environment, Porter's analysis of the five forces, PESTLE analysis.

JEL Classification: L10, L100

1 Introduction

Innovation is a key activity for the development of the company and for the improvement of the process activities of the company (Acuña-Carvajal et al, 2019, Chlopecký, Rolčíková and Kratochvíl, 2015). The authors (Chlopecký et al, 2019 and Hys, 2020, 2017) stated in the paper that from today's business point of view, trade limits are practically missing. One year after the outbreak of the COVID 19 pandemic and the related emergency situation worldwide, partial trade limits have been reintroduced (Kuckertz et al., 2020, Ivanov, 2020 and Dryhurst et al. 2020). The world is "flooded" with information and methods of analysis, for this reason or precisely because excessive analysis can lead to "paralysis of analysis", on the other hand, lack of information or its insufficient use can have far-reaching consequences for the company (Kozel et al, 2018, Kozel et al., 2017, and Michl, 2016, 2019). Consistent introduction of e.g., information systems into the waste management process can emphasize economic benefits (Kozel, Chuchrová 2015 and Kozel et al., 2017 and Ministr et al., 2019). In order to properly

[1] Moravská vysoká škola Olomouc, o.p.s., třída Kosmonautů 1288/1, 779 00 Olomouc, Ústav managementu a marketingu, CEVYKO a.s., Svornosti 86/2, 736 01 Havířov – Město, chlopecky@cevyko.cz
[2] VŠB Technical University of Ostrava, Faculty of Economics, Department of Applied Informatics, Sokolská třída 33, Ostrava, roman.danel@vsb.cz.
[3] VŠB – Technical University of Ostrava, Faculty of Materials Science and Technology, Department of Economics and Management in Industry, 17.listopadu 15, 708 33 Ostrava, sarka.vilamova@vsb.cz
[4] Moravská vysoká škola Olomouc, o.p.s., třída Kosmonautů 1288/1, 779 00 Olomouc, Ústav managementu a marketingu, omar.ameir@mvso.cz.
[5] Faculty of Management, Prague University of Economics and Business, Jarošovská 1117/II, CZ – 377 01 Jindřichův Hradec, Czech Republic, adam.pawliczek@vse.cz, Moravská vysoká škola Olomouc, o.p.s., třída Kosmonautů 1288/1, 779 00 Olomouc, Ústav managementu a marketingu, adam.pawliczek@mvso.cz

perform strategic analysis for business decision-making, it is necessary for the company to choose a rational approach to obtaining information and the scope of analytical work. (Chlopecký et al., 2020, and Chlopecký et al., 2019 and Chlopecký et al. 2018). Available literature sources describe that a wide variety of techniques are available for strategic management. However, numerous studies have shown that only a relatively small number of strategic management techniques are used in practice. A common technique that appears on a theoretical and practical level is, for example, the PESTLE method. (Chlopecký et al., 2019 and Chlopecký et al. 2018 and Anton, 2015). The main goal of the presented paper is to create an external analysis of a new municipal company CEVYKO, a.s. dealing with waste activities. The company was established at the end of 2019 and has not yet prepared a strategic document. The establishment of the company is a reaction to the change in legislation and the implementation of the European Commission's packages for the circular economy after 2014. (Kozel et al., 2018, Acuña-Carvajal, 2019). The year 2024 is a prerequisite for the completion of the construction of the entire CEVYKO project. The absence of a strategic document and the position of one of the authors in the company's management are the reasons why this article was submitted.

2 Characteristics of CEVYKO, a.s. (Joint Stock Company)

The company CEVYKO, a.s. is the result of project work to build a municipal waste utilization centre for the area of Havířov and its surroundings. The goal of CEVYKO, a.s. is to build a modern technological facility for efficient treatment of municipal waste in response to changes in Czech legislation in 2014. This facility will process separated (paper, plastic), mixed and high-volume (e.g., furniture) municipal waste. The CEVYKO project has overcome the incubation phase and is already "living" with its life towards responsible and modern municipal waste management meeting all the requirements of the 21st century in accordance with the strategy of the Moravian-Silesian Region in this area (Chlopecký et al, 2020).

The company CEVYKO, a.s. has three shareholders from the municipalities, and these are the statutory city of Havířov, the company ASOMPO, a.s. (unites 45 municipalities and towns of the region Nový Jičín) and the Association for Municipal Waste Management, z. s. (for municipalities and towns, especially in the Karviná region). The Statutory City of Havířov has 35 % of the shares of CEVYKO, a.s., ASOMPO, a.s. also has 35% of shares and the Association for Municipal Waste Management, z.s. has 30 % of the company's shares. Decision-making rights are divided between individual shareholders and their shares. Additional information about the company can be found at www.cevyko.cz (Chlopecký et al, 2020).

3 Used Methods and Methodical Part of the Paper

The authors focused on some of the most used methods of external and internal strategic management environment, which are still effective and quickly applicable for practical use. The results of the research are original and unique for a given type of business with a focus on the selected company and will help guide the creation of a strategy. Primary data for research and use in strategic analysis is obtained using a basic survey of the issue. These were mainly available internal materials of CEVYKO, a.s. and methodologies according to the paper:

External analysis for the purpose of strategic decision-making of a district heating company (Chlopecký et al., 2019).

The main goal was to find the key parameters of the analysis of either the external or internal environment of the company. These data provided additional data for expanding the information base. The methods used in the analysis are listed in Table 1.

Porter's analysis of the five forces	PESTLE analysis	SWOT analysis
• Strategic analysis of microenvironment	• Strategic analysis of the external environment	• Additional analysis following the results of the previous analysis of the external and internal environment

Table 1 Used methods of analysis of external and internal environment by CEVYKO, a.s.

The inspiration for this type of work was already published similar analysis, e.g., External Analysis for the Purpose of Strategic Decision-Making of Heating Company (Chlopecký et al., 2019, Porter, 2008). Selected methodology for strategic analysis of CEVYKO, a.s. is shown in figure 1.

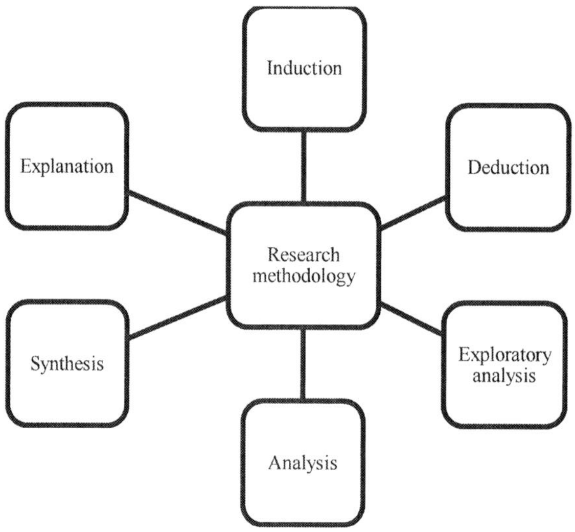

Figure 1 Methodology of information processing for analysis

Research induction can be defined as a judgment leading to an introduction to research. By deduction, one can mean a method in which new statements are reached from the accepted statements. The best possible explanation is in the exploratory analysis. Subsequent knowledge of phenomena and determination of specific results and their mutual relations and significance is defined as analysis. (Rolstadås, 1998, Rothaermel, 2008 and Michl, 2019) By synthesis in this analysis is meant a system summary and a combination of the information obtained, followed by an explanation of the results. *Additional information from the theoretical basis was also obtained from:*

- Foreign and domestic literature in the field of strategic management;
- Czech Statistical Office, WBO, Eurostat;
- Brainstorming with the company's statutory bodies and shareholder representatives;
- Foreign professional studies, analysis and studies. (Porter, 2008, Michl, 2016 and Chlopecký et al., 2019).

4 Own Research Methodology

The given methodology was initially elaborated by means of an orientation survey, the aim of which was to define the key parameters of the analysis (Ministr et al, 2015 and Ministr et al., 2019). The parameters led to a basic overview of the issue and helped to formulate a further approach to analytical work.

Above all, the method of brainstorming of authors with representatives of the company, shareholders, experts in the waste management sector and representatives of Technical Services Havířov, a.s.

The principle was to combine theoretical knowledge of the methodology of strategic analysis, which were the subject of our own research and practical experience of a functioning company. Brainstorming took place in several rounds, according to predefined rules, whether it was the preparatory phase of brainstorming until the evaluation of the results.

Brainstorming was performed on PESTLE, Porter and SWOT analysis (Pawliczek, Kozel and Vilamová, 2018). The results were processed in the basic MS Excel environment according to defined parameters. The given identified factors were evaluated by the weight of the given estimate of experts and authors on the basis of the product of the probability and the impact of the factor.

5 Empirical Findings

Empirical results of individual strategic analysis processed in the paper lead to the fulfilment of partial goals. These sub-objectives, resp. their evaluation is another basis for the main goal of the presented paper, namely the elaboration of a strategic analysis (Somosi, and Koczizsky, 2017 and Rozehnal and Novák, 2016).

This is one of the most important parts of the research work of the author's team.

5.1 PESTLE Analysis

For an overview, Table 2 shows the PESTLE analysis of CEVYKO, a.s. and described the individual most significant influences that were captured for the individual factors of the analysis.

Factors	Results
Political	**Political aspects of shareholders** Support for other forms of waste treatment Amendment to the Waste Act
Economic	**Commodity prices** CNB monetary indicators Basic macro data and robustness of pointer strength
Social	**Development of demography in the city** Unemployment and its amount in the city Unfavourable complex public opinion of waste companies Local place of work

Technological	**Technological development of waste processing** Waste treatment efficiency Purity of processed raw materials from waste Maximum use of commodities
Legislative	**Amendment to the Waste Act and EU requirements** Powers of municipalities within the pricing policy High environmental emphasis (circular economy)
Ecological	**Maximum recycling** Waste - free management Education

Table 2 PESTLE analysis of CEVYKO, a.s.

From the political point of view, the aspects of shareholders who are of a municipal nature have the main influence on the functioning and direction of the company. The most important factor that enters the analysis from an economic point of view is the price of waste output commodities. This factor is very difficult to predict over time because commodity prices in this sector are very volatile. Demography in the city of Havířov enters into one of the factors and is assessed by the authors as significant, because most of the income of CEVYKO, a.s. is based on the total population and unit price for waste treatment. Technological progress and new methods of waste treatment also affect the company and it depends on how the management will react to them. They can become a significant competitive advantage or also a negative phenomenon.

The legislative conditions for waste treatment have passed a new law, the question is how the legislation will be further developed not only from the perspective of the Czech Republic, but also the European Union. The influence of ecological factors is very high, because the principle of the circular economy and its trend in the world and Europe is considerable and is also related to the decarbonization of coal regions.

5.2 Porter's Model of Five Forces

The results of Porter's five-force model and the orientation of the individual effects of the model are shown in Table 3. The maximum possible number of points is five and the lowest zero.

Porter's model effects*	Score estimates/2021	Score estimates/2024
Existing competitors in the sector	2,88	4,88
Threat of entry of new competitors	2,01	2,91
Threat of substitutes	2,48	2,40
Bargaining effect of suppliers	2,12	4,58
Bargaining effect of customers	4,48	4,12

* Maximum 5 points, minimum 0 points.

Table 3 Porter's model of five forces of CEVYKO, a.s.

The summary of the results shows that the threat of substitutes is the least likely risk to competitiveness. The most significant risk appears to be existing competitors in the sector who have the necessary knowledge, technology and capital adequacy.

The bargaining power of suppliers is valued at 2.12 in 2021 and at an estimate of 4.58 in 2024. The higher rating is mainly due to a change in legislation and the conditions for limiting landfilling, etc. will be clear. Customers and their bargaining power are defined in 2021 as 4.48 and in 2024 by an estimate of 4.12 points.

5.3 SWOT Analysis

The construction of the SWOT analysis itself was based on the obtained analysis data, which are listed above. The results of the SWOT analysis are therefore the intersection of the data obtained. The SWOT analysis was evaluated by the so-called Kotler method, where the arithmetic product of the evaluation criteria defines the result of a given item in the analysis so that the measured values are compared. Figure 2 captures all four quadrants of the SWOT analysis and lists the most important parameters.

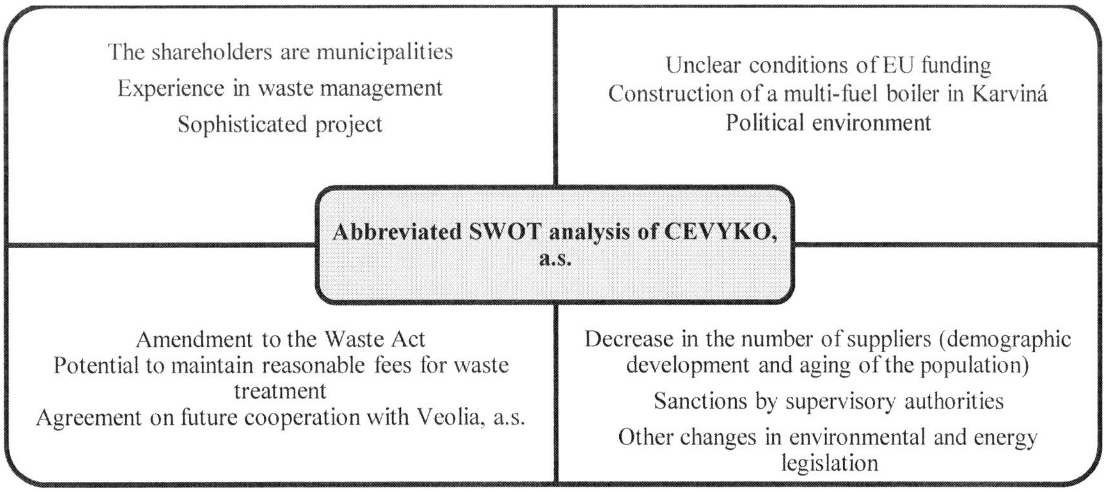

Figure 2 SWOT analysis and its quadrants

The most significant strengths of CEVYKO, a.s. related to the financing of the company's share capital, resp. financing of purely municipalities (involved municipalities). The strength of the involved municipalities and employees in the field of waste management is also a strong point. The last strong point, which was elaborated in the reduced SWOT analysis of the company CEVYKO, a.s. is already the beginning of the implementation of an elaborate project, which is unique in the territory of the Czech Republic due to its size, considered technology.

The authors identified the three weakest factors of the reduced SWOT analysis as follows. Unclear conditions of financing from EU sources, as the allocation period has ended and the following period and possible challenges are in the negotiations of interested parties such as the Ministry of the Environment, the State Environmental Fund, regions and the Government of the Czech Republic. On the occasion of CEVYKO, a.s. There are factors such as the amendment to the Waste Act in the current change, which is prepared for the second reading of the Parliament of the Czech Republic, the potential in maintaining reasonable fees for municipal waste treatment for citizens of participating municipalities and cities and the agreement on future cooperation with Veolia, a.s. for the supply of solid alternative fuel produced from waste and the possibility of further cooperation between the entities involved.

The biggest threats from the reduced SWOT analysis are: a decrease in the number of customers (demographic development and aging of the population), sanctions by supervisory authorities such as the Ministry of the Environment of the Czech Republic and others, other changes in environmental and energy legislation that are not possible at the same time. time to define and grasp relevant

6 Suggestion of Strategy

The possible size of the article limits the publication of all proposed strategies that were presented for CEVYKO, a.s. as one of the partial goals of the whole strategic analysis of the given company. For an overview, one strategy for the company is given, namely the strategy of applying strengths to seize opportunities.

SO Strategy – Applying Strengths to Take Advantage of Opportunities

Analysis show that regulations from the European Union are unlikely. A more likely opportunity for CEVYKO, a.s. is the final realization. The other three factors of opportunity concern both the potential of maintaining fees for waste treatment for citizens and the amendment to the Waste Act, resp. political will leading to the completion of the project across the political spectrum of the involved municipalities and cities.

Description of Goal Realization

Use of the strengths of municipalities, as shareholders of CEVYKO, a.s., to address the energy recovery of waste in connection with the amendment to the Waste Act, aimed at banning the dumping of municipal waste. Waste is the last commodity that municipalities and cities can handle, and therefore this goal and its implementation is a great opportunity not only for society. This goal is logically followed not only by the increase in the share capital of CEVYKO, a.s., but also by the agreement on the future contract with Veolia, a.s. as an investor in a multi-fuel boiler. Fulfilling this goal will suppress the rising price for waste treatment, but also the reasonable price of thermal energy for the city of Havířov.

From the results of external analysis, facts important for the company and its further strategic development can be deduced. In terms of strategic PESTLE analysis, the company is most influenced by the political aspects of shareholders, where shareholders' representatives may change in individual municipal elections. Another influence is the prices of commodities that arise throughout the waste treatment process. Porter's analysis of the five forces identifies significant risks in areas of existing competition in the industry, with a value of 2.88 points in 2021 and 4.88 points in 2024 out of five possible. The bargaining power of suppliers is also a significant risk from the value of 2.12 in 2021 by analysis, the authors arrived at a value of 4.58 points in 2024. At present, positive effects on a strong capital company prevail, with some promising opportunities for the future.

7 Discussion of the Results

From the results of external analysis, facts important for the company and its further strategic development can be deduced. In terms of strategic PESTLE analysis, the company is most influenced by the political aspects of shareholders, where shareholders' representatives may be changed in individual municipal elections. Another influence is the prices of commodities that arise throughout the waste treatment process. Porter's analysis of the five forces identifies significant risks in areas of existing competition in the industry, with a value of 2.88 points in 2021 and 4.88 points in 2024 out of five possible. The bargaining power of suppliers is also a significant risk from the value of 2.12 in 2021, the analysis of the authors reached a value of 4.58 points in 2024.

Not only these results, but the results of the overall strategic analysis are responded to the compilation of a SWOT matrix with a description of all four quadrants. Currently, the positive effects on a capital-strong company prevail with some promising opportunities for the future.

8 Conclusion

The waste sector is associated with a specific set of business aspects, especially with high investment intensity for projects of a similar type and legislative obligations of the waste manager. The aim of the paper was to achieve the design of suitable strategies based on the analysis performed for the specified area of interest of the Karviná region with acceptable investment and economic-operational conditions within a unique project in the Czech Republic. The set of these facts should be an impetus for the top management of waste companies, to develop intensive analytical activities with the aim of medium- and long-term strategic planning.

References

Acuña-Carvajal, F., Pinto-Tarazona, L., López-Ospina, H., Barros-Castro, R., Quezada, L. and Palacio, K. (2019). 'An integrated method to plan, structure and validate a business strategy using fuzzy DEMATEL and the balanced scorecard'. *Expert Systems with Applications*, 122, pp. 351-368

Anton, R. (2015). 'An Integrated Strategy Framework (ISF) for Combining Porter's 5-Forces, Diamond, PESTEL and SWOT Analysis'. *Open Science*, 4 (1), (2016), pp. 21-26.

Dryhurst, S., Schneider, C.R., Kerr, J., Freeman, A.L.J., Recchia, G., van der Bles, A.M., Spiegelhalter, D., van der Linden, S. (2020). 'Risk perceptions of COVID-19 around the world *Journal of Risk Research*', 23 (7-8), pp. 994-1006.

Hys, K. (2020). 'Identification of the Reasons Why Individual Consumers Purchase Dietary Supplements, w: Perspectives on Consumer Behaviour. Theoretical Aspects and Practical Applications / Sroka Włodzimierz (red.), *Contributions to Management Science*, ISBN 978-3-030-47379-2, pp. 193-209

Hys K. (2017). 'Performance marketing as a factor in the range of designing of modern business models, w: Strategic Performance Management'. New Concepts and Contemporary Trends, Management Science - Theory and Applications / Jabłoński Marek (red.), *Nova Science Publishers Inc.*, ISBN 978-1-53612-681-5, pp. 95-102.

Chlopecký, J., Moravec, L., Danel, R., Ameir, O. (2019). 'External analysis for the purpose of strategic decision-making of heating company'. *13th International Conference on Strategic Management and Its Support by Information Systems - SMSIS 2019*, pp. 33-41.

Chlopecký, J., Pawliczek, A., Ameir, O., Moravec, L., Hubáček, J. (2020). Project management in the field of modern municipal waste management related to the construction of a sorting line'. *International Multidisciplinary Scientific GeoConference Surveying Geology and Mining Ecology Management, SGEM*, 2020-August (5.1), pp. 639-646.

Chlopecký, J., Pawliczek, A., Vilamová, Š., Moravec, L., Hubáček, J., Ameir, O. (2018). 'Strategic risk management of an enterprise depending on external conditions'. *International Multidisciplinary Scientific GeoConference Surveying Geology and Mining Ecology Management, SGEM, 18* (1.3), pp. 855-861.

Chlopecký, J., Rolčíková, M. and Kratochvíl, M. (2015). 'Decision making influence of some macroeconomic factors concerning prospective sales of fine silicon carbide'. *15th International Multidisciplinary Scientific GeoConference SGEM*, Albena, Bulgaria, pp. 171-178.

Ivanov, D. (2020). 'Predicting the impacts of epidemic outbreaks on global supply chains: A simulation-based analysis on the coronavirus outbreak (COVID-19/SARS-CoV-2)' case Transportation Research Part E: *Logistics and Transportation Review*, 136, art. no. 101922.

Kozel, R. and, Chuchrová, K. (2015). 'Creation of System Support for Decision-Making Processes of Managers', *IDIMT-2015: Information Technology and Society - Interaction and Interdependence*: 23rd Interdisciplinary Information Management Talks, Poděbrady, Czech Republic, pp. 163-170.

Kozel, R., Podlasová, A., Šikýř, P. and Smelik, R. (2018). 'Innovations in Waste Management', *IDIMT-2018: Strategic Modeling in Management, Economy and Society: 26th Interdisciplinary Information Management Talks*, Kutná Hora, Czech Republic, pp. 119-126.

Kozel, Roman, Mikoláš, Milan, Vilamová, Šárka, Očko, Petr. (2017). 'New Methods of Designing the Balanced Scorecard Method for Management in Industrial Companies'. *Communications - Scientific Letters of the University of Zilina*. 2017, volume 19, issue 4, pp. 72-78. ISSN 1335-4205.

Kuckertz, A., Brändle, L., Gaudig, A., Hinderer, S., Morales Reyes, C.A., Prochotta, A., Steinbrink, K.M., Berger, E.S.C. (2020). 'Startups in times of crisis – A rapid response to the COVID-19 pandemic'. *Journal of Business Venturing Insights*, 13, art. no. e00169.

Michl, A. 'New euro convergence criteria' [Nová kritéria pro přijetí eura] (2016) Politicka Ekonomie, 64 (6), pp. 713-729.

Michl, A. 'Money and inflation: Lost cointegration [Peníze a inflace: Ztracená kointegrace] ' (2019) Politicka Ekonomie, 67 (4), pp. 385-405.

Michl, A. 'Ten Years Later: Lessons for DSGE Builders and Czech Policy Makers' (2019) Review of Economic Perspectives, 19 (3), pp. 159-174.

Ministr, J., Pitner, T. (2015). 'Use of non-investment subsidies in academic and business cooperation'. *IDIMT 2015: Information Technology and Society - Interaction and Interdependence - 23rd Interdisciplinary Information Management Talks*, pp. 141-146.

Ministr, J., Pitner, T., Danel, R., Chaplyha, V. (2019). 'Information Support of Daily Scrum Meetings'. *13th International Conference on Strategic Management and Its Support by Information Systems - SMSIS 2019*, Ostrava, Czech Republic, pp. 379-385.

Pawliczek, Adam, Kozel, Roman, Vilamová, Šárka. (2018). 'Strategic management and performance of enterprises evaluated using chaid decision tree analysis.' *Scientific Papers of the University of Pardubice*, Series D: Faculty of Economics and Administration, volume 26, issue 44, pp. 196-208. ISSN: 1211-555X.

Porter, M. (2008). 'The five competitive forces that shape strategy', *Harvard Business Review*, Harvard University, 86(1), pp. 79-93.

Rolstadås, A. (1998). 'Enterprise performance measurement', *International Journal of Operations & Production Management*, 18 (9/10), pp. 989-999.

Rothaermel, F. (2008). 'Competitive advantage in technology intensive industries', Chapter 7 in Technological Innovation: ' Generating Economic Results (Advances in the Study of Entrepreneur-ship, Innovation & Economic Growth, Volume 18), *Emerald Group Publishing Limited*, pp. 201-225.

Rozehnal, P., Novák, V. (2016). 'The approach to the integration of the IT governance frameworks for SME'. *IDIMT 2016 - Information Technology, Society and Economy Strategic Cross-Influences - 24th Interdisciplinary Information Management Talks*, Poděbrady, Czech Republic. Linz: Trauner, 367-374.

Somosi, M. and Kocziszky, G. (2017). 'Performance-based management of public utility organizations'. *12th International Conference on Strategic Management and its Support by Information Systems* 2017, Ostrava, Czech Republic, pp. 105-111.

Czech Stock Market Volatility before and during the Covid-19 Crisis

Michaela Chocholatá[1]

Abstract. This paper deals with the analysis of the Czech stock market characterized by the Prague PX stock returns using the weekly data between January 1, 2017 and January 21, 2021 in order to investigate the impact of the Covid-19 pandemic. Two different approaches were applied, the asymmetric EGARCH model and the two-state Markov switching model. Both approaches confirmed the time-varying behaviour of stock returns and corresponding volatility during the analysed period reflecting the higher volatility not only during the Covid-19 period, but during the last quarter of 2018 attributable to the global economic slowdown, as well. Since the EGARCH model enabled to capture the volatility persistence and higher impact of negative shocks in comparison to positive shocks of the same magnitude, with the presented Markov switching model we were able to identify the probabilities with which each state occurred at each point in time.

Keywords: PX stock returns, volatility, EGARCH model, two-state Markov switching model.

JEL Classification: G10, C22, C58

1 Introduction

Since the end of 2019 the world has been facing the global COVID–19 crisis caused by the coronavirus SARS-CoV-2. The crisis outbreaks in Wuhan, Hubei province, China and during the short time it rapidly spread to other countries worldwide. On March 11, 2020 the World Health Organization (WHO) declared the new coronavirus pandemic. The increasing number of the COVID-19 cases over time heavily influenced the economic environment including the financial markets all over the world. There have been published plenty of studies documenting the impacts of this pandemic on the various stock markets.

Baker et al. (2020) proved the much more serious effects of the Covid-19 pandemic on the US stock market in comparison to previous pandemics in 1918-19, 1957-58 and 1968. Analysing the reasons of such extraordinary stock market reaction they pointed out that not only the lethality of the virus, but especially the role of the government restrictions on individual mobility and commercial activity plus recommended social distancing provide a more promising explanation. Liu et al. (2020) confirmed a significant negative effect of the Covid-19 outbreak on stock market returns across all affected countries and areas. Just and Echaust (2020) investigated the relationship between the US stock market returns (S&P500), volatility, correlation and liquidity during the COVID-19 crisis based on the two-regime Markov switching model. Czech et al. (2020) applied the TGARCH (Threshold Generalized Autoregressive Conditional Heteroscedasticity) model to analyse the impact of COVID-19 cases on the exchange rates and stock market volatility in the Visegrad Group (V4) countries. They confirmed a negative correlation between the ongoing pandemic spread and the value of

[1] University of Economics in Bratislava, Faculty of Economic Informatics, Department of Operations Research and Econometrics, Dolnozemská cesta 1, 852 35 Bratislava, Slovakia, michaela.chocholata@euba.sk.

the Czech koruna, the Hungarian forint and the Polish zloty. Their TGARCH model results furthermore proved that there is a significant and negative link between the analysed stock market indices and the COVID-19 spread.

The aim of this paper is to assess the development of the Czech stock market characterized by the Prague PX stock returns using the weekly data between January 1, 2017 and January 21, 2021 in order to capture the impact of the Covid-19 pandemic. Both the EGARCH (Exponential GARCH) and the two-state Markov switching approach were used as a model framework for the analysis.

The rest of the paper is organized as follows. Section 2 introduces the data and the descriptive statistics, section 3 is devoted to the model framework used in this paper, including EGARCH model and Markov switching model. The empirical estimation results are outlined in section 4 and section 5 concludes.

2 Data and descriptive statistics

The analysed data set consists of weekly data of the PX stock price index spanning from January 1st, 2017 to January 21th, 2021 (i.e. 213 observations)[2]. The data were retrieved from the web-page Stooq (2021), the whole analysis was carried out in econometric software EViews.

Figure 1 shows the movement of the PX stock prices (PX) and of corresponding PX stock returns (D(LOG(PX))). The stock returns were calculated as the difference between the natural logarithms of the stock price index in time t and t-1. The development of both series clearly reflect the impact of the Covid-19 pandemic. Since the prices indicated a substantial downward movement beginning at the end of February 2020, the corresponding stock returns showed huge instability during the first months of 2020 following the Covid-19 outbreak. However, another substantial fall in the PX stock prices and higher volatility of stock returns could be observed during 2018 (especially during the last quarter) – this can be attributed e.g., to the global economic slowdown, to the uncertainty about the Brexit issues as well as to stagnating price competitiveness of the Czech exports (Ministerstvo průmyslu a obchodu, 2019).

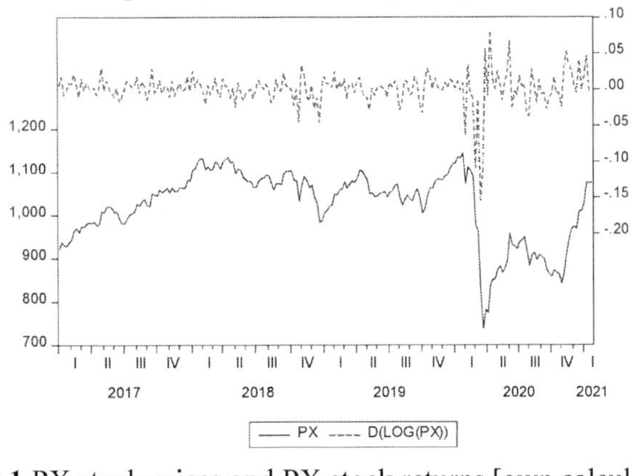

Figure 1 PX stock prices and PX stock returns [own calculations]

Data´s descriptive statistics for the whole analysed period are gathered in Table 1. Since the paper is focused on modelling of PX stock returns, we have to concentrate on the column

[2] Using the weekly data, the day-of-week effects were eliminated.

D(LOG(PX)) indicating the positive mean (weekly percentage return) of 0.726 % confirming the bullish run of the Czech market over the analysed period as a whole. The standard deviation indicates the volatility of 2.31%, the analysed series are negatively skewed with higher kurtosis than the normal distribution. Based on the values of the Jarque-Bera test statistics, the null hypothesis that the weekly return follows the normal distribution, can be rejected. The results of the Augmented Dickey-Fuller (ADF) test for log returns (t = -12.295) enable to reject the null hypothesis of the unit root, i.e. log returns can be considered as stationary. The Ljung-Box Q-statistics of Q (1) = 5.586 indicates that the AR (1) term will be used to explain the behaviour of log returns. To capture the turbulent development of the PX log returns, two types of approaches will be used in the paper - the asymmetric EGARCH model and the two-state Markov switching model.

	PX	**D(LOG(PX))**
Mean	1022.348	0.000726
Maximum	1142.950	0.081486
Minimum	738.8000	-0.154374
Std. Dev.	81.01313	0.023130
Skewness	-0.994591	-2.144062
Kurtosis	3.462011	16.76180
Jarque-Bera	36.83768	1835.347
Probability	0.000000	0.000000

Table 1 Descriptive statistics of the PX prices (PX) and of PX stock returns (D(LOG(PX))) [own calculations]

3 Model framework – EGARCH model and Markov switching model

In general, it can be supposed that the continuously compounded returns r_t (i.e. log returns) can be modelled as a Box-Jenkins ARMA (Autoregressive Moving Average) model. During the last three decades the ARCH-class models have become very popular in capturing the time-varying volatility of log returns. The ARCH model introduced by Engle (1982) and its extension to the GARCH model presented by Bollerslev (1986) have been followed by an extensive amount of modifications. With regard to the empirical part of this paper we will briefly introduce the exponential GARCH model, i.e. EGARCH model, introduced by Nelson (1991), enabling to capture both the volatility persistence and the asymmetric effects.

The corresponding conditional volatility EGARCH (p, q, r) model enabling to capture that good news and bad news have different effects on the conditional variance is given as follows:

$$\ln(h_t) = \alpha_0 + \sum_{i=1}^{q} \alpha_i \frac{|\varepsilon_{t-i}|}{\sqrt{h_{t-i}}} + \sum_{j=1}^{p} \beta_j \ln(h_{t-j}) + \sum_{k=1}^{r} \gamma_k \frac{\varepsilon_{t-k}}{\sqrt{h_{t-k}}} \tag{1}$$

Concerning the exponential form of the conditional variance function h_t there are no restrictions on parameters in order to ensure the non-negativity of the h_t. The leverage effect for the k-th order is present in case that $\gamma_k < 0$, the impact of news is asymmetric if $\gamma_k \neq 0$.

Different model specification that enables to capture processes driven by heterogeneous states of the world is represented by Markov switching model popularized by Hamilton (1989). Hamilton (1989) formulated a two-state Markov switching model in which the mean growth rate of the U.S. GNP is subject to regime switching, and where the errors followed a regime-invariant AR (4) process (EViews, 2020). As pointed out e.g., by Linne (2002) who examined the contagion effects of currency crises on several emerging stock markets in Central and Eastern Europe using the Markov switching model, the basic model distinguishes only two states of the world – calm periods with normal behaviour of stock returns and turbulent (crisis) periods in which the behaviour of stock returns changes dramatically characterised by high volatility and falling stock prices. Consideration of two different regimes, also known as bull and bear markets, capturing the "positive mean-low volatility" period and "negative mean-high volatility" period is well documented by e.g., Kośko (2006), Reiff (2018) and Almonares (2019). Following Hamilton (2010) and with regard to the empirical part of the paper, we will suppose that the historical behaviour of the stock returns r_t could be described with a first-order autoregression[3]

$$r_t = c_{S_t} + \emptyset r_{t-1} + \varepsilon_t, \qquad \varepsilon_t \sim N(0, \sigma^2_{S_t}) \tag{2}$$

where S_t denotes an unobserved state indicator following the two-state Markov chain (i.e., $S_t = 1$ indicates that the process is in regime 1 at time t and $S_t = 2$ means that the process is in regime 2 at time t – see e.g., Brooks, 2008; Franses and van Dijk, 2000) with

$$P\{S_t = j | S_{t-1} = i, S_{t-2} = k, \dots, r_{t-1}, r_{t-2}, \dots\} = P\{S_t = j | S_{t-1} = i\} = p_{ij} \tag{3}$$

The specification in (3) assumes that the probability distribution of the state at any time t depends only on the state at time $t-1$ (Hamilton, 2010; Brooks, 2008). Model (2) enables to capture both the changes in the mean values c_{S_t} as well as changes in the variance between individual regimes. Symbol $\{p_{ij}\}_{i,j=1,2}$ denotes the transition probability for the two-state Markov chain, i.e. probability that the state i (at time $t-1$) will be followed by the state j (at time t). The probability is non-negative and in case of the two-state Markov chain it holds that

$$p_{i1} + p_{i2} = 1, \qquad i = 1, 2 \tag{4}$$

4 Empirical estimation results

In the first step the log returns were modelled as an AR (1) model however with highly correlated squared residuals indicating the presence of the ARCH effect (with ARCH LM test value of $TR^2 = 11.619$). From the various types of ARCH-class models the EGARCH (4, 1, 1) model was chosen to be the most appropriate one. The values of estimated parameters from the conditional mean (AR (1))[4] equation and conditional variance equation together with the diagnostic tests of standardized residuals are gathered in Table 2. All the parameters were statistically significant at 5% significance level, there was neither autocorrelation in the standardized residuals nor in the squared standardized residuals till the lag 200 at the 1% significance level. The statistically significant and negative value of γ_1 parameter confirms

[3] The corresponding autoregressive parameter is denoted as $\emptyset$.

[4] $r_t = \mu + \emptyset r_{t-1} + \varepsilon_t$

higher impact of negative shocks compared to positive shocks of the same magnitude. The ARCH-LM test results confirmed no remaining heteroscedasticity. With regard to the non-normality of standardized residuals, the estimates were consistent only as quasi-maximum likelihood estimates.

Estimated parameters of AR (1) + EGARCH (4, 1, 1) model								
μ	$\emptyset$	α_0	α_1	β_1	β_2	β_3	β_4	γ_1
0.002 **	0.146 ***	-0.802 ***	0.370 ***	1.966 ***	-2.200 ***	1.689 ***	-0.516 ***	-0.080 **
Diagnostic test results of standardized residuals								
Q(200)		$Q^2(200)$		ARCH-LM		Jarque-Bera		
161.97		161.69		0.422		10.234***		

Table 2 Estimated parameters of AR (1) + EGARCH (4, 1, 1) model and diagnostic test results. Note: Symbols *** and ** denote rejection of the null hypothesis at the 1% and 5% significance level, respectively. [own calculations]

Figure 2 depicts the static forecasts of PX log returns together with the ± 2 conditional standard deviation clearly indicating the time-varying behaviour of conditional variance across the analysed period. The forecast evaluation is presented as well.

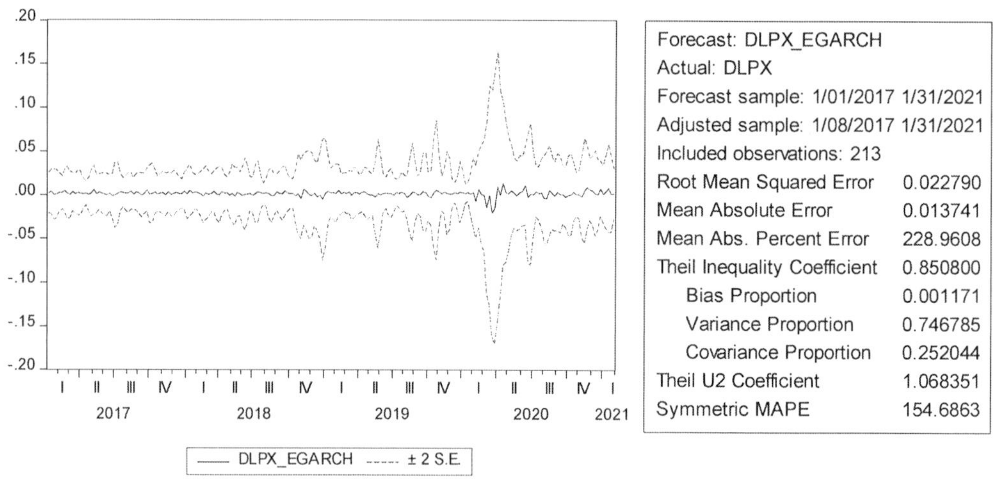

Figure 2 Static forecasts of PX stock returns – EGARCH model [own calculation]

The second approach, the two-state Markov switching model, enables to describe the switching behaviour of the stock returns during the analysed period. The estimation results of this model including transition probabilities and expected durations are outlined in Table 3. The statistical significance of estimated parameters indicates that not all estimated parameters were statistically significant. Regime 1 is characterized by negative mean return and high volatility (0.048), i.e. bear market; whereas regime 2 shows positive mean return and low volatility (0.012), i.e. bull market. The probabilities of staying in regime 1 and regime 2 are 0.751 and 0.949, respectively, indicating that the regime 2 is much more persistent than the regime 1. The transition probability from the high volatility regime 1 to the low volatility regime 2 of 0.249 is higher in comparison to transition probability of 0.051 from regime 2 to regime 1. The corresponding expected durations in a regime are approximately 4.014 and 19.420 weeks, respectively.

Regime 1		Regime 2		Common	Transition Matrix Parameters	
c_1	$\log(\sigma_1)$	c_2	$\log(\sigma_2)$	$\emptyset$	p_{11}	p_{21}
-0.006	-3.029 ***	0.002 *	-4.458 ***	0.072	1.103	-2.913 ***
Constant transition probabilities: P(i, k) = P(s(t) = k | s(t-1) = i) (row = i / column = j)				**Constant expected durations:**		
	1	**2**			**1**	**2**
1	0.750888	0.249112			4.014263	19.42006
2	0.051493	0.948507				

Table 3 Estimation results of two-state Markov switching model, transition probabilities, expected durations. Note: Symbols *** and ** denote rejection of the null hypothesis at the 1% and 5% significance level, respectively. [own calculation]

Markov switching smoothed regime probabilities in Figure 3 enable to assess the probabilities that regime j occurs at time t given all observations in the entire sample (Franses and van Dijk, 2000). The presented results show high probabilities of being in regime 1 (bear market) during two separate periods in the fourth quarter of 2018 as well as during several short periods in 2020 indicating the turbulent development during the Covid-19 pandemic. Reversely, regime 2 corresponding to the calm periods with normal behaviour of stock returns (bull market) is the most likely from the beginning of the analysed period till the end of the third quarter of 2018, during some few weeks in the fourth quarter of 2018, during the 2019 as well as during some periods in 2020.

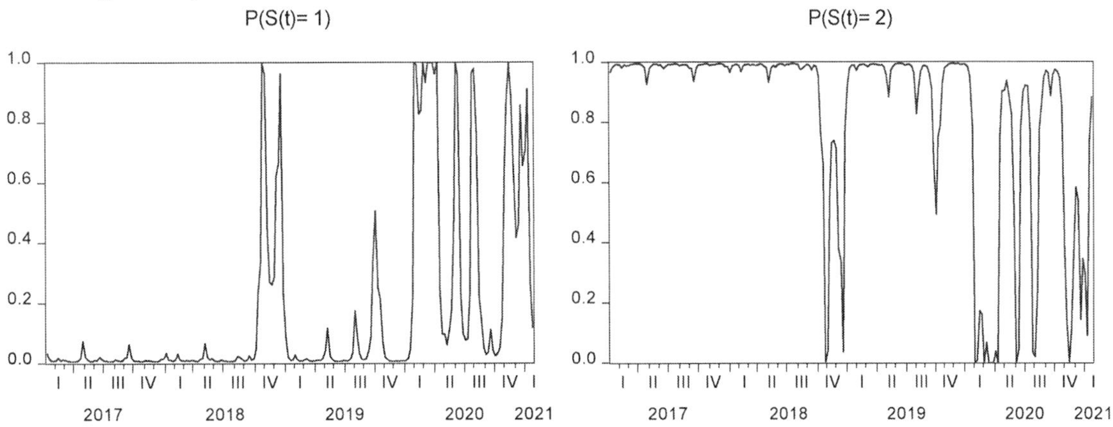

Figure 3 Markov switching smoothed regime probabilities [own calculation]

Figure 4, based on the estimated two-state Markov switching model, depicts the static forecasts of the analysed log returns together with the forecast evaluation. The graphic development captures the volatile behaviour during the last months of 2018 as well as during the first quarter of 2020 corresponding to the Covid-19 pandemic outbreak.

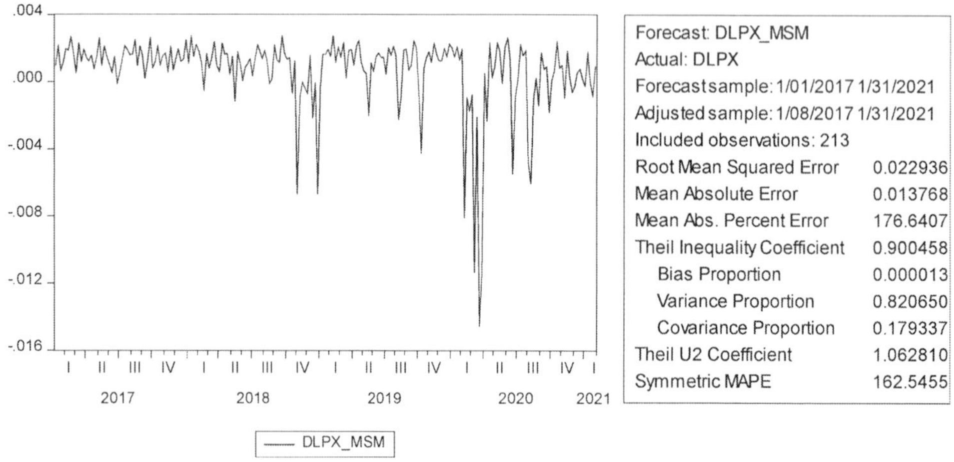

Figure 4 Static forecasts of PX stock returns – Markov switching model [own calculation]

5 Conclusion

The paper analysed the weekly log returns of the Czech PX stock index during January 2017 – January, 2021 period with concentration to assessment of the Covid-19 pandemics' impacts. Two different approaches were adopted – estimation of the EGARCH model and estimation of the two-state Markov switching model. The results proved considerably unstable development of stock returns as well as of corresponding volatility. Estimation of AR (1)-EGARCH (4, 1, 1) model enabled to assess the time-varying character of volatility, volatility clustering as well as asymmetric volatility reaction to the positive and negative shocks. The one-step ahead forecasts together with the corresponding standard error bands provide further insights into the stock returns and volatility behaviour.

The results from the Markov switching model show positive mean return during normal times (calm periods, bull market) while in crisis periods (bear market) the mean return is negative. The transition probability of remaining in calm periods is 0.949, while the transition probability of staying in a crisis period is lower (0.751) and statistically insignificant. As pointed out e.g., by Wang (2009), one of the reasons may be that the duration of the crisis periods is quite short and the probability of staying in this period varies. Based on the estimation results, the expected duration of staying in a calm period is 19.420 weeks in comparison to expected duration of a crisis period of 4.014 weeks. The estimated results furthermore proved that the two regimes have different volatilities, since both the parameters were statistically significant at the 1 % level. The estimated static forecasts enable to assess the clearly time-varying behaviour of analysed stock returns.

Acknowledgements

This work was supported by the Grant Agency of Slovak Republic – VEGA grant no. 1/0193/20 „Impact of spatial spillover effects on innovation activities and development of EU regions ".

References

Almonares, R. A. L. (2019). 'Markov Switching Model of Philippine Stock Market Volatility'. *DLSU Business & Economics Review*, 29 (1), pp. 24-30.

Baker, S. R., Bloom, N., Davis, S. J., Kost, K. J., Sammon, M. C. and Viratyosin, T. (2020). 'The unprecedented stock market impact of Covid-19'. [Online]. Available at: https://www.nber.org/system/files/working_papers/w26945/w26945.pdf [cited 2021-01-24].

Bollerslev, T. (1986). 'Generalized Autoregressive Conditional Heteroscedasticity'. *Journal of Econometrics*, 31 (3), pp. 307-327.

Brooks, C. (2008). *Introductory Econometrics for Finance*. 2nd ed. Cambridge: Cambridge University Press.

Czech, K., Wielechowski, M., Kotyza, P., Benešová, I. and Laputková, A. (2020). 'Shaking Stability: COVID-19 Impact on the Visegrad Group Countries' Financial Markets'. *Sustainability*, 12(15), 6282.

Engle, R. F. (1982). 'Autoregressive Conditional Heteroscedasticity with Estimates of the Variance of United Kingdom Inflation'. *Econometrica*, 50 (4), pp. 987-1007.

EViews. (2020). 'Switching Regression: Examples', [Online]. Available at: http://www.eviews.com/help/helpintro.html#page/content%2Fswitching-Examples.html%23ww190610 [cited 2021-01-24].

Franses, P. H. and van Dijk, D. (2000). *Non-linear time series models in empirical finance.* Cambridge: Cambridge University Press.

Hamilton, J. D. (1989). 'A New approach to the economic analysis of nonstationary time series and the business cycle'. *Econometrica*, 57 (2), pp. 357-384.

Hamilton, J. D. (2010). Regime switching models. In: Durlauf, S.N. and Blume, L.E. (eds). *Macroeconometrics and Time Series Analysis*. The New Palgrave Economics Collection. London: Palgrave Macmillan, pp. 202-209.

Just, M. and Echaust, K. (2020). 'Stock market returns, volatility, correlation and liquidity during the COVID-19 crisis: Evidence from the Markov switching approach'. *Finance Research Letters,* 37 (2020), 101775.

Kośko, M. (2006). 'An Application of Markov-switching Model to stock Returns Analysis'. *Dynamic Econometric Models*, 7, pp. 259-268.

Linne, T. (2002). 'A Markov Switching Model of Stock Returns: An Application to the Emerging Markets in Central and Eastern Europe'. In: Charemza, W.W. and Strzała, K. (eds). *East European Transition and EU Enlargement. Contributions to Economics*. Heidelberg: Physica, pp. 371-384.

Liu, H. Y., Manzoor, A., Wang, C. Y., Zhang, L. and Manzoor, Z. (2020). 'The COVID-19 Outbreak and Affected Countries Stock Markets Response'. *International Journal of Environmental Research and Public Health*, 17(8), 2800.

Ministerstvo průmyslu a obchodu. (2019). Analýza vývoje ekonomiky ČR duben 2019, [Online]. Available at: https://www.mpo.cz/assets/cz/rozcestnik/analyticke-materialy-a-statistiky/analyticke-materialy/2019/4/Analyza-vyvoje-ekonomiky-CR_duben-2019.pdf [cited 2021-01-24].

Nelson, D. (1991). 'Conditional heteroskedasticity in asset returns: A new approach'. *Econometrica*, 59 (2), pp. 347-370.

Reiff, M. (2018). *Analýza parametrov skrytého Markovovho modelu finančných časových radov*. Bratislava, Edícia: Habilitačné a inauguračné prednášky.

Stooq. (2021). [Online]. Available at: https://stooq.com/q/d/?s=^px [cited 2021-01-24].

Wang, P. (2009). *Financial econometrics*. 2nd ed. London and New York: Routledge.

Multiple p-Facility Location Problem with Randomly Emerging Demands

Jaroslav Janáček[1]

Abstract. Host of public service system models are based on the assumption that each demand is satisfied from the nearest service center. This assumption together with absence of center capacity limits lead to the proposition that each of the located centers is equipped with only one facility. This contribution deals with a more realistic situation, when the currently emerged demand may not be satisfied from the nearest center due to its occupancy by a former emerging demand. In this case, the current demand is served from the closest available center. To model these situations, probabilities of availability of the r nearest service centers must be taken into account and embedded into model. Under the assumption, locating of more than one facility at one service center may appear to be advantageous. In this contribution, we suggest two models for the latter more general case. The first one makes use of co called allocation variables and the other is based on radial formulation.
We verify the hypothesis that the radial formulation considerably accelerates convergence of the branch-and-bound method used for solving of service system design problem even for the generalized case.

Keywords: Public service system, multiple facility location, radial formulation, generalized disutility.

JEL Classification: C61, C63

1 Introduction

Public service systems are created and operated to provide inhabitants of a concerned geographical region with various kinds of necessary. The public service system design problem was studied as a task of selection of p center locations from a set of possible service center locations so that the average distance from a demand to the nearest service center is minimal.

The original approaches (Brotcorne, Laporte and Semet, 2003), (Doerner et al, 2005), (Jánošíková and Žarnay, 2014), (Guerriero, Miglionico and Olivito 2016) evaluated quality of the p- center deployment by the average response time of the system on a user's service request. These approaches modelled the problems as the weighted p-median problem and made use of exact and heuristic tools for the problem solving. An important success in large-size p – median problem solving was achieved by application of the radial approach (Eloumi et al. 2004); (Garcia et al. 2011); (Janacek 2008), (Sayach and Irnich 2016). The min – sum weighted p –median problem formulation was generalized to capture characteristic of a real public service system with random emerging demands and limited capacity of the service centers by introducing probability values of the situations, when the nearest, second nearest and so on up to r – nearest service center is the nearest available center due to occupation of the closer centers by earlier demands (Drezner and Drezner 2007). The radial approach to this

[1] Prof. RNDr. Jaroslav Janáček, CSc., University of Žilina, Faculty of Management Science and Informatics, Univerzitná 8215/1, 010 26 Žilina, Slovakia, e-mail: jaroslav.janacek@fri.uniza.sk

generalized p – median problem was developed and tested by (Janacek and Kvet 2013), (Kvet 2014), (Kvet 2015), (Kvet and Janáček 2018). The associated objective function is referred as the generalized disutility.

The above approached locate centers at some of possible center locations. The original model based on the p-median problem formulation does not allow locating more than one facility at one center location, because each additional center brings a lower objective function value. Nevertheless, the notion of generalized disutility admits more advantageous solutions of the p-facility location problem, where several facilities are placed at one center location.

This contribution deals with various formulations of the multiple p-facility location problem with generalized disutility objective function by means of integer programming. These models can be used together with an IP-solver as a solving approach to the problem. The suggested models will be submitted to testing with the goal to prove the hypothesis that the radial model will perform better than the allocation one when applied to the multiple p-facility location problems.

The remainder of the paper is organized as follows: Section 2 is devoted to the radial and allocation formulations of the multiple p-facility location problems. The associated numerical experiments are reported in Section 3. The results and findings are summarized in Section 4.

2 Radial and allocation formulations of the multiple *p*-facility location problem

In the text below, we consider set J of user locations spread over a serviced region. Each user location $j \in J$ is connected with population b_j, which is proportional to the number of demands arising at location j. User's demands are serviced from centers, which can be located only at some locations of a finite set I of possible service center locations. Together p facilities are at disposal to be distributed in the set I. A service center $i \in I$ can contain several facilities. The distance between a location $i \in I$ and a location $j \in J$ is denoted by d_{ij}. Furthermore, a sequence $q_1, \ldots, q_r$ of r descending probability values is given, where q_k is probability that the k-th nearest service center to a user j is the first available service center, which is able to provide the user with service. The objective of the problem is to design such a deployment of p facilities that the average distance from a user to the nearest available service center is minimal.

To describe the facility deployment in the both formulation, we introduce a series of integer location variables $y_i \in Z^+$ defined for each $i \in I$. The value of variable y_i gives the number of facilities located at location i.

To complete the location-allocation model, we introduce series of allocation variables $z_{ijk} \in \{0, 1\}$ for $i \in I$, $j \in J$ and $k=1, \ldots, r$, where $z_{ijk} = 1$ if user demand located to j is assigned to a possible service center i as to the k-th service center. After these preliminaries, a linear integer programming model of the problem can be formulated as follows.

$$Minimize \sum_{j\in J} b_j \sum_{k=1}^{r} q_k \sum_{i\in I} d_{ij} z_{ijk} \quad (1)$$

$$Subject\ to \sum_{i\in I} y_i = p \quad (2)$$

$$\sum_{i\in I} z_{ijk} = 1 \ \ for\ j \in J,\ k = 1,...,r \quad (3)$$

$$\sum_{k=1}^{r} z_{ijk} \le y_i \ \ for\ j \in J, i \in I \quad (4)$$

$$y_i \in Z^+ \ \ for\ \ i \in I \quad (5)$$

$$z_{ijk} \in \{0, 1\} \ \ for\ i \in I,\ j \in J,\ k = 1,\ ...,\ r \quad (6)$$

The objective function (1) expresses the expected value of traversed distances from users to the nearest available center. As the series of $\{q_k\}$ is decreasing, the optimization process will assign a demand of a user j to the nearest located center i for the case $k = 1$. Similarly, the demand will be assigned to the second nearest located center for the case $k = 2$, etc.

Constraint (2) limits the number of facilities, which are at disposal. Constraints (3) assure that demand of user j is allocated to exactly one center for the case k, which means that the k-th nearest center is the first available one. Constraints (4) enables to assign a demand of user j to a possible service center i at most y_i times.

Radial formulation of the problem uses above introduced integer location variables y_i and furthermore, it uses auxiliary zero-one variables x_{jtk} for $j\in J$, $t= 0, ..., m-1$ and $k= 1, …, r$ to model the distance of the k-th nearest service center to the user j. The variable x_{jtk} takes the value of 1 if the distance from the k-th nearest service center to the user location $j\in J$ is greater than t and it takes the value of 0 otherwise. Then the sum $x_{j0k} + x_{j1k} + ... + x_{jm-1k}$ corresponds to the smallest distance from the user j to the k-th nearest located center. The constant m corresponds to the greatest relevant distance in the problem.

To complete the model, we introduce coefficients a_{ijt} for each triple i, j, k $i\in I$, $j\in J$ and $t =$ 0, …, m-1, where $a_{ijt} = 1$ if and only if $d_{ij} > t$ and $a_{ijt} = 0$ otherwise for $t = 0, …, m$-1. Then, the radial model of the problem can be formulated as follows.

$$Minimize \sum_{j\in J} b_j \sum_{k=1}^{r} q_k \sum_{t=0}^{m-1} x_{jtk} \quad (7)$$

$$Subject\ to \sum_{i\in I} y_i = p \quad (8)$$

$$\sum_{k=1}^{r} x_{jtk} + \sum_{i\in I} a_{ijt} y_i \ge r \ \ for\ j \in J, t = 0,\ ...,\ m-1 \quad (9)$$

$$y_i \in Z^+ \ \ for\ \ i \in I \quad (10)$$

$$x_{jtk} \in \{0, 1\} \ \ for\ j \in J, t = 0,\ ...,\ m-1,\ k = 1,\ ...,\ r \quad (11)$$

The objective function (7) expresses the expected value of traversed distances from users to the nearest available center. In this formulation, the sum of x_{jtk} over subscript t stands for the distance from user j to the k-th nearest service center. Constraint (8) ensures that the number placed facilities equals to p.

Constraints (9) are the constraints, which link-up location variables y_i to the variables x_{jtk} so that the sum of variables x_{jtk} is greater than or equal to the value of complement of the number of located service centers in the radius t from the customer j to the number r. In other words, the optimization process will cause that the sum takes the value of difference of r and the number of located service centers in the radius t from the customer j if the difference is positive; otherwise it takes the value of zero.

3 Numerical experiments

The main goal of the following computational study is a comparison of the presented approaches to the multiple p-facility location problems with generalized disutility with the goal to find the most efficient implementation. The study has been performed using the benchmarks, which were derived from some of the Slovak self-governing regions. The individual instances of the benchmarks are denoted by the following names: Bratislava (BA), Nitra (NR), Trenčín (TN), Trnava (TT), Žilina (ZA), Banská Bystrica (BB), Košice (KE) and Prešov (PO). The sizes of the individual benchmarks are determined by integers m and p. The number m gives the number of possible center locations, i.e. the cardinality of set I, and p gives the number of facilities to be located. The number n of users is the same as the number m, because each user location was admitted as a possible service center location. The generalized disutility objective function was computed for $r = 3$. The coefficients q_k for k=1 … r has been obtained from statistics presented in (Jankovič, 2016) and their values are: $q_1 = 77.063$, $q_2 = 16.476$ and $q_3 = 100 - q_1 - q_2$. The instance sizes m and p are reported in Table 1

Benchmark	BA	BB	KE	NR	PO	TN	TT	ZA
p	25	46	38	36	44	26	22	36
m	87	515	460	350	664	276	249	315

Table 1 Description of the instances

The numerical experiments were run on a PC equipped with the Intel® Core™ i7 8565U processor with the parameters: 1.80 GHz and 12 GB RAM. Solutions of described problems were found by the optimization software FICO Xpress 8.3 (64-bit, release 2017).

Experiments with the approaches, which differ in implemented models, were organized so that each implementation was applied to each problem instance and the resulting service system designs obtained for the same instance were compared. In each case, the same service center deployment was achieved but the computational times considerably differed. This is why we report separately only computational times for radial and allocation approaches and denote these times as *CTrad* and *CTall* respectively. These entries are given in seconds in the Table 2. The table is organized so that each column corresponds to one instance and each row contains values of one characteristic of the resulting public service system design. Excepting computational times *CTrad* and *CTall*, we report the objective function value denoted by *Obj*, the number of located service centers (*noCenter*) and the numbers of centers with one and two located facilities (*noCent_1f* and *noCent_2f* respectively). In the designs, there was no center with more than two facilities.

Benchmark	BA	BB	KE	NR	PO	TN	TT	ZA
Obj	18450	38008	40711	40987	46884	31260	36401	36929
CTrad	0.36	5.19	5.08	3.78	9.49	1.93	9.46	2.17
CTall	2.97	228.93	173.02	907.08	418.45	312.74	227.37	970.79
noCenter	24	44	37	34	41	24	21	35
noCent_1f	23	42	36	32	38	22	20	34
noCent_2f	1	2	1	2	3	2	1	1

Table 2 Description of the optimal results

4 Conclusions

The research reported in this contribution is focused on exact solving techniques for the multiple p-facility location problems with the generalized objective function, which takes into account r nearest centers for user's demand service. The studied techniques are based on usage of a common commercial IP-solver, which employs a sophisticated version of the branch-and-bound method. The techniques differ in the models, which describe the generalized p-facility location problem. Two different problem formulations were submitted to the presented research. The first of them is the radial formulation and the second one is denoted as the allocation model. The presented results confirm the hypothesis that the radial approach considerably outperforms the allocation approach, even if it is applied on the more complex location problem than the original ones.

A future research in this field will focus on the approaches to the public service system design in a region with stochastically heterogeneous sources of service demands.

Acknowledgements

VEGA 1/0089/19 "Data analysis methods and decisions support tools for service systems supporting electric vehicles" and VEGA 1/0216/21 "Designing of emergency systems with conflicting criteria using tools of artificial intelligence". This work was supported by the Slovak Research and Development Agency under the Contract no. APVV-19-0441.

References

Brotcorne, L., Laporte, G., Semet, F. (2003). 'Ambulance location and relocation models'. *European Journal of Operational Research* 147, pp. 451–463.

Doerner, K. F., Gutjahr, W. J., Hartl, R. F., Karall, M., Reimann, M. (2005). 'Heuristic Solution of an Extended Double-Coverage Ambulance Location Problem for Austria'. *Central European Journal of Operations Research*, vol. 13, no 4, pp. 325-340.

Elloumi, S., Labbé, M., Pochet, Y. (2004). 'A new formulation and resolution method for the p-center problem', *INFORMS Journal on Computing* 16, pp. 84-94.

García, S., Labbé, M., Marín, A. (2011). 'Solving large p-median problems with a radius formulation'. *INFORMS Journal on Computing*, vol. 23, no 4, pp. 546-556.

Guerriero, F., Miglionico, G., Olivito, F. (2016). 'Location and reorganization problems: The Calabrian health care system case'. *European Journal of Operational Research* 250, pp. 939-954.

Drezner, T., Drezner, Z. (2007). 'The gravity p-median model'. *European Journal of Operational Research 179*, pp. 1239-1251.

Janáček, J. (2008). 'Approximate Covering Models of Location Problems'. In Lecture Notes in Management Science: Proceedings of the 1st International Conference ICAOR, Yerevan, Armenia, pp. 53-61

Janáček, J., Kvet, M. (2013). 'Public service system design with disutility relevance estimation'. *Proceedings of Mathematical Methods in Economics* 2013, Jihlava, Czech Republic, pp. 332-337.

Jankovič, P. (2016). 'Calculating Reduction Coefficients for Optimization of Emergency Service System Using Microscopic Simulation Model'. In: *17th International Symposium on Computational Intelligence and Informatics*, pp. 163-167.

Jánošíková, Ľ., Žarnay, M. (2014). 'Location of emergency stations as the capacitated p-median problem'. *International scientific conference: Quantitative Methods in Economics-Multiple Criteria Decision Making* XVII, Virt, Slovakia.

Kvet, M. (2014). 'Computational Study of Radial Approach to Public Service System Design with Generalized Utility'. *Digital Technologies 2014: Proceedings of the 10th International IEEE Conference*, pp. 198-208.

Kvet, M. (2015). 'Advanced Radial Approach to Resource Location Problems'. *Studies in Computational Intelligence: Developments and Advances in Intelligent Systems and Applications*, Springer, pp. 29-48.

Kvet, M., Janáček, J. (2018). 'Reengineering of the emergency service system under generalized disutility'. *Proceedings of the ICORES 2018: 7th International Conference on Operations Research and Enterprise Systems*, Madeira, Portugal, pp. 85-93.

Sayah, D., Irnich, S. (2016). 'A new compact formulation for the discrete p-dispersion problem'. *European Journal of Operational Research*, vol. 256, no 1, pp. 62-67.

Shop Floor Management with Self Service Business Intelligence applications

Pavel Jančálek [1]

Abstract. The main tool of the Shop Floor Management (SFM) is a structured system of meetings at all levels of the production hierarchy. The meeting participants, who are managing the production, need to be clearly, and self-servicely informed about the production data. This article describes the possible structuring of the SFM system and the use of Power Pivot as a product of Self-Service Business Intelligence (SSBI) that connects or confronts the production plans with the actual production. The connection is graphically displayed based on the multidimensional modelling and the possible online visualization of data from the SFM meetings is described.

Keywords: Shop Floor Management, Self Service Business Intelligence, production processes, multidimensional model.

JEL Classification: C81, M11

1 Introduction

The production is the most specific and often unique for each company and every member of the top and middle management in the given company should be familiar with it, Tomek and Vávrová (2014). To manage such an often time-varying production process, it is necessary to use appropriate tools that will be understood and respected across the production management and employees in the production, Jurová et al (2016).

This statement applies especially for the structured custom production of a wide portfolio of technically sophisticated products composed of many manufactured components and the necessary cooperation. This work describes the main elements of Shop Floor Management (SFM) in a manufacturing company, in terms of creating and using data modelling in Power Pivot, as a software tool for preparing Self Service Business Intelligence (SSBI) reporting applications.

Online data is provided using SQL views from the transactional databases of the Enterprise Resource Planning (ERP) and Manufacturing Execution Systems (MES) production modules for production planning and data collection in production. The SQL view is a fast and efficient way, built on the standard query commands, to retrieve and further process online data from transactional databases. This work does not deal with the description of the creation of SQL view, i.e., the internal structure of the query command text and the connection string.

The attention in this article is paid mainly to the data model in Power Pivot and subsequent data visualization for the SFM from the perspective of a data analyst in production controlling.

[1] VŠB – Technical University of Ostrava, Department of Applied Informatics, Sokolská tř. 33, Ostrava 70200, Czech Republic, pavel.jancalek@vsb.cz.

2 Theoretical background

The theoretical background is mainly in the possibility of applying SSBI in the creation of reporting applications and the main pillars of SFM.

Suzaki (2010) argues that everyone should learn to run their own "mini-company," where everyone is considered president of their area of responsibility. Hertle et al (2015) argue that the principle of the SFM should be to reduce the depth of the organizational hierarchy and integrate a competency management system.

To involve every employee in the management, it is necessary to have available data drawn from information systems, which after processing provide clear information, Laberge (2011). Howson (2014) concluded that the Business Intelligence (BI) gives people at all levels of the organization access to interact and analyses data to manage the business, improve performance, discover opportunities, and work effectively.

The SSBI thus appears to be a time- and cost-effective variable tool for creating reporting applications. Mainly are focused on the individual needs of users or their smaller groups and the use of the SSBIs leads to an overall greater satisfaction with information technology, which is transformed into a flexible helper that can better meet business requirements, Pour et al (2018).

"Power Soup" is the existence of at least six MS Data products prefixed with "Power" and Power Pivot is the central engine that enhances their usefulness for the mix of all BI solutions, Collie and Singh (2015).

3 Shop Floor Management in the hierarchy of production

The Production management in the monitored company is organized according to the technological chronology and parallels of in-house flows of materials, services, semi-finished and subsequently finished products.

The SFM is a system to support the management process, based on setting up and following regular quick meetings to pass the information about the course of the production process at various stages of production.

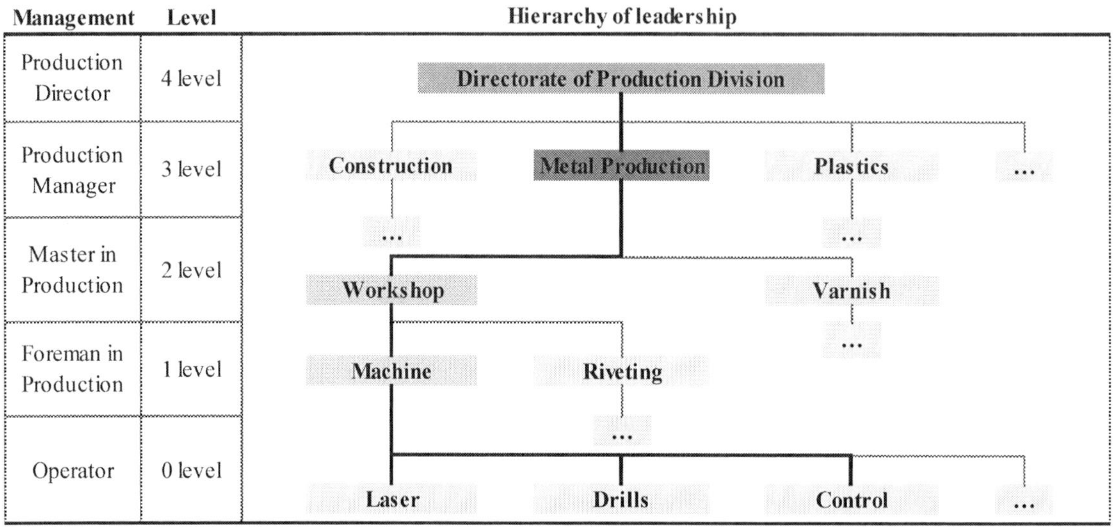

Figure 1 Hierarchy of production and SFM levels [Author]

Figure 1 shows the connection of the production management hierarchy with SFM levels. The hierarchy of the SFM is illustrated by the example of the Metal Production department.

Figure 2 shows the control elements of the SFM. The lower the SFM level, the more frequent, shorter, and more operational meetings. Meetings at level 0-1 are from 1-5 minutes, levels 1-2 are 5-10 minutes long, levels 2-3 are 10-30 minutes long and levels 3-4 are 30-60 minutes long. The leaders of given levels (or their temporary representatives) are always present at the meetings. The meetings are as specific as possible and focused directly on the fulfilment and course of production and cooperation. These main topics are communicated on the meetings: the fulfilment of orders, operations, and cooperation (it's also displayed on monitors located in workshops, corridors, and meeting rooms).

Management	Level	Frequency of meetings	Monitored values
Production Director	4 level	1 per week	Confrontation of production and sales plan Meeting the deadline for the centre's orders Filling capacity and meeting standards
Production Manager	3 level	Daily on at the beginning morning shifts	Meeting the deadline for orders of the department Filled to capacity and performance standards Off-schedule work and scrap
Master in Production	2 level	Daily on the end every shift	Meeting the deadline for workshop orders Filled to capacity and performance standards Off-schedule work and scrap
Foreman in Production	1 level		
Operator	0 level	Continuously during shifts	Meeting the deadline for workplace orders Filled to capacity and performance standards Off-schedule work and scrap Material transfer, daily surgery

Figure 2 Control elements of the SFM system [Author]

The lower the SFM level, the more detailed the reporting on the implementation of orders is. While operators and foremen (levels 0-1) monitor and solve a minute fulfilment of operations and cooperation between them at the workplace, the production management solves daily the order fulfilment with workshop masters (levels 2-3) and the production director solves with production managers (levels 3- 4) the fulfilment of the entire weekly plan and its connection to the sales department (once a week).

Custom manufacturing is very dynamic in accepting and subsequently meeting requirements and must maintain its tenacity to cope with the change in action.

4 Self Service Business Intelligence from separate databases

The SSBI and Power tools seek to resolve the conflict between two opposing business forces, the need for fast and inexpensive flexibility to turn data into information and a robust database base, providing accurate but separated and difficult-to-accessed data, MICROSOFT (2021).

Technological procedures, task plans and the course of the production process are recorded in various information systems or spreadsheets. In the production process, we work mainly with Enterprise Resource Planning (ERP) and Manufacturing Execution Systems (MES). The data and information flows in the production process are shown in Figure 3.

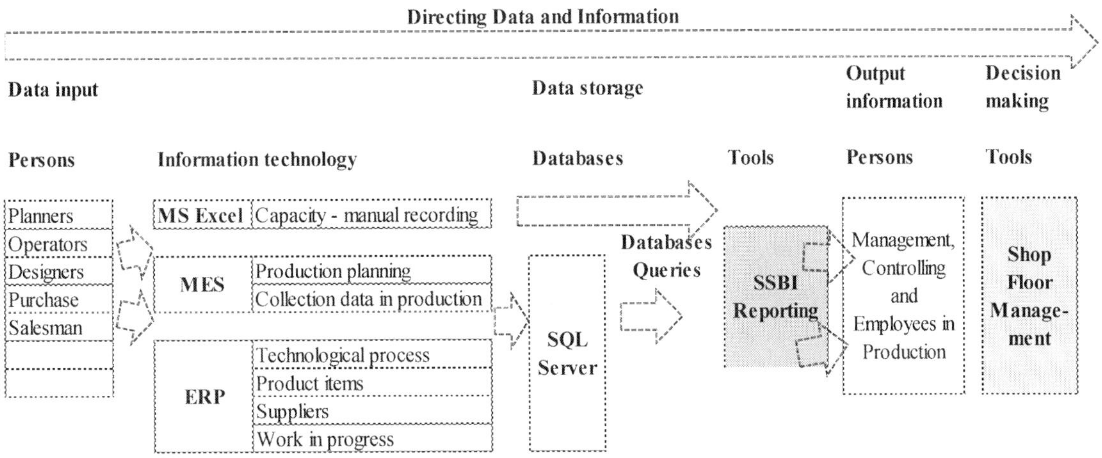

Figure 3 Flow of data and information through the production process [Author]

The ERP is a broad modular system for complex economic management of a company. Production module is containing code lists and the necessary procedures in the production process. The most important are the code lists of material, semi-finished and finished products. Each product is broken down into a BOM, which contains the material and various semi-finished products, which are further broken down into material or cooperative activities carried out by subcontractors. Each unique entity, i.e. the finished product, semi-finished product, cooperation and material, has its own unique number in the code list. By the material and cooperation entering the creation of semi-finished products, the individual production operations have their technological procedures with time standards for production. These technological procedures are entered into the ERP system by designers based on the finished development of a new product.

When a salesperson from the sales department enters a received order into the system to deliver a certain quantity of finished products to a customer, then the production requirement is broken down in the system and the individual finished products or semi-finished products are assigned a unique order number. At the same time, buyers in the company's purchasing department are alerted to keep the material warehouse sufficiently stocked. The simulation of the production plan or the time schedule of the sequence of individual operations realizable within the production capacities is then processed in the MES. Only completed data on the end of the production order and possible storage in intermediate warehouses in the case of semi-finished products or in the dispatch warehouse in the case of already finished products are returned to the ERP.

MES is also a broad modular information system or set of information systems that work with production data. The planner in the planning system simulates the implementation of individual orders and their operations over time. The planner must consider, for example, the maximum available capacities and missing material. The result in this case is a generated weekly plan, based on which task sheets, cutting plans and other documents necessary for operators to work on the implementation of the production order are prepared. As part of the fulfilment of the production plan, the operator in production records the start and completion of individual production operations in the system for data collection.

Figure 3 also shows MS Excel as a source for recording daily used human capacities at individual workplaces. This data is entered by the workshop master into a pre-set table in relational form, which is in a shared network folder because it has not been possible to place this data properly in any of the information systems yet.

ERP and MES are database information systems installed on a dedicated SQL server that manages databases and shares applications for clients on the network. Currently, only the necessary data transfer integration is performed between ERP and MES within the integration database in SQL server. Such as the code list of production orders and related products and their production operations or the code list of workplaces. This is transmitted by the data pump to both the planning system and the data collection system. This is the data transfer direction: ERP => MES. The data pump transfers data also from the MES => ERP direction in the interval of 15 minutes for data collection from production about the end of the operation of the order, i.e. manufactured, resp. the remaining pieces, or pieces of scrap.

Within the individual information systems, only partial data and users are available, i.e., especially workshop masters and production managers would need to open multiple individual systems to find out the information about each individual order and it would repeat with each order. With a daily volume of several hundred production operations within the monitored Metal Production department, it was almost impossible to manage everything clearly and predict possible problems and delays. This situation had to be addressed.

The use of the SSBI tools was chosen for a fast self-service, cheap, variable, easily changeable, replenishable, reliable and because it is an online solution system for working with the data. First, a procedure was chosen to identify the needs for reporting and, with the help of IT administration, gradually create fast SQL queries as a source basis or synthesis between databases and other relational connections in SSBI applications. The basis for integrated data processing is the Power Pivot functionality.

Table	Basic destription of table content	Master identif
Capacity	Record of the planned use of human capacity in the shift and workplace.	Dimension
Mat_Tran	Wiews of data collection in production, with necessary foreign keys for 6 relationships.	Fact table
Person	Code list of human capacities.	Dimension
Order	Code list of orders and operations with output quantity and number of scraps.	Dimension
Ok_Data_Metal	Code list of start and end times of laser cutting plan with human capacity codes.	Dimension
Plan_ShopFloor	Wiews of the production plan with the necessary foreign keys for 4 relationships.	Fact table
Laser_Order	Wiews of laser cutting plans with necessary foreign keys for 2 relationships.	Fact table
Work_Shift	Code list of shifts	Dimension
Machines	Code list of workplaces and machines, including their groups	Dimension
Work_Center	Code list of workplaces, machines and codes of subcontractors for cooperation.	Dimension
Suppliers	Code list of subcontractors for cooperation.	Dimension
Nav_Order	Code list of orders and operations with technological times of standards.	Dimension
Item	Code list of product, with number and description and assigned order 1: 1.	Dimension
Ok_End_Order	Code list of the last logged operations. Internal integration of MES - CPD and ERP.	Dimension
Nav_Flow_Order	Auxiliary code list of orders and operations.	Dimension
Calendar	Table of calendar data in Power Pivot. Auxiliary code list.	Dimension

Figure 4 Tables for Power Pivot [Author]

16 tables or more precisely 15 tables and 1 table is a calendar generated directly by Power Pivot. For a complete overview of the philosophy of the data model, Figure 4 will help, where the basic description of individual tables is given. Figure 5 schematically shows the session diagram created in Power Pivot and the individual resources are highlighted for better orientation.

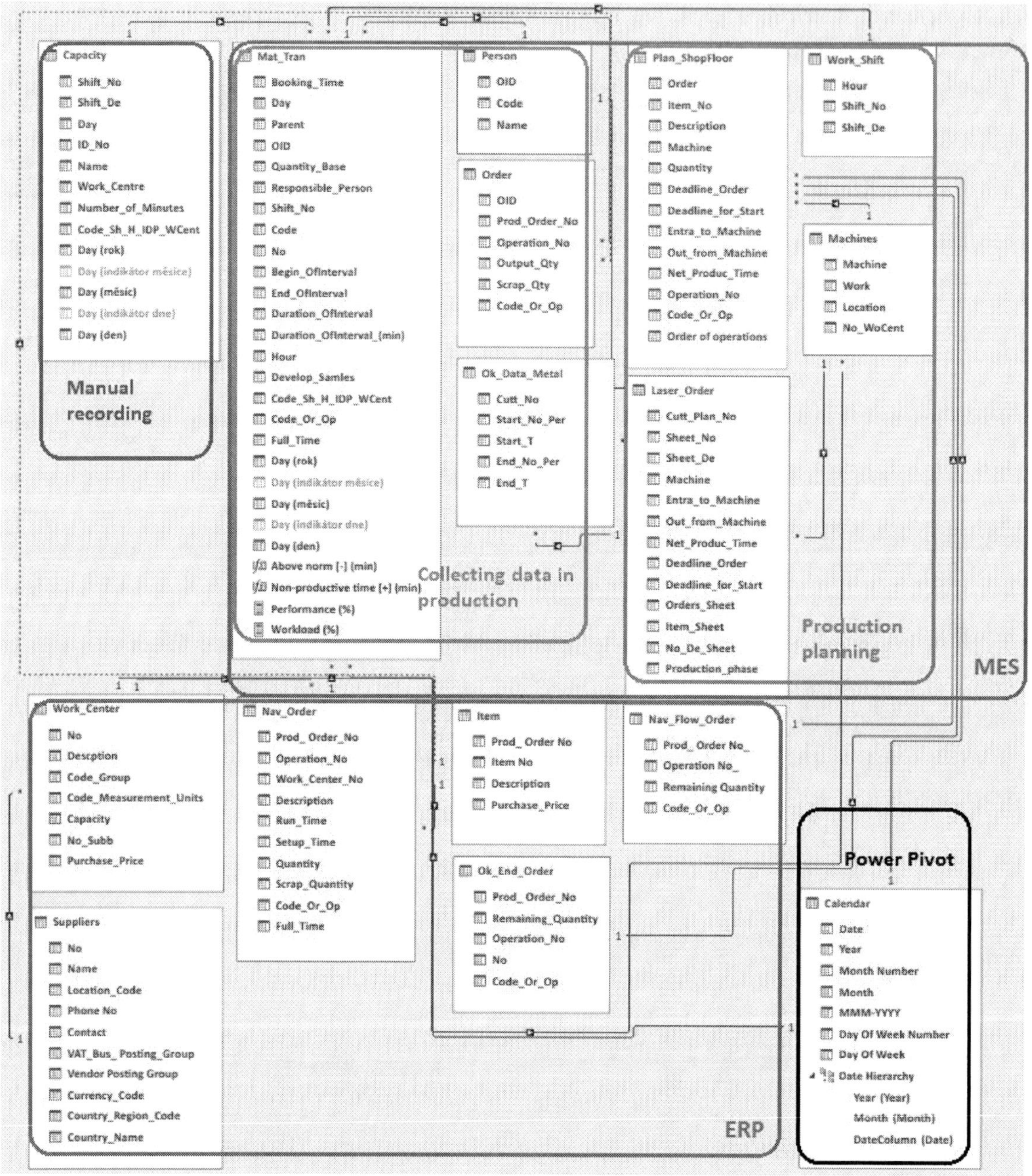

Figure 5 Diagram with table relations in a multidimensional model [Author]

The tables in the data model have 5 sources. There are 3 sources from the transaction information systems: ERP, MES - Production planning (MES-PP) and MES - Collection data in production (MES - CDP). Next source is created directly in MS Excel as a manual recording and the last source is the Calendar from Power Pivot. The attribute names within the tables from information systems are the original system names. Figure 6 shows session management in the Power Pivot, complete with source information systems.

Source Tab.FK	Tab.and Column FK	Relation	Tab. and Column PK	Source_Tab.PK
MES - PP	Laser_Order [Machine]	M:1 (*:1)	Machines [Machine]	MES - PP
MES - PP	Machines [No_WoCent]	M:1 (*:1)	Work_Center [No]	ERP
MES - CDP	Mat_Tran [Code_Or_Op]	M:1 (*:1)	Nav_Order [Code_Or_Op]	ERP
MES - CDP	Mat_Tran [Code_Sh_H_IDP_WCent]	M:1 (*:1)	Capacity [Code_Sh_H_IDP_WCent]	Manual recording
MES - CDP	Mat_Tran [Day]	M:1 (*:1)	Calendar [Day]	Power Pivot
MES - CDP	Mat_Tran [Hour]	M:1 (*:1)	Work_Shift [Hour]	MES - PP
MES - CDP	Mat_Tran [Responsible_Person]	M:1 (*:1)	Person [OID]	MES - CDP
ERP	Nav_Order [Prod_ Order_No]	M:1 (*:1)	Item [Prod_ Order No]	ERP
ERP	Nav_Order [Work_Center_No]	M:1 (*:1)	Work_Center [No]	ERP
MES - PP	Laser_Order [Cutt_Plan_No]	M:1 (*:1)	Ok_Data_Metal [Cutt_No]	MES - CDP
MES - CDP	Ok_Data_Metal [Start_No_Per]	M:1 (*:1)	Person [Code]	MES - CDP
MES - CDP	Mat_Tran [OID]	M:1 (*:1)	Order [OID]	MES - CDP
MES - CDP	Order [Prod_Order_No]	M:1 (*:1)	Item [Prod_ Order No]	ERP
MES - PP	Plan_ShopFloor [Code_Or_Op]	M:1 (*:1)	Nav_Flow_Order [Code_Or_Op]	ERP
MES - PP	Plan_ShopFloor [Code_Or_Op]	M:1 (*:1)	Ok_End_Order [Code_Or_Op]	MES - CDP
MES - PP	Plan_ShopFloor [Deadline_for_Start]	M:1 (*:1)	Calendar [Day]	Power Pivot
MES - PP	Plan_ShopFloor [Machine]	M:1 (*:1)	Machines [Machine]	MES - PP
ERP	Work_Center [No_Subb]	M:1 (*:1)	Suppliers [No]	ERP

Figure 6 Table relations in a multidimensional model [Author]

In the diagram, there were several columns linked between tables to create a key. These relations can even be 1: 1. In the Mat_Tran table, they are created using the DAX "measure" language, which are calculated fields at the PivotTable level and are associated with key performance indicators (KPIs), including graphical symbols to speed up user orientation.

5 Examples of visualization

The desired result of data modelling is with the help of PivotTable functionalities processed by online reports in MS Excel. Processed reports can be easily updated and customized.

The reports are not only available on the SFM meetings but are used across the Metal Production department. There is a screen in the hallway with a computer connection and the open files. The name "ShopFloor" is familiar among the workshop employees. They are able see how the goals were met anytime they need. An example of three reports is shown in Figures 7 to 9.

Because the monitored company in this article is a Czech company, the attributes in the reported contingency tables are translated into Czech. To bring the context closer to the reader, the selected attributes provide a description of which table in the model they belong to and what the sessions are.

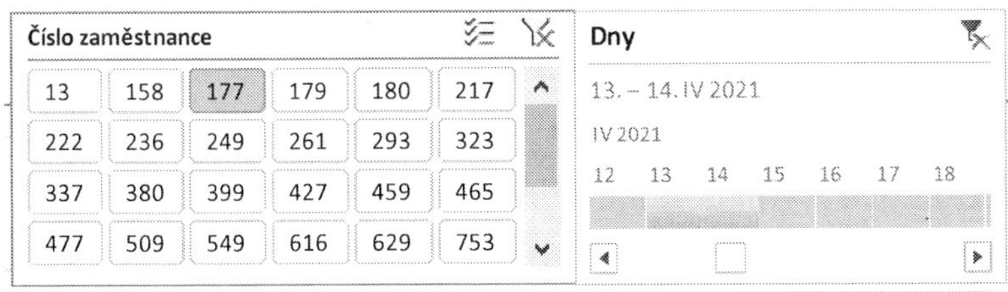

Pracovní centrum	Směna	Kapacita	Skutečnost (okdata)	Norma (nav)	Výkon (%)	KPI výkon	Pod normu [-] (min)	Vytíženost (%)	KPI zátěž	Neprodukt čas [+] (min)
⊟JEHLENI	1. ranní	520	485	522	108%		-37	93%		35
⊟JEHLENÍR	1. ranní	280	170	152	89%		18	61%		110
⊟ROVNÁNÍ	1. ranní	80	112	83	74%		29	140%		-32
Celkový součet		**880**	**768**	**757**	**99%**		**11**	**87%**		**112**

Figure 7 Report on compliance with standards and capacity utilization at workplaces [Author]

In Figure 7, the fact table is Mat Tran [Full_Time – "Skutečnost (okdata)"] and the associated dimensions Person [Code – "Číslo zaměstnance"], Capacity [Work_Center – "Pracovní centrum"]; Number_of_Minutes – ["Kapacita"] and Nav_Ordher [Full_Time - "Norma (nav)"]. The so-called "measure" and KPIs are also in the overview. This overview is not only evaluated on the SFM but is also continuously monitored by operators.

Lokace

Nýtovací dílna | Strojní dílna | Lakovna

Zakázka	Číslo_popis výrobku	Plán zahájení operace	Plán ukončení operace	Pracoviště	Zbývající množství	Odhlášení operace	Množství výrobků
M21012833	11016222 - Uložení osy X MP horní	13.04.2021 7:31	**13.04.2021 8:07**	Trumpf 5000	0	TRUMPF	54
		13.04.2021 8:07	**13.04.2021 8:21**	Jehlení	0	JEHLENÍR	54
		13.04.2021 11:50	**13.04.2021 12:01**	Rovnání	2	Ověřit!! Zmetky??	54

Figure 8 Report on the performance of work operations within one order, resp. product [Author]

In Figure 8, shows the Plan_ShopFloor main table with almost all attributes and the Nav_Flow_Order [Remaining_Quantity – "Zbývající množství"] and Ok_End_Order [NO – "Odhlášená operace"] dimensions appended to it. Within this overview, the numbers of scraps are also monitored.

Stroj

Laser_1 | Laser_2 | Laser_3 | TruLaser_1

Fáze výroby

dokončeno dle plánu | v plánu | další týden | dokončeno se zpožděn... | zpoždění

Plech	Číslo a popis materiálu	Výstup ze stroje	Ukončení v OkDa	Fáze výroby	Zakázky na plechu
070421K15	11100015 Plech Nerez, tl. 1,0mm - 2x1m	12.04.2021 14:04	12.04.2021 12:35	dokončeno dle plánu	M21012448
070421K16	11100015 Plech Nerez, tl. 1,0mm - 2x1m	12.04.2021 16:04	12.04.2021 14:39	dokončeno dle plánu	M21012448, M2101244
070421K11	11100002 Plech Fe, tl. 1,5mm - 2x1m	12.04.2021 16:25		v plánu	M21012443
070421K12	11100004 Plech Fe, tl. 2,0mm - 2x1m	12.04.2021 16:41		v plánu	M21012444

Figure 9 Report on the fulfillment of the laser cutting plan [Author]

In Figure 9, the main table is Laser_Order [Sheet_No - "Plech"] and others with almost all attributes. The attached dimension is Ok_Data_Metal [End_T - "Ukončení v OkData"]. The overview also informs whether the laser cutting was completed in the plan "dokončeno v plánu" or is in plan "v plánu".

With the help of the presented data model, it is possible to create several different reports for the operational needs of production management and workers.

6 Conclusion

This article describes of Shop Floor Management in terms of the use of information support tools Self Service Business Intelligence in a production company.

Neither SSBI nor Power Pivot is perfect and has its shortcomings. It is, for example, a increase in the size of the MS Excel files, which then work slowly or have limited possibility of data visualization. The SSBI tools can never completely replace BI tools like data warehouse in SQL server, OLAP (Online Analytical Processing) or visualization custom made application for reporting and data controlling. It is, however, a high-quality, quickly self-modifiable and inexpensive information tool, which on the based acquired knowledge and skills of people working with SSBI tools save mainly human, time and financial resources of the company.

References

Collie, R. and A. Singh. (2015). *Power Pivot and Power BI: The Excel User's Guide to DAX, Power Query, Power BI & Power Pivot in Excel 2010-2016.* Merritt Island: MrExcel.com. ISBN-13: 978-1615470396.

Hertle, C., Siedelhofer, C., Metternich, J. and E. Abele. (2015). *The next generation shop floor management-how to continuously develop competencies in manufacturing environments.* [Online]. ResearchGate. Available at: https://www.researchgate.net/publication/324731475_The_next_generation_shop_floor_management-how_to_continuously_develop_competencies_in_manufacturing_ environments [cited 21-04-27].

Howson, C. (2014). *Successful Business Intelligence. Unlock the Value of BI &Big Data.* New York: McGraf-Hill Education.

Jurová, M. and collective. (2016). *Výrobní a logistické procesy v podnikání.* Praha: Grada.

Laberge, R. (2012). *Datové sklady. Agilní metody a Business Intelligence.* Brno: Computer Press.

MICROSOFT (2021). *Power Pivot: Powerful data analysis and data modeling in Excel.* [Online]. Available at: https://support.microsoft.com/en-us/office/power-pivot-powerful-data-analysis-and-data-modeling-in-excel-a9c2c6e2-cc49-4976-a7d7-40896795d045 [cited 21-04-26].

Pour, J., Maryška, M., Stanovská, I. and Šedivá Z. (2018). *Self Service Business Inteligence. Jak si vytvořit vlastní analytické, plánovací a reportingové aplikace.* Praha: Grada. ISBN 978-80-271-0616-5.

Suzaki, K., (2010). *The New Shop Floor Management: Empowering People for Continuous Improvement.* London: Free Press.

Tomek, G. and V. Vávrová. (2014). *Integrované řízení výroby. Od operativního řízení výroby k dodavatelskému řetězci.* Praha: Grada.

The Digitalization of HR Processes: Success Factors and Consequences

Daniela Kharroubi[1]

Abstract. Research Background: As a result of the current unprecedented global changes due to Covid-19 pandemic, many organizations were obliged to face the reality, i.e., to keep a social distance and therefore to swap into the digital world, so that they can survive the current challenges.
Purpose of the article: The aim of this paper is to review recent publications, to analyze them and to provide an insight on the factors that determine the success of the digitalization process in HRM and define its consequences.
Methods: This paper provides a comprehensive review of quantitative, qualitative and theoretical studies published in journals and distinguishes articles that fall within the search criteria.
Findings and value added: Human resources management in most companies put an effort on the digital transformation of their processes in order to survive and grow. The author found that the existing literature focuses more on the study of the consequences of the digitalization of HRM than on the study of the factors that determine its success. We also distinguished three categories of factors, i.e., technological, organizational and people factors. This research is furthermore supplied with conditions to be respected in organizations to obtain a good HRM digitalization. These findings won't only benefit academicians but also managers and potential researchers, because they will be able to acknowledge the various aspects about the digital transformation of HRM.

Keywords: Human Resources Management (HRM), Digitalization, Factors, Consequences, Conditions.

JEL Classification: M12, O15, O33, Y3

1 Introduction

The Covid-19 pandemic forced many organizations to collectively swap the physical for the digital world in a matter of months. As retailers learn to operate without stores, business travelers without airplanes, and workers without offices, much of what started out as a temporary expedient is likely to become permanent. In this regard, investors in 2020 rewarded companies with digital-intensive such as Zoom Video Communications Inc. and Microsoft Corp. Thus, businesses are now spending less on office space and travel and more on cloud computing, collaboration software and logistics. In many ways, digitization is simply the next chapter of a process under way for a century, i.e., the dematerialization of the economy.

Many authors have mentioned that digitalization provides businesses with many advantages. Gassmann et al (2014) noted the ability of digitalization to transform existing products and services into digital variants and therefore offers advantages over the tangible product.

[1] VSB-Technical University of Ostrava, Faculty of Economics, Sokolska trida 33, 702 00 Ostrava, Czech Republic. E-mail: daniela.kharroubi@vsb.cz

Nöhammer and Stichlberger (2019) explained digitalization as an optimization tool that have positive consequences on the organization's future opportunities and trends.

However, the Covid-19 challenge required changes in many fields of businesses, one of them was Human Resources Management (HRM). Many HR processes, e.g., the recruitment and selection process, planning processes and performance management are no longer done by using traditional ways, but modified through the use of new digital technologies and information systems. Thus, digitalization influences the HR functions by innovating its individual processes from decision-making processes to problem solving (Manuti et de Palma, 2018). Cantoni and Mangia (2019) argued that digitalization requires the revamp of HR roles and the development of new competencies that will guarantee employee's wellbeing and organizational sustainability in the digital era.

The aim of this paper is to review recent literatures, analyse publications in the field of digitalization of HR practices and to provide an insight on the success factors of the digitalization process in HRM practices and its' consequences on organizations.

The second part of this paper provides a theoretical background into the concept of digitalization of HR. The third part describes the methodology used in this paper. The fourth part illustrates the results obtained from the analysis of publications, i.e., the factors that determine the success of the digitalization process in HRM practices and the consequences of digitalization. Subsequently, this part specifies information about important conditions in order to obtain a successful digitalization process. This paper ends up with discussions and conclusions.

2 Literature review

Although the definition to the term digitalization is absent in many articles, e.g., in Zeng, 2020; Ketolainen, 2018; Florea and Badea, 2013, but in many others it's inserted. Robert Wachel was the first to mention the term *digitalization* in his publication in 1971, who denoted it to the *digitalization of society* (Pieriegud, 2016). Stolterman and Fors (2004) defined *digital transformation* as a business model that is driven by the changes accompanied with the application of digital technologies in all aspects of human society. Westerman et al (2011) referred it to the use of technology that radically improves the performance or outcomes of an organization. Osipova (2019) analyzed the term *digitalization* to come up that it is necessary to see digitalization as a long-term process that involves not only technological changes but also strategic ones.

The digital evolution of the organization's business model and its processes takes place on two levels, i.e., the strategic and tactical level (Mazzone, 2014). In this regard, Ulrich and Dulebohn (2015) mentioned that HR are turning to be a strategic partner that ensure a long-term advantage to the organization in the era of digitalization.

Whereas the digitalization of HRM is understood as the integration of analytics, social and cloud technologies in different areas of HRM to deliver better productivity, redefined HR processes, work-life balance and decision-making processes and results (Stephan et al, 2016). The main idea behind the digitalization of HR processes is to modernize the HR processes, i.e., searching for talents, employee training and skills development, to streamline overall HRM solutions and functions by utilizing real-time interactive platforms, mobile applications, and integrated analytics (Galgali, 2017).

Likewise, the implementation of new technologies made HR professionals face many obstacles, from large amounts of data in spreadsheets, insufficient user experience, lack of IT functionality and many others challenges in recruiting, engaging and retaining employees. Thus, new technologies like big data, the internet of things, virtual reality, analytics, cloud, robots and AI brought the fact that it is needed to reskill or upskill the employees. All of this emphasizes the need of organizations to attract an agile workforce that will be dynamic and able to rapidly accept innovative ideas and responsibilities (Cantoni and Mangia, 2019). Therefore, digitalization strongly demands specific soft skills and an attitude towards the work which can't be performed or evaluated by digital systems (Mangipudi and Vaidya, 2018). The most important challenges faced by the HR department caused by digitalization are summarized in Table 1.

Challenges in HRM caused by digitalization
Creating new workforce planning strategy with redesigning job profiles
Changing the approach for recruiting new candidates
Addressing potential skill gaps among workforce due to robotization and automatization
E-learning with orientation on digital talent development
Performance management required advanced ICT skills
Potential work drawbacks such as stress, work-life imbalance and work insecurity
Developing new opportunities for talented workers and qualifying them for more complicated tasks
Minimizing the abrasion of highly skilled workers
Greater social responsibility

Table 1 Challenges in HRM caused by digitalization [Cantoni and Mangia, 2019]

Furthermore, it is important to address that the recruitment process was one of the most influenced areas during the pandemic. Since the companies had to focus on social media and other platforms in order to recruit new candidates. Bohmová and Chudán (2018) stated that social media networks in recruitment deliver a solution that is innovative and cost effective. Yet, social media networks are a space with huge potential candidates who voluntarily share their personal information, and which can be used by recruiters in order to contact them (Bohmova and Chudán, 2018). However, recruiters have to be aware of principles, and terms and conditions of social media networks.

Correspondingly, the ongoing development technologies in HR creates new tasks and requires the development of new HR technology competencies. In his study, Stracke (2011) draws the attention that HR competencies can't be observed directly but can be measured by the action aimed to achieve a specific objective. Based on the study of European Round Table of Industrialists (2017), the authors confirmed the following key digital HR competencies: digital literacy, digital communication, multitasking, data analytics, creativity, cloud technologies, critical thinking and long-life upskilling.

The next part of this paper concentrates on the methodology used, the results obtained from the analysis of publications, i.e., the factors that determine the success of the digitalization process in HRM practices in an organization and the consequences of digitalization. Subsequently, this part specifies information about important conditions in order to obtain a successful digitalization process.

3 Methodology

A systematic review of the literature on digitalization in HRM was carried out through a relevant search of keywords. Specific keywords like e- *HRM, digital HRM, digitalization of HRM* were searched, followed by certain criteria. Primarily, to access the relevant articles, the author searched relevant database Web of Science (WoS) and Google Scholar, limited to the period of 2010 - 2020. There were 2700 articles established by this search. By scanning the abstracts, 105 articles were related to the topic of the digitalization. By eliminating those articles not related to HRM, the author got a final sample of 32 articles. However, in order to identify the success factors for the digitalization of HRM practices and to derive an overview of consequences caused by it, the author had to analyze these publications and highlight the relevant factors and consequences.

4 Results

In this part, the results obtained from the analysis are represented. As previously mentioned, factors that determine the success of the digitalization process in HRM practices and the consequences of digitalization. Subsequently, it specifies information about important conditions in order to obtain a successful digitalization process.

4.1 Success factors

The results of the analysis revealed that factors that determine the success of the digitalization of HR practices are allocated into 3 categories as already suggested by Bondarouk's et al (2017) TOP model, i.e., technological, organizational and people factors.

The analyzed publications had shown as for technological factors that it is essential to take into consideration the application and its characteristics which are correlated to its usefulness and easiness to be used. In this regard, Njoku (2018) examined whether perceived usefulness and perceived ease of use have a positive relationship on the manager's attitude towards the value formed by the digital tools used in the organization. The results showed a strongly positive relationship in the case of perceived usefulness, and on the other hand, a weak negative relationship to the perceived ease of use. Other technological factors that affect the implementation of digital tools in HRM practices included data characteristics as mentioned by Nabila (2017) and data integrity and system integration as declared by Murphy (2018). Similarly, Bandarouk et al (2017) reported that standardization of HR processes is an important factor when adopting HR information systems (HRIS). However, whether adopting an in-house HRIS or outsourcing it would be more beneficial depends on the organization's specific needs, its expectations in the future and its risk orientations.

As for the organizational factors, the author distinguished two categories of factors. The first category included the organizational characteristics, i.e., size, sector, business area and the geographic location of the company. In this context, a study conducted by Kentainen (2018) proved that the type of approach adopted by an organization towards digitalization in HRM and its following success are strongly persuaded by the size, sector, business area and the geographic location where the organization operates. Correspondingly, Bondarouk et al (2017) stated that larger companies are more likely to implement e-HRM and that the successful adoption is more widespread among small organizations. Also, a study introduced by Hofmann et al (2018) showed that the private sector is able to better exploit the advantages of the digitalization of HRM in comparison to the public sector. Furthermore, they found that in the private sector, analytical skills are important for developing new business opportunities and in order to equip employees with the required competences, training plays an important role in both sectors (Hofmann et al, 2018).

As for the second category of the organizational factors, the author found that capabilities and resources of an organization have an impact on the successful adoption of HRIS. Firstly, the organizations can be tight on their budget due to economic recession which may lead for not implementing e-HRM or have unexpected the costs associated with it (Bondarouk et al, 2017; Murphy, 2018). Secondly, data access and privacy in regard to the organizational internal policies restrict the access and the possibility of the HRM employees to manipulate with or to edit the personal information which also influences the attitude of employees towards the implementation of HRIS (Zafar et al, 2015). Thirdly, unawareness of the potential of HRIS as introduced by Njoku (2018) as a result of a gap in technological knowledge may not admit the best use of the digital tools.

In people factors, the author underlined the following essential factors, i.e., the top management support, user acceptance, HR skills and, leadership and culture. Hazim (2019) stated that the support of the top management is one of the essential factors in defining the success of the digitalization process in HRM. In other words, HR managers play a vital role in making the employees understand the importance of the digitalization process. Zeng (2020) stated that the digital tools allow to make a user driven employee experience. Bondarouk et al (2017) emphasized that involving the HR employees in the implementation process of the IS positively influenced its successful adoption in HRM. Furthermore, Bondarouk et al (2017) claimed that HR managers are capable of solving micro-level problems, e.g., data entry, editing, etc., but have a lack to certain IT skills like solving macro-level technical problems while using HRIS. For this reason, it is important to address the vitality of training sessions in order to enhance the technical skills in HR employees. Also, Bondarouk et al (2017) added that IT friendly organizational cultures are more likely to successfully adopt the digitalization process in HRM practices.

4.2 Consequences of the digitalization of HRM practices

HR specialists as well as the organizations face merits and demerits as a result of digitalizing the HR practices. However, some of these consequences are often mentioned as a benefit, while others are considered as a risk. As for the positive/negative consequences, the following merits/demerits were distinguished (Table 2):

Positive consequences/benefits	Negative consequences/risks
Cost saving (cuts in HR costs).	Employees' resistance to change.
Increased operational efficiency.	Replacement by automation.
Time saving (speeding up processes).	Lack of ICT skills.
Paper eliminating.	Data security.
Better work quality with fewer errors.	Cyberattacks.
Data security.	Lack of investment in training employees.
Improvement of the decision-making process.	Difficulty in using new technologies.
Empowerment of the HR department.	Digital tools not fully utilized.
Improves employee's ICT knowledge.	Data integration of IT systems.
Better cognitive skills.	Changing the organizational structure.
Enables new employment forms.	Changing the employee and employer work relations.
Better employee motivation.	
Better employee communication.	

Table 2 Consequences of the digitalization of HR practices [Mangipudi and Vaidya, 2018; Mazurchenko and Maršíková, 2019; Saini, 2019]

Bondarouk et al (2017) explored that digitalization of HR practices have operational consequences in the form of HR effectiveness and efficiency, cost and time savings. However, Murphy (2018) claimed that digitalization increases the satisfaction of HR employees, but it is not clear whether it implicates a cutback in the operating costs of HRM. Furthermore, the author verified his claim in a research conducted to HR managers that digitalization does not reduce HR costs. Still, HR digital tools facilitated the administrative work of HR employees, not only by paper eliminating, but also by reducing the time needed to carry out certain tasks (Murphy, 2018).

Besides operational consequences, relational consequences were distinguished. Thus, the digitalization of HRM practices led for better employee motivation and communication. In this regard, Bondarouk et al (2017) observed that e-HRM enhances employees' awareness, appreciation and the use of HR programs. Murphy (2018) also found out that digitalization improves the employee's commitment.

Saini (2018) showed that the digitalization of HRM has a positive effect on three given variables. Thus, it improves the employee's ICT knowledge, cognitive skills and boosts their career development. In contrary, Bengtsson and Bloom (2017) showed in their study that there is a lack to suitable skills among HR managers.

On the other hand, some demerits have been connected to the implementation of HRIS, primarily were linked to data security that often includes a great deal of confidential data about employees, payrolls, performance appraisal data, etc. (Zafar, 2013).

4.3 Conditions to be respected in organizations during the digitalization of HR practices

Whilst studying most of the publication, the author distinguished three essential condition that must be taken into consideration by organizations in order to obtain a successful digitalization process of HRM. Murphy (2018) ensures that it is vital to have precise and well-defined objectives in the area of digitalization of HRM. In other words, the organization has to have a clear idea in which trend they want to direct its digital efforts and how could digitalization affect the roles of employees in it. Thus, the transformations process may need to redefine some employees' roles. Furthermore, it implies changes at the employee or the manager level, i.e., digitally enabling the workforce and the management (Saini, 2018).

As a second important condition is to identify the key personnel while working on the digital transformation. In this context, Bengtson and Boom (2017) argue that HR managers have to align their strategy with the organization's vision and have to have a digital awareness in order to extend the benefits of the digitalization of HR practices.

Thirdly, digital tools have to be seen as a complement to the traditional practices and as a way to facilitate them. Murphy (2018) added that in order to attain the highest level of efficiency and effectivity, traditional processes have to be modified so they adapt to the new technologies.

5 Discussion

Based on the acquired results, we can say that the existing publications primarily focus on the consequences of the digitalization of HR practices rather than on the success factors. The results of the analysis revealed that factors that determine the success of the digitalization of HR practices are nevertheless allocated into 3 categories as already suggested by Bondarouk's et al (2017) TOP model, i.e., technological, organizational and people factors. We also discovered that organizational factors comprehensively influence the eagerness of the HR department to adopt digital tools. On the other hand, technological and people factors affect the HR functions while adopting e-HRM. Ketolainen (2018) proved that organizational factors like size, sector, business area and the geographic location have an impact on the organization's attitude towards the adoption of digital tools. Besides that, we also found out other organizational success factors linked to budget limitations due to economic recession, unawareness of HRIS potential, and data security and privacy. As for the technological factors, we distinguished that the application and its easiness to be used, data characteristics and data integrity play an important role for the successful adopting of digital tools. Though, people factors seemed to have a significant increase in its relevance to the successful adoption of HRIS (Bondarouk et al, 2017). Thus, the employee's support and commitment are very important during its implementation. However, the various TOP factors were primarily linked to the internal factors of an organization. For this reason, it's essential to widen this model and to take into consideration the external factors of an organization.

In regard to consequences, merits and demerits were identified. In fact, digitalization contributed to a greater simplicity in administration practices, HR effectiveness, efficiency, cost and time savings. Thus, HRIS relieved the HR employees from bureaucratic tasks and increased their flexibility, allowing them to spend time on more important tasks. It was also found that

HRIS led to a better motivation, commitment and relationships among employees. On the other hand, negative consequences were also identified and primarily linked to data security, privacy and lack of ICT skills among employees. Which brings the fact that it is needed to reskill or upskill the employees.

We also observed that there was a significant number of publications released before the year 2010 indicating that e-HRM was covered by all different IS. However, new technologies have been evolved during the last decade and it is necessary to fill in the gap with new discoveries.

6 Conclusion

This paper reviewed publications released over the last decade and provided an insight on the success factors of the digitalization of HR practices, its consequences and conditions to be respected in organizations. Indubitably, this research confirmed that HRIS has the potential to simplify and enrich, support and steer, shorten and speed up the organizational process so that goals are accomplished (Bondarouk et al, 2017). It was also found that all factors, i.e., the organization, technological and people factors held responsible for the successful adoption of HRIS and that the positive consequences of the digitalization of HRM overweighted the negative consequences. And last not least, we concluded that digitalization is becoming the next chapter in HR practices, especially in the times of the COVID-19 pandemic.

Finally, the research concentrated on general e-HRM and didn't cover some functional areas of HRM such as e-recruitment which can be an initial point for future research studies.

Acknowledgements

This research was supported within the project of the Student Grant Competition at the Economic Faculty of VŠB-Technical University Ostrava SP2021/56.

References

Bloom, M., and Bengtsson, C. (2017). Human Resource Management in a Digital Era, [online]. Available at: http://lup.lub.lu.se/luur/download?func=downloadFile&recordOId=8914716&fileOId=8914717 [cited 2021-02-16].

Bondarouk, T., Parry, E., & Furtmueller, E. (2017). Electronic HRM: four decades of research on adoption and consequences. *The International Journal of Human Resource Management*, 28(1), pp.98-131.

Bohmová, L., and Chudán, D. (2018). Analyzing social media data for recruiting purposes. *Acta Informatica Pragensia*, 7(1), pp. 4-21.

Cantoni, F., and Mangia, G. (2019). *Human resource management and digitalization*. New York, Torino: Routledge.

European Round Table of Industrialists. (2017). Building and transforming skills for a digital world, [online]. Available at: https://www.ert.eu/document/building-and-transforming-skills-digital-world [cited 2021-01-31].

Florea, V. N., and Badea, M. (2013). Acceptance of new technologies in HR: E- recruitment in organizations. In *Proceedings of the European Conference on Information Management & Evaluation*, pp. 344-352.

Galgali, P. (2017). Digital transformation and its impact on organization's Human Resource Management, [online]. Available at:

https://www.academia.edu/35595152/Digital_Transformation_and_its_Impact_on_Organizations_Human_R esource_Management [cit. 2021-01-31].

Gassmann, O., Frankerberger, K., Csik, M. (2014). *The business model navigator: 55 models that will revolutionize your business group.* New Jersey: FT Press.

Hazim, H. H. (2019). The Power of Mentoring and Digitization as Processes of Strengthening the Human Resource Departments' Activity. *Journal of Economic Development, Environment and People*, 8(3), pp. 47-51.

Hofmann, S., and Ogonek, N. (2018). Different but Still the Same? How Public and Private Sector Organisations Deal with New Digital Competences. *The Electronic Journal of e-Government*, 16(2), pp. 127-135.

Ketolainen, N. (2018). Digitalization of human resources - the transformation journey into automated and data-driven service organization, [online]. Available at: https://www.theseus.fi/bitstream/handle/10024/149759/Ketolainen_Niina.pdf?sequence=1&isAllowed=y [cited 2021-02-07].

Mangipudi, M. R., and Vaidya, R. (2018). A study of digitalization in HRM and its effectiveness in execution of HR strategies and policies. *Helix*, 8(6), pp. 4220-4222.

Manuti, A., and De Palma, P. D. (2018). *Digital HR: a critical management approach to the digitalization of organization.* Cham: Palgrave Macmillan.

Mazzone, D. M. (2014). *Digital or death: Digital transformation – The only choice for business to survive smash and counter.* Mississauga: Smashbox Consulting.

Murphy, A. (2018). Can the digitisation of HR services alter employee perceptions of those services and the HR function at the same time as delivering HR operational cost savings to an organisation? [online]. Available at: https://esource.dbs.ie/bitstream/handle/10788/3516/mba_murphy_a_2018.pdf?sequence=1&isAllowed=y [cited 2021-02-07].

Nabila, Z. Z. (2017). Digital Trasformation: New Era of HR in perspective of Bata, [online]. Available at:http://dspace.bracu.ac.bd/xmlui/bitstream/handle/10361/8581/13104247_BBA.pdf?sequence=1&isAllowed=y [cited 2021-02-07].

Njoku, E., Ruel, H., Rowlands, H., Evans, L. and Murdoch, M. (2019). *An Analysis of the contribution of e-HRM to sustaining business performance.* Advanced Series in Management, Vol. 23, Emerald Publishing Limited.

Nöhammer, E., and Stichlberger, S. (2019). Digitalization, innovative work behaviour and extended availability. *Journal of Business Economics*, 89(8-9), pp. 1191-1214.

Osipova, O. (2019). Digital trasformation of personnel management services. In *International Conference on Digital Technologies in Logistics and Infrastructure (ICDTLI 2019).* Atlantis Press.

Pieriegud, J. (2016). Cyfryzacja gospodarki i społeczeństwa – wymiar globalny, europejski i krajowy. In *Cyfryzacja gospodarki i społeczeństwa. Szanse i wyzwania dla sektorów infrastrukturalnych,* pp. 11-38.

Saini, S. (2018). Digital HRM and its Effective Implementation: An Empirical Study. *The International Journal of management*, 7(2), pp. 62-66.

Stephan, M., Uzawa S., Volini, E., Walsh, B., and Yoshida, R. (2016). Digital HR: revolution, not evolution. In *Global Human Capital Trends 2016. The new organization: different by design,* pp. 97-101.

Stolterman, E. and A. C. Fors. (2004). *Information technology and the good life. In: Information Systems Research: Relevant Theory and Informed Practice.* London: Kluwer Academic Publishers.

Stracke, C. M. (2011). Competences and skills in the digital age: Competence development, modelling, and standards for human resources development. In *Proceedings of* the *5th International Conference on Metadata and Semantic Research,* pp. 34-46.

Ulrich, D., and Dulebohn, J. H. (2015). Are we there yet? What's next for HR? *Human Resource Management Review*, 25(2), pp. 188-204.

Westerman, G., Calméjane, C., Bonnet, D., Ferraris, P., and McAfee, A. (2011). Digital transformation: A roadmap for billion-dollar organizations. *MIT Sloan Management Review*, Cambridge, MA.

Zafar, H. (2013). Human resource information systems: Information security concerns for organizations. *Human Resource Management Review*, 23, pp. 105-113.

Zafar, H., and Stone, D. L. (2015). *HRIS security and privacy*. In Human Resource Information Systems: Basics, applications, and future directions (3rd Edition). Thousand Oaks, CA: Sage.

Zeng, H. (2020). Adaptability of artificial intelligence in Human Resources Management in this Era. *International Journal of Science*, 7(1), pp. 271-276.

Rectifying single sampling plans in acceptance sampling

Jindrich Klufa[1]

Abstract: Rectifying plans are sampling inspection plans in acceptance sampling when the remainder of rejected lots is inspected. These plans were introduced by Dodge-Romig for inspection by attributes (each inspected item is classified as either good or defective). Analogous rectifying plans for inspection by variables were introduced by author of this contribution. For inspection of separate lots are used the LTPD plans (LTPD is the lot tolerance percent defective), for inspection of series lots from the same producer are used the AOQL plans (AOQL is average outgoing quality limit). The sample size for inspection by variables is less than the corresponding sample size for inspection by attributes. On the other hand, the cost of inspecting an item by variables is usually greater than the cost of inspecting the same item by attributes. In this paper we shall solve the decision problem: inspection by variables or inspection by attributes?

Keywords: Acceptance sampling, inspection by attributes, inspection by variables, cost of inspection.

JEL Classification: C44, L15, C83

1 Introduction

The Dodge-Romig single sampling inspection plans by attributes are acceptance plans (n_a, c), where n_a is the number of items in the sample (the sample size), c is the acceptance number. Using this acceptance plan we decide as follows (see e.g., Hald (1981)):

The lot is rejected when the number of defective items in the sample is greater than c.

There are no assumptions for using these plans. The Dodge-Romig plans (n_a, c) minimize the mean number of items inspected per lot of process average quality, assuming that the remainder of rejected lots is inspected (denoted I_a) under the condition which protects the consumer against the acceptance of a bad lots:

the lots with the fraction defective $p \geq p_t$ (p_t is the lot tolerance proportion defective, the chosen parameter) are accepted with probability which is less or equal to β (β is consumer's risk, obviously β=0.10) - the LTPD plans by attributes,

or

the average outgoing quality (the mean fraction defective after inspection when the fraction defective before inspection was p) is less or equal to p_L for all values of input quality p, where p_L is average outgoing quality limit AOQL (the chosen parameter) – the AOQL plans by attributes.

These LTPD single sampling plans and also AOQL single sampling plans are tabulated in Dodge and Romig (1998).

1 Prague University of Economics and Business, Department of Mathematics, W. Churchill Sq. 4, 13067 Prague, e-mail: klufa@vse.cz

The corresponding single sampling inspection plans by variables are acceptance plans (n_v, k), where n_v is the number of items in the sample (the sample size), k is the critical value. Assumptions: Measurements of a single quality characteristic X are independent, identically distributed normal random variables with unknown parameters μ and σ^2. For the quality characteristic X is given either an upper specification limit U (the item is defective if its measurement exceeds U), or a lower specification limit L (the item is defective if its measurement is smaller than L). It is further assumed that the unknown parameter σ is estimated from the sample standard deviation s. Under the assumptions the lot is accepted when (see e.g. Klufa (2015))

$$\frac{U - \bar{x}}{s} \geq k, \qquad \text{or} \quad \frac{\bar{x} - L}{s} \geq k,$$

where

$$\bar{x} = \frac{1}{n_v} \sum_{i=1}^{n_v} x_i, \qquad s = \sqrt{\frac{1}{n_v - 1} \sum_{i=1}^{n_v} (x_i - \bar{x})^2}.$$

These plans (n_v, k) for inspection by variables minimize the mean number of items inspected per lot of process average quality, assuming that the remainder of rejected lots is inspected (denoted I_v) under the same conditions which protects the consumer against the acceptance of a bad lots (see Dodge-Romig plans). Calculation of these LTPD single sampling plans by variables using software Mathematica we can find in Klufa (2010) using software R in Kasprikova and Klufa (2011). Calculation of AOQL single sampling plans by variables we can find in Klufa (2014). Similar problems are solved in Yazdi and Nezhad (2017), Chen and Chou (2001), Aslam et al (2015), Kasprikova (2019), Wang and Lo (2016), Yazdi et al (2016), Kasprikova (2017), Balamurali et al (2014), Fallahnezhad et al (2018), Razmkhah et al (2021).

2 Inspection by attributes versus inspection by variables

The sample size for inspection by variables is less than the corresponding sample size for inspection by attributes. On the other hand, the cost of inspecting an item by variables is usually greater than the cost of inspecting the same item by attributes. Let us denote

$$C = \frac{c_v}{c_a},$$

where c_v is the cost of inspection of one item by variables and c_a is the cost of inspection of the same item by attributes. The parameter C is the fraction of the cost of inspection of one item by variables and the cost of inspection of the same item by attributes. Usually $C > 1$ (when $C \leq 1$, the rectifying plans for inspection by variables are always more economical than the corresponding attribute sampling plans). Under the notation the fraction

$$\frac{I_v}{I_a} C = \frac{I_v c_v}{I_a c_a}$$

is the fraction of the mean cost of inspection by variables per lot of process average quality $I_v c_v$ and the mean cost of inspection by attributes per lot of process average quality $I_a c_a$. Let us denote

$$C_L = \frac{I_a}{I_v}.$$

If $C = C_L$, then

$$\frac{I_v}{I_a} C = 1$$

and the mean cost of inspection by variables per lot of process average quality is the same as the mean cost of inspection by attributes per lot of process average quality, for $C < C_L$ is the inspection by variables preferable, for $C > C_L$ the rectifying plans for inspection by attributes are better than the corresponding plans for inspection by variables. The new parameter C_L, i.e. the fraction of the cost of inspection limit (denoted FCIL) we shall calculate according the formula

$$C_L = \frac{N - (N - n_a)\, L(\bar{p}; n_a, c)}{N - (N - n_v)\, L(\bar{p}; n_v, k)} \qquad (1)$$

where N is the number of items in the lot (the lot size, given parameter), $\bar{p}$ is the process average fraction defective (the given parameter) and $L(p)$ is the probability of accepting a submitted lot with fraction defective p (the operating characteristic, denoted OC). The operating characteristic is a decreasing function of the fraction defective p. For each acceptance sampling plan (n, c) is OC fundamental information of quality of this plan (therefore instead $L(p)$ we write $L(p; n, c)$). OC for inspection by attributes (see e.g. Hald (1981) is

$$L(p; n_a, c) = \sum_{i=0}^{c} \frac{\binom{Np}{i} \cdot \binom{N - Np}{n_a - i}}{\binom{N}{n_a}}$$

and OC for inspection by variables using noncentral t distribution (see e. g. Klufa (2010)) is

$$L(p; n_v, k) = \int_{k\sqrt{n_v}}^{\infty} g\left(t; n_v - 1, u_{1-p}\sqrt{n_v}\right) dt,$$

where $g\left(t; n_v - 1, u_{1-p}\sqrt{n_v}\right)$ is probability density function of noncentral Student t distribution with $(n_v - 1)$ degrees of freedom and noncentrality parameter $\lambda = u_{1-p}\sqrt{n_v}$ (u_{1-p} is quantile of standard normal distribution of order $1 - p$).

2.1 The LTPD single sampling plans

For these plans is chosen value p_t ($100p_t$ is the lot tolerance percent defective LTPD) and the consumer is protected against the acceptance of a bad lots through the condition $L(p_t) = 0.10$.

This condition guarantees that the lots with the fraction defective $p \geq p_t$ are accepted with probability which is less or equal to 0.10 (the operating characteristic is a decreasing function).

Example: We have chosen $p_t = 0.03$ (i.e. the LTPD is 3%). Let the lot size $N = 1000$ and the process average fraction defective $\bar{p} = 0.006$. We have to decide in this situation if the inspection by variables is better than the inspection by attributes or vice versa.

For these input parameters we can find in Dodge and Romig (1998) sampling plan for inspection by attributes

$$n_a = 170, \; c = 2.$$

The corresponding plan for inspection by variables we can compute using software Mathematica (see Klufa (2010)). We obtain

$$n_v = 89, \; k = 2.1271.$$

For decision inspection by attributes or inspection by variables we compute according to (1) the fraction of the cost of inspection limit FCIL. We obtain (see also Table 1)

$$C_L = 2.17 \,.$$

For example, if the cost of inspection of one item by variables c_v is two times greater than the cost of inspection of the same item by attributes c_a ($C = 2$) the LTPD plan for inspection by variables (89, 2.1271) is more economical than the corresponding LTPD plan for inspection by attributes (170, 2). Inspection by attributes is preferable when $C > 2.17$, i.e., $c_v > 2.17\, c_a$.

$\bar{p}\backslash N$	100	500	1000	4000	10000	50000	100000
0.00075	2.27	2.63	3.33	3.85	3.57	4.00	4.35
0.00150	1.92	2.56	2.78	3.13	3.03	3.23	3.33
0.00225	1.72	2.50	2.56	2.86	3.13	3.33	3.03
0.00300	1.61	2.50	2.50	2.78	3.57	4.35	3.45
0.00375	1.49	2.17	2.43	2.63	2.78	2.86	2.94
0.00450	1.43	2.08	2.33	2.63	2.70	2.78	2.78
0.00525	1.40	2.00	2.22	2.70	2.86	2.94	2.86
0.00600	1.32	1.96	2.17	2.78	3.13	3.33	3.33
0.00675	1.27	1.89	2.08	2.38	2.50	2.70	2.70
0.00750	1.23	1.85	2.00	2.38	2.50	2.70	2.56
0.00825	1.19	1.79	1.96	2.44	2.56	2.86	2.63
0.00900	1.16	1.75	1.92	2.50	2.63	3.23	2.86
0.00975	1.15	1.61	1.85	2.22	2.38	2.50	2.56
0.01050	1.12	1.56	1.82	2.17	2.33	2.44	2.50
0.01125	1.10	1.52	1.75	2.17	2.38	2.56	2.63
0.01200	1.09	1.47	1.72	2.22	2.44	2.78	3.03
0.01275	1.08	1.43	1.67	2.04	2.17	2.38	2.44
0.01350	1.06	1.39	1.61	2.00	2.13	2.33	2.44
0.01425	1.05	1.35	1.56	2.00	2.13	2.44	2.63
0.01500	1.04	1.32	1.54	2.04	2.17	2.63	3.03

Table 1 Values of the parameter C_L for $p_t = 0.03$ (source: own calculation)

2.2 The AOQL single sampling plans

For these plans is chosen value p_L, i.e. average outgoing quality limit AOQL. The AOQL plans guarantees that the average outgoing quality is less or equal to p_L for all values of input quality

p. The average outgoing quality AOQ is the mean fraction defective after inspection when the fraction defective before inspection was p. The average outgoing quality depends on input quality p, i.e. AOQ = AOQ(p) is a function of p. For this function is $AOQ(0) = AOQ(1) = 0$ and $AOQ(p) > 0$ for p in interval (0,1). When fraction defective p increases, the function $AOQ(p)$ a first increases. Then the lots are increasingly rejected, so $AOQ(p)$ begins to decline. For just one p in interval (0,1) the function $AOQ(p)$ has maximum. This maximum is chosen p_L for AOQL single sampling plans.

Example: We have chosen $p_L = 0.005$ (i.e. the AOQL is 0.5%). Let the lot size $N = 4000$ and the process average fraction defective $\bar{p} = 0.002$. We have to decide in this situation if the inspection by variables is better than the inspection by attributes or vice versa.

For these input parameters we can find in Dodge and Romig (1998) sampling plan for inspection by attributes

$$n_a = 160, \ c = 1.$$

The corresponding plan for inspection by variables is (see Klufa (2014))

$$n_v = 78, \ k = 2.3318.$$

For decision inspection by attributes or inspection by variables we compute according to (1) the fraction of the cost of inspection limit FCIL. We obtain (see also Table 2)

$$C_L = 3.13 .$$

It means for example, if the cost of inspection of one item by variables c_v is three times greater than the cost of inspection of the same item by attributes c_a ($C = 3$) the AOQL plan for inspection by variables (78, 2.3318) is more economical than the corresponding AOQL plan for inspection by attributes (160, 1). Inspection by attributes is preferable when $C > 3.13$, i.e. $c_v > 3.13\, c_a$. In most of practical situations, inspection by variables will be more economical than inspection by attributes and using AOQL plan for inspection by variables (78, 2.3318) instead AOQL plan for inspection by attributes (160, 1) can bring significant savings in inspection costs under the same protection of consumer.

Remark: The fraction of the cost of inspection limit FCIL depends for given LTPD or AOQL on the lot size N and the process average fraction defective $\bar{p}$, i.e., $C_L = C_L(N, \bar{p})$. Some values of the function are in Table 1 and Table 2. From numerical calculations it follows (see also Table 1 and Table 2) that value of the deciding point C_L increases when the lot size N increases and when the process average fraction defective $\bar{p}$ decreases.

$\bar{p}\backslash N$	100	500	1000	4000	10000	50000	100000
0.00025	2.86	3.23	3.45	5.26	4.76	6.25	5.88
0.00050	2.50	2.86	3.23	4.17	4.00	4.76	4.76
0.00075	2.27	2.70	3.13	3.70	3.85	4.35	4.76
0.00100	2.13	2.56	3.03	3.45	4.00	4.35	5.26
0.00125	2.04	2.44	3.03	3.23	3.70	4.17	4.55
0.00150	1.92	2.38	2.94	3.23	3.45	4.00	4.17
0.00175	1.85	2.33	2.94	3.13	3.33	4.17	4.17
0.00200	1.79	2.27	2.88	3.13	3.33	4.35	4.35

0.00225	1.72	2.17	2.44	2.86	3.23	3.70	3.85
0.00250	1.69	2.13	2.33	2.70	3.03	3.57	3.70
0.00275	1.64	2.08	2.22	2.63	2.94	3.45	3.70
0.00300	1.61	2.04	2.13	2.50	2.86	3.57	3.85
0.00325	1.56	1.96	2.08	2.38	2.70	3.13	3.33
0.00350	1.54	1.92	2.00	2.33	2.56	3.03	3.23
0.00375	1.52	1.89	1.92	2.22	2.44	2.94	3.13
0.00400	1.47	1.85	1.85	2.13	2.33	2.86	3.13
0.00425	1.45	1.69	1.79	2.00	2.13	2.50	2.63
0.00450	1.43	1.64	1.72	1.89	2.00	2.33	2.44
0.00475	1.41	1.61	1.67	1.79	1.89	2.13	2.17
0.00500	1.39	1.56	1.61	1.69	1.75	1.89	1.89

Table 2 Values of the parameter C_L for $p_L = 0.005$ (source: own calculation)

Conclusion

When the fraction of the cost of inspection limit FCIL is big, then acceptance sampling by variables is preferable. In this situation using the rectifying plans for inspection by variables instead of the corresponding plans for inspection by attributes can bring significant savings in inspection costs. This savings can be more than 50% under the same protection the consumer against the acceptance of a bad lots. On the other hand, if the fraction of the cost of inspection limit FCIL is near to 1, the rectifying plans for inspection by attributes are better than the corresponding plans for inspection by variables. From numerical calculations it follows that value of the fraction of the cost of inspection limit FCIL (see (1)) increases when the lot size N increases and when the process average fraction defective $\bar{p}$ decreases.

Acknowledgements

This paper was processed with contribution of long-term institutional support of research activities by Faculty of Informatics and Statistics, University of Economics, Prague, Czech Republic (IP400040).

References

Aslam, M., Azam, M., Jun, C.-H. (2015). 'A new lot inspection procedure based on exponentially weighted moving average'. *International Journal of Systems Science,* 46, pp. 1392–1400.

Balamurali, S., Azam, M., Aslam, M. (2014). 'Attribute-Variable Inspection Policy for Lots using Resampling Based on EWMA'. *Communications in Statistics – Simulation and Computation*, 45(8), pp. 3014–3035.

Chen, C. H. and Chou, C. Y. (2001). 'Economic design of Dodge-Romig lot tolerance per cent defective single sampling plans for variables under Taguchi's quality loss function'. *Total Quality Management,* 12, pp. 5–11.

Dodge, H. F.and Romig, H. G. (1998). *Sampling Inspection Tables: Single and Double Sampling*, 2nd ed. New York: John Wiley.

Fallahnezhad, M. S.; Qazvini, E.; Abessi, M. (2018) 'Designing an economical acceptance sampling plan in the presence of inspection errors based on maxima nomination sampling method'. *Scientia Iranica,* 25(3), pp. 1701-1711.

Hald, A. (1981). *Statistical Theory of Sampling Inspection by Attributes*, London: Academic Press.

Kasprikova, N. and Klufa, J. (2011). 'Calculation of LTPD Single Sampling Plans for Inspection by Variables and its Software Implementation'. *Proceedings of 5th International Days of Statistics and Economics, Prague*, pp. 266-276.

Kasprikova, N. (2017). 'Rectifying LTPD Plans Minimizing Mean Inspection Cost Per Lot of Process Average Quality Using EWMA Statistics'. *Journal of Testing and Evaluation*, 45, pp. 1436–1441.

Kasprikova, N. (2019). 'Economic Efficiency of Rectifying AOQL Plans Based on the EWMA Statistic'. *Journal of Testing and Evaluation*, 47(6), pp. 4263–4271.

Klufa, J. (2015). 'Economic aspects of the LTPD single sampling inspection plans'. *Agricultural Economics – Czech*, 61(7), pp. 326–331.

Klufa, J. (2010). 'Exact calculation of the Dodge-Romig LTPD single sampling plans for inspection by variables'. *Statistical Papers*, 51(2), pp. 297-305.

Klufa, J. (2014). 'Dodge-Romig AOQL Sampling Plans for Inspection by Variables - Optimal Solution'. *Procedia Economics and Finance,* 12, pp. 302-308.

Razmkhah, M.; Gildeh, B. S.; Ahmadi, J. (2021) 'An economic design of rectifying single sampling plans via maxima nomination sampling in the presence of inspection errors'. *Communications in Statistics – Simulation and Computation,* 50, pp. 217-233.

Wang, F. K. and Lo, S. C. (2016). 'Single Mixed Sampling Plan Based on Yield Index for Linear Profiles'. *Quality and Reliability Engineering International,* 32(4), pp. 1535–1543.

Yazdi, A. A. and Nezhad, M. S. F. (2017). 'Comparison between count of cumulative conforming sampling plans and Dodge-Romig single sampling plan'. *Communications in Statistics – Theory and Methods,* 46, pp. 189–199.

Yazdi, A. A., Nezhad, M. S. F., Shishebori, D., Mostafaeipour, A. (2016). 'Development of an Optimal Design for Conforming Run Length Sampling Methods in the Presence of Inspection Errors'. *Journal of Testing and Evaluation*, 44(5), pp. 1885–1891.

Selection of suitable measures for the application of age management goals in a selected organization

Terezie Krestová[1], Aleš Kresta [2]

Abstract. Age management allows the organization to use the potential of employees at every age and thus extend their working life and contribution to the organization. In order to apply age management effectively, there is a need to set age management goals in line with the organization's strategy and to establish appropriate age management measures to achieve the goals. In this paper, we propose the use of the analytic hierarchy process and illustrate how the method of can be applied to select the appropriate measures in the selected organization.

Keywords: Human Recourses Management, Age Management, Measures of Age Management, Analytic Hierarchy Process.

JEL Classification: J11, J14, M12

1 Introduction

Due to the trend of population aging and age structure changing change in the age structure (ČSÚ, 2019; Eurostat, 2019), this fact needs to be considered in the strategic management of the organization and adapted to human resource management. Human resource management will need to take into account both the increasing age of employees and later retirement, as well as the fact that there will be fewer graduates coming to the organization. In order for the organization to maintain its performance and competitiveness, creating conditions for employees of all ages will be a very important challenge. How to manage employees by age is engaged in age management. Many organizations have already noticed this trend and the application of age management is becoming a common part of HRM.

The aim of the paper is to select age management goals and measures for the selected organization.

At the beginning of the paper, age management is defined, then the benefits and application of age management are described. Then we deal with goals and measures used in age management. In the next part, the method of the analytic hierarchy process (hereafter AHP) is described and used for the selection of suitable measures in the selected organization. In the end, the total results are summarized.

2 Age management

Age management is the human resource management concerning age and specific needs at each stage of life. Ilamarinen (2012, p. 2) says that „*age-related factors should be taken into consideration in daily management, including work arrangements and individual work tasks, so that everybody, regardless of age, feels empowered in reaching their own and corporate*

[1] VŠB – TU Ostrava, Faculty of Economics, Sokolská tř. 33, Ostrava, 701 21, terezie.krestova.st@vsb.cz
[2] VŠB – TU Ostrava, Faculty of Economics, Sokolská tř. 33, Ostrava, 701 21, ales.kresta@vsb.cz

goals". Age management belongs to the concept of diversity management, which views diversity as a desirable element in the workplace because it allows increasing both the performance of human resources and the entire organization. In addition to age diversity, we also encounter, for example, racial, ethnic, sexual diversity, etc.

Age management is associated primarily with aging workers (50+). The first studies were really just focused on this group (Ilmarinen, 1997). Based on an extensive survey, the individual's ability to work and the factors that influence it have been defined (Ilmarinen, 2008). However, if we want to prolong an individual's career, the measure cannot be applied until he/she belongs to the category of older workers. And, it is not appropriate to prioritize only one category of employees. It is necessary to take care of employees in other stages of life so that their maximum potential is used at any age. This means that age management should affect all employees in the organization.

2.1 Benefits of age management

The application of age management has benefits for the organization, for individuals, but also the whole society. Individual benefits include, for example, the improvement of functional abilities, strengthening of health, an increase of competencies, and thus the improvement of working life and prolongation of the individual's working career. Societal benefits include reducing age discrimination, raising the retirement age, reducing the cost of unemployment, reducing the cost of health care. Thus the country's social system is less burdened and the national economy grows. From the point of view of organizational management, we will focus primarily on organizational benefits. This can be seen in increasing the overall productivity of the organization, increasing competitiveness, reducing absenteeism and turnover, increasing the professionalism of employees, and, last but not least, improving the image of the organization.

2.2 Goals and measures of age management in the organization

If the organization decides to apply age management, it is necessary to set goals in this area, what it wants to achieve in the field of age management. Before setting goals, it is appropriate to perform an initial audit, which will focus on, for example, the age structure of employees, turnover, sick leave and its length with respect to the employee's age, early retirement, how the organization's know-how is transferred, if there is a program to support work ability, etc. Furthermore, it is appropriate to analyse whether the organization has developed a program for recruiting graduates, what is the involvement of mothers who are currently on parental leave, whether it somehow supports workers who informally care for other family members, etc. It is appropriate to use the pillars of age management to perform the initial audit (Ilmarinen, 2012).

After the initial audit, it is appropriate to set individual goals of age management. The most common goals, resp. the expected benefits of age management that result from the audit may be the following (Urbancová and Vrabcová, 2020): retaining key employees, increasing employee performance, improving employee health, increasing employee motivation, improving education, developing employees' knowledge and skills, improving organizational culture, positive impact on employee values, improving the organization's name, acquiring new talent, reducing employee turnover and more.

Subsequently, specific proposals for age management measures are formulated. These measures must be linked to the organization's strategy for age diversity and the specifics of the organization must always be taken into account. In practice, we most often encounter the following activities that support the application of age management in the organization: employee health care, support of physical condition and healthy eating, workforce planning with regard to age diversity and support for a positive age policy, special forms of admission procedure for different age groups, reassignment of workers to another, suitable job position, adaptation of the work program, e.g. adjustment of the working environment or working hours, incentive programs according to the needs of different generations, the possibility of personal and career development, qualification growth at any age-adapted further education of older workers, creation of tools supporting intergenerational learning, development of health and safety measures and others.

To put age management into practice, the organization's management must show support for this concept. It is appropriate to support this with educational activities and workshops, and regular monitoring should also follow, e.g. again using age management pillars and monitoring improvements.

3 Selection of appropriate goals and measures for the application of age management in the organization

Each organization is unique and it is not possible to take a functional framework from another organization and just apply it to another. It is always necessary to consider the uniqueness of the organization. The application of age management is relatively new and organizations have often introduced it unconceptually and the measures taken are rather random (Urbancová, 2017).

The goals of age management are based on the age management audit and must be aligned with the strategic goals of the organization. However, the selection of appropriate measures for the set goals is rather intuitive and managers do not evaluate which measures really help to meet the goals of age management. A survey was conducted in 2020 on how age management is applied in practice. The aim was to find out what age management measures are applied, what are their benefits, what would be the consequences of not applying age management in the organization, etc. From the 65 signatories of the Diversity Charter addressed by survey, 54 organizations responded. Moreover, with one of these organizations, there was agreed on further cooperation. The human resource (HR) manager, who specializes in age management in this organization, was selected for cooperation.

The selected organization has been applying age management for 10 years and it is aware of its importance for the organization. The organization has defined age management goals, which should be achieved through various measures. To bring the greatest possible benefit to the application of these measures for both employees and the organization, these activities are regularly evaluated. The organization evaluates both the information from employees and the information from internal systems and documents.

In order to achieve the best results in this area, it is necessary to set priorities in terms of goals and, to that end, to select adequately the measures by which these goals will be achieved. Given that this is a decision-making problem, it seems appropriate to use the AHP method.

3.1 The AHP method

The AHP is a method of multicriteria decision-making, which enables the division of the decision-making problem into partial components and the subsequent connection of the solution of all sub-components into the overall solution (Ramík, 1999).

The procedure can be divided into the following steps. In the beginning, it is necessary to correctly determine the goal and the hierarchy of the solved problem. The basic elements are criteria and alternatives. The structure is shown in Figure 1.

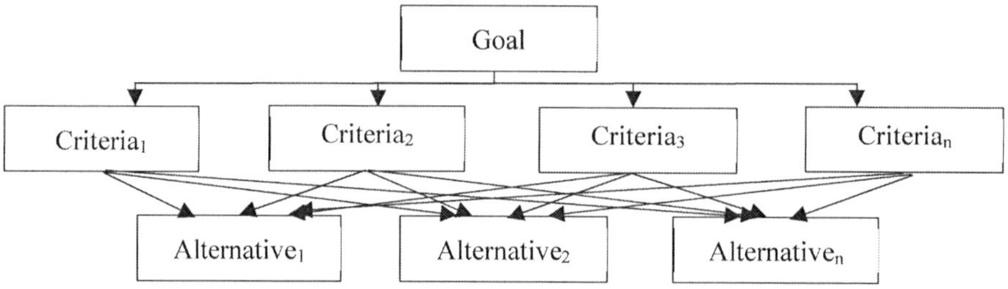

Figure 1 The general structure of hierarchy (Saaty, 1994)

In the next step, criteria are put into a reciprocal Saaty's matrix of size $n \cdot n$, where n is the quantity of criteria. Then criteria are pairwise compared and it is determined how many times is one more important than the other. To express the size of preference, Saaty (1994) recommends a point scale shown in Table 1. These values are applied if the criterion in the row (the first) is more important than the criterion in the column (second criterion). If the criterion in the column is preferred to the criterion in the row, reciprocal values are recorded (i.e. 1/9, 1/7, etc.). The elements of Saaty's matrix are utilized in the estimation of the weights of the criteria. Simply speaking there should be a relationship between the weight of ith criteria, w_i, the weight of jth criteria, w_j, and the elements of Saaty's matrix:

$$s_{ij} \approx \frac{w_i}{w_j}. \tag{1}$$

Point scale	Description
1	criteria are equally important
3	the 1st criterion is slightly more important than the 2nd
5	the 1st criterion is much more important than the 2nd
7	the 1st criterion is very much more important than the 2nd
9	the 1st criterion is absolutely more important than the 2nd

Table 1 Point scale (Saaty, 1994)

The sign of relevant evaluation is that Saaty's matrix is consistent, meaning the elements fulfill the condition of transitivity. The consistency can be evaluated by the coefficient of consistency CR (Consistency Ratio), where the consistency value is considered CR ≤ 0.1. Saaty defined the consistency ratio as

$$CR = \frac{CI}{RI}, \tag{2}$$

where CI is the consistency index and is expressed as

$$CI = \frac{\lambda max - n}{n-1}, \tag{3}$$

where n is the number of criteria (number of rows of the matrix) and λ_{max} is the characteristic number of the matrix - the eigenvalue and it is calculated as follows,

$$\lambda_{\max} = \sum_{i=1}^{n} \frac{(\mathbf{S} \cdot w)_i}{n \cdot w_i}, \tag{4}$$

where w is the vector of weights and **S** Saaty's matrix. RI is an index of randomness (random index) and assumes values in dependence on the number of selected criteria, respectively variants, and is derived from empirical research (Table 2).

N	1	2	3	4	5	6	7	8	9	10
RI	0	0	0.58	0.90	1.12	1.24	1.32	1.41	1.45	1.49

Table 2 RI values for different number of elements (Saaty, 1994)

In the last step, the weights w_i can be obtained via quadratic programming or logarithmic version quadratic programming. One of the simpler methods is the weighted geometric mean of the lines (Saaty, 1994),

$$w_i = \frac{[\prod_j^n s_{i,j}]1/n}{\sum_i^n [\prod_j^n s_{i,j}]1/n}. \tag{5}$$

After the computation of the weights of each alternative due to each criterion, final results can be set. The sum of the weights for every alternative is made and alternatives are ranked by order. On this basis, it can be decided which measures are beneficial for the fulfillment of set goals of age management.

3.2 Application of the AHP method to select appropriate measures

The aim is to select suitable measures for the application of age management in the selected organization. The criteria for selecting these measures are the age management goals of the organization, which were set by the HR manager of the organization as follows:

- retention of key employees (A),
- health prevention (B),
- improving education, development of knowledge and skills (competencies) of employees (C),
- improving the organization name and PR of the organization (D),
- reduction of employee fluctuation (E).

Then, possible measures to achieve these goals have been identified. These measures were formulated with the organization's HR manager based on the organization's practice and literature. These measures have been selected:

- employee health care, support of physical condition and healthy eating (I),
- adaptation of the work program, e.g. adjustment of the working environment or working hours (II),
- possibility of personal and career development, qualification growth at any age (III),
- development of health and safety measures (IV),

- reverse mentoring (V),
- reassignment of workers to another, suitable job position (VI),
- incentive programs according to the needs of different generations (VI).

Suggested goals and measures were discussed with the HR manager and it was stated that there is no relationship between the specified criteria and that the fulfillment of one of them is not affected by the others. At first sight, it may seem, that some measures may have any or just little effect on the achievement of certain goals. However, this is not a reason to exclude them from the comparisons. The impact of each criterion is taken into account in the final results.

These measures form alternatives in the AHP model. All evaluations were made with the HR manager of the selected organization he was the only evaluator. The structure of the problem is outlined in Figure 2.

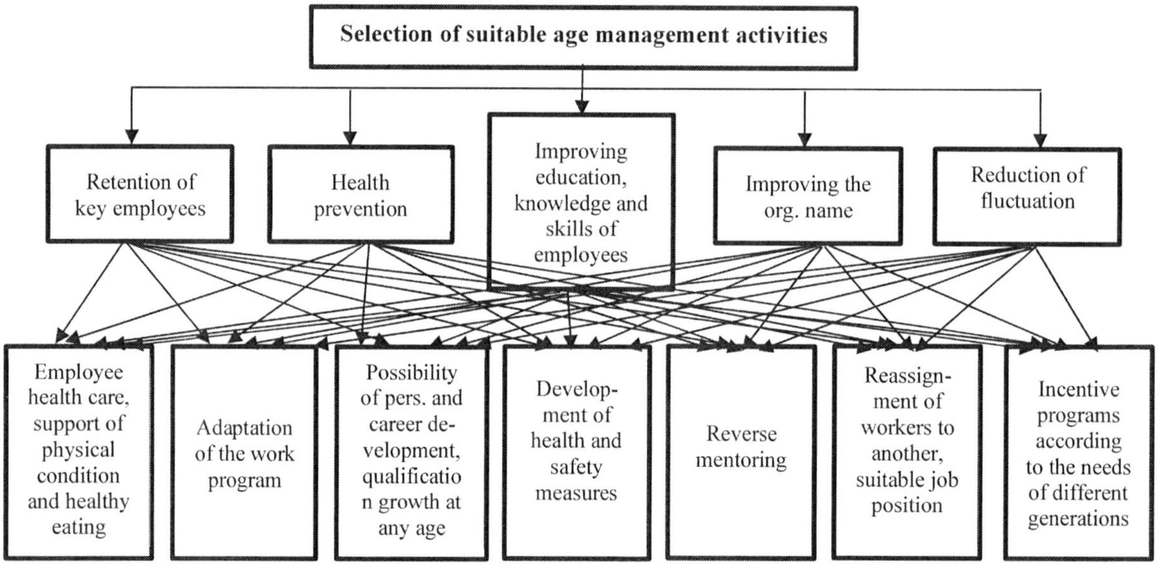

Figure 2 Graphical outline of the hierarchy (own elaboration)

First, goals of age management (A - E) are pairwise compared using Saaty's matrix (see Figure 3). The matrix is consistent (CR=0,0926).

Goals	A	B	C	D	E
A	1	5	3	5	1
B	1/5	1	1/3	1	1/3
C	1/3	3	1	3	3
D	1/5	1	1/3	1	1/5
E	1	3	1/3	5	1

Figure 3 Comparison of organizational goals (own elaboration)

By means of this procedure, the weight of each criterion is determined. Results are shown in Table 3. We can see that the most important criteria are the following three: retention of key employees (38.3 %), improving education, development of knowledge and skills (competencies) of employees (25.06 %), and reduction of employee fluctuation (22.28 %).

Then there are seven concrete age management measures (I - VII) evaluated concerning every criterion. Comparisons are shown in Figure 4. In all cases, the condition of consistency was fulfilled. The result is the weight of each alternative with respect to individual criteria.

In the end, the sum of weights is made to obtain the final result. Then we can set the rank of alternatives. Results ordered by rank are shown in Table 4.

Goals	Weight
Retention of key employees	0.3830
Health prevention	0.0754
Improving education, development of knowledge and skills of employees	0.2506
Improving the organization name and PR of the organization	0.0681
Reduction of employee fluctuation	0.2228

Table 3 Weights of criteria (own elaboration)

A	I	II	III	IV	V	VI	VII
I	1	1/3	1	5	3	7	5
II	3	1	3	3	4	6	5
III	1	1/3	1	1/3	2	5	2
IV	1/5	1/3	3	1	1	3	3
V	1/3	1/4	1/2	1	1	2	2
VI	1/7	1/6	1/5	1/3	1/2	1	1/5
VII	1/5	1/5	1/2	1/3	1/2	5	1

B	I	II	III	IV	V	VI	VII
I	1	2	5	2	5	3	6
II	1/2	1	3	3	3	1	3
III	1/5	1/3	1	1/5	1	1/3	1
IV	1/2	1/3	5	1	5	5	3
V	1/5	1/3	1	1/5	1	1/3	1
VI	1/3	1	3	1/5	3	1	3
VII	1/6	1/3	1	1/3	1	1/3	1

C	I	II	III	IV	V	VI	VII
I	1	1/5	1/5	1	1/5	1	1/3
II	5	1	1/3	3	1/3	1/2	1
III	5	3	1	5	1	5	3
IV	1	1/3	1/5	1	1/7	1	1
V	5	3	1	7	1	7	7
VI	1	2	1/5	1	1/7	1	1/5
VII	3	1	1/3	1	1/7	5	1

D	I	II	III	IV	V	VI	VII
I	1	1/3	1/3	1	3	5	1
II	3	1	1	1	3	3	1/2
III	3	1	1	3	3	3	3
IV	1	1	1/3	1	1	2	2
V	1/3	1/3	1/3	1	1	1	1/2
VI	1/5	1/3	1/3	1/2	1	1	1/2
VII	1	2	1/3	1/2	2	2	1

E	I	II	III	IV	V	VI	VII
I	1	1/3	1	3	2	1	2
II	3	1	1	3	1	3	3
III	1	1	1	3	1	5	3
IV	1/3	1/3	1/3	1	1/3	1/3	1/4
V	1/2	1	1	3	1	3	3
VI	1	1/3	1/5	3	1/3	1	1/3
VII	1/2	1/3	1/3	4	1/3	3	1

Figure 4 Comparison of alternatives due to each criterion (own elaboration)

Based on the results in Table 4 we can say that the organization should focus on four measures to fulfill the goals of age management. They are the adaptation of the work program, e.g. adjustment of the working environment or working hours (23.84 %), personal and career development and qualification growth at any age (18.98 %), reverse mentoring (17.1 %), and employee health care, support of physical condition and healthy eating (16.72 %). Less significant measures are then the development of health and safety measures (9.41 %), incentive programs according to the needs of different generations (8.41 %), and the reassignment of workers to another, suitable job position (5.54 %).

Alternatives	Weights					Total results
	Crit. A	Crit. B	Crit. C	Crit. D	Crit. E	
Adaptation of the work program, e.g. adjustment of the working environment or working hours	0.1337	0.0144	0.0257	0.0126	0.052	**0.2384**
Possibility of pers. and career development, qualification growth at any age	0.0472	0.0039	0.0719	0.019	0.0478	**0.1898**
Reverse mentoring	0.0326	0.0039	0.0893	0.0049	0.0403	**0.1710**
Employee health care, support of physical condition and healthy eating	0.0881	0.0247	0.0113	0.0093	0.0338	**0.1672**
Development of health and safety measures	0.0458	0.0153	0.0135	0.0090	0.0104	**0.0941**
Incentive programs according to the needs of different generations	0.0235	0.0041	0.0251	0.0090	0.0224	**0.0841**
Reassign-ment of workers to another, suitable job position	0.0121	0.0092	0.0139	0.0041	0.0161	**0.0554**

Table 4 Weights of alternatives (own elaboration)

4 Discussion

Age management is a current topic and due to the demographic trends will not lose its significance. Fabisiak and Prokurat (2012), Urbancová and Vrabcová (2020) or Blomé et al. (2020), for example, deal with the definition of the areas that age management includes and the goals that are set. However, not much space has yet been devoted to the question of how to choose appropriate measures for the application of age management. Frerichs et al. (2012) point out activities to fulfill age management goals (eg. training, lifelong learning and knowledge transfer, flexible working practices, the protection and promotion of health, workplace design, etc). and recommend applying more strategies to integrate workers of all ages into their jobs than to rely on isolated measures.

The authors of the paper are not aware of any other papers in which the issue of selecting appropriate measures would be solved and compared with the results. The authors think that the use of decision-making methods is a suitable way and other of them (ANP, WINGS) can be used if dependencies between the criteria or model alternatives are found. Further research will focus on which other measures the organization uses most often to achieve the goals of age management and which are suitable for the use in the implementation of age management in the organization.

5 Conclusion

The aim of the paper is to select age management goals and measures for the selected organization.

Age management is an approach to HRM concerning the age of employees. This approach is applied by HR managers in the organization in order to make the best use of the potential of each employee at any age. Age diversity in the organization is desirable, however, each age group needs a different approach.

Age management is defined in the paper, its benefits for individuals, organizations, and society as a whole are described. It is also mentioned how to apply it, including possible measures to achieve goals in this area. For the selected organization, goals are set in this area and possible measures to achieve these goals. The goals and measures are set on the basis of literature, own survey, and an interview with the HR specialist of the organization. The AHP method is chosen to select appropriate measures. The pairwise comparison is performed with the help of the HR manager from the organization.

Based on the results, it can be stated that in the selected organization it is appropriate to focus on the adaptation of the work program, e.g. adjustment of the working environment or working hours, personal and career development and qualification growth at any age, reverse mentoring and employee health care, support of physical condition and healthy eating in order to achieve the goals set in the field of age management.

This approach can also be an inspiration for other organizations that apply age management or are considering applying it. This method can be used both in setting the goals of age management and in the subsequent formulation of specific measures.

Acknowledgments

This paper is supported by the Student Grant Competition of the Faculty of Economics, VŠB-Technical University of Ostrava (project registration number: SP2021/15). All support is greatly acknowledged and appreciated.

References

Blomé, M.W., Borell, J., Håkansson, C. and Nilsson, K. (2020). Attitudes toward elderly workers and perceptions of integrated age management practices. *International Journal of Occupational Safety and Ergonomics*. 26(1), pp. 112-120.

ČSÚ. (2019). *Proměny věkového složení obyvatelstva.* 2019 [online]. Dostupné z: https://www.czso.cz/documents/10180/92011146/13015819a.pdf/1ef6814b-50bc-47d2-a63b-4781849d9e83?version=1.2 [cit. 2021-02-01].

Eurostat. (2019). *Ageing Europe. Looking at the lives of older people in the EU. 2019 edition.* [online]. Dostupné z: https://ec.europa.eu/eurostat/ documents/3217494/10166544/KS-02-19%E2%80%91681-EN-N.pdf/c701972f-6b4e-b432-57d2-91898ca94893 [cit. 2021-02-01].

Fabisiak, J. and Prokurat. S. (2012). Age Management as a Tool for the Demographic Decline in the 21st Century: An Overview of its Characteristics. *Journal of Entrepreneurship, Management and Innovation*. 8(4), pp. 83-96.

Frerichs, F., Lindley, R., Aleksandrowicz P., Baldauf, B. and Galloway, S. (2012). Active ageing in organisations: a case study approach. International Journal of Manpower. 33(6), pp. 666–684.

Ilmarinen, J. (2012). *Promoting active ageing in the workplace*. 2012. [Online] Dostupné z: https:// osha.europa.eu/cs/.../promoting-active-ageing-in-the-workplace [cit. 2021-02-02]

Ilmarinen, J. (2008). Ako si predĺžiť aktívny život. Starnutie a kvalita pracovného života v Európskej únii. Bratislava: Príroda.

Ilmarinen, J., Tuomi K. a M. Klockars. (1997). Changes in the Work Ability of Active Employees over an 11-Year Period. *Scandinavian Journal of Work, Environment & Health*. 23(1), pp. 49-57.

Ramík, J. (1999). *Vícekriteriální rozhodování – analytický hierarchický process (AHP).* Karviná: Slezská univerzita v Opavě.

Saaty, T. L. (1994). *Fundamentals of Decision Making and Priority Theory with the Analytic Hierarchy Process.* Pittsburgh: RWS Publications.

Urbancová H. and Vrabcová, P. (2020): Age management as a human resources management strategy with a focus on the primary sector of the Czech Republic. *Agric. Econ.* 66(6), pp. 251–259.

Microgenetic Training of an Artificial Neural Network for Predicting Currency Exchange Rate Based on Year Long High Frequency Data

Martin Maděra [1]

Abstract. Microgenetic algorithms are variants of genetic algorithms which, in general, converge faster. This paper discusses usage a microgenetic algorithm for training a neural network for predicting a currency exchange rate trained on a dataset consisting of more than 500,000 values. The microgenetic algorithm proved to be much faster in this case compared to a genetic algorithm while the same precision was achieved.

Keywords: Microgenetic algorithm, Neural network, Time series prediction, Exchange rate prediction.

JEL classification: C63, C61, C53

1 Introduction

The previous author's work proved that ARIMA (auto-regressive integrated moving average) models can be approximated successfully by artificial neural networks trained by genetic and microgenetic algorithms. Using these nature-inspired algorithms was faster than Backpropagation, an analytical algorithm based on partial derivatives (Marcek and Madera 2020).

This paper discusses modifying the techniques for usage on large datasets because computational complexity of prediction models can grow dramatically for larger data sets.

ARIMA models were constructed for the datasets in previous author's works alongside their approximations by artificial neural networks. There were no statistically significant differences between prediction results of ARIMA models and models based on artificial neural networks. No statistically significant differences between prediction results were observed between models based on artificial neural network trained by either genetic or microgenetic algorithms on a dataset of high frequency trading data representing a currency exchange rate between Euro (EUR) and Czech Koruna (CZK) for the 1st week of December 2018 (Marcek and Madera 2020).

The dataset used for this paper consists high frequency trading data representing a currency exchange rate between Euro (EUR) and Czech Koruna (CZK) for the whole year of 2018, 12 times the size of the previous one. Unfortunately, computational resources available to the author did not allow for construction of an ARIMA model for such a large dataset. Parameters of the ideal ARIMA model were determined (using techniques described in (Marček 2013) however the model itself was not constructed. These parameters were used to construct an approximation of the model using artificial neural networks. Networks were trained using both genetic and microgenetic algorithms (using own implementations). Precisions of these networks and their training times were compared.

---

[1]Technical University of Ostrava, Faculty of Economics, Ostrava, Czech Republic, Department of Applied Informatics, martin.madera@vsb.cz

2 Used data

The data used for research discussed in this paper were published by GAIN Capital company and are freely available at http://ratedata.gaincapital.com/.

2.1 Data description

The data comes in CSV (Comma Separated Values) format and data for exchange rate of EUR (Euro) to CZK (Czech Koruna) for year 2018 was used.

Date Time	Bid Rate
02/12/2018 18:29	25.9402
02/12/2018 18:30	25.938
02/12/2018 18:31	25.9377
02/12/2018 18:32	25.947
02/12/2018 18:33	25.9486
02/12/2018 18:34	25.9486
02/12/2018 18:35	25.9508
02/12/2018 18:36	25.9498
02/12/2018 18:37	25.9498
02/12/2018 18:38	25.9516

Table 1 Preview of used data, source: http://ratedata.gaincapital.com/

The data set starts at the 1st January 2018 17:01:00 and ends at the 31st December 2018 16:58:00. It contains 521,346 values. It should have 1-minute time resolution however some values are duplicate, some are missing. Table 1 shows a preview of the data.

2.2 Data pre-processing

For creating a prediction model for a time series, the series must be free of duplicate values and the values must be evenly spaced in time. A short Python script using the Pandas library was used for this purpose. The final number of values in the dataset was 525,600. The data shows an increasing trend. Figure 2.3.

For successful usage of the Box-Jenkins method for creating an ARIMA (autoregressive integrated moving average) model, the data should be stationary. If the time series is differentiated, the trend disappears, see Figures 2.3 (Marček 2013).

The pre-processed data were saved to a CSV file which was later used for training and evaluating the neural networks.

2.3 Box-Jenkins, ARIMA model

On 99% confidence, the autocorrelogram shows autocorrelations up to 19th value and the partial autocorrelogram up to 21st, see Figure 2.3 and Figure 2.3. According to the Box-Jenkins method, the ARIMA (ar=19, ma=21) model can be used. This model can be approximated using artificial neural networks (Marček 2013).

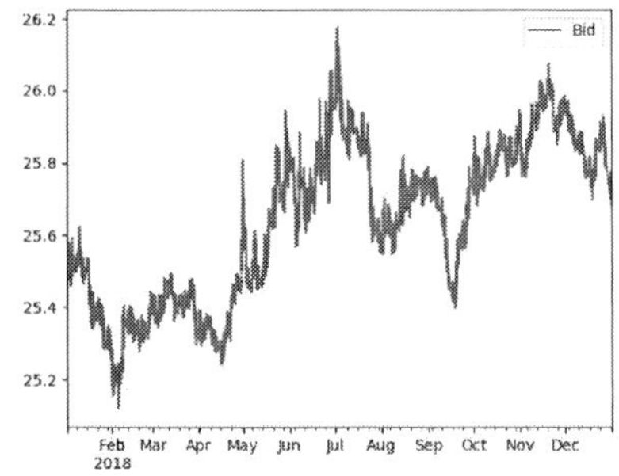

Figure 1 EUR/CZK exchange rate, without duplicates and missing values

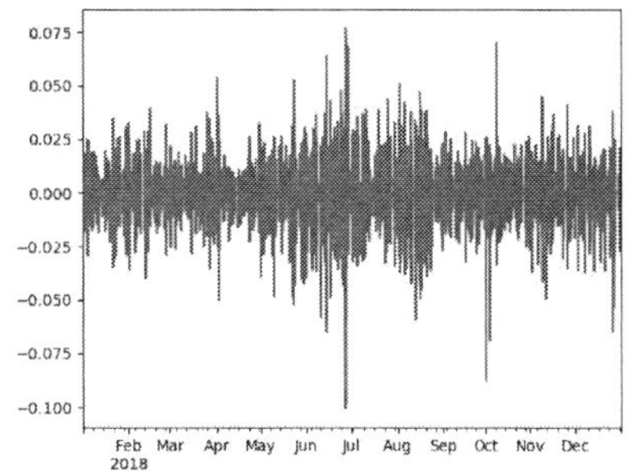

Figure 2 EUR/CZK exchange rate, differentiated - stationary.

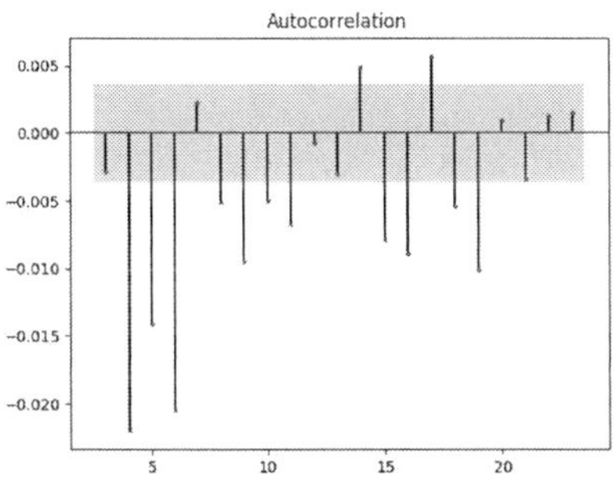

Figure 3 Autocorrelogram of differentiated exchange rate

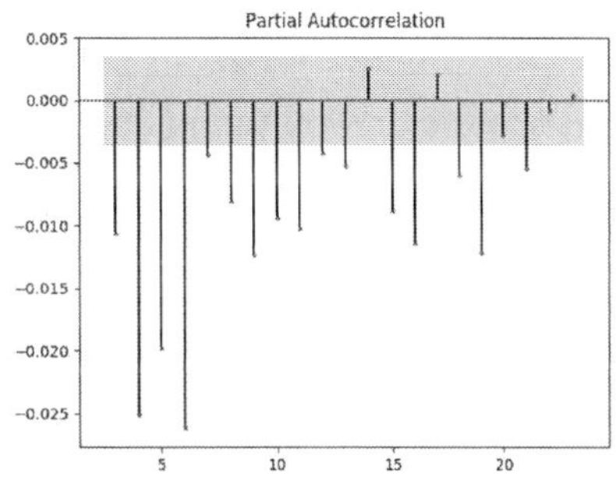

Figure 4 Partial autocorrelogram of differentiated exchange rate

2.4 Shape of the neural network

The ARIMA model for predicting this time series is based on 19 auto-regressive and 21 moving average values, as shown in section 2.3. Therefore, the network should have 21 neurons in the input layer.

The artificial neural network had 3 layers (input, hidden, output). The number of hidden layer neurons was found empirically, best results were achieved when the number was between 90 and 120. Pruning step was yet not implemented into the learning algorithm therefore the author do not claim this being the minimal number. Implementing pruning and other minimizing steps into the learning algorithm is subject of further author's work. Sigmoid function was chosen as an activation function for the hidden layer.

Since the networks should approximate a prediction algorithm which predicts one future value, the output layer has one neuron. Identity function was chosen as its activation function.

2.5 Training the network

Neural networks were trained using genetic and microgenetic algorithms and the loss function was Mean Squared Error.

The time series dataset was split into training and evaluation data so the training data consist of 75% of the original series. The training data were split into mini-batches of 1000 samples. Parameters of the network were changed after each mini-batch. After passing through all the original data, Mean Squared Error (MSE) was computed for evaluation data. When the MSE for evaluation data started to raise, the training was stopped because this is a usual sign of overfitting and overtraining (Marček 2013).

Predictions for the evaluation data was then calculated using the trained network and stored into a CSV file for further analysis.

3 Neural networks

Custom implementations of neural networks, genetic and microgenetic algorithms were used. Since the author have experience with implementing machine learning algorithms in LISP language, which was traditionally popular in machine learning and artificial intelligence, Clojure language was chosen for this implementation. Clojure is a modern dialect of LISP language, dynamically compiled to the Java bytecode (https://clojure.org/). Although it does not support all features of Common Lisp, all the libraries and frameworks used in Java can be seamlessly used form Clojure as well (and Clojure libraries can be used from Java).

3.1 Neural network implementation

Neural networks are represented as a collection of matrices of weights and biases. Clojure is a functional programming language, not object oriented – therefore there is no benefit in defining classes or interfaces (these features exist in Clojure mainly for interop with Java).

Each layer of the network is represented by a matrix of weights and vector of biases.

$$\begin{pmatrix} w_{11} & \cdots & w_{1n} \\ \vdots & \ddots & \vdots \\ w_{m1} & \cdots & w_{mn} \end{pmatrix} \times \begin{bmatrix} a_1 \\ \vdots \\ a_m \end{bmatrix} + \begin{bmatrix} b_1 \\ \vdots \\ b_m \end{bmatrix} = \begin{bmatrix} z_1 \\ \vdots \\ z_m \end{bmatrix} \tag{1}$$

$$W^L \times A^{L-1} + B^L = Z^L \tag{2}$$

$$A^L = \sigma(Z^L) \tag{3}$$

Where:

W is a matrix of weights,

W^L is a matrix of weights in the present layer (L and $L-1$ are indices, not powers),

A^{L-1} is a column vector of activations of the previous layer,

B^L is a column vector of biases of the present layer,

Z^L is a column vector of weighted input (sometimes referred to as potentials) of the present layer,

σ is the activation function (here: sigmoid or identity).

Equations 1 and 2 show the weighted input (z) of each layer in both expanded matrix form and using capital letters as matrices. This can be viewed as a vector of potentials of neurons in the layer. Note that weight matrix (W) is transposed compared to the most literature sources. This way it is easier to work with it in code. So w_{11} is the weight of the synapse from the 1st neuron of the previous layer to the 1st neuron of the current layer, w_{21} is the weight of the synapse from 1st neuron of previous layer to the 2nd neuron of the current layer. $\sigma(Z^L)$ is a simplified notation for applying an activation function to each element of Z vector, creating A vector. These equations are based on (Nielsen 2015).

3.2 Genetic algorithm implementation

The implementation of the genetic algorithm remained the same as in the previous author's work. Genetic algorithms traditionally work with genes either 0 or 1. For this application, this is inadequate, because this algorithm need to find weights and biases of a neural network, which can be an arbitrary floating point decimal numbers. On the other hand, for genetic algorithms to be efficient, the state space needs to be limited. Therefore, each parameter is transformed into interval [0, 1]. An individual for the genetic algorithm then consists of floating point numbers from [0, 1] interval and count of parameters in intervals equals to count of all weights and biases of the network. For a network with 21 input neurons and 90 neurons in the hidden layer, the number of genes of an individual is over 4,000.

$$
\begin{aligned}
i &= \frac{P - P_{min}}{|P_{max} - P_{min}|} \\
I &= (i_1 \dots i_n)
\end{aligned}
\tag{4}
$$

Where:

P is a parameter of the network (either weight or bias),

i is a gene

I is an individual expressed as a list of genes.

Genetic algorithms work with populations of individuals, which are then evolved using crossover, mutation and selection. Equation 4 shows the way an individual is constructed in this case. The individuals in each generation are crossed using single crossover point technique and mutation randomly mutates a gene, generating a new floating point number from interval [0, 1].

Selecting individuals for crossover uses a rank-selection technique (Saini 2017). Loss function of this algorithm reconstructs a neural network from each individual and uses the training data to compute predictions. Predictions are compared to expected (correct) values and Mean Squared Error is computed for each individual. This is the result of a loss function. The lower, the better (some genetic algorithms use vitality function – the higher, the better).

Next generation consist of elites which are preserved, crossed individuals, mutated individuals and couple of newly generated individuals. The genetic algorithm is created as a library therefore it can have more general use in the future.

Since computing the loss function for an individual does not affect the other individuals, its call is parallelized. The genetic algorithm does not define the loss function, it only defines a callback keeping it general. It is up to the calling code to ensure its thread-safety. (Marcek and Madera 2020)

3.3 Microgenetic algorithm

Microgenetic algorithms are genetic algorithms that use a very small population size (population size < 20) (Dozier, Bowen and Bahler 1994). However a diversity in population can be lost and therefore finding the best solution can get stuck. A restart is needed while retaining the elites in such case. The author's implementation of the genetic algorithms was modified to handle the smaller populations better and to allow automatic restarts when diversity is lost (when there are less unique individuals than threshold which is a configurable parameter of the algorithm, a restart is performed). When the population is restarted, only elites are retained.

Parameter	Genetic Algorithm	Microgenetic Algorithm
Population	1000	10
Elites	5 individuals	1 individual
Crossbreds	220 pairs	3 pairs
Mutants	1% chance either elite or crossbred	2% chance either elite or crossbred
Randoms	1000 – (elites + crossbreds + mutants)	10 – (elites + crossbreds + mutants)
Restart	–	diversity under 75%

Table 2 Genetic and microgenetic algorithm parameters

4 Performance evaluation and future work

40 networks were trained for the final performance evaluation, 10 of each of the 4 variants: trained by a genetic algorithm with 90 neurons in the hidden layer, trained by a genetic algorithm with 120 neurons in the hidden layer, trained by a microgenetic algorithm with 90 neurons in the hidden layer and trained by a microgenetic algorithm with 120 neurons in the hidden layer, see Table 3.

The computer used for these computations had 4 core AMD A8-6600K processor, 12GB of RAM, SSD and was running a linux-based operating system (Ubuntu 20.4).

Parameter	Genetic Algorithm 90n	Genetic Algorithm 120n	Microgenetic Algorithm 90n	Microgenetic Algorithm 120n
Elapsed time [min]	$4,104$	$4,350$	470	$1,686$
MSE of validation	4.51×10^{-6}	4.47×10^{-6}	4.41×10^{-6}	4.39×10^{-6}
Generations	$3,741$	$3,550$	$49,567$	$295,641$
Restarts	0	0	$2,027$	$6,965$

Table 3 Averages of results

5 Conclusion

Microgenetic algorithm was much faster than the traditional genetic for training neural networks for large datasets of high frequency trading data. The microgenetic training algorithm was thoroughly analyzed using profiling tools to find bottle necks. It was found that generation restarts had a significant impact on the performance, they effectively stopped the training for a short period of time each. Since the microgenetic algorithm needs a higher number of generations, implementing pruning and other minimizing steps into the training algorithm would probably be beneficial and will be a part of author's future work.

References

Dozier, G., J. Bowen, and D. Bahler (1994). "Solving small and large scale constraint satisfaction problems using a heuristic-based microgenetic algorithm". In: *Proceedings of the First IEEE Conference on Evolutionary Computation. IEEE World Congress on Computational Intelligence*, 1, pp. 306-311. DOI: 10.1109/ ICEC.1994.349934.

Marček, D. (2013). *Pravdepodobnostné modelovanie a soft computing v ekonomikey*. VŠB-TU Ostrava, 2013. ISBN: 978 80 248 2955-5.

Marcek, D. and M. Madera (2020). "Some statistical and CI models to predict chaotic high-frequency financial data". English. In: *Advances in Intelligent Systems and Computing*, 1029, pp. 1315-1323. ISSN: 2194-5357. DOI: 10.1007/978-3-030-23756-1_154.

Nielsen, M. A. (2015). *Neural Networks and Deep Learning*. Determination Press, 2015.

Saini, N. (2017). "Review of Selection Methods in Genetic Algorithms". In: *International Journal Of Engineering And Computer Science*, 6 (12), pp. 261–263. ISSN: 2319-7242. DOI: 10.18535/ijecs/v6i12.04.

Clever Prioritization of B2B Customers based on RFM analysis and Churn Prediction

Jan Manďák[1]

Abstract. Predicting churn from transactional data is not as common as predicting customer churn from subscription-based data, but represents a very valuable usage of this kind of data. Five years of invoicing data from Manufacturing Company were used in this study to predict if a given customer will place an order in the next 90 days. From just 4 columns of raw data (Invoice Date, Customer Name, Invoice Value, Invoice Code) several features were created, such as recency, frequency, monetary, customer lifetime or time between orders. Predictive model was then trained using the "base" and "histogram-based" Gradient Boosting algorithms. Cross-validated accuracy of both models was high (base 0.872, histogram based 0.866), as well as precision (base 0.896, histogram based 0.891) and recall (base 0.897, histogram based 0.892). Trained machine learning models were integrated directly into Power BI, where probabilities of churn together with input features of the model were provided to business decision makers in the form of well-arranged visualizations.

Keywords: Transactional Data, Churn Prediction, RFM Analysis, Gradient Boosting, Python, Power BI.

JEL Classification: M21, C88, C45

1 Introduction

There is no industry which won't be interested in keeping the current customers. From the cost perspective, it was many times shown that it is much cheaper to keep current customers than to acquire new ones. Prevent customer churn is also important based on the fact that nowadays customers have access to all kinds of information and therefore it is for them easy and less costly to switch between competitors. Companies know it and invest in finding ways how to prevent churn by targeting such customers with some kind of incentives. Utilization of various types of historical data to train machine learning models identifying churners is very well known use case of customer data analytics. There are two types of churn models – first one based on subscriptions and the second one based on transactional data. The latter one is the topic of this study and can be understood as „predicting if a given customer will place an order in the defined number of days (typically next 30 or 90 days)".

Various studies dealing with prediction of customer churn with the use of transactional data and RFM analysis have already been conducted. Li and Li (2019) applied combination of logistic regression and XGBoost algorithms to churn prediction problem in e-commerce and achieved accuracy 75.9 %. Aleksandrova (2018) took data from ERP system of Production Company from Bulgaria, calculated recency, frequency and monetary and used those to predict churn using several machine learning models in Azure ML Studio. She found out that Neural Networks performed better when RFM where continuous variables while Decision Trees were more accurate in usage of RFM scores (1-4) as input variables. Chen, Hu and Hsieh (2013)

[1] ENET Centre, VŠB – Technical University of Ostrava, 17. listopadu 2172/15, 708 00 Ostrava-Poruba, Czech republic, jan.mandak@gmail.com.

studied churn prediction of B2B customers in the logistic industry. Time between transactions, recency and monetary played the major role in churn prediction. The highest accuracy (0.93) was achieved by C4.5 decision tree algorithm. Another study was done by Jahromi, Stakhovych and Ewing (2014), who trained model for predicting churn based on transactional data of a major Australian Fast Moving Consumer Goods (FMCG) retailer. In their study boosting and logistic regression models outperformed both simple and cost sensitive decision tree models based on AUC.

This study is based on results of one proof of concept project made in a manufacturing company, but companies from various industries which collects transactional data can benefit from its findings and make a similar solution based on their data.

The originality of this study lies in the fact that it shows an end to end process, starting from the preparation for raw data in SQL Server through training a machine learning model in Jupyter notebook to calculation of probabilities of churn and visualizing predictions together with input data in Power BI. In the Fig. 1 you can see a simple architecture of the solution.

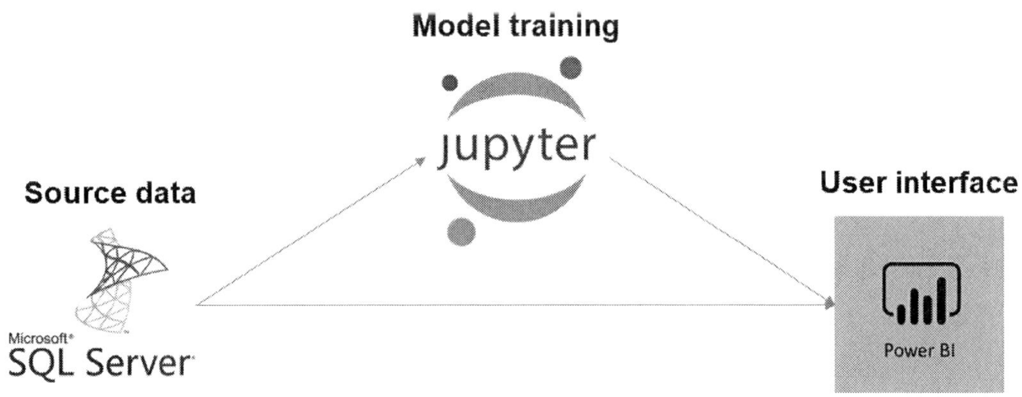

Figure 1 Solution architecture

2 Data Description

Data used for this project are stored in SQL Server database. Customer Name, Invoice Date, Invoice Value and Invoice Code are the "raw" data, which were further transformed into predictive features used for training of churn prediction model. The dataset contains 4409 customers, 2684 of them are churners, 1725 non-churners. Recency, frequency and monetary (Blattberg, Kim and Neslin, 2008) are three basic input variables:

- recency = number of days since latest invoice,
- frequency = count of invoices,
- monetary = sum of invoice value.

Example of SQL script to create RFM variables with definition of time period used for analysis can be found below:

```sql
-- Declare variables to be used
DECLARE @StartDate DATE, @EndDate DATE;

-- Initialize variables
SET @StartDate = '2019-01-01'
SET @EndDate = '2019-12-31'

-- Calculate recency, frequency and monetary
SELECT  raw_data.CustomerName
       ,DATEDIFF(day, MAX(raw_data.InvoiceDate), @EndDate) AS RECENCY
       ,COUNT(distinct raw_data.InvoiceCode) AS FREQUENCY
       ,SUM(raw_data.InvoiceValue) AS TOTAL_MONETARY
FROM

(SELECT
         B.[Date] AS InvoiceDate
        ,E.[CustomerName] AS CustomerName
       ,A.InvoiceValue
       ,A.InvoiceCode

FROM [wp].[FactInvoice] A
LEFT JOIN [dbo].[DimCalendar] B ON A.[InvoiceCalendarID] = B.[CalendarID]
LEFT JOIN [dbo].[DimCustomers] E ON A.[CustomerID] = E.[CustomerID]
WHERE A.InvoiceValue > 0 AND B.[Date] BETWEEN @StartDate AND @EndDate) as raw_data

GROUP BY CustomerName
```

Recency, frequency and monetary are not the only variables possible to compute from the raw data. These variables were also used to predict churn:

- Customer Lifetime (days since the first invoice),
- Number of Claims (count of negative invoices),
- Claimed Value (sum of negative invoices),
- Sales Cycle (average number of days between two subsequent invoices).

With the transactional data which are of non-contractual nature, there is no strictly defined end of contract e.g. like in Telecommunications. Therefore it is necessary to define churn by other technique. In our case churn is defined as no invoice in the next 3 months.

While presenting the solution to the business stakeholders, we found out that it won't be beneficial to predict which customer won't make any invoice in the next 3 months, but also to predict, which will. In the day-to-day business it can happen that there is more demand for some goods than supply and this information could be beneficial to serve mainly to customers with high likelihood to buy in the next 3 months.

3 Model training

Five years of invoicing data were used for training two types of Gradient Boosting models – base Gradient Boosting algorithm and algorithm based on division of continuous features into histograms. Gradient Boosting Models were used, because the author has a really good experience with their power from previous projects and they are together with LightGBM state-of-the-art models for tabular data. Two types of testing of predictive performance were then used to compare their performance – train/test split and 20 fold cross-validation.

3.1 Classification model

The range of possible classification algorithms is broad, it is possible to use simpler algorithms like logistic regression or decision trees, ensemble models like random forests or models based on gradient boosting and of course there are also many types of neural networks. As mentioned above, in this case an XGBoost algorithm (Chen and Guestrin, 2016) was used because of a very good performance in previous projects with tabular data and also based on the fact that it is considered as a state of the art model for tabular data among data professionals.

The output of *Gradient boosting* technique is an ensemble predictive model, which consists of several weak models. These weak models are typically decision trees. The final single strong learner combines weak learners in an iterative fashion. Steps of a *gradient boosting* procedure are the following. The goal is to find a model $\boldsymbol{F}$ to predict values of the form $\hat{y} = F(x)$ by minimizing some cost function. At each stage m, it is assumed that there is some weak learner F_m, which is improved by constructing a new model h. Formally we can define it as:

$$F_{m+1}(x) = F_m(x) + h(x) \quad (1)$$

The model h is fitted to the residual $y - F_m(x)$ and therefore each F_{m+1} tries to correct the errors of its predecessor F_m.

Python library *Scikit-learn* (Pedregosa et. al, 2011), a powerful library capable of handling all stages of data mining process, contains also implementation of gradient boosting technique. Two estimators were used in this project, *GradientBoostingClassifier* and *HistGradientBoostingClassifier*. The latter is as mentioned in the *Scikit-learn* documentation much faster than base *GradientBoostingClassifier*. *HistGradientBoostingClassifier* is inspired by *LightGBM* algorithm, which makes training faster because of the division of continuous features into bins.

3.2 Train and test data sets

In this proof of concept project, 5 years of historical data were used to calculate features for the training phase of predictive model, since the beginning of 2015 to the end of 2019. If a given customer had in the following 3 months (from 1.1.2020 to 31.3.2020) any invoice, then target variable Churn is set to 1, 0 otherwise, see Fig. 2. Training data set was also used to perform 20-fold stratified cross-validation, when the data set was randomly divided into 20 folds with equal number of customers in each one, and each fold was used just once as a testing data set. Stratified cross-validation ensures that the ratio of churners to non-churners is the same in all folds as it is in the whole dataset. This technique is used to test the stability of the trained model.

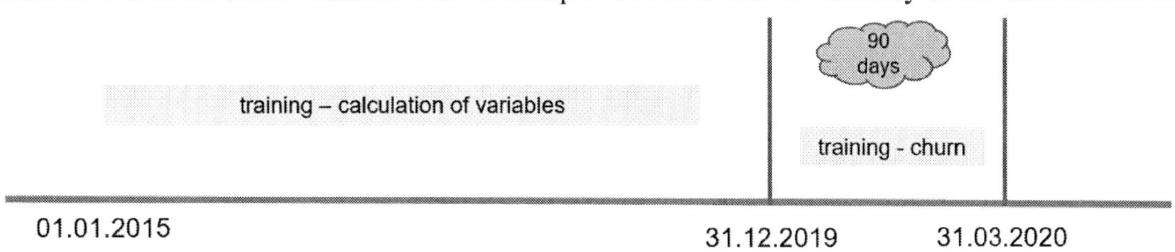

Figure 2 Training data set

Testing data set was created by prolonging the period for calculation of input variables by 3 months till the end of March 2020, see Fig. 3.

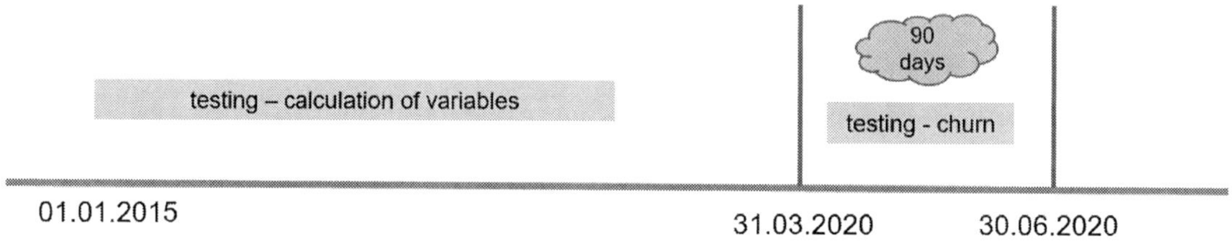

Figure 3 Testing data set

3.3 Results train/test data set

67 % of the data set were used for model training, it means 954 customers of out the all 4409 customers. The remaining 33 % were used for test size – 1455 customers. Values of accuracy, sensitivity and recall can be found in the Table 1.

Algorithm	Accuracy	Precision	Recall
GradientBoostingClassifier	0.913	0.921	0.931
HistGradientBoostingClassifier	0.964	0.966	0.972

Table 1 Results on test data set

3.4 Results cross-validation

The cross-validation is a useful technique for comparison of predictive performance of various algorithms and also for assessing of model overfitting. The whole data set is divided into 20 stratified folds, where each contains 1/20 of the customers and each one is used just once as a testing data set and 19 times used for model training. It means that we train 20 different models, compute predictive performance statistics and from these calculate mean and standard deviation. Mean values and standard deviations across 20 folds can be seen in the Table 2.

Model	Statistic	Accuracy	Recall	Precision
Base	mean	0.872	0.897	0.896
	std	0.022	0.030	0.022
Histogram	mean	0.866	0.892	0.891
	std	0.026	0.030	0.028

Table 2 Results of the 20-fold cross-validation

Predictive results of 20-fold cross-validation of both models are visualized using bar charts also in the Fig. 4. As you can see in the Fig. 4 and Table 2, there is almost no difference between predictive performance of the base and histogram based algorithm. Mean values of all metrics are close to 0.9, what suggests very good predictive performance, and very low standard deviation ranging from 0.022 to 0.030 suggests that there is no problem of model overfitting.

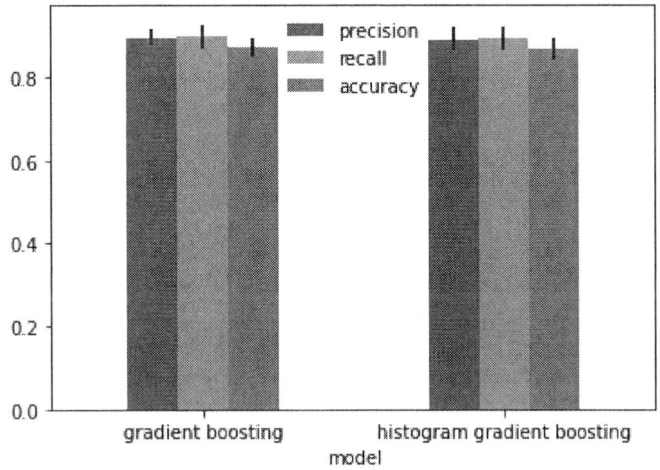

Figure 4 Comparison of base and histogram based model

4 Visualization for users

A great feature of Power BI (Powell, 2018) is the possibility to use Python code as a step in Power Query Editor (Transform data option in Power BI). In the Fig. 5 below there is an example of a small piece of Python code, where trained gradient boosting model saved to pickle format in Jupyter notebook is loaded, used to make predictions and probabilities, which are finally added as columns to the dataset.

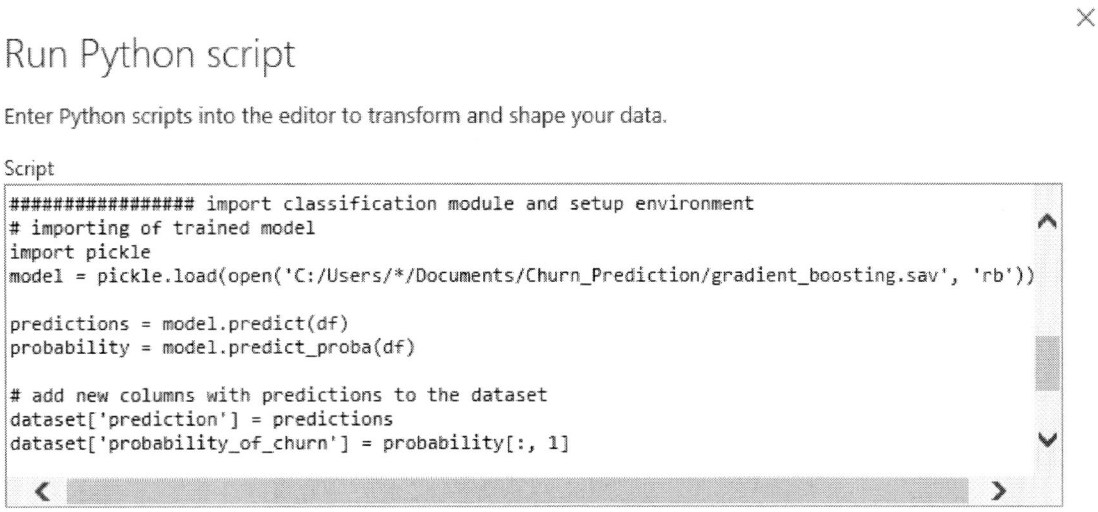

Figure 5 Python script in Power Query

These predictions and probabilities of churn are further combined with all features and RFM segments to provide an overall customer view to the business. The users can use various filters like Customer Name, Recency, Churn prediction or Country. In the Fig. 6 there is shown an example of usage of Power BI report. Recent customers which made invoice in the last 90 days and are predicted with a risk of churn are selected. Based on variables such as RFM segment, Monetary, Lifetime, SalesCycle or Probability of churn business can decide which customers should be prioritized. Customer names and monetary values are hided due to sensitivity reasons.

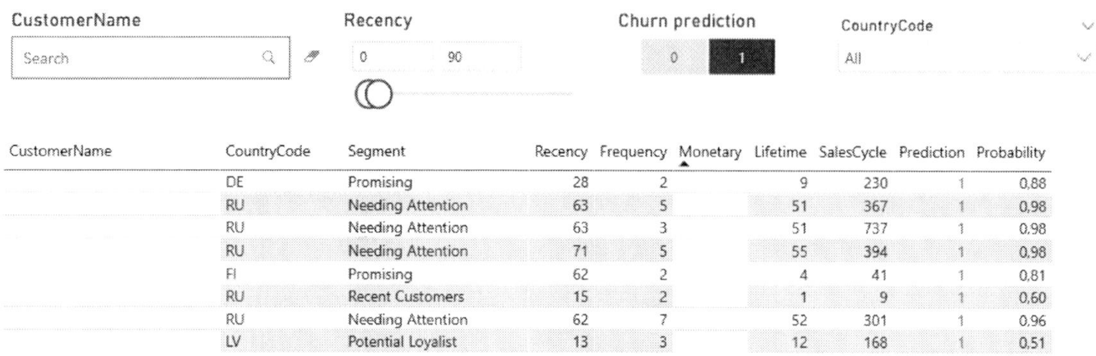

CustomerName	CountryCode	Segment	Recency	Frequency	Monetary	Lifetime	SalesCycle	Prediction	Probability
	DE	Promising	28	2		9	230	1	0,88
	RU	Needing Attention	63	5		51	367	1	0,98
	RU	Needing Attention	63	3		51	737	1	0,98
	RU	Needing Attention	71	5		55	394	1	0,98
	FI	Promising	62	2		4	41	1	0,81
	RU	Recent Customers	15	2		1	9	1	0,60
	RU	Needing Attention	62	7		52	301	1	0,96
	LV	Potential Loyalist	13	3		12	168	1	0,51

Figure 6 Visualization in Power BI

Power BI report for business users contains also one important chart for decision making – importance of variables used in model. Permutation importance algorithm (Breiman, 2001) was used, where each column is randomly shuffled and difference in predictive score between original model and model with corrupted data is computed. As we can see in the Fig. 7, Recency is the most important variable, followed by claimed valued and average time between orders. This definitely makes perfect sense, customers which ordered goods in recent times will most likely order in the next 3 months as well. When the claimed value is high, meaning that the customer was not satisfied with the goods, likelihood of churn is higher. Average time between orders tells us how often customer typically orders, e.g. once per month etc. This helps us to understand customer behavior and predict customer churn.

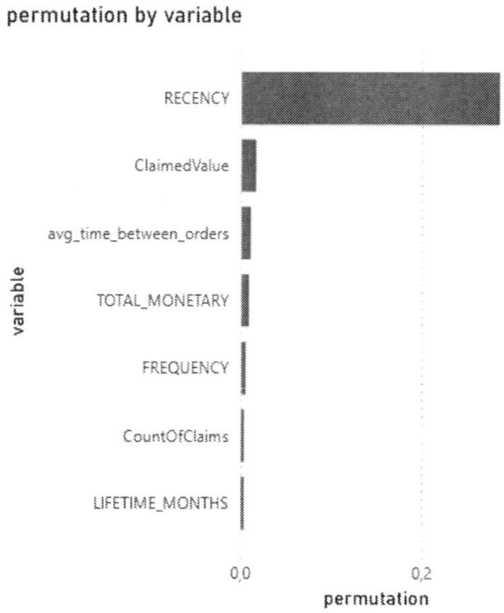

Figure 7 Permutation feature importance

Conclusion

This study has shown that from just 4 columns of invoice data (Customer Name, Invoice Date, Invoice Value and Invoice Code) it is possible to calculate various valuable features helpful not only for prediction of which customer won't make any invoice in the next 90 days, but also for data-driven based decisions of which customers to serve in order to keep the most valuable ones.

Although the predictive performance of the model is very good, we have seen in the previous section that there is one important variable which plays a major role. In the next phase of the model development it would be beneficial to create two separate models – one model for recent customers (e.g. those ones which made order in the previous 12 months) and second model for not so recent customers. It would be interesting to see the impact of other variables besides recency on churn of recent customers.

If we should highlight the difference of our solution in comparison with the solutions mentioned in the Introduction part, the biggest one is that this solution is not just a research paper, but a functional solution reviewed and used in a real world business use. From the point of view of used variables, here we used not just recency, frequency and monetary, like other studies, but also customer lifetime, number of claims, claimed value or average time between orders.

Solution is deployed to production Power BI Service of one division of a company and some additional features besides churn were added, e.g. sensitivity of customers to price changes or profitability. The solution was presented also to other divisions and stakeholders would like to have similar solution for their own divisions as well, what suggests that the solution has a real business value.

Acknowledgements

This work was supported by The Ministry of Industry and Trade within project CZ.01.1.02/0.0/0.0/17_176/0015702: "Výzkum a vývoj aplikace pro SMART řízení podniku".

References

Aleksandrova, Y. (2018). 'Application of machine learning for churn prediction based on transactional data (RFM analysis)'. *Proceedings of 18th International Multidisciplinary Scientific GeoConference SGEM 2018*, Albena, Bulgaria, pp. 125-132.

Blattberg, R. C., Kim, P.-D., and Neslin, S. A. (2008). *Database marketing: analyzing and managing customers*. New York: Springer.

Breiman, L. (2001). 'Random Forests'. *Machine Learning*, 45(1), pp. 5-32.

Chen, Tianqi and Carlos Guestrin (2016). 'XGBoost: A Scalable Tree Boosting System'. *Proceedings of the 22nd ACM SIGKDD International Conference on Knowledge Discovery and Data Mining*, San Francisco, California, USA, pp. 785-794.

Jahromi, Ali Tamaddoni, Stakhovych, Stanislav and Michael Ewing (2014). 'Managing B2B customer churn, retention and profitability'. *Industrial Marketing Management*, 43, pp. 1258-1268.

Kuanchin Chen, Ya-Han Hu and Yi-Cheng Hsieh (2015). 'Predicting customer churn from valuable B2B customers in the logistics industry: a case study'. *Information Systems and e-business Management*, 13, pp. 475-494.

Li, Xueling and Zhen Li (2019). 'A Hybrid Prediction Model for E-Commerce Customer Churn Based on Logistic Regression and Extreme Gradient Boosting Algorithm'. *Ingénierie des Systèmes d'Information*, 24(5), pp. 525-530.

Pedregosa, F. et al. (2011). 'Scikit-learn: Machine learning in Python'. *Journal of machine learning research*, 12(Oct), pp. 2825–2830.

Powell, Brett (2018). *Mastering Microsoft Power BI.* Birmingham: Packt Publishing.

Statistical/RBF NN framework for high frequency financial data

Dusan Marcek[1]

Abstract. In this paper, we develop and consider the accuracy of forecasting models based on statistical (stochastic) methods and two intelligent methodology based on SVM approach and neural networks by using novel activation function based on the cloud concept with parameters chosen by a grid search. The use of both intelligent methods is useful because there is no knowledge about the relationship between the inputs into the system and its output. The proposed approaches are applied to predict the high frequency time series of the daily EUR/USD exchange rate time series and assess their prediction performance. We showed that intelligent learning methods have more accurate outputs than the statistical one. On the other hand, the statistical GARCH-class models can identify the presence of the leverage effect and to react to the good and bad news.

Keywords: time series modelling and forecasting, SVM, RBF network, forecast accuracy, cloud concept.

JEL Classification: C13, G32

1 Introduction

Forecasting is a key element of management decision making. The ultimate effectiveness of any decision depends on the ability to predict the uncontrollable aspects of events following the decision. Over the past ten years statisticians and academics of computer science have developed new techniques based on probabilistic theory and latest information technologies help predict future values of high frequency financial data.

Many statistics based linear time series forecasting models have been proposed such as auto-regressive integrated moving average (ARIMA). Recently, artificial neural networks (ANNs) and other machine learning algorithms have been successfully applied to classification, regression and time series forecasting (Zivot, 2005). Besides ANNs, support vector regression (SVR) has shown its advantages. SVR is known as a strong predictor as it is more likely to achieve the globally optimal solution compared to a weak predictor such as ANN which is frequently trapped in a local minimum. In (Marcek, 2016) a forecasting model was reported, where a support vector machine (SVM) is employed. In addition, online learning was also implemented to offset the trend component in the time series. Jamimi (2011) has developed two different high-performance fault prediction models based on Support Vector Machines (SVMs) and Probabilistic Neural Networks (PNNs).

In this article we develop nonlinear forecasting models, analyze, discuss and compare the forecast accuracy from models which are derived from competing statistical and Radial Basic Function (RBF) neural network (NN) specifications. Our motivation for this comparative study lies in both the difficulty for constructing of appropriate statistical ARCH-GARCH and

[1] VŠB Technical University of Ostrava, Faculty of Economics, Department of Applied Informatics, Sokolská třída 33, Ostrava, dusan.marcek@vsb.cz.

SVR (Support Vector Regression) models to forecast high frequency financial time series data in ex post simulations and the recently emerging problem-solving methods that exploit tolerance for imprecision to achieve low solution costs (soft computing methods). Secondly SVR and RBF NN models are proposed and their forecasting performance is evaluated and compared with ARIMA/ARCH-GARCH models. Machine (artificial) intelligence systems as neural networks are dynamical trainable adaptive systems defined with arbitrarily many interacted differential or difference equations. Unlike statistical estimators they learn from experience with numerical sample data.

The aim of the paper is to explain and show achieved aspects of both statistical and soft approach for quantifying forecast accuracy applied to daily EUR/USD exchange rate time series and to assess their forecast performance. The paper is organized as follows. In Section 2 we briefly describe the basic ARMA/ARCH-GARCH methodologies, give review basic of SVM´s function estimation and introduce the architectures of RBF (Radial Basic Function) networks. Section 3 focuses on prediction using the data and statistical, SVR and RBF neural network with CA function framework. Finally, in Section 4 the difference among all prediction approaches is discussed.

2 Theoretical background

Traditional statistical/econometric models assume a constant one-period forecast variance. But, the financial time series features various form of nonlinear dynamics, the crucial one being the strong dependence of the instantaneous variability of the series in its own past. To predict the financial time series data an ARMA time series model is used with disturbances following GARCH type process (Gouriéroux, 1997).

2.1 ARMA time series models

Time series models have been initially introduced either for descriptive purposes like prediction or for dynamic control. In this paper we will use linear time series models so called ARMA which are very easy implement well-established methods for time series prediction (Box. 2013). They combine autoregressive (AR) and moving average (MA) part. AR is a linear combination of previous values, MA is a linear combination of previous errors. An ARMA(p, q) model of orders p and q is defined as

$$y_t = \phi_1 y_{t-1} + \phi_2 y_{t-2} + \cdots + \phi_p y_{t-p} + \varepsilon_t + \theta_1 \varepsilon_{t-1} + \theta_2 \varepsilon_{t-2} + \ldots + \theta_q \varepsilon_{t-q} \qquad (1)$$

where ϕ_i and θ_j are the parameters of the autoregressive and moving average parts respectively, and ε_t is white noise with mean zero and variance σ^2. We assume that ε_t is normally distributed, that is $\varepsilon_t \sim N(0,\sigma^2)$. The method of building an appropriate time series forecasting model is an iterative procedure that consists of the implementation of several steps. The main four steps are: identification, estimation, diagnostic checking, and forecasting.

2.2 Asymmetric GARCH type time series models

Among the field of application where the standard ARMA model fit is poor are financial and monetary problems. Exchanges rates, stock market return and other macroeconomic variables of generally high frequency are likely to originate from low complexity chaos. Detection of nonlinear hidden pattern in such time series provides important information about their behavior and improves the forecasting ability over short time. The generalized GARCH has been derived by Bollerslev (1986) for time sequence $\{y_t\}$ in the following form

$$y_t = y_t = v_t\sqrt{h_t}$$
$$h_t = \alpha_0 + \sum_{i=1}^{m}\alpha_i y_{t-i}^2 + \sum_{i=1}^{m}\beta_j h_{t-j} \tag{2}$$

where $\{v_t\}$ is a sequence of IID (Independent Identical Distribution) random variables with zero mean and unit variance. α_i a β_i are the ARCH and GARCH parameters, h_t represents the conditional variance of time series conditional on all the information to time t -1, I_{t-1}. There are another extensions of the classic GARCH model e.g. the exponential GARCH abbreviated as EGARCH proposed by Nelson (1991), PGARCH (power GARCH) proposed by Ding, Granger and Engle (1993), which allow for leverage effects.

3 Support vector regression (SVR)

Support vector machines (SVMs) can also be successfully applied in regression (nonlinear function estimation) problems (Drucker et al. 1997; Vapnik, Gollowich, and Smola 1997). A typical property of SVM´s is that, up to a small number of hyper-parameters, the solution is characterized by a convex optimization problem, more specifically a quadratic programming (QP) problem. Based on the reasons stated in works Cao et al. (2005), Kim (2003) as well as on base of Marcek (2019) we decided to choose support vector regression as a representative of artificial intelligence technique into high frequency data where classical statistical or econometrical methods could not be used due to computational or time (cost efficiency) reasons. Next, we give a brief introduction to the theory and methods of SVM´s for non-linear function estimation.

The SVR learning machine is given by n training data, from which it attempts to learn the input-output relationship $y = f(x)$ where $D = \{[x_i, y_i] \in \Re^p \times \Re, i = 1,2,...,n\}$ consists of n pairs $D = \{x_i, y_i\}_{i=1}^n$. The SVR considers approximation function of two forms

$$f(\mathbf{x},\mathbf{w},b) = \begin{cases} \sum_{i=1}^{n} w_i\mathbf{x} + b & \text{for linear regression,} \\ K(\mathbf{x}_i,\mathbf{x}_j)\mathbf{w} + b & \text{for non-linear regression,} \end{cases} \tag{3}$$

where $K(\mathbf{x}_i,\mathbf{x}_j)$ are so called kernel functions, w are the weights (parameters) and b represent the bias.

The optimal linear regression function is given by the minimum of the functional,

$$\Phi(w,\xi) = \frac{1}{2}\|w\|^2 + C\sum_i(\xi_i^- + \xi_i^+), \tag{4}$$

where C is a pre-specified value, and ξ^-, ξ^+ are slack variables representing upper and lower constrains on the output of the system.

Using an ε-insensitive loss function (see FIGURE 1c)

$$|y - f(\mathbf{x},\mathbf{w})| = \begin{cases} 0 & \text{if } |y - f(\mathbf{x},\mathbf{w})| \le \varepsilon, \\ |y - f(\mathbf{x},\mathbf{w})| - \varepsilon & \text{othewise,} \end{cases} \tag{5}$$

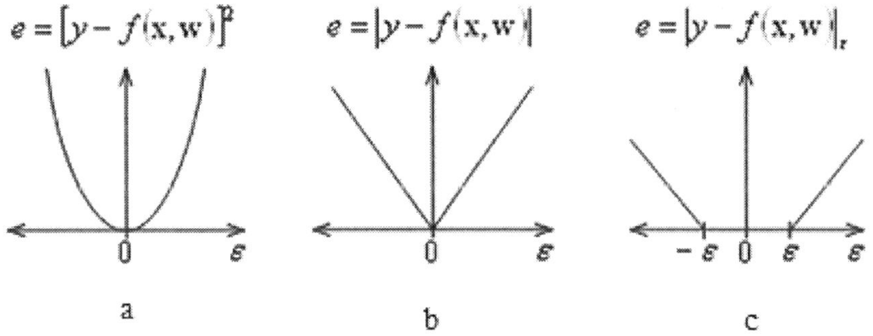

Figure 1 Loss function

solution is given by

$$\max_{\alpha,\alpha_i^*} \mathfrak{A}(\alpha,\alpha_i^*) = \max_{\alpha,\alpha_i^*} -\frac{1}{2}\sum_{i,j=1}^{n}(\alpha_i - \alpha_i^*)(\alpha_j - \alpha_j^*)\mathbf{x}_i^T\mathbf{x}_j - \varepsilon\sum_{i=1}^{n}(\alpha_i + \alpha_i^*) + \sum_{i=1}^{n} y_i(\alpha_i - \alpha_i^*) \tag{6}$$

with constrains,

$$\begin{gathered} 0 \le \alpha_i, \alpha_i^* \le C, \quad i = 1....,l \\ \sum_{i=1}^{l}(\alpha_i - \alpha_i^*) = 0. \end{gathered} \tag{7}$$

Solving Equation (4) with constrains (5) determines the Lagrange multipliers α_i, α_i^*, and the regression function, in the case of a linear model, is given by Equation (3), where

$$\begin{gathered} \mathbf{w} = \sum_{i=1}^{n}(\alpha_i - \alpha_i^*)\mathbf{x}_i \\ b = -\frac{1}{2}[\mathbf{w},(\mathbf{x}_r + \mathbf{x}_s)] \end{gathered} \tag{8}$$

The Karush-Kuhn-Trucker (KKT) conditions that are satisfied by the solution are,

$$\boldsymbol{\alpha}_i \boldsymbol{\alpha}_i^* = 0, \quad i = 1,...,l. \tag{9}$$

Therefore the support vectors are points where exactly one of the Lagrange multipliers is greater than zero.

In the case of a non-linear model is usually required to adequately model data. The non-linear SVR solution, using an ε-insensitive loss function, is given by,

$$f(\mathbf{x},\mathbf{w},b) = K(\mathbf{x}_i,\mathbf{x}_j)\mathbf{w} + b \tag{10}$$

$$f(\mathbf{x},\alpha,b) = \sum_{i=1}^{n}(\alpha_i - \alpha_i^*)K(\mathbf{x}_i,\mathbf{x}_j) + b, \tag{11}$$

where

$$\begin{cases} b = y_k - \sum_{i=1}^{n}(\alpha_i - \alpha_i^*)K(\mathbf{x}_i,\mathbf{x}_k) - \varepsilon & \text{for} \quad \alpha_k \in (0,C), \\ b = y_k - \sum_{i=1}^{n}(\alpha_i - \alpha_i^*)K(\mathbf{x}_i,\mathbf{x}_k) + \varepsilon & \text{for} \quad \alpha_k^* \in (0,C). \end{cases}$$

4 Neural networks architectures

In recent years, scientists try to incorporate other factors to increase the accuracy of neural networks, such as evolving RBF (Radial Basis Function) neural networks in which also genetic algorithms are implemented (Marcek and Kotillova, 2016, Marcek, 2019). Newday people talk above massive renaissance of neural networks - mainly thanks to publications about deep neural networks (Dietterich, 2000, Hinton, et al., 2006) and convolutional neural networks (Kang et al, 2019).

Neural networks can be understood as a system which produces output based on inputs the user has defined. It is important to say that user has no knowledge about internal working of the NN system. Neural networks work on the *Black Box* principle. According to some publications such as Gooijer, Hyndman (2006), NN are the prediction models which have the biggest potential in predicting time series and high-frequency financial time series data. In this section we firstly show an approach of function estimation for time series modelled by means of classic RBF trained by BP, then we introduce NNs with soft and hybrid architectures.

The architecture of classic RBF neural networks (see FIGURE 2) is defined by processing units and their interconnections, activation functions and learning methods. Potentials of hidden layers for the classic neural network of feedforward type neurons are simple linear operations of scalar product of vectors **w** and **x**. In RBF NN, the potential of the jth hidden neuron is counted as the difference of Euclidian distance given by vectors

$$u^j = \| \mathbf{x} - \mathbf{w}^j \|^2, \quad \text{for } j = 1,2, \ldots, n. \tag{12}$$

where s is the number of the RBF neurons. Note that for the RBF NN, the hidden layer weights $\mathbf{w}^j$ represent the centers $\mathbf{c}^j$ of activation function in the hidden layer.

RBF NN also uses different types of activation functions known as Gaussian or radial basis function. Activation function for j^{th} hidden neuron is defined as

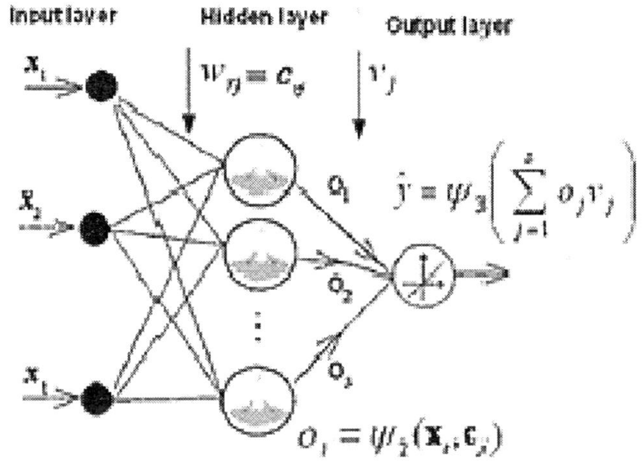

Figure 2 Classic RBF NN

$$\psi_2(u^j) = e^{\frac{-u^j}{2\sigma_j^2}} = e^{\frac{\|\mathbf{x}-\mathbf{w}^j\|^2}{2\sigma_j^2}} \quad (13)$$

for j = 1, 2, ..., s, where σ_j^2 is a variance of jth neuron. If the components of input vector are not orthogonal then the activation function looks like this

Computation of the input - output function can be described as

$$\psi_2(u^j) = e^{\frac{-(\mathbf{x}-\mathbf{w}^j)^T \Sigma^{-1} (\mathbf{x}-\mathbf{w}^j)}{2}} = o_j \quad (14)$$

$$\psi_2 = \exp\left[-(\mathbf{x}_t - \mathrm{E}(\mathbf{x}_j)/2(En')^2\right] \quad (15)$$

If the scalar output values $o_{j,t}$ from the hidden layer will be normalized, where the normalization means that the sum of the outputs from the hidden layer is equal to 1, then the RBF network will compute the "normalized" output $o_j^N = o_j / \sum_{j=1}^{s} o_j$ for j = 1, 2, ..., s (see FIGURE 3). The network according to Kecman (2001) with one hidden layer and normalized output values $o_{j,t}$ is the fuzzy logic model or the soft RBF network.

Our improvements neural networks are designed so that the classical activation functions for neurons in the hidden layer was replaced by a cloud activation function (CAF) in the form (see FIGURE 4)

$$\psi_2 = \exp\left[-(\mathbf{x}_t - \mathrm{E}(\mathbf{x}_j)/2(En')^2\right] \quad (16)$$

where En' is a normally distributed random number with mean (entropy) En and standard deviation (hyper-entropy) He, E is the expectation operator (Li, 2008).

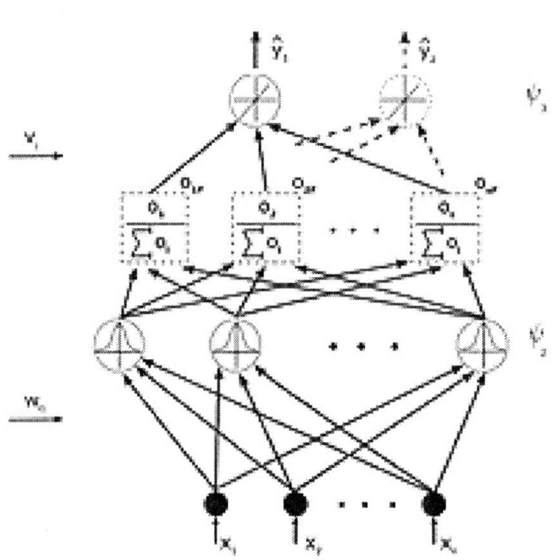

Figure 3 Soft RBF NN with cloud activation function

Note that for an RBF network, the hidden layer weights $\mathbf{w}_j$ represent the centers $\mathbf{c}_j$ of activation functions in the hidden layer. To find the weights $\mathbf{w}_j$ or centers of activation functions we used the adaptive (learning) version of K-means clustering algorithm for s clusters. The second parameter of the RB function, the standard deviation is estimated as K, (K $\geq$ 1) multiple of the mean value of quadratic distance among the input vectors and their cluster centers. The value of K is regarded as the rate of overlapping in the distribution of input data. To learn the weights v_j the first-order gradient procedure was used and these weights can be adapted by the error back-propagation algorithm. Back-propagation training is mathematically designed to minimize the mean square error (MSE) over all training data samples.

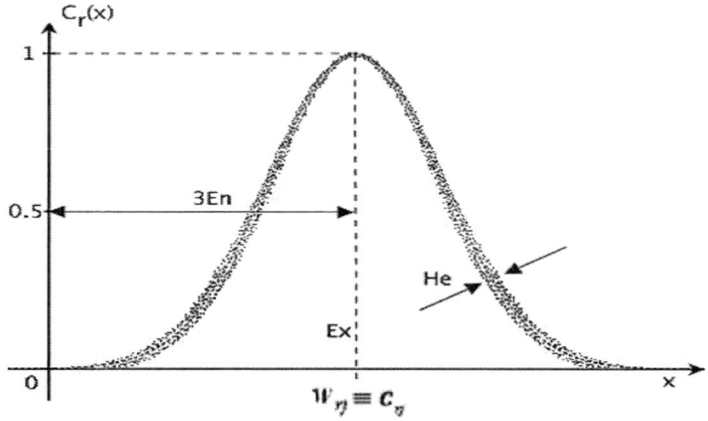

Figure 4 Cloud activation function

5 Data, development of forecasting models and comparison

There are the EUR/USD-exchange rate used time series dataset in order to forecast these exchange rate. Our dataset is composed of 4382 observations (from January 2, 2001 to December 31, 2012) of the average daily prices for EUR currency against the US dollar. As we would like to develop a time series model for one daily ahead forecast of the changes in the EUR/USD-exchanges, the sample period for analysis from January 2, 2001 to June 30, 2007 was defined, i.e. the period over which the forecasting model can be developed and the ex post forecast period from July 1, 2007 to December 31, 2012 (denoted as validation or ex-post data set).

The relevant lag structure of potential inputs was analysed using traditional statistical tools, i.e. using the autocorrelation function (ACF), partial autocorrelation function (PACF) and the Akaike/Bayesian information criterion (AIC/BIC). We looked to determine the maximum lag for which the PACF coefficient was statistically significant and the lag given the minimum AIC. According to these criterions the ARIMA(1,1,1) model was specified as

$$\Delta y_t = \xi + \varphi_1 \Delta y_{t-1} + \theta_1 \varepsilon_{t-1} + \varepsilon_t , \quad (17)$$

where ξ, φ_1, θ_1 are unknown parameters of the model, ε_t is independent random variable drawn from stable probability distribution with mean zero and variance σ_ε^2. The maximum likelihood procedure was used for estimation the parameters of an ARCH or GARCH model. To find the appropriate statistical model various procedures such as LM test, QQ plots, AIC and BIC criterions were used. The quantification of the model was performed by means of the R2.6.0 software at http://cran.r-project.org and resulted into the best ARIMA(1,1,1)+PGARCH(1,1) model with the following mean equation

$$\Delta y_t = 0.000126 + 0.079563 \Delta y_{t-1} + 0.041943 \varepsilon_{t-1} + \varepsilon_t , \quad (18)$$

and variance

$$h_t^{1.8365} = 2.26\ .10^{-7} + 0.03028\ \left(\left| \hat{\varepsilon}_{t-1} \right| + 0.008032 \hat{\varepsilon}_{t-1} \right)^{1.8365} + 0.96015 h_{t-1}^{1.8365} \quad (19)$$

To examine the accuracy of the prediction model, the Root Mean Square Error (*RMSE*) evaluation measure is used in this study. It is defined as $RMSE = \frac{1}{n} \sum_{n=1}^{n} (y_t - \hat{y}_t)^2$ where $\hat{y}_t$ is the predicted value of corresponding y_t.

The SVR application was conducted using the variables and data sets as the statistical model above. In this study, according to the previous result, polynomial kernel was used with the measure of error approximation, ε = 0.001, and the regularization parameter C = 1.8, which influences a trade-of between an approximation error and weights vector norm. These parameters were chosen by a grid search. The range of ε is [0.0001, 1], and the range of C is [1, 10]. The prediction of EUR/USD-exchange rate has been done using *WEKA* software (Hall, 2009).

In the RBF neural network with CA function framework, the non-linear forecasting function $f(\mathbf{x})$ was estimated according to the expressions (13) with RB function $\psi_2(./.)$ given by equation (16). This RBF NN assumes that the noise level of the entropy is known. Noise levels are indicated by hyper entropy. It is assumed that the noise level is constant over time.

We select, for practical reasons, that the noise level is a multiple, say 0.015 of entropy. For RBF NN, we choose the RBF activation function with parameters chosen by a grid search. The range of K parameter (the rate of overlapping in distribution of input data) [1.0, 4.0], and the range of s (number of hidden layer neurons) is [1, 10]. The size of the neural network is (2, 4, 1), which is a one hidden layer model.

From prediction results EUR/USD-exchange rate in TABLE 1, the effectiveness of all these prediction methods can be appreciated. By analyzing the forecasting outputs in TABLE 1, we can find that these methods also perform well for short-term time series exchange rate forecasting. Moreover, the NN learning methods have more accurate outputs than statistical one. However, SVR has a slightly better forecasting performance than artificial neural networks for these data sets. This phenomenon is probably caused by the reason that there is only one hidden layer in the neural networks used here (Crawley, 2007).

Model	**RMSE**
ARIMA(1,1,1)+PGARH(1,1)	0.00362
SVR	0.00087
RBF neuronal net	0.00181

Table 1 Statistical summary measures of model´s ex post forecast accuracy for ARIMA(1,1,1)+PGARCH(1,1), SVR models and soft RBF net

6 Conclusion

In this paper, we proposed three forecasting models based on statistical, SVR and neural networks. Prediction results for EUR/USD-exchange rate data set has been mutually compared. Based on RMSE, the proposed SVR and NNs learning methods have outperformed the statistical method. In addition, the proposed artificial intelligence methods haave potential ability to deal with massive and more complicated datasets. Artificial intelligence applications are a very efficient method for extremely big data sets where classical statistical or econometrical methods could not be used due to computational or time (cost efficiency) reasons (Hinton et al, 2006).

For future work, methods composed of different deep learning algorithms will be implemented and compared with various types of regression and time series datasets from financial institutions. Moreover, more advanced optimization algorithms for parameter selection will be developed to further enhance the prediction process.

Acknowledgements

This paper was supported by European Social Fund within Student grant competition EkF, VŠB-TU Ostrava as a part of project SP2019/81.

References

Box, G. E., Jenkins, G. M. and Reinsel, G. C. (2013) Time series analysis: forecasting and control. John Wiley & Sons.

Zivot, E., Wang, J. (2005) *Modeling Financial Time Series with S-PLUS®*, Springer Verlag, NY.

Marček, D., Kotillova, A. (2016) Statistical and Soft Computing Methods Applied to High Frequency Data. *Journal of Multiple-Valued Logic and Soft Computing* Vol.26(6), pp.593 -608.

Jamimi, H. A. and Ghouti, L. (2011) Efficient prediction of software fault proneness modules using support vector machines and probabilistic neural networks, *In 5th Malaysian Conference in Software Engineering*, pp. 251-255.

Gouriéroux, Ch. (1997) *ARCH Models and Financial Application*. Springer Verlag, NY.

Bollerslev, D. (1986) Generalized Autoregressive Conditional Heteroscedasticity, *Journal of Econometrics* 31 (1986), pp. 307-327.

Nelson, D. B. (1991) Conditional Heteroscedasticity in Asset Returns: a New Approach, *Econometrica* 59 (2), pp. 347–370.

Ding, Z., Granger, C. W., and Engle, R. F. (1993) A Long Memory Property of Stock Market Returns and a New Model. *Journal of Empirical Finance* 1, pp. 83-106.

Drucker, H., Burges, C. J. C., Kaufman, K., Smola, A., and Vapnik, V. N. (1997) Support vector regression machines. In *Advances in neural information processing systems*. Vol. 9, pp. 151-161. Cambridge, MA: MIT Press.

Vapnik, V. N., Glowich, N., and Smola, A. (1997) Support vector methods for function approximation, regression estimation, and signal processing. In Advances in neural information processing systems. Vol. 9. Cambridge, MA: MIT Press.

Cao, D. Z., Pang, S. L., Bai, Y. H. (2005) Forecasting Exchange Rate Using Support Vector Machines. Proceedings of the Fourth International Conference on Machine Learning and Cybernetics, China.

Kim, K. (2003) Financial Time Series Forecasting Using Support Vector Machines. *Neurocomputing*, 55, pp. 307-319.

Marček, D. (2019) Comparison of Predictive Statistical Learning Accuracy with Computational Intelligence Methods. *In INFORMATICS 2019 - IEEE 15th International Scientific Conference on Informatics,* Article number 9119308, pp. 317-322.

Marcek, D., Kotillova, A. (2016). Statistical and Soft Computing Methods Applied to High Frequency Data. *Journal of Multiple-Valued Logic and Soft Computing* Vol. 26(6), pp.593-608.

Dietterich, T., G. (2000) *Ensemble methods in machine learning, in Multiple classifier systems*. Springer, pp. 1-15.

Hinton, G., Osindero, S., and Teh, Y, W. (2006) A fast learning algorithm for deep belief nets, *Neural computation* 18(7), pp. 1527-1554.

Kang, W., Kenli, L. Liqian Z. Yikun H., Zhongyao, Ch., Jing, L., Cen, Ch. (2019) Multiple convolutional neural networks for multivariate time series prediction. *Neurocomputing* 360, pp. 107-119.

Gooijer, J., G., Hyndman, R., J. (2006) 25 Years of Time Series Forecasting,"International Journal of Forecasting, Vol. 22, pp. 443-473.

Kecman, V. (2001) *Learning and soft computing: support vector machines, neural networks, and fuzzy logic*, (Massachusetts: The MIT Press.

Li, D., Du, Y. (2008) *Artificial intelligence with uncertainty,* (Boca Raton: Chapman & Hall/CRC, Taylor & Francis Group.

Hall, M., Frank, E., Holmes, G. (2009) The WEKA Data Mining Software, 2009, [Online], Available at: www.weka.com.

Crawley, M. (2007) *The R Book*. Wiley, Chichester, 2007.

Chang, C., and Lin, C., J. (2011) Libsvm: a library for support vector machines. *ACM Transactions on Intelligent Systems and Technology (TIST)*, 2(3), p. 27.

Resource-Workflow Petri Nets with Time Tokens and Their Using in Process Management

Ivo Martiník[1], Daniel Klimsza[2]

Abstract. Resource-workflow Petri nets with time tokens (RWPNTT) are the newly introduced class of low-level process Petri nets in this article. RWPNTT are specifically designed for their use in the process management area for modeling processes consisting of individual time-dependent activities that must be synchronized with a given external time source and for determining their time-optimal critical paths. The concept of global network time is not explicitly introduced in the definition of the class of RWPNTT and this fact simplifies its implementation and the proof of its properties. The concept of global network time is then worked only implicitly within the mechanism of transition firing. The new RWPNTT class also enables the analysis of other process properties by using of well-known methods of Petri nets theory and it also has the possibility to determine the time-optimal critical path of the given process whose activities share a finite set of different resources that are necessary to successfully complete any of them. These properties of RWPNTT class are demonstrated on the process examples in this article.

Keywords: Resource-Workflow Petri Nets with Time Tokens, Critical Path Method, discrete time, process management, resource sharing.

JEL Classification: C610

1 Introduction

A number of defined classes of Petri nets are currently available (Diaz, 2000) for the needs of modeling generally parallel systems of all the types. When studying many types of systems in the area of energetics, modeling of time variables associated with individual system events, duration of activities, time history of the modeled system and many other time characteristics also play an important role. Time Petri nets and timed Petri nets (Popova-Zeugmann, 2013) (Diaz, 2000) are the two most important classes of low-level Petri nets that use the concept of discrete time in their definition. In the case of these and many other classes of discrete-time Petri nets (Furia et al., 2012) (van Hee and Sidorova, 2013) (Martos-Salgado and Rosa-Velardo, 2014) it can be stated that the most of them use only relative time variables usually related to the specific marking of a given Petri net. This can then cause problems, for example, when modeling complex time-synchronized energy systems in which their individual components must be synchronized with a given external time source.

Workflow Petri nets (WPN) (van der Alst and van Hee, 2004) were defined as the subclass of low-level process Petri nets (Huang at al., 2012) for their using primarily in the area of workflow management. WPN is a connected Petri net that includes within the set of all its places the unique input place with no input arcs and the unique output place with no output arcs. *Resource-workflow Petri nets with time tokens* (RWPNTT) are the newly introduced class of

[1] VSB-Technical University of Ostrava, Faculty of Economics, Department of Applied Informatics, Sokolská třída 33, Ostrava, Czech Republic, ivo.martinik@vsb.cz.

[2] VSB-Technical University of Ostrava, Faculty of Economics, Department of Applied Informatics, Sokolská třída 33, Ostrava, Czech Republic, daniel.klimsza.st@vsb.cz.

low-level process Petri nets whose definition and selected properties are the main topics of this article. RWPNTT are based in their definition on the concepts of the class of *workflow Petri nets with time stamps* (WPNTS) (Martiník, 2018) and the class of *resource-workflow Petri nets with time stamps* (RWPNTS) (Martiník, 2020). RWPNTT then represent the class of low-level process Petri nets and they are specifically designed for their use in the process management area for modeling processes consisting of individual time-dependent activities and for determining their time-optimal critical paths. The main difference between the RWPNTT class and the WPNTS and RWPNTS classes of Petri nets is the fact that the definition of global network time is not explicitly introduced in the definition of the class of RWPNTT, which greatly simplifies its implementation and also proof of its properties. The concept of global network time is worked only implicitly within the mechanism of the transition firing in this case. The critical path of the process is generally defined as the (temporally) longest possible path from the process start point to the process end point. Each critical path consists of the list of activities that the project manager should focus most on to ensure timely completion of the given process. The completion time of the last mission on the critical path is also the process completion time. The Critical Path Method (CPM) (O'Brien and Plotnick, 2016) is used by default to determine the critical path of the given process.

The new RWPNTT class of Petri nets allows not only modeling processes composed of individual time-dependent activities and determining their time-optimal critical paths, but, in addition to standard CPM method, it also enables the analysis of other process properties with using of standard methods of Petri nets analysis and it also has the possibility to determine the time-optimal critical path of the given process whose activities share a finite set of different resources that are necessary to successfully complete any of them. These properties of RWPNTT are demonstrated on the simple project example and its time-optimal critical path and other properties specification in this article.

The article is arranged into the following sections: in the section 2 the RWPNTT and their main properties are described; section 3 explains the concepts of time-optimal steps and time-optimal critical paths of RWPNTT and the simple examples of the presented ideas from the area of the process management are presented; section 4 then gives the conclusions of the research to conclude the article.

2 Resource-workflow Petri net with time tokens and their properties

Let N denotes the set of all *natural numbers*, $N := \{1, 2, \ldots\}$; N_0 denotes the set of all *non-negative integer numbers*, $N_0 := \{0, 1, 2, \ldots\}$; $\emptyset$ denotes the *empty set*; $N_\emptyset := N_0 \cup \{\emptyset\}$, i.e., $N_\emptyset := \{\emptyset, 0, 1, 2, \ldots\}$; $|A|$ denotes the *cardinality* of the given set A; $A \times B := \{(x, y) \mid (x \in A) \wedge (y \in B)\}$ denotes the *cartesian product* of the sets A and B; $\neg$ denotes the *logical negation* operator; $f\colon A \to B$ denotes the *function* f with the *domain* A and the *codomain* B; by the (non-empty finite) *sequence* σ over the non-empty set A we understand the function $\sigma\colon \{1, 2, \ldots, n\} \to A$, where $n \in N$, that is denoted by $\sigma := <a_1, a_2, \ldots, a_n>$, where $a_i = \sigma(i)$ for $1 \leq i \leq n$; if $\sigma := <a_1, a_2, \ldots, a_n>$ is the sequence, then the set $\boldsymbol{ELEMS}_\sigma := \{a \mid \exists i, 1 \leq i \leq n\colon a = \sigma(i)\}$. Let $(A \subset N_0) \wedge (\exists n \in N\colon |A| = n) \wedge (A \neq \emptyset)$, then $max(A) := x$, where $(x \in A) \wedge (\forall y \in A\colon x \geq y)$, $min(A) := z$, where $(z \in A) \wedge (\forall y \in A\colon y \geq z)$.

Definition 1. *Net NET* is the ordered triple $NET := (P, T, A)$, where P is finite non-empty set of the *places*; T is finite set of the *transitions*, $P \cap T = \emptyset$; A is finite set of the *arcs*, $A \subseteq (P \times T) \cup (T \times P)$. □

Some commonly used notations for the nets are $\bullet y = \{x \mid (x, y) \in A\}$ for the *preset* and $y\bullet = \{x \mid (y, x) \in A\}$ for the *postset* of the net node y (i.e., place or transition). The *path* leading from the node x_1 to the node x_k of the net is the non-empty sequence $<x_1, x_2, \ldots, x_k>$ of net nodes, where $k \in N$, which satisfies $(x_1, x_2), (x_2, x_3), \ldots, (x_{k-1}, x_k) \in A$. We will denote the set of all such paths of the given net NET by $\boldsymbol{PATHS}_{NET}(x_1, x_k)$. The path of the net leading from its node x to its node y is the *circuit* if $(y, x) \in A$. We will denote the set of all the circuits of the given net NET by $\boldsymbol{CIRCUITS}_{NET}$.

Definition 2. *Workflow net with time tokens* (WNTT) *WNET* is the ordered tuple $WNET := (P, T, A, TI, IP, OP)$, where:

1) (P, T, A) is the *net*,
2) TI: $(T \times P) \rightarrow \boldsymbol{N}_0$ is the *time interval function*,
3) IP is the *input place*, $(IP \in P) \wedge (\bullet IP = \emptyset) \wedge (|IP\bullet| = 1)$,
4) OP is the *output place*, $(OP \in P) \wedge (OP\bullet = \emptyset) \wedge (|\bullet OP| = 1) \wedge (OP \neq IP)$,
5) $\forall p \in (P \setminus \{IP, OP\})$: $(|\bullet p| = 1) \wedge (|p\bullet| = 1)$,
6) $\forall x \in (P \cup T)\ \exists \sigma \in \boldsymbol{PATHS}_{WNET}(IP, OP)$: $x \in \boldsymbol{ELEMS}_{\sigma}$,
7) $\boldsymbol{CIRCUITS}_{WNET} = \emptyset$. □

The WNTT *WNET* consists of the net (P, T, A); the *time interval function TI* then assigns with each arc of the type (*transition, place*) the non-negative integer number d (with the default value of 0 in the net diagram) that expresses the minimum time interval during which the token has to remain in the *place* instead of being able to participate in the next firing of some transition in its postset; the *input place IP* is the only one place of WNTT *WNET* with no input arc(s) and with one output arc; the *output place OP* that is the only one place of WNTT *WNET* with no output arc(s) and with one input arc. It must also be fulfilled for the WNTT *WNET* that every of its non-input and non-output places has exactly one input arc and one output arc (see 5 of Definition 2); every node x (i.e., place or transition) must be the element of some path σ from the input place IP to the output place OP (i.e., every WNTT is the connected net - see 6 of Definition 2); WNTT *WNET* must not contain any circuits that could cause a state of deadlock during its firing of the transactions (see 7 of Definition 2).

Definition 3. *Resource-workflow net with time tokens* (RWNTT) *RWNET* is the ordered tuple $RWNET := (P, T, A, TI, IP, OP, RP)$, where:

1) (P, T, A, TI, IP, OP) is the WNTT denoted by $\underline{RWNET}$,
2) RP is finite set of the *resource places*, $RP \subseteq (P \setminus \{IP, OP\})$, $\forall rp \in RP$: $\bullet rp = rp\bullet \neq \emptyset$.□

The RWNTT *RWNET* consists of the WNTT $\underline{RWNET} := (P, T, A, TI, IP, OP)$; the finite set RP of the *resource places* is used for expressing the conditions of the modeled process containing some initial resources and we use circles with the double line for their representation; the preset of the given resource place $rp \in RP$ is the same as its postset, i.e., RWNTT *RWNET* can contain so called *loops*, generally $\boldsymbol{CIRCUITS}_{RWNET} \neq \emptyset$ and therefore every circuit of the given RWNTT *RWNET* must contain at least one resource place rp.

Definition 4. Let $RWNET := (P, T, A, TI, IP, OP, RP)$ be the RWNTT. Then:

1) *marking* M of the RWNTT $RWNET$ is the function $M: P \rightarrow N_{\varnothing}$,
3) transition $t \in T$ is *enabled* in the making M of the RWNTT $RWNET$ that is denoted by t *en* M, if $\forall p \in \bullet t$: $M(p) \neq \varnothing$,
4) *firing of the transition* $t \in T$ results in changing the marking M of the RWNTT $RWNET$ into its marking M' that is denoted by $M\,[t\rangle\, M'$, where:
   a) $\forall p \in \bullet t \setminus t\bullet$: $M'(p) := \varnothing$,
   b) $\forall p \in t\bullet$: $M'(p) := max(\{M(p) \mid p \in \bullet t\}) + TI(t, p)$,
   c) $\forall p \in P \setminus (\bullet t \cup t\bullet)$: $M'(p) := M(p)$,
5) if the mutually different transitions $t_1, t_2, \ldots, t_n \in T$ are enabled in the marking M of the RWNTT $RWNET$ (i.e., $(t_1\ en\ S) \wedge (t_2\ en\ S) \wedge \ldots \wedge (t_n\ en\ S)$) we say that these transitions are *enabled in parallel* in the marking M that is denoted by $\{t_1, t_2, \ldots, t_n\}$ *en* M;
6) finite non-empty sequence $\sigma := <t_1, t_2, \ldots, t_n>$ of the transitions $t_1, t_2, \ldots, t_n \in T$ for which the following is valid in the marking M_1 of the RWNTT $RWNET$:
$$M_1\,[t_1\rangle\, M_2\,[t_2\rangle \ldots [t_n\rangle\, M_{n+1}$$
is called *step* σ and it is denoted by $M_1\,[\sigma\rangle\, M_{n+1}$,
7) we will say that the marking M' of the RWNTT $RWNET$ *is reachable* from its marking M if there exists the finite sequence $\sigma := <t_1, t_2, \ldots, t_n>$ of the transitions $t_1, t_2, \ldots, t_n \in T$ such that $M\,[\sigma\rangle\, M'$,
8) the set of all the markings M' of the RWNTT $RWNET$ that are reachable from its marking M will be denoted by $[M\rangle$,
9) the set of all the finite sequences $\sigma := <t_1, t_2, \ldots, t_n>$ associated with all the reachable markings $M' \in [M\rangle$ is denoted by $[M\rangle\rangle$, i.e.,
$[M\rangle\rangle := \{<t_1, t_2, \ldots, t_n> \mid \exists M' \in [M\rangle: M\,[t_1\,t_2 \ldots t_n\rangle\, M', n \in N\}$,
10) *input marking* M_i of the RWNTT $RWNET$ is such marking where $(\forall p \in (RP \cup \{IP\})$: $M_i(p) = 0) \wedge (\forall p \in (P \setminus (RP \cup \{IP\}))$: $M_i(p) = \varnothing)$,
11) *output marking* M_o of the RWNTT $RWNET$ that is reachable from its input marking M_i is every of its markings M_o where $(M_o \in [M_i\rangle) \wedge (\forall p \in (RP \cup \{OP\})$: $M_o(p) \neq \varnothing) \wedge (\forall p \in (P \setminus (RP \cup \{OP\}))$: $M_o(p) = \varnothing)$,
12) the set of all the output markings M_o of the RWNTT $RWNET$ that *are reachable* from its input marking M_i is denoted by $[M_i\rangle_o$.
13) the set of all the finite sequences $\sigma := <t_1, t_2, \ldots, t_n>$ associated with all the output markings $M_o \in [M_i\rangle$ is denoted by $[M_i\rangle\rangle_o$, i.e.,
$[M_i\rangle\rangle_o := \{<t_1, t_2, \ldots, t_n> \mid \exists M_o \in [M_i\rangle_o: M_i\,[t_1\,t_2 \ldots t_n\rangle\, M_o, n \in N\}$. □

Definition 5. *Resource-Workflow Petri net with time tokens* (RWPNTT) $RWPNET$ is the ordered couple $RWPNET := (RWNET, M_i)$, where $RWNET := (P, T, A, TI, IP, OP, RP)$ is the RWNTT and M_i is the input marking of the RWNTT $RWNET$.

Definition 6. Let $RWPNET := ((P, T, A, TI, IP, OP, RP), M_i)$ be a RWPNTT.

1) ETI: $[M_i\rangle\rangle_o \rightarrow N_0$ is the *execution time interval* function of $RWPNET$ defined as follows:
$\forall \sigma \in [M_i\rangle\rangle_o, M_i\,[\sigma\rangle\, M_o$: $ETI(\sigma) := M_o(OP)$,
2) $METI$ is the *minimum execution time interval* of $RWPNET$ defined as follows:

$METI := min(\{ETI(\sigma) \mid \sigma \in [M_i\rangle\rangle_o\})$,

3) *TOSTEPS* is the set of the *time-optimal steps* of *RWPNET* defined as follows: $TOSTEPS := \{\sigma \mid (M_i\,[\sigma\rangle\, M_o) \wedge (M_o(OP) = METI)\}$,
4) *TOCP* is the set of the *time-optimal critical paths* of *RWPNET* defined as follows: $TOCP := \{\rho \mid (\rho \in \boldsymbol{PATHS}_{\underline{RWPNET}}(IP, OP),\ \rho := \langle IP, t_1, p_1, t_2, p_2, \ldots, p_{n-1}, t_n, OP\rangle) \wedge (TI(t_1, p_1) + TI(t_2, p_2) + \ldots + TI(t_n, OP) = METI)$, where $\{p_1, p_2, \ldots, p_{n-1}\} \subset P$, $\{t_1, t_2, \ldots, t_n\} \subseteq T$, $n \in N_0\}$.

The above established concepts will be demonstrated on the simple example of the RWPNTT $RWPNET1 := ((P, T, A, TI, IP, OP, RP), M_i)$ that is shown in Figure 1, where $P :=$ {IP, P1, A, B, C, D, OP}; $T :=$ {T1, T2, T3, T4}; $A :=$ {(IP, T1), (T1, P1), (T1, B), (T1, D), (P1, T2), (B, T3), (T2, A), (T3, C), (A, T4), (C, T4), (D, T4), (R1, T2), (T2, R1), (R2, T2), (T2, R2), (R2, T3), (T3, R2), (T4, OP)}; $TI :=$ {((T1, P1), 0), ((T1, B), 2), ((T1, D), 5), ((T2, A), 4), ((T3, C), 6), ((T2, R1), 4), ((T2, R2), 4), ((T3, R2), 6), ((T4, OP), 0)}; $IP :=$ IP; $OP :=$ OP, $RP :=$ {R1, R2} (it should be noted here that *TI*(T2, R1) = *TI*(T2, R2) = *TI*(T2, A) = 4 and *TI*(T3, R2) = *TI*(T2, C) = 6).

RWPNTT *RWPNET1* is in its input marking $M_i := (M_i(\mathrm{IP}), M_i(\mathrm{P1}), M_i(\mathrm{A}), M_i(\mathrm{B}), M_i(\mathrm{C}), M_i(\mathrm{D}), M_i(\mathrm{R1}), M_i(\mathrm{R2}), M_i(\mathrm{OP})) = (0, \varnothing, \varnothing, \varnothing, \varnothing, \varnothing, 0, 0, \varnothing)$. Marking M of any RWPNTT expresses the current time state of the modeled system using the time stamp associated with each of its token. Individual values of the time stamps associated with the tokens, informally said, represent the values of the implicit net time (net time is not explicitly introduced in the definition of RWPNTT) at which the respective token can first participate in the firing of the selected enabled transition t of the given RWPNTT. The transition T1 is enabled in the input marking M_i of the RWPNTT *RWPNET1* because $\forall p \in \bullet\mathrm{T1}: M_i(p) \neq \varnothing$, i.e., $(\bullet\mathrm{T1} = \{\mathrm{IP}\}) \wedge (M_i(\mathrm{IP}) = 0 \neq \varnothing)$ (see 2 of Definition 3). Firing of the transition T1 changes the input marking M_i of the RWPNTT *RWPNET1* into its marking $M_1 = (\varnothing, 0, \varnothing, 2, \varnothing, 5, 0, 0, \varnothing)$ (i.e., $M_i\,[\mathrm{T1}\rangle\, M_1$), where (see 3 of Definition 3) $M_1(\mathrm{IP}) := \varnothing$; $M_1(\mathrm{P1}) := max(\{M_i(\mathrm{IP}) \mid \mathrm{IP} \in \bullet\mathrm{T1}\}) + TI(\mathrm{T1}, \mathrm{P1}) = max(\{0\}) + 0 = 0$; $M_1(\mathrm{B}) := max(\{M_i(\mathrm{IP}) \mid \mathrm{IP} \in \bullet\mathrm{T1}\}) + TI(\mathrm{T1}, \mathrm{B}) = max(\{0\}) + 2 = 2$; $M_1(\mathrm{D}) := max(\{M_i(\mathrm{IP}) \mid \mathrm{IP} \in \bullet\mathrm{T1}\}) + TI(\mathrm{T1}, \mathrm{D}) = max(\{0\}) + 5 = 5$.

The transitions T2 and T3 are enabled in the marking M_1 and so called *conflict* occurs at their enabling, i.e., both transitions T2 and T3 have at least one common (resource) place R2 in their presets, each of the these transitions is individually enabled in the marking M_1, but these transitions are not enabled in parallel in this marking (see 4 of Definition 3) and enabling of one of them will prevent enabling of the other (i.e., $(\bullet\mathrm{T2} \cap \bullet\mathrm{T3} \neq \varnothing) \wedge (\mathrm{T2}\ en\ M_1) \wedge (\mathrm{T3}\ en\ M_1) \wedge \neg(\{\mathrm{T2}, \mathrm{T3}\}\ en\ M_1)$). The term of conflict can be then obviously generalized for the case of the finite set $t_1, t_2, \ldots, t_n$ ($n \in N$) of the transitions of the given RWPNTT. Since no explicit rule has been defined which of the conflicting transitions T2 and T3 to fire in this case, we will randomly select the transition T2 to fire. Firing of the transition T2 changes the marking M_1 into the marking $M_2 = (\varnothing, \varnothing, 4, 2, \varnothing, 5, 4, 4, \varnothing)$ (i.e., $M_1\,[\mathrm{T2}\rangle\, M_2$), where (see 3 of Definition 3) $M_2(\mathrm{P1}) := \varnothing$; $M_2(\mathrm{A}) := max(\{M_1(\mathrm{P1}), M_1(\mathrm{R1}), M_1(\mathrm{R2}) \mid \bullet\mathrm{T2} = \{\mathrm{P1}, \mathrm{R1}, \mathrm{R2}\}\}) + TI(\mathrm{T2}, \mathrm{A}) = max(\{0, 0, 0\}) + 4 = 4$; $M_2(\mathrm{R1}) := max(\{M_1(\mathrm{P1}), M_1(\mathrm{R1}), M_1(\mathrm{R2}) \mid \bullet\mathrm{T2} = \{\mathrm{P1}, \mathrm{R1}, \mathrm{R2}\}\}) + TI(\mathrm{T2}, \mathrm{R2}) = max(\{0, 0, 0\}) + 4 = 4$; $M_2(\mathrm{R2}) := max(\{M_1(\mathrm{P1}), M_1(\mathrm{R1}), M_1(\mathrm{R2}) \mid \bullet\mathrm{T2} = \{\mathrm{P1}, \mathrm{R1},$

R2}}) + TI(T2, A) = max({0, 0, 0}) + 4 = 4 (see Figure 1). There is enabled transition T3 in the marking M_2 and firing of this transition changes the marking M_2 into the marking M_3 = (∅, ∅, 4, ∅, 10, 5, 4, 10, ∅) (i.e., M_2 [T3⟩ M_3). Finally, there is enabled transition T4 in the marking M_3 and firing of this transition changes the marking M_2 into the output marking M_o = (∅, ∅, ∅, ∅, ∅, ∅, 4, 10, 10) (i.e., M_3 [T4⟩ M_o).

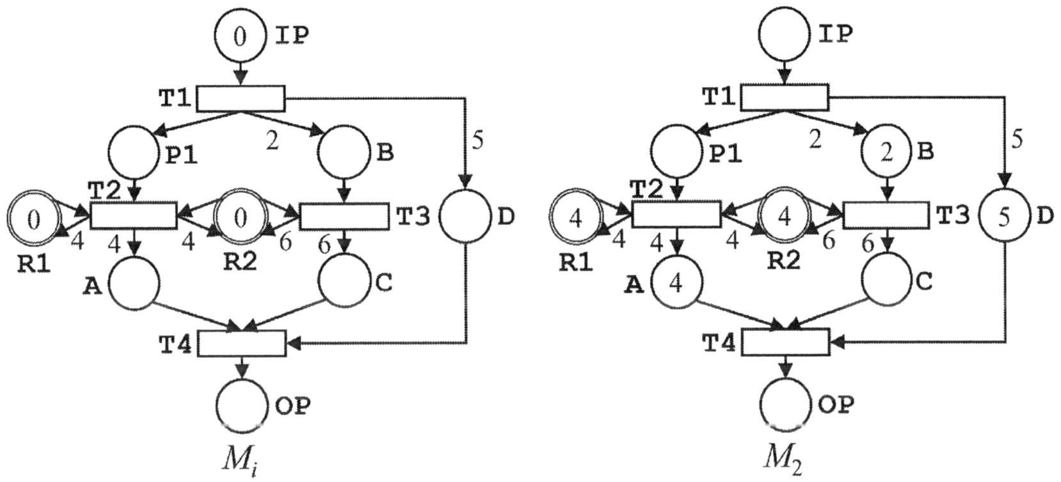

Figure 1 RWPNTT *RWPNET1* in its input marking M_i and in the marking M_2 (M_i [T1 T2⟩ M_2).

3 Time-optimal steps and time-optimal paths of resource-workflow Petri nets with time tokens

The critical path method (CPM) (O'Brien and Plotnick, 2016) is one of the basic deterministic methods of the network analysis. It is used in particular for the analysis of processes in which the duration of their individual activities of which these processes are composed can be estimated with a high degree of accuracy. Its aim is to determine the duration of a given process on the basis of the duration of the so-called critical path by which we mean a sequence of interdependent activities with no time reserve. The CPM method makes it possible to facilitate the effective time coordination of partial interrelated activities within a given process. Each process has at least one critical path that consists of the list of time-dependent activities on which the project manager should focus the most to ensure its timely completion. The time to complete the last activity on the critical path is also the time to complete the whole process. For the critical activities, their total time reserve, and thus also the leisure reserve, is equal to zero, i.e., the delay in starting such a critical activity or extending its duration will affect the duration of the whole process.

The theory of RWPNTT can then be successfully applied especially in modeling processes and in determining their time-optimal steps and time-optimal critical paths. We will further show that RWPNTT theory can also be used to generalize the original process model used by the CPM method in the following paragraphs, given that each activity may require a limited set of so-called resources (e.g., energy, financial, material, etc.) for its exclusive use and successful completion, with the proviso that each of these resources can also be used for other activities of the studied process. The simple resource sharing model based on RWPNTT will be described in which each of these resources is represented by a separate token 0 that is located at the appropriate resource place in the input marking M_i of the given RWPNTT (i.e., each of these resources is immediately available to the appropriate activity for its completion in the input marking M_i of the given RWPNTT and also for its further use by another activity once the previous activity has been successfully completed). The simple example of such process whose activities need to share selected resources for their successful completion is described in the following table of its activities (see Table 1) and it is represented by the RWPNTT *RWPNET1* in Figure 1.

Activity	Time Duration	Previous Activities	Shared Resources
A	4	-	R1, R2
B	2	-	R2
C	6	B	-
D	5	-	-

Table 1 Table of activities, their time durations, dependencies and shared resources

Places A, B, C, D and E in RWPNTT *RWPNET1* represent individual activities of the studied process. The respective values of the time interval function *TI* associated with the input arcs of these places then express the durations of individual activities (i.e., for example activity B is represented by the place B, its time duration is given by the value *TI*(T1, B) = 2 and it has no previous activities). The place P1 then has the character of an auxiliary activity with the duration of *TI*(T1, P1) = 0. Each of the tokens 0 located in the resource places R1 and R2 in the input marking M_i of the RWPNTT *RWPNET1* models the shared resource R1, resp. R2. Both resources can be used immediately after the whole process starts (because both are modeled by the token 0) and both of them will also be immediately available for further use by other process activities as soon as the respective activity using this shared resource is successfully completed (because *TI*(T2, R1) = *TI*(T2, R2) = *TI*(T2, A) = 4 and *TI*(T3, R2) = *TI*(T2, C) = 6). Therefore, if RWPNTT *RWPNET1* is in the current marking $M_2 = (\emptyset, \emptyset, 4, 2, \emptyset, 5, 4, 4, \emptyset)$, this marking then models the situation in which the activity A is performed using both R1 and R2 resources, activity B is waiting for the release of the resource R2 and activity C could be started. The token 4 at the place A expresses the fact that activity A may be terminated after 4 time units. The tokens 4 occurring at the resource places R1 and R2 that are shared by the activity A throughout this time interval have a similar meaning. The transition T3 may therefore be fired only after the (symbolic) expiration of these 4 time units and by its firing the RWPNTT *RWPNET1* will move into the marking $M_3 = (\emptyset, \emptyset, 4, \emptyset, 10, 5, 4, 10, \emptyset)$. The token 10 will be located in the place C (representing the activity C) in this marking expressing the fact that the transition T4 may be performed only after 10 time units have elapsed from the moment of the beginning of the whole process (and a similar meaning then they also have other tokens located in the respective places of the *RWPNET1*). The value of the single token that is located in the output place OP in the output marking M_o of the *RWPNET1* then expresses the value of the execution time interval required to implement the whole process, i.e., *ETI*(<T1, T2, T3, T4>) = 10 (see 1 of Definition 6).

Classic methods used for the analysis of Petri nets based on the study of the set of all the reachable states of the given RWPNTT can be used for determining the values of the minimum execution time interval *METI*, time-optimal steps *TOSTEPS* and time-optimal critical paths

TOCP (see Definition 6). It can be easily determined that the set $[M_i\rangle\rangle_o$ = {<T1, T2, T3, T4>, <T1, T3, T2, T4>}, i.e., M_i [T1⟩ M_1 [T2⟩ M_2 [T3⟩ M_3 [T4⟩ M_{o1} and M_i [T1⟩ M_1 [T3⟩ M_4 [T2⟩ M_5 [T4⟩ M_{o2}, where M_i := (M_i(IP), M_i(P1), M_i(A), M_i(B), M_i(C), M_i(D), M_i(R1), M_i(R2), M_i(OP)) = (0, ∅, ∅, ∅, ∅, ∅, 0, 0, ∅), M_1 = (∅, 0, ∅, 2, ∅, 5, 0, 0, ∅), M_2 = (∅, ∅, 4, 2, ∅, 5, 4, 4, ∅), M_3 = (∅, ∅, 4, ∅, 10, 5, 4, 10, ∅), M_4 = (∅, 0, ∅, ∅, 8, 5, 8, 8, ∅), M_4 = (∅, ∅, 12, ∅, 8, 5, 12, 12, ∅), M_{o1} = (∅, ∅, ∅, ∅, ∅, ∅, 4, 10, 10), M_{o2} = (∅, ∅, ∅, ∅, ∅, ∅, 12, 12, 12).

The presented result implies that:

- *ETI*(<T1, T2, T3, T4>) = M_{o1}(OP) = 10;
- *ETI*(<T1, T3, T2, T4>) = M_{o2}(OP) = 12;
- *METI* = *min*({10, 12}) = 10;
- *TOSTEPS* = {<T1, T2, T3, T4>};
- *TOCP* = ∅ (because ***PATHS***$_{RWPNET1}$ = {<IP, T1, P1, T2, A, T4, OP>, <IP, T1, B, T3, C, T4, OP>, <IP, T1, D, T4, OP>}, *TI*(T1, P1) + *TI*(T2, A) + *TI*(T4, OP) = 0 + 4 + 0 = 4 ≠ 10 = *METI*, *TI*(T1, B) + *TI*(T3, C) + *TI*(T4, OP) = 2 + 6 + 0 = 8 ≠ 10 = *METI*, *TI*(T1, D) + *TI*(T4, OP) = 5 + 0 = 5 ≠ 10 = *METI*).

It can therefore be stated that the sequence <T1, T2, T3, T4> represents the only one time-optimal step of RWPNTT *RWPNET1* associated with the minimal execution time interval of 10 time units. It is not without interest that in the case of RWPNTT *RWPNET1* no time-optimal critical path of the net can be found in the case of which its total time reserve is equal to zero. It is thus certainly worth noting that a given RWPNTT *RWPNET* := ((*P*, *T*, *A*, *TI*, *IP*, *OP*, *RP*), M_i) can contain *several different time-optimal critical steps* but it *does not have to contain any time-optimal critical path* (in the sense of the classic CPM method)!!!

An example of much more complicated process and the result of its analysis will be presented in the following example. The set of activities and their dependencies of this process is defined in Table 2 and its representation by RWPNTT *RWPNET2* can be seen in Figure 2. It can be shown that in the case of RWPNTT *RWPNET2*:

- *METI* = 15;
- *TOSTEPS* = {<T1, T4, T3, T7, T6, T2, T5, T8>, <T1, T4, T7, T3, T6, T2, T5, T8>, <T1, T4, T7, T3, T2, T6, T5, T8>, <T1, T4, T7, T3, T2, T5, T6, T8>};
- *TOCP* = {<IP, T1, P3, T4, C, T7, D, T6, F, T8, OP>} (because *TI*(T1, P3) + *TI*(T4, C) + *TI*(T7, D) + *TI*(T6, F) + *TI*(T8, OP) = 0 + 2 + 5 + 8 + 0 = 15 = *METI*).

From these facts then immediately follows that the process represented by the RWPNTT *RWPNET2* will be optimally finished after the time interval of 15 time units. Furthermore, it is clear that the order of sharing the resources R1, R2 and R3 by the individual activities of the given process is very important for achieving the time time-optimal critical path <IP, T1, P3, T4, C, T7, D, T6, F, T8, OP>, i.e., first, the resource R3 must be available to the activity C, then the resources R2 and R3 must be available to the activity B, and finally, the resources R1 and R2 will be shared by the activity A.

Activity	Time Duration	Previous Activities	Shared Resources
A	6	-	R1, R2
B	3	-	R2, R3
C	2	-	R3
D	5	C	-
E	4	A	R1, R2
F	8	B, D	-
G	7	C	-

Table 1 Table of activities, their time durations, dependencies and shared resources

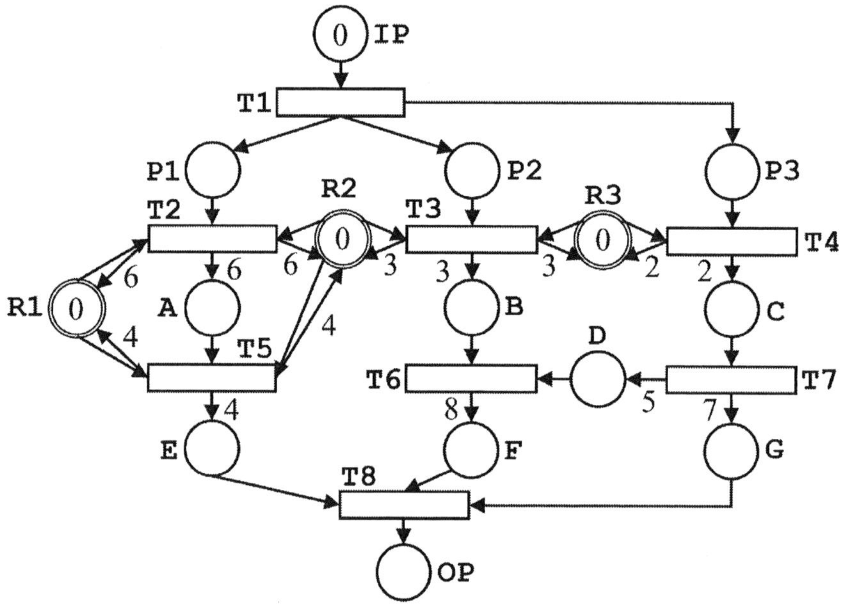

Figure 2 RWPNTT *RWPNET2* in its input marking M_i.

4 Conclusions

The definition of RWPNTT presented in this article can be further generalized and their modeling capabilities for applications in the area of processes control and their optimization can be extended, especially for modeling the temporary unavailability of individual shared resources, the ability to enter lower and upper limits of individual process activities, the possibility to enter the duration of individual process activities in the form of fuzzy numbers, etc. Finding the time-optimal critical path of such a process and verifying the properties of the RWPNTT that models this process is generally not a trivial problem and the use of Petri net theory plays a crucial role here.

Acknowledgements

This paper was supported by the Student Grant Competition project No. SP2021/86 by the Ministry of Education, Science, Research and Sport of the Czech Republic.

References

van der Alst, W. and van Hee, K. (2004). *Workflow Management: Models, Methods and Systems*. 1st ed. Massachusetts: MIT Press.

O'Brien, J., J. and Plotnick, F., L. (2016). *CPM in Construction Management*. 8th ed. New York: McGraw-Hill.

Diaz, M. (2009). *Petri Nets: Fundamental Models, Verification and Applications*. 1st ed. London: John Willey & Sons.

Furia, C. A., Mandrioli, D., Morzenti, A. and Rossi, M. (2012). *Modeling Time in Computing*. 1st ed. Heidelberg: Springer-Verlag.

van Hee, K. and Sidorova, N. (2013). 'The Right Timing: Reflections on the Modeling and Analysis of Time'. Colom, J. and Desel, J. (eds.) *Application and Theory of Petri Nets and Concurrency 2013*, Lecture Notes in Computer Science, vol. 7927, pp. 1-20.

Huang, H., Jiao, L., Cheung, T. and Mak, W., M. (2012). *Property-Preserving Petri Net Process Algebra In Software Engineering*. 1st ed. Singapore: World Scientific Publishing.

Lin, Ch-P. and Dai, H-L. (2014). 'Applying Petri Nets on Project Management'. *Universal Journal of Mechanical Engineering*, 2(8), pp. 249-255.

Martiník, I. (2018). 'Workflow Petri Nets with Time Stamps and Their Using in Project Management'. *Computer Information Systems and Industrial Management.* Lecture Notes in Computer Science, vol. 11127. pp. 193-206.

Martiník, I. (2020). 'Resource-Workflow Petri Nets with Time Stamps and Their Using in Process Management'. *Proceedings of 38th International Conference on Mathematical Methods in Economics, 9th-11th September 2020, Brno, Czech Republic, EU.* Brno, Czech Republic, pp. 364-370.

Martos-Salgado, M. and Rosa-Velardo, F. (2014). 'Dynamic Networks of Timed Petri Nets'. Ciardo, G., Kindler, E. (eds.) *Application and Theory of Petri Nets and Concurrency 2014*, Lecture Notes in Computer Science, vol. 8489, pp. 294-313.

Popova-Zeugmann, L. (2013). *Time and Petri Nets*. 1st ed. Heidelberg: Springer-Verlag.

Project Management Skills: Hard Versus Soft. Is It Enough? Technical Tools That Really Work

Lukáš Melecký[1], Michaela Staníčková[2]

Abstract. A project may be well-conceived and adequately financed, the resources may be specialists, and consultants may be highly experienced. Still, suppose the efforts of all the participants are not skillfully coordinated and managed. In that case, the project may overrun the budget, fail to meet the schedule, or fall short in functional and technical quality. The larger and more complex the project, the more critical this overall management function becomes. In general, project managers have no formal authority, though they are held responsible for the project's overall success. They are responsible for managing all stakeholder groups' interaction, each with its expectations and project success criteria. The project manager is often well served by putting their egos aside and keeping a necessary emotional distance from their work. Summarized, the position of project manager demands a comprehensive defined skill set and personality profile. The paper aims to briefly introduce the project manager's skills and specifically focus on the successful technical tools necessary for his work in today's digital age.

Keywords: Hard Skills, Project Management, Project Manager, Soft Skills, Technical Skills, Tools.

JEL Classification: C67, H43, M11, O22.

1 Introduction

Problems arise in every organization. Such issues as what products/systems to develop, should capacity be expanded, or should a computer be purchased are just a few of an endless number of continuing problems about which management must concern itself if the firm is to survive. These problems and their alternative solutions establish some elements of change around which the organization must adapt. Projects are generally found to carry out these changes, and someone is always responsible for each project's successful completion. This person is usually the **project manager**.

Every project is unique in terms of the problems that arise, the priorities and resources assigned to it, the environment in which it operates, and the project manager's attitude and style to guide and control project activities. The success of a project thus depends to some extent on the skills of the project manager. What does it mean to be a great project manager? It's not about qualifications or degrees (but those are good too, of course). It's not about merely delivering on a project manager's classic duties and responsibilities (although obviously, that's a big part of it). Those things are essential. But being a great project manager isn't just about tasks and timings. Some of the crucial project manager skills – the ones that will team the project manager feel valued, motivated, and trusted – are divided into hard and soft skills.

[1] VŠB-Technical University of Ostrava/ Faculty of Economics, Department of International Economic Relations, Sokolská třída 33, 702 00 Ostrava 1, Czech Republic, lukas.melecky@vsb.cz.

[2] VŠB-Technical University of Ostrava/ Faculty of Economics, Department of International Economic Relations, Sokolská třída 33, 702 00 Ostrava 1, Czech Republic, michaela.stanickova@vsb.cz.

In this context, it is necessary to distinguish two project management lines, i.e. **hard and soft project management**. In project management, theory and practice exist concocted debate about hard versus soft project management merits. Besides hard and soft project management skills, we must talk about **technical skills of project managers**. In today's day and age, project management is all about using the right tools and techniques. Having these two things in order can help to each project manahager manage the projects quickly and effectively. In many surveys, it has been found that using the right project management tools and techniques can increase the overall performance, productivity, and happiness-levels at work.

In this paper, we want to assess the terms hard and soft mean and why they are not in opposition to each other. Beyond these essentials, in this paper, we will discuss powerful tools and techniques to make project management much more comfortable than before. Both project management tools and techniques go together; it's important to have in-depth knowledge of both.

The above mentioned is realized through the method of literature review. A literature review is a survey of scholarly sources on a specific topic. It provides an overview of current knowledge, allowing identifying relevant theories, methods, and gaps in the existing research. A good literature review doesn't just summarize sources – it analyzes, synthesizes, and critically evaluates to give a clear picture of the state of knowledge on the subject. Such a result of the literature review is part of the paper, project management skills were introduced (hard and soft project management skills), many project management tools and techniques were further analyzed, the most relevant ones were compared and evaluated, including partial specifications and advantages and disadvantages of each of them. This comparison is made on the basis of the comparative method. Comparative research is a research methodology in the social sciences that aims to make comparisons across different topics and areas of research interest. Comparison is a fundamental tool of analysis. It sharpens powers of description, and plays a central role in concept-formation by bringing into focus suggestive similarities and contrasts among cases.

2 Project Management Competencies and Certifications

About 97% of organizations believe that adequate knowledge of project management is critical to organizational success. Unfortunately, barely over half of the project managers are certified and skilled in their tenure and career in the project management domain. Believe it or not, project management certifications can massively help you advance in your career. Organizations prefer to recruit certified professionals, but they also get to helm better projects in the future.

There are famous institutes and online portals known to offer world-class education and certifications to aspiring professionals. Once you get a certificate from a reliable institute, you become qualified to showcase your skills and expertise to companies worldwide. Being a recognized and sought-after name in an industry, you get the global acceptance and acknowledgement to work wherever you want. Let's look at some competencies as defined within different leading project management organizations.

The Project Management Institute (PMI®) identifies three different competency dimensions: knowledge, personal and performance. The knowledge as performance competencies is organized around the nine project management knowledge areas described in the Guide to the Project Management Book of Knowledge (PMBOK® Guide). The personal competencies are broken up into six areas: achievement and action, helping and human service, impact and influence, managerial, cognitive, personal effectiveness (PMI, 2017).

The European based International Project Management Association (IPMA) assesses various qualifications and competences concerning knowledge, experience, and personal attitude. The IPMA Competency Baseline (ICB) identifies 42 key competencies for knowledge and experience as well as 8 aspects for personal attitude and 10 for general impression (IPMA, 2018).

The Australian Institute for Project Management (AIPM) developed the National Competency Standards for Project Management (NCSPM) in consultation with the industry and under the auspices of the Australian National Training Authority (ANTA). The AIPM has adopted the PMBOK® Guide as the knowledge base for the NCSPM and depicts the competencies around the nine knowledge areas (AIPM, 2021).

The Japanese Engineering Advancement Association of Japan (ENAA), together with the Project Management Professionals Certification Center (PMCC) has issued a new project management Body of Knowledge (BoK) in August of 2002, the P2M Guidebook, a guidebook for Project and Program Management for Enterprise Innovation. This new project management standard is quite different from PMI's and IPMA's body of knowledge. The new standard's vision is based on "how project management can best stimulate innovation and generate improved business value." The P2M Guidebook, based on a "tower structure", is according to the Japanese Standard Committee, more aligned to the business of "management of projects" than to the European and North American BoK dedicated to the management of a single project (PMFORUM, 2000).

The different project management organizations use certification as a measure of project management competence. Certification is seen as a method to measure demonstrated ability in managing projects. There are several project management certifications in the market. PMI has two certification levels - Certified Associate in Project Management (CAPM™) and Project Management Professional (PMP). IPMA has a four-level certification program - Project Management Practitioner (PMF), Registered Project Management Professional (PMP), Certificated Project Manager (CPM), and Certificated Program Director (CPD). The Australian AIPM certification, the RegPM, is available in three levels - project team member/project specialist (QPP), project manager (RPM) and project director/program manager (MPD). P2M is the basis of Japan's certification system for project and program managers. Certification is classified according to levels of positional missions, responsibilities, and experience: Project Management Specialist (PMS), Project Manager Registered (PMR), and Project Management Architect (PMA) (PMCC, 2002).

Certification, by itself, does not qualify a candidate as a project manager. It can be used to demonstrate a commitment to the profession and evidence of a certain level of knowledge. A project management certification is a good indicator of a person's knowledge but is never guaranteed quality (Udo and Koppensteiner, 2004).

3 Hard and Soft Project Management Skills

Defining skills as either hard or soft is slightly misleading. It implies that one might be more difficult or the other less important. The truth, as always, has a nuance that the jargon misses. Anyone who has spent time in a work environment understands that the distinction between hard skills and soft skills is an artificial one, as they often overlap. Yes, the difference differentiates types of skills, and they are categorically different in many ways. However, they're two sides of the same coin. To carry that metaphor perhaps to an absurd end, that coin is the admission price into professionalism. People don't only work with technical tools but with other flesh-and-blood individuals. A combination of hard skills and soft skills is ideal for understanding methodologies and teamwork – one being useless without the other.

What are hard and soft project management skills? At its simplest, the terms hard and soft project management are usually referring to method/technique-oriented and people-oriented skills. In Figure 1 are the skills broken down into hard skills, soft skills, and traits. Combinations may arise great project manager.

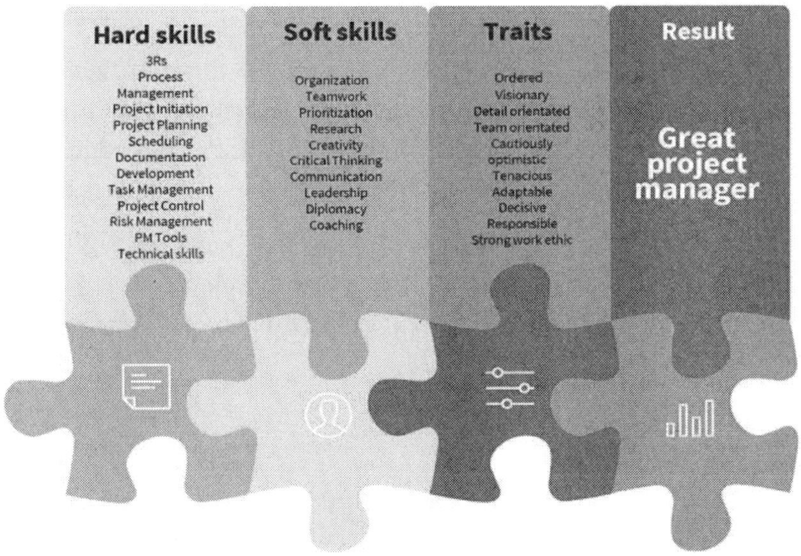

Figure 1 Project management skills list [Own elaboration, 2021]

Hard project management skills, i.e., the technical skills of analysis, planning, tracking, and problem-solving. These skills are highly project management focused and are often numerical, logical, and data-oriented. The kind of personality traits that support implementing them well are discipline, rationality, and cool rigour.

Soft project management skills, i.e., the people-oriented skills of empathy, collaboration, influence, and leadership. These skills tend to have a much broader business and social application. They are marked by high levels of' emotional intelligence', which is usually taken to be a combination of self-awareness, self-control, empathy for others' feelings and social skills. So, the sort of personality we see here is gregarious or caring, but undoubtedly good with people and enjoys being and working with them.

Don't these two personalities conflict? This is an obvious question to ask. Many models of nature set up four types:

- the hard-driving getting-things-done person
- the coldly analytical rational-thinking person
- the socially alert caring-sharing person
- the openly gregarious influential-networker person

It is easy to see hard and soft project management skills in the top two and the bottom two. But none of those models (when explained adequately) seek to place you firmly into one box. Many people do have a style that makes us more most comfortable. That's true, but each project manager can be flexible and happily adopt more than one personality style. Sometimes project manager prefers different types in different situations. The project manager can also move from one type to another. Maybe the project manager 'style' is a combination.

What seems to be true is this: *Good project management is hard and soft project management*. If the project manager wants to be a good project manager, he or she needs to deploy hard and soft project management skills. The project manager needs to be able to choose which ones to focus on at any time. And project manager also needs to switch quickly or even combine hard and soft project management approaches, as the situation merits.

Experts in project management are not sure that hard and soft project management skills truly represent two different things. Instead, they prefer to think of them as two ends of a spectrum. Like red and blue, they are easy to distinguish. But there is stuff in between that may start as hard but have a bit of soft, or seem soft, but with a little hard edge. And some project management skills are certainly both logical and emotional.

To summarize the above mentioned, a list of project management skills places them on a spectrum (Figure 2). This is not an attempt at an exhaustive list. Nor is putting on the range anything more than subjective assessment. The purpose is purely to illustrate this point of view.

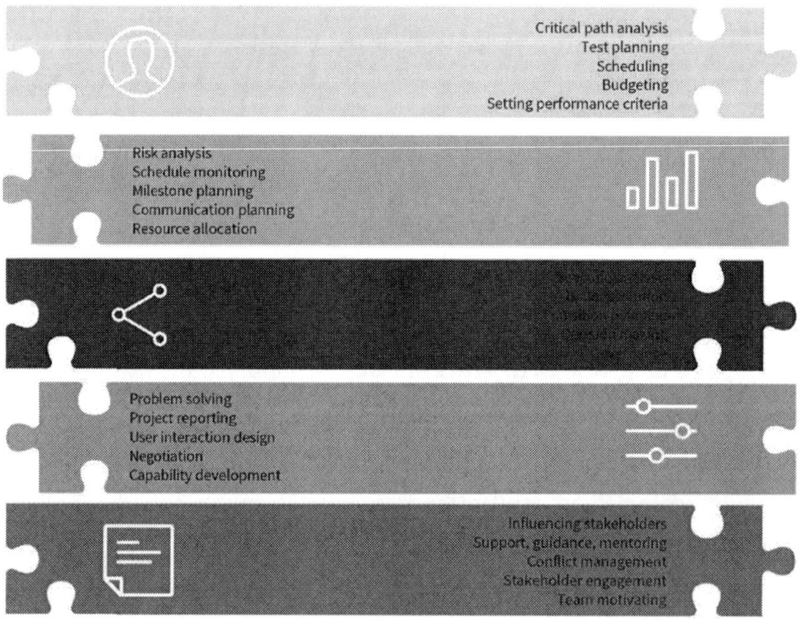

Figure 2 Project Management Skills Spectrum [Own elaboration, 2021]

4 Techniques and Practical Tools

Project management is a challenging task with many complex responsibilities. In today's day and age, project management is all about using the right tools and techniques. Having these two things in order can help to project manager manage the projects quickly and effectively. In many surveys, it has been found that using the right project management tools and techniques can increase your overall performance, productivity, and happiness-levels at work.

Fortunately, there are many tools available to assist with accomplishing the tasks and executing the responsibilities. Some require a computer with supporting software, while others can be used manually. Initially, however, some questions arise here. Why do project manager need project management techniques (and what's the difference anyway)? Why should the project manager have technical skills? At the beginning of the project, there are so many unknown variables that it's easy to feel overwhelmed. And this is where having a procedure helps: *Project management techniques are the procedure = they are the roadmap.*

When the project manager uses project management techniques, they will organize all the moving parts of the project into a logical set of tasks, leaving nothing to chance. When the project manager follows it step-by-step, they will ensure that they complete the project successfully. However, not all project management techniques were made alike. Depending on the project type and the team, the project manager will choose some of the following. He or she will not opt for the same technique every time manage a project, and that's completely fine! The preferred technique should adapt to the project – not the other way around.

Project management techniques have helped change the way project managers tackle different projects. Using a specific project management technique can help finish a project more efficiently. Before diving into tools, it should remember that all these methods will help organize and structure the project. There's no correct answer. The chosen method depends on the project manager and the project. Let's look (Figures 3a, 3b, 3c) at some leading project management tools – comparison based on Aston (2021), Kashyap (2021), Leis (2021), TechnologyAdvice (2021). Nowadays, project management tools expand their functions and cross boundaries with their combination of features, further complicating the user's selection process.

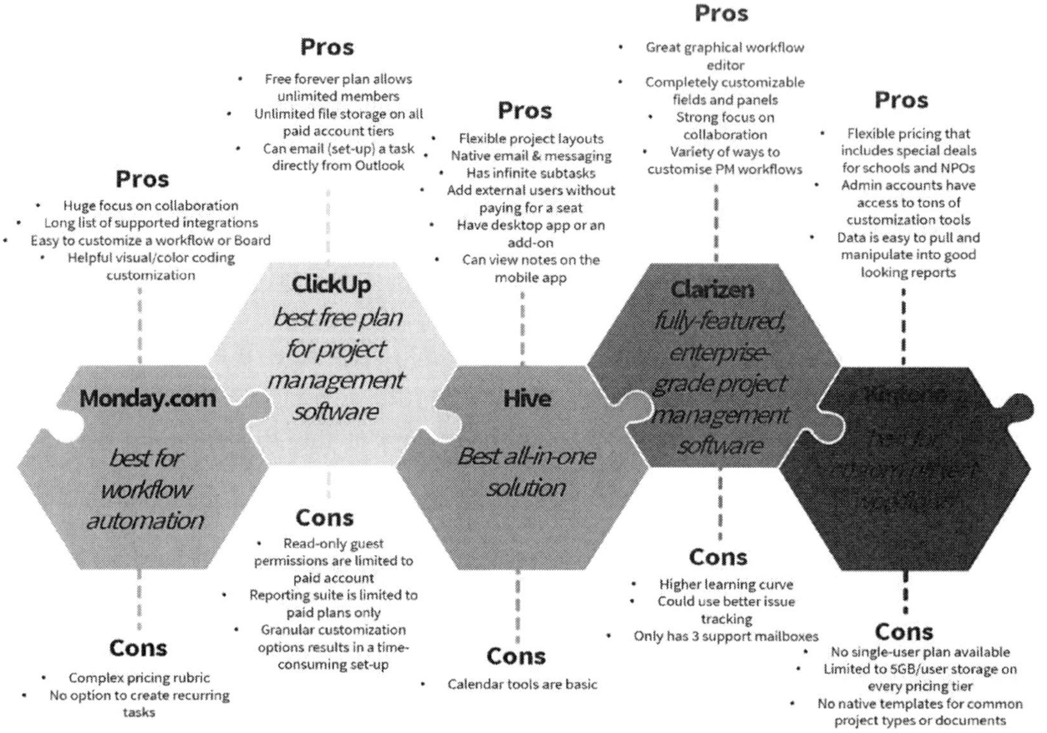

Figure 3a Project Management Software List – Part no. 1 [Own elaboration, 2021]

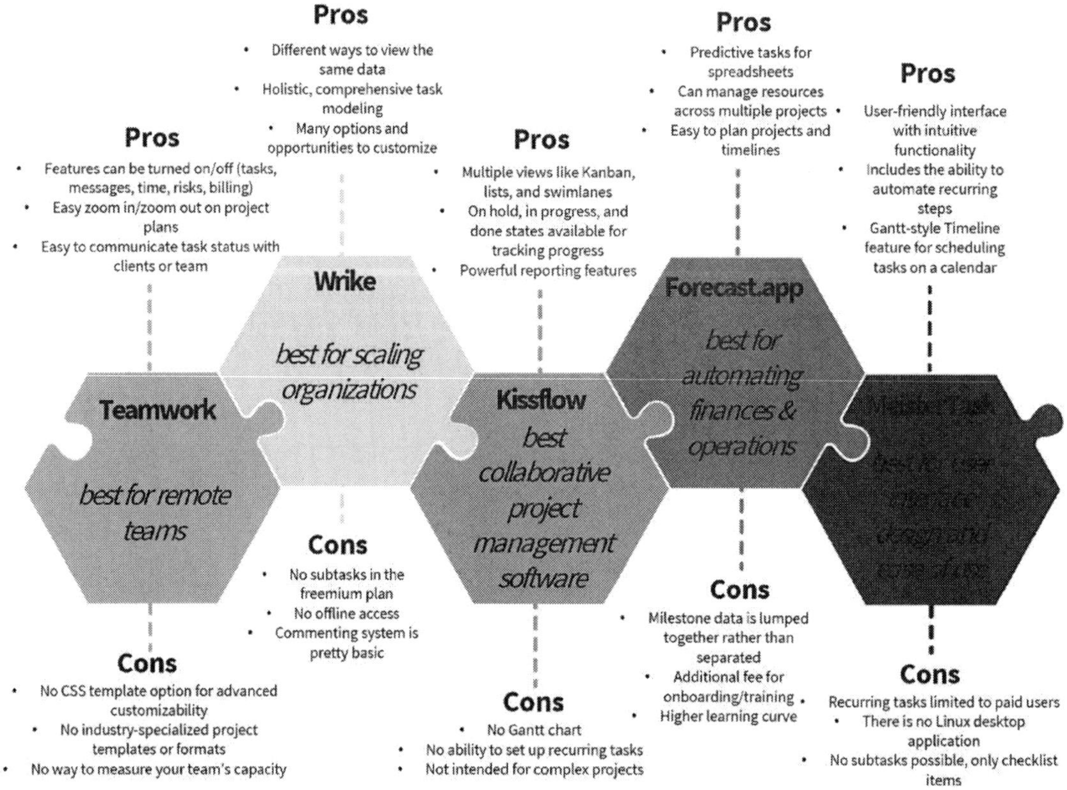

Figure 3b Project Management Software List – Part no. 2 [Own elaboration, 2021]

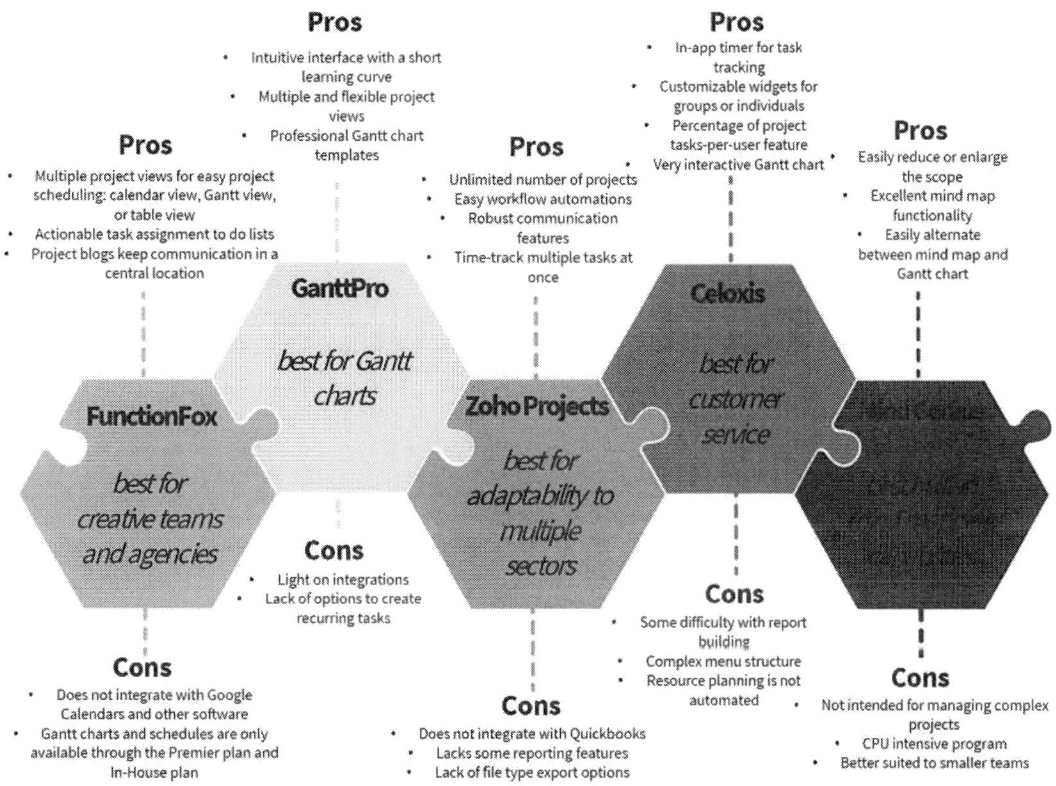

Figure 3c Project Management Software List – Part no. 3 [Own elaboration, 2021]

5 Conclusion

Different roles in project management will require other competencies. The project management environment is characterized by change, responsibilities, and required knowledge and skill levels, continuously transforming. One of the key competencies is, therefore, to be flexible and adaptive in any situation. Although certification does not qualify a project manager by itself, it indicates the candidate's knowledge of concepts and methodologies. It also shows that the candidate is dedicated to the profession. The kind of project management certification is not of primary importance.

Successful project managers can or may better demonstrate the unbiased fairness of a judge, the skills of a diplomat, the authority of a general, and the parent's understanding (McNamara, 2003).

Acknowledgements

This paper was created under "Innovation project management course" – Project 2019-1-CZ01-KA203-061373.

References

Aston, B. (2021). Compare The 15 Best Project Management Software Of 2021. [Online]. Available at: https://thedigitalprojectmanager.com/best-project-management-software/ [cited 2021-02-20].

Australian Institute of Project Management (AIPM) (2021). The 9 essential project management skills you need to be successful in 2021. [Online]. Available at: https://www.aipm.com.au/project-management-career-path/skills [cited 2021-02-20].

International Project Management Association (IPMA) (2018). *Individual Competence Baseline for Project Management*. Amsterdam: International Project Management Association.

Kashyap, V. (2021). 53 Best Project Management Tools & Software for 2021. [Online]. Available at: https://www.proofhub.com/articles/top-project-management-tools-list [cited 2021-02-20].

Leis, M. (2021). 42 Best Project Management Software and Tools (2021 Update). [Online]. Available at: https://www.scoro.com/blog/best-project-management-software-list/ [cited 2021-02-20].

McNamara, J.P. (2003). The "Neutral" Project Manager. [Online]. Available at: https://www.pmi.org/learning/library/core-competencies-successful-skill-manager-8426 [cited 2021-02-20].

PMFORUM (2000). Project Management Standards and Professional Certification. [Online]. Available at: http://www.pmforum.org/prof/standard.htm#APM [cited 2021-02-20].

Project Management Institute (PMI) (2017). *Project Manager Competency Development Framework*. Newton Square, PA: Project Management Institute.

Project Management Professionals Certification Center (PMCC) (2002). A Guidebook of Project & Program Management for Enterprise Innovation. [Online]. Available at: http://www.pmcc.or.jp/english/p2m/P2M_Summary.pdf [cited 2021-02-20].

Udo, N. and Koppensteiner, S. (2004). What are the core competencies of a successful project manager? [Online]. Available at: https://www.pmi.org/learning/library/core-competencies-successful-skill-manager-8426 [cited 2021-02-20].

TechnologyAdvice (2021). TechnologyAdvice Project Management Software Buyer's Guide. [Online]. Available at: https://technologyadvice.com/project-management/ [cited 2021-02-20].

Modern Approaches to Endpoint Protection

Jan Ministr[1], Tomas Pitner[2], Vyacheslav Chaplyha[3]

Abstract. Protecting of the endpoints has never been more important and challenging. The threat actors are becoming more and more sophisticated in their ability to exploit vulnerabilities, breach organizations' IT infrastructures, and hack into sensitive data. One of the main drivers for this phenomenon comes from the fact that in time of the coronavirus, the global workforce is pre-dominantly at home which means that work is happening at the endpoint (in the third quarter of 2020, Check Point Research saw a 50% increase in the daily average of ransomware attacks com-pared to the first half of the year). The article deals with problematic of the process of making endpoint security decisions. The article deals with the issue of determining a strategy for an effective approach to endpoint security. In the introductory part, the article deals with determining the necessary prerequisites for effective endpoint security. It then describes the key principles for choosing the right solution.

Keywords: Cyber security, endpoint, Endpoint Detection and Response (EDR), ransomware, zero-day at-tacks.

JEL Classification: M15

1 Introduction

Endpoint security is the practice of securing endpoints or entry points of end-user devices such as desktops, laptops, and mobile devices from being exploited by malicious actors and campaigns. The ensuring of cyber security is now increasingly costly for organizations. Malware threats are becoming more complex. According of Sophos study the 87% of IT managers agree that organizations lose an average of seven working days per month identifying and repairing infected computers (Sophos, 2020). In organizations, there is growing pressure to provide adequate endpoint security solutions (Moravec et al.,2017). Only 16% of information security executives today are able to collect, analyze, and respond to 75% or more of their telemetry security events today (Forbes.com, 2019). Based on these trends in recent months, the company and their security team must develop their skills and methodologies to avoid these ways of disrupting business and causing both financial and reputational damage (Danel et al, 2015). Older antivirus solutions offer insufficient protection against today's advanced threats and insufficient response rates, nor do they provide the ability to show the root cause or the damage caused (La Porte et al, 2020).

Endpoint security systems protect endpoints on a network or cloud from cyber security threats. Endpoint security can include a variety of approaches. It is important that the personnel responsible for endpoint security properly understand the threats they are trying to prevent. To determine appropriate access to security endpoints, it is essential that those responsible for cybersecurity in the organization provide the necessary initial conditions for an effective endpoint security solution (Pitner & Ministr, 2020). Based on the evaluation of the initial

[1] VSB - Technical University of Ostrava, Czech Republic; jan.ministr@vsb.cz.
[2] Masaryk University, Czech Republic; tomp@fi.muni.cz
[3] Lviv National Agrarian University, Ukraine; 4vyach@gmail.com.

conditions, it is then possible to determine the required properties of the future endpoint protection solution.

2 Necessary Prerequisites for Effective Endpoint Security

Security executives are responsible for protecting endpoints from attacks while al-lowing access from any device to any application on any network with minimal impact on the user experience (Zumerle & Smith, 2020). A solution that can protect an organization and its ever-growing number of endpoints from any attacks without disrupting business continuity requires securing the necessary prerequisites in the following 5 areas.

2.1 Anti-phishing

Current phishing emails involve highly sophisticated social engineering techniques that are designed to force endpoint users to detect sensitive data or enable fraudulent financial transactions. Anti-phishing solution enables organizations to stay ahead of cybercriminals and remove the burden of detection from the manipulated endpoints user.

Whether the field of anti-phishing meets the requirements of a modern solution, it is necessary to find out its following attributes:

- preventing proactively complex and sophisticated attacks such as zero-day phishing, impersonation, copy phishing, and business e-mail compromise;
- perform full scans of web pages and forms and in-depth heuristic analysis;
- preventing employees from reusing corporate data on non-corporate websites.

2.2 Anti-Ransomware

Ransomware, especially zero-bottom ransomware, can be very malicious because it attacks endpoints without warning, leaving the security team unprepared. In addition, ransomware can infiltrate an organization through multiple entry points, including the Web, e-mail, and removable media devices. In the United States alone, there was a 98% increase in ransomware attacks during the 3rd quarter of year 2020 (Check Point, 2020). An endpoint protection solution with advanced anti-ransomware features will allow an organization to mitigate risk and prevent a successful attack.

Whether the field of anti-ransomware meets the requirements of a modern solution, it is necessary to find out its following attributes:

- protection of the organization against sophisticated ransomware attacks on the zero day;
- an anti-ransomware module that tracks changes to files on user drives and identifies ransomware behavior, such as illegitimate file encryption;
- attack blocking and automatic recovery of encrypted files.

2.3 Content disarm and reconstruction

Here it is necessary to balance on the one hand the delay, which is caused by the control of each file that is attached to the incoming e-mail, and on the other hand their download without checking directly into the memory of endpoints. This is why an endpoint security solution must include an automatic file sanitization capability, also known as content disarm and deconstruction or threat extraction.

Whether the field of content disarm and reconstruction meets the requirements of a modern solution, it is necessary to find out its following attributes:

- ensuring that all incoming files are safe without compromising employee productivity;
- remove exploitable content from documents by disinfecting them from potentially harmful elements (cleans them and delivers a 100% sanitized version within 100 seconds).

2.4 Anti-bot capabilities

Bots represent an impressive security threat. They are often used by hackers in an Advanced Persistent Threat (APT) attack on a specific person or organization. Hackers connect bots to the organization's control servers, where they remotely control the robot and instruct it to perform illegal activities. Such robot attacks can cause data theft - personal, financial, intellectual or organizational data. To prevent these attacks, endpoint protection must include the necessary anti-bot features.

Whether the field of anti-bot capabilities meets the requirements of a modern solution, it is necessary to find out its following attributes:

- automatic detection of bot driven infection before sensitive data is exposed;
- continuous monitoring of outgoing traffic and identification of communications that take place on command and control servers to detect infected computers;
- block infected traffic, repair after the attack and isolate infected computers to prevent the possible spread of lateral infection.

2.5 Automated post-preach detection, remediation, and response

While traditional endpoint detection and response (EDR) solutions can detect suspicious behaviors, they typically have very few out-of-the-box rules nor can they perform automatic remediation. Lacking automation means that the risk of attack residuals is greater, not to mention that manual processes are time consuming and can potentially lead to greater impact. Lack of automation means that the risk of residual attacks is greater, not to mention that manual processes are time consuming. Automation is a major differentiator where security staff are scarce and there is a need for rapid detection of advanced persistent threats and to provide the fastest remediation of these (La Porte et al, 2020).

Whether the field of automated post-breach detection, and response meets the requirements of a modern solution, it is necessary to find out its following attributes:

- automatic analysis, contextualization and incident correction;
- automatic identification of the actual attack, the way the hacker got in, the impact on the business and the way the systems should be cleaned.

3 Key principles for choosing an effective endpoints protection solution

After a careful evaluation of the necessary prerequisites, it is possible to proceed to the selection of key features of the proposed effective endpoints protection solution. For a specific effective solution, it is important to go through the next key principles in detail, which can be divided into the following 5 areas.

3.1 A Prevention-first approach

Network intrusion prevention will always trump detection and remediation. Pre-venting an attack will save the organization a lot of time and money. For example, the cost of a malware attack is estimated at an average of $ 2.6 million per company (check Point, 2020). There is also always a risk of damaging brand justice and customer trust.

Whether the field of a prevention-first approach meets the requirements of a modern solution, it is necessary to find out its following attributes:

- Preventive protection with anti-phishing features, including unknown phishing sites, anti-ransomware, Content disarm a reconstruction, abuse prevention, and anti-bot features.;
- Prevention mode (except detection mode) in cases where the threat is clear and the risk is high;
- Alerting and providing users with information and knowledge in the event of detected cyber threats.

3.2 Artificial intelligence driven multilayered security

Traditional solutions, including antivirus, isolation, and legacy endpoint protection products, offer limited control and lack the structure required for such complexity. About 91% of cyber security professionals fear that hackers will use artificial intelligence in cyber-attacks against their society, which are more sophisticated and more difficult to detect. (TechRepublic, 2020). There are millions of strains of unknown malware and many sophisticated escape techniques. This means that stopping today's most dangerous attacks requires controlling more than one layer. To successfully eliminate computer criminals, the end-point protection solution must be controlled by artificial intelligence. an effective solution must be able to control every other attack area and go beyond traditional detection methods such as signatures and rules.

Whether the field of an artificial intelligence driven multilayered security meets the requirements of a modern solution, it is necessary to find out its following attributes:

- inclusion of artificial intelligence engines that perform static analysis of files and executable files to identify unknown malware before startup;
- use the collaborative knowledge base to gain access to dynamic real-time security information to provide knowledge and insights;
- the ability of the artificial intelligence engine for behavioral analysis to collect behavioral indicators from the device to correlate these indicators;
- Validity of behavior heuristics, rules and machine learning models for optimizing malware identification and classification.

3.3 Post-infection remediation and recovery

In practice, it cannot be assumed that the organization will not be affected by a cyber-attack. About 77% of more than 3,600 security and IT professionals surveyed, suggesting they do not have a cyber security incident response plan (Hardcastle, 2019). Therefore, it is essential for the organization to be prepared with the latest capabilities after infection for repair and recovery.

Whether the field of post-infection remediation and recovery meets the requirements of a modern solution, it is necessary to find out its following attributes:

- automatic quarantine of infected computers to prevent the attack from spreading by lateral movement across the corporate network;
- continuous monitoring and recording of endpoint events. This would be a phase involving the affected files, running processes, changes to the system registry, and network activities;
- automatic remediation and sterilization of the entire cyber kill chain in order to re-store the device to the last clean point;
- inclusion of advanced incident response algorithms and the possibility of deep analysis of raw forensic data;
- complete recovery of ransomware encrypted files;
- proactive threat detection with a mechanism for recording endpoint events for long-term preservation.

3.4 Unified and cloud-based management

Securing endpoints becomes more complex when multiple solutions from multiple vendors must be managed. By 2022, 60% of organizations that use Endpoint Detection and Response (EDR) capabilities will use endpoint protection solutions from the same vendor or managed detection and response services. (Firstbrook, 2020). In a recent survey, 99% of security experts agree that using solutions from several security vendors poses unnecessary challenges. And 69% agree to prioritize consolidation of vendors to achieve better security (Glesson, 2020).

Whether the field of unified and cloud-based management meets the requirements of a modern solution, it is necessary to find out its following attributes:

- integration into the network;
- integration into the cloud infrastructure;
- integration into the mobile security infrastructure.

3.5 Consolidated security and threat intelligence architecture

The benefits of the cloud are well known - from flexibility to flexibility, scalability and speed. An endpoint protection solution that serves as a single unified agent simplifies processes, simplifies management, and reduces total cost of ownership. By 2025 cloud solutions will grow from 20% of new business to 95% (BCSG, 2015). The benefits of the cloud are well known - from flexibility to scalability and speed.

Whether the field of consolidated security and threat intelligence architecture meets the requirements of a modern solution, it is necessary to find out its following attributes:

- unification of endpoint protection, data protection and web browsing protection solutions;
- cloud establishment and monitoring of devices and policies;

- ensuring complete redundancy;
- flexible deployment options for the cloud;
- on-Premise, where the software runs on computers, which allows greater control over the availability of the entire system.

4 Characteristics of modern security endpoint solutions

4.1 Assessment of option the techniques of endpoint protection

Antivirus solutions are proven to be very effective against known threats. But there are two groups of techniques which we can use in innovation:

- Traditional techniques with endpoint protection solutions.
- New techniques which identify unknown threats, such as malware that has never been seen before, have become more and more common. The combination of both above techniques, often referred to as "next-gen", appears as optimal solution of end point security.

When organization evaluates endpoint innovation, they should not just prefer for one primary feature. Relying on one dominant feature, even if it is best-in-class, means that the innovation solution is vulnerable to single point of failure. Conversely, a defense-in-depth approach, where there is a collection of multiple strong security layers, will stop a wider range of threats. This is what it often refers to as "the power of the plus", as a combination of foundational techniques with machine learning, anti-exploit, anti-ransomware, EDR, plus much more.

4.2 Comparison and evaluation of available endpoint characteristics

Comparing products with different features is hard enough, but comparing their performance in simulated attacks, where an attacker's actions are potentially infinite and unknown, is nearly impossible (Doucek et al, 2018b). Therefore, many organizations choose to rely on third party assessments to aid their buying decisions.

Various evaluations are available to organizations in the selection of endpoint innovation solutions in the form of comparative tables and graphs, as shown in Table 1.

Supplier	Malware protection rate
Avast, Bitdefender, Panda, Sophos, SparkCognition	99,9%
Cisco, Symantes, Trend Micro	99,8%
K7, McAfee	99.7%
Segride	99.6%
FireEis, Microsoft, ESET	99.5%

Table 1 Test of AV-Comparatives Business Security, source: according Intercept X.

One of the possible and simple ways to evaluate the endpoint innovation solution is to obtain answer to the following 10 questions (criteria) about the evaluated products:

1) Does the product rely on foundational techniques, modern techniques, or a combination of both? Which specific features are core to the technology?
2) How does the product detect unknown threats? Does it utilize machine learning?
3) For products claiming to leverage machine learning, what type of machine learning is used? Where does the training data come from? How long has the model been in production?
4) What technology exists to prevent exploit-based and file-less attacks? What antiexploit techniques are leveraged, and what types of attacks can they detect?
5) Does the product have technology specifically designed to stop ransomware?
6) Does the vendor have third party results validating their approach?
7) Does the product have an acceptable level of false positives? If a false positive is detected, how easy is it to reduce its impact?
8) What visibility into an attack does the vendor provide, such as root cause analysis?
9) Does the product automatically respond to a threat? Can it automatically clean up a threat and respond to an incident?
10) What level of effort is involved in the deployment and use of the innovation solution?

The importance of individual criteria is based on specific security needs as well as the customer's financial capabilities. The above described criteria can be for example evaluated using the method of pairwise comparison and alternatives will be evaluated by maximize utility evaluation. The product that best meets the given security criteria is then the most suitable for the given customer.

4.3 The endpoint solution value

The endpoint innovation solution should add value to the whole business and an effective solution that will enable:

- reducing cyber risk so that reduce attack exposure and significantly increase response time in case of infection (Caravelli & Jones, 2019), (Nyemkova et al., 2020);
- increasing visibility with gaining deeper and wider insight into safety of property, it allowing to make informed and accurate decisions (Diogenes & Ozkala, 2019);
- increasing productivity so that it reduces the impact of computer security on the IT team and users throughout the organization (Doucek et al, 2018a);
- saving money by switching from point products to a computer security system what allows to reduce on-board costs, integration and training, as well as day-to-day system management overhead. Reseller consolidation also benefits from non-IT functions such as purchasing and legal;
- displaying security value what reduce time spent solving everyday problems, a computer security system can free up IT teams to work on business-oriented projects. Increased protection and resulting reduction of user downtime also allows a wider organization to appreciate the value of security (Pavlicek & Střížová, 2017).

5 Discussion

The endpoint protection domain is one that is full of complexity and challenges. The number and complexity of endpoints is constantly growing. There is also a growing number of technically proficient cybercriminals using increasingly sophisticated attacks. They have never been more sophisticated. Therefore, it is necessary to use midpoint protection of endpoints.

By combining and adopting the attributes of the modernized endpoint protection approach described in chapters 3 and 4, security teams can be confident that they are using the most robust approach.

The list of 10 basic security criteria in Chapter 4.2 is open and can be expanded based on new security threats. Another open research problem, which is based on this concept, is the design of a simple decision-making method of evaluating a suitable security solution for the customer.

6 Conclusion

The company's organizational management should now consider innovating the protection of the entire digital environment. When addressing and implementing end-point security, management must know that this is only one part of the overall security strategy. Some specific technologies that need to be considered along with endpoint protection innovations include full disk encryption, mobile device management, mobile device security, etc.

From a customer perspective, it is good for one vendor to provide innovative solutions that together create consistent protection and enforcement solutions across the organization. Working with a vendor can provide better security, reduce management, and reduce costs.

References

BCSG. (2015). The small business revolution: trends in SMB cloud adoption, [Online]. Available at https://www.bcsg.com/wp-content/uploads/2015/03/The-small-business-revolution-trends-in-SMB-cloud-adoption.pdf [cited 2020-12-10].

Caravelli, J.; Jones, N. (2019). *Cyber Security Threads and responses for Government and Business*. Santa Barbara, USA: Prageger.

Check Point. (2020) Check Point Software Technologies Reports Third Quarter 2020 Financial Results, [Online]. Available at https://www.checkpoint.com/press/2020/check-point-software-technologies-reports-third-quarter-2020-financial-results/ [cited 2021-1-1].

Danel, R. et al. (2015). 'Information Support for Sales Management in the Company OKD a. s.' *Proceedings of 11th International Conference on Strategic Management and its Support by Information Systems*, Uherské Hradiště, Czech Republic, pp. 46-54.

Diogenes, Y.; Ozkala, E. (2019). *Cyber security - attack and Defense Strategies, 2nd edition*. Birmingham: UK: Pakt Publishing.

Doucek, P.; Kuncová, M. and Nedomová, L. (2018a). 'The penetration of ICT into the economy - technical infrastructure in the V4 countries '. *Proceedings of 12th IFIP WG 8.9 Working Conference on Research and Practical Issues of Enterprise Information Systems: CONFENIS 2018*, Poznan, Poland, pp. 69-78.

Doucek, P, Pavlicek, A. and Luc, L. (2018b). 'Internet of thigs or surveillance of things?' *Proceedings of 1th IFIP WG 8.9 Working Conference on Re-search and Practical Issues of Enterprise Information Systems, CONFENIS 2017*, Shangai, China, pp. 45-55.

Firstbrook, P. (2020). Market Guide for Endpoint Detection and Response Solutions, [Online]. Available at https://www.gartner.com/en/documents/3894086/market-guide-for-endpoint-detection-and-response-solutio [cited 2021-1-21].

Forbes.com. (2019) Chief information security officer priorities for 2019, [Online]. Available at https://www.forbes.com/sites/oracle/2019/01/17/chief-information-security-officer-priorities-for-2019/#62641d8a6937 [cited 2020-10-1].

Gleeson, B. (2020). Cutting complexity to strengthen security: why consolidation matters, [Online]. Available at https://blog.checkpoint.com/2020/06/12/cutting-complexity-to-strengthen-security-why-consolidation-matters/ [cited 2020-12-3].

Hardcastle Lyons, J. (2019). IBM: 77% of Enterprises Don't Have a Cybersecurity Incident Response Plan, [Online]. Available at https://www.sdxcentral.com/articles/news/ibm-77-of-enterprises-dont-have-a-cybersecurity-incident-response-plan/2019/04/ [cited 2021-1-15].

La Porte, B. et al. (2020). Market Guide for Endpoint Detection and Response Solutions, [Online]. Available at https://www.gartner.com/en/documents/3978685/market-guide-for-endpoint-detection-and-response-solutio [cited 2020-10-20].

Moravec, L. et al. (2017) 'Application of the Cyber Security Act in Havířovská teplárenská společnost, a.s'. *In Proceedings of the 12th International Conference on Strategic Management and its Support by Information Systems, (SMSIS 2017).* Ostrava: VSB – Technical University of Ostrava, pp. 425-433.

Nyemkova, E. et all; (2020). 'Advanced Methods and Means of Authentication of Devices'. *In: Lecture Notes on Data Engineering and Communications Technologies: Business Information Data-Centric Business and Applications.* Cham, Germany, 205-228.

Pavlicek, A. Střížová, V. (2017). 'Cross culture differences on Facebook'. *Proceedings of 25th Interdisciplinary Information Management Talks: Digitalization in Management, Society and Economy, IDIMT 2017.* Podebrady, Czech Republic, pp. 137-146.

Pitner, T., Ministr, J. (2020). 'Innovations for future energy security'. *Proceedings of 28th Interdisciplinary Information Management Talks: Digitalized Economy, Society and Information management, IDIMT 2020.* Kutna Hora, Czech Republic, pp. 85-92.

Sophos. (2020). The Dirty Secrets of Network Firewalls, [Online]. Available at https://www.insight.com/en_US/content-and-resources/brands/sophos/the-dirty-secrets-of-network-firewalls-infographic.html [cited 2020-10-20].

TechRepublic, (2020). 91% of cybersecurity pros fear hackers will use AI to attack their company, [Online]. Available at https://www.techrepublic.com/article/91-of-cybersecurity-pros-fear-hackers-will-use-ai-to-attack-their-company/ [cited 2021-1-10].

Zumerle, D, Smith, R. (2020). Hype Cycle for Endpoint Security, [Online]. Available at https://www.gartner.com/en/documents/3987589/hype-cycle-for-endpoint-security-2020 [cited 2020-10-29].

Impact of the first wave of Covid-19 on the trends of ICT Professionals' wages in the Czech Republic

Lea Nedomova[1], Petr Doucek[1]

Abstract. The article discusses the impact of the first wave of Covid-19 on the trend of ICT Professionals' wages in the Czech Republic. The first goal of the article is to analyze the impact of the first wave of Covid-19 on the trend of ICT Professionals' wages in the Czech Republic. We analyzed also gender pay gap also based on it as the second goal of the article. For analyzing the wage trend, we used data from Trexima, a.s. for the years 2016-2020. We used standard MS Excel tools to analyze the obtained time series data. The results show that the impact of the first wave of Covid-19 on the nominal gross wages of ICT Professionals was minimal. We have also found out that the gender gap pay still exists. However, the positive information is that the gender pay gap decreased during the analyzed time period and that the trend lines also indicate its decrease in the future - the average wage by 3.7 percentage points and the median wage by 3.7 percentage points as well.

Keywords: ICT Professionals, nominal gross wages in ICT, Gender Pay Gap, first wave of Covid 19.

JEL Classification: C82, E24, E64, J16, L86

1 Introduction

The relatively harmonious trend of the world global economy was disrupted at the end of 2019 and the beginning of 2020 by the Covid-19 pandemic that impacted the economy and all its industries (Cotula, 2021; Leach et al, 2021). Many industries were hit hard by the pandemic, while other industries not so much (Dutta and Fischer, 2021). The impact of the pandemic on economies is discussed in various articles and studies, such as (Cvetkovic, Nesovic and Terzic, 2021; Chudik et al, 2020; Adam, Henstridge and Lee, 2020; Ozili and Arun, 2020) analyzing the impact on world global economy and (Albu et al, 2020) analyzing the impact on the Czech economy. Covid-19 was at the forefront of interest in healthcare (Gautam and Hens, 2020), energy supply (Cvetkovic, Nesovic and Terzic, 2021) as well as in ICT, where the majority of articles discussed the ethical handling of information and the dissemination of fake news (Gonzales, Cueva and Tafur, 2021) or hoax (da Silva, Medeiros and Correo, 2021). The economic impact of the pandemic will also be felt in human resources, unemployment and employees' remuneration. New emerging trends, such as home office, require less transport and transport services (Ortiz et al, 2021) and save employees' commute time that can be spent on other things.

The specific impact of Covid 19's impact is on employees' wages and on the labor market. Let's start with the analyzes (O'Keeffe, Johnson and Daley, 2021) - the analysis dealt with the impact of Covid 19 on employment and income of young generation, (Wong and Wong, 2021) - the analysis deal with the change in financing state projects due to the Covid 19 epidemic and

[1] Prague University of Economics and Business, Department of System Analysis, W. Churchill sq. 1938/4, Prague, Czech Republic, doucek@vse.cz, nedomova@vse.cz

last but not least analysis (Ranchhod and Daniels 2021) that addressed the impact of Covid 19 on the labor market.

In relation to those above mentioned analyzes, we formulated more questions related to the first wave of the epidemic, which we wanted to answer in our research. One part of them focused on the development of wages at ICT Professionals ICT Managers (CZ_ISCO 133), ICT Specialists (CZ_ISCO 25) and ICT Technicians (CZ_ISCO 35). The specifications and job descriptions of individual groups of ICT Professionals are available in (CZSO, 2020a). Another group of questions were focused on the gender pay gap. The problem of equal pay for equal work has been the subject of studies by Western society for over seventy years.

2 Problem Formulation

Given the changes in the functioning of the Czech economy, especially during the first wave of the pandemic in the spring, we wanted to know how the first closure of the Czech economy affected employees working in information and communication technologies (ICT) - ICT Professionals. In our article, which is based on our research, we formulated the following Research Questions:

- **RQ1 – How did the first wave of Covid-19 impact the trend of gross wages of ICT Professionals?**

When processing the data, we have discovered a significant gap in wages of ICT Professionals working in the business sector and those working in the non-business sector. This is why, we formulated our second Research Question.

- **RQ2 – How big is the gap in wages of ICT Professionals working the business sector and the non-business sector?**

When analyzing the wages of men and women, we formulated our third Research Question for a very similar reason. Our workplace has focused on this issue for a long time, and RQ 3 was thus only a logical consequence of our previous analyses.

- **RQ3 – What is the trend of the gender pay gap among ICT Professionals?**

3 Methodology a Data Collection

In the area of methodology, two areas were decisive, namely the **collection of data** for our analyzes and **the tools and procedures** with which we analyzed the data.

3.1 Data Collection

The data we used for our analysis come from Trexima, a.s. that processes i.e. AEIS (Average Earnings Information System) (ISPV, 2020). The survey is harmonized with the European Union's structural survey called „The Structure of Earnings Survey ", conducted based on Commission Regulation no. 1916/2000. The file contains data about earnings in the second quarter of each year because it includes the highest number of available workhours and a minimum number of national holidays and thus these earnings reflect the most the basic salaries or wages. This annual survey is managed by the Ministry of Labor and Social Affairs. In our analyses, we worked with a sample of data for ICT Professionals ranging from 53,473 records in 2016 to 70,494 records in 2020. Every record provides information about the wage of an employee – ICT Professional – in the Czech Republic.

3.2 Used Methodology

We analyzed the data extracted from the AEIS for the entire group of ICT Professionals (CT Managers, ICT Specialists and ICT Technicians). We also have partial analyses for groups of profession, but - due to the limited space for our article - we may present them during our own conference. When analyzing the trend of wages of ICT Professionals, we came across a significant difference between wages in the business sector and the non-business sector, and therefore we added this dimension to our analyses. Gender, i.e. the pay gap between women and men, is another dimension that we analyzed. We performed the entire analysis for the years 2016–2020, mainly due to the consistency of data obtained in this structure starting the year 2016.

The analyzed data include gross wages in Czech Crowns. We analyzed both the average wage and the median wage since the median wage better reflects the actual situation in wages because the average wage can be skewed by a relatively small number of high wages (this is mainly true for ICT Managers). Another limitation of the data file is that it includes wages up to 100,000 CZK. Any monthly income exceeding this amount is included in the 100,000 CZK bracket. We analyzed the obtained data using MS Excel tools and statistical functions.

4 Results

The presented results of our time series analysis are divided into three main sections, which correspond to our Research Questions, and there is then a summary discussion in the Discussion section.

4.1 Trend of gross wages of ICT Professionals

The data answering RQ1 are provided in Figure 1.

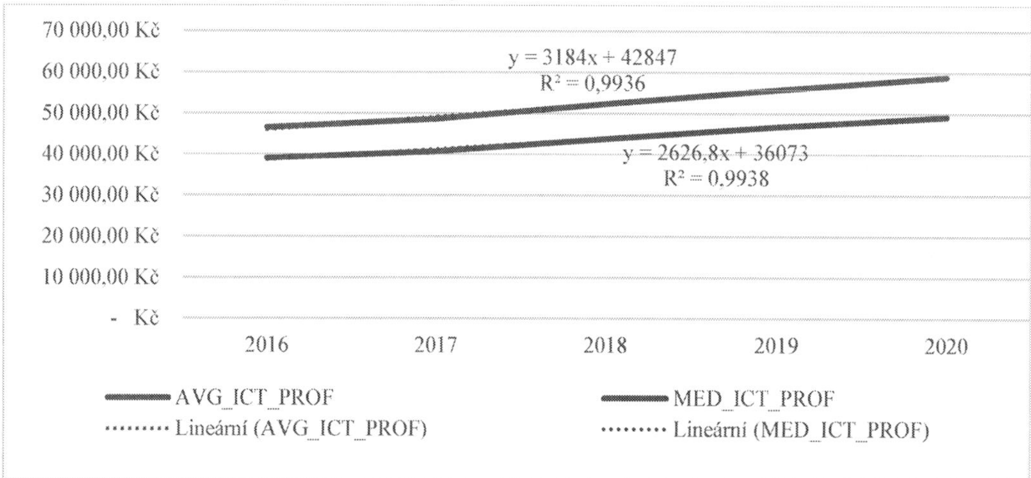

Figure 1 Trend of gross wages of ICT Professionals during 2016–2020

Figure 1 clearly shows a constantly growing trend of wages of ICT Professionals in the CR since 2016. And we can see that the average wage is higher than the median wage.

4.2 Trend of a gap in wages of ICT Professionals working in the business section and the non-business section

As we can see from Figure 2, the business sector is the main driver of the growing wages of ICT Professionals.

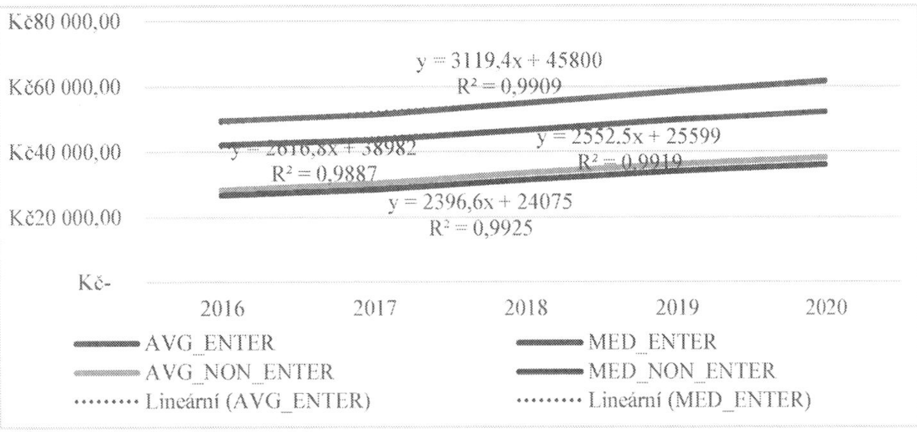

Figure 2 Trend of a pay gap in the business sector and the non-business sector during 2016–2020

Figure 2 again shows the trend of the average wage and the median wage over time. At first glance, it is clear that wages in the business sector significantly exceed wages in the non-business sector. A more detailed analysis shows that wages in the non-business sector represent only 60% of the business sector in terms of the average wage and approximately 67% in terms of the median wage. We did not see any significant change in the wage trend due to the first wave of Covid-19 at the beginning of 2020. Wage growth, i.e. the interpolated line has an upward slope (positive coefficient) and the estimate confidence level is above 0.98 for all functions.

4.3 Trend of the gender pay gap among ICT Professionals

Another relatively often analyzed quantity is the gap between men's and women's wages - the so-called gender pay gap. Let's look at this issue from two different perspectives. The first one is the trend of men's and women's wages in the years 2016–2020. The trend is clear - the wages of men and women keep growing (Figure 3). The actual trend of the Gender Pay Gap is shown in Figure 4.

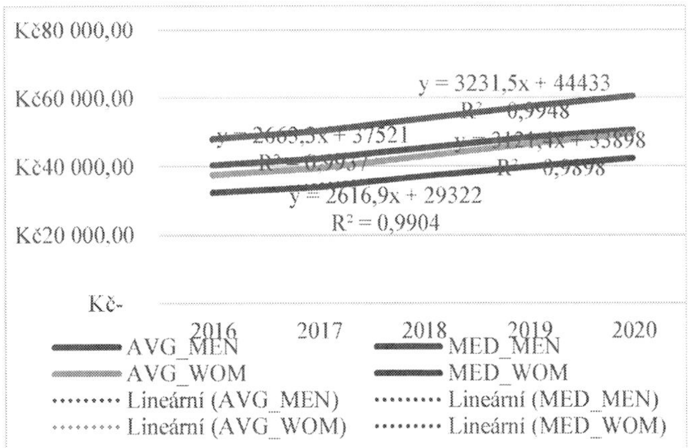

Figure 3 Trend of the gender pay gap among ICT Professionals during 2016–2020

Both the average wage and the median gross wage clearly show a gender pay gap. The trend of time series data shows that wages are steadily growing – the estimate confidence level is always above 0.98. Interestingly, the trend of the median wage of men slowed down in comparison to the average wage in 2020 and approached the average wage of women. The trend line slope of women's average wages is also higher than that of men's median wages. Thus, we can assume that these two quantities will be the same in a very short time – approximately in the year 2023.

The trend of the gender pay gap is shown in Figure 4.

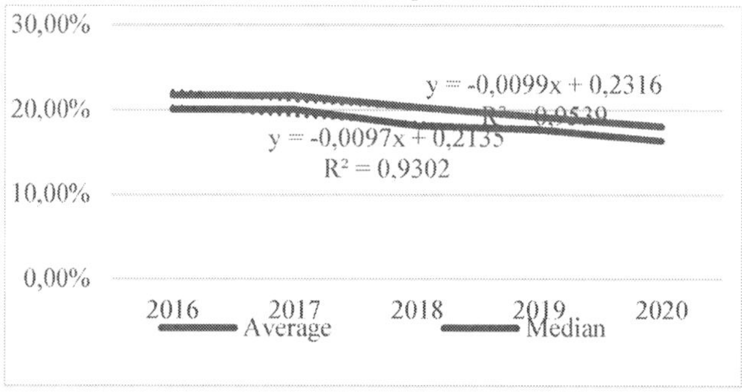

Figure 4 Trend of the gender pay gap among ICT Professionals during 2016-2020

There is an obvious positive trend that is gradually moving towards the equalization of wages of female and male ICT Professionals. It is also important to add that the Czech Republic is one of the countries with the highest gender pay gap and has failed to reduce this gap at the national level for quite some time. The ICT profession is one of the few professions that are slowly but surely improving this unfavorable situation.

5 Discussion

When working with the data, we realized some of their limitations. The ISPV file contains data for more than 2,000,000 employees for each year of the analyzed time period, which provides a very good picture of wages in the Czech economy. We have approximately 50,000 to 70,000 records for ICT Professionals for each year, which represents approximately 2.5% - 3.5% of the entire sample. According to the latest CZSO data (CZSO, 2020b), ICT Professionals represent approximately 3.9% of all employees in the Czech Republic (in 2018, more current data are not available). Thus, the ICT Professionals sample very well represents their share in the total number of employees.

The data for the non-business sector represent approximately 12.5% of all records, which presents some problem for analyzing the gap between the non-business sector and the business sector. Based on the data from the Czech Statistical Office, employees in the non-business sector in the CR represent approximately 17.72% (CNB, 2021). Thus, the business sector is significantly more represented, and the aggregates for ICT Professionals are thus closer to the values of the business sector.

Another problem is the number of records for women. Our previous surveys (Nedomova, Maryska and Doucek, 2017) show that women currently represent about 10% of all ICT Professionals. The file that we obtained for our analysis included 16.14% of records concerning women.

Our detailed analyses are mainly limited by the fact that wages are placed into brackets by 500 CZK from 0 to 100,000 CZK. Wages exceeding 100,000 CZK are lumped into one bracket "over 100,000 CZK." Therefore, it is impossible to separate the trend of monthly wages over 100,000 CZK since we can analyze only an increase in the number of records in this bracket and not records for, e.g. wages over 200,000 CZK and any potential higher wages. Interestingly, in 2020 there was 1.66% of such records for the Czech economy.

The first wave of Covid-19 did not have any impact on the trend of wages of ICT Professionals, mainly due to the fact that the data were collected too close to this first wave. Organizations did not respond to the change because they believed it was a short-lived episode that would not last long. Besides, the first wave resulted in an increase, rather than a decrease, in demand for the work of ICT Professionals. Therefore, the wages of ICT Professionals are expected to grow in 2021.

Gender pay gap is one of the most important priorities of the European Union's social policy. Our previous surveys show that the gender pay gap in the Czech Republic in 2018 was approximately 20% (Eurostat, 2020). The gender pay gap in the European Union in 2018 was around 10%. The gender pay gap among ICT Professionals is roughly the same in terms of the average wage and lower by two percentage points in terms of the median wage. Another survey, which we conducted and which focuses on the gender pay gap by age in three categories up to 30 years, 30-50 years and over 50, shows that the gender pay gap is significantly lower among younger ICT Professionals - around 0% - 5%. This fact is good news for a further reduction in the gender pay gap among ICT Professionals.

6 Conclusions

The conclusions of our article recapitulate and summarize the findings to our Research Questions in the Results section.

RQ1 – How did the first wave of Covid-19 impact the trend of gross wages of ICT Professionals?

Based on our findings, the first wave of Covid-19 did not have any impact on the trend of gross wages of ICT Professionals, both in terms of the average wage and the median wage. The wage trend followed the trend that started in 2016. This fact is also supported by the 0.99 confidence level of the interpolated linear function.

RQ2 – How big is the gap in wages of ICT Professionals working the business sector and the non-business sector?

The trend of the percentage of the non-business sector's wages in the business sector's wages is shown in Table 1. The two identified perspectives are provided here.

Table 1 shows that the absolute gap between the average wage and the median wages in the business sector and the non-business sector is increasing, but given the steady increase of wages in both categories, it is clear that percentage-wise wages in the non-business sector are very slowly approaching wages in the business sector. During the analyzed time period, the gap in terms of the average wage decreased by 4.66 percentage points and in terms of the median wage by 5.42 percentage points. However, the gap between the non-business sector and the business sector widened in terms of absolute numbers, as the last two columns in Table 1 indicate.

Year	Percentage		Absolutely	
	Average	Median	Average	Median
2016	57,21%	63,47%	21 181,48 Kč	15 385,25 Kč
2017	58,79%	64,99%	21 169,62 Kč	15 272,40 Kč
2018	60,99%	67,42%	21 436,46 Kč	15 164,76 Kč
2019	61,91%	68,24%	22 238,56 Kč	15 792,63 Kč
2020	61,87%	68,89%	23 481,81 Kč	16 225,95 Kč

Table 1 Trend of wages of ICT Professionals working in the business sector and the non-business sector

RQ3 – What is the trend of the gender pay gap among ICT Professionals?

Table 2 (Figure. 4) shows that the trend of the gender pay gap slowly diminished during 2016–2020. During the analyzed time period, the gender pay gap among ICT Professionals dropped by 3.69 percentage points in terms of the average wage and by 3.67 percentage points in terms of the median wage.

Year	Average	Median
2016	21,75%	20,02%
2017	21,68%	20,04%
2018	20,32%	18,09%
2019	19,15%	17,67%
2020	18,06%	16,35%

Table 2 Trend of wages of ICT Professionals – Gender Pay Gap

This conclusion is positive because the equalization of wages of women and men is one of the main objectives of the European Union's social policy. This year, we will expand the obtained data for the data from the second quarter of 2021 and analyze the impact of the second wave of the Covid-19 epidemic. The data from 2021 will show us the future trend.

Acknowledgements

Paper was processed with contribution of long-term support of scientific work on Faculty of Informatics and Statistics, University of Economics, Prague (IP 400040).

References

Adam, C., Henstridge, M. and Lee, S. (2020). The impact of global economic disruption is as big a threat to low-income countries as the direct effects of COVID-19, [Online]. Available at: https://voxeu.org/article/impact-global-economic-disruption-big-threat-low-income-countries-direct-effects-covid-19 [cited 2021-01-20].

Albu, L. L., Preda, C. I., Lupu, R., Dobrotă C. E., Călin, G. M. and Boghicevici, C. M. (2020). Estimates of Dynamics of the Covid-19 Pandemic and of Its Impact on the Economy. *Romanian Journal of Economic Forecasting,* 23 (2), pp. 5-17.

Chudik, A., Mohaddes, K., Pesaran, M. H., Raissi M. and Rebucci, A. (2020). Economic consequences of Covid-19: A counterfactual multi-country analysis, [Online]. Available at:

https://voxeu.org/article/economic-consequences-covid-19-multi-country-analysis [cited 2021-01-20].

CNB. (2021). *Nepodnikatelská sféra (Průměrný evidenční počet zaměstnanců-osob, roční data) - ekonomika ČNB.* [Online]. Available at: https://www.kurzy.cz/cnb/ekonomika/osob-rocni-data/nepodnikatelska-sfera/ [cited 2021-01-14].

Cotula, L. (2021). Towards a political economy of the COVID-19 crisis: Reflections on an agenda for research and action. *World Development*, 138, DOI: 10.1016/j.worlddev.2020.105235

Cvetkovic, D., Nesovic, A. and; Terzic, I. (2021). Impact of people's behavior on the energy sustainability of the residential sector in emergency situations caused by COVID-19. *Energy and Buildings,* 230, DOI: 10.1016/j.enbuild.2020.110532

CZSO. (2020a). *Klasifikace zaměstnání (CZ-ISCO).* [Online]. Available at: https://www.czso.cz/csu/czso/klasifikace_zamestnani_-cz_isco- [cited 2021-01-14].

CZSO. (2020b). *Digitální ekonomika v číslech – 2020.* [Online]. Available at: https://www.czso.cz/csu/czso/digitalni-ekonomika-v-cislech-2020

da Silva, M. A., Medeiros, F. B. and Correo, K. A. C. (2021). Covid-19 and fake news: analysis of the veryfyed news at the website "Fact or fake". *CHASQUI-REVISTA LATINOAMERICANA DE COMUNICACION,* 145, pp. 119-136

Dutta, A. and Fischer, H. W. (2021). The local governance of COVID-19: Disease prevention and social security in rural India, *World Development*, 138, DOI: 10.1016/j.worlddev.2020.105234

Eurostat. (2020). *Gender pay gap in unadjusted form by NACE Rev. 2 activity - structure of earnings survey methodology. online data code: EARN_GR_GPGR2.* Available at: https://ec.europa.eu/eurostat/databrowser/view/EARN_GR_GPGR2/default/table?lang=en [cited 2021-01-14].

Gautam, S. and Hens, L. (2020). COVID-19: impact by and on the environment, health and economy. *Environment, Development and Sustainability*, 22, pp. 4953–4954. DOI: 10.1007/s10668-020-00818-7.

Gonzales, M. M. P., Cueva, M. A. L. and Tafur, R. D. A. (2021). The health network and its participation in the dissemination or containment of fake news and hoaxes related to COVID-19: the case of Lima-Peru. *Chasqui-Revista Latinoamericana de Comunicacion,* 145, pp. 89-114.

ISPV. (2020). *Informační systém o průměrném výdělku.* Retrieved from https://www.ispv.cz /

Leach, M., MacGregor, H., Scoones, I. and Wilkinson, A. (2021). Post-pandemic transformations: How and why COVID-19 requires us to rethink development. *World Development*, 138, DOI: 10.1016/j.worlddev.2020.105233

Nedomova, L., Maryska, M., & Doucek, P. (2017). Unequal wage of men and women in ICT in the Czech Republic? *Gender, Technology and Development,* 21(1–2), 116–134. DOI: 10.1080/09718524.2017.1385317.

O'Keeffe, P., Johnson, B. and Daley, K. (2021). Continuing the precedent: Financially disadvantaging young people in "unprecedented" COVID-19 times. *Australian Journal of Social Issues*, Early Access: FEB 2021, DOI: 10.1002/ajs4.152.

Ortiz, F. C., Aguaded, I., Civila, S. and Dias, A. P. (2021). MIL cities, smart campus and e-health: Prevention of Covid-19. *Chasqui-Revista Latinoamericana de Comunicacion,* 145, pp. 197-213.

Ozili, P. and Arun, T. (2020). *Spillover of COVID-19: impact on the Global Economy.* [Online]. Available at: SSRN: https://ssrn.com/abstract=3562570 or DOI: 10.2139/ssrn.3562570.

Ranchhod, V. and Daniels, R. C. (2021). Labour Market Dynamics in South Africa at the Onset of the COVID-19 Pandemic. *South African Journal of Economics*, 89(1), 44-62. DOI: 10.1111/saje.12283.

Wong, J. and Wong, N. (2021). The economics and accounting for COVID-19 wage subsidy and other government grants. *Pacific Accounting Review*, Early Access: FEB 2021, DOI: 10.1108/PAR-10-2020-0189.

In-memory data processing in Microsoft Excel

Vítězslav Novák [1], Petr Rozehnal [2]

Abstract. Microsoft Excel is a spreadsheet where it is usual to have data stored in worksheet cells. Nevertheless, in many cases it is more efficient not to have the data stored directly in the workbook sheets or to process them there, but to move them to the operating memory for their processing. These options are provided by the Power Pivot add-in within Excel, but application developers in Excel can also use the Visual Basic for Applications programming language. This article should not only show ways how to process data in Excel in-memory, but should also demonstrate the benefits of in-memory data processing by comparing the performance of data stored in sheet cells and in-memory.

Keywords: Microsoft Excel, Power Pivot, Visual Basic for Applications, in-memory, operating memory, array.

JEL Classification: M15

1 Introduction

Spreadsheets as a software category appeared in 1979. Namely, it was the VisiCalc spreadsheet (Bricklin, 2018). Although the size of the tables grew from a possible 254 rows and 63 columns of the VisiCalc spreadsheet to the current 1,048,576 rows and 16,384 columns of the Microsoft Excel spreadsheet, the basic principles of use remained unchanged. The data is still stored in table cells and calculations are performed using formulas referring to cells with input values. However, the amount of data is growing exponentially and therefore the traditional form of calculations using references to worksheet cells is already beginning to reach its performance limits in the case of a large amount of data. Calculations with processing times in the order of seconds or even minutes are not exception.

Calculation time is not the only recent performance limitation in spreadsheets. Other limitations include the number of rows in the worksheet, limited ability to create relationships between tables, and others. Microsoft is already trying to solve some of the limitations in Excel spreadsheet. An interesting representative of such solutions is the Power Pivot add-in. Probably the most important feature of Power Pivot is that it does not store data in worksheet cells, but uses so-called data models. Data model's data are processed by the VertiPaq in-memory database. This eliminates the limitations of a limited number of rows in a worksheet, but also increases application performance because addressing data in RAM is much more efficient in performance than addressing it in worksheet cells.

However, developers of Microsoft Excel applications using the Visual Basic for Applications (VBA) programming language can also significantly affect the performance of their applications. The solution is basically similar to the solution used by the Power Pivot add-in, namely the transfer of processing data from worksheet cells to the computer's operating

[1] VŠB - Technical university of Ostrava / Faculty of Economics, Department of Applied Informatics, Sokolská třída 33, 701 21 Ostrava 1, vitezslav.novak@vsb.cz.
[2] VŠB - Technical university of Ostrava / Faculty of Economics, Department of Applied Informatics, Sokolská třída 33, 701 21 Ostrava 1, petr.rozehnal@vsb.cz.

memory, in the language of the VBA programming language, this means the transfer of data to two-dimensional arrays.

This article should not only show ways how to in-memory process Excel workbook data, but should also demonstrate the benefits of in-memory data processing by comparing the processing of data stored in worksheet cells and in-memory. All measurements will be performed on a table with two columns: Category (containing randomly generated values of 4 categories), Value (containing random numbers between 1 and 9). 1,000, 10,000, 100,000 and 1,000,000 table rows will be processed sequentially. The configuration of the computer is as follows: CPU – Intel Core i5 1.60 GHz, RAM – 8.00 GB, disk storage – 1.00 TB, software – OS: MS Windows 10, MS Office 2019.

2 In-memory Data Processing using Power Pivot

According to (Microsoft, 2020), Power Pivot is an Excel add-in you can use to perform powerful data analysis and create sophisticated data models. With Power Pivot, you can mash up large volumes of data from various sources, perform information analysis rapidly, and share insights easily.

It is important for this article that the data model data in the Power Pivot add-in is processed by the VertiPaq database engine. According to Russo and Ferrari (2015), VertiPaq is an in-memory columnar database. Being in-memory database means that all of the data handled by a data model reside in operating memory. This has a huge effect on the speed of calculations processing.

The speed of the calculations processing is also affected by the fact that VertiPaq is a columnar database. According to Holubová, Kosek, Minařík and Novák (2015), for columnar databases, the basic data structure is not a table, for columnar databases, each column has its own data structure and it is physically separated from the other columns. On this data structure, the aggregation of values in the column is much easier because database engine doesn't have to scan other columns, what is needed when using relational database.

2.1 Using Power Pivot

According to Russo and Ferrari (2015), Power Pivot is available in Excel as an add-in since 2010 version. However, data stored in Excel worksheets are not placed in data models automatically, it is necessary to add them there in one of several ways.

The most common way to add data to a data model is to check the given checkbox when creating a PivotTable. A similar option also exists when importing data into Excel. However, the use of a data model is not necessary for these options.

The use of a data model in Excel is necessary when creating relationships between several tables (similar to relationships between tables in relational databases). However, the relationships of Excel data models do not reach the possibilities of relationships used in relational databases (e.g. they allow only inner joins, not outer joins). In order to create relationship between tables in Excel, the tables must be structured tables.

In addition to improving the performance of calculations and the ability to use relationships between multiple tables, using Power Pivot also provides to Excel users other benefits, such as:

- possibility to import tables with more than 1 million rows, because the data is not stored in worksheets, but in-memory,
- the distinct count function in Excel pivot tables,
- use of DAX (Data Analysis Expressions) language to create more sophisticated formulas, so-called measures, usable in Excel pivot tables.

It might seem that Excel is not a suitable tool for storing large data, that it might be more appropriate to keep the data in the original storage, today most often a relational database, and only connect to this date. In this case, however, you lose the specific capabilities and performance of the VertiPaq columnar database when performing aggregations on table columns and the associated DAX language. As written by Němec and Zapletal (2017), the traditional relational databases slowly lose their dominant place, mainly due to inherent limits in context of processing complex data and are being replaced by other types of databases.

2.2 Efficiency of using Power Pivot in data processing

The following section will demonstrate that the use of a data model (Power Pivot) to store data has a great impact on the speed of processed calculations. We will create a pivot table of sums of values for individual categories and will compare two ways to perform this operation. The first way will be to use the data stored in the Excel worksheet (i.e. without using the Power Pivot add-in), the second way will be to use the data stored in the data model (i.e. using the Power pivot add-in). In order to measure the time of the calculation processing, we will create pivot tables using VBA procedures that allow time measurement.

The following procedures were used to measure the effectiveness of using Power Pivot in data processing (in the code sample, only the key statements that create the pivot table whose execution speed was measured are used):

```
Sub createPivotTableFromWoksheet()
    myTime = Timer
    Set myPivotTable = ThisWorkbook.PivotCaches.Create(SourceType:=xlDatabase, _
        SourceData:=mySourceWorksheet.Name & "!" & mySourceData).CreatePivotTable( _
        TableDestination:=myDestinationWorksheet.Name & "!" & myDestinationRange, _
        TableName:="PivotTableExistingSheet")
    With myPivotTable
        .PivotFields("Category").Orientation = xlRowField
        With .PivotFields("Value")
            .Orientation = xlDataField
            .Position = 1
            .Function = xlSum
        End With
    End With
    Debug.Print Timer - myTime
End Sub
```

Code 1 Procedure for creating a pivot table from worksheet data

```
Sub createPivotTableFromDataModel()
    myTime = Timer
    Set myPivotTable = ThisWorkbook.PivotCaches.Create(SourceType:=xlExternal, _
        SourceData:=ActiveWorkbook.Connections("ThisWorkbookDataModel"), _
        Version:=6).CreatePivotTable( _
        TableDestination:=myDestinationWorksheet.Name & "!" & myDestinationRange, _
```

```
        TableName:="PivotTableExistingSheet")
    With myPivotTable
        .PivotCache.RefreshOnFileOpen = False
        .RepeatAllLabels xlRepeatLabels
        .AddDataField myPivotTable.CubeFields("[Measures].[SumOfValue]"), "Soucet Value"
        With .CubeFields("[Table].[Category]")
            .Orientation = xlRowField
            .Position = 1
        End With
    End With
    Debug.Print Timer - myTime
End Sub
```

Code 2 Procedure for creating a pivot table from data model

Each of the procedures was executed on a given number of processed rows five times, while the execution time of the procedure was measured. The times in the table are given in seconds.

Power Pivot	Rows	Attempt 1	Attempt 2	Attempt 3	Attempt 4	Attempt 5	Average Time
No	1,000	0.0391	0.0273	0.0273	0.0352	0.0234	0.0305
	10,000	0.0352	0.0430	0.0430	0.0352	0.0391	0.0391
	100,000	0.1133	0.1016	0.1211	0.1133	0.1172	0.1133
	1,000,000	1.0898	1.0430	1.0313	1.0156	1.0547	1.0469
Yes	1,000	0.1289	0.1289	0.1250	0.1250	0.1289	0.1273
	10,000	0.1250	0.1094	0.1250	0.1250	0.1172	0.1203
	100,000	0.1328	0.1250	0.1094	0.1328	0.1094	0.1219
	1,000,000	0.1211	0.1094	0.1289	0.1250	0.1250	0.1219

Table 1 Measured times when performing procedures from Code 1 and Code 2

From the measured values it is evident that if the data in the worksheet was used to create pivot tables (i.e. Power Pivot was not used), then with the increasing number of processed rows, the time for calculation processing also increased in direct proportion. However, this does not apply if the workbook data model was used to create pivot table. The time required to create a pivot table with the increasing number of processed rows remained the same. From this, it is clear that for the VertiPaq database engine, 1 million rows in a table is not performance significant.

It is also clear from the table that with larger volumes of data (in our example more than 100,000 rows) it is more advantageous to place the data in the data model of the workbook. In addition to saving time when processing the calculation, you will also get the other benefits mentioned above. With a limited use of the number of rows of the worksheet (i.e. one million rows), calculations using the data model are about 10 times faster.

3 In-memory Data Processing using Visual Basic for Application

According to Microsoft (2019), Visual Basic for Applications (VBA) is an event-driven programming language that enables you to extend Office applications. VBA helps to develop automation processes, Windows API and user-defined functions. It also enables you to manipulate the user interface features of the host applications.

3.1 Using two-dimensional arrays in VBA

The VBA traditionally uses a Range object to work with worksheet cells. Using this object, it is possible to address cells directly and make any modifications to them. However, making these modifications is relatively slow because VBA must address worksheet cells, which are relatively complex objects. To change cell values, it is much more convenient to transfer these values to two-dimensional arrays stored in RAM and then address these values only using the integer indexes of the array items.

According to Král (2010), moving data from an Excel spreadsheet to a two-dimensional array stored in RAM is very easy. All you have to do is save the table addressed using a Range object in a VBA variable of Variant data type and thus a two-dimensional array is automatically created. You will then perform all data operations in this array. Then you save this array back to an object of Range data type (see example below).

3.2 Efficiency of using arrays in data processing

The following section will demonstrate that making changes of values in arrays instead of making direct changes in worksheet cells has a huge impact on the speed of the changes. We will add the value 1 to the second column of the table, measuring the duration of the operation. We will compare two ways to perform this operation. The first way will be to make changes directly in the worksheet cells. The second way will be to transfer the cell values into a two-dimensional array, perform the desired operation in the array, and then transfer the values from the array back to the worksheet cells.

The following procedures were used to measure the effectiveness of using arrays when changing data in worksheet (in the code sample, only key statements whose execution speed has been measured are used):

```
Sub incrementInSheet()
    myTime = Timer
    For Each cl In mySourceData
        cl.Value = cl.Value + 1
    Next cl
    Debug.Print Timer - myTime
End Sub
```

Code 3 The procedure that increases the value of cells by one directly in a worksheet

```
Sub incrementInMemory()
    myTime = Timer
    myArray = mySourceData
    For i = 1 To UBound(myArray, 1)
        For j = 1 To UBound(myArray, 2)
            myArray(i, j) = myArray(i, j) + 1
        Next j
    Next i
    mySourceData = myArray
    Debug.Print Timer - myTime
End Sub
```

Code 4 The procedure that increases the value of cells by one using a two-dimensional array

Each of the procedures was executed on a given number of processed rows five times, while the execution time of the procedure was measured. The times in the table are given in seconds.

Array	Rows	Attempt 1	Attempt 2	Attempt 3	Attempt 4	Attempt 5	Average Time
No	1,000	0.0547	0.0352	0.0508	0.0430	0.0391	0.0445
	10,000	0.3789	0.3672	0.3633	0.3633	0.3555	0.3656
	100,000	3.4922	3.5625	3.4883	3.5508	3.4766	3.5141
	1,000,000	33.6953	33.1836	34.0508	33.9805	34.3125	33.8445
Yes	1,000	0.0078	0.0078	0.0078	0.0039	0.0039	0.0063
	10,000	0.0195	0.0156	0.0156	0.0156	0.0117	0.0156
	100,000	0.0977	0.0977	0.0938	0.0938	0.0977	0.0961
	1,000,000	0.9180	0.8984	0.9180	0.9063	0.9063	0.9094

Table 2 Measured times when performing procedures from Code 3 and Code 4

From the measured values it is evident that the processing time increases in direct proportion to the number of processed values both without the use of the array and with its use. At the same time, however, it is also clear that with the number of processed values, the efficiency of the use of array also increases. Processing 1,000 values was 7 times faster in an array than without using the array, 10,000 values 23 times faster, and more than 100,000 values 37 times faster. As a result, Excel application developers should almost always prefer to use arrays instead of a Range object when processing data.

4 Conclusion

In-memory data processing is one of ways how to process an ever-increasing amount of data in a reasonable amount of time. This method of data processing is used by many manufacturers of newly developing NoSQL databases, as well as manufacturers of traditional enterprise applications, such as SAP with its SAP HANA database. Another traditional application where in-memory data processing can be used is also Excel. Excel already includes tools that use in-memory data processing, such as the Power Pivot add-in. However, Excel application developers using VBA can increase the performance of their applications by processing the data of their applications using two-dimensional arrays instead of processing them directly in worksheet cells.

This article aimed not only to show how to in-memory process Excel data, but also to demonstrate the performance benefits of in-memory data processing. Measurements have shown that the difference in the data processing speed outside the RAM or in the RAM is large and increases with the number of processed rows.

References

Bricklin. D. (2018). VisiCalc: Information from its creators. Dan Bricklin and Bob Frankston. [Online]. Available at: http://www.bricklin.com/visicalc.htm [cited 2020-12-17].

Holubová. I.. Kosek. J.. Minařík. K. and Novák. D. (2015). *Big Data a NoSQL databáze*. Praha: Grada.

Král. Martin. (2010). *Excel VBA. Výukový kurz*. Brno: Computer Press.

Microsoft (2019). *Office VBA Reference.* [Online]. Available at: https://docs.microsoft.com/en-us/office/vba/api/overview/ [cited 2020-12-18].

Microsoft (2020). *Power Pivot: Powerful data analysis and data modeling in Excel.* [Online]. Available at: https://support.microsoft.com/en-us/office/power-pivot-powerful-data-analysis-and-data-modeling-in-excel-a9c2c6e2-cc49-4976-a7d7-40896795d045 [cited 2020-12-15].

Němec. R. and Zapletal. F. (2017). 'On the determination of query execution patterns of the application of the Anchor Data modeling method using machine-learning methods '. In: *Proceedings of the 12th International Conference on Strategic Management and its Support by Information Systems*. Ostrava. Czech Republic. pp. 55.

Russo. M. and Ferrari. A. (2015). *The Definitive Guide to DAX: Business Intelligence with Microsoft Excel. SQL Server Analysis Services and Power BI.* Redmond: Microsoft Press.

Russo. M. and Ferrari. A. (2017). *Analyzing Data with Microsoft Power BI and Power Pivot for Excel*. Redmond: Microsoft Press.

Optimizing municipal solid waste collection using GIS: A case study in Jablunkovsko region

Lucie Orlíková[1], Jiří Horák[2], Petr Kozel[3]

Abstract. Municipal waste collection is an important logistic activity within any city. Mathematical programming approaches maximize or minimize an objective function for improvement in the collection procedure, to ensure operational efficiency and also serve as decision support tools. Geographic information system approaches allow processing of additional considerations, often ignored in other methods, such as the street network modeling. This paper deals with the application of the two approaches (sweep algorithm and p-median approach) for a basic decomposition of a set of vertices. The experiment is carried out on the real-world solid waste data of Jablunkovsko region. The results indicate that using p-median approach for a decomposition can be used for the vehicle routing problem.

Keywords: waste management, route optimization, GIS, vehicle routing problem.

JEL Classification: C44, C65, R42

1 Introduction

The management of municipal solid waste (MSW) has become a major environmental issue (Kanchanabhan et al., 2010, Sulemana et al., 2018) due to its negative consequences on the society and environmental systems if not properly executed. Solid waste management involves the processes of generation, collection, transport, treatment, value recovery, and subsequent disposal. Bad design of any of these processes increases operational costs and can result in environmental pollution (Kyessi et al., 2009).

The optimization problem of MSW collection can be described by a vehicle routing model including some basic components such as the vehicles, nodes, and their relations in order to ensure predefined goals (Son, 2014). Several vehicle routing models for different cities were presented in the literature. For example, Ghose et al. (2005) presented a GIS model for the Asansol Municipality Corporation (AMC) of West Bengal State (India). The model uses information on population density, waste generation capacity, road network and the types of road, storage bins and collection vehicles. Tavares et al. (2009) integrated some factors such as the driving situations, vehicle load and road gradient to the vehicle route models of the city of Praia, the capital of Cape Verde. Sulemana et al. (2018) reviews studies in the area of applying optimization systems in the collection process of solid waste with particular interest in systems that are based on mathematical programming and geographic information system (GIS). A total of 100 peer-reviewed journal articles, books, and reports were accessed and it was found that the studies should focus on improving the efficiency of the vehicle routing systems through modification of companies delivery schedules, optimizing the feet of trucks' routes, and

[1] VSB-TU Ostrava, Dep. of geoinfomatics, 17.listopadu 2172/15, 708 00 Ostrava-Poruba, lucie.orlikova@vsb.cz
[2] VSB-TU Ostrava, Dep. of geoinfomatics, 17.listopadu 2172/15, 708 00 Ostrava-Poruba, jiri.horak@vsb.cz
[3] VSB-TU Ostrava, Dep. of mathematical methods in economics, 17. listopadu 2172/15, 708 00 Ostrava-Poruba, petr.kozel@vsb.cz

incorporating information related to traffic conditions into the models in order to avoid generating traffic congestions. Another example is municipal solid waste collection optimization in Singapore (Xue et al., 2015). This paper developed a specific waste collection allocation model to answer the following question: where to send our waste from different waste generation points.

This paper deals with the application of the sweep algorithm and p-median approach for a basic decomposition of a set of vertices to partial subsets, where service vehicle routes are identified by using of a suitable algorithm. The mathematical experiments presented in this paper were implemented in Jablunkovsko region during the optimization of routes for service vehicles for the municipal waste collection.

2 Methodology

Vehicle route planning is an inherent part of decision-making process of all subjects providing the transport network service. Waste collection problems are, however, one of the most difficult operational problems to solve. The initial task for vehicle route designing while the service of vertices in a transport network is considered, is the Traveling Salesman Problem requiring the most efficient Hamiltonian cycle. The following basic requirement must be fulfilled to determine the minimum Hamiltonian cycle (MHC): the sum of requirements located at the vertices of a transport network is less than or equal to the service vehicle capacity.

There are a whole range of methods for dealing with the vehicle routing problem (Alonso et al. (2008), Buhrkal et al. (2012), Bagheri et al. (2020)), but we will primarily focus on the decomposition approaches. Firstly, the two-step decomposition Cluster-First Route-Second method can be used to generate clusters of vertices so that the sum of requirements in each cluster does not exceed the service vehicle capacity. Secondly, the Traveling Salesman Problem is subsequently solved in individual clusters using some of heuristic algorithms. The presented contribution is devoted to the mathematical programming of the Cluster-First Route-Second method, namely using the p-median approach.

Alternatively, a Sweep Algorithm for clustering can be applied. This method discussed in detail in Renaud and Boctor (2002), Yu and Hung (2015), Pomp et al. (2017).

2.1 The p-median problem

The p-median problem is a special case of the capacitated location-allocation problems and it can be used for clustering (Upchurch and Kuby (2010), Kozel et al. (2018)).

The principle of this approach is following: two sets J, I are given; the set of customers $J = \{1, ..., n\}$ and the set of possible location of centers $I = \{1, ..., m\}$. Each customer j of the set J defines own service requirement (the size of this requirement is denoted as b_j). Each of centers, which will be located in some place of the set I, has the capacity K. A maximum predetermined number of the centers p may be located in the set I. The following condition must be met: the sum of capacities of all centers is greater than or equal to the sum of requirements of all customers:

$$\sum_{j=1}^{n} b_j \leq K * p \tag{1}$$

The distance between location of the center i and the customer j can be modelled by the distance matrix d_{ij}. The goal is to design a location of p centers in a set of vertices I so that the sum of distances between the customer j and the nearest center i is minimal and the capacity of any center is not exceeded.

2.2 Mathematical model of the capacitated p-median problem

The allocation model of the described problem was described in (Janacek and Kvet, 2016, García et al., 2011). It can be formulated as follows:

$$min\ \sum_{i=1}^{m} \sum_{j=1}^{n} x_{ij} * d_{ij} \tag{2}$$

$$\sum_{i=1}^{m} x_{ij} = 1, for\ j = 1, \dots, n \tag{3}$$

$$x_{ij} \leq y_{i,}\ for\ i = 1, \dots, m, j = 1, \dots, n \tag{4}$$

$$\sum_{i=1}^{m} y_i \leq p \tag{5}$$

$$\sum_{j=1}^{n} x_{ij} * b_j \leq K, for\ i = 1, \dots, m \tag{6}$$

$$x_{ij} \in \{0,1\}, for\ i = 1, \dots, m, j = 1, \dots, n \tag{7}$$

$$y_j \in \{0,1\}, for\ i = 1, \dots, m \tag{8}$$

The variable x_{ij} represents an assignment of the customer j to the location i and in a similar way, the bivalent variable y_i represents an assignment of the center in the location i. The objective function (2) gives the total distance travelled among customers and assigned centers. The conditions (3) ensure that each customer will be assigned to just one location. Furthermore, the conditions (4) express that each customer can be assigned only to a location with the assigned center. The condition (5) means that only just p of centers will be located. What is more, the conditions (6) put the following constraint: the sum of customer requirements assigned to one center does not exceed the specified capacity K. The obligatory conditions (7) and (8) define a domain of variables.

The above-mentioned model (2) – (8) can be used for already described clustering with following small adjustments. First of all, the set of customers J corresponds to the set of vertices of the graph V, from which the depot $\{d\}$ is removed, thus $J = V - \{d\}$. Moreover, it should be considered that the set of possible locations of centers is equal to the set of customers: $I = J$. In addition, the number of located centers p corresponds to the number of created clusters and the capacity of centers K corresponds to the sum of customer requirements, which are assigned to the individual clusters $S_1, \dots, S_p$ (Kozel et al., 2018).

3 Study area and data

Numerical experiments with the mathematical model (2) – (8) were implemented on the real problem of the municipal waste collection in Jablunkovsko region (NE of Czechia). The specific commercial company ensures municipal waste collection in Bystřice nad Olší, Písek, Písečná, Hrádek, Dolní Lomná and Hrčava. The following data were provided for each area: the number of customers and their addresses, the number of collection routes, the vehicle capacity, the collection container capacity and the frequency of waste collection.

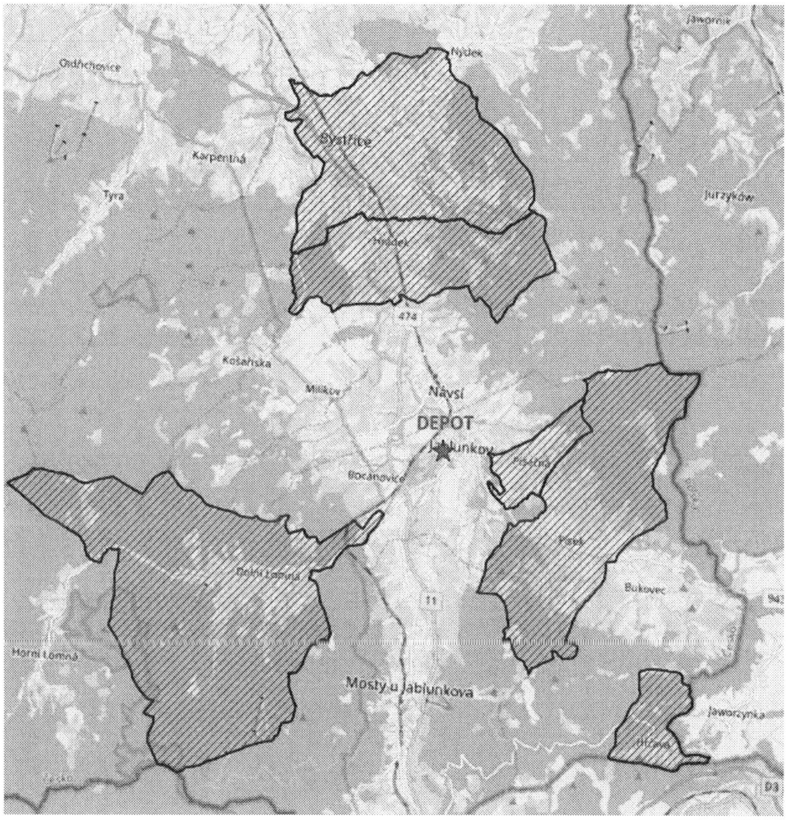

Figure 1 The location of the selected municipalities

Geodatabase StreetNet CZE (CEDA) was used for numerical experiments. Geodatabase StreetNet is made of 16 data layers – the core layer represents seamless and fully routable road network supplemented by additional topographic layers and layers of administrative boundaries. The majority of information can be found in the roads layer (road) – its descriptive information (number, international number and class of the road, street name etc.), attributes describing technical and functional state of individual segments and basic attributes for movement on the network.

3.1 Data preprocessing

Recorded customer´s addresses are not standardized and contain misspelling, missing or superfluous parts. Geocoding or address matching allows for the connection of coordinates to their records localized through the address by connecting to the file that contains the addresses and coordinates. Geocoding services are provided mainly by web search engines (Fojtík et al., 2016).

Geocoding of individual customers were performed using Geocode by Awesome Table (https://workspace.google.com/marketplace/app/geocode_by_awesome_table/904124517349) and OpenCage Geocoder (https://opencagedata.com/). The results were compared with the Registry of Territorial Identification, Addresses and Real Estate (RÚIAN).

Geocode by Awesome Table is a tool that helps to get latitudes and longitudes from addresses in a Google Sheet. Geocoding can be restricted by a bounding box or a region. The limits (Standard Usage) for free geocoding are 1000 requests per day.

OpenCage Geocoder is a simple and consistent geocoding library written in Python. The API combines multiple geocoding systems in the background. Each system is optimized for different parts of the world and types of requests.

The RÚIAN project is the most extended project in the frame of the Czech public administration civil service basic registries system. Address information administered in RÚIAN are binding for the whole civil service.

Results of both geocoding services are compared in Table 1. The Google Geocode by Awesome Table outperforms the Open Cage Geocoder service in all cases except of Dolni Lomna. There are many recreational facilities with a registration number in Dolni Lomna and this can cause a geocoding problem. This data set indicates the lowest geocoding success for GAT and the 2nd worst result for OCG. The most successful geocoding provides addresses in Pisecna (both for GAT and OCG).

Data set	No. of entries	Google Awesome Table	Open Cage Geocoder
Bystřice nad Olší	1495	1296 (86.7%)	1168 (78.1%)
Písek	427	378 (88.5%)	365 (85.4%)
Písečná	262	234 (89.3%)	226 (86.2%)
Hrádek	457	403 (88.1%)	371 (81.1%)
Dolní Lomná	214	136 (63.5%)	167 (78.0%)
Hrčava	49	35 (71.4%)	34 (69.3%)

Table 1 Number of localized addresses for geocoding tools

The randomly selected samples from each data set for a manual check contain 110 addresses. The correctly geocoded addresses were considered to be within 10 meters of the RÚIAN location. Summary results show that the best accuracy was achieved by OpenCage Geocoder, which detected the correct address for a total of 64.8% located objects. A lower accuracy was obtained in the case Google Geocode by Awesome Table (57,2%).

Geocoding of individual customers was followed by calculation of the origin-destination (OD) matrix (Table 2), which specifies the travel demands between the origin and destination nodes in the network.

ID	NAME	ORIGIN	DESTINATION	TOTAL LENGTH (M)
1	1 – 1	1	1	0
2	1 – 2	1	2	3180.6
3	1 – 3	1	3	3851.3
4	1 – 4	1	4	4333.2
5	1 - 5	1	5	4889.5

Table 2 An example of origin-destination matrix (Bystřice nad Olší)

4 Results and discussion

The data sets for each area were decomposed into subsets corresponding to the service vehicle routes with respect to the given average filling of containers. The mentioned decomposition was conducted by the Sweep Algorithm and the p-median approach. Finally, the individual vehicle cycles, represented by the minimum Hamiltonian cycles in clusters, were found using the heuristic algorithm (the Lin-Kernighan method (Lin, Kernighan 1973) in the computational environment Wolfram Mathematica.

The Table 3 contains information about numbers of vertices in clusters, which were generated using the Sweep algorithm and the p-median approach in Bystřice nad Olší. The routes have been optimized by using Dijskra´s algorithm (a route starting and ending at the same depot). The table below contains information about the optimized route lengths of MHC (individual vehicle cycle) in each cluster and length differences between both methods. If the Sweep algorithm is used for clustering, the total distance 159.9 km will be travelled while serving the territory. However, if the p-median approach is used for generating clusters, the total distance travelled is 139.7 km which means 20.2 km less (12.5%).

Cluster Number	Vertices$_s$	Route length$_s$ (km)	Vertices$_m$	Route length$_m$ (km)	Difference (m-s) (km)
1	499	48.8	500	57.2	+8.4
2	499	54.1	496	44.8	-9.3
3	499	57.0	500	37.7	-19.3
SUM	1496	159.9	1496	139.7	-20.2

Table 3 Comparison of sweep algorithm (s) and p-median (m) approach (Bystřice nad Olší)

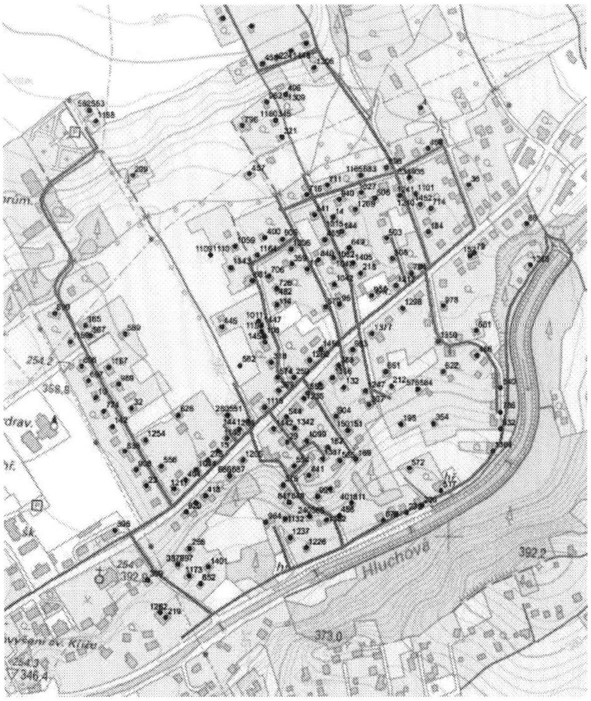

Figure 2 The optimal route to visit all customer´s addresses in Bystřice nad Olší

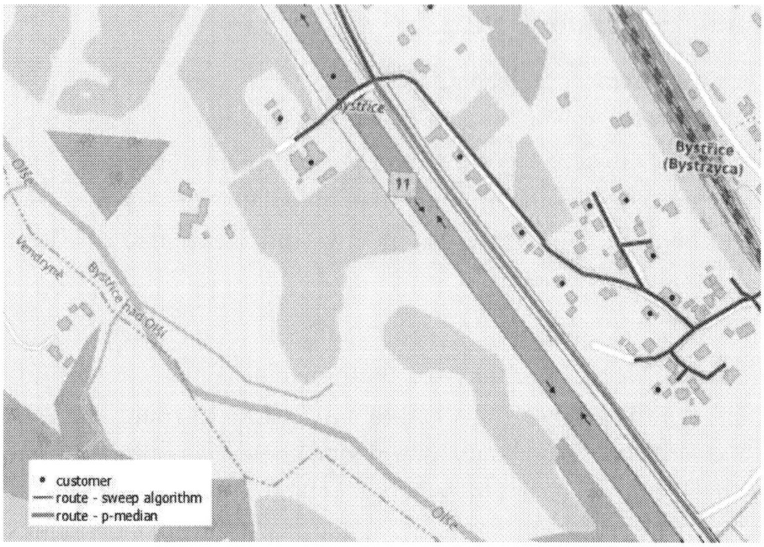

Figure 3 The optimal route after decomposition by the Sweep Algorithm and the p-median approach

Similar results were achieved in other municipalities in the Jablunkov region. Route length shortage thanks to p-median optimization is between 1.8 km and 20.2 km (4.3% to 12.5%). The largest saving using p-median approach is indicated for Bystřice nad Olší village.

5 Conclusion and future work

The performance of solid waste collection systems is measured by indicators such as travel distances, quantity of collected waste, number of truck trips and operating cost. In this paper, the usage of the sweep algorithm and p-median approach for the basic decomposition of the customer´s addresses to optimize service vehicle routing is demonstrated. A real-world dataset based on the waste disposal behavior of residential grids in Jablunkov region was used. Utilization of p-median approach shorten optimized route lengths by 4.3% to 12.5%. The future direction could be the extension of this work to automate the route searching on municipality servers including information about contemporary traffic issues and give notification if there is any route that has overflow or the possibility of overflow (simulation of different container filling, utilization of sensor measurements etc.).

Acknowledgements

The authors gratefully acknowledge the financial support from the grant SP2021/35.

References

Alonso F., Alvarez MJ., Beasley JE. (2008) A tabu search algorithm for the periodic vehicle routing problem with multiple vehicle trips and accessibility restrictions. *Journal of the Operational Research Society*; 59: 963-976.

Bagheri K., Neysani Samani N., Jolokhani Niyaraki M R. (2020) Routing Vehicle of Urban Waste Collection Utilities GIS. JGST. 9 (3) :85-95, URL: http://jgst.issge.ir/article-1-783-en.html

Buhrkal, K., Larsen, A., & Ropke, S. (2012) The Waste Collection Vehicle Routing Problem with Time Windows in a City Logistics Context. *Procedia - Social and Behavioral Sciences, 39*, pp. 241-254. doi:10.1016/j.sbspro.2012.03.105.

Fojtík, D., Horák, J., Kocich, D., Orlíková, L., Inspektor, T. (2016) *Smart geocoding of objects*. 2016 17th International Carpathian Control Conference (ICCC), Tatranska Lomnica, 2016, pp. 200-205, doi: 10.1109/CarpathianCC.2016.7501093.

García, S., Labbé, M., Marín, A. (2011) Solving large p-median problems with a radius formulation, *INFORMS Journal on Computing*, 23 546-556.

Janáček, J., Kvet, M. (2016). Sequential approximate approach to the p-median problem. *Computers & Industrial Engineering*, 94, 83–92.

Kanchanabhan, T. E., Mohaideen, J. A. (2010) Using GIS in solid waste management planning for tambaram municipality in South Ohennai. *Journal of the Institution of Engineers* (India): Environmental Engineering Division, vol. 90, no. MARCH, pp. 37–44.

Kozel, P., Orlíková, L., Pomp M., Michalcová, Š. (2018) Application of the p-Median Approach for a Basic Decomposition of a Set of Vertices to Service Vehicles Routing Design. Conference: *36th International Conference on Mathematical Methods in Economics (MME)*. Location: Jindrichuv Hradec, CZECH REPUBLIC Date: SEP 12-14, 2018 Sponsor(s): Univ Econ, Fac Management; Czech Soc Operat Res; Czech Econometr Soc.

Kyessi, A., Mwakalinga, V. (2009) GIS application in coordinating solid waste collection: the case of Sinza Neighbourhood in Kinondoni municipality, Dar es Salaam city, Municipality and Natural Resources Management, pp. 3–8.

S. Lin and B. W. Kernighan (1973) An effective heuristic algorithm for the traveling-salesman problem, Oper. Res., vol. 21, no. 2, pp. 498–516, doi: 10.1287/opre.21.2.498.

Pomp, M., Kozel, P., Michalcová, Š., Orlíková, L. (2017). Using the Sweep Algorithm for decomposing a set of vertices and subsequent solution of the traveling salesman problem in decomposed subsets. In: *Proceedings of 35th International Conference Mathematical Methods in Economics 2017*, pp. 584–589. Uherské Hradiště.

Renaud, J., Boctor, F.F. (2002) A sweep-based algorithm for the fleet size and mix vehicle routing problém. *European Journal of Operational Research*, 140(3), pp. 618-628, ISSN 0377-2217, https://doi.org/10.1016/S0377-2217(01)00237-5.

Son, L. H. (2014) Optimizing Municipal Solid Waste collection using Chaotic Particle Swarm Optimization in GIS based environments: A case study at Danang city, Vietnam. *Expert Systems with Applications*, 41(18), pp. 8062-8074. ISSN 0957-4174, https://doi.org/10.1016/j.eswa.2014.07.020.

Sulemana, A., Donkor, A.E., Forkuo, E.K., Oduro-Kwarteng, S. (2018) Optimal Routing of Solid Waste Collection Trucks: A Review of Methods. *Journal of Engineering*, vol. 2018, Article ID 4586376, 12 pages. https://doi.org/10.1155/2018/4586376.

Tavares, G., Zsigraiova, Z., Semiao, V., Carvalho, M.G. (2009) Optimisation of MSW collection routes for minimum fuel consumption using 3D GIS modelling, *Waste Management*, Volume 29, Issue 3, Pages 1176-1185, ISSN 0956-053X, https://doi.org/10.1016/j.wasman.2008.07.013.

Upchurch, Ch., Kuby, M. (2010) Comparing the p-median and flow-refueling models for locating alternative-fuel stations, Journal of Transport Geography, Volume 18, Issue 6, 2010, pp. 750-758, ISSN 0966-6923, https://doi.org/10.1016/j.jtrangeo.2010.06.015.

Xue, W., Cao, K., Li, W. (2015) Municipal solid waste collection optimization in Singapore, *Applied Geography*, Volume 62. pp. 182-190, ISSN 0143-6228, https://doi.org/10.1016/j.apgeog.2015.04.002.

Yu,X., Hung, J. Y. (2015) Coverage path planning based on a multiple sweep line decomposition," IECON 2015 - *41st Annual Conference of the IEEE Industrial Electronics Society*, Yokohama, pp. 004052-004058, doi: 10.1109/IECON.2015.7392731.

New MS Project Add-in for Task Threatness Evaluation

Petra Pavlíčková[1], Helena Brožová[2], Jan Rydval[3], Josef Havlíček[4], Tomáš Šubrt[5]

Abstract. The analysis of project tasks using the criticalness potential defining the criticalness of tasks and using the failureness potential defining the possibility of various tasks failure is important due to possibility to find the threatening tasks already during their implementation in project. Criticalness potential of task means evaluation of time, topological, slack, cost and work criticalness of task and failureness potential is analyzed based on project management triangle. The aggregation of the evaluation of these two potentials expresses the tasks threatness assessment displayed in the task threatness matrix.

In this paper, we introduce Microsoft Project VSTO add-in "Task Threatness Matrix Add-In" (TTM) created by our authors' group which allows analysis of the criticalness and failureness potential of the project tasks. The main advantage of this add-in is its implementation into Microsoft Project and its easy application.

Keywords: Project management, task threat, task criticalness, task failureness, task threatness matrix.

JEL Classification: O22, O30

1 Introduction

Microsoft Project is designed to assist a project manager in developing a schedule, assigning resources to tasks, resource levelling of schedules, tracking progress, creating budgets based on tasks and its resources, and analysing workloads. All these Microsoft Project tools are based on the critical path schedules. Some third-party add-ons also are available, covering for instance tools for critical chain and event chain methodology. These tools are well supported by theory, so Microsoft Project can be characterized as a very useful quantitative tool for project managers, however, such tools do not cover all phases of project management.

Given that most projects do not end successfully and fail or end up with more or less problems (Aschman, 2018, Betz, 2018), there is a great lack of, for example, tools for analysing project risks and also analysing project tasks in terms of their failure. The main problem factors of the projects falling are budget overspending, schedule slipping, quality of project outputs due a lot of project changes gradually requested by customers, and/or severe and continuing operational problems holding for at least one year.

[1] Czech University of Life Sciences Prague, Fac. of Economics and Management, Dept. of Systems Engineering, Kamýcká 129, 165 21 Praha 6 – Suchdol, CZ, pavlickovap@pef.czu.cz

[2] Czech University of Life Sciences Prague, Fac. of Economics and Management, Dept. of Systems Engineering, Kamýcká 129, 165 21 Praha 6 – Suchdol, CZ, brozova@pef.czu.cz

[3] Czech University of Life Sciences Prague, Fac. of Economics and Management, Dept. of Systems Engineering, Kamýcká 129, 165 21 Praha 6 – Suchdol, CZ, rydval@pef.czu.cz

[4] Czech University of Life Sciences Prague, Fac. of Economics and Management, Dept. of Systems Engineering, Kamýcká 129, 165 21 Praha 6 – Suchdol, CZ, havlicekjosef@pef.czu.cz

[5] Czech University of Life Sciences Prague, Fac. of Economics and Management, Dept. of Systems Engineering, Kamýcká 129, 165 21 Praha 6 – Suchdol, CZ, subrt@pef.czu.cz

Theoretical background for risk analysis is work up only for methods and processes related to projects as a whole and many authors suggest new, more exact approaches (Williams, 2017, APM, 2008). Almost no authors are interested in analysis of the individual project tasks failing or threating due their time parameters, costs and work. However, Microsoft Project is creating a project schedule (evaluating critical tasks based on critical path) or determining the budget and resource requirements but it is not aimed at analysis of potential fails or threats of tasks. Because the failure of projects is due not only to problems of projects as a whole but also to problems with successful implementation of individual project tasks, it is important for project managers to analyse possible threats of the individual tasks, their realization, timelines, quality costs and so on. Combination of task criticalness and failureness potential will enable project managers to assess a task role as potentially risk on the project. This allows the findings of such tasks and focusing on their management, control and support in order for their successful implementation.

For these reasons we introduced the task threatness matrix based on the Winterlink's matrix and we suggested and created Microsoft Project VSTO add-in "Task Threatness Matrix Add-In" as a result of our OPPR project (see Acknowledgements). This Add-In allows analysis of the criticalness and failureness potential of the project tasks and created the Task Threatness Matrix. The main advantage of this add-in is its implementation into Microsoft Project environment and easy application.

The aim of this paper is to present our methodology of task threatness and our tool "Task Threatness Matrix Add-In". The following text is organized as follows: The chapter 2 consists of methodology description. The chapter 3 consists of description of our Add-In and shows the basic steps of its application.

2 Task criticalness, failureness and threatness concept

The "Task Threatness Matrix Add-In" is based on the newly proposed criticalness, failureness and threatness concept (Brožová et al., 2019a, 2019b). The concept of threatness of project tasks combines two views – task criticalness and task failureness (Figure 1).

The task criticalness concept is much wider then criticality of project tasks defined from a time perspective only. The *task criticalness potential* (Brožová et al., 2014, 2016) is suggested to provide the overall evaluation of the task criticalness using quantitative crisp evaluation without soft knowledge about character of the tasks using following indicators:

- Duration – longer task duration means higher value of time criticalness indicator,
- Slack – shorter task slack means higher value of slack criticalness indicator,
- Cost – higher task cost means higher value of cost criticalness indicator,
- Work – higher task work means higher value of work criticalness indicator, and
- Topology – higher probability the activity will lie on critical pass related to the project topology means higher value of topological criticalness indicator.

The task criticalness potential is based on the multiple attribute decision making method using mentioned indicators which are based on objective values from project schedule and are transformed using linear utility function and fuzzified using fuzzy linguistic scale.

The *task failureness potential* (Brožová et al., 2019a, 2019b) is based on the expert estimation of the possibility of task fails from the project triangle view and the human factor view. The task failureness indicators are expressed using fuzzy linguistic scale respecting three key indicators:

- Duration – higher possibility of task duration extension means higher value of time failureness indicator,
- Cost – higher possibility of task cost increasing means higher value of cost failureness indicator,
- Quality – higher possibility of task quality deterioration means higher value of quality failureness indicator.

The task failureness potential is also based on the multiple attribute decision making method using mentioned indicators evaluated using fuzzy linguistic scale.

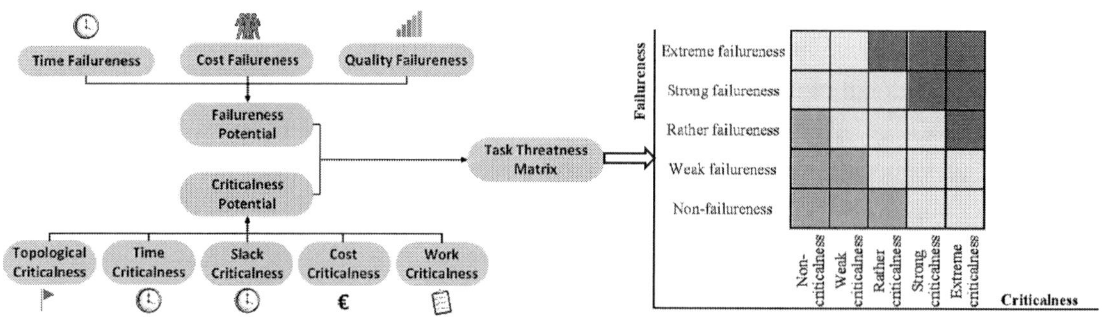

Figure 1 Factors of task threatness and task threatness matrix

The evaluation of all indicators (five criticalness and three failureness indicators) has fuzzy form using the six step non-uniform fuzzy scale (Table 1).

Linguistic terms		**Fuzzy number** $M(T_j) = (t_{1j}, t_{2j}, t_{3j}, t_{4j})$
Not at all critical	Not at all failing	(0; 0; 0; 0.1)
Usually not critical	Usually not failing	(0; 0.1; 0.2; 0.3)
Rather not critical	Rather not failing	(0.2; 0.3; 0.4; 0.6)
Rather critical	Rather failing	(0.4; 0.6; 0.7; 0.8)
Usually critical	Usually failing	(0.7; 0.8; 0.9; 1)
Always critical	Always failing	(0.9; 0.1; 1; 1)

Table 1 Fuzzy linguistic terms describing intensity of task criticalness and failureness indicators

The criticalness and failureness potentials are calculated using multiple criteria decision methods and using linguistic approximation are mapped into five step non-uniform fuzzy scale (Table 2).

Linguistic terms		**Fuzzy number** $M(V_j) = (v_{1j}, v_{2j}, v_{3j}, v_{4j})$
Non-criticalness	Non-failureness	(0; 0; 0.05; 0.15)
Weak criticalness	Weak failureness	(0.05; 0.15; 0.25; 0.35)
Rather criticalness	Rather failureness	(0.25; 0.35; 0.5; 0.6)
Strong criticalness	Strong failureness	(0.5; 0.6; 0.75; 0.85)
Extreme criticalness	Extreme failureness	(0.75; 0.85; 1; 1)

Table 2 Fuzzy linguistic terms describing the task criticalness and failureness potential

The *task threatness matrix* is obtain using the fuzzy linguistic evaluation of the task criticalness and failureness potentials as two-dimensional evaluation of task. The fuzzy values of criticalness and failureness potential are used for placing of the tasks into cells of task threatness matrix (Figure 1) which is inspired by Winterlink's matrix.

3 Task Threatness Matrix Add-In

Task Threatness Matrix Add-In (TTM) was developed in Visual Studio Tools for Office (VSTO). This method of add-on development allows easier distribution, the user then installs it, for example using the .exe file. To install the "Task Threatness Matrix Add-In", you must have Microsoft Project version 2019 or 2016 installed. The TTM is not tested with older versions of MS Project. The TTM has two language versions – English and Czech. Installation, uninstallation, activation and deactivation of this add-on is performed in full accordance with the common procedures of these actions in the MS Windows environment.

After successful installation and possible activation of the TTM, the "*Task Threatness*" tab will appear in the Microsoft Project tab bar. Clicking on this tab will open the new tab bar with individual functions of the add-on (Figure 2) organized into three sections "*Task Criticalness*", "*Task Failureness*" and "*Task Threatness Matrix*".

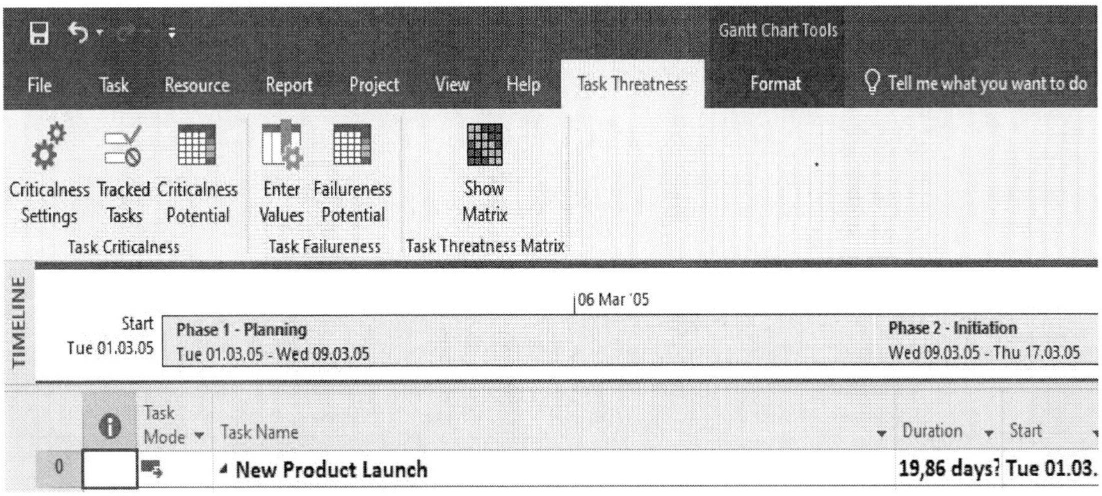

Figure 2 Task Threatness tab and its menu

The first step in analysing tasks based on criticality indicators is to check the weights of these indicators with the "*Criticalness Settings*" tab. The default setting of the weights values results from the performed expert estimation (Brožová, 2014). If the user wants, he/she can change these weights (Figure 3).

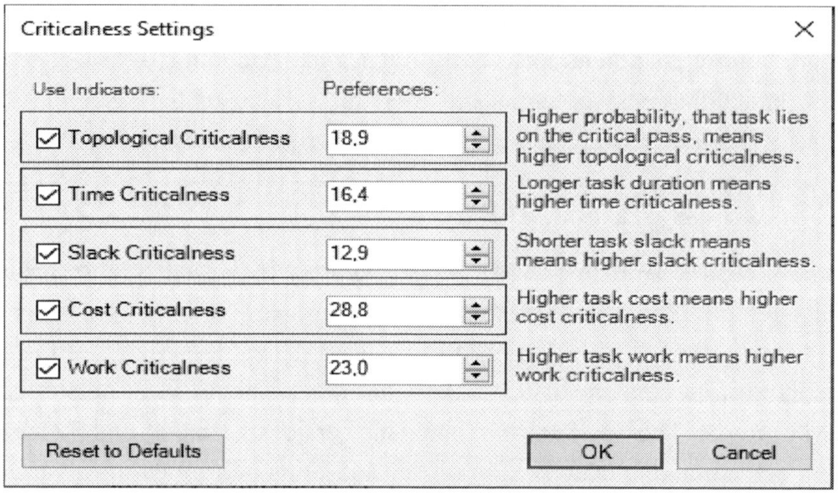

Figure 3 Table for setting weights for criticalness indicators

The next step is to decide which tasks to analyse with this method. Clicking the "*Tracked Tasks*" tab inserts a "*Skip when tracking*" column, in which a green square indicates that criticalness analysis has been performed and a red square indicates that it has not been performed for individual task (Figure 4).

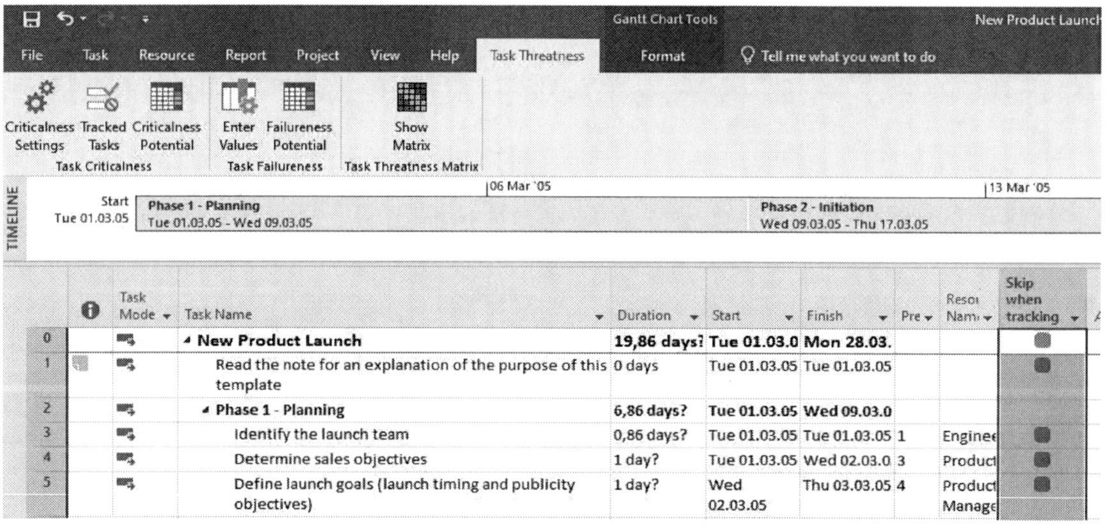

Figure 4 Inserted column "Skip when tracking"

Clicking the "*Criticalness Potential*" tab performs all necessary calculations and the window with table of fuzzy linguistic values of the criticalness indicators and criticalness potential for selected (or all) project tasks is opened (Figure 5).

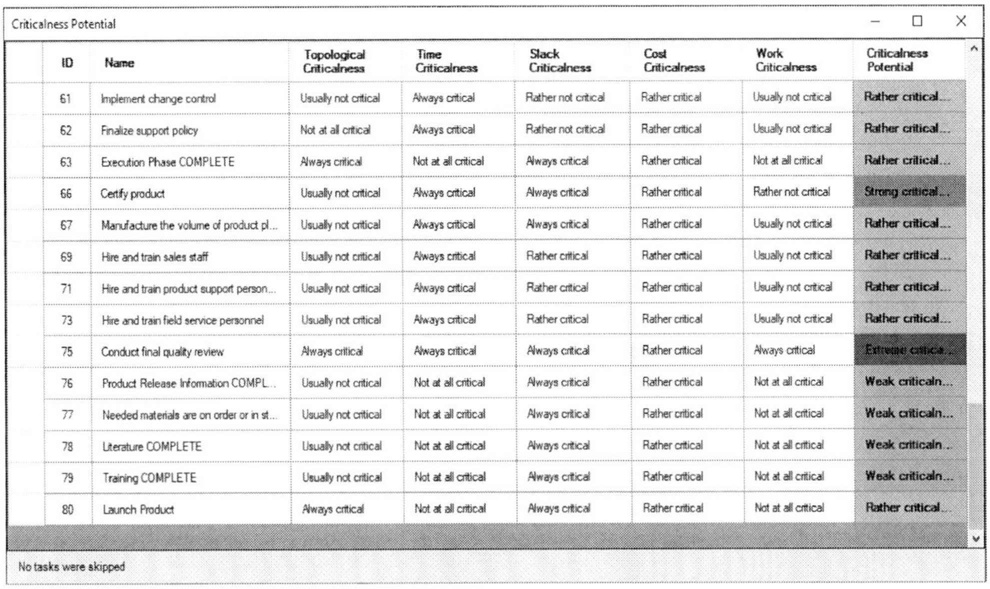

Criticalness Potential

ID	Name	Topological Criticalness	Time Criticalness	Slack Criticalness	Cost Criticalness	Work Criticalness	Criticalness Potential
61	Implement change control	Usually not critical	Always critical	Rather not critical	Rather critical	Usually not critical	Rather critical...
62	Finalize support policy	Not at all critical	Always critical	Rather not critical	Rather critical	Usually not critical	Rather critical...
63	Execution Phase COMPLETE	Always critical	Not at all critical	Always critical	Rather critical	Not at all critical	Rather critical...
66	Certify product	Usually not critical	Always critical	Always critical	Rather critical	Rather not critical	Strong critical...
67	Manufacture the volume of product pl...	Usually not critical	Always critical	Always critical	Rather critical	Usually not critical	Rather critical...
69	Hire and train sales staff	Usually not critical	Always critical	Rather critical	Rather critical	Usually not critical	Rather critical...
71	Hire and train product support person...	Usually not critical	Always critical	Rather critical	Rather critical	Usually not critical	Rather critical...
73	Hire and train field service personnel	Usually not critical	Always critical	Rather critical	Rather critical	Usually not critical	Rather critical...
75	Conduct final quality review	Always critical	Always critical	Always critical	Rather critical	Always critical	Extreme critica...
76	Product Release Information COMPL...	Usually not critical	Not at all critical	Always critical	Rather critical	Not at all critical	Weak criticaln...
77	Needed materials are on order or in st...	Usually not critical	Not at all critical	Always critical	Rather critical	Not at all critical	Weak criticaln...
78	Literature COMPLETE	Usually not critical	Not at all critical	Always critical	Rather critical	Not at all critical	Weak criticaln...
79	Training COMPLETE	Usually not critical	Not at all critical	Always critical	Rather critical	Not at all critical	Weak criticaln...
80	Launch Product	Always critical	Not at all critical	Always critical	Rather critical	Not at all critical	Rather critical...

No tasks were skipped

Figure 5 Window with table of fuzzy linguistic values of criticalness potential

To analyse tasks in terms of their failure, it is first necessary to enter the failureness rate in terms of time, cost and quality. Clicking the "*Enter Values*" tab in the "*Task Failureness*" section adds three columns to the task table with Undetermined values filled in by default. The user then fills in the values of failureness indicators from the linguistic scale for the chosen (or all) tasks (Figure 6).

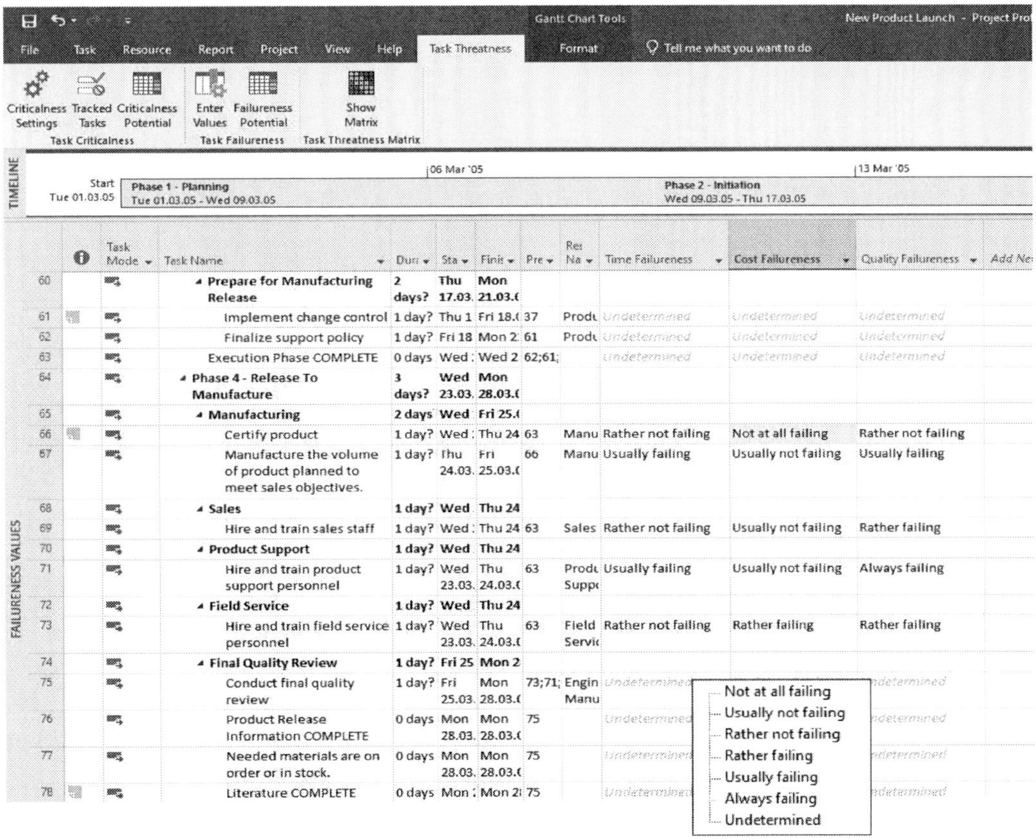

Figure 6 Inserted columns "Time, Cost, Quality Failureness"

Clicking the "*Failureness Potential*" tab performs all the necessary calculations and the user obtains a table of fuzzy linguistic failureness potential values for all evaluated project tasks (Figure 7).

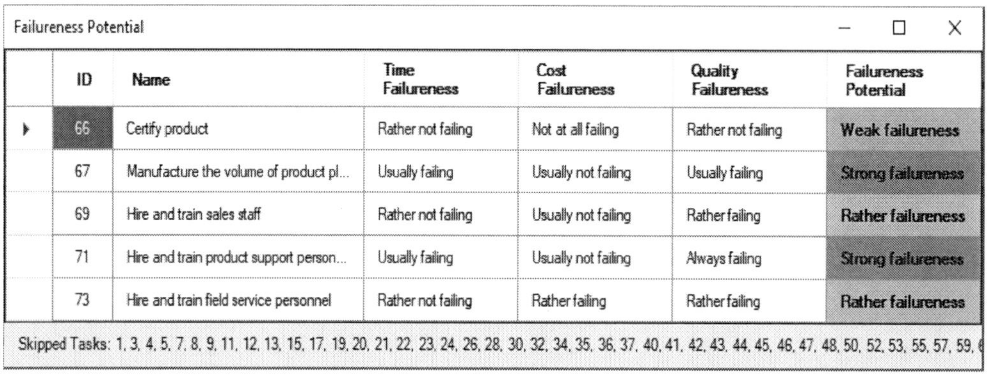

ID	Name	Time Failureness	Cost Failureness	Quality Failureness	Failureness Potential
66	Certify product	Rather not failing	Not at all failing	Rather not failing	Weak failureness
67	Manufacture the volume of product pl...	Usually failing	Usually not failing	Usually failing	Strong failureness
69	Hire and train sales staff	Rather not failing	Usually not failing	Rather failing	Rather failureness
71	Hire and train product support person...	Usually failing	Usually not failing	Always failing	Strong failureness
73	Hire and train field service personnel	Rather not failing	Rather failing	Rather failing	Rather failureness

Figure 7 Window with table of fuzzy linguistic values of failureness potential

Clicking the last tab "*Show Matrix*" in the "*Task Threatness Matrix*" section displays a window with a table of evaluation of tasks in terms of criticalness and failureness potentials and a task threatness matrix (Figure 8).

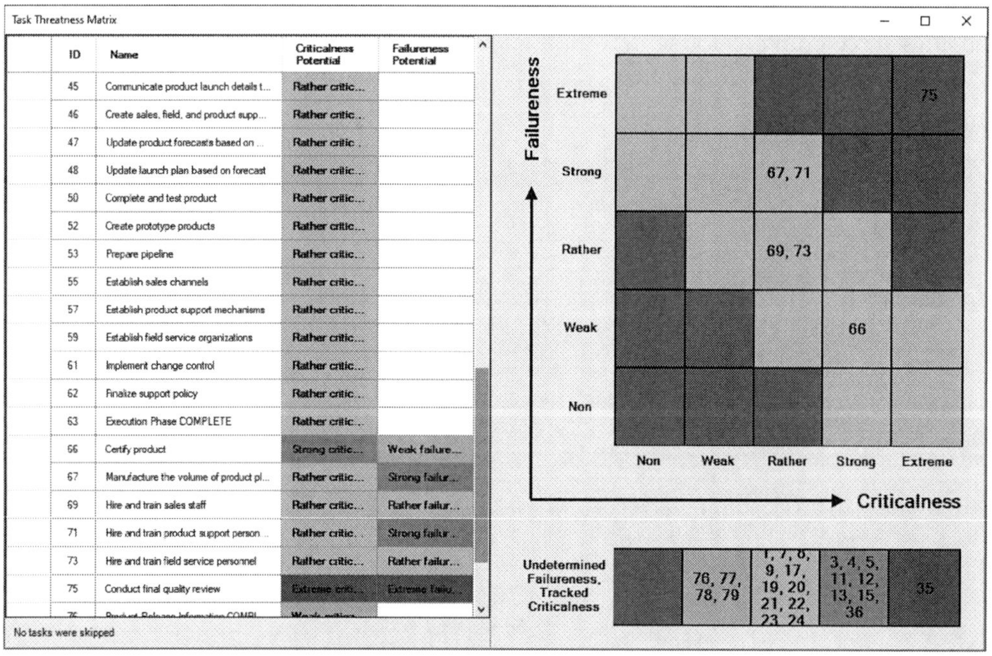

ID	Name	Criticalness Potential	Failureness Potential
45	Communicate product launch details t...	Rather critic...	
46	Create sales, field, and product supp...	Rather critic...	
47	Update product forecasts based on ...	Rather critic...	
48	Update launch plan based on forecast	Rather critic...	
50	Complete and test product	Rather critic...	
52	Create prototype products	Rather critic...	
53	Prepare pipeline	Rather critic...	
55	Establish sales channels	Rather critic...	
57	Establish product support mechanisms	Rather critic...	
59	Establish field service organizations	Rather critic...	
61	Implement change control	Rather critic...	
62	Finalize support policy	Rather critic...	
63	Execution Phase COMPLETE	Rather critic...	
66	Certify product	Strong critic...	Weak failure...
67	Manufacture the volume of product pl...	Rather critic...	Strong failur...
69	Hire and train sales staff	Rather critic...	Rather failur...
71	Hire and train product support person...	Rather critic...	Strong failur...
73	Hire and train field service personnel	Rather critic...	Rather failur...
75	Conduct final quality review	Extreme criti...	Extreme failu...

Figure 8 Window with task threatness matrix

This matrix shows the positions of the individual project tasks. The green bottom left part displays tasks at low threatness potential, the orange part consists of the tasks at medium threatness, and the red top right part shows the tasks at high threatness potential. A row is added to bottom of this matrix showing the position of tasks evaluated only according to the criticalness potential. This table indicates to the project manager which tasks need more attention using traffic light label, those in the red areas require urgent solutions.

4 Conclusion

There are a number of software products for project management (eg MS-Project, Primavera, etc.). These are oriented on critical path and cost and resources analysis of the whole projects, but do not contain a module for analyzing the criticalness and failureness of project tasks. The introduced Add-In solution for MS-Project is therefore unique. Our "Task Threatness Matrix Add-In" was presented to a number of project managers who evaluated it as an interesting, usable, and useful tool to support project management. This approach is useful for tasks risk analysis with respect to the project schedule, cost and resources and the project management triangle. The project tasks failureness or criticalness potential have undoubtedly an impact on the project success. In the large projects, the failureness can be evaluated only for selected tasks and remaining tasks can only be arranged according to the criticalness potential in the additional row bellow the task threatness matrix. Important advantage of this add-on is simple work with it and well-arranged displaying of results.

Acknowledgements

The research is supported by the Operational Programme Prague – Growth Pole of the Czech Republic – Implementation proof-of-concept activities CULS to promote technology transfer and knowledge into practice, No: CZ.07.1.02/0.0/0.0/17_049/0000815 – KZ10.

References

APM – Association for Project Management (2008). *Prioritising project risks*. Princess Risborough, UK: Association for Project Management.

Aschman, A. (2018). Why Capital Project Systems Succeed or Fail, IPA, [Online]. Available at: https://www.ipaglobal.com/news/article/why-capital-project-systems-succeed-or-fail-2/ [cited 2020-08-24].

Betz, J. (2019). 27+ Impressive Project Management Statistics in 2019, [Online]. Available at: https://learn.g2.com/project-management-statistics [cited 2020-08-26].

Brožová, H., Bartoška, J. and Šubrt, T. (2014). 'Fuzzy Approach to Risk Appetite in Project Management', *Proceedings of the 32st International conference on Mathematical Methods in Economics*, Olomouc, Czech Republic, pp. 61-66.

Brožová, H., Bartoška, J., Šubrt, T. and Rydval, J. (2016). 'Task Criticalness Potential: A Multiple Criteria Approach to Project Management', *Kybernetika*, 52, pp. 558-574.

Brožová, H., Šubrt, T. Rydval, J. and Pavlíčková, P. (2019a). 'Task Threatness Matrix in the Project Management', *Proceedings of the 32nd International conference on Mathematical Methods in Economics*, České Budějovice, Czech Republic, pp. 234-239.

Brožová, H., Šubrt, T. Rydval, J. and Pavlíčková, P. (2019b). 'Fuzzy Threatness Matrices in Project Management', *Proceedings of the 15th International Symposium on Operational Research in Slovenia,* Bled, Slovenia, pp. 581-586.

Williams, T. (2017). 'The Nature of Risk in Complex Projects', *Project Management Journal*, 48, pp. 55–66.

Influence of Incoterms 2020 on Strategic Decision-making of Entrepreneurs

Michaela Petrová[1], Martina Krügerová[2], Michal Kozieł[3]

Abstract. The transaction of international trade also brings with it the possibility of misunderstandings and costly disputes, unless purchase contracts are thoroughly concluded. Incoterms help manage these risks. The main purpose of the Incoterms rules is to define mutual roles, duties, responsibilities, and the transfer of risks. The aim of the article is to identify the benefits of Incoterms conditions in concluding purchase contracts. The authors conclude that the use of Incoterms clauses brings more advantages than disadvantages. Both for individual contracting parties and for international trade. An important aspect, however, is the correct use of a suitable condition. The authors also draw attention to possible impacts under inappropriately used conditions, such as ineffective risk allocation or abuse of a dominant position.

Keywords: Incoterms, International Trade, Purchase Contract, Risks, Transaction costs.

JEL Classification: K12, K33, F23, M16

1 Introduction

Imports and exports are key components in international trade and concern all sectors, especially those related to production, where the production process requires the import of products or raw materials for the export of final products abroad. Due to the large number of suppliers and customers, the negotiation of business agreements is complicated and diverse. Things such as delivery, shipping costs, shipping risk and commitments need to be agreed upon. Negotiating all the terms for the transaction may take time, and sometimes the contract may not be accepted at the end of the negotiation. And it is the mutual trade of the two entities that is facilitated by the general conditions, but they also speed it up and reduce the cost of contracting. In international trade, the contracting parties may use established and their own compiled business conditions. The general terms and conditions of a more general nature are the UNIDROIT Principles of International Commercial Contracts, which represent a set of principles for the area of international trade applicable regardless of the legal, economic, and political conditions of a particular country. The general terms and conditions used in concluding the purchase contract include the Incoterms (International Commercial Terms). Specialized or interest organizations may develop other specific trading conditions (like the paradigmatic conditions of the ISDA - International Swaps and Derivative Association, used in trading in derivatives on the capital markets; or the FIDIC conditions used in international practice, mainly in construction industry). In the article we will focus on the importance of business

[1] VSB – Technical University of Ostrava, Faculty of Economics, Sokolská třída 33, 701 21 Ostrava, Email: michaela.petrova@vsb.cz, ORCID 0000-0003-0979-3046.
[2] VSB – Technical University of Ostrava, Faculty of Economics, Sokolská třída 33, 701 21 Ostrava, Email: martina.krugerova@vsb.cz, ORCID 0000-0001-5049-8183.
[3] VSB – Technical University of Ostrava, Faculty of Economics, Sokolská třída 33, 701 21 Ostrava, Email: michal.koziel@vsb.cz, ORCID 0000-0001-8561-0358.

conditions in concluding purchase contracts in international trade and their influence on the strategic decision-making of entrepreneurs, therefore the business conditions of Incoterms are selected for closer examination.

Incoterms are regulations or conditions of delivery of a product which are a set international standard for the conclusion of a purchase contract between a buyer and a seller and which have been published by the International Chamber of Commerce (ICC) and are in compliance with United Nations (UN) trade principles. Within the framework of international trade, a fundamental change was made this year, representing the issuance of new basic business conditions for the sale of goods - INCOTERMS 2020. The new version of Incoterms 2020 rules issued by ICC entered into force on 1 January 2020 and is thus the eleventh version. Since the first publication of the rules in 1936, the ICC has constantly maintained and developed them. (ICC, 2020).

The Incoterms rules are paradigmatic contractual conditions from which the contracting parties can choose a combination of rules that suit them for a given contractual relationship and incorporate it into the contract. The Incoterms rules are intended for use only in purchase contracts (Bejček et al, 2016). Incoterms have a global reach, so it is important to pursue this issue. In particular, the practical impact of Incoterms is invaluable. By being an international standard, they take international contracting to a completely different level. It thus creates a unifying element across the various legal regulations of individual states and language barriers.

The process of concluding a purchase contract, the choice of Incoterms conditions affects transaction costs. The autonomy of the will of the parties in the contracting process contributes greatly to this. It is thus the will of each party to assess the risks associated with the contract, the specific choice of business conditions and its impacts (benefits) on the transaction. The aim of the article is to explain the importance of Incoterms delivery conditions for risk management, to identify the benefits of Incoterms conditions in concluding purchase contracts and thus the importance for strategic decision-making of entrepreneurs. International trade relations can be very complicated and the delivery of goods to another state can be associated with many complications. By choosing the right Incoterms, the entrepreneur can avoid various risks associated with transportation, liability for damage, taxation, etc. He can also significantly affect and reduce the transaction costs associated with a given business transaction.

2 Literature review

The number of contracts of a certain type that the entity concludes during its activities leads the entities to rationalize this process. Entities conclude contracts in a given formalized manner and with a certain content. To do this, they often choose business conditions, which become a form of standardization of contracting. One of the types of business conditions are the Incoterms delivery conditions, which are used in international trade. Incoterms are a set of rules that are commonly included in international purchase contract for the above reasons (Bejček et al, 2016), and which are a binding standard in terms of international and national law (Rozehnalová, 2015; Dobiáš and Malacka, 2019). The use of Incoterms also influences the behaviour of the entrepreneur. Bergami (2013), Smejkal and Rais (2013) consider correctly used Incoterms 2010 as an effective tool for risk management. Stojanović and Ivetić (2020), in turn, see delivery rules as a kind of "channel" that connects trade and logistics.

It must be taken into consideration that the ICC is not an instrument of government and therefore cannot legislate. It must be borne in mind that the ICC is not an instrument of government and therefore cannot legislate. But as Bergami (2013) states, it can and does do rules that the parties involved can follow voluntarily, as is the case with the Incoterms rules, which are accepted by their explicit inclusion in the purchase contracts. It is also important to note that Incoterms are not an entire contract, but only one important part of the overall sales contract.

The Incoterms are used to determine the key responsibilities of sellers and buyers with respect to different delivery methods, risk transfer and costs. They help entities determine the roles, responsibilities, liability for transportation and compensation that are accepted and thus form an agreement between buyer and seller (Debattista, 2020; Suraraksa, Amchang and Sawatwong, 2020). It provides the parties with a guarantee which, according to Smejkal and Rais (2013), consists precisely in the uniform interpretation of the clause included in the purchase contract, and substantially reduces various subsequent ambiguities and disputes. But it is necessary to realize that the conditions do not represent the whole contract. The Incoterms only address the relationship between seller and buyer. It does not address the relationship with forwarders, carriers, insurance companies and banks. Ramberg (2011) recalls that the parties must also determine which rules apply if the contract is not performed as expected due to different circumstances and how disputes between the parties should be resolved.

The application of Incoterms business conditions in international business practice can bring several advantages and disadvantages and can significantly affect a particular business. However, the condition is that a specific condition is selected and used correctly. Vogt (2018) states that if the conditions are used correctly, they can speed up logistics and bring cost savings, and logically, when misunderstood conditions, they cost money, time, and lead to bad contracts. The authors state that correctly used Incoterms are an effective tool for risk management. The article evaluates the conditions under which they will be beneficial for risk management.

3 Analysis of conditions - input data

Incoterms are product delivery conditions. This is an international standard for concluding a purchase contract between a buyer and a seller. The conditions must be in accordance with United Nations (UN) trade principles. Buyers and sellers must recognize the extent of the cost and risk commitment to reach an understanding between the two parties that may have a different culture (Suraraksa, Amchang and Sawatwong, 2020).

The Incoterms set out the obligations of buyers and sellers in the supply of goods for the purchase of goods worldwide. The costs and risks between the parties are clearly identified. Incoterms contain ICC rules for the use of 11 commercial clauses. In 2020, there are some changes in conditions compared to the 2010 version.

The intention of the changes was to make the terms and conditions more accessible and easier to use. (Durdağ et al., 2020)A revision was desirable. Already Bergami (2013) pointed out some problematic and outdated business and banking practices in Incoterms 2010. The most important initiative behind the new version of Incoterms was to focus on improving the presentation so that users are guided to the right rule for their contract. Thus, design adjustments have been made to help the international trading community move towards smoother export / import transactions. This is a clearer explanation of the definition and connection between the purchase contract and the ancillary contracts, with explanations for each rule and the possibility of re-ordering in accordance with the rules (Debattista, 2020). In addition to these "cosmetic" changes, there have been more significant changes compared to the previous version of Incoterms 2010. Debattista (2020) summarizes the most important changes:

- Bills of lading with an on-board notation and the FCA rule,
- Costs, where they are listed,
- Different levels of insurance cover in CIF and CIP,
- Arranging for carriage with seller's or buyer's own means of transport in FCA, DAP, DPU and DDP,
- Change in the three-letter initials for DAT to DPU,
- Inclusion of security-related requirements within carriage obligations and costs,
- Explanatory Notes for Users.

Changes in business rules are so far processed in the articles to a very limited extent, as well as studies focused on the analysis of the use of Incoterms between buyer and seller, which is confirmed in their study by Vogt and Davis (2020). The author's team will deal with the changes in detail in a separate article regarding their scope, as this issue is not directly related to the topic of this article. For the purposes of the articles, we will be based on the Incoterms 2020 rules, although their meaning is generally applicable to all versions of the rules.

The Incoterms describe and regulate three main areas (obligations, risks, and costs) in a total of 11 conditions, which are shown in Table 1 for a comprehensive view of the issue (ICC, 2020).

Mode of transport	**INCOTERMS 2020**	
Rules for any mode of transport	**EXW**	Ex Works
	FCA	Free Carrier
	CPT	Carriage Paid To
	CIP	Carriage and Insurance Paid To
	DAP	Delivered at Place
	DPU	Delivered at Place Unloaded
	DDP	Delivered Duty Paid
Rules for sea and inland waterway transport	**FAS**	Free Alongside Ship
	FOB	Free on Board
	CFR	Cost and Freight
	CIF	Cost, Insurance and Freight

Table 1 Incoterms 2020 table [ICC, 2020]

It can be seen from Table 1 that the Incoterms describe and regulate three main areas - obligations, risks, and costs. It sets out the obligations of the seller and the buyer - who does what, such as who arranges the transport, insurance of the goods, who obtains the transport documents and export or import licenses. The conditions determine where and when the seller delivers the goods. That is, cases where the risk passes from the seller to the buyer. And which party is responsible for what costs (transport, packaging, loading or unloading costs and inspection or security costs). Thus, according to Bergami (2013), it becomes an effective tool for risk management.

4 INCOTERMS and strategic decision-making

The application of business conditions in international business practice has several advantages and disadvantages, and thus impacts on the strategic decision-making of economic entities that can significantly affect a particular trade.

Using Incoterms has many benefits for both the buyer and the seller. The advantage is that Incoterms are concluded worldwide and are used in more than 30 different languages. There is a reduction in contract negotiation times and transaction costs are reduced. From the economic definitions, transaction costs include the costs of finding potential buyers and sellers, negotiating, drawing up a contract, determining whether a partner is complying with the contract, costs of enforcing a contract that the partner does not comply with, costs caused by non-compliance. Excessive transaction costs can prevent certain exchange acts. If the state introduces legal norms that protect property rights and enforce well-executed contracts well, then transaction costs will be reduced, and exchange will be encouraged. Due to internationally agreed business conditions, these transaction costs are reduced in connection with the negotiation and conclusion of contracts. (Holman et al., 2017)

As far as transaction costs are concerned, there is clearly a reduction in the costs associated with concluding the contract as the contract time is shortened. The time that the parties must spend in the contracting process is also reduced. One-time transaction costs are thus spread over time and into other similar contracts. Finally, the costs of reloading and legal services are falling. The rules of Incoterms are elaborated in detail in many language versions, where even a layman can understand from these rules and their explanations what rights and obligations apply to him when choosing a particular clause. In addition, these are very widespread rules and therefore information on them is generally available. However, as Bejček et al (2016) point out, in case of incorrect setting of conditions or their abuse, they can then be a tool for abuse of a dominant position on the relevant market (the dominant partner forces acceptance by the other party if the conditions are disproportionate). In the opposite sense, the authors consider the right choice of condition to facilitate non-discriminatory behaviour in the market, and thus a significant benefit for international trade.

As we have stated, the indisputable advantage of using the Incoterms conditions for a strategic manager as a contractor can be the saving of legal services (of course, we consider the assumption of the correct choice of the clause). The conditions can bring legal certainty, make the private law environment in which the parties operate more transparent and formalize business practices, thus indirectly leading to a more transparent and proportionate regulation of relations.

A disadvantage can be considered a situation where, due to the use of conditions and the clause, the risks can be distributed inefficiently. Depending on which Incoterms clause the parties choose, they bear a specific degree of risk. Although the relative degree of risk is difficult to determine due to the high number of variables, Bergami (2013) categorized Incoterms into risk bands based on the relationship between risk factor and cost.

The risk of loss of or damage to the goods and the obligation to bear the costs pass from the seller to the buyer as soon as the seller fulfils his obligation to deliver the goods. All clauses stipulate that the transfer of risk and costs may occur even before the delivery of the goods, if the buyer does not take over the goods as agreed. This is so that the buyer is not allowed to delay the moment of the transfer of risk and costs. Thus, in addition to determining the methods of delivery, all 11 rules indicate when delivery costs and risks are transferred from one participant to another. The rules thus determine who will deal with the insurance company in the event of damage to the goods, or who will bear the risk of financial loss in the event of a refusal by the culprit or the insurance company. However, the Incoterms clauses do not address the issue of the transfer of ownership of the goods, they only address the transfer of the right of disposal to the consignment.

As mentioned above, Incoterms have the character of business conditions. This means that, if permitted by law, they replace or supplement statutory provisions. The advantage of Incoterms is their comprehensibility and uniform interpretation between the contracting parties, which eliminates possible disputes regarding the interpretation of individual provisions of the contract, which are replaced by these international rules. On the other hand, if the legal provision is mandatory, then it is not possible to deviate from it, nor will the best business conditions be applied here, as the legal regulation will always take precedence over the contractual regulation. However, in the case of commercial relations, the legal provisions are largely dispositive. This means that if the parties want to deal with these issues differently in the contract, they have the opportunity. If the contracting parties do not want to regulate these issues, they are governed by a specific provision of the law. This can cause problems in practice, when the issue of choosing the law, or determining the law applicable to the legal relationship with the international element. However, many national laws directly provide that part of the contractual relationship will be governed by or only by reference to the terms and conditions. In this way, the Incoterms rules can be implemented into the contract without much difficulty.

Disputable aspects may arise in the conclusion of contracts, in the use of commercial terms and their adequate inclusion in private law, and in the distinction between situations related to the implementation of trade between entrepreneurs and the participation of consumers in international private law. When using Incoterms in practice, we must keep in mind that the conditions tell the parties what to do, but no longer explain the situation if one of the parties does not do so. Therefore, such unexpected events need to be set out directly in the contract or in the form of an amendment in a clear and convincing manner. This will prevent possible future disputes due to unexpected events.

Another crucial aspect is the fact that these are voluntary rules that the parties may or may not choose. It is therefore purely up to the parties to apply these rules in their contract. Of course, there may be situations where one of the parties insists on the introduction of these rules and the other rejects them. However, this is rather a question of contractual freedom and contracting, which was not the subject of this article.

5 Conclusion

Incoterms' terms and conditions make economic sense primarily by having their content professionally prepared in advance, recognized worldwide, and used in more than 30 different languages. In addition, these clauses are drafted in such a way that their content does not cast doubt on their interpretation. Of course, this does not necessarily mean that the contract corresponds to their requirements or it may not be completely ideal. However, we can conclude that the conditions will be entirely positive. When deciding to conclude a contract, the conditions will be beneficial.

There are several advantages to using Incoterms. This is a relatively complex adjustment, as the clauses cover not only the transfer of the risk of loss and damage to the goods, but also any subsequent claims related to the transport of the goods. They are easily revised and are regularly reviewed every 10 years. Incoterms are very sophisticated, and the individual clauses differ in the methods and details of transport and adapt the transfer of danger accordingly. We must also not forget the fact that we are still moving within the framework of private law, even with an international element. This means that even if the parties choose a specific clause, they can further modify or refine it according to their own needs, for example to the exclusion of a specific rule. Other benefits included a reduction in transaction costs, translation and legal costs, greater legal certainty in concluding contracts or a faster and in many ways simpler contracting process. The authors consider the situation of inefficient risk distribution due to inappropriate use of conditions and the given clause to be a disadvantage, which can be avoided by a certain standardization of business cases. Of course, the wrong choice of condition will always be a disadvantage for a particular party and an advantage for the other party. When can it become a tool to abuse a dominant position in the relevant market (Bejček et al, 2016). However, the authors conclude that, when the conditions are used correctly, Incoterms lead to non-discriminatory market behaviour and benefit international trade.

The aim of this article was to identify the benefits of business conditions in concluding purchase contracts. In conclusion, the use of Incoterms has more advantages than disadvantages. Another crucial aspect is the fact that these are voluntary rules that the parties may or may not choose. And in the final stage, they can also influence the choice of the contractor.

In 2020, there are some changes in the conditions compared to the version from 2010. The intention of the changes was to make the business conditions more accessible and easier to use. Some key changes significantly change the contractual balance and impose new rights and obligations on the parties. Regarding their scope, the author's team in the next article will focus on the analysis of individual Incoterms delivery conditions and the comparison of changes to identify the benefits of the new conditions.

Acknowledgements

This research was financially supported within the VŠB–Technical University SGS grant project No. SP2021/74 (Minimization of Risks Related to the Delivery of Goods Against the Background of the Use of INCOTERMS 2020).

References

Bergami, R. (2013). 'Managing Incoterms 2010 risks: tension with trade and banking practices.' *Int. J. Econ. Bus. Res.*, 6 (3), pp. 324-338.

Bejček, J. et al. (2016). *Obchodní podmínky*. Brno: Masarykova univerzita.

Debattista, Ch. (2020). Introduction to Incoterms® 2020. [Online]. In INCOTERMS® 2020; ICC.

Dobiáš, P. and Malacka, M. (2019). *Obchodní podmínky v mezinárodním obchodním styku*. Praha: Leges.

Durdağ, C. et al. (2020). 'The past, today and future of incoterms in international delivery: A review on the innovations in logistics.' *Journal of Economics Library*, 7, pp. 201–207.

Available at: https://iccwbo.org/publication/incoterms-2020-introduction/ [cited 2020-01-10].

Holman, R. et al. (2017). *Dějiny ekonomického myšlení*. 4nd ed. Praha: C.H. Beck.

ICC (2020). Incoterms® 2020, [Online]. Available at: https://iccwbo.org/resources-for-business/incoterms-rules/incoterms-2020/ [cited 2020-01-16].

Ramberg, J. (2011). *ICC Guide to Incoterms 2010: Introduction.* ICC.

Rozehnalová, N. et al (2015). Czech private international law. 1st edition. Brno: Masaryk University, Faculty of Law

Smejkal, V. and Rais, K. (2013). *Řízení rizik ve firmách a jiných organizacích*. 4nd ed. Praha: Grada.

Stojanović, Đ. and Ivetić, J. (2020). 'Possibilities of using incoterms clauses in a country logistics performance assessment and benchmarking.' *Transport Policy*, 98, pp. 217-228.

Suraraksa, J., Amchang Ch. and Sawatwong, N. (2020). 'Decision-Making on Incoterms 2020 of Automotive Parts Manufacturers in Thailand.' *Journal of Asian Finance, Economics and Business*, 7 (10), pp. 461-470.

Vogt, J. (2018). 'The Use and Misuse of Incoterms in Movement of Goods.' [Online] Supplychainbrain.com. June 2018, pp. 44-47. [cited 2020-02-01].

Vogt, J. and Davis, J. (2020). 'The state of incoterm® research.' *Transportation Journal*, 59(3), pp. 304-324.

Volatility spillover effect in Asian stock markets

Petr Seďa[1], Lorena Caridad Lopéz del Río [2]

Abstract. An understanding of the processes of volatility spillovers among stock markets and its consequences is important for asset valuation, risk management, portfolio construction, hedging strategies and economic policy in general. This paper aims to estimate and interpret volatility spillover effects in selected Asian stock markets using multivariate GARCH models. More precisely, there will be investigated the linkages between four developed and four emerging Asian stock markets and two developed world stock markets (USA, Germany). In this paper, we employ a VAR-GARCH-BEKK model. Our investigations cover the period from January 2007 to December 2018 which includes the phase of the global financial crisis. Achieved results confirmed significant impact of the volatility spillover effect coming from the US stock market. This effect is greater in the period of the global financial crisis.

Keywords: spillover effects, stock market, VAR-GARCH-BEKK model, volatility transmission.

JEL Classification: C13, C39, C55

1 Introduction

Institutional investors and individuals make investment decisions that are affected by the perceived higher risk arising from significant volatility and its spillover between markets. As a result, if stock returns do not correlate too much and there is no significant spillover of volatility, the international diversification of investment portfolios would bring benefits, as investors can reduce risk without affecting returns (Sucháček et al., 2017). Contrary to that, if stock markets move together and there is a significant volatility spillover, then the advantages from diversification may be small.

The speed of global financial market integration around the world has led to many studies that have examined the mechanism by which movements between stock markets are transferred. The authors found that while correlations between stock markets are generally growing, there are still profitable opportunities for investors to benefit from portfolio diversification by investing in stock markets in different countries (Yavas and Dedi, 2016). Not surprisingly, since the Asian crisis in 1996–1997, both economists and politicians have begun a debate on capital controls, and several countries have introduced an input tax on short-term capital inflows (Ostry et al, 2011). Following the end of the global financial crisis in 2007-2009, stock markets around the world responded to the policy measures of major countries. In particular, the quantitative easing of the Federal Reserve Bank, the European Central Bank and the Bank of Japan resulted in historically lowest interest rates.

[1] VSB-Technical University of Ostrava, Faculty of Economics, Department of Mathematical Methods in Economics, Sokolská třída 33, 702 00 Ostrava 1, Czech Republic, petr.seda@vsb.cz.

[2] University of Cordoba, Department of Statistics and Econometrics, Agrifood Campus of International Excellence ceiA3, E-14001 Cordoba, Spain, lcaridadlr@gmail.com

Volatility modeling in financial time series has been the subject of much attention since the introduction of the ARCH model (Engle, 1982). While the economic integration of international stock markets was evident, the relationship between the volatility and co-volatility of different markets gradually came to the fore.

Li (2012) examined the impact of China's stock market reforms on stock market ties between China, the United States, Korea and Japan. His results show that the Chinese stock market is linked to non-Chinese markets, and the implemented reforms allow volatility to spillover from China to these markets. Some researchers have also investigated the extent of volatility transmission in different markets during a particular political or economic event, such as the global financial crisis (Neaime, 2012). Li and Giles (2015) studied stock market links in the United States, Japan, and six Asian emerging countries. Their results confirm a significant one-way shock and a spillover of volatility from the US market to emerging markets in Asia, and Japan. They also showed that the spillover effects of volatility between the US market and other Asian markets were stronger during the Asian financial crisis and also two-way.

The main goal of this paper is to examine the volatility spillovers between the two world developed stock markets (USA and Germany) and four developed (Japan, Singapore, South Korea and Hong Kong) and four emerging (Malaysia, Thailand, Indonesia and mainland China) Asian stock markets using information based on the main indices of those markets. In this paper, the VAR-GARCH-BEKK model will be utilized.

The novelty of this paper consists of the following aspects:

- the volatility spillover effect is investigated in both developed and emerging main Asian stock markets in relation to the global stock market and the eurozone.
- the basic testing period is divided into two different sub-periods that include different stages of development of stock markets (e.g. the global financial crisis),
- the multivariate VAR-GARCH-BEKK model is applied.

Our paper is organized in the following way. In the Introduction, where the motivation was explained, the added value of this paper was stressed, and a short review of the literature including the current state of the research topic on an international scale is delivered. The second chapter is providing a brief description of the research objective. Moreover, the methodology applied in this paper is described and explained and the data sample analyzed as well. In the third chapter, the empirical results are expressed in the form of tables. In addition, outcomes are interpreted in an economic manner. The conclusion summarizes the outcomes of this paper. It is evaluated whether the aim of the paper was fulfilled and the main findings of the research are presented.

2 Methodology

In this chapter, the multivariate VAR-GARCH-BEKK model is described and explained. Further, the data sample used in this article is described and analyzed as well.

2.1 Multivariate Volatility Transmission VAR-GARCH-BEKK Model

In order to estimate the multivariate volatility model, it is necessary to find the models used for both the mean and the variance-covariance equations. For the mean equation, the VAR(k)

model is utilized (Hamilton, 1994). However, the modelling time-varying second-order moments is crucial (Engle, 1982). Bauwens et al. (2006) proposed three mutually non-exclusive possible multidimensional GARCH type models that are based on different specifications of the variance-covariance matrix H_t. Bollerslev et al. (1988) proposed a general VEC model in which each element of the variance-covariance matrix H_t is expressed as a linear function of the delayed square errors, the cross-products of the errors, and the delayed values of the elements of that matrix. However, the VEC model is not able to capture the effects of volatility spillovers between different markets, and also the extended diagonal DVEC model still cannot guarantee that the variance-covariance matrix H_t is positively definitive. To overcome these shortcomings, Engle and Kroner (1995) proposed a new BEKK model that ensures a new parameterization of H_t.

$$H_t = C'C + A'\varepsilon_{t-1}\varepsilon_{t-1}'A + G'H_{t-1}G, \tag{1}$$

where each element of H_t is a linear function of the lagged squared errors and cross-products of errors and lagged values of the elements of H_t. Moreover, **C** is $(N \times N)$ lower triangular matrix for constant, **A** and **G** represent $(N \times N)$ parameters matrices.

The BEKK model ensures positive semi-definiteness by working with quadratic forms. As empirically observed, stock prices volatility tends to have greater effect in response to negative shocks than positive ones. Kroner and Ng (1998) extended the BEKK model to capture this asymmetric effect of the time-varying variance-covariance by adding the matrix **D**:

$$H_t = C'C + A'\varepsilon_{t-1}\varepsilon_{t-1}'A + G'H_{t-1}G + D'\epsilon_{t-1}\epsilon_{t-1}'D, \tag{2}$$

where ϵ_t is the same as ε_t if ε_t reaches negative value and zero if otherwise. In the trivariate case, the model can be rewritten as follows:

$$\begin{aligned} H_t &= C'C \\ &+ \begin{bmatrix} a_{11} & a_{12} & a_{13} \\ a_{21} & a_{22} & a_{23} \\ a_{31} & a_{32} & a_{33} \end{bmatrix}' \begin{bmatrix} \varepsilon_{1,t-1}^2 & \varepsilon_{1,t-1}\varepsilon_{2,t-1} & \varepsilon_{1,t-1}\varepsilon_{3,t-1} \\ \varepsilon_{2,t-1}\varepsilon_{1,t-1} & \varepsilon_{2,t-1}^2 & \varepsilon_{2,t-1}\varepsilon_{3,t-1} \\ \varepsilon_{3,t-1}\varepsilon_{1,t-1} & \varepsilon_{3,t-1}\varepsilon_{2,t-1} & \varepsilon_{3,t-1}^2 \end{bmatrix} \begin{bmatrix} a_{11} & a_{12} & a_{13} \\ a_{21} & a_{22} & a_{23} \\ a_{31} & a_{32} & a_{33} \end{bmatrix} \\ &+ \begin{bmatrix} g_{11} & g_{12} & g_{13} \\ g_{21} & g_{22} & g_{23} \\ g_{31} & g_{32} & g_{33} \end{bmatrix}' H_{t-1} \begin{bmatrix} g_{11} & g_{12} & g_{13} \\ g_{21} & g_{22} & g_{23} \\ g_{31} & g_{32} & g_{33} \end{bmatrix} \\ &+ \begin{bmatrix} d_{11} & d_{12} & d_{13} \\ d_{21} & d_{22} & d_{23} \\ d_{31} & d_{32} & d_{33} \end{bmatrix}' \begin{bmatrix} \epsilon_{1,t-1}^2 & \epsilon_{1,t-1}\epsilon_{2,t-1} & \epsilon_{1,t-1}\epsilon_{3,t-1} \\ \epsilon_{2,t-1}\epsilon_{1,t-1} & \epsilon_{2,t-1}^2 & \epsilon_{2,t-1}\epsilon_{3,t-1} \\ \epsilon_{3,t-1}\epsilon_{1,t-1} & \epsilon_{3,t-1}\epsilon_{2,t-1} & \epsilon_{3,t-1}^2 \end{bmatrix} \begin{bmatrix} d_{11} & d_{12} & d_{13} \\ d_{21} & d_{22} & d_{23} \\ d_{31} & d_{32} & d_{33} \end{bmatrix}. \end{aligned} \tag{3}$$

The diagonal elements of the matrix **A** (a_{ii}) measure the effect of shocks on its own country's volatility, while the off-diagonal elements of the matrix **A** (a_{ij}) in the matrix express the effect of country *i*'s shock on country *j*'s volatility. We can omit asymmetric terms in equations (2) and (3) since the parameter matrix **D** has a similar expression to the matrix **A**. The parameters of the matrix **D** can measure the asymmetric response to the negative shocks. The past volatility effects are expressed by the matrix **G**. The diagonal elements of the matrix **G** (g_{ii}) measure its own past volatility effect on its conditional variance, while the off-diagonal elements of the matrix **G** (g_{ij}) gauge the effects of past volatility of market *i* on market *j*'s conditional variance. It is also known as "volatility spillover" (Li and Giles, 2015).

2.2 Data Sample Description

The data used in this article include the stock indices of the four developed and four developing Asian countries, along with the stock indices of the United States and Germany, which represent the two developed stock markets. The four Asian emerging stock market indices are the Shanghai SSE index in mainland China, the KLCI index in Malaysia, the SET index in Thailand and the IDX index from Indonesia. The four developed Asian markets represent the STI index from Singapore, the KOSPI index from South Korea, the HANG SENG index from Hong Kong and the Japanese NIKKEI225 index. The S&P500 index was chosen as the representative of the US stock market, and the DAX30 index represents the developed stock market in the euro area. The data sample was obtained from https://www.investing.com/indices. The whole reference period of the sample is from October 9, 2007 to December 31, 2018. The reason for choosing this period is that both the global financial crisis and following economic recovery is covered so that in addition to the long-term examination of volatility developments we can also explore dynamic links between countries in the short term.

To figure out the volatility spillover effect dynamics, the basic testing period was divided into two sub periods. The development of prices of S&P 500 index was chosen as a benchmark for the splitting of the basic testing period:

1) The first testing period (09/10/2007-30/06/.2009) is also known as a crisis period. On October 9, 2007 the American stock market started to fall down. After the housing bubble and subprime crisis, the bank sector collapsed partially and the US economy fell into recession. The global financial crisis ended on the 30th of June 2009 according to The National Bureau of Economic Research (NBER).
2) The second testing period (01/07/2009-31/12/2018) is also called a post-crisis period. The US economy was recovering and taking on a growth trajectory.

The data are daily and therefore include five trading days a week, bringing more than 2,800 observations. When using daily data, we can capture more information than with weekly or monthly data. For statistical reasons, it is appropriate to work with time series of returns instead of prices (Brooks, 2002). In addition, the revenues have the additional advantage of being reported without units. Continuously compound daily returns r_t for each stock market are expressed by the first difference of the logarithm of the stock market indices, respectively their prices P_t:

$$r_t = \ln \left(P_t / P_{t-1}\right). \qquad (4)$$

3 Empirical Results

In this chapter, the main results and findings achieved with respect to the aim of this paper will be described and presented in the form of tables. In the modelling, we use the numbers 1, 2 and 3 to stand for the US, German and one of the Asian markets, respectively. Based on the Schwarz-Bayesian Information Criterion and Hannan-Quinn Information Criterion, for the mean equation we adopted the VAR(2) model for both sub-sample analysis, and asymmetric GARCH-BEKK(1,1) model for the variance-covariance equation for all eight groups of stock markets. To sum up, in this paper the VAR(2)-GARCH-BEKK(1,1) model was applied.

Due to the limited extent of the paper, the complete results of all eight estimated VAR(2)-GARCH-BEKK(1,1) models will not be presented. We will focus only on the parts of the models that estimate volatility and its transmission between markets. This is in line with the goal of our article. Most of the coefficients of the main equation of the estimated VAR models are statistically significant. It can be concluded that the impact of the US market returns is much greater than in the case of the German market. This is especially true in times of crisis. As for the residues, the only problem was that their distribution did not correspond to normal.

	NIKKEI	STI	KOSPI	HANGSENG	KLCI	SET	IDX	SSE
Panel A								
a_{11}	1.38E-06	0.000191	0.005427	0.000669	1.94E-11	0.001156	1.16E-06	0.000115
a_{12}	4.92E-07	0.000280	0.000551	0.000596	1.75E-11	0.001609	4.29E-07	0.000153
a_{13}	4.69E-07	0.001943	0.012401	0.005136	2.64E-12	0.006974	5.01E-07	0.001321
a_{22}	1.76E-07	0.000412	5.75E-05	0.000530	1.58E-11	0.002240	1.58E-07	0.000213
a_{23}	1.67E-07	0.002851	0.001276	0.004571	2.38E-12	0.009710	1.85E-07	0.001802
a_{33}	1.60E-07	0.019795	0.028332	0.039407	3.59E-13	0.042089	2.16E-07	0.015219
Panel D								
d_{11}	**0.122992**	**0.135926**	**0.132909**	**0.133106**	**0.145763**	**0.126612**	**0.152409**	**0.152539**
d_{12}	**0.093629**	**0.098726**	**0.107244**	**0.093958**	**0.096116**	**0.090039**	**0.104875**	**0.106088**
d_{13}	0.044856	**0.098256**	**0.174550**	**0.121512**	0.041777	**0.091329**	0.075306	0.014291
d_{22}	**0.108371**	**0.112180**	**0.115859**	**0.112865**	**0.108109**	**0.105595**	**0.115483**	**0.112347**
d_{23}	0.059255	0.063814	0.008991	**0.109044**	**0.120524**	0.073763	0.051529	0.048233
d_{33}	**0.175334**	**0.155116**	**0.204903**	**0.234964**	**0.205235**	**0.101485**	**0.530785**	**0.135591**
Panel G								
g_{11}	**0.907961**	**0.898539**	**0.894238**	**0.890583**	**0.891564**	**0.902994**	**0.889702**	**0.893905**
g_{12}	**0.313942**	**0.205657**	**0.305541**	**0.198555**	**0.202862**	**0.210813**	**0.200763**	**0.204822**
g_{13}	**0.801324**	**0.797220**	**0.778501**	**0.822197**	**0.433080**	**0.786244**	**0.695920**	**0.790696**
g_{22}	**0.919961**	**0.912851**	**0.916987**	**0.906598**	**0.914396**	**0.918700**	**0.911962**	**0.915872**
g_{23}	0.107260	0.104637	0.089605	0.029564	**0.139349**	0.093918	**0.204574**	0.001573
g_{33}	**0.894735**	0.901044	**0.863102**	**0.759062**	**0.701413**	**0.869804**	**0.544345**	**0.887499**

Table 1 Estimation of VAR-EGARCH-BEKK model in crisis period

The volatility spillovers among countries may change in time. In addition, the subprime financial crisis may affect spillovers significantly. Table 1 shows the estimation of selected parameters of the VAR-GARCH-BEKK model in the crisis period. Statistically significant values are in bold. Panel A contains parameters of matrix **A**, panel D then parameters of matrix **D** and finally panel G parameters of matrix **G.**

One can see all the estimated parameters in Panel A are not significant. As for diagonal parameters, the effects of each market shock on its own volatility are not obvious. Regarding the off-diagonal parameters, the non-significant parameters mean that the effects of each market´s shocks on other markets´ volatility are not observed.

With regard to Panel D, all the estimated parameters in diagonal are statistically significant. All the markets are affected by their own past negative shocks. As for the magnitudes of effect, we calculated the average values of d_{11} (0.1378), d_{22} (0.1114) and d_{33} (0.2179). Hence, we can see that the Asian markets responded to the bad news more intensely than the German and US markets. As for the off-diagonal parameters in matrix **D**, only d_{12} parameters are significant. It indicates negative shock transmission from the US market to the German market during the crisis period. However, we cannot prove there is the transmission of the bad news from the US market to Asian markets except for Hong Kong, Singapore, South Korea and Thailand. Parameters d_{23} are significant only for Hong Kong and Malaysia.

Finally, for the volatility spillovers in Panel G, it is clear that almost all the parameters are statistically significant except for some values of g_{23} and g_{33}. The diagonal parameters are significant except for the Singaporean market. Almost all those parameters in diagonals are close to one, which indicates a high degree of volatility persistence. In addition, the degree of volatility persistence is slightly higher in the case of the USA and Germany than in Asian markets so that the Asian markets are driven relatively less by persistence from own past volatilities. Nevertheless, since the parameters g_{13} are significant, it can be concluded that the volatility from the US market transmitted to all Asian markets with a relatively high magnitude. Last, we cannot prove there is obvious volatility spillover effect from German market to Asian markets.

To sum up, during the crisis period, it is evident that since all the Asian markets are rather affected by volatility transmitted from the US stock market. It can be also said that the negative shocks that occurred in the US market spread to other markets (Germany and 4 Asian markets).

Further, we will analyze the effect of volatility spillovers during the post-crisis period. The results are demonstrated in Table 2. Having suffered the world-wide global financial crisis, the linkage between three groups of markets may change. Moreover, the extend of volatility spillovers may also change to a different degree.

As for the parameters in Panel A, it is obvious that only coefficients in a_{33} are significant in a 5% significance level except for the Shanghai market. This implies that almost all the Asian markets are affected by their own past shocks significantly. As for the off-diagonal parameters, the non-significance means that none of the markets´ shocks affected volatility of another country.

As for the Panel D, most of the estimated parameters in diagonal are significant so that almost all the markets are affected by its own past negative shocks. As for the magnitudes of effect, we calculated the average values of d_{11} (0.1605), d_{22} (0.0958) and d_{33} (0.0575). It indicates that the US market responds to bad news more intensely than the German and Asian markets. However, the magnitudes of those effects are lower in the post-crisis period than in crisis period. Moreover, in the post-crisis period, Asian markets seem to be more stable than the German and US markets. With respect to the off-diagonal parameters in matrix **D**, most of the coefficients in d_{12}, d_{13} and d_{23} are significant. That means there are significant negative shocks spillovers from the US market to German and Asian markets except for the Korean, Malaysian, Thai and Chinese markets, and from the German market to the Hong Kong market.

	NIKKEI	STI	KOSPI	HANGSENG	KLCI	SET	IDX	SSE
Panel A								
a_{11}	0.003597	4.76E-06	0.006858	3.04E-05	0.001459	4.42E-06	0.001825	0.003949
a_{12}	0.001709	0.000102	0.005548	0.000279	0.000745	5.93E-05	0.001012	0.002268
a_{13}	0.014912	0.000373	0.014108	0.000722	0.010202	0.000352	0.008494	0.013005
a_{22}	0.000812	0.002387	0.004488	0.002570	0.000380	0.000794	0.000566	0.001303
a_{23}	0.007083	0.008325	0.011412	0.006637	-0.00521	0.004712	0.004730	0.007473
a_{33}	**0.061821**	**0.029039**	**0.029020**	**0.017140**	**0.071428**	**0.027962**	**0.039550**	0.042836
Panel D								
d_{11}	0.003597	**0.176058**	**0.173523**	**0.188406**	**0.186016**	**0.191226**	**0.176783**	**0.188522**
d_{12}	**0.001709**	**0.113612**	**0.112685**	**0.120125**	**0.119083**	**0.126447**	**0.120343**	**0.125163**
d_{13}	**0.144912**	**0.120795**	0.032532	**0.090810**	0.053681	0.055048	**0.096070**	0.046908
d_{22}	0.000812	**0.102080**	**0.100322**	**0.106110**	**0.109055**	**0.121462**	**0.110911**	**0.115706**
d_{23}	0.007081	0.052627	0.018232	**0.090189**	0.058314	0.060736	0.045408	0.029579
d_{33}	0.061821	0.064022	0.064188	0.051313	0.045454	**0.093390**	0.067874	0.011747
Panel G								
g_{11}	**0.873700**	**0.874443**	**0.872637**	**0.868174**	**0.868941**	**0.868586**	**0.875019**	**0.870113**
g_{12}	0.097943	0.097540	**0.198460**	0.093652	0.095824	0.091660	0.097752	0.095327
g_{13}	0.097943	0.097540	**0.198460**	0.093652	0.095824	0.091660	0.097752	0.095327
g_{22}	**0.861111**	**0.797720**	**0.884218**	**0.911464**	**0.861983**	**0.790586**	**0.787582**	**0.816905**
g_{23}	0.085005	0.020871	**0.309326**	0.027919	0.088652	0.014244	0.010641	0.033184
g_{33}	**0.922858**	**0.921610**	**0.925079**	**0.919877**	**0.923540**	**0.915346**	**0.921076**	**0.921271**

Table 2 Estimation of VAR-EGARCH-BEKK model in post-crisis period

Finally, we focus on the Panel G. It is obvious that almost all the diagonal parameters are significant at 5% significance level. It means that all the markets are influenced by the own past volatilities significantly. Moreover, almost all the coefficients in diagonals are close to one. It confirms high level of volatility persistence. The degree of volatility persistence is higher in the Asian markets than in US or German markets. At last, since the parameters g_{13} and g_{23} are only significant for the Korean market, it can be proved that the increased volatility in the US and German markets transmitted to the Korean market with a relatively large magnitude.

In short, in the post-crisis period, the effects of shock that occurred in the US market are not so significant in Asian markets as in the crisis period. In addition, the Asian markets seem to be more integrated with each other.

Achieved results are in line with paper of Li and Giles (2015) who applied VAR-GARCH-BEKK to investigate links among stock markets of the United States, Japan, and six Asian emerging countries. Their observed a significant one-way spillover of volatility from the US market to all emerging markets in Asia. They also showed that the spillover effects of volatility between the US market and other Asian markets were stronger during crisis period. Rao, Meng and Li (2020) studied the impact of Shenzhen-Hong Kong Stock Connect (SHSC) on the complex co-movements' relation between the stock markets of Shenzhen and Hong Kong from the aspects of dynamic correlation and volatility spillover using BEKK-GARCH model. Their results show that the opening of Shenzhen-Hong Kong Stock Connect (SHSC) caused that the volatility spillovers of stock markets in Shenzhen and Hong Kong have shifted from one-way spillover to two-way spillovers, which indicates that the SHSC mechanism has strengthened the correlation degree and has improved the ability of risk spillover in the two stock markets. Other articles that were published focused on the application of the VAR-GARCH-BEKK model in the field of energy commodities market in combination with stock markets (Lin and Chen, 2019).

4 Concluding Remarks

In this paper, we investigated the volatility spillovers in four developed and four emerging Asian stock markets in relation to the US and German stock market in the period of 2007-2018. The results of the multivariate VAR-GARCH-BEKK model indicated that during the crisis period, it is evident that all the investigated stock markets from Asia have been rather affected by volatility spillovers from the US stock market. The shocks especially the negative ones that occurred in the US market spread to other markets in Asia to a large extend. However, during the post-crisis period, the effects of shock that occurred in the US market are not so significant in the Asian market as in the crisis period. Moreover, the Asian markets seem to be more integrated with each other having more associations in general. The effects of the German stock market were significantly smaller compared to the US market. In addition, bad news affected rather developed Asian markets in both testing sub-periods.

Acknowledgements

This paper was supported by the Operational Programme Education for Competitiveness – project No. CZ.1.07/2.3.00/20.0296.

References

Bauwens, L., Laurent, S. and Rombouts, J. V. K. (2006). 'Multivariate GARCH models: A survey'. *Journal of Applied Econometrics*, 21(1), pp. 79-109.

Bollerslev, T., Engle, R. F. and Wooldridge, J. M. (1988). 'A capital asset pricing model with time-varying covariances'. *Journal of Political Economy,* 96(1), pp. 116–131.

Brooks, C. and Henry, Ó. T. (2000). 'Linear and non-linear transmission of equity return volatility: Evidence from the U.S., Japan and Australia'. *Economic Modelling*, 17(4), pp. 497-513.

Engle, R. F. (1982). 'Autoregressive conditional heteroscedasticity with estimates of the variance of United Kingdom inflation'. *Econometrica*, 50(4), pp. 987-1007.

Engle, R. F. and Kroner, K. F. (1995). 'Multivariate simultaneous generalized ARCH'. *Econometric Theory.* 11(1), pp. 122-150.

Hamilton, J. D. (1994). *Time series analysis*. Princeton, N.J: Princeton University Press.

Kroner, K. F. and Ng, V. K.. (1998). 'Modeling asymmetric comovements of asset returns'. *The Review of Financial Studies*, 11(4), pp. 817-844.

Li, H. (2012). 'The impact of China's stock market reforms on its international stock market linkages'. *Quarterly Review of Economics and Finance*, 52(4), pp. 358-368.

Li, Y. and Giles, D. E. (2015). 'Modeling Volatility Spillover Effects between Developed Stock Markets and Asian Emerging Stock Markets'. *International Journal of Finance & Economics,* 20(2), pp. 155-177.

Lin, B. Q. and Chen, Y. F. (2019). 'Dynamic linkages and spillover effects between CET market, coal market and stock market of new energy companies: A case of Beijing CET market in China'. *Energy*, 172(C), pp. 1198-1210.

Neaime, S. (2012). 'The global financial crisis, financial linkages and correlations in returns and volatilities in emerging MENA stock markets'. *Emerging Markets Review*, 13(3), pp. 268-282.

Ostry, J. D., Ghosh, A. R., Chamon, M. and Qureshi, M. S. (2011). 'Capital controls: When and why?' *IMF Economic Review*, 59(3), pp. 562–580.

Rao, C., Meng, Y. and Li, P. (2020). 'Dynamic correlation and volatility spillover between the stock markets of Shenzhen and Hong Kong'. Scientia Iranica, Articles in Press, [Online]. Available at: http://scientiairanica.sharif.edu/article_21903_080ca859c8745fab13b008978c97de67.pdf [cited 2021-03-10].

Sucháček, J., Seďa, P., Friedrich, V. and Koutský, J. (2017). 'Regional aspects of the development of largest enterprises in the Czech Republic'. *Technological and Economic Development of Economy*, 23(4), pp. 649-666.

Yavas, B. F. and Dedi, L. (2016). 'An investigation of return and volatility linkages among equity markets: A study of selected European and emerging countries'. *Research in International Business and Finance*, 37(C), pp. 583–596.

Conditional predictability of assets returns: a dynamic approach

Petr Seďa [1], Lorena Caridad López del Río [2]

Abstract. The efficient market hypothesis is one of the approaches to explain asset price movements in stock markets. However, the reality empirically observed in stock markets is rather in line with the adaptive market hypothesis. Statistical tests, which are aimed at verifying the properties of efficient market models, are mainly focused on testing the predictability of returns. The BDS test is one of the strongest nonlinear tests that verify the first type random walk model. When using this test, it is possible to verify whether the returns are conditionally predictable. The object of this paper is the stock markets in the Czech Republic and Poland, which are approximated by their main indices. This paper aims to verify the conditional predictability of the returns of the PX and WIG20 indices using the BDS test. The dynamics of development over time in the period 2004-2017 will be monitored. The results show that there were identified periods when returns are conditionally predictable, but also periods when they are not predictable. The results differ for both indices. Based on the results, it would be possible to define a potentially profitable trading strategy.

Keywords: adaptive market hypothesis, BDS test, bootstrap, dynamics, efficient market hypothesis, stock market.

JEL Classification: C12, C22, G14

1 Introduction

This paper is motivated by the fact that it has been empirically found that stock returns can be predicted based on information on past prices and returns. This fact contradicts with the efficient market (EMH) hypothesis. The weak form of EMH states that stock prices fully reflect all available information, which is limited to past prices, and as a result, stock returns are purely unpredictable based on past prices (Fama 1970).

It has been empirically found that stock returns have predictive power and the EMH does not always apply. This fact calls into question the validity of EMH. Most previous work on market efficiency has also followed the conventional approach of testing the efficiency of a weak form over a specific period, which has two main problems. First, as Campbell, Lo and MacKinlay (1997) noted, this approach determines whether a market is efficient throughout the whole period as an "all or nothing" condition and ignores the notion of relative efficiency. Second, the conventional approach assumes that the level of market efficiency is constant over a predetermined period. However, this is highly unlikely, as many factors will lead to market efficiency changes over time (Lim and Brooks 2011). Lo (2004) formulated the adaptive market hypothesis (AMH) as an alternative to the EMH. This hypothesis contains elements of evolutionary psychology. Compared to other alternatives, the AMH is a new approach. It is

[1] VSB-Technical University of Ostrava, Faculty of Economics, Department of Mathematical Methods in Economics, Sokolská třída 33, 702 00 Ostrava 1, Czech Republic, petr.seda@vsb.cz.
[2] University of Cordoba, Department of Statistics and Econometrics, Agrifood Campus of International Excellence ceiA3, E-14001 Cordoba, Spain, lcaridadlr@gmail.com.

gaining more and more attention from the academic public. It is undeniable that such an interdisciplinary approach to market interaction should provide an invaluable view of the internal functioning of the market. The supremacy of the AMH can be understood in terms of reconciliation with the existing theoretical framework and consistency, assuming equilibrium in an efficient market.

The AMH is given increased attention in the academic literature. There is evidence of adaptive stock returns behavior. Urquhart and Hudson (2013) examined whether the US, UK, and Japanese stock markets matched AMH, using linear and nonlinear independence tests. They show strong evidence in favor of AMH, suggesting that AMH provides a better explanation of stock returns behavior than EMH. Noda (2016) found that the level of market efficiency in Japanese stock markets changes over time, which is consistent with AMH. Ito, Noda and Wada (2016) defined a non-Bayesian time-varying model and showed that the US stock market developed over time in line with the AMH.

The object of this paper is the stock markets in the Czech Republic and Poland, which are approximated by their main indices PX and WIG20. The goal of this paper is to verify the conditional predictability of the logarithmic returns of the PX and WIG20 indices using the nonlinear BDS test. The empirical analysis will cover the data sample from May 2004 to December 2017.

The added value of this paper consists of two aspects:

- the *p*-values of the BDS test will be estimated with a help of bootstrap;
- conditional predictability of assets returns was investigated dynamically only in developed stock markets, not in emerging markets in Central Europe;

Our paper is organized in the following way. After the Introduction, where the motivation of the paper was explained, a short review of literature provided, and the added value of this paper was stressed, the second chapter delivers a comparison of the EMH with the adaptive market hypothesis and the BDS test is compactly described. The third chapter is providing a brief description of the data sample and an estimation of the *p*-values of the BDS for two nesting dimensions using the bootstrap. Moreover, the empirical results will be expressed in the form of figures that clearly show the development of predictability over time. The conclusion summarizes the outcomes of this paper. Outcomes of this paper will be also discussed with regard to similar and related works of other authors.

2 Methodology

In this chapter, the adaptive market hypothesis will be described in relation to the EMH. Next, the meaning of statistical tests for testing the predictability of asset returns will be explained with emphasis on the nonlinear BDS test.

2.1 Efficient market hypothesis versus adaptive market hypothesis

The EMH is one of the possible approaches to explain the movement of asset prices in financial markets. However, it has been empirically observed and proofed that this theoretical concept is often in contradiction with the real behaviour of stock markets (Veselá, 2011).

Evolutionary psychology examines how beings adapt to their environment. The purpose is to show that behavioral economics can coexist with the EMH. The main idea of the AMH is that market agents are driven by evolutionary tendencies of competition, adaptation, and natural selection. Asset prices reflect all these individualistic tendencies, as well as the environmental characteristics of the market. The AMH is based on the limited rationality hypothesis.

Thus, the market trading process is an adaptive process formulated by the tendency to optimize the behavior of individual market agents through a trial and error process that incorporates previous experience into the current decision-making process. In this way, a system of heuristic knowledge is created, which is used to solve a problem associated with various market circumstances. Since these circumstances change continuously, the primary requirement for gaining optimality is the ability to adapt heuristics to a new set of circumstances (Tseng, 2006). The price of an asset is therefore the result of environmental conditions as well as the number and nature of market participants.

The AMH recognizes that emotional, irrational, and cognitive prejudices can be introduced into the adaptation process of individual market agents. However, these are only agents who can learn from their mistakes and adapt their behavior (Lo, 2005). If we apply this hypothesis, markets move towards effective market equilibrium through the process of adaptation. Theoretically, the adaptive market hypothesis is not excluded from the EMH. According to Lo (2004), the AMH implies a dynamic nonlinear relationship between risk and return, which is based on current market conditions. Lo (2004) also identified new information as a predictor of survival, as it provides tools to improve market adaptability.

2.2 BDS test

One of the empirical features of efficient markets is the randomness of price changes. Price developments should therefore not be predictable. To verify randomness, several linear and nonlinear statistical tests have been defined in the literature. These tests are related to the first or third type of random walk models. The BDS test is one of the strongest nonlinear tests of the first-type random of walk hypothesis (Seďa, 2020). The predictability of returns will be verified by this test.

The BDS independence test is a nonparametric test of the null hypothesis that the data are independent and equally distributed (Brock et al., 1996). The rejection of the null hypothesis means that returns are conditionally predictable. This test is based on the concept of correlation integral. The BDS test is used to test the first type of random walk hypothesis. An important characteristic of the BDS test is its sensitivity to a wide range of alternative hypotheses. It can identify different types of processes that are not independently and equally divided:

- linear dependence;
- chaos;
- nonlinear stochastic processes.

On the one hand, this feature can be considered as an advantage; on the other hand, it is not possible to determine directly from the BDS test which of the alternatives led to the rejection of the null hypothesis. It is then necessary to use special statistical tests that are sensitive to only one type of dependence. The BDS test is based on the concept of correlation integral, which is a measure of the spatial correlation between two points of m-dimensional space. For the case of a series of logarithmic returns r_t that contains n observations, it is possible to write the correlation integral for m dimensions:

$$C_{m,n}(\varepsilon) = \frac{2}{(n-m+1)\cdot(n-m)} \cdot \sum_{s=1}^{n-m} \sum_{t=s+1}^{n-m+1} \prod_{j=0}^{m-1} H_\varepsilon(r_{s+j}, r_{t+j}), \tag{1}$$

where ε is small enough preset distance, m is a nesting parameter and H represents the Heaviside function, for which the following holds:

$$H_\varepsilon(r_i, r_j) = \begin{cases} 1 \text{ if } |r_i - r_j| \leq \varepsilon \\ 0 \text{ for other cases.} \end{cases} \tag{2}$$

Brock et al. (1996) defined test statistics:

$$W_{m,n}(\varepsilon) == \frac{\sqrt{n-m+1}\cdot\left[C_{m,n}(\varepsilon) - \left(C_{1,n-m+1}(\varepsilon)\right)^m\right]}{\hat{\sigma}_{m,n}(\varepsilon)} \sim N(0,1), \tag{3}$$

where $\hat{\sigma}_{m,n}(\varepsilon)$ is an estimate of the asymptotic standard deviation $C_{m,n}(\varepsilon) - \left(C_{1,n-m+1}(\varepsilon)\right)^m$.

The distance ε is usually chosen as a proportion of the sample standard deviation of the data. For $n \rightarrow \infty$, the BDS statistic converges in its distribution to a normalized Gaussian distribution. Brock et al. (1996) stated that the selection distribution approximates the asymptotic distribution already for values $n > 500$.

As stated in the Introduction of this paper, we will focus on the dynamics of asset returns predictability. That is why, a time window with a fixed length (20 months) was chosen to describe the development of predictability of returns over time. This time window will be always slid one month forward (Urquhart and McGroarty, 2014). The process of the shift by one month was repeated the end of testing period. Every time window contains enough observations to generate reliable results. At the same time, it provides sufficient results to analyze how the level of conditional predictability has evolved over time.

3 Empirical Results

In this chapter, the data sample utilized for empirical analysis and the main results and findings achieved with respect to the aim of this paper will be described and presented in the form of figures and tables.

3.1 Data sample

In this article, we will not test the predictability of individual stocks but just indices that approximate the development of the entire market. Indexation expresses the risk and return of the overall market. In the long run, the market is expected to outperform any stock selection. The object of this paper is the stock markets of the Czech Republic and Poland. Testing the predictability of asset returns will be performed on the daily data of the most representative stock indices of these countries. Specifically, these are the PX index of the Prague Stock Exchange and the WIG20 index traded on the Warsaw Stock Exchange. Both indexes are total return type. The data sample was downloaded from the official websites of the relevant exchanges (www.pse.cz and www.gpw.pl).

The basic testing period was defined from the beginning of May 2004 to the end of December 2017. In this paper, we will work with closing values for each business day. It is therefore a nearly 14-year time series of daily logarithmic returns of selected indices. The total number of observations is therefore about 3500 and varies according to the number of trading days in each market. The basic test period includes the various phases of the business cycle, i.e. both the growth and decline phases including the global financial crisis. It also includes phases of decline, growth, and stagnation of the stock market. The start of the time series is set for the 1st of May 2004 due to the accession of the Czech Republic and Poland to the European Union.

3.2 Evaluation of conditional predictability of returns

In the empirical analysis, the nonlinear BDS independence test was applied. To verify just the presence of a nonlinear dependence, the linear dependence was removed from the returns of the individual indices using the AR(p) model. The optimal length of the delay was based on the Ljung-Box test (Ljung and Box, 1978) up to 10 delays. In addition to a linear dependence, also the heteroskedasticity usually occurs in financial market data.

Since the BDS test has much greater power than the test of ARCH effects, where the presence of nonlinearity is tested only in the form of conditional variance, the AR(p)-Component GARCH(1,1) model (Engle and Lee, 1999) was estimated on the returns of all indices. The standardized residuals of these models were then tested using the BDS independence test. Thus, if a statistically significant dependence is identified on the residuals filtered by the AR(p)-Component GARCH(1,1) model using the BDS independence test, it is a non-linear dependence.

A time window with a fixed length was chosen to describe the development of predictability of returns over time. In this paper, the first period of 20 months was defined from May 2004 to December 2005. This time window will be always slid one month forward. The first test statistic was therefore calculated in the interval from the first business day of May 2004, when the testing period begins, to the last business day of December 2005. The next step was a shift from June 2004 to January 2006 and so on. The process of the shift by one month was repeated until December 2017, when the testing period ends.

One of the problems of the BDS test is the fact that the test statistic is based on asymptotic estimates, which can lead to erroneous conclusions especially for smaller samples (Richardson and Stock, 1989). To avoid this problem, the method of bootstrap was applied. This method involves the calculation of individual and combined statistical tests using T-observation samples generated by weighing the original data with average random variables with a zero mean and a variance of 1. These results were used to generate bootstrapped distributions of test statistics. Bootstrapped p-values are calculated directly from a fraction of replications that fall outside the limits defined by the estimated statistics. The number of replications was set at 2500.

Figures 1 and 2 show the evolution of the p-values of the non-linear BDS independence test statistics for the returns of the PX and WIG20 indices. The values of BDS statistics were calculated for nesting dimensions 2 and 3, which are described in the graphs by the symbols

BDS2 and BDS3. The statistical significance of BDS tests will again be evaluated on the 5% significance level, which is indicated in the graphs by a red horizontal line.

The p-values were obtained based on a time series lasting 20 months. Thus, for example, the p-value as of October 2006 corresponds to the data sample for the period from February 2005 to September 2006. The obtained p-values are of course variable over time and differ between both indices and nesting dimensions.

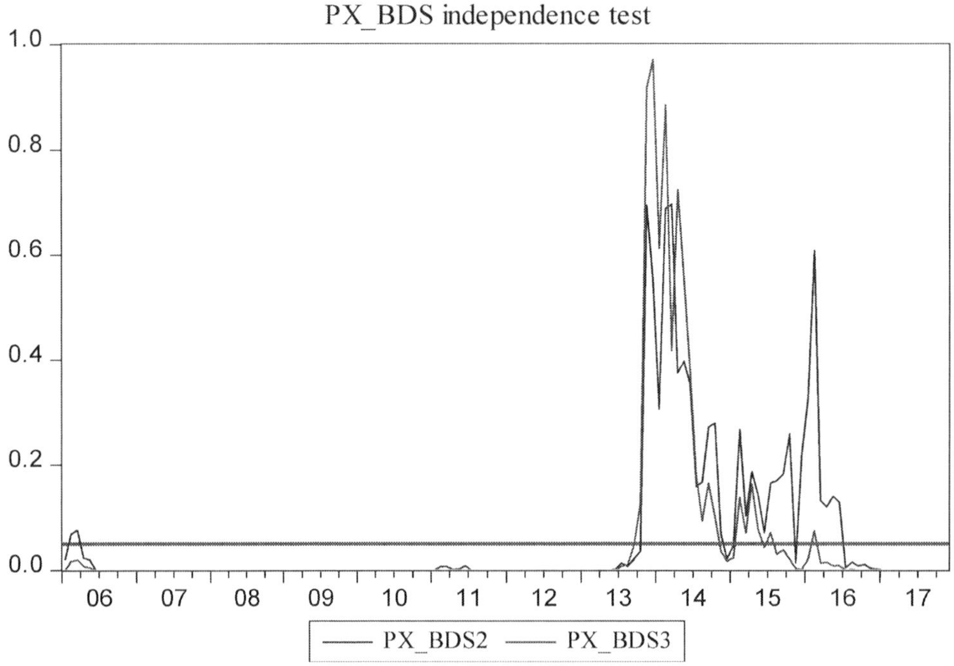

Figure 1 Bootstrapped p-values of the BDS independence test with nesting dimensions 2 and 3 for PX index returns

In the case of the PX index, the values of BDS statistics are statistically insignificant only in February and March 2006 (for nesting dimension 2), then there is a long period when the values of BDS statistics are significant. This period lasts until November 2013 (for nesting dimension 2) and October 2013 (for nesting dimension 3), respectively. The BDS statistics are statistically insignificant for the nesting dimension 2 in the period from December 2013 to June 2016. This stability is disturbed only in three cases. In the case of nesting dimension 3, the period of statistical insignificance of BDS statistics is significantly shorter. It lasts from November 2013 to July 2015. However, during this period, the null hypothesis was rejected four times. From mid-2016 until the end of the testing period, the returns of the PX index were again statistically significantly predictable.

As for the WIG20 index, the results differ significantly from the PX index. The BDS statistics for the nesting dimension 2 are not statistically significant in the period from January 2006 to November 2010. Similar results can also be identified for the nesting dimension 3. However, the stability of the results is disturbed nine times, especially at the beginning of 2009. From July 2011 to April 2013, the returns are again conditionally predictable, the same applies in the period from March 2014 to July 2015. In the period from May 2013 to February 2014, the BDS statistics are again not statistically significant, which also applies in the period from August 2015 to the end of the testing period.

The obtained results show that for each index, there were identified periods when returns are statistically significantly predictable, but also some periods when returns are not statistically significantly predictable. These changing levels of predictability depend on the tests used, as the tests vary in their strength. Therefore, a direct comparison can only be made if the testing procedure is consistent. It is advisable to examine the results also relatively.

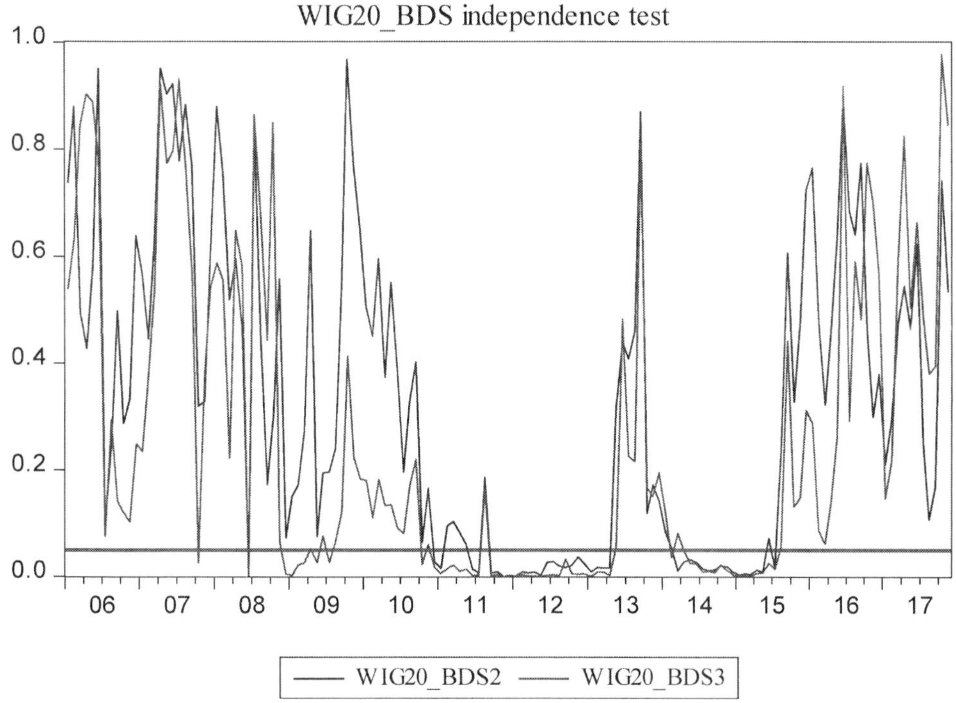

Figure 2 Bootstrapped p-values of the BDS independence test with nesting dimensions 2 and 3 for WIG20 index returns

Since the graphic outputs are not completely clear, it is advisable to create an overview of the results also in the form of a clear table. Table 1 shows the percentage of test statistics that do not reject the null independence hypothesis for the BSD test with nesting dimensions 2 and 3. The results are confronted with a 5% level of significance. Table 1 shows that the WIG20 index can be considered less predictable than the PX index. Overall, it can be stated that for both indices the periods when returns are predictable alternate with those when they are not predictable. This fact is consistent with the AMH, not the EMH.

Index	BDS2	BDS3
PX	22.22%	13.89%
WIG20	71.53%	62.50%

Table 1 Relative predictability based on a comparison of the percentage of non-rejection of the null hypothesis in the case of the BDS test against the 5% level of significance

Another logical step of the analysis is the proposal of a possible trading strategy, which would be based on the results of the BDS test (Seďa, 2020). Such a strategy could, for example, be based on a quantitative relationship between the p-values of the BDS tests and the stage of market development. It would also be possible to create a model of the dependence of random-behavior rejection on economic, political shocks or other external influences. If such a model were statistically significant, it would be in line with the adaptive market hypothesis. However, a trading strategy, where signals for buying or selling will be generated on the basis of the non-linear nearest neighbor (NN) method, seems to be a more suitable option. This method is based on the selection of geometric segments of historical values of the time series, which are similar to the last segment, which precedes the observation that must be predicted (Fernández-Rodríguez et al., 1999). This approach is philosophically different from the Box-Jenkinson methodology. The NN method selects the relevant previous observations on the basis of their levels and geometric trajectories, not their location in time. This method is based on similar principles as the nonlinear BDS test of independence (correlation integral, nesting dimension). This would lead to a direct link between the results of statistical tests and the proposed trading strategy. In case of application of this strategy based on the NN method, it would be appropriate to compare the results with other strategies. For example, a prediction-based strategy based on the ARIMA model or a risk-adjusted buy-and-hold strategy is offered (Allen and Karjalainen, 1999).

4 Concluding Remarks

In this paper, we investigated the hypothesis of whether the main indexes of Czech and Polish stock markets are conditionally predictable or not. The basic testing period was defined from May 2004 to December 2017. It covers different market stages of development of stock markets including the global financial crisis. In this article, the data of daily frequency are utilized. The conditional predictability of asset returns was investigated with the help of a nonlinear BDS test. Empirical results are carried out and compared in a dynamic way. The predictability of returns is rejected most often in the case of the Polish WIG20 index, while the Czech PX is predictable often. To secure the significance of applied BDS tests, the methods of bootstrapping were utilized. It seems that the behaviour of the Czech and Polish stock market approximated by their main indices is rather in harmony with the adaptive market hypothesis than the efficient market hypothesis. Based on dynamic results, the potentially profitable investment strategy based on nonlinear features of returns can be proposed as well. Our outcomes are in accordance with the results of other authors and theoretical expectations.

Acknowledgements

This paper was supported by the Operational Programme Education for Competitiveness – project No. CZ.1.07/2.3.00/20.0296.

References

Allen, F. and Karjalainen, R. (1999). 'Using genetic algorithms to find technical trading rules'. *Journal of Financial Economics,* 51(2), pp. 245–271.

Brock, W., Dechert, D., Scheinkman, J. and LeBaron, B. (1996). 'A test for independence based on the correlation dimension'. *Econometric Reviews,* 15(3), pp. 197–235.

Campbell, J. Y., Lo, A. W. and MacKinlay, A. C. (1997). *The Econometrics of Financial Markets*. 1st ed. Princeton University Press, Princeton.

Engle, R. and Lee, G. (1999). *A permanent and transitory component model of stock return volatility.* In: Engle, R. & White, H. (eds.): Cointegration, causality, and forecasting: A festschrift in honor of Clive W.J. Granger. 1st ed. New York: Oxford University Press.

Fama, E. (1970). 'Efficient capital markets: a review of theory and empirical work'. *The Journal of Finance*, 25(2), pp. 383-417.

Fernández-Rodríguez, F., Sosvilla-Rivero, S. and Andrada-Félix, J. (1999). 'Exchange-rate forecasts with simultaneous nearest-neighbour methods: Evidence from the EMS'. *International Journal of Forecasting,* 15(4), pp. 383–392.

Ito, M., Noda, A. and Wada, T. (2016). 'The evolution of stock market efficiency in the US: a non-Bayesian time-varying model approach'. *Applied Economics*, 48(7), pp. 621-635.

Kim, J. H., Shamsuddin, A. and Lim, K. (2011). 'Stock return predictability and the adaptive markets hypothesis: Evidence from century-long U.S. data'. *Journal of Empirical Finance*, 18(5), pp. 868–879.

Lim, K-P. and Brooks, R. (2011). 'The evolution of stock market efficiency over time: A survey of the empirical literature'. *Journal of Economic Surveys*, 25(1), pp. 69-108.

Ljung, J. M. and Box, G. (1978). 'On a measure of lack of fit in time series models'. *Biometrika,* 65(2), pp. 297–303.

Lo, A. W. (2017). *Adaptive Markets: Financial Evolution at the Speed of Thought.* 1st ed. Princeton: Princeton University Press.

Lo, A. W. (2004). 'The adaptive market hypothesis: Market efficiency from an evolutionary perspective'. *Journal of Portfolio Management*, 30(5), pp. 15–29.

Noda, A. (2016). 'A test of the adaptive market hypothesis using a time-varying AR model in Japan'. *Finance Research Letters*, 17, pp. 66-71.

Richardson, M. and Stock, J. (1989). 'Drawing inferences from statistics based on multiyear asset returns'. *Journal of Financial Economics,* 25(2), pp. 323–348.

Seďa, P. (2020). *Teoretické aspekty hypotézy efektivního trhu a empirie na akciových trzích v zemích střední Evropy*, SAEI, vol. 65, 1st ed. Ostrava, VSB-TU Ostrava.

Tseng, K. (2006). 'Behavioral finance, bounded rationality, neuro-finance, and traditional finance'. *Investment Management and Financial Innovations,* 3(4), pp. 7–18.

Urquhart, A. and McGroarty, F. (2014). 'Calendar effects, market conditions and the adaptive market hypothesis: Evidence from long-run U.S. data'. *International Review of Financial Analysis,* 35(C), pp. 154–166.

Veselá, J. (2011). *Investování na kapitálových trzích.* 1st ed. Praha: Wolters Kluwer.

Capturing Uncertainty in Opinions on Distance Learning Using Fuzzy Sets

Miloš Švaňa [1] , František Zapletal [2] , Miroslav Hudec [3] , Radek Němec [4]

Abstract. Due to the COVID-19 pandemic, distance learning has become a hot topic in education. Universities worldwide were forced to replace traditional learning with distance learning without deeper preparation. The focus was mostly put on technical solutions. However, the opinions and feelings of the groups involved - mainly teachers, students, and IT staff, should be also considered. Given the novelty of the situation, it is unreasonable to expect that the collected answers are without vagueness and hesitance. To solve this problem, this work proposes a method of capturing and aggregating such answers. At the first level, the answers of a single respondent are represented as fuzzy numbers whose mean is then calculated to represent their overall opinion. At the second level, the aggregation by the relative quantifier *most of* reveals whether the majority of members of a group inclines towards a positive or negative opinion. In this way, the uncertainties in answers and non-equal sizes of groups are covered. This model is illustrated by a numerical example followed by discussion and concluding remarks.

Keywords: Flexible survey, distance learning, hesitance and vagueness, aggregation, fuzzy sets.

JEL classification: C83, D83

1 Introduction

Due to the COVID-19 pandemic, universities are currently adapting to the process of distance learning. The focus is mainly put on the technical solutions. The opinions and feelings of the groups involved - mainly teachers, students, and IT staff, should be also considered. Each group can contribute to the adaptation of the teaching process with their opinions on various aspects regarding the distance learning experience. The members of each group, however, should not be surveyed in the same way. In addition, considering the novelty of the situation, it is unreasonable to expect that the collected answers are without vagueness and hesitance. Both these aspects of collecting and evaluating opinions should not be neglected. For instance, students' technical skills are on different levels and therefore a question regarding the efficiency of implementing a certain on-line tool supporting the teaching process can be viewed with a certain degree of uncertainty.

The user experience is both observable and measurable (Albert and Tullis, 2013), thus can be collected. When conducting a survey in an academic environment, the following issues should be considered:

[1]VSB-Technical unversity of Ostrava, Faculty of Economics, Department of Systems Engineering, Sokolská 33, Ostrava, Czech Republic, milos.svana@vsb.cz

[2]VSB-Technical unversity of Ostrava, Faculty of Economics, Department of Systems Engineering, Sokolská 33, Ostrava, Czech Republic, frantisek.zapletal@vsb.cz

[3]VSB-Technical unversity of Ostrava, Faculty of Economics, Department of Systems Engineering, Sokolská 33, Ostrava, Czech Republic, miroslav.hudec@vsb.cz

[4]VSB-Technical unversity of Ostrava, Faculty of Economics, Department of Systems Engineering, Sokolská 33, Ostrava, Czech Republic, radek.nemec@vsb.cz

1) Groups with different levels of expertise and skills.

2) Unequal size of groups and/or not all participants are cooperative in the survey.

3) Some participants do not fill in the questionnaire carefully (e.g., select the neighboring value).

4) Due to the novelty of this situation, it is unreasonable to expect that the collected answers are without vagueness and hesitance.

The authors address these issues and offer a possible solution by designing and demonstrating a robust aggregation method for the evaluation of survey answers.

Collecting and evaluating opinions in education is a well-established field. These activities were devoted to various aspects for improving education, e.g., (Flegl and Rosas, 2019; Vnoučková et al., 2016; Yildizli, 2019). After almost a year of continuous distance learning, the environment is more or less stable and should be evaluated from diverse perspectives.
The focus of this paper is on a new approach for evaluating uncertain opinions from different groups involved in the teaching process. Two groups of crucial importance are students and teachers. The definition of groups depends on the issue being addressed and the approach itself does not rely on any specific group definition (and number of groups).
Two main contributions of the approach are the formalization of vagueness and hesitance in individual answers using fuzzy sets and aggregation of answers within a group using relative fuzzy quantifiers like *most of*.

The remainder of the paper is as follows: Section 2 introduces the aggregation process of the respondents' answers. Section 3 is focused on the numeric example to demonstrate the proposed process regarding distance learning, whereas Section 4 is devoted to the discussion. Section 5 concludes the paper and provides an outlook for further research.

2 Aggregation process

The proposed aggregation of individual respondents' answers and answers within a respondent group is based on the theory of fuzzy sets to cover fuzziness in answers. Thus, at the beginning of this section, the basic concepts of the fuzzy set theory are elaborated.

2.1 Preliminaries of fuzzy set theory

A fuzzy set $\mathcal{F}$ is a subset of universe $\mathbb{X}$ described by the membership function $\mu_{\mathcal{F}}(x)$, which assigns the membership degree from the unit interval to each $x \in \mathbb{X}$ (Zadeh, 1965) where $\mu_{\mathcal{F}}(x) = 1$ says that an element x without any doubt is member of fuzzy set F, whereas a value from the open interval $(0, 1)$ indicates the partial membership.

In this paper, triangular fuzzy numbers (TFN) (see Fig. 1) capture the vagueness and hesitance of respondents' opinions, i.e., the answer is most likely $m_{\tilde{A}}$, but due to hesitance the neighbouring values should also be considered with lower intensities.

The addition of fuzzy sets and multiplying fuzzy sets with a real number are necessary for aggregating respondents' answers by the arithmetic mean of fuzzy sets. If $\tilde{A}$ and $\tilde{B}$ are TFNs

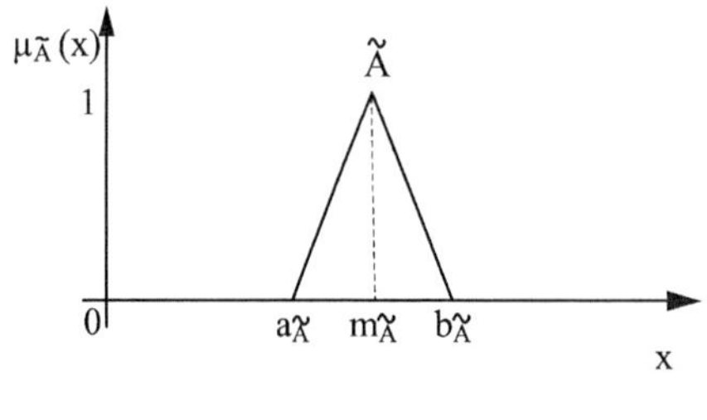

Figure 1 Triangular fuzzy number $\tilde{A} = (a_{\tilde{A}}, m_{\tilde{A}}, b_{\tilde{A}})$.

defined by the triplets $(a_{\tilde{A}}, m_{\tilde{A}}, b_{\tilde{A}})$ and $(a_{\tilde{B}}, m_{\tilde{B}}, b_{\tilde{B}})$, respectively (the notation is in line with Fig. 1), the addition of fuzzy sets can be written as (Zimmermann, 2001)

$$\tilde{A} \oplus \tilde{B} = (a_{\tilde{A}} + a_{\tilde{B}}, m_{\tilde{A}} + m_{\tilde{B}}, b_{\tilde{A}} + b_{\tilde{B}}). \tag{1}$$

The multiplication of a TFN by a real number is expressed as:

$$p \cdot \tilde{A} = (p \cdot a_{\tilde{A}}, p \cdot m_{\tilde{A}}, p \cdot b_{\tilde{A}}), \tag{2}$$

where $p \in \mathbb{R}$. The arithmetic mean of TNFs is obtained by their sum (1) and consequently multiplied by $p = \frac{1}{n}$ where n is the number of TNFs.

Next, the linear gamma function, depicted in Fig. 2, formalizes the relative quantifier *most of*. The concepts *negative opinion* and *positive opinion* are shown in Fig. 3.

The possibility under which a fuzzy set (in this case a TFN) $\tilde{A}$ belongs to the fuzzy set (in this case concept *positive opinion* PO) is expressed as (see Fig. 4) (Galindo et al., 2006)

$$\text{Pos}(\tilde{A}, \tilde{PO}) = \sup_x \min\big(\mu_{\tilde{A}}(x), \mu_{\tilde{PO}}(x)\big). \tag{3}$$

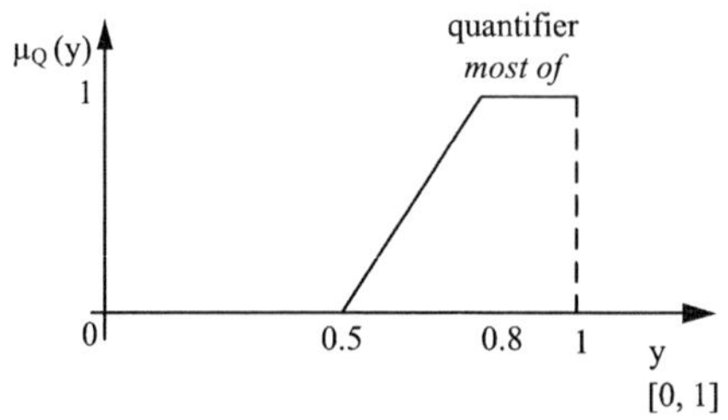

Figure 2 Relative quantifier *most of*.

2.2 Aggregation of individual respondent's answers

At this level, the goal is to aggregate the answers provided by an individual respondent into a single fuzzy number, capturing the opinions and hesitance of all answers.

First, the fuzzy representation of each answer is constructed. An individual answer is represented by a TFN whose parameters are given by (4), a_{ij} denoting the answer of respondent i to question j chosen from a discrete scale ranging from a_{min} to a_{max} and h_{ij} representing the level of hesitance for this answer from $[0, h_{max}]$.

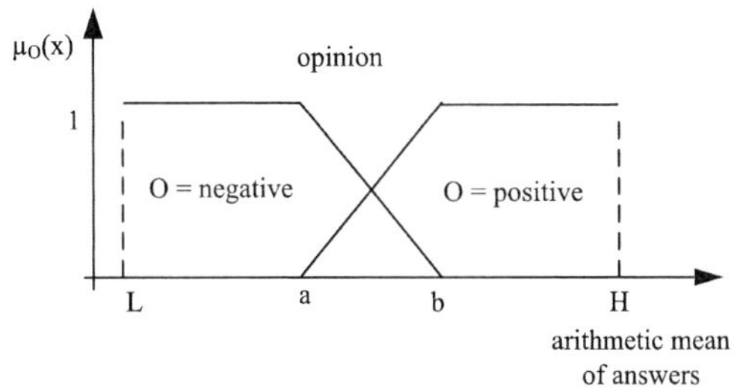

Figure 3 Concepts *positive* and *negative* opinion expressed by overlapping sets.

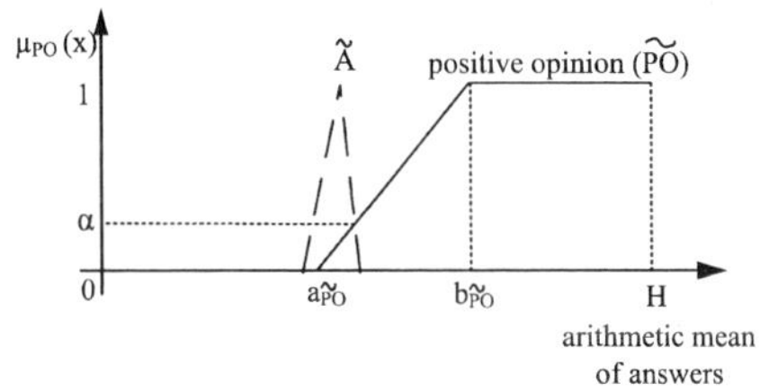

Figure 4 Possibility measure of an answer to the positive opinion .

$$\tilde{a}_{ij} = \Big(\max\left(a_{\min}, a_{ij} - h_{ij}\right); a_{ij}; \min\left(a_{\max}, a_{ij} + h_{ij}\right)\Big) \tag{4}$$

If the respondent does not feel any hesitance, the fuzzy representation collapses into a singleton. Moreover, the support of the fuzzy representation is limited to the interval $[a_{min}, a_{max}]$.

Arithmetic mean is then used to aggregate all answers of a single respondent. This aggregation function is considered a suitable choice as it does not introduce any bias towards positive or negative opinions. This is not true for other common aggregation functions, such as the geometric mean. As one could infer from (1) and (2), arithmetic mean of TFNs can be easily determined by calculating the the arithmetic mean of each element of the TFN triplet.

2.3 Aggregation within Groups

This aggregation calculates the opinion regarding the distance learning for each respondent group. Aggregation by the relative quantifier *most of* reveals, whether the majority of respondents has positive or negative inclination. In this aggregation step, the influence of careless answers is mitigated (i.e., respondents who provide neighbouring values instead of desired ones are evaluated similarly). This method also deals with the problem of the imbalanced group sizes and different number of questions for each group (Rakovská and Hudec, 2019).

The formal structure of the summarized sentence is *Q entities have P*, where *Q* is a relative quantifier (e.g., *most of*) and *P* is a fuzzy predicate. The validity of such sentence is calculated by (Yager, 1982):

$$v\Big(Qx\big(P(x)\big)\Big) = \mu_Q\left(\frac{1}{n}\sum_{i=1}^{n} \mu_P(x_i)\right) \tag{5}$$

where n is the number of respondents in a group, $y = \frac{1}{n}\sum_{i=1}^{n}\mu_P(x_i)$ is the proportion of respondents that satisfy predicate P (e.g., *positive opinion*), μ_Q and μ_P formalize the chosen relative quantifier and predicate, respectively, by membership functions.

The quantifier *most of* is an increasing function $\mu_Q(x) : [0,1] \to [0,1]$ where $\mu_Q(0) = 0$ and $\mu_Q(1) = 1$ hold (Fig. 2). According to (Kacprzyk and Zadrozny, 2005), it can be expressed as

$$\mu_Q(y) = \min\left(1, \max\left(0, \frac{y - 0.5}{0.3}\right)\right) \tag{6}$$

where y is the proportion of respondents having a positive (or negative) opinion.

The solution expresses the intensity of inclination of the whole group towards the positive (or negative) opinion. Thus, the evaluated groups can be compared, whether they share the similar opinion or have significantly different opinions. The next section demonstrates the proposed approach on the numeric example.

3 Numerical example

In this section, the proposed method is demonstrated with a numerical example. In the introduced example, the two most important groups are considered - students and teachers. They evaluate their satisfaction with distance teaching during the current academic year from different perspectives. Each group gets five questions, some of them are identical, the others are specific for the given group. The list of questions are summarized in Tab. 1. To make the evaluation easier for the respondents, all questions were formulated in such a way that value 5 corresponds with the absolute satisfaction (value 1 with absolute dissatisfaction, value 3 expresses the neutral opinion). For each non-neutral evaluation, the respondents were required to add the hesitance level (0 = no hesitance, 1 = weak hesitance, 2 = strong hesitance).

Question	**Group**
Do you consider your internet connection sufficient for online learning?	S
Do you consider your HW equipment sufficient for online learning?	S, T
Do you consider the SW platforms used SW platforms good for online learning?	S
Do you consider the support of the teachers and faculty management sufficient for online learning?	S
Do you think that online lectures and seminars are of at least the same quality than the in-class lectures?	S, T
Do you consider the support of the faculty management sufficient for online learning?	T
Do you consider your skills and knowledge of the used SW platforms sufficient for online learning?	T
Do you consider the activity of students during the lectures sufficient?	T

Table 1 The list of questions for the included groups.

It is worth emphasizing that this example is not built as a thorough survey. It is rather a demonstration how the proposed method can be applied. Thus, only a small sample of respondents were addressed (one study group of 30 students and 10 teachers from the home university of the authors). On the other hand, their answers are real and more or less follow the results of a large survey realized at the end of 2020.

Starting with the first level of aggregation, the answers are firstly transformed into triangular fuzzy numbers (or singletons for the answer without any hesitation) using (4). Then the arithmetic mean of all answers of each individual respondent is calculated by (2). Fig. 5 provides a graphical representation of this fuzzification process for a single student.

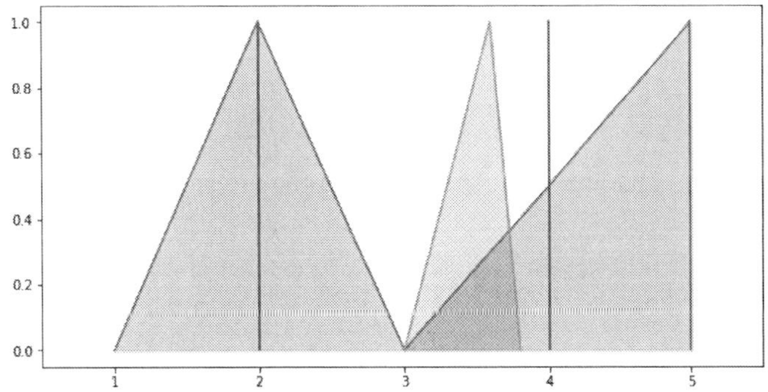

Figure 5 Aggregation of answers (blue) from a single respondent using arithmetic mean (orange).

At the second level, the conformance between the mean value of the individual respondent's answers and a fuzzy set representing positive opinion is calculated by (3). The fuzzy set positive opinion (Fig. 3) is a trapezoidal set with core [4, 5] and support [2, 5]. The calculation of conformity for a single student is illustrated in Fig. 6.

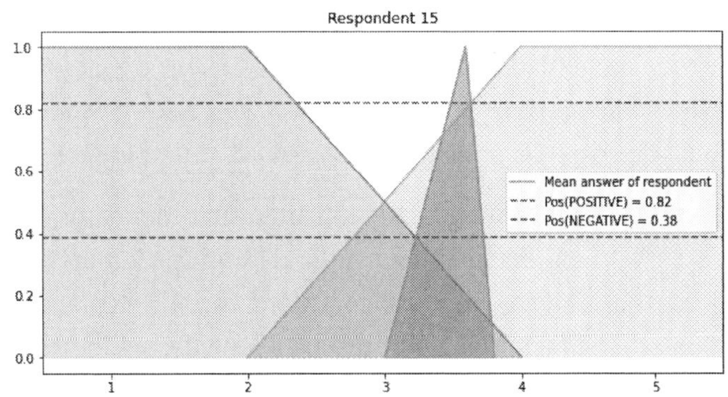

Figure 6 Degrees of conformity with positive and negative opinions for a single respondent.

Levels of conformity are then used to determine the overall degree of positive or negative opinion in a student group. Finally, using (6), the validity of a statement *the most of students have a positive opinion* is determined. Results of this final step for both groups in the context of positive opinion are compared in Fig. 7.

Considering the degree of positive opinion from Fig. 7, that is 0.64 for students and 0.13 for teachers, as well as the degrees of negative opinion which are 0 and 0.29 for students and teachers respectively, one could conclude that the opinion of students on distance learning is

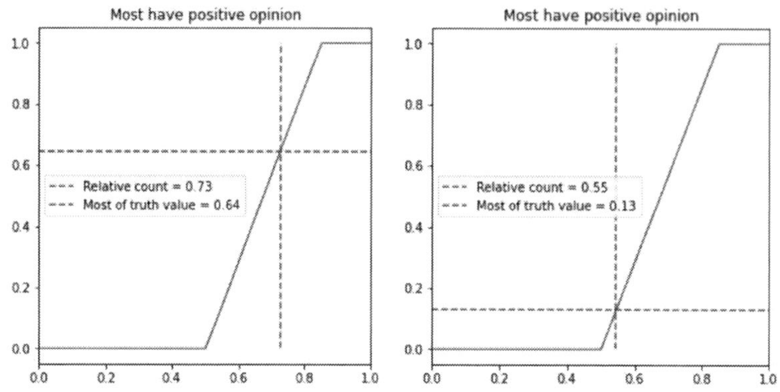

(a) Students (b) Teachers

Figure 7 Results of the second level of aggregation

overwhelmingly positive. Teachers, on the other hand, are mildly negative while still perceiving at least some positive aspects.

4 Discussion

The proposed approach has been illustrated on an example. The first level, aggregating individual answers, is realized by the arithmetic mean of fuzzy numbers. It covers the aggregation of equally relevant uncertain answers. When the questions differ in relevancy, weights can be applied. However, the other averaging functions might not be suitable as they incline their answers towards the minimal or maximal individual answer.

At the second level, the relative quantifier *most of* is applied to reveal whether the majority of respondents in a group share positive or negative opinion. Additional relative quantifiers like *few* or *about half* can also be straightforwardly applied. Quantifies with the highest validity for a given group can be then combined into a "short story" such as *about half of all teachers share negative opinion, most students have positive opinion and few members of the IT staff share negative opinion*. Such descriptions are easily understood at first glance.

The numeric example is used to merely demonstrate that this theory works and can be applied in full-featured surveys on distance learning. The proposed approach is not limited to this application and can be easily transferred and used for surveys on other topics in higher education, as well as in other educational institutions. Considering the setting of an elementary school, parents, for example, also play a crucial role and their opinions should be considered. Local governance usually manages elementary schools in a region. Such survey could be valuable insight into the problems and strong points of distance learning in these schools.

5 Conclusions

Due to the COVID-19 pandemic, distance learning has become a hot topic. Alongside technical aspects, opinions and feelings of the main groups like teachers, students, and IT staff should be considered. To cover the new situation, this work has proposed an approach for handling vagueness and hesitance in survey answers, as well as differences between these groups, including different sets of questions and number of respondents.

The approach can be split into two stages. At the first stage, each answer is transferred into a fuzzy number, capturing the hesitance of the respondent. Answers of each individual respondent are then aggregated using the arithmetic mean, the result representing their overall opinion. At the second level, the opinion of all respondents from a given group is aggregated and expressed by the relative quantifier.

The approach was demonstrated on a numerical example using a small sample of respondents. The results suggest that the opinion on distance learning is positive among students, but mildly negative among teachers. This result was surprising as the authors expected more criticism from students.

The proposed approach is flexible and can be applied to different contexts. It can be also used to describe the survey results linguistically.

Future research should be focused on examining the usefulness of the approach in a more complex setting, with a larger number of respondents and improved set of questions. Alternative ways of capturing respondent uncertainty should also be considered. These include, for instance, type-II or intuitionistic fuzzy sets.

Acknowledgements

This work was supported by the SGS project No. SP2021/86. This support is gratefully acknowledged.

References

Albert, W. and Tullis, T. (2013). *Measuring the User Experience, Collecting, Analyzing, and Presenting Usability Metrics (Interactive Technologies)*, 2nd ed. Elsevier, Dodrecht.

Flegl, M. and Rosas, L. (2019). Do professor's age and gender matter or do students give higher value to professors' experience? *Quality Assurance in Education*, 27(4):511–532.

Galindo, J., Urrutia, A., and Piattini, M. (2006). *Fuzzy databases: Modeling, Design and Implementation*. Idea Group Publishing Inc., Hershey.

Kacprzyk, J. and Zadrozny, S. (2005). Linguistic database summaries and their protoforms: towards natural language based knowledge discovery tools. *Information Sciences*, 173(4):281–304.

Rakovská, E. and Hudec, M. (2019). A three–levelled aggregation model for evaluating software usability by fuzzy logic. *International Journal of Applied Mathematics and Computer Science*, 29(3):489–501.

Vnoučková, L., Urbancová, H., Smolová, H., and Šmejkalová, J. (2016). Students' evaluation of education quality in human resource management area: Case of private czech university. *Journal of Efficiency and Responsibility in Education and Science*, 9(2):45–41.

Yager, R. (1982). A new approach to the summarization of data. *Information Sciences*, 28(1):69–86.

Yildizli, H. (2019). Structural relationships among teachers' goal orientations for teaching, self-efficacy, burnout and attitudes towards teaching. *Journal of Efficiency and Responsibility in Education and Science*, 12(4):111–124.

Zadeh, L. A. (1965). Fuzzy sets. *Information and Control*, 8:338–353.

Zimmermann, H. (2001). *Fuzzy Sets Theory - ad its Applications*. Kluwer, Dordrecht.

Sharing information on social networks

Jana Syrovátková[1], Jiří Korčák[2], Antonín Pavlíček[3]

Abstract. Along with the extensive use of information and communication technology gains importance also the issue of sharing personal information on social networks. The main questions are what are people sharing on the social networks, with whom, and if there are differences between experienced and inexperienced IT users.

The research took place in the Czech Republic in October 2020 through 471 correctly and fully answered questionnaires. Respondents were primary first-year university students (324 respondents). For comparison and completion, an older student was also invited among the respondents, or other people were invited through a call on social networks (147 respondents).

The answers are further differentiated according to the IT experience. The hypothesis was that more experienced users are sharing less information. We have found that there is information like exact date of birth, that is shared twice more often entirely publicly in inexperienced user group than in experienced group.

Keywords: social networks, sharing personal information, IT experience, survey.

JEL Classification: O35, D83

1 Introduction

Humans are social beings. People have an inner need to interconnect; it is clear from everyday life as well as from scientific studies of the brain. Even our neurons connect to each other and are doing their best to connect even more. Small kids try to befriend everyone they meet. It all comes together and we as humankind are inseparably tied to each other. (Lieberman, 2013).

It is then clear that with the rise of the internet and online communication we will try to connect via computers as well. That is where social networks come into play. People come to social networks and connect with each other. They communicate and together create the content of social networks. As in the real world, in the online environment, smaller groups of people will begin to emerge, in addition to large communities. (Harris and McCabe, 2017). Thus, small communities can thrive even in bad times like today. However, whether one wants to or not, to participate in such communication, one must share certain information.

1.1 Sharing information

The very concept of sharing is difficult to deal with in scientific research because everyone understands it in their own way (Lampinen, 2015). It is thus necessary to focus on the subject of sharing, which may differ and may assist in further analysis of sharing as such.

[1] Prague University of Economics and Business, Department of Information Technologies, W. Churchill Sq. 4, 130 67 Prague 3, jana.syrovatkova@vse.cz

[2] Prague University of Economics and Business, Department of Information Technologies, W. Churchill Sq. 4, 130 67 Prague 3, xkorj58@vse.cz

[3] Prague University of Economics and Business, Department of Information Technologies, W. Churchill Sq. 4, 130 67 Prague 3, antonin.pavlicek@vse.cz

Kümpel, Karnowski & Keyling (2015) talk about news sharing as a unifying concept that is understood most easily. However, it is not just news and innovations that people share on social networks.

From the very beginning, social networks have grown and gained popularity thanks to the sharing of information about people themselves. According to Alhabash and Ma (2017), sharing information is one of the five most common reasons to visit the social network Facebook and one of the eight most common reasons to visit Twitter, Instagram, and Snapchat. Information sharing is thus clearly the domain of social networks, regardless of whether it is the sharing of personal information and data or news.

Confirmation of this statement can also be proof that social networks are user-generated sites. At least social networks can be defined as so according to Carr and Hayes (2015), who specifically claim that social media are: "Internet-based, disentrained, and persistent channels of masspersonal communication facilitating perceptions of interactions among users, deriving value primarily from user-generated content". Thus, information sharing is not only an integral part of social networks, but it is the very basis on which social networks are built.

1.2 Sharing news

Sharing news is becoming more and more common on social networks. The reason is undoubtedly the speed of the flow of information and access to it. However, on social networks, everyone is a content creator, and if someone does not have complete information about the shared news, problems can arise. This can lead to misinformation, which is untrue but did not occur purposefully or for the wrong intention. The second possibility is that people share the news that arose out of resentment and intending to harm or damage someone. In this case, it is disinformation. (Ireton, Posetti and Unesco, 2018). Batchelor (2018) also states that fake news is not the domain of today's social networks but has been in society long before. However, he also says that the fight against false messages is problematic if in the system there are still people with more influence and who spread such information. He presents everything on the example of a well-known artist and his beliefs in a flat Earth while influencing his surroundings by sharing such information. As long as such "weak links" appear to be in the chain of information, disinformation and misinformation will also spread.

1.3 Personal information

Sharing personal information is an issue that has recently become more and more discussed. Waters (2011) created research on why people publish private information and discover several interesting dimensions of the problem. One is the so-called "usual behavior", so people are just used to sharing information. The second is to "keep up with trends", it is important for people to stay up to date and the metaphorical mirror that is offered to them through others on social networks is necessary for them to "stay cool". Other reasons can be found as well, a common one is presented by Solove (2012). He finds out, that people when asked about disclosure of their personal information, say "I have nothing to hide."

On the other hand, sharing personal information is closely related to privacy, which is inherent in people's untouchable spheres of their lives. Nissenbaum (2010) talks widely about what information people share and talks about contexts that influence people in their decisions whether to disclose certain information or not.

2 Methodology

We collected data from October to November 2020. It was a part of the bigger survey focused on social networks and privacy. We started with Introductory ICT course students of Prague University of Economics and Business, Faculty of Finance and Accounting (336 respondents, mostly first-year students), then we have asked other students and through social networks (135 respondents).

We have had analyzed the degree of sharing personal data on social networks. In the user analysis section there is information about users and the answers are further differentiated according to experience with the ICT. In Sharing information analysis section we analyse user answers about sharing. For statistical analysis we had used t-test with H0: $\mu_1 = \mu_2$ against H_A: $\mu_1 \neq \mu_2$. While H_0 was defined as: "There is no difference in sharing information on social networks between experienced and non-experienced IT users" and H_A defined as: "Both groups share information differently".

2.1 Survey questions

In addition to basic statistics (gender, age, country of birth, stage, size of the city in which the respondents live), we also asked respondents which social networks they use and how often. The offer included Facebook, Instagram, Twitter, LinkedIn, In contact, Snapchat, WhatsApp, Skype, Tinder, and Viber. Frequencies of use were online (still connected), once a day, once a week, once a month, I have an account, I do not use it, I do not have an account.

For basic statistical analysis, we use information about the respondents' IT knowledge – none, small, medium, advanced, and expert.

The basic topic of the research was which of the listed data users share and how often:

Number of shared information	Shared information
S1	Surname and name
S2	Personal photo (face)
S3	Name of the school where they are/were studying
S4	Date of birth
S5	Year of birth only
S6	e-mail address
S7	Employer
S8	Partnership status
S9	Phone number
S10	Address
S11	Location sharing

Table 1 Respondends answers numbered as used in research

Possible answers were: completely public, only for „friends", I do not disclose, and I am not sure.

3 User analysis

There were 227 men and 244 women, 371 of them were born in the Czech Republic, 100 in other countries. 379 people were undergraduate students, 11 master's degree students, 6 postgraduate students and 75 absolvents (any type of school). Age and urbanization of respondents in the charts.

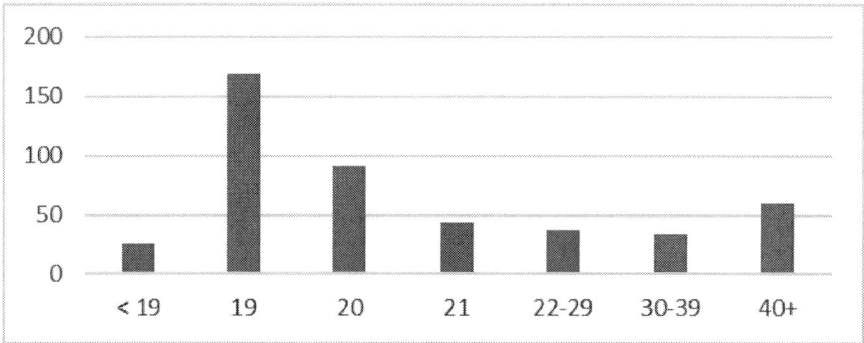

Figure 1 Age distribution of respondents.

As it can be seen most of the respondents are between the ages of 19 and 21. In the second charter it can also be seen that most of respondents come from larger cities (more than 100,000 inhabitants). These two facts are only a logical result of data collection mainly at Prague university.

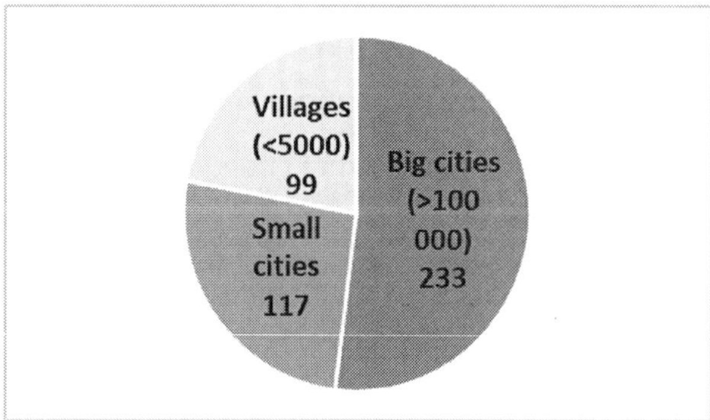

Figure 2 Urbanization of respondents.

IT experience of users is very important for the analysis. In the Figure 3 you can see the distribution of IT experience among respondents. It should be mentioned, but it is not surprising that there were zero users among the respondents without knowledge of working with computers. The largest number of users has a medium experience.

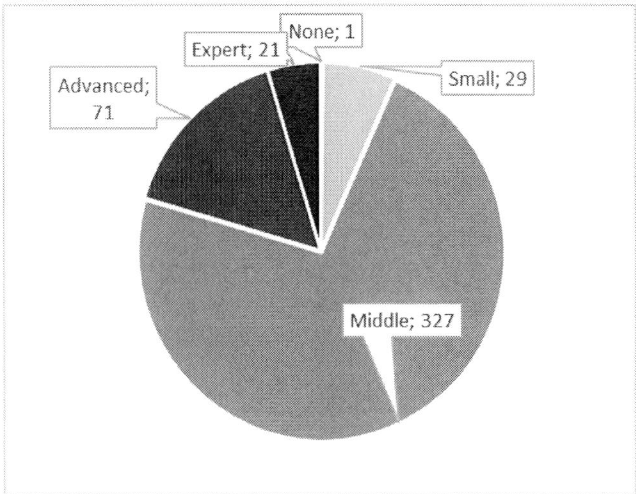

Figure 3 Respondents' ICT experience

3.1 Social networks usage

Although it is said that Facebook is a social network more for older and younger people use other social networks, our survey showed that respondents most often use the social network Facebook (at least once a day are there 87% of respondents), followed by Instagram and WhatsApp. Interesting is the number of users who have an account on Skype and do not use it. This probably stems from its great popularity before the advent of Facebook. The following chart shows the ratio of usage of individual social networks:

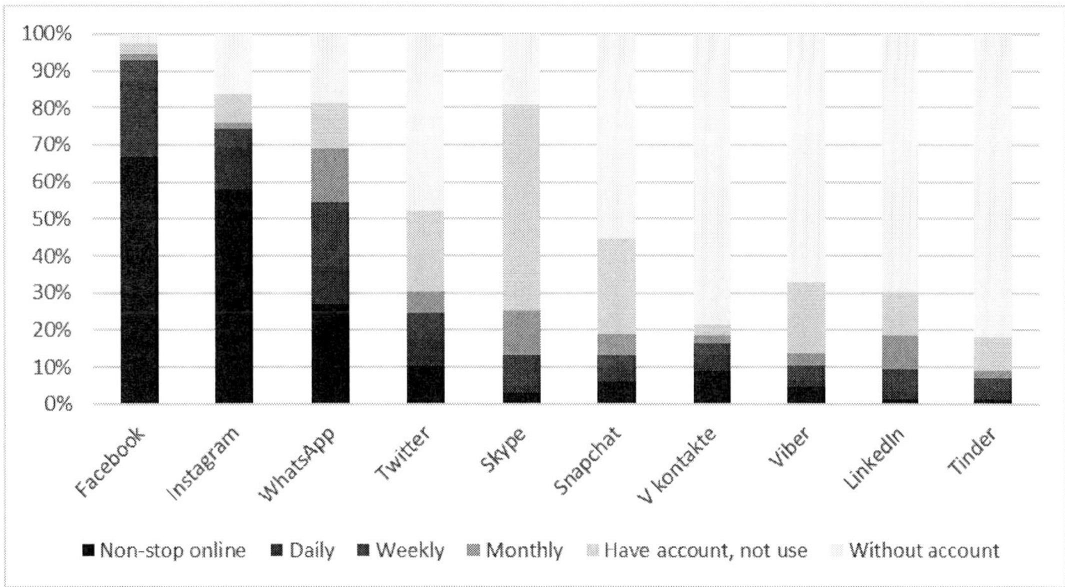

Figure 4 All social networks - frequency of usage

We also picked up three most popular social networks and in following chart is presented summed usage of individuals of these networks.

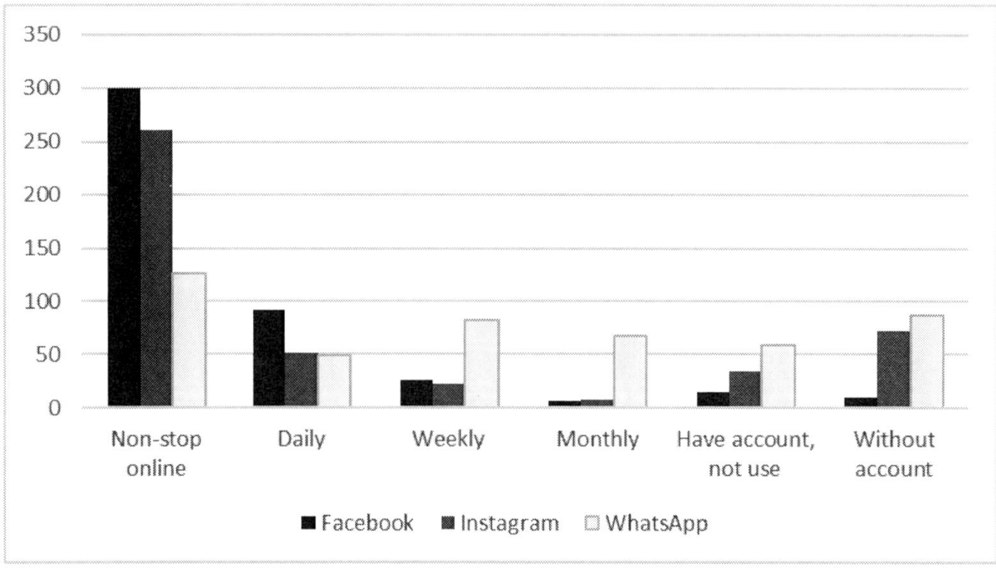

Figure 5 Three most popular social network

4 Sharing information analysis

First of all, we looked at the answers of all respondents together. Most often, first and last names and personal photos are shared. This may also be because the most common Facebook requires the real name and surname of users to register, and many groups require a photo to enter. More than 60% of respondents share this data incomplete publicity and more than 90% at least for friends. Another often shared figure is the respondent's school, less employment for those who are employed. The date of birth is often shared only with friends. E-mail, phone number, address of residence, or location, but also the partner status are little shared.

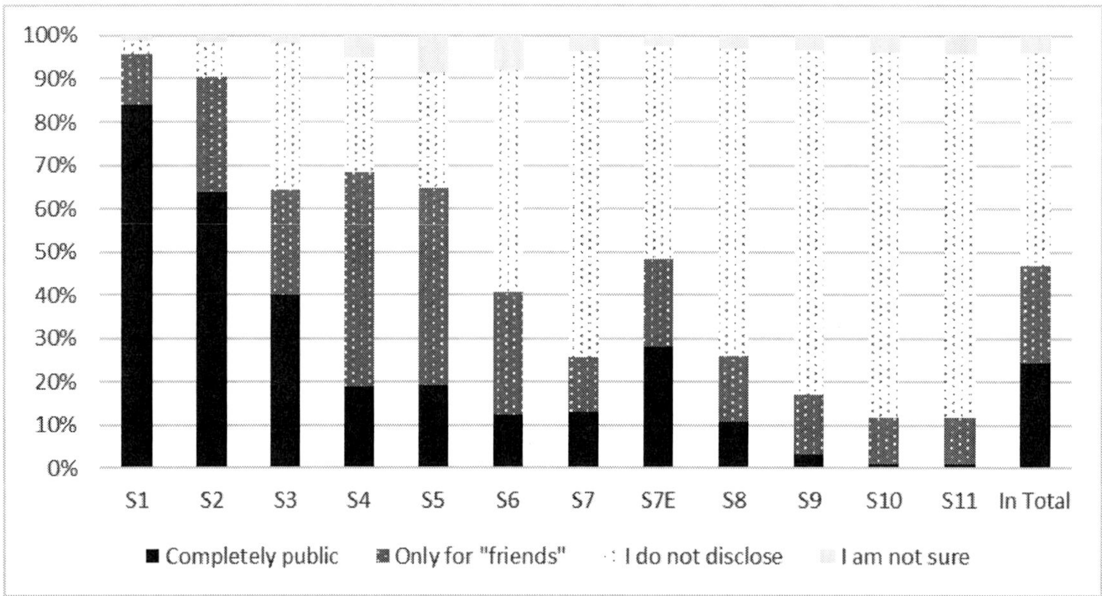

Figure 6 What types of data are shared with whom, S7E stands for sharing for employed respondents only

Next, we have differentiated users by categories – Experienced users are users with advanced or expert knowledge of ICT, not experienced are users with small and middle knowledge of ICT.

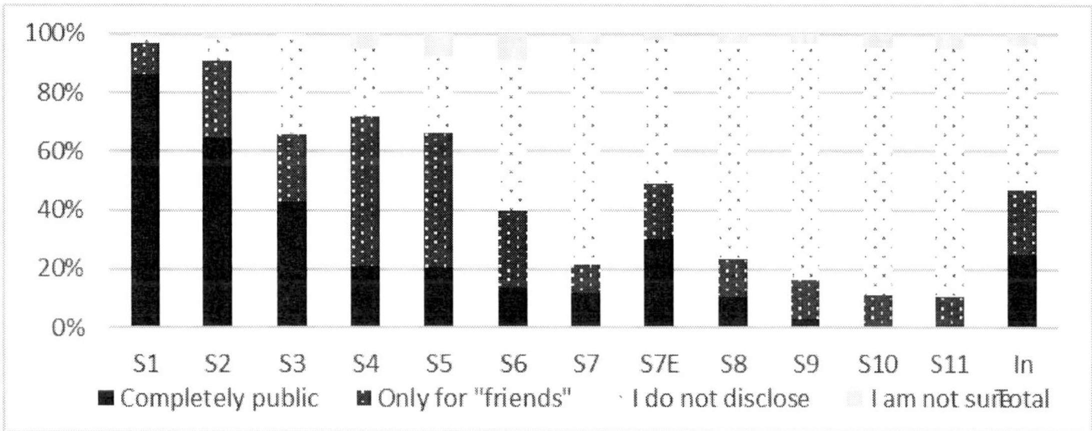

Figure 7 What types of data are shared and how often – Not experienced users only

Previous and following chart show numbers of respondends's answers as introduced in Table 1. For better understanding we present separately not experienced users and experienced ones.

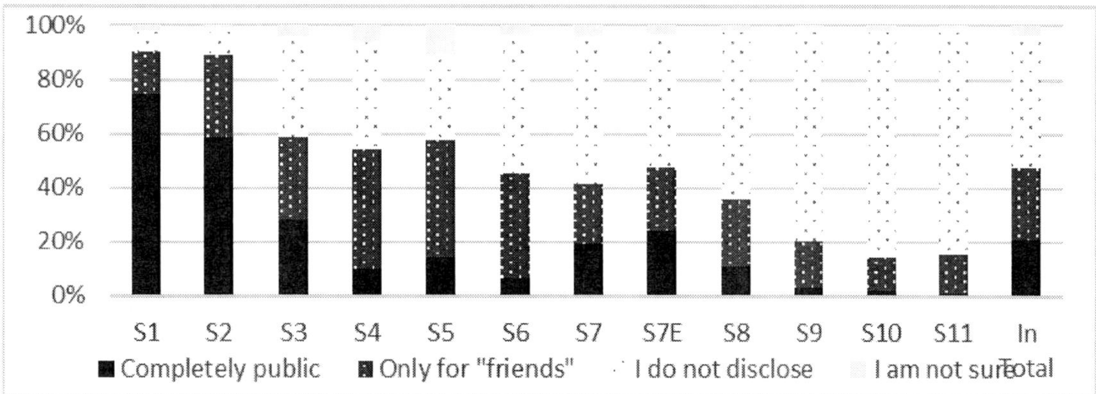

Figure 8 What types of data are shared and how often – Experienced users only

We have two groups of users – experienced and not experienced. We did not mentioned people, who do not know, whether they are sharing or not. We encoded the remaining answers to a numerical scale – we coded zero sharing as 0, sharing "for friends only" to 1 and public sharing to 2. For these answers, we further compare how willing people are to share their private data. Because they are different people and the data are independent we can use a two-sample t-test to compare the mean values of the willingness of sharing the data. We can compare t-statistics with the critical value of normal distribution 1.96. For better comparison we have added the p-value too.

	Experienced user			Not experienced user			*t*-statistics	*p*-value
	N	Mean	Sample variation	*N*	Mean	Sample variation		
S1	90	1.69	0.37	375	1.85	0.17	-2.95	0.003
S2	91	1.49	0.45	372	1.59	0.39	-1.23	0.220
S3	88	0.91	0.68	374	1.10	0.76	-1.86	0.064
S4	86	0.69	0.43	360	0.98	0.47	-3.58	0.000
S5	82	0.80	0.48	349	0.95	0.50	-1.63	0.104
S6	89	0.54	0.39	344	0.59	0.55	-0.56	0.575
S7	88	0.64	0.65	365	0.35	0.47	3.46	0.001
S7E	59	0.75	0.71	94	0.81	0.78	-0.44	0.664
S8	90	0.48	0.48	367	0.35	0.45	1.55	0.121
S9	91	0.24	0.25	364	0.20	0.23	0.73	0.466
S10	90	0.17	0.19	362	0.12	0.13	0.97	0.333
S11	91	0.16	0.16	359	0.13	0.13	0.91	0.336
In Total	**1035**	**0.71**	**0.64**	**4085**	**0.75**	**0.71**	**-1.41**	**0.157**

Table 2 Value of two-sample *t*-test for comparison sharing on experienced and not experienced users

From the table we can see that hypothesis H_0 we can reject (on a significance level 0.05) at S1, S4 and S7. However, if we exclude respondents who do not even have a job, then we cannot reject S7. Although t-statistics is very close to 1.96 at S3, S5 and S8, we cannot reject these hypothesis.

5 Discussion

Although social networks are popular mainly for sharing information (Alhabash and Ma, 2017), research has shown that users are not reluctant to share names, surnames, photos or schools. They already protect their employer or date of birth. And e-mail addresses, phone numbers, residence and partner status are already considered to be private.

6 Conclusion

Most respondents were included in the group of medium computer experience. However, there were still enough experienced users that these groups could be compared. It has been shown that less experienced users are more likely to share first and last names and exact dates of birth. The names of the school or the sharing of the year of birth were also more frequent, but this occurrence was no longer statistically significant. Experienced users, on the other hand, more often share Partnership status, but again this was not statistically significant.

Acknowledgments

This paper was processed with a contribution from the University of Economics in Prague, IG Agency, OP VVV IGA/A, CZ.02.2.69/0.0/0.0/19_073/0016936, grant number 05/2021.

References

Alhabash, S., & Ma, M. (2017). A Tale of Four Platforms: Motivations and Uses of Facebook, Twitter, Instagram, and Snapchat Among College Students? *Social Media + Society*. https://doi.org/10.1177/2056305117691544

Batchelor, J. (2018). Fighting fake news. Science World, 74(10), 14

Carr, C. T., & Hayes, R. A. (2015) Social Media: Defining, Developing, and Divining, *Atlantic Journal of Communication*, 23:1, 46-65, DOI: 10.1080/15456870.2015.972282

Harris, K and McCabe, A. (2017). Community Action and Social Media: Trouble in Utopia?", Third Sector Research Centre.

Ireton, C., Posetti, J., & Unesco. (2018). Journalism, fake news & disinformation : UNESCO,. http://digitallibrary.un.org/record/1641987

Kümpel, A. S., Karnowski, V., & Keyling, T. (2015). News Sharing in Social Media: A Review of Current Research on News Sharing Users, Content, and Networks. *Social Media + Society*. https://doi.org/10.1177/2056305115610141

Lampinen, A. (2015). Deceptively Simple: Unpacking the Notion of "Sharing." *Social Media + Society*. https://doi.org/10.1177/2056305115578135

Lieberman, M. D. (2013). *Social: Why our brains are wired to connect.*

Nissenbaum, H. F. (2010). Privacy in Context: Technology, Policy, and the Integrity of Social Life. Stanford, Calif: Stanford Law Books.

Solove, D. J. (2012). Nothing to hide: The false tradeoff between privacy and security. Yale University Press

Waters, S. & Ackerman, J. (2011), Exploring Privacy Management on Facebook: Motivations and Perceived Consequences of Voluntary Disclosure. Journal of Computer-Mediated Communication, 17: 101-115. https://doi.org/10.1111/j.1083-6101.2011.01559.x

Chatbot33 to Increase Students' Interest in University Study

Markéta Šindlerová[1], Ivo Martiník[2]

Abstract. Chatbot33 is a specific chatbot that will be primarily used to promote and provide information on study programs accredited and offered at the Faculty of Economics VSB-Technical University of Ostrava for all those interested in studying at this faculty. In addition to this basic function for applicants Chatbot33 will also serve faculty students for whom it should be able to define and explain basic and important terms and concepts they will encounter during their studies. Chatbot33 is operated on the website of the student organization Sokolska33, it is implemented in the form of neuro-fuzzy expert system in the IBM Watson Assistant programming environment and its basic features and functionalities are the main topic of this article.

Keywords: chatbot, Natural Language Processing, neuro-fuzzy expert system, IBM Watson Assistant.

JEL Classification: C63, D83

1 Introduction

The worldwide pandemic of coronavirus COVID-19 caused the closure of the schools of all the types in a total of 185 countries and a sudden worldwide transition to distance form of education that affected approximately 90% of all the pupils and the students worldwide. The impossibility of the full-time contact between the teacher and the student is reflected not only in the change of the way of teaching, but also in other areas. One of them is also the promotion of accredited study programs and the provision of detailed information on studying at individual universities for secondary school students. These activities are usually performed in the form of open days at individual universities, promotional fairs, events held directly on the premises of the relevant secondary school and other methods that cannot be carried out during the coronavirus pandemic in the full-time form, but only remotely with using of the information technologies. One of the projects in this area that was solved at the Faculty of Economics VSB-Technical University of Ostrava was the pilot implementation of the programming system ensuring the continuous provision of information about the studies and the study programs at this faculty. The aim of this project was not only to ensure the provision of information about the studies only in the standard passive form of websites with relevant information, but also in the form of active dialogue with secondary school students that is conducted in the Czech language. The special chatbot called *Chatbot33* was therefore designed, implemented and put into operation for these purposes and it is also the *very first chatbot* available on the faculty's websites.

Chatbot is a software system used to conduct online chat conversations through text or text-to-speech in real time instead of in direct contact with a living person. The chatbots are designed and implemented to convincingly simulate the way a person would behave in a natural

[1] VSB-Technical University of Ostrava, Faculty of Economics, Sokolská třída 33, Ostrava, Czech Republic, marketa.sindlerova.st@vsb.cz.

[2] VSB-Technical University of Ostrava, Faculty of Economics, Department of Applied Informatics, Sokolská třída 33, Ostrava, Czech Republic, ivo.martinik@vsb.cz.

conversation. Chatbots therefore usually require constant debugging and testing from a programmer point of view (Burden and Savin-Baden, 2019). The term "ChatterBot" was originally coined by Michael Mauldin (creator of the first Verbot) in 1994 to describe class of these conversational programs. People have been trying to communicate with computers through natural language since the first computers. The first chatbot (Eliza) was created at Massachusetts Institute of Technology in 1966 (i.e., before the creation of personal computer). Eliza worked on the principle of searching for keywords in the input text and performed appropriate actions based on them (Das and Khan, 2018). Over time and with the development of new technologies and methods in natural language processing, chatbots have slowly become full-fledged, voice-controlled personal assistants, such as Siri from Apple, Alexa from Amazon, Google Assistant from Google, and more.

Chatbots are typically used in online web dialog systems for a variety of purposes, including customer service, request routing or information gathering. While some chatbot applications use extensive word classification processes, natural language processors and sophisticated artificial intelligence applications, others simply search for general keywords and generate answers using common phrases obtained from an associated library or database. Most chatbots are accessible in real time through website pop-ups windows or through virtual assistants. They can be further divided into use categories which include business (e-commerce via chat), education, entertainment, finance, health, news and productivity (Biswas, 2018). Although chatbots are used in a variety of areas they still have a lot of limits and limitations. Unlike humans, chatbots still have problems, for example, with recognizing emotions, managing complex and complicated conversations, they are limited by the properties and quality of the system used to process natural language and knowledge bases, etc. A big limitation of chatbots is also their limitation to only a certain conversational domain (i.e., it is very complicated to create a chatbot capable of conversing on any topic and in the case of chatbots having rules-based conversational logic it is even impossible). However, this problem can be expected to be overcome in the future, as shown by IBM's experiment where their Project Debater2 can converse on complex topics, which was demonstrated on 12th February 2019, when Debater was able to debate with a professional debater on topics such as "They had would we subsidize kindergartens?”, none of which knew these topics in advance (IBM, 2019).

The main topic of this article is a description of the design and implementation of the chatbot called Chatbot33 that will be primarily used to promote and provide information on study programs accredited and offered at the Faculty of Economics VSB-Technical University of Ostrava for all those interested in studying at this faculty. In addition to this basic function for applicants the Chatbot33 will also serve faculty students, for whom it should be able to define and explain basic and important terms and concepts they will encounter during their studies.

The article is arranged into the following sections: in the section 2 natural language processing and its main properties are described; section 3 explains the Chatbot33, its selected properties and functionalities and the simple example of its conversation; section 4 then gives the conclusions of the research to conclude the article.

2 Natural Language Processing and Its Properties

There are used two sub-areas of *natural language processing* (NLP) when designing and implementing chatbots (see Figure 1) - *natural language understanding* (NLU) and *natural language generation* (NLG) (Traum, 2009). NLU is a sub-area of NLP that examines the methods by which a software application can "understand" natural language inputs, "understand" their meaning and respond adequately to them. The goal of understanding natural language is therefore to process an unstructured text in natural language into a structured form so that it can be further worked with. For this purpose, so-called language models are created, the task of which is to predict the probability distribution of expressions in the relevant language for a specific area of interest (i.e., for the area of a specific solved problem). Depending on the specific solved problem, various types of statistical language models are used in practice which differ from each other in the way and complexity of modeling. For example, for the area of communication, where the whole sentence structure is important, language models based on so-called probabilistic context-free grammars proved to be suitable. However, along with advances in artificial intelligence research in recent years, language models can also be found that are not based on the above-mentioned classical static methods, but they are based on deep learning methods (Heaton, 2015) (Kim, 2017) that use forward multilayer neural networks or deep reinforcement learning methods to represent the language model (Deng and Liu, 2018).

NLG is a sub-area of NLP that is the exact opposite of NLU. The subject of research in this area is not methods for converting unstructured text in natural language into structured form, but, on the contrary, methods for converting data in structured form into text in natural language. However, because the process of generating natural language is very complicated, almost all current systems for generating natural language are based on predefined rules (or so-called "if-then-else" logic) and templates, and these templates and rules must be defined by man. Based on the defined rules, the NLG system then finds a suitable template for the entered input and then only inserts the necessary data into this found template or compiles the resulting text from various parts (Shevat, 2017).

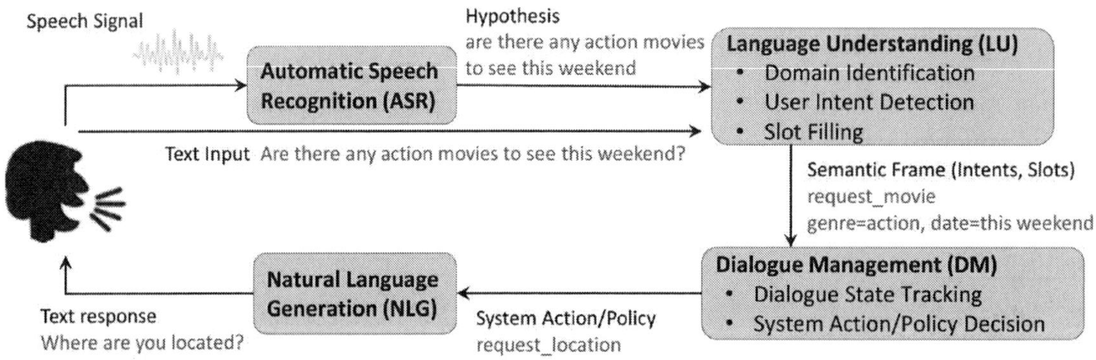

Figure 1 Natural Language Processing [Deng and Liu, 2018]

Among the basic NLP methods in building chatbots the following can be mentioned:

- *part-of-speech tagging* - this is the process of dividing unstructured text into so-called tokens (sometimes this process is called tokenization); tokenization is then important in identifying the entities and intentions that the user query contains;

- *stemming* - this is the process of converting inflected words to their basic form (i.e., for example, the form of the word "saying" is converted to the infinitive "say");
- *lemmatization* - this is an algorithmic process of determining the basic form of a word or phrase (= lemma) through morphological analysis of words and vocabulary;
- *named-entity recognition* (NER - sometimes also entity identification or traction) - this is the process of finding and classifying named entities that exist in a user's entered text;
- *stop words filtering* - "stop words" (the equivalent of parasitic words is used in the Czech language) are high-frequency words that do not form the meaning of sentences and these are usually words with little lexical content; it is necessary to try to filter these words from the document before processing the text (i.e., in English these are, for example, the words "a", "an," the ", etc.). (IBM NLP, 2020)

3 Chatbot33 and Its Properties

Chatbot33 is primarily intended for the promotion and provision of information on study programs accredited and offered at the Faculty of Economics VSB-Technical University of Ostrava for all those interested in studying at this faculty. The Chatbot33 is operated on the website of the student organization Sokolská33 (Sokolska33, 2021) and hence its name.

One of the key problems of the Chatbot33 analysis phase was, of course, the determination of its conversational domains, which are currently:

- offer of study fields for individual types of study (i.e., bachelor, master, doctoral) and description of their individual study programs;
- base information on MBA and U3V studies;
- definition of basic terms and relations used at the Faculty of Economics (e.g., Edison, eduroam, LMS, Sokolská33, etc.);
- opening hours of selected places at the Faculty of Economics (e.g., canteen, library, study room, study department, etc.);
- verbal description and picture of the map of the floors of the faculty buildings with an indication of where the selected place is located;
- information on internships and studies abroad;
- information about the student organization Sokolská33 and possible involvement in it.

The most important criteria in deciding on the choice of a software platform for creating the Chatbot33 included the support of the Czech language, the availability of the platform in the form of a service and the support of the classification of intentions and entities. There are currently a number of NLP platforms on the market. As part of the decision on the selection of the most suitable platform, an analysis of four selected platforms was performed:

- IBM Watson Assistant (IBM Watson, 2021);
- DialogFlow (Google, 2021);
- Wit.ai (Facebook, 2020);
- Luis (Microsoft, 2021).

The analysis focused mainly on the necessary support of the Czech language, the functionality of the platforms and the possibility of future expansion of the Chatbot33 for working with voice inputs. However, the friendliness of the development environment and the implementation of system entities were also taken into account. According to official documentation, only two of the above platforms support the Czech language, namely IBM Watson Assistant and Wit.ai, owned by Facebook. Although it is possible to create Czech-converting chatbots using DialogFlow platforms from Google or Luis from Microsoft, it would be necessary to subject the message to machine translation before processing the natural language of the message, which carries a greater risk of misunderstanding and determining the intended purpose. The price factor of provided services was also analyzed. All of the above platforms offer a free version, but this is subject to the maximum number of messages processed per minute (in the case of Luis and DialogFlow) or in total (in the case of IBM Watson Assistant). Unlimited message processing is provided by paid versions, whose costs are around $0.002 per processed message. The paid version is not only offered by Wit.ai. All analyzed platforms implement the ability to work chatbot with voice inputs. This factor was taken into account when deciding on the most suitable platform, mainly due to the planned intention to expand the Chatbot33 functions with this capability in the future. Due to the lack of support for the Czech language, only the IBM Watson Assistant and Wit.ai platforms were considered for their use. The biggest advantage of the Wit.ai platform is its zero cost of using this service, but although this platform is very popular with developers, it has a number of disadvantages. Above all, these are limited functionalities and only limited support for voice inputs. Due to the fact that the developed chatbot is in a way to represent the work of students of the educational institute, the IBM Watson Assistant platform was chosen for its implementation. Another reason for choosing this platform was a subjectively more friendly environment for the chatbot's own development.

We will focus on the software architecture of the Chatbot33 in the next paragraphs. As already mentioned, the NLP chatbot consists of parts of the NLU and NLG. The design and implementation of the Chatbot33 was therefore implemented in the form of a neuro-fuzzy expert system (Singh and Lone, 2019), where:

- part of the NLU uses the IBM Watson NLU service (IBM NLP, 2020) and it is designed and implemented in the form of a deep neural network that is trained in the field of machine learning of text input including its understanding through grammar and context that allows to determine the intended meaning of a sentence; knowledge from the field of semantic and syntactic analysis is used to determine the meaning and understanding of a sentence with the NLU also introducing an appropriate ontology, i.e., the data structure with the specification of the relationships between words and phrases; a combination of these two analyzes is necessary for a machine understanding of the meaning of text input in natural language;
- part of the NLG is designed and implemented in the form of the expert system, which seeks to find an answer to a specific query using a knowledge base composed of defined queries and known values that can be acquired by declared entities.

IBM Watson NLU service seeks to recognize the appropriate category and concept, familiar entities and keywords in user input, as well as message sentiment so that the chatbot is able to respond effectively to user needs. IBM Watson NLU service is built on a machine learning area called *Transfer Learning*. Transfer Learning is a deep learning approach in which one of the pre-created models with an already learned neural network is used as a starting point for the development of a specific model (IBM NLU, 2020).

The NLG part of the Chatbot33 was implemented in the IBM Watson Assistant environment (IBM Watson, 2021) in the form of the expert system in which:

- the *facts base* consists of the set of declared entities and their values including synonyms and the set of defined intentions together with so-called *utterances*, by which the given intention can be expressed. (note: these are examples of questions that users can ask about the purpose - e.g., with the intention of finding out study fields, users can ask, for example, "What are the study programs at the faculty?", etc.);
- the *knowledge base* is realized by declaring the so-called *dialogue nodes*, which can be interconnected into larger structures through standard logical operators AND and OR;
- the *inference mechanism* is designed to generate a suitable chatbot response, where after recognizing the intent and individual entities of the query stored in the fact database, the knowledge base (so-called dialogue) is searched to find a dialogue node whose conditions will be met and provide the user with an answer defined of this dialogue node.

The dialog node definition then also contains the conditions to be met in order for its body's commands to be executed. The condition of the dialog node can therefore be, for example, in the following (symbolic) form:

IF (intention == "study programs") AND (place == "Faculty of Economics")
THEN execute dialogue node "Study Programs of Faculty of Economics"

If the user input contains, for example, clicks or errors, it is then possible to use the so-called *Fuzzy Matching* for better recognition of searched entities. Fuzzy Matching in the IBM Watson environment (Cobus Greyling, 2019) consists of three components (functions) when declaring a dialog node:

- *stemming* - a function for recognizing the stem part of a given word;
- *misspeling* - this function is able to map user input to the corresponding entity despite the presence of spelling errors or small syntactic differences, including the form of plural words, etc.;
- *partial match* - this feature attempts to automatically suggest synonyms to defined entity values. (Greyling, 2019).

The following diagram (see Figure 2) graphically shows the principle of the operations of the Chatbot33. The user has the option to choose from the offered questions or define his own question when opening the Chatbot33 dialog. If the user selects the question "What can I study?", the Chatbot33 will then recognize the intention of this question as "Study Programs". The inference mechanism then encounters the dialogue node of the same name (see Figure 3) which meets the condition of recognizing this intention. The single-choice question is then generated as to what type of study the user is interested in. The user then selects one of the selected options. If the user is interested in studying a bachelor's or master's degree then in the next response the chatbot will again receive a single-choice offer of individual study programs of the selected level of study. A more detailed description of the selected study program will take place when selecting the study program. If the user selects a different type of study than the bachelor's or master's degree then he will receive a description of the selected type of study in the next reaction. The chatbot will wait for another user response in either case. The user will then receive a text response in both cases. If the Chatbot33 does not recognize any intent or value of a known entity then the commands of the "anything_else" dialogue node will be filled in, the user will receive an apology for not understanding the query and he is asked to try to reformulate the query or select one of frequently asked questions that might interest him. The "anything_else" dialogue node is executed even if the intent and entities are recognized but no other node is found that meets the defined conditions. The commands defined in the corresponding node will be executed in the case of recognizing the intention and finding the node fulfilling the conditions. The next step then depends on the possible reaction of the user.

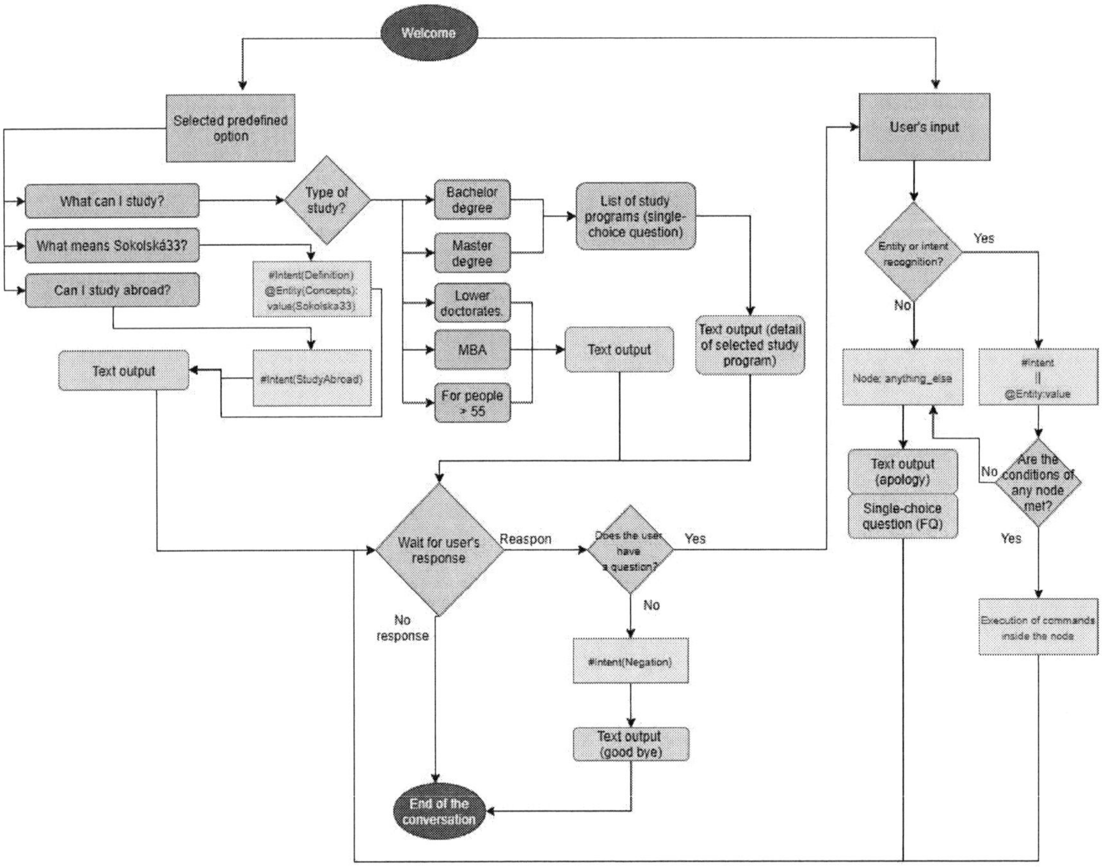

Figure 2 Chatbot33 functionalities

An example of a conversation with the Chatbot33 (in the Czech language) when searching for information about study programs for applicants is shown in the following Figure 4.

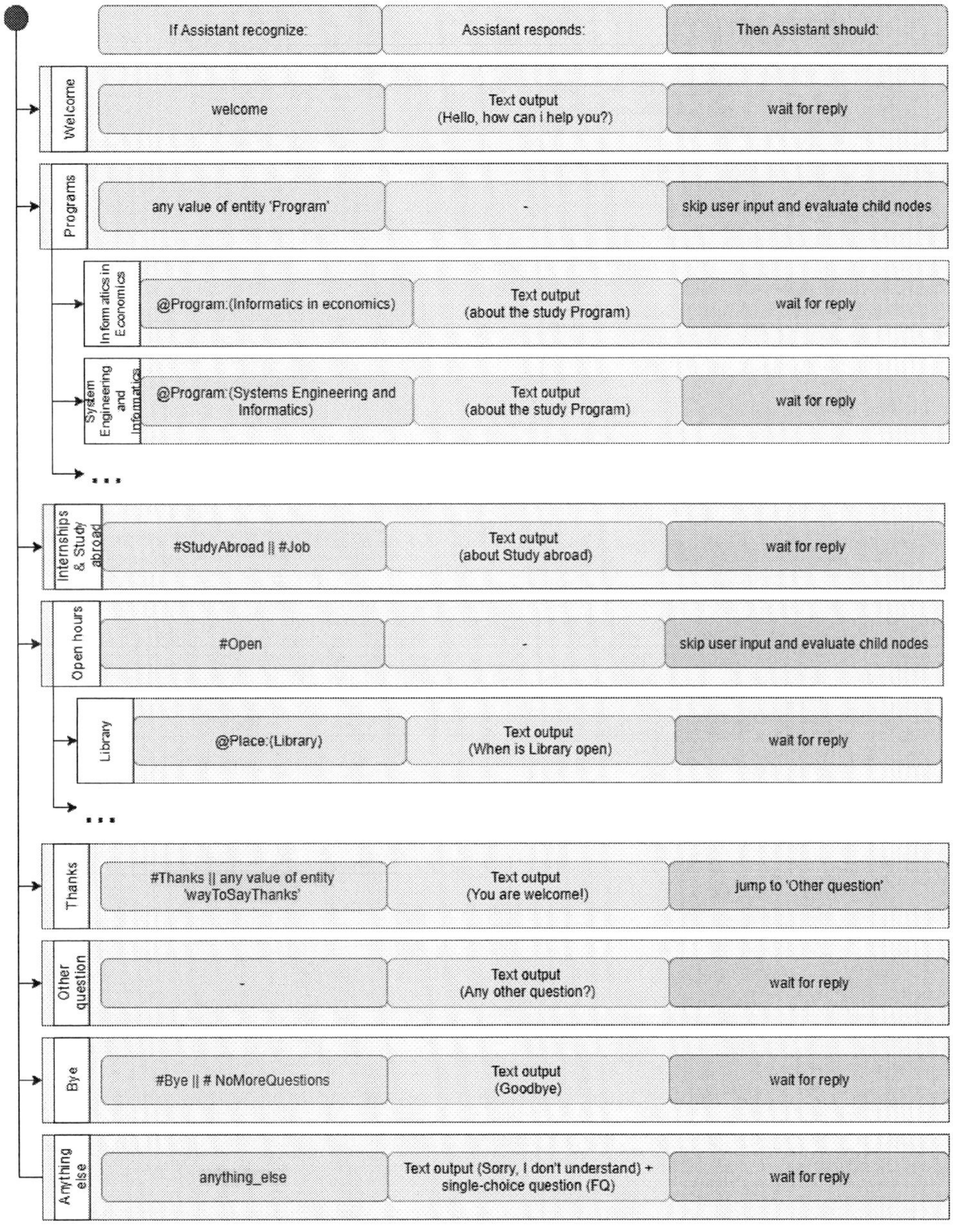

Figure 3 Chatbot33 dialogue nodes

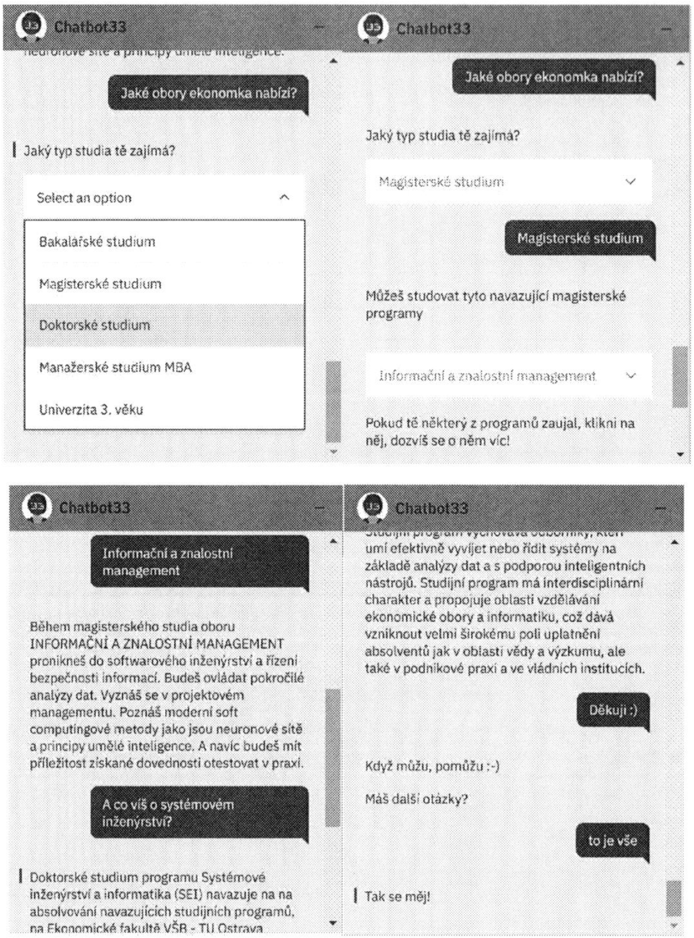

Figure 4 Chatbot33 conversation example

4 Conclusions

The Chatbot33 was officially launched on the website of the student organization Sokolská33 on 1st March 2021. For example, the Chatbot33 had a total of 26 conversations in the week of 22nd - 29th March 2021 according to the analytics tool that is part of the IBM Watson Assistant environment (see Figure 5). It received an average of 4.69 messages per conversation and it reached the maximum number of conversations on 25th March 2021, when it led 7 conversations per day. The Chatbot33 was able to provide an adequate response in 99 cases out of a total of 122 received messages and it provided a choice of topics in response to the remaining 23 user questions (i.e., referred to as "not covered" in IBM Analytics). The Chatbot33 thus currently understands 81.2% of user queries.

Further development of the Chatbot33 will be directed primarily to the implementation of the possibility of voice communication with the chatbot. The IBM Watson environment was chosen for the further development of the Chatbot33 for this reason that it also offers the Speech-to-Text service (based on the machine learning) for the conversion of voice input to text. Speech recognition and its conversion into textual data is a demanding process mainly due to the existence of specific intonations and accents in most individuals and often also due to fast and grammatically incorrect speech. The scope of the Chatbot33 knowledge base should also be expanded in further development. This goal is mainly to increase the number of known entities and the intentions of the Chatbot33. Specifically, it could be information about admission procedures to study at the VSB-Technical University of Ostrava, the possibilities of scholarships and subjects that are taught within the study of individual fields of study.

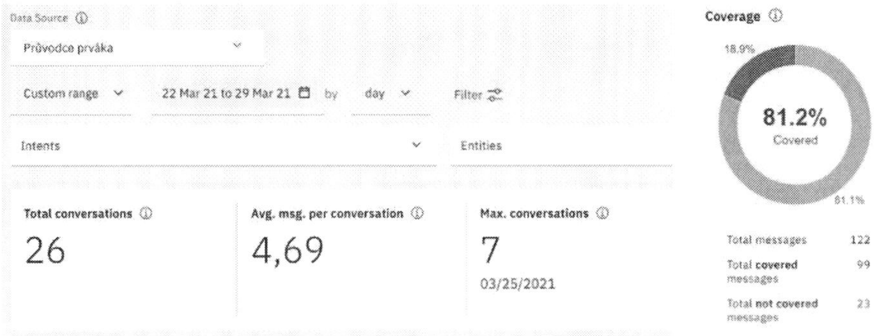

Figure 5 Analysis of the use of Chatbot33 for a selected week

Acknowledgements

This paper was supported by the Student Grant Competition project No. SP2021/86 by the Ministry of Education, Science, Research and Sport of the Czech Republic.

References

Biswas, M. (2018). *Beginning AI Bot Frameworks: Getting Started with Bot Development*. 1st ed. Kolkota: Apress.

Burden, D. and Savin-Baden, M. (2019). *Vitual Humans: Today and Tomorrow*. 1st ed. New York: CRC Press.

Cobus Greyling. (2019). *IBM Watson Assistant: Fuzzy Matching* [online]. Available at: https://cobusgreyling.medium.com/fuzzy-matching-in-chatbots-36063a7af027 [cited 2021-02-12].

Das, A. and Khan, R. (2018). *Build Better Chatbots: A Complete Guide to Getting Started with Chatbots*. 1st ed. Bangalore: Apress.

Deng, L. and Liu, Y. (2018). *Deep Learning in Natural Language Processing*. 1st ed. Singapore: Springer Nature.

Facebook. (2020). *Wit.ai – Service Documentation* [online]. Available at: https://wit.ai/docs/ [cited 2021-02-12].

Google. (2021). *Google DialogFlow – Service Documentation* [online]. Available at: https://cloud.google.com/dialogflow/docs [cited 2021-02-12].

Heaton, J. (2015). *Artificial Intelligence for Humans, Volume 3: Deep Learning and Neural Networks*. 1st ed. Chesterfield: Heaton Research.

IBM. (2019). *Think 2019 Kicks Off with Live Debate Between Man and Machine. IBM Research Blog* [online]. Available at: https://www.ibm.com/blogs/research/2019/02/ai-debate-recap-think-2019/ [cited 2021-02-12].

IBM NLP. (2020). *Natural Language Processing* [online]. Available at: https://www.ibm.com/cloud/learn/natural-language-processing [cited 2021-02-12].

IBM NLG. (2020). *NLP vs. NLU vs. NLG: the differences between three natural language processing concepts* [online]. Available at: https://www.ibm.com/blogs/watson/2020/11/nlp-vs-nlu-vs-nlg-the-differences-between-three-natural-language-processing-concepts/ [cited 2021-02-12].

IBM Watson. (2021). *IBM Watson Assistant – Service Documentation* [online]. Available at: https://cloud.ibm.com/docs/assistant?topic=assistant-getting-started&_ga=2.21935803.1272816929.1603116070-718699761.1602794626#getting-started [cited 2021-02-12].

Kim, P. (2017). *MATLAB Deep Learning: With Machine Learning, Neural Networks and Artificial Intelligence*. 1st ed. Seoul: Apress.

Microsoft. (2021). *LUIS – Language Understanding (LUIS) documentation* [online]. Available at: https://docs.microsoft.com/en-us/azure/cognitive-services/luis/ [cited 2021-02-12].

Shevat, A. (2017). *Designing Bots: Creating Conversational Experiences*. 1st ed. Sebastopol: O'Reilly Media.

Singh, H. and Lone, Y. A. (2019). *Deep Neuro-Fuzzy Systems with Python*. 1st ed. New York: Apress.

Sokolska33. (2021). *Sokolská33* [online]. Available at: http://www.sokolska33.cz/ [cited 2021-02-12].

Traum, D. (2009). *Models of Culture for Virtual Human Conversation*. 1st ed. Berlin: Springer.

Sustainable entrepreneurship in small and medium-sized enterprises in the Czech Republic

Hana Štverková[1], Michal Pohludka[2]

Abstract. Sustainable entrepreneurship is a phenomenon of recent years. It should be implemented using a business model aligned with sustainability principles. Entrepreneurship is widely understood as an engine of progress that brings growth to the economy, increases market competitiveness, increases the productivity of individual companies through technological change, and creates jobs and added value and prosperity for members of society. This paper focuses on identifying factors whose impact supports the sustainable transformation of small and medium-sized enterprises in Czech Republic. Through research in innovative small and medium-sized enterprises, the application of the principles of sustainable business was evaluated. Awareness of sustainable business is widespread among owners and managers of small and medium-sized enterprises, who apply the principles of sustainability to their corporate philosophy and strategy.

Keywords: corporate philosophy, development, environment, small and medium-sized enterprises, sustainable entrepreneurship.

JEL Classification: M10, Q01, L20

1 Introduction

Sustainable entrepreneurship is one of the most current topics in recent times in today´s global society, especially today when the pandemic of COVID 19 efficiently slowed down economic development and brought uncertainty to the business environment. This issue is becoming a key in tackling climate change, eliminating poverty, overcoming global economic crises, protecting the environment, and the fight against terrorism. All governmental and non-governmental organizations deal with its component organizations of the world. Not only is the sustainability an issue addressed by transnational and national organizations, it is increasingly being addressed, it is also dealt with by business entities themselves.

Sustainable entrepreneurship is a way of doing business that is not only focused on short-term profit, but also takes into account the principles of long-term sustainability and is based on the principles of sustainable development. Its basic premise is environmental friendliness, both locally and globally. Sustainable entrepreneurship represents a new way of management where economical as well as environmental, social, and ethical factors are concerned. Its aim is to generate a long-term income, contribute to society, and protect the environment.

Sustainability can be understood as the perseverance of the system, and it focuses on meeting the needs of the present without compromising the ability of future generations to meet their needs.

[1] VŠB- TU Ostrava, Faculty of Economics, Department of Business Administration, 17. listopadu 2172/155, 708 00 Ostrava, Czech Republic, hana.stverkova@vsb.cz.
[2] ZKV Career, s.r.o., Chomutovská 38/10, Ruzyně, 161 00 Praha, Czech Republic, michal@zkvcareer.com.

The aim of this article is to discuss the awareness and application of the principles of sustainable business by small and medium-sized enterprises in the Czech Republic. It is necessary to identify the factors whose impact supports the sustainable transformation of small and medium-sized enterprises. The purpose of this article is to show the situation in small and medium-sized enterprises in terms of application of the principles of sustainable entrepreneurship.

1.1 Literature review

Sustainability comes from sustainable development and is closely connected with corporate social responsibility. Sustainable development was defined by Brundtland (1987) as development that meets the needs of the present without compromising the ability of future generations to meet their own needs. Even this concept is somewhat vague, it aims to maintain economic advancement and progress while protecting the long-term value of the environment. Although many definitions abound, the most often used definition of sustainable development is that proposed by the Brundtland Commission (Brundtland, 1987; Cerin, 2006; Dernbach, 2003; Stoddart, 2011 etc.). This is the broadest definition.

Elkington (1997) introduced the concept of the Triple Bottom Line (TBL), or 3P (People, Planet and Profit). This definition attempts to provide a more practical direction suggesting to balance the three dimensions of sustainability: economical, human and environmental systems. The concept of sustainable entrepreneurship is reminiscent of the corporate social responsibility (CSR) model, although they intersect in many ways, some authors see differences in them. Thus, sustainable entrepreneurship is based on the same three pillars shown on Figure 1 - economic, ecological, and social.

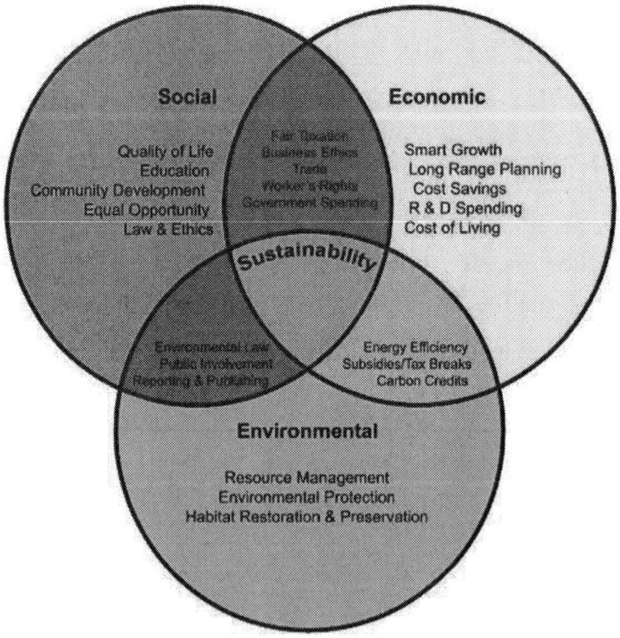

Figure 1 Relationships between Social, Environmental and Economic Sustainability [Mensah, 2019]

The economic pillar should look for ways to achieve steady growth in society's wealth without damaging the environment or disrupting national economies. The aim is to use modern environmentally friendly technologies and constant technical progress (Baruah, 2020, Haessler, 2020). Panwar et al. (2006) argue that the economic pillar should ensure that economic development is stable and efficient. According to Panwar et al. (2006) the second pillar, the social pillar, is based on social sustainability, which should give individuals control over their lives. It should be compatible with people's culture and values and preserve their identity originality. (Laszlo, 2008)

Sustainable entrepreneurship refers to the discovery, creation, and exploitation of entrepreneurial opportunities that contribute to sustainability by generating social and environmental gains for others in society (Hockerts and Wüstenhagen, 2012; Miethlich and Šlahor, 2018). Sustainable entrepreneurship is perceived as a concept that endeavors to balance the economic, social, and environmental aspects. Therefore, it is necessary to address the competitiveness of the company, taking into account the environmental and socio-economical aspects of business. Economic aspects of the entrepreneurship should be pursued in the aspects of the circular economy, diversity of the labor market, and sustainable communities.

Based on Shane and Venkataraman (2007), sustainable entrepreneurship is defined as the teleological process aiming at the achievement of sustainable development, by discovering, evaluating and exploiting opportunities and creating value that produces economic prosperity, social cohesion and environmental protection. Achieving sustainability at the global level through a strategic approach, which is a long-term perspective and is interested in combining different development models (Mets, Holbrook and Läänelaid, 2021). In addition to the classic three-pillar model, there is, for example, a prism model by Spangenberg (2013). There are also alternative models, one was created by Holden, Linnerud and Banister (2016). In the model, instead of the classical three pillars, they use moral ways such as meeting human needs, ensuring social justice, and respecting the environment limits. This model is mainly based on economic aspects. Emphasis is placed on human, social, productive, financial, and natural capital. The main idea is that if the total capital is growing, the development is considered as sustainable.

Small and medium-sized enterprises have a pivotal position in national economics in light of formation healthy entrepreneurial environment. Existence of small and medium-sized enterprises stabilize society. Each marked political insecurity and radical current situation could be for SMEs recourse threat. SMEs are essential for the growth of the national economy and the whole society. Small and medium-sized enterprises form healthy entrepreneurial environments. In this paper, SMEs are viewed in EU Recommendation 2003/361; see Table 1.

Company category	Staff	Turnover	Balance Sheet Total
Medium-sized	<250	≤ € 50 m	≤ € 43 m
Small	< 50	≤ € 10 m	≤ € 10 m
Micro	< 10	≤ € 2 m	≤ € 2 m

Table 1 Typology of SMEs [EU Recommendation 2003/361]

As small and medium-sized enterprises form the backbone of the national economy, therefore it is necessary to address their relationship to sustainable entrepreneurship. In the field of sustainable entrepreneurship, different methods are adopted depending on whether scientists want to deal with the theories or the phenomenon that characterized the discipline of sustainable entrepreneurship. Authors focus on the phenomenon of sustainable entrepreneurship, so they used the questionnaire survey and interviews.

2 Research and results

This survey was conducted among innovative small and medium-sized enterprises in the Czech Republic at the end of 2020. The choice of answers was used in questionnaire and used to collect data by measuring the opinion of the respondents. Authors utilized an interview with some of the respondents to enable interaction to improve quality of the research as well as response rate. There were 150 small and medium-sized enterprises contacted for a questionnaire survey. In the first part, it was necessary to identify sustainable entrepreneurship principles and its components as perceived by small and medium-sized owners and managers. There were used the combination of three parts of sustainable entrepreneurship, firstly – the labor market – diversity, preparedness for demographic change, equal opportunities, work flexibility, education, secondly, basic 7 principles of circular economy for the evaluation of sustainable entrepreneurship by SMEs and thirdly sustainable communities - corporate volunteering, corporate giving, shared economy, cooperation with cities, cross-sectoral partnerships. In second part of the questionnaire, it was evaluated if the SMEs incorporated these aspects into the corporate's philosophy and strategy and whether they are introduced to the employees by companies' managers and owners. Small and medium-sized enterprises owners and managers were the respondents since they have the relevant information concerning the entrepreneurship investigated. For the identification of respondents, the largest group consisted of respondents over 50 years old (45%), 24 % age group in 30-49 years old, and 31% young entrepreneurs under 30 years. Females made up 43% of the respondents and the majority group were men 57%. There were 32% of SMEs respondents operation in service, 27% in supply chain management, 23% in production, 18% in manufacturing.

The results further show that most owners and managers of small and medium-sized enterprises were aware of the issues of sustainable business, 97 % of all respondents were knowledgeable in the issues of sustainable entrepreneurship. However, only 49 % confirmed the conscious use of the principles of sustainability.

7 principles of sustainable entrepreneurship	Use	Considering to used	Do not used
Comply with environmental standards	29 %	16 %	55 %
Innovate	96 %	3 %	1 %
Quality of production and services	89 %	4 %	7 %
They are certified	37 %	8 %	55 %
They recycle and cycle	74 %	23 %	3%
Use renewable resources	53 %	11 %	36 %
Use shared economy (tools, cars)	26 %	39 %	35 %

Table 2 Use of 7 principles of circular economy by small and medium enterprises

Table 2 shows the seven elements of the circular economy that are important for sustainable entrepreneurship. It can be stated that most of the interviewed small and medium-sized enterprises apply these principles or are starting to think about them. Certification and use of environmental standards according to additional interviews are considered by owners and managers of SMEs to be costly in terms of certification, but the principles of environmental standards are followed.

From the point of view of the labor market, where employees interact with employers and each others (employers compete to select the most trustworthy, and the employees strive for the most satisfying workplace), it is appropriate to start from the principles of market diversity. In general, we can refer to the term diversity as accepting differences between people and supporting and appreciating this diversity by increasing the number of employees from disadvantaged groups in companies, especially in management positions. The surveyed small and medium-sized enterprises apply the principles of education (93 %), equal attitude (89 %), diversity (89 %) from a demographic point of view and from the point of view of different age groups of employees. The problem in some researched companies is organizational changes (in research understood as readiness to make changes of an organizational nature due to changing conditions and already used in 24 % of companies) and therefore the flexibility of work cannot be processed (42 %), which is shown in Table 3.

Labor market	Use	Considering to be used	Do not used
Diversity	89 %	7 %	4 %
Education	93 %	1 %	6 %
Equal opportunities	89 %	4 %	7 %
Organizational changes	24 %	39 %	37 %
Preparation for demographical changes	46 %	38 %	16 %
Work flexibility	42%	14 %	44 %

Table 3 Use of labor market elements in small and medium-sized enterprises

The column "Use" means that this procedure is already applied in the surveyed companies; "Considering to be used" means that companies know about these concepts and are ready to include them in their business activities, "Do not used" means that the surveyed companies are not interested in these concepts.

The last examined area was a sustainable community, where it was found out whether small and medium-sized enterprises participate in volunteering, create value for the local community, are involved in networks or clusters or associations. From this point of view of sustainable entrepreneurship, small and medium-sized enterprises are mainly dealing with sponsorship (87 %) and activities for the local environment (62 %), see Table 4.

Sustainable community	Use	Considering	Do not used
Activities for local community	62 %	14 %	24 %
Networking	56 %	11 %	33 %
Sponsorship	87 %	7 %	6 %
Volunteering	47 %	21 %	32 %

Table 4 Sustainable community

All 87 % of the surveyed small and medium-sized enterprises have activities related to sustainable entrepreneurship integrated into their corporate philosophy, 76 % into the corporate strategy, and these companies regularly acquaint their employees with their corporate philosophy and vision.

Small and medium-sized enterprises do not feel the need to formally name the direction they are heading as a sustainable entrepreneurship. Based on the survey, the economic pillar is in the small and medium-sized enterprises built on:

- the corporate's philosophy by identity and vision,
- corporate strategy,
- human resources – integrity and their needs.

According to the research, social sustainability lies both in close connection with the local community and in contributing to the employment and the economic prosperity of the region in general, or targeted support for charitable projects in the corporate environment.

The expectations of employees, customers, and regulators, as well as the changing conditions for the business, force them to respond and build their activities on the principles of sustainable entrepreneurship.

It is also necessary to pay attention to the soft factors of competitiveness, which in small and medium-size enterprises form a four-leaf clover of business manifestations, namely corporate philosophy with company´s identity, people with their skills and integrity, business strategy, and communication with the ecosystem. Doing business in contexts of sustainable entrepreneurship help companies predict and manage risk, reduce costs, increase success by helping customers live more responsibly, gain new markets, etc., through product innovation.

3 Discussion

Small and medium-sized enterprises also need to become a much more active player and, together with others, participate in creating solutions for important areas such as the labor market, diversity, education, and the use of natural resources. However, small and medium-sized companies should in some way comprehensively cover the topic of responsible business and have a long-term strategy with specific goals and steps.

Based on the research of Eurobarometr (2017), it can be stated that in the Czech Republic, sustainable business is beginning to blend into the normal life of society. The survey revealed the following findings:

- 4% of Czech companies minimize waste to use resources more efficiently,
- 3% of Czech companies have invested 11 percent or more of their turnover in more efficient use of resources,

- 45% of Czech companies slightly reduced production costs thanks to measures for more efficient use of resources.

These conclusions were to some extent confirmed by the authors' research, as it was found that most owners and managers of small and medium-sized enterprises were aware of the issues of sustainable business. At the same time, they look at the labor market in terms of principles characteristic of sustainability. On the other hand, half of them confirmed the intended use of sustainability principles, which is seen as a space for improvement.

On the other hand, the society in the Czech Republic starts to understand the importance of sustainable entrepreneurship from the point of view of the principles of circular economy, sharing economy and diversity of the market as the research shows (Horenská, 2018):

- 29% of Czechs know the concept of shared economy,
- 25% of Czechs have ever tried the services of a shared economy,
- 8% of people in the Czech Republic offer their services or property in a shared economy,
- 64% of people use these services due to financial savings,
- 41% of people support the regulation of a shared economy,
- 74% of respondents know Zonky thanks to a massive advertising campaign. It is thus the best known of the companies providing shared economy services.

This concept was also confirmed by the author's research, as it was found that they are mainly dealing with sponsorship and activities for the local environment. This would not be possible without the involvement of the general public.

Responsibility and sustainability thus become one of the important elements of the precondition for business success. In recent years, most multinational and purely Czech companies are aware that the world in which they do business is changing radically. Thus, small and medium-sized enterprises combine their social responsibility and sustainability programs with how to respond to demographic change, labor market situation, declining availability of resources, climate change, changing customer and public expectations. All this brings small and medium-sized enterprises not only a competitive advantage, but also economic savings, and is reflected in their reputation.

4 Conclusion

Tough competition is the generator of changes in the market. In this area, there is a fundamental influence on marketing and is associated with a satisfied, stable, and loyal customer. The key element is therefore the customer in today's dynamic and competitive environment. Monitoring its satisfaction is essential, it determines the value of this satisfaction and its development at a time when it is identified by the preferences of clients who are the final source of income of the company. The income increase or decrease affects, among other things, satisfaction of the customers, and this has an impact on reducing interest in society itself and may weaken the company economically. Then it is logical that it reduces customer satisfaction and can discourage the functioning of all other internal processes of the company.

The concept of sustainable entrepreneurship is nothing new, in a sense, it can be understood as a return to the roots. It is not enough to look at the company's competitiveness only in financial health, production, marketing, management, etc., it is necessary to examine competitiveness in terms of new dimensions, especially in terms of long-term business sustainability.

References

Baruah, P. (2020). 3 pillars of sustainability [Online]. Available at: https://planningtank.com/environment/3-pillars-of-sustainability [cited 2021-01-24].

Brundtland, G. H. (1987). *Our Common Future.* Oxford University Press.

Cerin, P. (2006). 'Bringing economic opportunity into line with environmental influence: A discussion on the Coase theorem and the Porter and van der Linde hypothesis'. *Ecological Economics*, 56 (2), pp. 209-225.

Dernbach, J. C. (2003). 'Achieving Sustainable Development: The Centrality and Multiple Facets of Integrated Decisionmaking'. *Indiana Journal of Global Legal Studies,* 10 (1), Article 10.

Elkington, J. (1997). *Cannibals with forks: the triple bottom line of 21st century business*. Oxford: Capstone Publishing Ltd.

Eurobarometr (2017). Ochrana životního prostředí a klimatu je důležitá pro více než 90 % evropských občanů. [Online]. Available at: https://ec.europa.eu/czech-republic/news/200303_eurobarometer_cs [cited 2020-02-10].

EU Recommendation 2003/361. Entrepreneurship and Small and medium-sized enterprises (SMEs): SMEs definition, [Online]. Available at: https://ec.europa.eu/growth/smes/sme-definition_en [cited 2020-02-10].

Haessler, P. (2020). Strategic Decisions between Short-Term Profit and Sustainability, *Administrative Sciences,* 10 (3), pp. 63.

Hockerts K. and Wüstenhagen R. (2012) 'When David Meets Goliath: Sustainable Entrepreneurship and the Evolution of Markets'. In: Nicholls A. and Murdock A. (eds) *Social Innovation*. Palgrave Macmillan, London.

Holden, E., Linnerud, K., & Banister, D. (2017). 'The imperatives of sustainable development'. *Sustainable Development*, 25 (3), pp. 213–226.

Horenská, P. (2019). Sdílenou ekonomiku využívá téměř čtvrtina Čechů. Stoupá podpora

regulace. [Online]. Available at: https://www.ipsos.com/sites/default/files/ct/news/documents/2018-04/tz_ceska_asociace_sdilene_ekonomiky_ipsos_12.4.2018.pdf [cited 2020-02-10].

Laszlo, C. (2008). *Sustainable value: How the world's leading companies are doing well by doing good.* Stanford University Press.

Miethlich, B. and Šlahor, Ľ. (2018). 'Employment of persons with disabilities as a corporate social responsability initiative: necessity and variants of implementation'. *International Conference Proceedings 2018 : Innovations in Science and Education*. Praha, Czech republic, pp. 350-355

Mensah, J. (2019). Sustainable development: Meaning, history, principles, pillars, and implications for human action: Literature review. *Cogent Social Sciences*, 5 (1), 1653531.

Mets T, Holbrook J and Läänelaid S. (2021). Entrepreneurship Education Challenges for Green Transformation. *Administrative Sciences*. 11(1):15.

Panwar, R., Rhine, T., Hansen, E., and Juslin, H. (2006). 'Corporate responsibility: Balancing economic, environmental, and social issues in the forest products industry'. *Forest Products Journal*, 56 (2), pp. 4–12.

Shane S., Venkataraman S. (2007). 'The Promise of Entrepreneurship as a Field of Research'. In: Cuervo Á., Ribeiro D., Roig S. (eds) *Entrepreneurship*. Springer, Berlin, Heidelberg.

Spangenberg, J. H. (2013). 'Pick simply the best: Sustainable development is about radical analysis and selective synthesis, not about old wine in new bottles'. *Sustainable Development*, 21 (2), pp. 101–111.

Stoddart, P. (2011). 'Development through fair trade: candour or deception'? *Economic Affairs*, 31 (1), pp. 131-134.

Empirical Evidence of Dependency Between Check-Out Times

Petra Tomanová [1] , Vladimír Holý [2] , Ondřej Sokol [3]

Abstract. We analyze a wide range of retail datasets and investigate the dependence structure of customer check-out times. Naturally, times between successive check-outs exhibit strong seasonal and diurnal patterns. For their adjustment, we use the cubic splines model estimated by the weighted least squares method. More interestingly, even after the adjustment, times between successive check-outs possess an autocorrelation structure. We capture it by the autoregressive conditional duration model based on the generalized gamma distribution with score dynamics estimated by the maximum likelihood method.

Keywords: Check-Out Times, Autoregressive Conditional Duration Model, Generalized Autoregressive Score Model, Retail Business.

JEL classification: C41, C44, M11

1 Introduction

In retail business analytics, times when customers check out are often considered random but independent. This is for example a common assumption in queueing systems in which check-out times represent arrival times into processing. For a textbook treatment of the queueing theory, see e.g. Stewart (2009).

In this paper, we let times between successive check-outs be dependent on the time of the day and season as well as on their past values. We closely follow the methodology of our previous work Tomanová and Holý (2021)and analyze check-out times in two phases.

First, we adjust times between successive check-outs for diurnal and seasonal patterns. For this purpose, we utilize a linear regression model with *cubic splines* and linear trend. To account for irregularly spaced observations, we estimate the model by the *weighted least squares (WLS)* method. For a practical guide to polynomial and spline regressions, see e.g. Bruce and Bruce (2017).

Second, we model dynamics of the adjusted times between successive check-outs by the *autoregressive conditional duration* (ACD) model of Engle and Russell (1998). The ACD model originates in finance but can be successfully utilized in retail business analytics as well. We use a particular form of the ACD model based on the *generalized gamma distribution* with score-driven dynamics. Such model belongs to the class of the *generalized autoregressive score* (GAS) models of Creal et al. (2013). We estimate the model by the *maximum likelihood* method. For a literature review of the ACD literature, see Pacurar (2008) and Saranjeet and Ramanathan (2018). For a comprehensive list of the GAS literature, see `www.gasmodel.com`.

[1]Prague University of Economics and Business, Department of Econometrics, Winston Churchill Square 1938/4, 130 67 Prague, Czechia, petra.tomanova@vse.cz.

[2]Prague University of Economics and Business, Department of Econometrics, Winston Churchill Square 1938/4, 130 67 Prague, Czechia, vladimir.holy@vse.cz.

[3]Prague University of Economics and Business, Department of Econometrics, Winston Churchill Square 1938/4, 130 67 Prague, Czechia, ondrej.sokol@vse.cz.

The goal of this paper is to demonstrate that the approach of Tomanová and Holý (2021) to modeling times between successive check-outs is applicable to a wide range of retail datasets. Besides the empirical study of an online bookstore by Tomanová and Holý (2021), we also present applications to an online jewelry store, an online electronics store, an online gift store, and a brick and mortar drugstore.

2 Datasets

The selected real datasets include both online and brick and mortar stores with a various business focus. The datasets differ in the length of the monitored period as well as the frequency of visits and other characteristics.

Online Bookstore. For comparison, we start by reviewing the results of Tomanová and Holý (2021) for a Czech online bookstore. This dataset is obtained from the database of an online bookstore based in Prague. The data cover the period from June 8 to December 20, 2018, resulting in 204 days and 5753 observations. The precision of the timestamp is one minute. In line with Bauwens (2006), we set zero values of times between successive check-outs to 0.5 minutes as our model requires strictly positive values. The median of the raw check-out times is 24 minutes, the mean is 49 minutes, and 29 orders arrive in the system per day on average – see Tomanová and Holý (2021) for further details.

Besides Tomanová and Holý (2021), this dataset is also analyzed by Tomanová (2018) who performs a process quality assessment based on process simulation. Tomanová (2019a) further shows that clustering of arrivals into a queueing system increases the probability of weeks with an extreme number of arrivals. Finally, Tomanová (2019b) makes recommendations for the management based on previous results.

Online Jewelry Store. The second dataset contains purchase data of a Middle East medium-sized online jewelry store[1] from November 29, 2018, to November 11, 2020. The dataset of anonymized behavior is collected by the behavior tracking service of the REES46 marketing stack. However, we analyze a slightly shorter period starting from January 15, 2019, due to structural break. The resulting sample includes 676 days with 84577 observations. Due to the higher precision of one second, zero values of times between successive check-outs are set to 0.01 minutes instead of 0.5. The median of the raw check-out times is 5 minutes, the mean is 11 minutes, and 125 orders arrive in the system per day on average.

Online Electronics Store. The third dataset contains purchase data of large home appliances and online electronics store[2] from May 1 to November 21, 2020. Our sample consists of 930131 timestamps of transactions with a time precision of one second and includes 205 days. Zero values are set to 0.01 minutes. The median of the raw check-out times is 0.08 minutes, the mean is 0.32 minutes, and 4537 orders arrive in the system per day on average. Data was collected using a behavior tracking system on a large eCommerce store in a Middle East country.

Online Gift Store. The data comes from a UK-based online retail focusing mainly on unique all-occasion gifts[3]. We used 23631 transactions from January 4, 2010, to December 9, 2011,

[1] https://www.kaggle.com/mkechinov/ecommerce-purchase-history-from-jewelry-store
[2] https://www.kaggle.com/mkechinov/ecommerce-purchase-history-from-electronics-store
[3] https://www.kaggle.com/hellbuoy/online-retail-customer-clustering

resulting in 285 analyzed days. The time precision is one minute and zero values are set to 0.5 minutes. The median of the raw check-out times is 3 minutes, the mean is 6 minutes, and 83 orders arrive in the system per day on average. The dataset is presented in Chen et al. (2012).

Brick and Mortar Drugstore. Finally, we analyze a dataset from a brick and mortar retail drugstore that contains 72723 timestamps of transactions from the cash register. The dataset spans from January 1 to December 31, 2017, and includes 362 days. The precision is one minute and zero values are set to 0.5 minutes. The median of the raw check-out times is 2 minutes, the mean is 3 minutes, and 201 orders arrive in the system per day on average. Holý et al. (2017), Sokol et al. (2020) and Sokol and Holý (2020) describe the dataset in more detail.

3 Diurnal and Seasonal Patterns

3.1 Methodology

In the first phase of our approach, we capture the non-linear behavior of the diurnal and seasonal patterns using cubic splines. A *cubic spline* is a piecewise cubic polynomial with continuous derivatives up to order two at knots ξ_k, $k = 1, \ldots, K$ (see e.g. Bruce and Bruce, 2017). Let raw times between successive check-outs $\tilde{y}_i$, $i = 1, \ldots, n$ follow

$$\log \tilde{y}_i = \beta_0 + \beta_1 b_1(x_i) + \beta_2 b_2(x_i) + \cdots + \beta_{K+3} b_{K+3}(x_i) + \gamma t_i + \varepsilon_i, \tag{1}$$

where β_j and γ are parameters to be estimated, ε_i is a disturbance term, t_i is the trend variable, b_j are the basis functions, and x_i is the time difference of the i-th observation and the beginning of the week. The basis functions are equal to (i) the variable x_i, $b_1(x_i) = x_i$; (ii) its square, $b_2(x_i) = x_i^2$; (iii) its cube, $b_3(x_i) = x_i^3$; and (iv) truncated power functions, $b_{k+3}(x_i) = \max\{0, (x_i - \xi_k)^3\}$, $k = 1, \ldots, K$. Note that the trend variable t_i is not linear in observations but linear in time.

The parameters in (1) are estimated by the *weighted least squares (WLS) method.* Weights are equal to raw times between successive check-outs to account for an uneven number of observations in time. The diurnally and seasonally adjusted times between successive check-outs y_i are then obtained as exponentiated residuals from regression (1).

3.2 Results

The first three datasets – Online Bookstore, Online Jewelry Store, and Online Electronics Store – exhibit strong diurnal patterns due to the long check-out times at night, see Figure 4.1. The rest two datasets do not contain data during the night (e.g. the brick and mortar drugstore closes at 8 PM), however, we can still observe the diurnal pattern in terms of shorter check-out times during rush hours in the middle of the day than in the morning and evening. Moreover, strong weekly and monthly seasonal patterns are observed for all datasets, especially for Online Gift Store and Brick and Mortar Drugstore that exhibit much lower frequency during weekends (the first one is even closed on Saturday).

To obtain the diurnally and seasonally adjusted and detrended inter-arrival times, we estimate the regression equation (1) in the same manner as Tomanová and Holý (2021): (i) we select one knot for every 90 minutes, which results in appropriate fit in all cases, (ii) we use weekly aggregation in (1), (iii) we stack the sample three times consecutively to ensure continuity between Sundays and Mondays and compute the adjusted inter-arrival times based on the second sub-sample, (iv) we estimate the parameters by the WLS method.

Figure 4.1 shows the check-out times and their fitted diurnal and seasonal patterns with the trend. The diurnally and seasonally adjusted and detrended inter-arrival times are computed as the exponentiated residuals of estimated equation (1) and for convenience, they are standardized to have unit mean.

4 Score-Driven Dynamics

4.1 Methodology

In the second phase of our approach, we model the adjusted times between successive check-outs y_i, $i = 1, \ldots, n$. Let y_i follow the *generalized gamma distribution* proposed by Stacy (1962). It is a continuous probability distribution for non-negative variables with three parameters – the scale parameter α and the shape parameters $\psi > 0$ and $\varphi > 0$. Special cases include the gamma distribution (when $\varphi = 1$), the Weibull distribution (when $\psi = 1$) and the exponential distribution (when $\varphi = 1$ and $\psi = 1$). The probability density function is given by

$$f(y|\alpha, \psi, \varphi) = \frac{1}{\Gamma(\psi)} \frac{\varphi}{e^{\alpha}} \left(\frac{y}{e^{\alpha}}\right)^{\psi\varphi - 1} e^{-\left(\frac{y}{e^{\alpha}}\right)^{\varphi}}, \qquad y \in (0, \infty), \tag{2}$$

where $\Gamma(\cdot)$ is the gamma function.

Next, we consider that the scale parameter α is time-varying, i.e. we use α_i, $i = 1, \ldots, n$. Let parameter α_i follow recursion

$$\alpha_{i+1} = c + b\alpha_i + a\nabla_{\alpha}(y_i, \alpha_i, \psi, \varphi), \qquad i = 1, \ldots, n, \tag{3}$$

where c is the constant parameter, b is the autoregressive parameter, a is the score parameter, and $\nabla_{\alpha}(y_i, \alpha_i, \psi, \varphi)$ is the score given by

$$\nabla_{\alpha}(y, \alpha, \psi, \varphi) = \frac{\partial \log f(y|\alpha, \psi, \varphi)}{\partial \alpha} = \varphi \left(y^{\varphi} e^{-\varphi\alpha} - \psi\right), \qquad y \in (0, \infty). \tag{4}$$

This is an observation-driven model which belongs to the class of the *generalized autoregressive score (GAS) models* of Creal et al. (2013).

We estimate the model by the *maximum likelihood method*. The estimated parameters $\hat{c}$, $\hat{b}$, $\hat{a}$, $\hat{\psi}$, and $\hat{\varphi}$ are obtained by maximizing the log-likelihood function given by

$$\left(\hat{c}, \hat{b}, \hat{a}, \hat{\psi}, \hat{\varphi}\right) \in_{c,b,a,\psi,\varphi} \sum_{i=1}^{n} \log f(y_i|\alpha_i, \psi, \varphi), \tag{5}$$

where $f(y_i|\alpha_i, \psi, \varphi)$ is given by (2) and α_i by (3). Due to the recursive nature of the model, we set the initial value α_0 to the long-term mean value $c/(1 - b)$ and the initial score to zero.

4.2 Results

After the seasonal and diurnal adjustment, the analyzed check-out times of all datasets still tend to cluster over time. To capture the autocorrelation, we estimate the parameters of the

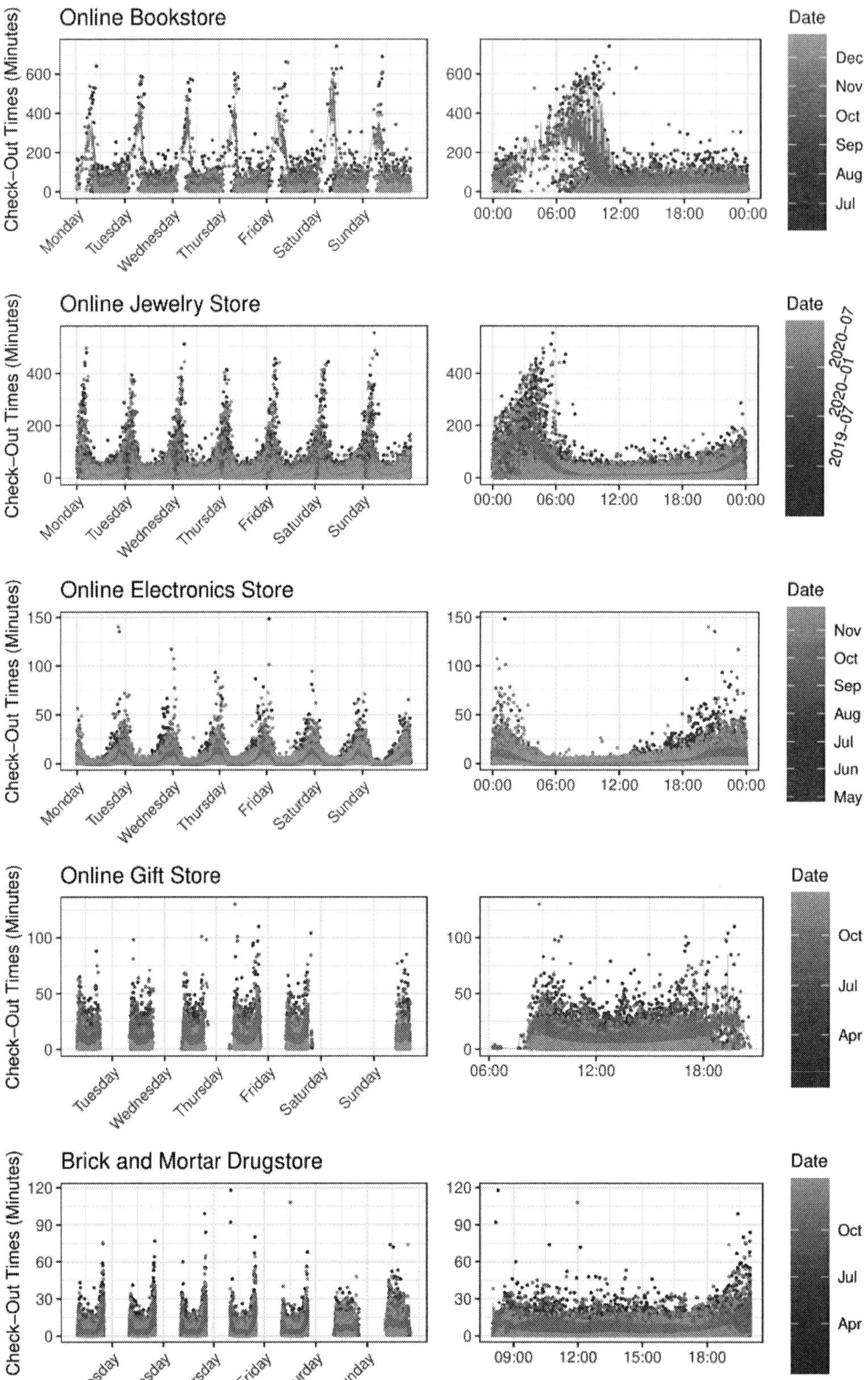

Figure 1 Intra-week (left) and intra-day (right) view of raw check-out times and their fitted diurnal and seasonal pattern.

	Model		Estimate					Model Fit	
	Spec.	Dist.	c	b	a	ψ	φ	Lik.	AIC
Online Bookstore	Static	Exp.	0.000	0.000	0.000	1.000	1.000	−5 753.0	11 508.0
	Static	Weibull	-0.013	0.000	0.000	1.000	0.971	−5 748.9	11 501.9
	Static	Gamma	0.041	0.000	0.000	0.959	1.000	−5 749.8	11 503.5
	Static	G. G.	-0.118	0.000	0.000	1.081	0.926	−5 748.4	11 502.8
	Dyn.	Exp.	-0.001	0.761	0.059	1.000	1.000	−5 728.3	11 462.6
	Dyn.	Weibull	-0.004	0.751	0.059	1.000	0.974	−5 724.9	11 457.8
	Dyn.	Gamma	0.007	0.761	0.061	0.966	1.000	−5 726.0	11 460.0
	Dyn.	G. G.	-0.057	0.720	0.073	1.147	0.896	−5 723.3	11 456.6
Online Jewelry Store	Static	Exp.	0.000	0.000	0.000	1.000	1.000	−84 577.0	169 156.0
	Static	Weibull	-0.063	0.000	0.000	1.000	0.885	−83 427.5	166 858.9
	Static	Gamma	0.168	0.000	0.000	0.845	1.000	−83 742.6	167 489.2
	Static	G. G.	-0.856	0.000	0.000	1.579	0.679	−83 150.4	166 306.8
	Dyn.	Exp.	0.000	0.998	0.023	1.000	1.000	−79 216.2	158 438.4
	Dyn.	Weibull	0.000	0.998	0.026	1.000	0.940	−78 934.1	157 876.1
	Dyn.	Gamma	0.000	0.998	0.025	0.920	1.000	−79 018.1	158 044.2
	Dyn.	G. G.	-0.001	0.998	0.029	1.270	0.816	−78 850.6	157 711.2
Online Electronics Store	Static	Exp.	0.000	0.000	0.000	1.000	1.000	−930 131.0	1 860 264.0
	Static	Weibull	0.000	0.000	0.000	1.000	1.000	−930 068.3	1 860 141.0
	Static	Gamma	0.000	0.000	0.000	1.000	1.000	−930 111.6	1 860 227.0
	Static	G. G.	0.000	0.000	0.000	1.000	1.000	−930 025.0	1 860 056.0
	Dyn.	Exp.	0.000	0.999	0.023	1.000	1.000	−736 214.5	1 472 435.0
	Dyn.	Weibull	0.000	0.999	0.021	1.000	1.051	−734 245.2	1 468 498.0
	Dyn.	Gamma	0.000	0.999	0.020	1.141	1.000	−731 273.1	1 462 554.0
	Dyn.	G. G.	-0.003	0.999	0.024	4.355	0.469	−718 547.4	1 437 105.0
Online Gift Store	Static	Exp.	0.000	0.000	0.000	1.000	1.000	−23 631.0	47 264.0
	Static	Weibull	-0.036	0.000	0.000	1.000	0.931	−23 521.4	47 046.7
	Static	Gamma	0.052	0.000	0.000	0.950	1.000	−23 610.2	47 224.4
	Static	G. G.	-35.913	0.000	0.000	57.187	0.114	−22 580.6	45 167.2
	Dyn.	Exp.	-0.001	0.956	0.049	1.000	1.000	−23 255.2	46 516.4
	Dyn.	Weibull	-0.002	0.951	0.059	1.000	0.942	−23 177.0	46 362.0
	Dyn.	Gamma	0.001	0.956	0.050	0.972	1.000	−23 249.1	46 506.2
	Dyn.	G. G.	-3.982	0.897	0.123	64.804	0.110	−22 061.8	44 133.7
B&M Drugstore	Static	Exp.	0.000	0.000	0.000	1.000	1.000	−72 723.0	145 448.0
	Static	Weibull	0.048	0.000	0.000	1.000	1.122	−71 868.1	143 740.1
	Static	Gamma	-0.313	0.000	0.000	1.367	1.000	−70 721.8	141 447.5
	Static	G. G.	-26.416	0.000	0.000	52.634	0.152	−66 389.4	132 784.8
	Dyn.	Exp.	0.000	0.992	0.022	1.000	1.000	−71 756.3	143 518.7
	Dyn.	Weibull	0.000	0.993	0.015	1.000	1.141	−70 652.1	141 312.1
	Dyn.	Gamma	-0.003	0.992	0.016	1.409	1.000	−69 380.1	138 768.1
	Dyn.	G. G.	-0.240	0.986	0.027	30.234	0.204	−65 145.9	130 301.8

Table 1 Parameter estimates of the inter-arrival time models with the log-likelihood value (Lik.) and the Akaike information criterion (AIC).

dynamic model based on the generalized gamma distribution with the GAS dynamics. For comparison, we also present the results for static and dynamic models based on special cases of the generalized gamma distribution (G.G.), namely, the exponential (Exp.), Weibull, and gamma distributions.

In all cases, the best performing model in terms of the *Akaike information criterion* (AIC) is the dynamic GAS model using the generalized gamma distribution, see Table 1. On the other hand, the worst performing model is the static exponential model. In three cases – Online Bookstore, Online Jewelry Store, Brick and Mortar Drugstore – the dynamic models are substantially better than their static counterparts. The difference of AIC values are at least 43.6 in the case of Online Bookstore, however, the difference is even more profound in the other two cases (8595.6 in case of Online Jewelry Store and 391643.0 in case of Brick and Mortar Drugstore). In the rest two cases – Online Electronics Store and Online Gift Store – the static generalized gamma model performs better than the dynamic models based on exponential, Weibull, and gamma distributions.

5 Conclusion

We demonstrate that a wide range of retail datasets exhibits dependence of times between successive check-outs on the time of the day and season as well as on their past values. We also show that the former dependence can be captured by the cubic splines model and the latter by the autoregressive conditional duration model. The methodology is flexible enough to fit all analyzed datasets – it works well for (i) both shorter and longer datasets, (ii) data with very low and very high frequency, (iii) check-out times with different precisions, (iv) both continuous check-out times and those that occur in certain opening hours, and for (v) both online and brick and mortar retail stores. Our results have implications on subsequent analysis of times between successive check-outs, namely on the queueing theory. As discussed and studied by Tomanová and Holý (2020), ignoring the dependence structure in queueing systems leads to significantly underestimated performance measures and consequently suboptimal decisions.

Acknowledgements

The work on this paper was supported by the Internal Grant Agency of the Prague University of Economics and Business under project F4/27/2020.

References

Luc Bauwens. Econometric Analysis of Intra-Daily Trading Activity on the Tokyo Stock Exchange. *Monetary and Economic Studies*, 24(1):1–24, 2006. ISSN 0288-8432.

Peter Bruce and Andrew Bruce. *Practical Statistics for Data Scientists: 50 Essential Concepts*. O'Reilly Media, Sebastopol, 2017. ISBN 978-1-4919-5295-5.

Daqing Chen, Sai Laing Sain, and Kun Guo. Data Mining for the Online Retail Industry: A Case Study of RFM Model-Based Customer Segmentation Using Data Mining. *Journal of Database Marketing & Customer Strategy Management*, 19(3):197–208, 2012. ISSN 1741-2439. doi: 10.1057/dbm.2012.17.

Drew Creal, Siem Jan Koopman, and André Lucas. Generalized Autoregressive Score Models with Applications. *Journal of Applied Econometrics*, 28(5):777–795, 2013. ISSN 0883-7252. doi: 10.1002/jae.1279.

Robert F. Engle and Jeffrey R. Russell. Autoregressive Conditional Duration: A New Model for Irregularly Spaced Transaction Data. *Econometrica*, 66(5):1127–1162, 1998. ISSN 0012-9682. doi: 10.2307/2999632.

Vladimír Holý, Ondřej Sokol, and Michal Černý. Clustering Retail Products Based on Customer Behaviour. *Applied Soft Computing*, 60:752–762, 2017. ISSN 1568-4946. doi: 10.1016/j.asoc.2017.02.004.

Maria Pacurar. Autoregressive Conditional Duration Models in Finance: A Survey of the Theoretical and Empirical Literature. *Journal of Economic Surveys*, 22(4):711–751, 2008. ISSN 0950-0804. doi: 10.1111/j.1467-6419.2007.00547.x.

Kaur Bhogal Saranjeet and Thekke Variyam Ramanathan. Conditional Duration Models for High-Frequency Data: A Review on Recent Developments. *Journal of Economic Surveys*, 33 (1):252–273, 2018. ISSN 0950-0804. doi: 10.1111/joes.12261.

Ondřej Sokol and Vladimír Holý. The Role of Shopping Mission in Retail Customer Segmentation. *International Journal of Market Research*, 2020a. ISSN 1470-7853. doi: 10.1177/1470785320921011.

Ondřej Sokol, Vladimír Holý, and Tomáš Cipra. Customer and Product Clustering in Retail Business. In *Proceedings of the 7th World Conference on Soft Computing*, pages 529–537, Baku, 2020. Springer. ISBN 978-3-030-47123-1. doi: 10.1007/978-3-030-47124-8.

E. W. Stacy. A Generalization of the Gamma Distribution. *The Annals of Mathematical Statistics*, 33(3):1187–1192, 1962. ISSN 0003-4851. doi: 10.2307/2237889.

William J. Stewart. *Probability, Markov Chains, Queues, and Simulation: The Mathematical Basis of Performance Modeling*. Princeton University Press, Princeton, Oxford, 2009. ISBN 978-0-691-14062-9. doi: 10.1515/9781400832811.

Petra Tomanová. Measuring Intensity of Order Arrivals and Process Quality Assessment of an Online Bookstore: A Case Study from the Czech Republic. In *Proceedings of the 7th International Conference on Management*, pages 768–773, Prešov, 2018. Bookman s.r.o. ISBN 978-80-8165-301-8.

Petra Tomanová. Clustering of Arrivals and Its Impact on Process Simulation. In *Proceedings of the 15th International Symposium on Operations Research in Slovenia*, pages 314–319, Bled, 2019a. Slovenian Society Informatika. ISBN 978-961-6165-55-6.

Petra Tomanová. Business Process Simulation and Process Quality Assessment of Czech Online Bookstore. In *Proceedings of the 3rd International Conference on Advances in Business and Law*, pages 1–4, Dubai, 2019b. Dubai Business School.

Petra Tomanová and Vladimír Holý. Clustering of Arrivals in Queueing Systems: Autoregressive Conditional Duration Approach. *Central European Journal of Operations Research*, 2021. ISSN 1613-9178. doi: 10.1007/s10100-021-00744-7.

Time dependent decision alterations due to the changing priority of criteria

Rijad Trumić[1]

Abstract. Decision making is a subject to a lot of people, and a lot of companies. A lot of methods deal with the subject of finding and making the best possible decision in a secure, as well as insecure environments, but in the real world a lot of decisions are time based and limited because the environment changes and evolves. Everyone knows the saying „If I knew what I know now, I would have chosen the other way!". The aim of this paper is to demonstrate the problem of the dynamic decision-making on a real-world example taken out of the car manufacturing industry.

The example will demonstrate where the problem lies and what it is when the base conditions are static and non-time adaptive. If we take „adaptive base conditions into consideration, the decision-making process and preferences change as well. In section 4.1 we use the AHP method to decide at a static, or rather, specific point in time. In section 4.2 we extend the AHP method with the dynamic decision-making process, which we will refer to as AHP-Dynamics. As another, further extension of this dynamic AHP point of view, we also talk about how the sensitivity of time efficiency can play a role in the decision efficiency. Taking decision volatility into account can serve as a motivation and benefit so save a lot of money in many industries.

Keywords: Analytical Hierarchy Process (AHP), AHP-Dynamics, change catalogue, overhead, technical requirements.

JEL Classification: C61, C62

1 Introduction

A vehicle development usually takes 5 years before it goes into serial production. It begins with a so-called "early phase" which lasts about 1 year. Then the "concept phase" begins, which lasts approx. 2 years and where attempts are made to define the conceptualize the entire vehicles. Specification sheets are written for all the vehicle components. These specification sheets are sent to the suppliers with a request to make the cost estimation and reply with an offer. In addition to the specification sheets, the requirements also contain further information such as an estimated volume, installation space for the respective components in the vehicle, as well as other quality and logistics requirements. The supplier nomination usually takes place after the concept work, 3 years before the start of production. Achieving the best costs and best prices for the nomination of a supplier through the entire production time and up to the aftersales is one of the most important goals. At the time of supplier nomination, the vehicle manufacturers try to have mature technical concepts, stable premises, requirements for the components and the entire vehicle, and an as informed estimate of the production volume as possible. After the supplier has been selected, in the remaining 3 years, the vehicles and also individual components are further improved and changed by the supplier, which is often caused by different base conditions, such as laws, buyer preferences of the vehicles or competition that repeatedly forces

[1] VSB-Technical university of Ostrava, Faculty of Economics, Department of Business Management, Sokolská 33, Ostrava, Czech Republic, rijad.trumic.st@vsb.cz

the vehicle manufacturer to react to external influences. The components often have to be redesigned because the supplier realizes in the production phase that he cannot meet the requirements after all. The cause of the change can come from the manufacturer, supplier or even legislature.

2 Problem description

As we can see in chapter 1, the car manufacturer only has a rough idea of the actual base conditions. It is possible that even at the start of the serial production, the car manufacturer only has a final technical description of the components available. The production volume as well as possible legislative changes (i.e., change in CO2 emission limits), are continuously changed. At the time of nomination of the supplier, predictions must be made, but in most cases, they do not materialize as described. With these very vague predictions, the manufacturer must sign a contract with the supplier which can have a duration of up to 25 years. Those 25 years include the 3 years of development, 7 years of production, and another 15 years of spare part production.

All car manufacturers nominate suppliers for vehicle components a few years before the SOP. This means that the technical procurement status of these components does not have the same technical status as for the SOP because the components face technical changes due to the development phase after a nomination. However, since the suppliers are already nominated and contractual obligations already exist, the changes are, in many cases, implemented at higher prices, dictated by the suppliers. Car manufacturers often have no option to negotiate the costs or to even withdraw from the contract, as the development has already been performed and the security of supply has the utmost priority. In the end, the high costs are mostly accepted because the car manufacturer does not have any negotiation leverage.

Nevertheless, changes are an integral part of the development process. Changes are required to continuously improve vehicles and develop them up to market maturity. They are also required to stay competitive by implementing necessary changes, but we also need to be competitive on the cost side of things, despite the changes. Figure 1 shows the general cost path and the problem during the whole life cycle of one component.

Unfortunately, good nomination results are often forfeit because of changes in the component development process. The nomination has the largest impact on costs during the whole process. The changes after the nomination are a significant cost driver for OEMs and they often have to be negotiated in a single-source environment. Change requests are never entirely avoidable in a vehicle development process, certainly the efforts in concept plausibility must be intensified and the quality specifications must be improved.

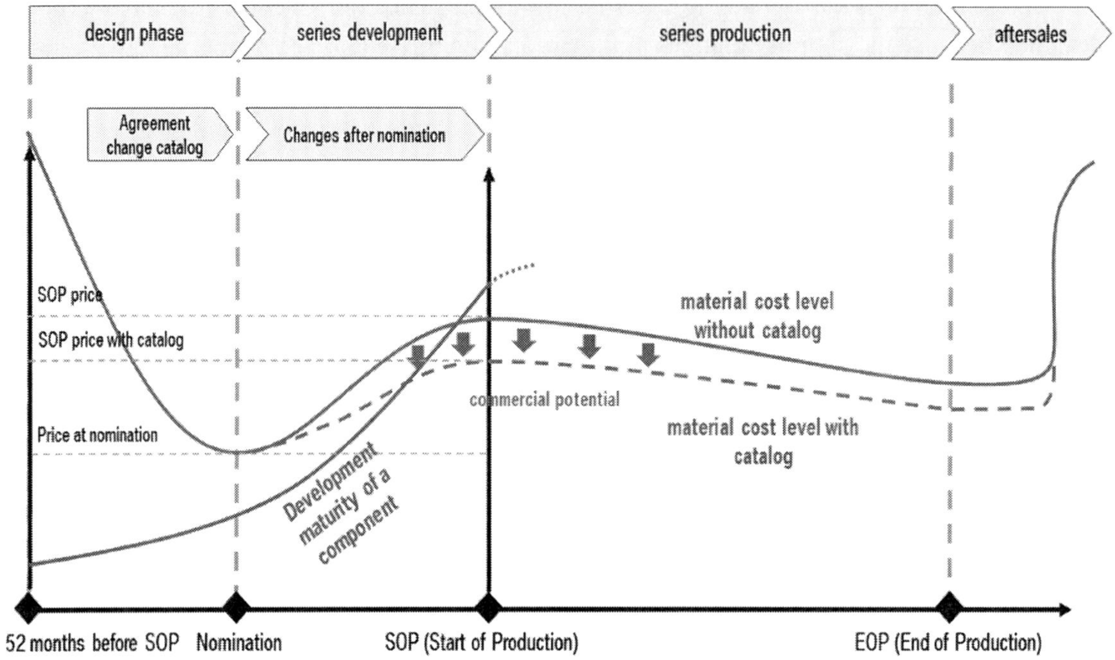

Figure 1 Cost diagram before and after supplier nomination

The main goal is to reduce the cost of changes. The focus of this paper is to observe the change in the decision-making process and the prioritization of the appropriate alternative options through the lifecycle of the project. Here the focus is on the change in the prioritization of the alternative options, before and after the nomination of a supplier.

3 Project work methodology

On the top level we have defined the reduction in the cost of change. On the second level we have described the decision-making criteria, which have a significant influence on the alternative options at the time of change. The decision-making criteria change over time or depending on the situation/phase the car manufacturer is in at the time. Through work experience as well as in coordination with a group of experts, the following decision-making criteria were defined:

- Speed of implementation,
- complexity,
- capacity effort,
- setting of premises,
- internal know-how,
- output.

The speed of implementation is an important factor in the selection of the tools. It is especially important how fast each topic can be implemented in practice; how complex the topics are in the preparation phase and how much manpower and time it would require.

Furthermore, it is also quite important whether specific requirements can be set for the respective topic. For example, if requirements are kept too rough and general in a change catalogue, the costs cannot be precisely defined. A precise and detailed definition of the requirements also enables a detailed statement of costs for a specific change action.

It is also important whether the know-how is available within the company itself because, the experience of the employees is also an essential aspect. Employees from the development and purchasing department can take all the topics from lessons learned bring them into the toolset and give them to the supplier for a cost evaluation.

Finally, output is the last, but not least important criteria. It may be that everything can be implemented extremely fast, with low-capacity requirements and high know-how, but if the output is small or it brings little savings, the focus is usually redirected to another topic.

As already mentioned, these decision criteria have a significant influence on the alternative options, that were defined by the expert group during the brainstorming process. These alternative options are:

- Change catalogue or pre-negotiation of possible changes in the future,
- Improvement of the technical requirements and specifications,
- A decrease of the overhead and profit surcharge or a question whether the used „Surcharge calculation" by many OEMs, is future-oriented.

The use of a cost catalogue after a nomination can be useful in many cases, amongst others to negotiate changes better and more effectively. Increasing product requirements are an important part of a nomination. A good change catalogue is developed in close coordination between the purchasing and development teams. In the second step, the contribution of a cost calculator is of course important in order to calculate the measures or changes requested in the change catalogue. This leads to better negotiation results.

By improving the detail and quality of the specifications, we can avoid many changes through the development of the series, so that the change catalogue can be made redundant or at least greatly reduced in complexity; however, this improvement is most often not possible in the early phase or at the time of nomination because the requirements for the component and the development goals are mostly still unknown, and because of that the requirements and conditions are often kept very general at the time of nomination.

The third main aspect in avoiding costs in series development, but even more importantly in series delivery, is a decrease of overhead and profit surcharges. Many OEMs use a surcharge calculation as a calculation base. The calculation uses the botton-up approach to calculate the cost components and then add the overhead and profit surcharges as a percentage of the material and production costs. This is primarily determined during the nomination and agreed with the supplier.

3.1 Application of the AHP method

The Analytical Hierarchy Process (AHP) presented by Saaty (1994) is a method for solving multi-criteria decision problems. In this method, a problem is broken down hierarchically into sub-problems, thus reducing complexity. The sub-problems are solved step by step. The evaluation of the alternatives in the AHP procedure takes place with regard to their importance to a superordinate element or criterion and is compared in pairs (see Saaty, 2000). The criteria are compared at one level in the hierarchy of the problem (see Saaty, 2001). If a problem is divided into several levels, the pair comparisons are continued first on the criteria level and then successively for the other criteria levels. The results of all comparisons are presented in an evaluation matrix. The priorities are calculated through an iterative process with the so-called eigen value method. There are three steps. In the first step, the evaluation matrix is squared (Dolan et al., 1989). In a second step, the matrix is normalized, and the local weights are determined. In the third step, this process of squaring and normalization is repeated in an iterative process until the calculated weights have an insignificant deviation compared to the values determined by the previously calculated matrix (Saaty, 1980).

$$A = \begin{pmatrix} a_{11} & \dots & a_{1j} & \dots & a_{1n} \\ \dots & \dots & \dots & \dots & \dots \\ a_{i1} & \dots & a_{ij} & \dots & a_{in} \\ \dots & \dots & \dots & \dots & \dots \\ a_{n1} & \dots & a_{nj} & \dots & a_{nn} \end{pmatrix} \quad \text{with}$$

$$\forall i = 1, \dots, n \quad \forall j = 1, \dots, n{:}\; a_{ij} > 0 \qquad \forall i = j{:}\; a_{ij} = 1 \qquad \forall i = 1, \dots, n$$

$$\forall j = 1, \dots, n{:}\; a_{ij} = {a_{ji}}^{-1}$$

Each element of the comparison shows how much an element is more significant with respect to the element of the overlying level (Saaty, 1994). The following scale is used for this.

AHP Scale of Importance for comparison pair (a_{ij})	**Numeric Rating**	**Reciprocal (decimal)**
Extreme Importance	9	1/9 (0.111)
Very strong to extremely	8	1/8 (0.125)
Very strong Importance	7	1/7 (0.143)
Strongly to very strong	6	1/6 (0.167)
Strong Importance	5	1/5 (0.2)
Moderately to Strong	4	1/4 (0.25)
Moderate Importance	3	1/3 (0.333)
Equally to Moderately	2	1/2 (0.5)
Equal Importance	1	1 (1.0)

Table 1 Relative meaning of the criteria for the superior element

In order to determine the inconsistency between the pairs, Saaty (2000) has developed a consistency index (*CI* = *Consistency Index*) and a consistency value (*CR* = *Consitency Ratio*). The largest eigenvalue λ_{max} of the evaluation matrix is equal to the dimension n of the matrix for the consistency of the pairs. The consistency of the matrix can be checked using the largest eigenvalue λ_{max}.

$$CI = \frac{\lambda_{max} - n}{n - 1}$$

The necessity of revising the evaluation matrix can be checked with the consistency value (*CR*). A *CR* value < 0.1 is permissible. SAATY indicates that for $CR \geq 0.1$ a revision of the pair comparisons in the evaluation matrix should be made (Saaty, 1994).

$$CR = \frac{CI}{RI}$$

The Random Index (*RI*) is an average consistency index that was randomly generated from reciprocal matrices. SAATY shows in table 2 the determined values.

n	2	3	4	5	6	7	8	9	10	11	12	13	14	15
RI	0.00	0.52	0.89	1.11	1.25	1.35	1.40	1.45	1.49	1.51	1.54	1.56	1.57	1.58

Table 2 Random Index (Saaty, 2000)

This method is worth doing because in the practical example, one can also use the sensitivity method to, in the end, determine how stable the decision was before and after an event.

The paper of Gonzales-Prida (2012) already shows that there can be differences in the decision making at different points in time, but Gonzales-Prida does not show a real-world example and it also does not go in depth into the efficiency of the decision. Chapter 4 is focusing on this extension to the method. The paper written by Nguyen Tho Thong (2019) also describes the problem with the dynamic decision making of the Topsis method in detail and with in-depth mathematical explanations, but it does not have and is not based on a practical example.

4 Application and results of the method

Figure 2 depicts a summary of the problems with the AHP decision tree. The second level lists the criteria that are most important for this problem. The third level shows the individual alternatives or tools that can be taken into consideration. The AHP method is also well suited to solve the problem because the assessment is quantitative in nature.

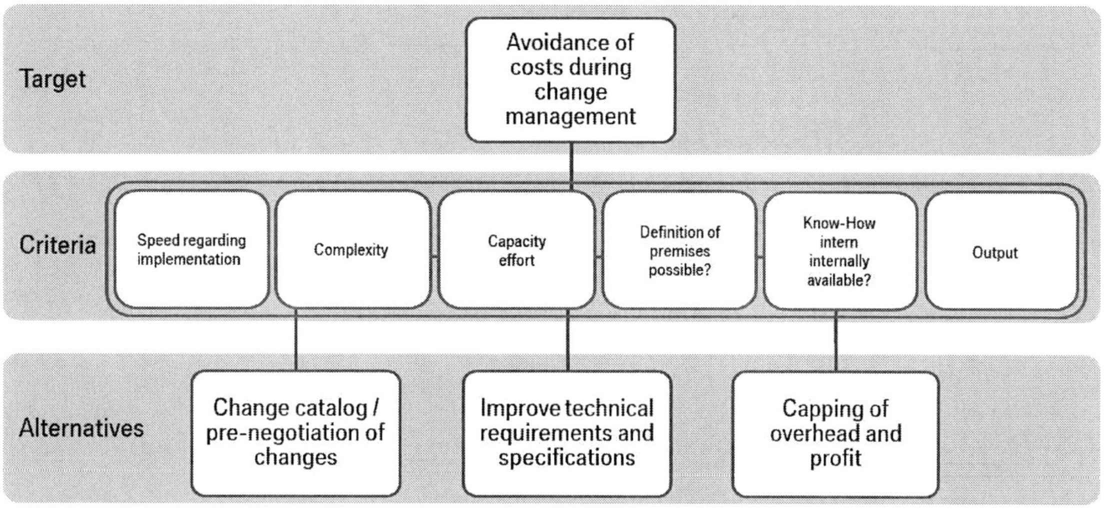

Figure 2 Presentation of the problem

4.1 Input data and model quantification of criteria before supplier nomination

To rate the content, a group of experts has been chosen. The group works for a big, German car manufacturer, and they already have real life experience with the topic at hand.

In phase one, we will base the rating on the assumption that our position of power is much higher before we initially chose a part supplier.

	Speed	Complexity	Capacity	Premises	Know How	Output
Speed	1	0.333	3	0.143	0.25	0.2
Complexity	3	1	3	0.25	0.2	0.111
Capacity	0.333	0.333	1	0.143	0.2	0.2
Premises	7	4	7	1	1	1
Know How	4	5	5	1	1	0.5
Output	5	9	5	1	0.2	1

Table 3 Evaluation matrix of all criteria in the second decision level

The result for the evaluation matrix in Table 1 is $\lambda_{max} = 6.35$.

Consistency-Index *CI* ($n = 6$)

$$CI = \frac{6.35 - 6}{6 - 1} = 0.07$$

Calculation of the consistency rate *CR* (*Random-Index RI= 1.25*)

$$CR = \frac{0.07}{1.25} = 0.056 < 0.1$$

Since the *CR* value is 0.056, it is not necessary to revise the evolution matrix.

After calculation of alternatives in terms of speed, complexity, capacity, premises, know-how and output we have the following results.

	Weights	Ranking
Change cataloge	0.283	2
Technical Requirements	0.111	3
Overhead	0.606	1

Table 4 Ranking of final results

In this summary, the importance or priorities are clearly visible. The top priority is overhead, followed by the change catalogue. In contrast, the subject of specifications is at the last place, which is also reflected in reality.

4.2 Input data and model quantification of criteria after supplier nomination

Now in phase two, we will base the rating on the assumption that the supplier has already been chosen, and that our position of power is much lower. We have used the same rating criteria for all alternative methods, the only differences are the changed "points of interest" within the base conditions.

	Speed	Complexity	Capacity	Premises	Know How	Output
Speed	1	3	2	7	2	2
Complexity	0.333	1	0.5	7	1	2
Capacity	0.5	2	1	7	2	2
Premises	0.143	0.143	0.143	1	0.5	0.333
Know How	0.5	1	0.5	2	1	3
Output	0.5	0.5	0.5	3	0.333	1

Table 5 Evaluation matrix of all criteria in the second decision level

The result for the evaluation matrix and calculation of the consistency rate CR is acceptable and calculated as shown in chapter 4.1. After calculation of alternatives in terms of speed, complexity, capacity, premises, know-how and output we have the following results.

	Weights	Ranking
Change cataloge	0.205	2
Technical Requirements	0.627	1
Overhead	0.166	3

Table 6 Ranking of final results

Table 4 shows the difference in decision making over a time period. The topics change their priority, which proves that a decision is not a constant, but rather that it is based on time. In this example it is "logical" that, after selecting the part supplier, the technical requirements are not changed, to avoid "cost of change", independent of the fact if a Change catalogue exists or not. The fact that the overhead cost is the least important part is comprehensible, because a part supplier, after the selection process, would never agree to a limit of overhead cost, because it is one of their biggest sources of profit. The creation of a change catalogue is possible after the appointment, but the conditions are significantly worse compared to the conditions before the appointment of the supplier.

As you can see, the results as well as the decision-making process has clearly changed and created different base conditions. Base conditions change over time, so we can say, that decision making is also based on time, except the base condition does not change at all, which in real life is rarely the case.

A sensitivity analysis is used to check to what extent changes in the weighting of the criteria have an impact on the final result of the alternatives. Through these changes, limits can be defined at which the ranking of the alternatives suddenly changes. If the final result does not change during the small changes on the criteria, the final result is stable. In return, there is an unstable result if the ranking of the alternatives is given even with small changes. This means that the first AHP evaluation has to be checked in detail and the result can be scrutinized (Saaty and Vargas, 2000).

5 Conclusion

One of the biggest issues with the application of methods like the AHP method, based on subjective input, is the relevance of time. It is also quite interesting to examine the change of behavior, and priorities, and discover why they changed, and which factors played a role in the process. In this context we can also for example perform the Topsis method or the Fuzzy analysis, which would be possible extensions to this paper. Currently we are using the sensitivity analysis. In this practical example we can observe that, even the time, when the contract is signed with the supplier, plays a role in the behavior of both parties. This fact changes the position of power in an instant after which they result in different interests and goals.

It is possible to go a step further and show the comparison of the efficiency between the used method (new base conditions) and the original method (old base conditions) in form of a ratio or deviation chart. With this, it is also possible to create an entry for "change of base conditions" and consider it as an insecurity for the calculation of future projects, as well as a point for lessons learned for all projects of a similar nature. In this regard we can conclude that the time factor is changing the decisions made, depending on the time when they are made, and they vary. This sensitivity factor should be implemented into the actual AHP method, which can also serve as a topic for the next case study.

Acknowledgement

This work was supported by the SGS project No. SP2021/86. This support is gratefully acknowledged.

References

Brunelli, M. (2015). *Introduction to the Analytic Hierarchy Process.* Heidelberg: Springer Briefs in Operations Research.

Dolan, J., Isselhardt, B. and Cappuccio, J. (1989). *The analytic hierarchy process in medical decision making* – a tutorial. Med Decis Mak., 9 (1), pp. 40–50.

Gonzales-Prida, V. (2012). *Dynamic Analytic Hierarchy Process: AHP method adapted to a changing environment.* 2nd IFAC Workshop on Advanced Maintenance Engineering, Services and Technology. Universidad de Sevilla, Spain. November 22-23.

Nguyen Tho, T., Luu Quoc, D., Le Hoang, S. (2019). *Dynamic interval valued neutrosophic set: Modeling decision making in dynamic enviroments.* Elsevier.

Saaty, T. (1980). *The analytic hierarchy process: planning, priority setting, resource allocation.* 2. Aufl. New York: McGraw-Hill; S. XIII, 287.

Saaty, T. (1994). *How to Make a Decision: The Analytic Hierarchy Process.* In: Interfaces, Vol. 24, No. 6, pp. 19-43.

Saaty, T., and Vargas, L. (2000). *Models, Methods, Concepts and Applications of the Analytic Hierarchy Process,* 2nd ed. International Series in Operations Research and Management Science.

Saaty, T. (2000). *Fundamentals of Decision Making and Priority Theory with the Analytic Hierarchy Process.* 2. Aufl., Pittsburgh.

Corporate Social Responsibility and Financial Performance: The Moderating Role of Internal Control in Chinese Appliance Listed Companies

Xiaojuan Wu[1 2]

Abstract. Corporate social responsibility (CSR) is one of the tools comprehensively representing the competitiveness of a company. A large number of studies have commonly found that CSR can positively affect corporate financial performance (CFP). However, there are also negative or neutral relationships, so some literature reviews suggest studying this relationship in different contexts. The objective of this paper is to study and verify whether the CSR level of companies with different internal controls (IC) has a comparable impact on CFP in Chinese appliance listed companies. The regression results show for the firm with low IC, the relationship between CSR and CFP is positive, while for the firm with high IC, this relationship is negative. This findings enable management to have a clearer understanding of the relationship between CSR and CFP, thereby helping them to make strategic decisions related to CSR.

Keywords: CSR, CFP, IC, moderating effect.

JEL Classification: M14, C31, M19

1 Introduction

With the increasingly fierce competition between companies, what factors would affect the corporate financial performance (CFP) has attracted the attention of many scholars and the public. The impact of corporate social responsibility (CSR) as one of the company's main competitive methods on CFP has naturally become one of the hot topics of researchers. Although a lot of literature review (Endrikat, Guenther and Hoppe, 2014; Van Beurden and Gössling, 2008) found that most existing research supports the positive relationship between CSR and CFP, there are still some studies that proving the negative, mixed or non-influencing relationship (Alshehhi, Nobanee and Khare, 2018). Therefore, Alshehhi, Nobanee and Khare (2018) suggest that further research should focus on the effect of moderating variables on the relationship between CSR and CFP. As the company's risk management system, internal control (IC) is a powerful guarantee for the successful implementation of CSR-related strategic actions. Therefore, as a follow-up study, this research takes the Chinese appliance listed companies in 2018 as a sample to investigate the impact of CSR on CFP under different IC context.

The objective of this paper is to study and verify whether the CSR of companies with different IC level will have different impacts on the CFP of Chinese appliance listed companies. The results of regression model indicate that for the firm with low IC, the relationship between CSR and CFP is positive, while for the firm with high IC, this relationship is negative. Although these results are out of our expectation, after careful consideration, they are more in line with reality. For companies with low IC, they are usually in the early stages. Their relatively small

[1] Technical University of Ostrava, Department of business administration, Sokolská 33 Ostrava, xiaojuan.wu@vsb.cz.
[2] Hebei GEO University, faculty of management, Huai'an Road 136 Shijiazhuang, China.

scale leads to relatively low CSR costs, but this helps the company win a good reputation, which is beneficial to the company. As the company grows, it invests more and more in CSR, which has a negative impact on CFP. This research not only enriches the existing literature but also contributes to practice, which enables company management to have a clearer understanding of the impact of CSR on CFP at different stages of the company's development, thereby helping them to make CSR-related strategic decisions.

The study is structured as follows. Section 2 reviews the existing literature on the relationship between CSR and CFP as well as the moderating effect of IC on this relationship, and hypotheses are proposed. In Section 3, input data are introduced, and the regression models with and without interactive variables are formulated. Section 4 describes the empirical results of the models, which are interpreted and discussed. In the last section, Section 5, we provide conclusions and a summary of our findings.

2 Literature review

Firstly, the concept of IC and CSR adopted in this study are introduced. Secondly, the existing literature on the relationship between CSR and CFP as well as the moderating effect of IC on this relationship, and hypotheses are proposed.

2.1 Internal control

From 2008 to 2010, Chinese five ministries and commissions, including the Ministry of Finance, successively issued the "Basic Norms for Enterprise internal control" and the "Supporting Guidelines for Enterprise internal control", which promoted the development of IC construction. The five components of IC stipulated in Basic Norms are the same as the concept defined by COSO, including the internal environment, risk assessment, control activities, information and communication, and internal supervision. As an institutional arrangement, the purpose of IC is to reasonably ensure legal operation and compliance, asset security and reliability of financial information, improve operating efficiency and effectiveness, and thereby promote the realization of corporate development strategies.

In recent years, as people have gradually realized the important role of IC in company activities related to CSR, more and more empirical studies use IC as a moderating variable to explore its impact on company development. Hao, Qi and Wang (2018) found IC had a significant and partial moderating effect on the relationship between CSR and stock price crash risk. Guo and Shen (2019) study the role of IC quality in the impacts of managerial shareholding on CSR performance.

2.2 CSR

Academic research on CSR began to take form in the 1950s. A lot of scholars and organizations strive to define the concept of CSR. So far, there is still no commonly accepted definition of CSR. This paper adopts the concept of CSR advocated by Elkington in 1997 based on the triple bottom line principle. He assumes that if an enterprise forms an economic and social system, then its development objectives should constitute a triple beam, which relates to the profit, the people associated with the company, and cares for the planet.

Existing CSR literature indicates CSR disclosure significantly reduces the firm-level cost of capital (Michaels and Grüning, 2017), and CSR has a positive effect on competitive advantage, reputation and customer satisfaction, further influence on firm performance positively (Saeidi et al.,2015).

2.3 Association between CSR and CFP

Regarding the impact of CSR on CFP, there are two completely opposite theories: value creating and value destroying (Yu and Zhao, 2015). Value creation theory argues that incorporating environmental and social responsibility into company strategies and practices is conducive to reduce company risks and promote long-term value creation. On the contrary, the value destruction theory predicts that companies engaged in environmental and social responsibility may not attach great importance to profitability and therefore benefit stakeholders at the expense of shareholders.

A large number of empirical research results support the positive correlation between CSR and CFP. Endrikat, Guenther and Hoppe (2014) find that there is a positive and partially bidirectional relationship between corporate environmental performance (CEP) and CFP by meta-analytically integrating the findings of 149 studies. Alshehhi, Nobanee and Khare (2018) studied 132 papers from top journals and found that 78% of publications report a positive relationship between corporate sustainability and CFP. Similarly, Peloza (2009) reported that of the 159 studies reviewed, 63% of the relationships were positive, 22% were mixed or neutral, and 15% were negative.

Based on the above analysis, the following research hypothesis is proposed.

Hypothesis 1. The impact of CSR on CFP is positive.

2.4 CFP and CSR: the moderating role of IC

IC facilitates the optimization of capital allocation efficiency, thereby promoting the realization of sustainable growth of enterprises (Li, 2020). The "Application Guidelines for IC No. 4—Social Responsibility" clearly states that enterprises should fulfill their social obligations and responsibilities in the process of operation and development, including production safety, product quality, environmental protection, resource conservation, promotion of employment, and protection of employees' rights and interests. From this directive, it is clear that IC is an important guarantee for the implementation of CSR. The risk derived from CSR aggravate the company's risk level and broaden the company's risk boundaries (Li, 2020). Generally, IC can be regarded as an institutional system of risk management. When the company's IC level is at a low level, it is difficult to prevent improper behavior from damaging the company's reputation and image, and avoid adverse events that damage CSR practices. This low-level risk control makes it tough for CSR activities to proceed smoothly, thus posing a potential threat to the achievement of CFP. In contrast, if the company's operations are under effective IC, the risks associated with CSR can be identified and reduced as much as possible, so as to protect the legitimate rights and interests of stakeholders to the greatest extent. This high-level risk control promotes the successful realization of CSR strategic goals, which is further conducive to the improvement of CFP. Therefore, we believe that high-level IC can enhance the positive impact of CSR on CFP, while low-level IC will weaken the positive impact of CSR on CFP.

Based on the above analysis, the following research hypothesis is proposed.

Hypothesis 2. The positive impact of CSR on CFP is stronger for companies with higher levels of IC than for companies with lower levels of IC.

3 Data and methodology

First, the sample employed is described; second, how to measure the critical independent variable (CSR) is illustrated; then, the data source of the moderator of IC is interpreted; finally, the specific regression model to test our hypotheses are developed.

3.1 Sample selection

This study aims to explore the moderating effect of IC on the relationship between CSR and CFP in the Chinese appliance industry. Thus, the study selects the Chinese home appliance listed companies for the year 2018 as the research object. The companies list is taking over from the Iwencai database. After excluding the companies listed in 2018 and 2019, ST companies and companies with missing data, a sample of 53 listed companies is left. Precisely, it consists of 25 companies listed on the Main Board, 21 companies listed on the Small and Medium Enterprise Board, and 7 companies listed on the Growth Enterprise Market. All data are collected from Iwencai database, DIB database (dedicated to IC research of Chinese enterprises), annual financial statements and CSR reports (if any).

3.2 Independent variable

Vast previous literature on China's CSR research has selected the overall evaluation score published by Rankins CSR Ratings (RKS). It is a reliable CSR rating agency that measures the performance and disclosure of CSR in China. However, there is a flaw in its rating results that it cannot cover all listed companies. It is because RKS evaluates the CSR of listed companies based on the CSR reports issued by the companies, but not every listed company is able or willing to disclose its CSR report. Given the fact that the necessary sample data in this study cannot be obtained from this reliable rating report, this study constructs an evaluation criteria system based on the characteristics of China's appliance industry to assess the CSR implementation status of the appliance companies. With the aid of the analytic hierarchy process, the evaluation criteria system is established from the three aspects of economics, environment and society according to the aforementioned triple bottom line principle. All the criteria selected, the assignment of the specific weights for each criterion and the original data for each sample company can be found in the author's another paper (Wu, Dluhošová and Zmeškal, 2021). The majority of the original data is manually collected by the author from the annual report and CSR report; the rest of the data used is from Iwencai database.

3.3 Moderating variable

This study takes IC as the moderator. The IC index comes from the DIB database which is a professional agency dedicated to the research on IC and risk management of Chinese listed companies. This IC index is obtained from the basic IC index corrected by IC defects. The basic IC index is designed by this agency according to the degree of realization of the above IC objectives. The range of this IC index is 0 to 1000. The larger the index, the higher the IC level.

3.4 The research model of the study

Since the data in this study only involve a cross-sectional dimension, a multiple linear regression model is proposed to test the hypotheses formulated in the previous section. Hence, this study develops the following regression specifications to test the association between CSR and CFP (test of H1).

$$ROE = \beta_0 + \beta_1 CSR_C + \beta_2 FS + \beta_3 LEV + \beta_4 FT + \varepsilon, \quad (1)$$

where β_0 is the intercept, $\beta_{1,...,}\beta_n$ represent the regression coefficient, ε is the error term.

In the above equation, ROE denotes CFP—measured as the ratio of net profit to equity. In order to unify the expression with Equation (2), we also use CSR_C, which is the centred CSR, in Equation (1). Following the prior literature (Hao, Qi and Wang, 2018), we controll for several firm-level factors that may affect CFP. Firm size (FS) is the natural logarithm of total assets. The ratio of total debt to total assets (LEV) is used as a proxy for financial leverage. Firm type (FT) is a dummy variable, which is 1 for family business and 0 otherwise.

To test H2, we regress ROE on CSR, IC, their interactive terms and control variables in Eq. (2). This allows us to examine the moderating effect of IC on the link between CFP and CSR.

$$ROE = \beta_0 + \beta_1 CSR_C + \beta_2 IC_C + \beta_3 CSR_C \times IC_C + \beta_4 FS + \beta_5 LEV + \beta_6 FT + \varepsilon, \quad (2)$$

where IC_C is the centred moderating variable of IC, and $CSR_C \cdot IC_C$ is the interaction variable. The introduced centring procedure does not affect the regression results of the model; however, it eliminates the multicollinearity between independent variables (Hasan and Habib, 2017).

4 Results and discussion

First of all, we present the descriptive statistics of all variable involved in the model and model verification result; then, regression of model are shown; finally, we discuss the results.

4.1 Descriptive statistics and model verification

Table 1 provides the descriptive statistics for the variables used in the regression models. ROE ranges between −70.41% and 34.79%, with a mean of 4.454% and a standard deviation of 22.8636%. The CSR level varies from 0.1832 to 0.7163, with a mean of 0.4848 and a standard deviation of 0.1149. CSR_C fluctuates from -0.3016 to 0.2315, with a mean of 0 and a standard deviation of 11.49. The variation range of IC is 339.8175 to 783.83, with a mean of 652.1419 and a standard deviation of 78.8256. IC_C shifts from -312.3244 to 131.6881, with an average of 0 and the same standard deviation as IC.

Variables	Minimum	Maximum	Mean	Std. Deviation
ROE	-70.41%	34.79%	4.454%	22.8636%
CSR	0.1832	0.7163	0.4848	0.1149
CSRc	-0.3016	0.2315	0.0000	0.1149
IC	339.8175	783.8300	652.1419	78.8256
ICc	-312.3244	131.6881	0.0000	78.8256
Firm size	20.2696	26.2981	22.5002	1.4592
Financial leverage	0.1473	0.7935	0.4655	0.1771
Firm type	0.0000	1.0000	0.6226	0.4894

Table 1 Descriptive statistics

Table 2 presents Pearson's correlation analysis results among all variables with their significance level. The maximum coefficient of the Pearson correlations is 0.645. Therefore, it is apparent that there is no multicollinearity among independent variables from the correlation coefficient values.

	ROE	CSR	IC	CSRc·ICc	FS	LEV	FT
ROE	1						
CSR	0.202	1					
IC	0.613**	0.209	1				
CSRc·ICc	-0.239	0.117	0.308*	1			
FS	0.1549	0.499**	0.315*	0.434**	1		
LEV	-0.377**	0.357**	-0.122	0.357**	0.645**	1	
FT	-0.024	-0.315*	-0.094	-0.089	-0.441**	-0.364**	1

Note: ** and * indicate statistical significance at the levels of 0.01 and 0.05, respectively.

Table 2 Correlation matrix

4.2 Regression results

The regression results for the two analysed equations are shown in Table 3. The estimated coefficients should be compared. R-squared of Equation (1) is 0.443, which means that all the independent variables in Equation (1) together explain about 44.3% of the variance in the CFP of the Chinese appliance listed companies. For Equation (2), the p-value of change in R-squared is less than the 1% significant level, which means that the moderating variable of IC plays an essential role in explaining the association between CFP and CSR.

Variable	Equation (1)					Equation (2)				
	Coef.	**S.E.**	**t**	**Sig.**	**Sig.b**[1]	**Coef.**	**S.E.**	**t**	**Sig.**	**Sig.b**[1]
Constant	-151.818	52.191	-2.909	0.005	0.008	-123.779	44.835	-2.761	0.008	0.061
CSR_C	40.798	24.919	1.637	0.108	0.184	19.507	19.197	1.016	0.315	0.414
IC_C						0.156	0.029	5.308	0.000	0.002
$CSR_C \cdot IC_C$						-1.055	0.232	-4.539	0.000	0.002
FS	9.158	2.448	3.740	0.000	0.002	6.943	2.123	3.270	0.002	0.026
LEV	-106.809	18.324	-5.829	0.000	0.005	-58.905	16.094	-3.660	0.001	0.028
FT	-0.104	5.685	-0.018	0.986	0.993	2.242	4.342	0.516	0.608	0.705
R^2				0.443				0.694		
F-statistic				9.553 **				17.390**		
Change in R^2 (ΔR^2)								0.251		
F-statistic (ΔR^2)								18.852**		

Note: 1 Sig.b represents the bootstrap results which are based on 1000 bootstrap samples;
2 ** indicates statistical significance at the level of 0.01

Table 3 Regression results

The results reported in Table 3 show that in Equations (1) and (2), both coefficients of CSR_C are not significant ($p > 0.05$), which indicates CSR is not related to the variation in ROE in general. Hypothesis 1 was not proven in this study. However, the more useful information can be found when we look at the coefficient of interaction $CSR_C \cdot IC_C$, which is negative and significant ($p < 0.01$). It means the IC plays a significant but weakening role in the relationship between CFP and CSR, rather than an enhancing role as we expected in Hypothesis 2. This moderating effect of IC is visibly depicted in Figure 1. Combined with Table 4, we can see that the conditional effect is positive and statistically significant when the level of IC is lower, as shown by the blue line in Figure 1. And when the level of IC is higher, the conditional effect is negative and statistically significant, as shown by the red line in Figure 1. It is the combination of the positive and negative conditional effect that results in the insignificant relationship between CFP and CSR on the whole.

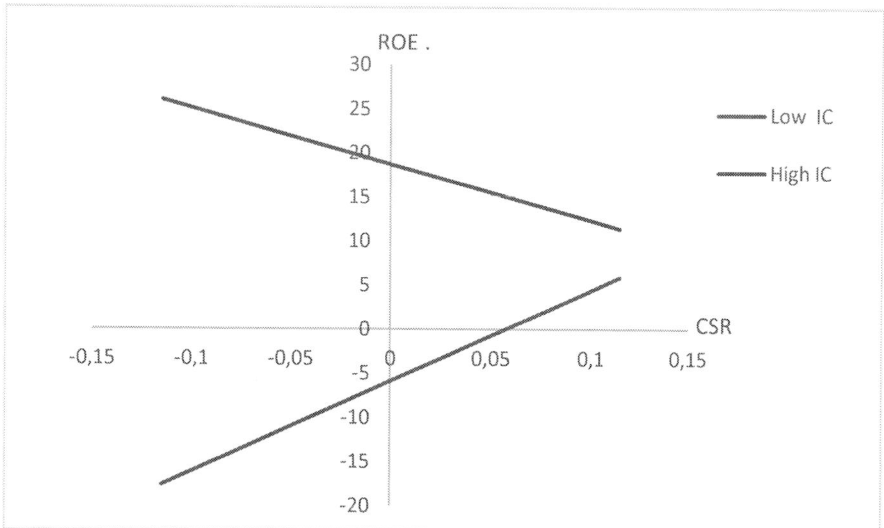

Figure 1 Graph of moderating effect of IC on the relationship between CSR and CFP

IC	Effect	S.E.	t	p	LLCI	ULCI
-78.8256	102.683	24.3868	4.2106	0.0001	53.5945	151.7715
0	19.5069	19.1971	1.0161	0.3149	-19.1352	58.149
78.8256	-63.6693	28.5307	-2.2316	0.0306	-121.099	-6.2395

Table 4 Conditional effects of the focal predictor at values of the moderator

In addition, we notice that the coefficient of IC in Equations (2) is significant ($p < 0.01$) and positive, which means IC is one of the positive factors affecting the CFP. We can get the same answer from the position of two lines in Figure 1, where the red line representing the companies with high IC is always above the blue line representing the companies with low IC.

4.3 Discussion

This positive correlation between CFP and CSR in companies with low levels of IC proves Hypothesis 1 to some extent. It indicates that for the companies with limited IC, CSR is a vital factor which can influence the CFP positively. Generally, companies with low IC levels are associated with early-stage companies. Therefore, this result is consistent with the reputational and strategic values associated with CSR involvement, that is, "although CSR is costly, the marginal benefit of CSR investments may be greater for younger companies than their mature counterparts"(Hasan and Habib, 2017).

This negative correlation between CFP and CSR in companies with high levels of IC can be explained by the empirical results of Barnett and Salomon (2012). They studied samples from KLD (which comprises largely S&P 500 companies and the Russell 3000 index companies) and found that the relationship between CFP and CSR is negative during the range of low to moderate CSR. "Because it is costly to be socially responsible, those companies with higher corporate social performance (CSP) have higher costs than do those firms with lower CSP" (Barnett and Salomon, 2012) . Due to the relatively short development time of CSR in China, the overall status of CSR implementation in China is still in its infancy according to the "CSR Blue Book (2018)" published by the Chinese Academy of Social Sciences. Therefore, the sample company, even with high IC which can ensure the effective completion of activities related to CSR in accordance with the strategic plan, still lacks sufficient stakeholder influence capacity (SIC) to create gains that will offset the costs, so the CSP-CFP relationship is negative over this range (Barnett and Salomon, 2012).

5 Conclusion

The study surveyed whether IC moderates the association between CSR and CFP in the specific and unique conditions of Chinese appliance listed companies. When we test the relationship between CSR and CFP of all sample companies as a whole, this relationship was insignificant. However, when considering the impact of the moderator of IC on the relationship between CSR and CFP, we unexpectedly found that for the firm with low IC, the relationship between CSR and CFP is positive, while for the firm with high IC, this relationship is negative. Therefore, these findings indicate that the early-stage firms (usually with low IC) obtain higher profits from the investment in CSR due to the greater marginal benefit; as the company matures, various systems (including IC) are becoming sound, but the profit will decrease as the increase in CSR since the investment in CSR is costly and the SIC is not sufficient to offset the costs.

This conclusion can help management of Chinese companies at different stages to clearly understand the relationship between CSR and CFP. Especially for early-stage companies, it will encourage them to engage in more CSR to acquire more profits. At the same time, it also told the management that as the company grows, profits will decrease with the increase in CSR, but this is only temporary. When the company obtains sufficient SIC, profits will increase as CSR increases again (Barnett and Salomon, 2012).

Future studies can extend the research in a number of ways. First, after obtaining the data, more periods can be investigated with the aim of discovering dynamics. Second, analysis of other sectors in China with specificities can also provide broader evidence.

Acknowledgements

The research was supported by SGS project SP2020/124, Financial Modelling and Decision-making of Companies and Financial Institutions under Risk, Flexibility and Interaction.

References

Alshehhi, A., Nobanee, H. and Khare, N. (2018). 'The impact of sustainability practices on corporate financial performance: Literature trends and future research potential', *Sustainability (Switzerland)*, 10(2).

Barnett, M. L. and Salomon, R. M. (2012). 'Does it pay to be really good? Addressing the shape of the relationship between social and financial performance', *Strategic Management Journal*, 33(11), pp. 1304–1320.

Endrikat, J., Guenther, E. and Hoppe, H. (2014). 'Making sense of conflicting empirical findings: A meta-analytic review of the relationship between corporate environmental and financial performance', *European Management Journal. Elsevier Ltd*, 32(5), pp. 735–751.

Guo, M. and Shen, S. (2019). 'Managerial shareholding and CSR: Does internal control quality matter?-Evidence from China', *Sustainability (Switzerland)*, 11(15).

Hao, D. Y., Qi, G. Y. and Wang, J. (2018). 'Corporate social responsibility, internal controls, and stock price crash risk: The Chinese stock market', *Sustainability (Switzerland)*, 10(5).

Hasan, M. M. and Habib, A. (2017). 'Corporate life cycle, organizational financial resources and corporate social responsibility', *Journal of Contemporary Accounting and Economics. Elsevier Ltd*, 13(1), pp. 20–36.

Li, X. (2020). 'The effectiveness of internal control and innovation performance: An intermediary effect based on corporate social responsibility', *PLoS ONE*, 15(6).

Michaels, A. and Grüning, M. (2017). 'Relationship of corporate social responsibility disclosure on information asymmetry and the cost of capital', *Journal of Management Control. Springer Berlin Heidelberg*, 28(3), pp. 251–274.

Peloza, J. (2009). 'The challenge of measuring financial impacts from investments in corporate social performance', *Journal of Management*, 35(6), pp. 1518–1541.

Saeidi, Sayedeh Parastoo et al. (2015). 'How does corporate social responsibility contribute to firm financial performance? The mediating role of competitive advantage, reputation, and customer satisfaction', *Journal of Business Research*, 68(2), pp. 341–350.

Van Beurden, P. and Gössling, T. (2008). 'The worth of values - A literature review on the relation between corporate social and financial performance', *Journal of Business Ethics*, 82(2), pp. 407–424.

Wu, X., Dluhošová, D. and Zmeškal, Z. (2021). 'Corporate Social Responsibility and Profitability: The Moderating Role of Firm Type in Chinese Appliance Listed Companies', *Energies*, 14(1).

Yu, M. and Zhao, R. (2015), 'Sustainability and firm valuation: an international investigation', *International Journal of Accounting & Information Management*, 23(3), pp. 289-307.

On Impact of Economic Development on Attitude to Sustainable Development Goals in Automotive Industry

František Zapletal [1] , Radim Lenort [2] , Pavel Wicher [3]

Abstract. Sustainable development goals (SDGs) adopted by all United Nations Member States in 2015 provide an opportunity for the automotive industry to create value for both shareholders and all other stakeholders. The aim of the paper is to research the SDGs preferences in the worldwide automotive industry from the point of view of the economic country conditions in which the individual automotive companies operate. The comparison of preferences was carried out for three broad economic condition categories - G7, developed economies, and developing economies. The PROMETHEE ranking method and its GAIA tool were used as the main research methodology. The obtained results show that the SDGs preferences of automotive companies significantly depend on the country economic conditions in which they operate.

Keywords: Automotive, sustainability, PROMETHEE, GAIA, multi-criteria decision making.

JEL classification: C44, Q56, M14

1 Introduction

Sustainability is a fundamental business strategy in the automotive industry today. Corporate sustainability is a wise balance among economic development, environmental stewardship, and social equity (Sikdar, 2003) and represents an opportunity for automotive companies to bring value for both their shareholders and all other stakeholders. One of the key approaches to increasing corporate sustainability is to follow the Sustainable Development Goals (SDGs) announced by the United Nations in 2015. An ever-growing number of companies declare these efforts in their sustainability reports. The aim of the paper is to research the SDGs preferences in the worldwide automotive industry from the point of view of the economic country conditions in which the individual automotive companies operate. The research seeks to confirm the hypothesis that the SDG preferences will be different in companies operating in countries with different levels of economic strength.

Problems where similarities in behaviour are explored are often solved by clustering methods (Aggarwa et al., 2015; Lu and Weng, 2007). However, the authors of this paper chose a different approach based on ranking multi-criteria decision-making methods, namely, the PROMETHEE method and its graphical tool GAIA. The main reason is that only a very small number of alternatives (clusters) is considered here (this number is given by the levels of economic development), which would cause troubles when clustering. Moreover, the PROMETHEE method as well as the graphical tool GAIA are more user-friendly, computationally easy, and well trace-

[1]VŠB-Technical unversity of Ostrava, Faculty of Economics, Department of Systems Engineering, Sokolská 33, Ostrava, Czech Republic, frantisek.zapletal@vsb.cz

[2]ŠKODA AUTO University, Department of Production, Logistics and Quality Management, Mladá Boleslav, Na Karmeli 1457, Czech Republic, radim.lenort@savs.cz

[3]VŠB-Technical unversity of Ostrava, Faculty of Materials Science and Technology, Department of Ecomomics and Management in Industry, 17. listopadu 15, Ostrava, Czech Republic, pavel.wichert@vsb.cz

able (Behzadian et al., 2010; Hayez et al., 2009).

2 Sustainable development goals

In 2015, member States of the United Nations adopted the 2030 Agenda for Sustainable Development. This Agenda is a plan of action for people, Planet, and prosperity, and it also seeks to strengthen universal peace in larger freedom (United Nations General Assembly, 2016). Organizations worldwide can play a significant role in the advancement of the Sustainable Development Agenda (Rosati and Faria, 2019). As part of the the Agenda, the United Nations announced 17 Sustainable Development Goals – SDGs (United Nations, 2021):

1) No poverty: End poverty in all its forms everywhere.
2) Zero hunger: End hunger, achieve food security and improved nutrition and promote sustainable agriculture.
3) Good health and well-being: Ensure healthy lives and promote well-being for all at all ages.
4) Quality education: Ensure inclusive and equitable quality education and promote lifelong learning opportunities for all.
5) Gender equality: Achieve gender equality and empower all women and girls.
6) Clean water and sanitation: Ensure availability and sustainable management of water and sanitation for all.
7) Affordable and clean energy: Ensure access to affordable, reliable, sustainable and modern energy for all.
8) Decent work and economic growth: Promote sustained, inclusive and sustainable economic growth, full and productive employment and decent work for all.
9) Industry, innovation and infrastructure: Build resilient infrastructure, promote inclusive and sustainable industrialization and foster innovation.
10) Reduced inequalities: Reduce inequality within and among countries.
11) Sustainable cities and communities: Make cities and human settlements inclusive, safe, resilient and sustainable.
12) Responsible consumption and production: Ensure sustainable consumption and production patterns.
13) Climate action: Take urgent action to combat climate change and its impacts.
14) Life below water: Conserve and sustainably use the oceans, seas and marine resources for sustainable development.
15) Life on land: Protect, restore and promote sustainable use of terrestrial ecosystems, sustainably manage forests, combat desertification, and halt and reverse land degradation and halt biodiversity loss.
16) Peace, justice and strong institutions: Promote peaceful and inclusive societies for sustainable development, provide access to justice for all and build effective, accountable and inclusive institutions at all levels.
17) Partnerships for the goals: Strengthen the means of implementation and revitalize the global partnership for sustainable development.

Awareness of sustainable development goals is constantly increasing among stakeholders and companies (Yamane and Kaneko, 2021). The SDGs stress the necessity of private businesses' active participation, appealing for their creativity and innovation to create value for the common good, such as reducing poverty, eradicating hunger, and protecting biodiversity (van der Waal and Thijssens, 2020).

3 Methodological background of PROMETHEE method

The PROMETHEE method has been introduced by Mareschal et al. (1984) and it is widely used to solve various decision-making problems from different fields (Behzadian et al., 2010). The main reason why this method is applied in this paper is that it provides, besides the ranking of alternatives, the graphical tool called GAIA plane (Geometrical Analysis for Interactive Assistance), see Hayez et al. (2009). This tool enables to explore the relationships among criteria and alternatives' performance profiles without considering the weights of criteria (i.e., objectively). This section provides a brief mathematical description of the main ranking PROMETHEE algorithm (PROMETHEE II), and thc GAIA planc.

All PROMETHEE algorithms are based on the same idea. Alternatives are pair-wisely compared in terms of each considered criterion. This comparison is done using the preference function P_i chosen for each criterion i. The preference function assigns the preference degree (in $[0, 1]$) according to the difference in performance between two options and expresses to what extent we prefer one alternative to another with respect to the given criterion. The choice of the preference function shape is usually essential for further results. For the sake of simplicity, a piece-wise linear function (Fig. 1) is mostly used in the published studies (Behzadian et al., 2010).

The PROMETHEE II algorithm brings the complete ranking of the alternatives. Its condensed description can be found in (1).

$$\phi(A_t) = \frac{\sum_{j=1,j\neq t}^{s} \sum_{i=1}^{k} w_i \cdot P_i(v_{i,t} - v_{i,j})}{s-1} - \frac{\sum_{j=1,j\neq t}^{s} \sum_{i=1}^{k} w_i \cdot P_i(v_{i,j} - v_{i,t})}{s-1}, \ \forall t, \tag{1}$$

where

- $v_{i,t}$ is the performance value of t-th alternative in terms of i-th criterion;
- k stands for the number of criteria;
- s stands for the number of alternatives;
- w_i represents the weight of i-th criterion;
- $\phi(A_t)$ is a net flow of the t-th alternative.

The graphical output GAIA is not based on the aggregated net flows $\phi(A_t)$, but on the so called unicriterion net flows $\phi_i(A_t)$, see (2). The relationship between the aggregated and unicriterion flow of an alternative is straightforward: $\phi(A_t) = \boldsymbol{w} \cdot \bar{\boldsymbol{\phi}}(A_t)$, where $\boldsymbol{w} \in \mathbb{R}^k$ is the vector of weights and $\bar{\boldsymbol{\phi}}(A_t) \in [-1, 1]^k$ is the vector of unicriterion net flows.

$$\phi_i(A_t) = \frac{\sum_{i\neq t} \big(P_i(v_{i,t} - v_{i,j}) - P_i(v_{i,j} - v_{i,t})\big)}{s-1}, \ \forall t \tag{2}$$

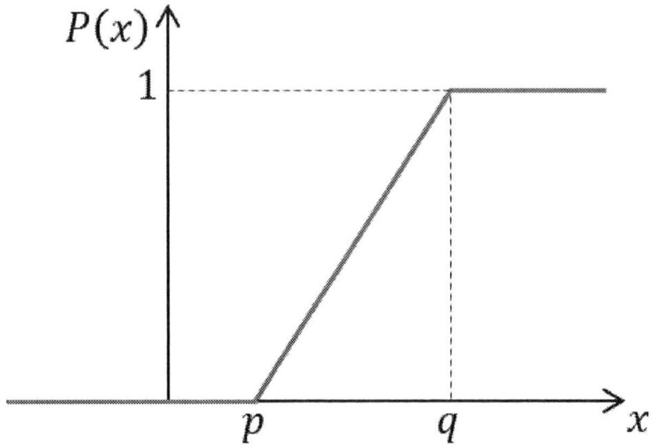

Figure 1 Linear shape of the preference function Mareschal et al. (1984)

Note 1. The formulas (1) and (2) hold for the maximizing criteria (the greater performance values are preferred to lower values). For minimizing criteria, the order of the performance values $v_{i,t}$ and $v_{i,j}$ in the subtraction would be switched.

Using (2), we obtain s points in k-dimensional space, which are projected onto the (2-D) plane using Principal Component Analysis (Hayez et al., 2009; Abdi and Williams, 2010). According to Hayez et al. (2009), it is necessary to check the quality of the projection (i.e., if the result is not too much distorted by the loss of data). Brans and Mareschal (2005) mention the threshold of 80% to consider the projection reliable enough.

The GAIA plane includes the projection of all k axes (criteria) and s points (alternatives). The following conclusions can be deduced from the plane:

- if two alternatives lie close to each other, they have a similar profile of performance (and vice versa);
- if two projected axes (criteria) are oriented in the similar/opposite direction, they express similar/opposite preferences, accordingly;
- if two projected axes are orthogonal, the corresponding criteria are not mutually related in terms of preferences;
- the longer the projected axis is, the stronger distinguishing power the criterion has.

4 Input data

The input data were obtained from the United Nations (UN) Global Compact database. The UN Global Compact is a voluntary initiative based on CEO commitments to implement universal sustainability principles and to take steps to support UN goals (United Nations, 2021). The database works from 2000 and provides sustainability information and documents about more than 16,000 participants (companies and non-business signatories) from 160 countries around the world. Main output is the Communication on Progress (COP), which is an annual disclosure through which participants inform stakeholders about their efforts to implement the principles of the United Nations (UN) Global Compact (United Nations Global Compact, 2013). The participants are divided by the following characteristics: type, tier, platform, initiative, country, sector, and status.

Our research is focused on Companies and Small or Medium-sized enterprises (SMEs) in Automobiles Parts sector, in which the database has 220 participants. 195 of them are active and, according to our analysis, 136 provides information for the following question: "Which of the following Sustainable Development Goals (SDGs) do the activities described in your COP address?" This section of COP delivers the binary output, that declares to which SDGs the participant contributes.

It is worth noting that the data, which were used for analysis, were declared by the participants in the past and do not necessarily coincide with the preferences expressed in the current management of the participants. However, only 4 participants did not have actual COP (published before 2019).

For this article, a further classification of participants is needed. The main idea is to classify them according to the economic country conditions of their headquarters. Standard UN classification into four broad categories (United Nations, 2020): G7, developed economies, economies in transition, and developing economies were used. Only one participant was included in category economies in transition and was therefore excluded from the analysis.

To get the performance values for the categories, we used the arithmetic mean of the obtained binary values, i.e., the relative frequency with which the participants in a particular category follows the given SDG (e.g., the value of 0.25 means that 1 out of 4 participants in the category follows the SDG). The resulting input data are summarized in Table 1.

	Count	SDG1	SDG2	SDG3	SDG4	SDG5	SDG6	SDG7	SDG8
TotDD	32	0.13	0.09	0.78	0.63	0.72	0.19	0.34	0.84
TotDG	49	0.47	0.29	0.69	0.67	0.69	0.43	0.33	0.84
TotG7	54	0.3	0.24	0.7	0.69	0.74	0.52	0.46	0.78

	SDG9	SDG10	SDG11	SDG12	SDG13	SDG14	SDG15	SDG16	SDG17
TotDD	0.53	0.38	0.44	0.78	0.75	0.13	0.19	0.41	0.5
TotDG	0.47	0.43	0.45	0.61	0.57	0.16	0.39	0.39	0.39
TotG7	0.69	0.52	0.56	0.78	0.76	0.28	0.37	0.43	0.46

Table 1 Input data for the analysis. Source: own processing.

5 Results and discussion

The analysis was performed in Visual PROMETHEE software[1]. Since the relevant data are missing, all criteria (SDGs) were considered equally important (the weights w_i were set equal for all of them for PROMETHEE II ranking analysis).

All criteria were handled using the linear shape of the preference function (see Fig. 1) with the indifference threshold $p = 0$ and the preference threshold $q = 1$. In other words, every, even small, difference in performance matters. On the other hand, the maximum preference would occur only if all companies from the first group follow the given SDG and, the other way

[1]Available at: `http://www.promethee-gaia.net/vpa.html`

around, none of the companies belonging to the second group follow this SDG. Such settings can cause smaller distances in the final ranking, but it brings better comparability between the criteria.

One can intuitively expect that the higher economic strength, the greater awareness of the needs of sustainable growth and, thus also a better ranking. This opinion is confirmed for G7 countries (1st position), see the results of PROMETHEE ranking in Tab. 5. On the other hand, the developing countries (DG) outrank the developed countries (DD). The main reason is that the developed countries do not tend to follow the goals like no poverty (SDG1), and zero hunger (SDG2) simply because they consider them obvious and not worthy of special attention. It is worth noting that the resulting net flows are quite similar (as a result of the preference threshold value of the preference functions), and the rank reversal phenomenon can potentially occur if the set of groups would change (Mareschal et al., 2008).

	G7	DD	DG
ϕ value	0.0725	-0.0559	-0.0166

Table 2 Results of the PROMETHEE ranking (G7 = G7 countries, DD = developed countries, DG = developing countries.

The structure and dependencies of the problem are revealed in the GAIA plane, see Fig. 2. The quality of projection calculated by Visual PROMETHEE is 100%, no information was lost at all by the projection.

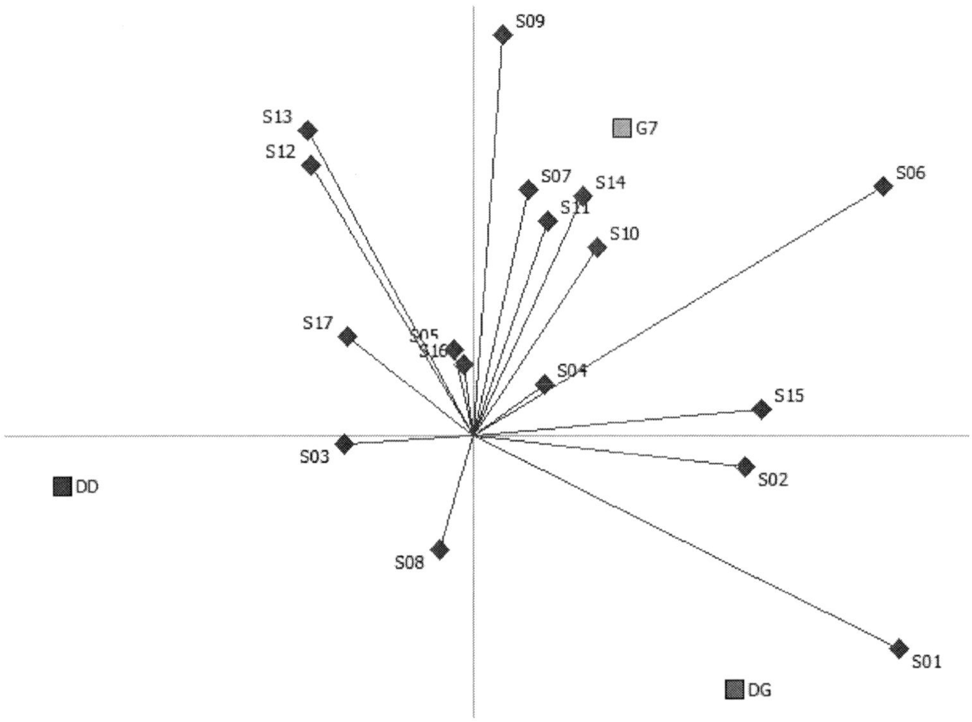

Figure 2 Resulting GAIA plane

The positions of all groups in the GAIA plane are completely different, which reports that they have very different profiles (the companies within each group focus more on specific

SDGs). It can be seen that the excellent ranking of the G7 group is caused by its tendency to follow SDG6 (clean water and sanitation), SDG7 (affordable and clean energy), SDG9 (industry, innovation and infrastructure), SDG10 (reduced inequalities), SDG11 (sustainable cities and communities) and SDG14 (life below water). On the other hand, SDG3 (good health and well-being) and SDG8 (decent work and economic growth) can be regarded as weaknesses of this most rich group. Both these goals are the only (weak) advantages of the developed countries (DD) in comparison with others.

The longer the projected axis of a criterion, the stronger distinguishing power. From this point of view, SDG9 and SDG6 bring the key value to the G7 group and SDG1 (no poverty) to the developing countries.

6 Conclusions

This paper explored the patterns of behaviour of automotive companies in terms of SDGs depending on the economic strength of the residential country. The results showed that the key goals for the automotive industry (i.e., the most often followed goals are decent work and economic growth, good health and well-being, gender equality, responsible consumption and production, climate action, and quality education. On the other hand, the overall structure of the goals strongly depends on the economic strength of the residential country.

When comparing the G7 countries with developed countries, the companies belonging to G7 tend to prefer no poverty, zero hunger, clean water and sanitation, industry, innovation, and infrastructure life below water as well as on land. A deeper analysis showed that this difference is caused mainly by the Japanese companies, which are often very large and tend to follow all (or almost all) SDGs unlike the rest of G7 countries (in Europe and USA).

The main difference between the developing countries and the other two groups is that the developing countries focus more on no poverty and zero hunger, which are the most burning issues in there.

The results indicated also other influencing factors (not only the economic strength) like, e.g., size of the companies and geographical location. These factors also reflect the national as well as the corporate culture of the companies. Therefore, further research will be focused on the extension of the presented model by other factors.

Acknowledgements

This work was supported by the SGS projects No. SP2021/86 and SP2021/43. This support is gratefully acknowledged.

References

Abdi, H. and Williams, L. J. (2010). Principal component analysis. *Wiley interdisciplinary reviews: computational statistics*, 2(4):433–459.

Aggarwa, C. C. et al. (2015). Data classification: Algorithms and applications.

Behzadian, M., Kazemzadeh, R. B., Albadvi, A., and Aghdasi, M. (2010). Promethee: A comprehensive literature review on methodologies and applications. *European journal of Operational research*, 200(1):198–215.

Brans, J. and Mareschal, B. (2005). Chapter 5: Promethee methods. *Multiple Criteria Decision Analysis: State of the Art Surveys*, pages 164–189.

Hayez, Q., Mareschal, B., and De Smet, Y. (2009). New gaia visualization methods. *In 2009 13th International Conference Information Visualisation*, pages 247–251. IEEE.

Lu, D. and Weng, Q. (2007). A survey of image classification methods and techniques for improving classification performance. *International journal of Remote sensing*, 28(5):823–870.

Mareschal, B., Brans, J. P., Vincke, P., et al. (1984). Promethee: A new family of outranking methods in multicriteria analysis. Technical report, ULB–Universite Libre de Bruxelles.

Mareschal, B., De Smet, Y., and Nemery, P. (2008). Rank reversal in the promethee ii method: some new results. *In 2008 IEEE International Conference on Industrial Engineering and Engineering Management*, pages 959–963. IEEE.

Rosati, F. and Faria, L. G. (2019). Addressing the sdgs in sustainability reports: The relationship with institutional factors. *Journal of cleaner production*, 215:1312–1326.

Sikdar, S. K. (2003). Sustainable development and sustainability metrics. *AIChE journal*, 49(8):1928–1932.

United Nations (2020). World economic situation prospects. New York, Available at `https://www.un.org/development/desa/dpad/wp-content/uploads/sites/45/WESP2020`$_{A}$*nnex.pdf*.

United Nations (2021). The 17 goals. Cited: 2021-02-05, Available at `https://sdgs.un.org/goals`.

United Nations General Assembly (2016). Resolution adopted by the general assembly on 19 september 2016. a/res/71/1. The New York Declaration.

United Nations Global Compact (2013). Un global compact policy on communicating progress. Cited: 2020-03-08, Available at `https://www.unglobalcompact.org/docs/communication`$_{o}n_{p}rogress/COP_{P}olicy.pdf$.

van der Waal, J. W. and Thijssens, T. (2020). Corporate involvement in sustainable development goals: exploring the territory. *Journal of Cleaner Production*, 252:119625.

Yamane, T. and Kaneko, S. (2021). Impact of raising awareness of sustainable development goals: A survey experiment eliciting stakeholder preferences for corporate behavior. *Journal of Cleaner Production*, 285:125291.

VŠB - Technical University of Ostrava
17. Listopadu 15/2172
708 33 Ostrava - Poruba
Czech Republic

ISBN 978-1-7138-4230-9

CURRAN ASSOCIATES INC.
proceedings.com